Teaching the Humanities

Selected Readings

Sheila Schwartz

State University College, New Paltz

The Macmillan Company

Collier-Macmillan Limited, London

First Printing

Library of Congress catalog card number: 70-93286

THE MACMILLAN COMPANY
COLLIER-MACMILLAN CANADA, LTD., TORONTO, ONTARIO

PRINTED IN THE UNITED STATES OF AMERICA

Acknowledgments and Credits

PART I

William R. Clauss, "What Is Education in the Humanities?"
Unpublished speech reprinted by permission of the author.

Walter Feinberg, "To Define the Humanities," *The Journal of Aesthetic Education* (June 1969), 1-13.
Reprinted with the permission of Ralph A. Smith, editor, and Walter Feinberg.

Fred T. Wilhelms, "The Unexpected Inch," *Educational Leadership* (January 1963), 225-229.
Reprinted with permission of the Association for Supervision and Curriculum Development and Fred T. Wilhelms. Copyright © 1963 by the Association for Supervision and Curriculum Development.

Harold Taylor, "The Spirit of Humanism," *Music Educators Journal* (September 1966), 51-110.
Reprinted with permission of the Music Educators Journal and Harold Taylor. Copyright © Music Educators Journal, September 1966. Reprinted with permission.

Bureau of Secondary Curriculum Development, New York State Education Department, "Rationale and Definition of the Humanities," *The Humanities: A Planning Guide for Teachers.* Albany, N.Y.: the Department, 1966, pp. viii-xii.
Reprinted with permission of Dr. Vivienne Anderson and The Bureau of Secondary Curriculum Development, New York State Education Department.

Jerry L. Walker, "Humanities: A Question of Values."
Unpublished speech reprinted with permission of the author.

R. F. Arragon, "Encounter with the Humanities." *The Key Reporter* (Summer 1967).
Reprinted from *The Key Reporter* volume 32, number four, Summer 1967: By permission of the publishers and the author. Permission granted for material from "The Contribution of the Humanities," *Journal of General Education,* Vol. IX (October 1955).

Prudence Dyer, "The Creative Expressions of Man."
Unpublished speech given at the Conference on High School Humanities Programs sponsored by the Department of Public Instruction and Drake University, November 2, 1967.
Reprinted with permission of the author.

Ralph A. Smith, "Aesthetics and Humanities Education," Unpublished article.
Portions reprinted from *Studies in Art Education* and *The Record,* with their permission. Printed by permission of Ralph A. Smith.

Charles R. Keller, "Humanities in the High School: The Wave of the Present," *English Journal* (March 1965), 171-174.
Reprinted with permission of the National Council of Teachers of English and Charles R. Keller.

Marguerite V. Hood, "Non-Performance Music Classes in Secondary Schools," *Music Educators Journal* (May 1967), 75-79.
Reprinted with permission of the Music Educators Journal and Marguerite V. Hood. Copyright © Music Educators Journal, May 1967. Reprinted with permission.

Ewald B. Nyquist, "Keynote Address," *Encounter with the Performing Arts*. Albany, N.Y., State Education Department, 1968, pp. 17-32.
Reprinted with permission of Dr. Vivienne Anderson and The Division of the Humanities and the Arts.

Alan Sapp, "Keynote Address," *Encounter with the Performing Arts*. Albany, N.Y.: State Education Department, 1968, pp. 33-39.
Reprinted with permission of Dr. Vivienne Anderson and The Division of the Humanities and the Arts.

PART II

George T. Prigmore, "Philosophy and Content in a Comprehensive Humanities Program," *Proceedings of the Tenth Annual Directors of Instruction Conference on the Improvement of Teaching*. Santa Fe, N.M.: New Mexico State Department of Education, January 19-20, 1968, pp. 13-18.
Reprinted with permission of the editor and author George T. Prigmore.

Lawrence K. Frank, "Why Modernize the Humanities?" *Educational Leadership* (January 1963), 220-224.
Reprinted with permission of the Association for Supervision and Curriculum Development and Mrs. Lawrence K. Frank. Copyright © 1963 by the Association for Supervision and Curriculum Development.

William H. Cornog, "Teaching Humanities in the Space Age," *The School Review* (Autumn 1964), 377-393.
Reprinted with permission of The University of Chicago Press, Publisher, and William H. Cornog. Copyright 1964 by The University of Chicago Press. All rights reserved.

Excerpt from T. S. Eliot, "Ash Wednesday," *Collected Poems 1909-1962*. By permission of Harcourt, Brace & World, Inc., the publishers.

Maxine Greene, "The Humanities and the Public School: 'You Must Change Your Life,' " *The Record* (February 1966), 338-342.
Reprinted with permission of *The Record* and Maxine Greene.

Excerpt from T. S. Eliot, "The Waste Land," *Collected Poems 1909-1962*. By permission of Harcourt, Brace & World, Inc., the publishers.

Eugene J. Fox, "An Administrator Looks at the Fine Arts and Humanities," *Proceedings of the Tenth Annual Directors of Instruction Conference on the Improvement of Teaching*. Santa Fe, N.M.: New Mexico State Department of Education, January 19-20, 1968, pp. 26-34.
Reprinted with permission of George T. Prigmore, editor, and Eugene J. Fox.

Neille Shoemaker, "Seven Aspects of the Humanities Movement." With permission of the author and the NAHE Journal.

G. Bruce Dearing, "Education for Humane Living in an Age of Automation," *School and Society* (October 31, 1964), 305-309.
Reprinted with permission of *School and Society* and G. Bruce Dearing.

PART III

Sheila Schwartz, "Essential Ideas for Secondary School Humanities Courses," *The English Record* (December 1968).
Reprinted with permission of *The English Record*.

Harris L. Dante, "The Humanities, History, and the Goals of the Social Studies," *Social Education* (May 1967), 401-404.
Reprinted with permission of the National Council for the Social Studies and Harris L. Dante.

Carolyn A. Glass and Richard I. Miller, "Humanities Courses in Secondary Schools," *Educational Theory* (July 1967), 227-235.
Reprinted with permission of *Educational Theory* and Richard I. Miller.

Francis Shoemaker, "New Dimensions for World Cultures," *The Record* (April 1968), 685-697.
Reprinted with permission of *The Record* and Francis Shoemaker.

Leon C. Karel, "Allied Arts: An Approach to Aesthetic Education," *The Journal of Aesthetic Education* (Autumn 1966), 109-119.
Reprinted with permission of *The Journal of Aesthetic Education* and Leon C. Karel.

Thayer S. Warshaw, "Studying the Bible in Public School," *English Journal* (February 1964), 91-100.
Reprinted with the permission of the National Council of Teachers of English and Thayer S. Warshaw.

Frank Manchel, "Movies and Man's Humanity."
Unpublished article. Printed with the permission of Frank Manchel.

Robert M. Diamond, "Instructional Resources in the Teaching of Art History," *School Arts* (June 1967), 24-28.
Reprinted with the permission of *School Arts* and Robert M. Diamond.

Bernard S. Miller, "The Quest for Values in a Changing World," *Social Education* (February 1965), 69-73.
Reprinted with permission of the National Council for the Social Studies and Bernard S. Miller.

Adele Stern, "Humanities: From Aeschylus to Antonioni," *English Journal* (May 1969).
Reprinted with the permission of the National Council of Teachers of English and Adele H. Stern.

Walter J. Hipple, Jr., "Humanities in the Secondary Schools," *Music Educators Journal* (February 1968), 85-161.
Reprinted with permission of the *Music Educators Journal* and Walter J. Hipple.

Courtenay V. Cauble, "Humanities: Why and How," *The English Record* (December 1965), 2-7.
Reprinted with permission of *The English Record*.

Carl Ladensack, "Brooklyn Bridge: A Good Jumping-Off Place."
Unpublished speech. Printed with permission of Carl Ladensack.

"To Brooklyn Bridge." From *Complete Poems and Selected Letters and Prose of Hart Crane*. Permission of LIVERIGHT, Publishers, New York. Copyright 1933, 1958, 1966 by Liveright Publishing Corp.

Elmer Moore, "The Dobbs Ferry Humanities Program."
Unpublished report. Printed with permission of Elmer Moore.

Richard Calisch, "Humanities at Elk Grove," *Illinois Education* (May 1968), 1-9.
Reprinted with permission of *Illinois Education* and Richard Calisch.

Owen J. Murphy, Jr., "A High School Humanities Program," *Catholic School Journal* (November 1966), 61-65.
Reprinted with permission of the *Catholic School Journal* and Owen J. Murphy, Jr.

Max Bogart, "Literature and the Humanities Ideal," *Educational Leadership* (January 1963), 230-33, 289.
Reprinted with permission of the Association for Supervision and Curriculum Development and Max Bogart. Copyright © 1963 by the Association for Supervision and Curriculum Development.

Sandra Izquierdo, "A Synopsis of the Auburn High School Humanities Program."
Unpublished paper. Reprinted with permission of Sandra Izquierdo.

Roy York, Jr., "Notes on Starting a Humanities Course," *The Journal of Aesthetic Education* (April 1968), 109-116.
Reprinted with permission of *The Journal of Aesthetic Education* and Roy York, Jr.

Robert N. Kirk, "English and the Arts," *English Journal* (February 1967), 229-234.
Reprinted with the permission of the National Council of Teachers of English and Robert N. Kirk.

Bessie Stuart and Muriel Hunt, "The Good, the True, the Beautiful," *Educational Leadership* (December 1963), 167-170.
Reprinted with permission of the Association for Supervision and Curriculum Development and Bessie Stuart and Muriel Hunt. Copyright © 1963 by the Association for Supervision and Curriculum Development.

Harry S. Broudy, "The Role of the Humanities in the Curriculum," *The Journal of Aesthetic Education* (Autumn 1966), 17-27.
Reprinted with permission of *The Journal of Aesthetic Education* and Harry S. Broudy.

PART IV

William A. Jenkins, "The Humanities and Humanistic Education in the Elementary Grades," in A. H. Marckwardt, ed., *Literature in Humanities Programs*. Champaign, Ill.: National Council of Teachers of English, 1966, pp. 31-41.
Reprinted with the permission of the National Council of Teachers of English and William A. Jenkins.

Henry W. Ray, "The Humanities in Elementary Education," *Social Education* (December 1964), 459-460.
Reprinted with the permission of *Social Education* and Henry W. Ray.

G. E. Beckett, "The CHum Program for the Elementary School."
Unpublished report. Printed with permission of G. E. Beckett.

PART V

Sheila Schwartz, "Teacher Training for the Humanities," *Teaching the Teacher of English* (December 1968), 9-14.
Reprinted with the permission of the National Council of Teachers of English.

Eldridge Cleaver, "The Guru of San Quentin," *Esquire* (April 1967).
© Copyright 1967, 1968 by Eldridge Cleaver.

Leon C. Karel, "Teacher Education in the Related Arts," *Music Educators Journal* (October 1966), 38-41.
Reprinted with permission of the *Music Educators Journal* and Leon C. Karel.

Katherine Kuh, "The Art Education Myth," *Saturday Review* (September 1968), 66-67, 80.
Reprinted with permission of the *Saturday Review* and Katherine Kuh. Copyright 1968 Saturday Review, Inc.

Carl Ladensack, "Teacher Workshop in the Humanities."
Unpublished report. Reprinted with permission of Carl Ladensack.

Elaine C. Block and Janet Lieberman, "An NDEA Humanities Institute: Developing Arts Core Curricula in the Elementary School," *Impact* (Spring 1968), 13-17.
Reprinted with permission of *Impact* and Elaine C. Block and Janet Lieberman.

Raymond W. Houghton, "The Focus of Humanism and the Teacher," in Robert R. Leeper, Ed., *Humanizing Education: The Person in the Process.* Washington, D.C.: Association for Supervision and Curriculum Development, 1967, pp. 53-63.
Reprinted with permission of the Association for Supervision and Curriculum Development and Raymond W. Houghton. Copyright © 1967 by the Association for Supervision and Curriculum Development.

PART VI

Lawrence C. Howard, "Teach Them the Arts of Freedom," *Saturday Review* (June 18, 1966), 66-67, 80.
Reprinted with permission of the *Saturday Review* and Lawrence C. Howard. Copyright 1966, Saturday Review, Inc.

Marjorie B. Smiley, "Humanities and the Disadvantaged," *Impact* (Spring 1968), 8-12.
Reprinted with permission of *Impact* and Marjorie B. Smiley.

Sheila Schwartz, "Humanities for All Students," in *Forum on the Humanities.* Albany, N.Y.: State Education Department, Division of the Humanities and the Arts, 1969.

Judith Murphy and Ronald Gross, "Can the Arts 'Turn On' Poor Kids to Learning?" *The Record* (March 1968), 581-586.
Reprinted with the permission of *The Record* and Ronald Gross and Judith Murphy.

Glendy Culligan, "High School and the Cultural Illiterate," *American Education* (November 1966), 1-5.
Reprinted with the permission of *American Education.*

Miriam B. Goldstein and Edward C. Martin, "Humanistic Education for the General Student: A Progress Report," *The English Leaflet* (Fall 1964), 8-30.
Reprinted with the permission of *The English Leaflet.*

APPENDIXES

American Council of Learned Societies, "Statement and Recommendation," *Report of the Commission on the Humanities.* New York: the Council, 1964, pp. 1-15.
Reprinted with the permission of the American Council of Learned Societies.

Barnaby C. Keeney, "The National Endowment for the Humanities and the Classroom," in A. H. Marckwardt, ed., *Literature in Humanities Programs.* Champaign, Ill.: National Council of Teachers of English, 1966.
Reprinted with the permission of the National Council of Teachers of English and Barnaby C. Keeney.

Robert V. Denby, "An NCTE/ERIC Report on Humanities Instruction in Secondary Schools," *English Journal* (February 1969), 272-280.
Reprinted with the permission of the National Council of Teachers of English and Robert V. Denby.

Contents

Part III: Humanities in the Secondary School 139

Part IV: Humanities in the Elementary School 285

Part V: Teacher Education and the Humanities 305

Part VI: Humanities and the Disadvantaged   345

Appendixes   393

Part I
Definition of the Humanities

The 1964 Report of the Commission on the Humanities,[1] *a report designed to increase federal support for the humanities, defined the area of focus as follows:*

The humanities are the study of that which is most human. Throughout man's conscious past they have played an essential role in forming, preserving, and transforming the social, moral, and aesthetic values of every man in every age. One cannot speak of history or culture apart from the humanities. They not only record our lives; our lives are the very substance they are made of. Their subject is every man. . . .

The humanities may be regarded as a body of knowledge and insight, as modes of expression, as a program for education, as an underlying attitude toward life. The body of knowledge is usually taken to include the study of history, literature, the arts, religion, and philosophy. The fine and the performing arts are modes of expressing thoughts and feelings visually, verbally, and aurally. The method of education is one based on the liberal tradition we inherit from classical antiquity. The attitude toward life centers on concern for the human individual: for his emotional development, for his moral, religious, and aesthetic ideas, and for his goals—including in particular his growth as a rational being and a responsible member of his community.

The articles in this section amplify the above definition. Clauss identifies three terms in common use—the humanities, *the* humanization of education, *and* humanities education. *He provides a workable definition for today's schools by selecting* humanities education, *which will aid the student in making developmental choices, as the desirable goal for all of contemporary education.*

[1] See Appendix A.

1

Both Feinberg and Wilhelms define the humanities as an approach to a variety of subjects rather than as a specific body of subject matter. "They are a set of purposes," says Wilhelms, "which have the power to help a young person find out what he wants to live for, *to hammer out a set of values for himself, to work through to purposes that give him a personal meaning. . .and. . .help him identify with what is best in this old world of ours. . . ."*

Taylor, rejecting the view of the humanities as "culture containers" or "value containers," sees traditional humanities courses as basically an administrative convenience. The spirit of humanism, which pervades all aspects of the curriculum and which makes "all social, moral, and cultural questions a matter for new continuing enquiry," should replace the traditional view of the humanities.

The New York State Department of Education "Rationale" sees the humanities as the activities that define one's relationship to self and society. Walker suggests that "the proper study of the humanities are those uniquely human activities, the creation and use of symbols." Because man creates "things" to symbolize his "values," Walker further defines the humanities as the study of values.

Arragon, tracing the humanities historically, sees them in terms of the creation of humanistic objects that are both more and less than life. It is through the interpretation of these tangible objects that man engages in the humanistic discovery through which he can learn to understand his own and other societies.

Dyer defines the humanities as the creative expressions of man, thus echoing the ideas of Arragon. Students of the humanities must, therefore, be exposed to the skills essential for creating these expressions and also to the skills necessary for understanding and interpreting them.

Smith sees the humanities as "aesthetic exemplars," in contrast to the subjects of history, philosophy, religion, mathematics, or the physical and social sciences. His method is to initiate students into "the aesthetic forms of understanding. . .[that]. . .draw on a number of arts and sciences but. . .cannot be reduced to any one of them."

Keller defines the humanities as embracing literature, languages, history, music, art, and philosophy, but Hood defines them in terms of purpose. The common purpose of the humanities is the development in students of the knowledge of the relationship between the fine arts, music, literature, and dance.

Nyquist, seeing the humanities as those experiences that lead to cultural democracy, uses the words humanities *and* performing arts *interchangeably. A major goal of the humanities is, to Nyquist, the development of future audiences who will be enthusiastic supporters of the performing arts.*

Last, Sapp defines humanities as "the great world of letters, the great world of verbal communication, and the great world of man's efforts, in language and letters, to say what he has to say."

What Is Education in the Humanities?

William R. Clauss

Current interest at all levels of schooling seems to revolve around three terms—the humanities, the humanization of education, and humanities education. Each may have its own definition.

1. *The humanities* usually refer to a select number of disciplines. There are arguments about which are to be included.
2. *Humanization of education* means to apply the techniques derived from the behavioral sciences to all areas of the education process. To make it more humane—that is, enlightened and compassionate.
3. *Humanities education,* I believe, seeks to provide the student with means by which he comes to know himself through an examination of the expressive works of man and through the execution of self-initiated expressions affirming that which he values.

Any discussion of this last term must take the other two into consideration. They affect what experiences one is to include in humanities education and how one performs in the teaching-learning situation.

For teachers the interest in humanities education is burgeoning. The motivation for this interest derives from several factors—the imbalance of emphasis in the curriculum, the current student value revolution, the need to extend one's sensitivity to all means of expression, and the realization that a sense of self can be developed through humanities education.

The call for change came soon after World War II. Some voices, as Alberto Moravia's, called for all of society to reexamine humanism. In 1946 he wrote:

The world urgently needs to be brought back to man's measure. Only in a world made to his measure can man rediscover, through contemplation, an adequate idea of himself, cease to be a means and propose himself as an end. . . . A modern world made to the measure of man needs to be made on the one hand to his physical measure, that is according to his physical capacity to move, see, embrace, and understand, and on the other to his intellectual and moral measure, that is according to his capacity to enter into a relationship with ideas and moral values.[1]

During the ensuing decade a great debate developed between those who supported science and technology as the force to better man's life and others who saw dangers in the materialism and alienation it seemed to be fostering. Among these supporters of the humanistic studies are Ralph Barton Perry, Ronald S. Crane, Harry S. Broudy, Charles R. Keller, and Moody E. Prior. Prior sums up their position in his *Science and the Humanities.*

[1] Moravia, Alberto, *Man as an End* (New York: Farrar, Straus and Giroux, 1966), p. 63.

3

The humanities are concerned with man and the human condition. They are therefore preoccupied with the choices which are open to men, the goals men set for themselves, and the means they choose to gain them; and they are consequently further preoccupied with how these affect the character and the quality of an individual's life, and to what extent and in what ways they make possible the full realization of the capacities which appear to distinguish men from other forms of sentient life.[2]

Heretofore, elementary and secondary schools in New York State have not had to provide a rationale for humanities education—nor did they have to deal in any way with the term. Although languages, literature, history and the other fine arts were taught, few were the programs which saw them as means to humanistic ends. "Humanities" seemed to fit the educational lexicon at the college level where such subjects were conveniently administered as a divisional unit.

For the public school teacher the intent and the extent of the term constitute some major concern and debate. At least one distinguishing factor can be made, however, and that contrasts the methods by which the humanities and the sciences arrive at their goals of human understanding. For the sciences unite in the effort to explain some aspect of human behavior by applying the scientific method—that is the procedures of generalizing from selected data and constructing explanatory hypotheses to be tested by the data. In contrast, the humanities are an accumulation of human achievements that can be known through skills of language (including all symbolic media), analysis (philosophical, historical, and critical) and through empathy. They posit more questions of value than of fact. Man acquires knowledge and understanding of himself and other men by introjection of the values inherent in the human expressions that are the vehicles of the humanities. Such introjections are made freely. Scientific criteria for proof are not always demanded. One example, two people may arrive at the same empathic state for minority groups through the two different routes—one by coming to certain realizations through collecting sociological data about such groups and developing a compassionate attitude as a result, and the other person can arrive at a similar end by reading E. M. Forster's *A Passage to India.*

Humanities Education as Process. Schools have the capabilities today to aid youth in attaining higher levels of human integration and function. The 1970's and 80's will require of individuals greater capacities for challenge, openendedness, and an integration of the whole being—body, mind and spirit.

The educational process that will foster such goals must change from the "molding" or "shaping" processes of the past to a developmental "choice-making" process whereby the individual prepares himself to live confidently and creatively in the free society we envision for him. To this end, humanities education must apply itself. It must develop processes in the realms of inquiry, subjectivity, curricula, teaching, and valuing.

[2]Prior, Moody E. *Science and the Humanities* (Evanston: Northwestern University Press, 1962), p. 58.

Inquiry. The process of inquiry is a search for truth. In it the learner seeks to arrive at the relevant answer. To perform well in this process the student will need to be able to create and to evaluate. Humanities education, in its focus on the human condition, relies on a great body of human achievement (literature, in all of its genre, visual and aural arts.) It offers, as well, the media for a creative affirmation of truth as seen by the individual. The interdisciplinary aspects of humanities education tend to open-up rather than fragment knowledge for inquiry purposes. Through its philosophic, historical and aesthetic analysis methods humanities education provides for evaluation—evaluation using what may be new standards of measurement and objectives.

Subjectivity. A traditional concept of the objectivity-subjectivity dichotomy is that where one is the mainstay of the sciences the other, subjectivity, properly belongs to the arts. In our technologically oriented society the emphasis given to the rational-objective point of view has placed in question all reactions based on feeling, emotion and intuition.

The report of the Educational Policies Commission of the NEA on "The Role of the Fine Arts in Education"[3] states:

A newly emerging rationale in favor of the arts suggests that they provide a setting in which people can learn to accept their own limited abilities to be totally objective about anything. This may seem at first to be either unimportant or unwise. It may be felt that acceptance of one's own irrationalities is not such a good thing, if it means no longer trying to be more rational. The strains of argument here are delicate, and they often are discussed in a self-defeatingly garbled manner.

Most will agree that no man is perfectly objective about anything, and is likely to be quite nonobjective about himself. This realization, however, seems to be insufficient to keep some people from trying always to be as objective as they can about everything. They consciously submerge everything uncontrolled within them in order to squeeze out one more degree of objectivity.

There is a growing awareness today of the benefits brought to living a fulfilled life by following the bent of the subjective aspects of one's mind. In the words of the Commission, "It is rather a mature, calm acceptance of the realization that one will continually be doing, thinking, feeling, being, and becoming things which could not possibly be predicted, controlled, or avoided."

The need for the humane individual to be compassionate necessarily involves the emotions. Learning experiences involving value choices can be enriching to one's humanness if feelings are used. Issues of the human condition dealt with in humanities education therefore provide a youth with opportunities to discover his feelings and, hopefully, those issues about which he can do something with compassion. The subjective aspects of such learning experiences are a barrier that many teachers cannot cross but, to many others, these experiences open-up broader avenues to the teacher-student relationship.

[3] Educational Policies Commission. ' The Role of the Five Arts in Education," *Art Education*, October 1968, Vol. 21, no. 7, p. 4.

Curricula. The objectives of humanities education invite an opening up of the school curriculum. Much has already been said by others of the weaknessess of education caused by the lock-step, course-centered, fragmented or closed curriculum. Their criticisms are presently being met in some schools which have found in humanities education the orientation to foster those habits of mind which are the real goal of education—a capacity of intellectual wonder and artistic delight.

A humanities based curriculum places much emphasis on the uniqueness of each child. No mere lip service is given to the principles of individuation! Teachers and child form a professional, humane working team in their search for inter-relationships from among many areas of knowledge and many human experiences. The child's accumulated experience forms the base from which each succeeding learning experience evolves. He proceeds in his own unique way and at his own unique pace.

Teaching. When a student is considered to be individual and unique, then a main task of the teacher is to assist in the developing uniqueness of each student. Such a task asks for a teacher who can discern potentials in the student and encourage them to evolve. Thus, in humanities education where the primary objective is the discovery of self, a teacher who dispenses preformed answers is a contradiction. The teaching role here is not one of knowledge dispenser but, rather, the role of guide or of catalyst, one who is secure, confident and creative in his relationship with the student.

Value. Various positions have been taken in the current value dilemma. Some segments of our society are attempting to work out a new set of values, others believe that older values simply need renewal. There are those who believe that teachers should not impose values (most especially certain varieties) and there are others who claim that *that* is exactly what certain students need!

Psychotherapists point out, however, that all these arguments miss the point of the central problem—that we have to a great extent lost the power to affirm the values that we espouse. What everyone needs is a prior capacity—the opportunity to act upon that which we cherish, prize, or value.

A very large part of humanities education is concerned with ethics. Perhaps it is the most important part, the most relevant for youth today. Ethical judgment and choice-making must be grounded in the person's freedom to place a value on a position and to test it through action. Only as he affirms reality through an act, a deed, will the value affect his living. When placed in the learning situation such acts aid in the discovery of responsibility, the possiblityof change, and a belief in what one is doing. In addition, one tends to also discover that what is good, true, and beautiful for one is not totally dissimilar from what others have discovered.

Louis E. Raths[4] has written extensively of a means by which a student can be confronted with a values based situation and then is impelled to discover and declare himself in the face of it. His "process of valuing" is applied in the classroom in this way—

---

[4]Raths, Louis E. *Values and Teaching* (Columbus: Charles E. Merrill Co., 1966).

An issue requiring human evaluation is posed and the students perform the following steps:

1. Choosing from alternatives.
2. Choosing after careful consideration of the consequences of each alternative.
3. Choosing freely.
4. Prizing, being glad of one's choice.
5. Prizing, being willing to publicly affirm one's choice.
6. Acting upon one's choice, incorporating choices into behavior.
7. Acting upon one's choice repeatedly, over time.

The implications of this process are clear for the humanities teacher. When a student is inquiring about a particular human social issue, the positions taken by other men on the issue constitute the alternatives. The student may find *his* answer or may be drawn on to pose further questions. In either case he finds the expressive work of man relevant to his needs and in the process may discover other relevancies to which he should attend.

It must be remembered that the humanities develop through cumulation and are not a sequential development such as the sciences. Aquinas can be as relevant as Tillich, Euripides as O'Neill, Praxiteles as Moore.

Humanities education provides a vision of the past and present and can aid in projections for the future. Through it man can choose the greater good for the moment or the future. By feeling oneself in another's needs and desires, through empathy and introjection, one can realize selfhood and make choices with the good of one's fellowman as well as oneself in mind.

To Define the Humanities

Walter Feinberg

There are some areas which by all rights should be above criticism and therefore in need of no defense. To the common man, God, motherhood, and country usually occupy such a status. To the university professor, it is either the sciences or the humanities. While God, mother, country, and science are usually able to maintain their prestige, the humanities are not. The problem for the humanities is that unlike the others, which everyone can recognize, few people can agree upon the meaning of humanistic study. The humanities require a defense, but a defense seems to demand first an identification.

Identification may seem like an easy task. We may point to the philosophy student reading Kant, or to the English professor analyzing Yeats, or to the historian discussing Gibbons and then assert that all are engaged in humanistic activity. But what does this pointing mean and why is it that we point to the student reading Kant, but not to the one working out a problem in mathematical logic? Why do we point with some certainty to the man with the *Critique of Pure Reason* under his nose, but with much less certainty to the one staring down the pages of *The Origin of Species?* The act of pointing, while disconcerting to some, may nevertheless be accurate, but its accuracy is only temporary. It does not reveal a principle of identity which might allow the inclusion of some future activities under the rubric of humanistic study and the exclusion of others.

To most people "the humanities" suggest a set of academic subjects such as literature, history, and philosophy, and while different people may want to include different subjects in the set, most believe that there is a definite relationship between them. If such a relationship can be established, then the problem of identification has been solved.

Some believe the humanities are tied together by a common origin. Literature, philosophy, history, and even art are seen to have had their beginnings in the mythology of more primitive man. Here, it is said, fiction and reality merged in the created history of a given tribe only later to be separated as man began to keep records of his activities. But if the humanities are to be identified in this way, then it would seem that mathematics and indeed science itself should be included. For the mathematical principles developed by such groups as the early Pythagoreans were, as much as history, a part of their myth-making activity.

If the identifying principle of the humanities is not to be found in a common origin, then perhaps it may arise from a similar object of concern. It is sometimes said that science deals with the physical universe and the humanities with man. Included in the concept of man are all of those attributes of human existence which some believe are not amenable to measurement, the most important being found in the realm of values. It is argued that the behavior of physical objects can be determined because such behavior is nothing more than the sum of forces on the object. Human behavior is believed to be different because it is self-determined, making it possible for human beings to transcend the forces impinging upon them. This is said to be the only possible meaning of human choice. Whether or not this argument has any validity, it should be clear that the object of concern does not alone separate the humanities from other activities. Even if it were the case that the humanities restricted themselves to statements about man and his values, the fact is that other areas are concerned about this too. The social and behavioral sciences could be identified in the same way.

It has sometimes been suggested that the social and behavioral sciences share a specific method which is not the method of the humanities. While such a statement demands much qualification, it is perhaps the case that these sciences do demand that statements about human behavior be tested against evidence grounded in human behavior. If this is the case, then the implication may be that the humanities share a method too, but that this method is different from that of the sciences.

Because it is required that scientific statements be grounded in experience, it is sometimes suggested that the humanities depend more heavily upon intellect and imagination. When this point of view is taken, the areas usually mentioned for its support are literature and the arts. Problems arise, however, when it is recognized that the conceptual framework of a scientific system also involves the imagination and that areas of humanistic study, such as history, have an empirical dimension to them. To the scientist, the theory which accounts for the data is as important as the collection of the data. The fact that there are times when more than one theory can adequately explain the data and then derive accurate predictions is an indication that imagination plays a part in scientific activity. Moreover, the historian's dependence upon the records of actual events is so obvious that any suggestion that the humanities are not concerned with the empirical world is questionable.

If imagination is not unique to the humanities and concern with the accuracy of the data is not unique to the sciences, then perhaps the difference lies in the uses to which such imagination and concern are put and in the ways they are expressed. It is sometimes suggested that the humanities rely more heavily upon a written, nonmathematical language; that scientific statements are predictive and humanistic one are not. However, the first suggestion is not very useful and the second is not true. If the humanities were to be identified by the kind of language used, then there would be no way to distinguish a work by Shakespeare from a committee report or a telephone book. To say that all scientific statements are predictive is to exclude from the realm of science definitional statements, statements of classification, and laws. Furthermore, the number of systems, now classified under the humanities, but modeled after science, are too numerous to allow the distinction to go unquestioned. To one degree or another, Hobbes's *Leviathan, Spinoza's Ethics,* and Marx's general "sociology" and "economics" were created in this light.

Regarding the humanities, it may be that the very search for an identifying principle is misleading. Some plural nouns take their meaning not because they indicate an identity but because they indicate objects which cannot be included under another identity. The yiddish "goyum" is such a word indicating those people not related by the quality of Jewishness. The word "masses" is similar in this respect for it indicates a classification for those human relationships that cannot be subsumed under normal social categories of class, caste, race, religion. If "humanities" is this kind of word then it would indicate areas of study related to one another simply by virtue of the fact that they are not related to anything else. If this were the case, then there would be no possible defense of the humanities in general, but merely arguments that attempted to reveal the value of a number of very different and discrete areas of study. Thus, for example, philosophy could be defended because of its contribution to computer technology even though in this respect it would have little or nothing to do with history or literature. It is important therefore to decide whether "the humanities" is similar in function to a phrase like "the masses" or whether there is a *significant* relationship between its members.

The word "masses" is able to perform its function because every time it is uttered there is understood an implied and possible set of relationships, such as "class" or "caste," and it is only in relation to the implied set that "masses" is able to highlight the nonrelatedness of the objects included under its rubric. However, both "mass" and "class" assume a certain kind of relatedness. But "class" not only assumes one kind, it highlights another which the term "mass" does not. For example, both "mass" and "class" assume people related to one another socially through certain institutions. However, "class" also implies people related by virtue of a certain status, a certain income or a certain frame of mind. "Mass" suggests people who are not related in that way, and the significance of the term lies in the very fact that its members are thus not related. If "the humanities" is similar to "the masses" in function then there would be first an assumed relationship implied by both the humanities and at least one other term and second, a relationship highlighted by the other term but not by "the humanities."

"The sciences" and "the humanities" mark off areas of study and inquiry from areas of feeling or action. But the sciences suggest also an area concerned with the quantification of phenomena and a set of operating procedures that can cut through qualitative differences. If "the humanities" indicates a set of nonrelated subjects, then it would include those areas that could not be classified under the sciences. If, however, "the humanities" not only assumes one identity, in common with "the sciences," but highlights another, then it will have established its own principle of inclusion.

The humanities and the sciences are related by virtue of the fact that both indicate areas of study and the product of such an area is something called knowledge. The question for the humanities is whether there is such a thing as nonscientific knowledge and if there is, whether it is one thing or many. It can be argued, for example, that humanistic knowledge is not essentially different from scientific knowledge, but rather that it is a primitive scientism. If one takes this point of view, then there is only one kind of knowledge and that is best expressed by science.

Monroe Beardsley takes this position in his essay "The Humanities and Human Understanding."[1] Focusing on literature, Beardsley argues that the knowledge it provides is not essentially different from that of a science such as psychology. Psychological knowledge differs from literary insight only because the psychologist forms his generalizations from empirical evidence while the generalizations we form through fiction may exist only as possibilities which may or may not be manifested in actual behavior. It is not clear from Beardsley's essay whether this is the only kind of insight provided by humanistic study, but there are times when he seems to suggest that it is not. However, he fails to reveal any other and he also fails to mention whether another kind of insight could be classified as knowledge.

Although his essay includes the word "Humanities" in the title, Beardsley's argument is primarily concerned with literature, and the reason for his focus is somewhat peculiar. After suggesting that most people would like to include philosophy, literature, and history under the rubric of humanistic study, he then proceeds to eliminate philosophy and history because these areas are relevant to both the sciences and the humanities. The philosophy or the history of science is as significant as the philosophy or history of literature or art.[2] Beardsley fails to realize that by taking this step, he has made his paper irrelevant to its topic. A more

---

[1] In Thomas B. Stoup (ed.), *The Humanities and the Understanding of Reality* (Lexington, Kentucky: University of Kentucky Press, 1966), pp. 1-31.

[2] *Ibid.,* pp. 12-13.

apt title would have been "Literature and Human Understanding." Beardsley avoids the problem of identity by eliminating all but one of the items that needs to be related suggesting that the class of items called the humanities contains but one member and that member is literature. While his procedure may or may not be legitimate, it certainly is odd.

Beardsley's assumption seems to be that there is but one type of knowledge for which the paradigm example is science of one kind or another. The humanities can, however, approach the paradigm, even suggesting areas for science to pursue, but they cannot surpass it. The problem with Beardsley's argument is that it merely demonstrates that value can be found *in* humanistic activity, but it does not demonstrate the value *of* such activity. If the value of literary insight is seen to lie in its closeness to psychology and the difference between the two lies only in the fact that psychology builds and tests its notions against real cases, then in fact, literature has been dismissed as second-class psychology. Its value is thus measured by the degree to which it approaches in insight the more sophisticated area of study.

In defense of Beardsley, it should be noted that he had set about to reveal the contribution of the humanities to human understanding and was thus emphasizing the cognitive function of literature. He also says, however, that

Even if literature contributed nothing to our understanding of human nature... its existence might still be thoroughly justified, and its appearance in the world very welcome. As a pattern of actions interwoven and shaped into something worthy of intense contemplation for the sake of its expressiveness and beauty, a literary work can hold up its head. Something can be said on its behalf by a reasonable aesthetic.[3]

Thus, for Beardsley there are two ways in which a literary work may be of value. First, because of the general understanding of human nature that it may provide, and second, because of the aesthetic pleasure which may be derived from it. But for him, these are two very different things.

Beardsley makes the mistake of beginning his essay backwards by first asking what should be included under the humanities and then by posing the question of what value this subject matter can serve. Because the problem of identification is so difficult, it may be better to deal with the question of value and to ask whether there is any cognitive value which the sciences alone cannot provide and whether there is another kind of study which may be able to produce it. To begin in this way avoids a commitment to a pre-established subject area.

The mistake made by most defenders of the humanities is to ask first what subject should be called humanistic and then to ask what values such subjects might serve. This approach does not always lead to a serious examination of the humanities. In identifying the subject areas, the author's commitment has usually been revealed, and he must then find something of value in the subjects identified. But what is being defended when history is cited for its contribution to military

---

[3] *Ibid.,* p. 28.

science or philosophy for its aid to computer technology? When literature is cited for its contribution to psychology, then psychology has become the ground of value and literature only rests on its foundation.

However, if we assume for the moment that in literature we have a correct paradigm for humanistic study, then we may examine this paradigm for any unique value it may reveal. Instead of looking at fiction, as Beardsley does, let us concentrate the analysis on biography. Recall Beardsley's conclusion that literary insight differs from scientific insight because the statements of the former need not be tested in the arena of empirical evidence. But biography, no matter how small a sample it may be, is a statement drawn from that arena. Scientific insight may be gleaned from biographical works, but the question is whether such insight is relevant to the intent of the work and whether other values may be contained in that intent. Examining the *Autobiography of Malcolm X,* it is possible to extract a number of insights of psychological importance, but for the sake of brevity I will limit this discussion to some of those that are concerned with learning theory.

The story of Malcolm is the story of a black man as he moves from a childhood in the schools and reformatories of Lansing, Michigan, to the bars and dance halls of Boston, to the flophouses of Harlem, the confinement of prison, and finally to a position of importance in the Muslim religion. It is the story of a man who found in prison a school and in a religious fanatic a teacher. But most of all, it is the story of a man who had a remarkable capacity for growth derived from an uncommon ability to admit error and change his mind. Embodied in the book, however, are other things, not the least of which are some general principles about how people learn. These are the principles that will be examined for their scientific importance and then related to their humanistic significance.

One of the first and obvious instances of learning occurs when young Malcolm, after expressing a desire to become a lawyer, is told by an English teacher: "But you've got to be realistic about being a nigger. You're good with your hands . . . why don't you plan on carpentry." The effect of this and other similar situations initiates Malcolm's life as a hustler and thief. And, if we look at this episode "scientifically," it could be said that an organism, cut off from one set of rewards, tends to seek out another.

Other episodes reveal other principles. In prison, Malcolm's family is initially unsuccessful in its attempts to convert him to the Muslim religion until his brother, Reginald, prescribes to Malcolm a mode of behavior guaranteed to set him free. Malcolm thus refuses to eat pork, he gives up smoking and swearing, and eventually he adopts the Muslim religion. The situation suggests clearly that resistance to large scale changes in behavior may be overcome by series of programmed steps and the promise of forseeable rewards.

Such insights may or may not be psychologically significant, but if they are, they are better located in an elementary psychology text. To concentrate upon the universal and abstractly significant laws distorts completely the relevance of the story. Malcolm's life was not governed by the laws of psychology. Psychological factors were present, but their presence was contained within the context of a situation. To abstract the universal is to lose sight of the concrete, to examine the work for its psychological relevance is to lose sight of the situation in which that relevance operated. The book is psychologically significant and it could be looked at in that way, but its psychological significance should not be mistaken for its humanistic significance.

If this work does reveal psychological principles and if these principles have the empirical support that the life of one man can give them, then what is it that places the biography out of the realm of psychology and into the realm of literature? The answer is that the work *can* be placed in the realm of psychology, but this was not the author's intent. When psychological principles are expressed, it is the reader who is expressing them and, when he does this, no one should deny to him the fact that he is doing psychology, however unsophisticated. To defend the humanities on the grounds that they can do in a primitive way what the sciences can do in a sophisticated way is not to defend them at all. The autobiography is not humanistically significant because of the scientific insights it may yield, even though it does yield them. Its humanistic significance is to be found only in the fact that it says something about a man which science cannot say very well. The autobiography is a vehicle that takes the reader into the life experience and the frame of reference of another human being. Its value is not to be judged by the categories of truth or falsity (the categories of science), nor by the categories of validity or invalidity (the categories of logic).

Many of the statements Malcolm makes, many of the beliefs he holds, from the "objective" point of view, would be patently false, but this is irrelevant. As we touch his experience, we come to understand that his statements and beliefs are more than credible and that if his experience were ours we might very well believe and say the same things. A frame of reference is not truth, it is the foundation for *truths* and Malcolm's life shows us how we too might believe "the unbelievable." Given Malcolm's experiences, his beliefs are true. They are the most coherent explanations for those experiences, and science can do no better. If the scope of his early experience is narrow then his later beliefs explain very well why it is so.

The categories that are relevant for a work in the humanities are the categories of credibility or incredibility, and these can be applied only in the light of the phenomena or the experiences that are being explained. Nor is it inconceivable that two quite different interpretations may be offered to account for the same phenomena or experiences. This is simply a recognition of the limits of human intelligence and is quite consistent with the quality of humility that is sometimes cited as an effect of humanistic study. To study a work humanistically is to learn something about man's finitude, for each work provides a mode of interpretation that may be challenged by another work of perhaps equal credibility.

When the humanities are understood in this way then it becomes clear that no work can, on its merits alone, be classified as belonging to the humanities just as few works can, on the same grounds, be excluded from membership. The student impresses his purpose on a work. He can view it for its "objective" merits, judging how well it conforms to the data as he knows the data, or he can decide to take its frame as his own, judging each response in light of the author's "reality."

Literature, therefore, cannot be singled out as the only living member of the humanities and neither can philosophy or history. Newton and Galileo, Darwin and Freud have given man ways to understand his experience that are as significant as Leibniz or Goethe.

When studied humanistically literature undertakes to develop and display a world view and then to attach the readers' emotions to it. It is not obligated to argue for the view by laying bare the reasons that support it or by refuting the possible arguments against it. It serves only to remove the many layers of fog that may becloud and obscure the obvious so that the reader, if he chooses, can see more clearly. What the reader finally sees is not the universal and abstract laws of science, but rather the concrete behavior of man, aspects of which those laws attempt to explain.

But humanism has other dimensions to it. As literature displays, philosophy, *studied humanistically,* unfolds, examines, and sometimes develops a world view. It takes the obvious, unravels it, reveals the assumptions it entails, and maps out the possibilities it hides. Unlike literature, its aim is not to display the view of a finite number of people but to develop a species view or to suggest the limiting conditions of any species view. The expression of the limits of man's possible systems are found not only in the traditional philosophies, such as the categories of Kant, the irony of Socrates, or the absurd of Kierkegaard. It is found in any system that places a limit on Man's rationality and on his capacity to know. Freud's *id* is as much an expression of this limitation as is Kierkegaard's absurd.

To study a system humanistically does not mean that the system must assert that man's knowledge is limited, but the student's recognition of the limitations of a system introduces an element of objectivity into the study. But because this kind of objectivity, when generalized, says something about the student as well as the system, it is not without emotional significance.

Although works of literature and philosophy lend themselves to humanistic study, the objects of humanistic study are not exhausted by them. Scientific works whose truths have been superceded can also be approached in this way. They too have established models for thinking and feeling.

A defense of the humanities does not require a definition that embraces all of the traditional humanistic subjects. To ask whether there is a kind of knowledge which is not scientific is simply to ask whether there are some functions which science alone cannot perform. To say that a scientific work can be studied humanistically is to say that it can reveal more than it procedures and its findings contain.

Just as the humanities reveal some of the limitations of past systems, so too can they reveal the sophistication that science and philosophy have built into our own view of the world. They can help us to understand that what we believe and see is not always believed by an unbiased mind or seen by an uncluttered eye. Humes's treatment of causation is an outstanding example of a return to "naive" understanding. It strips away one of the sophisticated constructs that intellectual history, in its widest meaning, has led us to take for granted. Philosophical study can be especially useful uncovering some of the sophistication that science and intelligence have build into thoughts and our language. For one of the functions of philosophy has been to show that our ideas and our language could be other than they are. It has done this by developing other models of human intelligence or by showing the credibility of past models.

For the student of the humanities to understand something about his own thought and that of his contemporaries, he needs a point of reference. Philosophy can show the development of the system of ideas, but history can show the power held by the system and the way it may have captured the minds and the behavior of a group of people. And history can show a once powerful idea enfeebled by an overextension in time and an overgeneralization in institutions.

More than a set of subjects then, the humanities indicate an approach to a variety of subjects. They suggest an openness to the frame of reference of the work under consideration and a willingness to try and weave that frame into one's own. If some works enjoy preference over others it may be only because these have captured the imagination and extended the thinking of man. The student who takes seriously this course of study learns to accept his own times and his own beliefs only tentatively and to respect both the achievements and the mistakes of the past, recognizing that each is defined in the context of an unstable present. Science approaches an event from the point of view of the present. It attacks a problem with the powers, the instruments, and the ideas that it has inherited, and only on rare occasions does an event so stubborn arise as to initiate a reinterpretation of these ideas. At its best, the study of the humanities develops men capable of reinterpreting ideas in light of stubborn events.

The Unexpected Inch

Fred T. Wilhelms

We learn humanity from humanity.

No one is born civilized. We learn our humanity from humanity. Surrounded by decent, kindly people, a child slowly learns to subdue the savagery of his impulses. He learns to play and to work with his fellows, even to be considerate of them. He picks up a sense of what is good and what is to be cherished. In his head and heart an image forms of what life is and can be. And over the years he grows into a truly human person.

But alas! Many babies are born into the midst of all that is cheap and tawdry. The people they depend upon are coarse and gross, or even twisted and malign.

And even we luckier ones, we too live out our lives mostly in the mild company of mediocrity.

Yet every baby is capable of growing to some touch of greatness in his soul. Nor is this much a matter of the quality of his brain. Bright, or not-so-bright, a human being can grope his way toward a satisfying fineness in the values he holds dear. Even a meager brain can support some cultivated joy in what is lovely—in things, in people, and in human relationships. It is not the intelligent alone whose character can shine forth in faith and truth and simple goodness. Those haunting potentialities that make man truly human are not the sole gift of high intellect. In these terms no man need settle for a low star to steer by.

Only—and this I think is the humanities idea—something from beyond must be brought into a life that is to rise. We can learn to be ordinary—no small thing!—from the ordinary people around us. But only the extraordinary can help us to go higher.

And the extraordinary is in short supply. With reasonable fortune a young person may be close to a few adults who can lift him—a parent or relative of rare quality, a great teacher or two, a friend in his church or neighborhood. But even for those who are this fortunate it is still too little. We simply cannot learn enough from those who happen to be nearby.

A Way of Approach. Ultimately, to learn humanity at its higher levels, we must all lean heavily upon *vicarious* contacts, still *learning from people*, but reaching out to them—to the fine and the great in all times and places—through whatever media will bring us closest. To establish this contact is the function of the humanities.

Interpreted thus, the humanities are not a body of subject matter. They are, rather, a way of approach, a set of purposes. Some subject fields, notably literature and music and the arts, have obvious and direct opportunities to serve the purposes. For poems and songs, sculpture and painting, and the novel and biography and drama have the capacity to move people enormously. Yet mere technical instruction in these fields may have little to do with the humanities ideal. Conversely, in our times, the physical and social sciences and the burgeoning behavioral sciences such as psychology and anthropology may be taught so as to have tremendous humanizing values. And guided experience, through school activities or through service in the community, may for some be most significant of all.

For the humanities are never solely of the intellect, even though they will stretch the intellect to its furthest reaches; always they have to do also with emotions and feelings and ideals, with commitments to goals and cherished values. To "appreciate" a poem is never simply to know what it means, though that is involved; there is always some overtone of moving with the poet in the depth of one's being.

The power to reach the emotions is not peculiar to a few subjects. Science may look more plainly intellectual, while music plays more clearly to the feelings. Yet it is in the sciences that many a youngster, left cold by art, will make his real response to beauty, form his lifelong commitment to truth, or even dedicate himself to serving mankind. If new fire enters a young spirit, what does it matter whether it comes from the lifework of Socrates, Michelangelo, or Beethoven—or from Madame Curie, Lincoln, or Churchill?

What this all adds up to is that we have a tremendous pool of new curricular resources to use for humanities purposes. To see the contrast, put yourself in the shoes of an educator in the centuries before our own. He had almost nothing to use but a handful of classics. Books were scarce, few students had even seen a great work of art or heard a symphony. The natural sciences were rudimentary. Except for history—and that not well developed—the social sciences were virtually untouched. The behavioral sciences were still to be conceived. A meager curriculum it seems. Yet it could produce a Thomas Jefferson with such breadth of mind that at the height of violent crisis, he could lean back and see the whole thing as one phenomenon of the universal: "When, in the course of human events, it becomes necessary for one people. . . . ."

Now we no longer need to depend on literature alone. Even if we did, what a new wealth of resources we should have! The literature of the world lies open before us—all the great heritage of minds and spirits that transcend our own—in the original or in excellent translation. It includes an unprecedented wealth of nonfiction of every conceivable sort, rooted in science, in social thought, and in a steady, reexamination of morality. New, too, is an unequalled resource of materials written directly to children and youth.

The excellent reproduction of art has become so inexpensive that its treasures can be brought to the schoolroom. The splendors of music find their way to us even more easily. Motion pictures and television open out still other resources. If we cannot get from the humanities a greater harvest than they have ever yielded before, it is not that we lack tools for their cultivation. One has a tantalizing sense that a great renaissance should be so easy!

Beyond an Elite. Yet it will not be easy. For we must face up to a task our forefathers never tried. In the spirit of their times they never thought to go beyond an elite. In the spirit of ours we must do our work with all. We must because our experience with democracy and universal education has given us at least some dawning intuition of what the common man can rise to. Yet we also know more than ever before about the great ranges of abilities and interests, and about the impact of social class and every aspect of background. To reach all with the humanities we shall have to make bold use of a tremendous diversity of means.

We have not tried that very much. All too often we act as if the only way to humanities goals is through a few dozen time-hallowed works. If great masses of our children do not hear the message of Shakespeare, we surrender altogether—often on the specious argument that we must not "lower the standards"—and just let them sit there in their alienation. Or we divert them into a curriculum of the ordinary and the "practical." Now it is time to see that the authentic carriers of the humanities are not few, but very numerous; not coming to us only in a few esoteric forms, but rather in immense variety, attuned to children and youth of every shape of ability and interest and background.

Even if we stick to traditional forms, our new teaching devices can open them out to many more students. We have many ways of building easy gradients to the lofty heights. For instance, the boy who gets little from reading *Macbeth* may tune in to it fairly well if he first hears one of the great recordings, or had his imagery stimulated by a motion picture.

But—and this is more fundamental—we must not limit ourselves to the traditional means. We need to hunt for the *moral equivalents* of the great, traditional vehicles.

For instance, week after week on television "The Defenders" presents a powerful plea for our institutions at their best, for freedom and justice and mercy. Does it not have a high element of moral equivalence to, say, the *Areopagitica,* for those who cannot read that lofty work—or even for those who can?

Or, if that is still too far up for some of the urchins who dawdle through our classes, how about "Bonanza"? Yes, I know, it contains violence. But, looked at thoughtfully, it is also a study of maturity and immaturity, of weakness and strength, of the tragedies that spring from twists in human character. It just might "work" as a starting point for some youngsters who can't see why the endless analysis of Hamlet's waverings so fascinates his teacher.

Closer to the school's usual offerings, every librarian knows books for a wide range of tastes. Owen Wister's exciting Western, *The Virginian,* is not generally classed among the hundred great books, but it is a classic study of a fellow who matures into a man. The adult model that emerges would not be bad for many a youngster to grow by, for a while. Or take *And Now Miguel,* the simple and beautiful story of a teen-age farm boy trying to join up with the menfolks. His struggle is a universal of adolescent life. Maybe there are more suitable versions of it for boys from the pavements, but boys and girls need *something* as they work to find themselves.

If even these easy stories are too hard for some—and I suppose they are—where do we look next? I am sure the media are there, waiting for us to use. We can find them if only we can shake off the stereotypes of "greatness" and start thinking of *validity*—validity for a given youngster as he now is.

Outside literature, there are media that make their demands less upon abstract intelligence. We ought to be grateful that one need not be academically smart to fall in love with music. Its resources are infinite, and it is not only the great symphony that has power to lead a person toward beauty and sensitivity and universal truth. Art, too, goes where verbal ability need not follow. Generations of Americans have taken their bearings on Abraham Lincoln, because they had sensitive photographs of that great man.

But one can also go completely outside the "cultural"—even to so lowly a subject as consumer education. You start talking about how to buy a bicycle or a dress and all at once the class can be pondering what's worth working for in the first place. Suddenly, one day, you find yourself in a thoughtful analysis of the place of recreation in life, and how to develop a rich and balanced program. And that may lead to a realistic appraisal of what is possible in the poor part of town; then your "apathetic" adolescents blaze out in righteous indignation on behalf of the underdog. Thus a philosophy of life can be got at in toughly realistic ways, with youngsters who are on poor terms with abstraction.

In Touch with Mankind. The truth is, it is dangerous to stereotype the humanities as a set body of subject matter. When we do, we often fall into mere technical instruction in that subject matter, teaching it for its own sake. We turn the almost-sacred field of literature into an arid waste of analysis and criticism, forgetting what the stuff was written for in the first place. We require everyone to read certain standard pieces, forgetting what good adult reading proves—that there is no one thing in all the world's literature everybody has to like. We fall into serio-comic dogmas about no one's really being educated until he can think in at least two languages. And, altogether, we get into a precious posture that no real writer would have anything to do with.

The humanities have work to do, real work, in a real world, with real people—all of them.

They have the power to help a young person find out what he wants to live *for*, to hammer out a set of values for himself, to work through to purposes that give him a personal meaning. They can help him identify with what is best in this old world of ours, and commit himself.

The humanities can lead a person toward taste and a sense of beauty, toward cherishing the beautiful in at least some of its varied forms. They can help him build resources for a rich inner life, toward inner dignity coupled with recreative fun.

They can help a young person get to know himself, with all his faults and virtues, to dig down into the less conscious wellsprings of his behavior. Getting acquainted with his emotions and his impulses can generate a new acceptance of the whole affective side of his nature and make it available to him as a source of strength. He can win through to a solid self-respect, and he will be free to love and be loved.

The humanities can do this by putting him in touch with all mankind in its whole sweep through history, helping him to identify with the human condition, with all that implies of bliss and sorrow, of success and failure. They can help him get in perspective. With their help he can develop a tough inner fiber to carry him through times of trouble.

They can help him to see things in the large, to hunt for the general answer in the confusion of specifics.

Capacity for Growth. The list could go on, but already the words disappoint me, as they probably do you. It is hard to catch the magic of the humanities in simple sentences. We get highflown, when we mean we just want to help youngsters understand and accept themselves and the people around them, get a better vision of what's possible for themselves and their society, build resources for a life with purpose and true pleasure and quit settling for mediocrity.

Yet maybe it is not altogether bad to give voice to some very high purposes—if we really mean them. For we are not going to get anywhere till we genuinely see that just such things are perfectly, practically possible. The potential for all of them is there, in our children. That is how human beings are. More of them showed it, for a while, in Athens, when the conditions were right. More of them showed it again in the bustling days of the Renaissance and in Elizabethan England. They showed it marvelously when they came to these free shores and moved out on the frontiers and built this nation. It was never any accident, any more than it is an accident that with better nutrition each generation of our babies grows an inch taller.

An inch per generation in all the other dimensions of human goodness would not be a bad goal. Our babies are born with plenty of capacity for the growth. Our job is to see that the conditions are right for growing that unexpected inch.

The Spirit of Humanism

Harold Taylor

The present crisis is less a crisis of culture than of the position we have given to culture. We have set it before and above life, when it ought to be behind and below life—because it is a reaction to life. We must now stop putting the cart before the horse. *Ortega y Gasset*

We have not stopped putting the cart before the horse. We have simply put more into the cart, and we have called it science and the humanities. A culture consists of a body of ideas and values at work within a society, a body of ideas which are assumed to be true and according to which the citizens live. To keep the ideas, that is, the culture, alive and growing, it is necessary that the ideas be re-thought, re-shaped, re-experienced, and placed in a new perspective from year to year and generation to generation by each new entrant into the world. It is the function of education to create the conditions out of which there can be a constant renewal of insight and a re-formulation of ideas and experiences in the personal lives of the young.

The nature of justice for example, has its perennial necessities and modes; these can be found in the classical texts. But justice for the Negro, to choose an idea at random, has its immediate meaning in the lives and attitudes of contemporary Negroes and whites within the context of contemporary society. It is an activity, a series of feelings, ideas and acts which take place in a personal and social context.

To choose another example, the nature and form of the beautiful can be read about and seen in the classical texts and models, but the true nature of art can only be found through immediate experiences, feelings, ideas, and acts that take place in a cultural context.

I want to point to these obvious things before reiterating that Ortega's remark is true and that the American system of education has given a position to culture that divorces it from the living experience of the young. Having separated the world of fact from the world of value, having separated learning from doing, thought from action, science from art, the useful from the liberal, it is then necessary for educators to have a category into which all the values can be put, that is, the humanities. The facts can be assembled into accumulations called the sciences. The values, God help them, go into the humanities.

I suggest that the first thing we have to do is to refuse to make those distinctions and to redefine what is meant by the humanities. The humanities are not culture-containers or value-containers or courses in the higher things. In fact there is no such thing as the humanities, unless one is willing to accept the idea that science is not a humanistic discipline, and that facts have nothing to do with values. Science is an activity of thought whose main characteristic is an insistence on understanding, more precisely than is possible by any other means, the nature of a reality which would otherwise be perceived only dimly and imprecisely. It is a branch of philosophy, the branch that makes theories and investigates phenomena.

It therefore has a great deal to do with philosophy, and it is no accident that the great philosophers of the 19th and 20th centuries have been scientists and that their predecessors thought of science as a form of natural philosophy.

On the other hand, we do have to do something about the kind of raw material of human experience which does not lend itself to being organized into the concepts and categories of the scientific disciplines; we have to deal with matters of the heart, of the senses, of the deepening of consciousness itself. There is a need here for looser categories and less precision of reference, there is a need for ways of putting together the results of personal insight and of spontaneous perception into forms through which one can enter straight into the common experience of man. The artists and writers find forms and categories to do this; the scholars and educators then have to find ways in which the work of artists and writers can be opened up to those who have not thought about what the artists have been thinking about, or have not been interested in what they have been doing.

In this sense the scholars and educators are organizers of experience. At their best, they are sensitive enough and informed enough to put their students into situations in which the ideas and images of painters, playwrights, designers, philosophers, historians, or dancers have a full chance to enter fully the consciousness of the students. This means the engagement of students in the practice of the arts themselves and the confrontation of the student with genuine issues involving genuine intellectual and moral options. The student must face the fact that it is he who must decide the quality of his own response to an object of art, it is he who must judge the worth of an idea within a framework of his own which he must learn how to construct for himself.

The trouble is that in the schools and colleges he is very seldom allowed to do so. Except for a sprinkling of experimental schools and colleges—Putney, Rocky Mountain, Sarah Lawrence, Antioch among them—where the educational program is built explicitly around the idea of personal involvement and confrontation with the issues and ideas, education consists of packaged and supervised learning out of textbooks, anthologies, lectures, surveys, outlines, and other obstacles to thought and insight. All the answers are given before the student has a chance to ask about anything. The organization of knowledge becomes more a matter of administrative convenience than of natural forms which the knowledge itself would take if it were considered to be the creation of ideas by the process of thought and imagination.

We can use the words art, science, history, philosophy, sociology, and literature to describe certain bodies of knowledge which are grouped together by convention, and we can separate the arts and the humanities from science and technology simply by naming them as separate and assembling materials under the proper headings. But these are administrative devices used by scholars and educators for purposes of organization; the names of the subjects do not correspond to the areas of experience which first created them.

Was Socrates talking political science, psychology, Greek literature, or philosophy? He was known as a philosopher but he talked about everything, including education. The point is that he did not think or talk in separate categories. He talked and thought about whatever interested him, and he was interested in enquiry of all kinds. He pursued answers wherever his mind took him. So do novelists, painters, playwrights, and so should students.

I mention Socrates at this point because I can recall a controversy at the University of Wisconsin, when I taught in the philosophy department there, about whether the political science department should be allowed to teach Plato and Hobbes, since Plato and Hobbes belonged to the philosophy courses and it was held that the political science people should stick to their own authors. I suggested that we trade Hobbes for Marx and that we would probably come out ahead.

Then the absurd question for the curriculum becomes, would Plato, taught in the political science department, be part of the student's education in the humanities, or would that just be plain old science, with the student robbed of the exquisite philosophical insight available only in the philosophy department—an agency of learning properly certified as a legitimate source of values rather than of facts? (I occasionally slipped a fact or two into my lectures and discussions, as a gesture of bravado.)

We are face to face here with the idea of education as the administration of courses, an idea at the source of so much educational subversion, with the student standing at the counter of the educational bureaucracy counting up his credits in the humanities so as to be certified as having been made properly aware of the great questions of life and history.

Here is the same cart before the same old horse. The achievement of insight, the ability to distinguish truth from falsehood, to deal seriously with the intricacies and ambiguities of good and evil, beauty and ugliness, is the prime purpose of education in every field. The gigantic body of knowledge accumulated through the ages must be divided, sub-divided, classified, and organized if it is to be at all manageable. But it is the *result* of individual and collective effort, not its cause; it is the means through which new knowledge is created and understood, new and old concepts are re-created, and the purpose in presenting classified parts of it (subjects) to the young is to provide them with the means through which they can learn to enter the stream of cultural and social history without having to collect the entire body of knowledge all over again. That body is the instrument for creative and analytical thinking. It exists as the material for learning, not merely as material to be learned.

My proposal is, therefore, that we return to the root of the matter, in the quality and intensity of experience available to the race, and that we consider the problem of education in the humanities not to be a problem in the administration of a separate set of courses in a separate section of a curriculum of study, but as the creation and enhancement of the spirit of humanism throughout the whole curriculum and the entire environment of the school, college, and surrounding culture. In the time of the Renaissance, it was the creation of new modes of perception and sensibility by poets, writers, painters, composers, architects, and thinkers which broke the chains of orthodox philosophy and the conventional social wisdom. The spirit of humanism, then as now, is found in the sensibility of the artist, the scholar, the student, and the citizen, all of them combined as creator, critic, audience, and learner, each with his own true function, each learning from the other, each willing to accept anything human as the proper study and concern of man.

Herbert Read has a clear way of putting it when he speaks of the necessity to preserve the natural intensity of all modes of perception and sensation. The sheer delight in perceiving objects and ideas which delight, the intellectual excitement of apprehending ideas which make a difference to the way one looks at oneself and at the world, the aesthetic elation of carrying out work of one's own in science, in art, in society, or organizing a body of knowledge which has personal meaning—these are the values which the schools must seek and around which the curriculum must be formed. The curriculum is the whole atmosphere; it is not subjects and a syllabus. Its qualities are determined by what the students are encouraged to do and how the teacher teaches, how he chooses the variety of experiences through which his students move. These decisions on his part are determined by the quality of his own sensibility and the intensity of his own concern.

I am speaking here not necessarily about 'inspiring' teachers although we certainly need them in profusion, but of teachers who are themselves sensitive to the values and inner meanings of the arts and sciences and who can find their own ways to involve the student in the process of developing his own sensibility. In this case there is no reason, within certain limits, why every student should possess the same body of knowledge. What each man knows is what he has paid a price for learning, what he has invested himself in knowing, what he has found for himself, and this can, should, and does vary from person to person, depending on his personal circumstances and the influences surrounding him. The task is to surround the young with beneficent and provocative influences, the kind which incite the intellect and feelings into action.

Accordingly, when we talk about the arts and the humanities in America, and speak of organizations of government like the National Endowment for the Arts and the Humanities, we are saying in general terms that new forms of organization are now necessary if the arts and sciences are to flourish in the spirit of humanism and not in terms of the accumulation and distribution of information about objects and ideas. The only place in which a fundamental attitude to the arts and the humanities in America can be created and long-run support can be developed lies in the educational system. When we examine it closely, we can see that one of our difficulties lies in anti-aesthetic and, in many ways, anti-intellectual content of the curricula of the high schools and universities. The creative arts are pushed out of the high school curriculum in favor of those subjects necessary for gaining admission to college from high school and to graduate school from college. Students whose talents lie in the creative arts are systematically excluded from instruction in the American high school and college.

Where is there room for the students whose gifts are not purely scholastic? Where is there room for the child who loves to paint, to sculpt, to sing, to act, to compose, to write, to dance, to celebrate his personal joy? Or, for that matter, where is there in the educational system a concern for the majority of American children whose interest and aptitudes in the arts are not yet formed and who need for their personal development that kind of direct experience with the arts which alone can nourish their sensibilities and cultivate in them a devotion to cultural values?

Instead of that concern in the schools, we find barren wastes of academic subject matter and a system of academic rewards for those who can do the tests. We select for further education those who possess certain verbal skills which have a partial correlation with intelligence. When the educational system is reviewed year by year from nursery school to graduate school, we find a continuing and mounting attack on the possibility of aesthetic education. Almost the last chance for the child to enjoy the arts in an educational institution lies in the nursery school, and, even here, there are people who are entering the field armed with tests and devices to see how quickly the children can be taught to read, in preparation for taking more of the tests which depend on reading and determine one's degree of that kind of scholastic aptitude which is currently identified with intelligence. Very early in the elementary grades, the external values of the socity begin to impose themselves on the curriculum and the children, and the child who wishes to be successful must adapt himself to certain norms determined by the demands of the society. None of these demands, at this point, has to do with the demonstration of aesthetic sensitivity.

The point is made with much elegance by William Stafford in a poem entitled simply, "Lit Instructor."

> Day after day, up there beating my wings
> With all of the softness truth requires
> I feel them shrug whenever I pause.
> They class my voice among tentative
> things,
> And they credit fact, force, battering.
> I dance my way toward the family of
> knowing,
> Embracing stray error as a long-lost boy
> And bringing him home with my flut-
> tering . . .

The truth of the artist does require softness, sympathy, concern, and a certain kind of attention which, if not given, renders his truth unavailable to his audience. That this attention is seldom given in the high school and colleges is to be explained by the fact that it is so seldom asked for. One can imagine the examination questions which would afflict the student who has "studied" Stafford's poem. Why is error like a long-lost boy? Compare Stafford's style with Robert Frost's. Can you feel a shrug?

The course of instruction in the literary arts is a continual stream of interruptions in the student's learning, interruptions to enquire of him what he has remembered. The student therefore becomes accustomed to listening and thinking in one dimension, from which the aesthetic is excluded.

Confirmation of these conditions is to be found when we look at the curriculum of the American high school as it now exists. Professor Richard Miller, of the University of Kentucky, has given us a brief survey of the role of the humanities in the high schools through two questionnaires, one sent to each of the departments of education in the separate states, the other to each school listed by the state departments as schools which offer work in the humanities.

The questionnaire to the state departments asked three questions. The first was whether the departments were publishing materials for the schools about the humanities; five of the departments replied "yes," 47 replied "no," and two did not answer the question. The five were Florida, Missouri, Pennsylvania, Puerto Rico, and Virginia. It is fair to deduce from this that the state departments have not taken an active part in establishing humanities programs in their high schools.

The second question had to do with whether the state department knew of humanities programs in the schools of their states and, if so, which schools they considered as offering good courses in the field. Thirty-one states answered "yes," twenty replied "no," and three indicated that they had no knowledge of such a course being taught in their state. Of the thirty-one states where courses are offered, most of them lie in the eastern half of the country, mainly in the northeastern section.

The third question asked for an estimate of the direction in which interest in the humanities is moving, particularly since 1960. Thirty-seven answered "increased"; thirteen states answered "about the same"; four states made no indication. Another part of the question asked for the interest expected from 1965 to 1970. Forty-three states answered that an increase was expected; five, "about the same"; six states gave no indication. Of the thirty-one states which replied "yes" to the question of whether humanities courses were being taught within their school systems, all noted an increase in the interest either at present or in the future.

Some reasons for the increased interest were given; for example, more attention is being paid to the needs of individual students, national publicity, and conferences reflecting new interests in the humanities in general, and a need to bring about a better balance in the present curriculum. While these reasons were dominant, others said that materials from the humanities were being read and discussed in greater measure as a result of Project English; a new emphasis upon literature and history was coupled with a tendency to identify the "educated man" as one who was familiar with the great books; more school systems were now asking for information about the humanities. One state department replied that "apparently this is another of those cycles that education and society must go through. Usually it takes a decade to get it out of their system." We can be happy that at least in one state we can count with certainty on the American habit of throwing out the baby with the bath water.

When we turn to the actual humanities courses in the schools, we find several things; first that the courses are to be found mainly in the larger schools, those between 1700 and 1800 students, where there is greater faculty specialization and more flexibility in the teaching programs; second, that the definition of the humanities as an educational category is in need of serious criticism and reformation. Since the questionnaire itself assumed that the definition of the humanities had to do with course offerings in the field of philosophy, history, art, or the great books, it was natural that the replies would be put in those terms. The listing of other course titles were, for example, "Society and the Arts," "American Civilization," "Arts and Man," "Essential Ideas," and "History of Western Thought." For the majority of the schools, the humanities course is defined as a study of the allied arts, or a combination of the allied arts, concepts, and philosophy. Most of the courses have been initiated since 1960.

A further analysis of the replies shows that only a small minority of the students were enrolled in the humanities courses, usually they were electives for those going on to college and they were elected by juniors and seniors considered to be superior students. The courses were for the most part taught by English teachers. Those in philosophy were taught usually by teachers who had taken a major in history or philosophy, or had had some graduate or undergraduate work in philosophy. The great books teachers have usually taken their major field as English literature, and the average course in the humanities was taught by four teachers, most frequently with majors in English, art, music, and history of the social sciences.

According to Professor Miller, the obstacles to an expansion of the humanities curriculum consist mainly in the inadequate preparation of teachers, the fact that the high school curriculum is already jammed to the full with existing subjects, and that most teachers think of the humanities in terms of loosely related anthologies containing fragments of literature, philosophy, and social criticism. In those cases in which new work in the field could be identified as promising and relevant, teachers had developed programs similar to those now being developed by Educational Services Incorporated, where the main emphasis is shown by titles such as "A Pilot Project in the Study of Mankind," "Myth and Art as Teaching Materials," "Society and the Arts."

It is clearly time to reconsider the entire matter of the high school curriculum, not merely as an exercise in the re-adjustment of course offerings to achieve a "better balance," but as a means of going deep in cultural and social questions which concern the development of a modern American society. Our national goals have been, and are being, determined not by the creative thinking and actions of statesmen, politicians, social scientists, philosophers, or educators but by the exigencies of short-term national reactions to events and the forces of economic, political, and military history. When the Second World War ended and the societies of the world fell into a new era, it was at first assumed that the role of the United States was one in which the ideas of liberal democracy could be established on a world-wide scale. The hostility of the Soviet Union to those ideas and the mutual antagonisms between states in a revolutionary period of world history forced the United States into a defensive posture from which it has not yet recovered. The educational system and the entire society were put to work to sustain a national goal of economic, political and military security. That goal, as imposed upon the society by a variety of means, has in my judgment badly damaged the ability of the American people to respond generously, imaginatively, and creatively to the reality of America's position in the world and to the circumstances of world politics.

The schools and universities have thus become instruments of national policy rather than innovators of social change. In a culture dominated by the mass media presently used as tools in the engineering of various kinds of consent—in matters of taste, political ideology, foreign policy, and cultural values—the educational system has seemed powerless to set in motion a flow of ideas and programs which can counteract the trend toward social and political conservatism. It is this phenomenon which I see reflected in the present curriculum of the American high school, and it is here that a major reform must begin, stretching back into the teachers' colleges, the universities, and into their supporting political institutions.

When we speak of the humanities we are speaking of an area of concern which makes all social, moral, and cultural questions a matter for new and continuing enquiry. It involves the application of science to the use and benefit of man, not to his manipulation and destruction. It involves the liberation of new powers of the intellect and imagination by the enjoyment of the infinite varieties of art. It involves some relatively simple things in education, for example the involvement of the American students in the arts themselves, involvement in the making of political decisions through which the national goals can be reshaped in a manner more in keeping with the claims of American democracy.

We can take hope in the fact that already there are new forces stirring on the campuses and in the schools. They are the forces of a new generation impatient of its elders, prepared to protest, ready to take initiatives. Theirs is a protest against the whole standardized pattern of American values, for which the standardized, sterilized educational system is the main transmission agent. Some members of that generation have left college and school in order to act as members of a reform movement for the whole of society, the arts and all. They are the ones who already have a serious interest in the arts which they did not get from the educational system. They are writing their own poems, building their own curriculum for Negro children, composing and playing their own music, organizing their own theater to play before audiences in the South who have never seen live theater, mimeographing their own literary magazines, writing their own research on social and political problems. I see no reason why, with the variety and wealth of talent in the arts displayed daily by the younger generation, we cannot do them the honor of including these vital aspects of their present lives in the curricula of our schools and colleges. They should not be forced to give up art and creative thinking simply because they enter an institution of education.

Rationale and Definition of the Humanities

New York State Education Department

In our society, as in many before ours, the members are attempting to define and illuminate the fundamental aspirations and ideals of mankind.

We have seen, in recent years, a renewed interest on the part of the public in those areas which have to do with the expression of man's ideals—the humanities. Some thinkers despair of the democratic opening of academic and cultural opportunities to the masses. They fear that it will result in the debasement and destruction of man's great works. Neither are they confident of the ability of the schools to help the new pursuers of knowledge to understand, appreciate, and respect man's achievement. By making *man's expressive works in all its forms* available to an unprecedented extent and by providing all of our people with at least the basic intellectual equipment to understand and respond to it, many of us expect the realization of a fulfilled life.

We Americans are basically healthy minded people. We know that we have accomplished miracles and we live in the confident expectation that we will accomplish many more. The extent to which our schools rise to the issue will determine whether the people will enjoy the best that we have to offer, or obliterate cultural values by demanding less.

According to Alfred North Whitehead, "Culture is activity of thought, and receptiveness to beauty and humane feeling." While one's own thought activity is important, an interest in that of others is essential. Likewise the humane feeling must be toward others.

The second aspect of "activity of thought" is the ability to use one's mind as a critical and analytic tool, a tool capable of probing evidence and arriving at sound conclusions, sound in terms not only of positive or negative answers but also of *suspended judgment.*

What we know about anything directly relates to the way we behave about it. *It is important to know, but it is even more important to know what to do with what we know.* It is for this reason that many have found enriching experiences in the humanities. There are few, if any, subjects which are things in themselves. *Everything that a human being learns should be a vital part of that system which forms the framework of his personal culture.*

In most schools the different subjects are generally taught as if they were unrelated to each other, and as if the principal purpose of learning the subject was to pass examinations. The humanities approach acts on broader terms and seeks to acquaint the student with the thoughts, creations, and actions of his predecessors and contemporaries. It interrelates every area of knowledge to *form a comprehensive and vital whole.* The purpose is not the mere accumulation of factual material, but the determination of Self by the student.

The humanities approach leads the student to think about *values.* It establishes principles of freedom and responsibility. He learns that, within certain limits, men have choices among alternatives; that these choices should be made carefully and thoughtfully; that making a choice is an act; and that acts have consequences.

Definition. Before a school establishes a humanities program, a working definition of the humanities should be agreed upon. While each definition will be similar, none need be identical. Following is a catalogue of definitions which should encourage the processes of browsing, sorting, discussing, selecting, and ultimately deciding upon a definition suitable for one particular program.

The literature, past and present, abound in a variety of interpretations. One can discover the poetic ". . . life itself, caught on the wing by those superlative marksmen we call poets, thinkers, historians, painters, and composers" (Clifton Fadiman); the specific ". . .negatively, the humanities are those areas which are not included in the sciences, mathematics, and the social sciences. . .the humanities embrace literature, languages, history, music, art and philosophy" (Charles Keller); the curt ". . . humanities education is values education"; and the humorous ". . . we believe in something we cannot delimit." Probably the only safe working definition of the humanities is this: "You know horses–cows are different." (Howard Mumford Jones)

One accepted fact is that the "humanities" derive from a philosophical concept "humanism." Humanism, according to Ralph Barton Perry, ". . . is a gospel, cultural movement or educational program which originated in Europe in the twelfth century and idealized man." In practice, humanism considers man and his expressive works deserving of admiration and study. Historically, it was inspired by the renewed interest in antiquity and a rejection of some concepts of the Middle Ages.

The term "humanities" was first used in the Renaissance to describe the works of the classic writers, *letterae humaniores,* more humane literature. Humanism turned man away from the relative Medieval disregard for external human accomplishment, which he undervalued especially when it stood in contrast to God-orientated virtuous accomplishment.

The education of modern man was centered in the humanities until the present century when a materialistic society brought about an emphasis on specialized and technological studies. Very recently, concern over world tensions has promoted a re-examination of the values generally held by man. It is believed by many that the curriculum of our educational institutions should be redirected to a strengthening of the humanities as a means of giving meaning and purpose to life today.

To this end, contemporary thinkers are attempting a redefinition of the word. Man has the individualistic and ambiguous nature indicative of his versatility; therefore, we need not be surprised at the variety of definitions and the controversy they promote.

In the *Report of the Commission on the Humanities,* the definition of the humanities holds that they may be regarded. . .*as a body of knowledge and insight*–which usually includes the study of languages, literature, history, and philosophy; the history, criticism, and the theory of art and music; and the history and comparison of religion and law; the natural sciences and the social sciences are considered as natural allies; *as modes of expression*–the fine and the performing arts (painting, sculpture, cinema-photography, architecture, music, dance, and drama)–are modes of expressing thoughts and feelings visually, verbally, and aurally; *as a program for education*–the method is one based on the liberal tradition we inherit from classical antiquity; and *as an underlying attitude toward life*–which centers on concern for the human individual: for his emotional development, for his moral, religious, and aesthetic ideas, and for his goals–*including in particular his growth as a rational being and a responsible member of his community.*

We can see, in the broad interpretation, several of the problem areas that concern present-day speakers for the humanities; i.e., the relationship of the physical and social sciences; the emphasis on a study of works from antiquity; the inclusion of Far-Eastern studies; the difference in approaches to understanding–through performance or vicarious experience; feelings versus ideas; and the ultimate goal of humanistic studies–the individual *or* society or both.

For Ralph Barton Perry the humanities embrace "...whatever influences conduce to freedom,...any agency or relationship or situation or activity which has a humanizing, that is, a liberalizing effect, which broadens learning, stimulates imagination, kindles sympathy, inspires a sense of human dignity, and imprints that bearing and form of intercourse proper to a man...."

In his definition there can be no limitation in terms of discipline. In fact, we should no longer use such curriculum construction terms as "fusion," "correlation," and "broad fields" when discussing methods of subject matter integration in the humanities. There is no discipline without meaning in the study of Man and they constitute a whole rather than a fragmented association. The "sciences" are a part of the "matrix from which he springs...this he surveys and appropriates by knowledge, utilizes for the realization of ideals, adorns and enjoys through his sense of beauty, stands upon and peers beyond."

Wolfgang Stechow supports this stand when he discusses art as a humanity, "...there is no such thing as bringing art down to the human level, but only an elevating of art to the human level, since mystic vagueness is surely not to be considered on a superhuman level. A humanistic approach to art therefore involves familiarity with many other aspects which are indissolubly connected with the human realm, such as technical problems, problems of individual interpretation...."

President Kennedy eloquently spoke for the arts in these words:

It's hardly an accident that Robert Frost coupled poetry and power. For he saw poetry as the means of saving power from itself. When power leads man toward arrogance, poetry reminds him of his limitations. When power narrows the areas of man's concern, poetry reminds him of the richness and diversity of his existence. When power corrupts, poetry cleanses. For art establishes the basic truths which serve as the touchstones of our judgment. The artist, however faithful to his personal vision of reality, becomes the last champion of the individual mind and sensibility against an intrusive society and an officious state.

To those who would exclude a study of the effects of the sciences on man a traditional definition of a man "devoted to seeking out and restoring to general esteem the humane letters of antiquity..." would seem to apply. In the extreme, proponents of this view restrict themselves to a study of the history of art, music, and certain literary works. If the goal of a humanistic education is to increase one's capacity for freedom, his "...exercise of enlightened choice," then any definition that excludes such important areas as science and the Eastern civilizations considerably weakens humanism.

The problem of "feeling-knowing," emotions versus ideas, the subjective and the objective has been presented by Earl S. Johnson in his discussion of the common subject matter of the social studies and the humanities. They are the feelings, sentiments, opinions, standards, and ideals of man. The difference between the social studies and humanities approaches is in the bringing of "...particular men and women to our direct acquaintance through intimate understanding" by the humanities and the seeking "to convert such understandings into formal generalizations" by the social studies. He finds support for the primacy of emotions in human conduct in quotations from: David Hume, "reason ought to be the slave of the passions"; Santayana, "ultimate truths are more easily and more adequately conveyed by poetry than by analysis"; Pascal, "the heart hath its reasons which reason doth not know"; William James, "our judgments concerning the worth of things, big or little, depend on the *feelings* the things arouse in us. Where we judge a thing to be precious in consequence of the idea we form of it, this is only because the idea is itself associated already with a feeling...wherever there is a conflict of opinion and difference of vision, we are bound to believe that the truer side is the side that feels the more, and not the side that feels the less"; and finally John Dewey has said: "There is no thought lest it be enkindled by an emotion."

Ralph Barton Perry finds a basis for resolving the polarity of views in this argument just as he found one for the inclusion of the sciences. He says: "In the design of natural man the head and the heart are not only parts of a whole, they are functionally interdependent. Neither means anything without the other, anymore than a steering gear means anything without an engine or an engine without a steering gear. The real issue is not intellect versus emotion, but intellect *and* emotion—the one for the benefit of the other...."

Obviously, the humanities can serve as a source for introspective study of the Self or as a source for defining one's relationship to Society or for both. There are speakers for all points of view. Marguerite V. Hood's definition seems to take the individualistic view, "the humanities are subject areas which deal with *man as a human being,* with the development of his ideas through the successive periods in the history of the world, with the things which influenced those ideas and with the cultural creations, intellectual or artistic, which grew out of those ideas." And Nathan M. Pusey considers "...true mental growth, it seems, can come duly from contact with great and original ideas as they have operated in the minds of exceptional individuals...every human being needs direct personal contact with the great stories, myths, and fictions of the human race, and with history, to begin to know himself and to sense the potentialities that lie within his reach...." The "search for self" aspects of the humanities are summed up in the oft-quoted questions *"Who am I? Where have I come from? Where am I going? Why? What is the meaning of life?"*

The humanities as a solution to societal problems is advocated by Gerald Else in his principles of (1) the political idea—that men engage in free discussion to determine the nature of the political institutions by which they choose to live; (2) the free operation of the mind; and (3) moral responsibility: a concept which limits freedom of men and institutions to actions that are good.

For most, though, the benefits that accrue from a humanistic study are seen in both the individual and the society in which he interacts. As Clifton Fadiman says, "It has become terrifyingly apparent that, not a few, but enormous numbers of citizens must be so educated that they can take their places in a fantastically complex world, and help, each in his own way, to run it. The problems of production and distribution are, clearly enough, going to be solved; it is the problems of *government* and *self-development* that will engage the attention of tens of millions during the coming century."

Humanities: A Question of Values

Jerry L. Walker

In his new book, *Urban Schooling* (Harcourt, 1968), Herbert Rudman wrote the following:

> Today, the role of the American school in society is clear. The society must provide equal opportunity for all members to participate responsibly and productively, while the school must equip its students with the knowledge and skills needed to function productively and must cooperate with other social agencies to instill the values that will allow the fruitful participation of all the people. Anything short of this invites disaster and the end of America as we know it. (p. 4)

I will readily admit that there are days when I would just as soon see an end to the "America as we know it," given its easy tolerance of the discrepancy between the American dream and the American reality and its grass-roots acceptance of racism, materialism, and militarism. With all of its weaknesses, though, I still believe America offers mankind the greatest hope of fulfillment and is therefore worth saving. But if it is to be saved and its potential realized, the schools must indeed accomplish the tasks that Rudman named—the teaching of knowledge and skills and the teaching of values.

Contrary to what our critics say, we have done a rather good job of teaching productive knowledge and skills to the majority of our youth. Our technology has not sprung from ignorance and ineptitude. That is not to say that we could not do a more efficient job of reaching a larger percentage of our population. We could, and we are working on that. Where we have failed—and failed miserably—is in the teaching of values. Oh, we have rewarded students who demonstrated that cleanliness is next to Godliness, that silence is golden, or that patience is a virtue. We have even punished those who thought otherwise. But we have not taught our students how to identify their values, how to evaluate them, or how to change them. As a result, we have produced a lot of learned bigots.

This is where a humanities program can make its greatest contribution. The proper studies of the humanities are those uniquely human activities, the creation and use of symbols. So far as we know, man is the only animal capable of symbol-making. It is that ability that allows him to reflect on his past, record his present, and imagine his future. The aim of it all is control. Man can control what he can order, and he orders through the use of symbols. Man orders in a preferred way, and his symbols reflect that preference. Any study of man's symbols will therefore be a study of what he prefers, that is, what he values.

Whatever man invents can be viewed as a symbol: his language, his artifacts, his institutions, his forms of recreation, and his means of subsistence. As symbols, they necessarily reflect values or preferences. Take language, for instance. There are some Indian tribes and South Sea Islanders whose languages contain no means of expressing past or future tense. That does not mean, as some people assume, that theirs are underdeveloped languages. It means only that those people have developed languages that express the way they prefer to think of time. There is no past for them, only the present. In those cultures, there is little evidence of remorse, or even hope. How could there be, with no past or future to contend with? One has to assume that those people have developed languages that express their values, and to them the present is of great value.

Take our own language, which contains several ways to signal past, present, and future. We obviously prefer to think in those terms. We believe in the continuity of time, and we value it. If we did not, Original Sin would not be such a lingering spiritual malaise. How many times did we hear Hubert Humphrey speak about the continuity in government? Consider also our language preference for the active voice. English teachers are constantly telling students to recast a passive construction into an active one. Certainly that is a reflection on our values. We would rather do than be done. We value the active man.

If you consider our homes as symbols, it becomes clear that we value convenience, comfort, privacy, cleanliness, easy upkeep, and moderate durability. A look at our schools shows that, among other things, we value tradition, role authority, book learning, sports, punctuality, perseverance, and neat classes of people and material. Our games reveal competing values—cooperation and competition. We urge people to work together on a team and then pit the teams against one another. Our institution of marriage shows that we value possession, responsibility, security, male authority, and contractual commitment. Take a look at our jobs, and you find we value ingenuity, speed, convenience, and coffee breaks. In whatever we arrange, we express our values.

Usually we accept the values of the group or groups to which we belong, but not always. Nowhere is this clearer than in the art we produce. Considering art can be a fascinating study in values, for you find in it not only group values, but the artist's comment on those values. That is true whatever the medium and whatever the period. Whether a work of art be a painting, a play, a sculpture, or a dance, it reveals something about the values men held at the time. Put a Mondrian next to a Rembrandt and the contrasting values become obvious, as they would if you contrasted a Shakespearean sonnet with an e. e. cummings' poem.

Not only does man create things to symbolize his values; he also selects objects from the natural world and gives them symbolic value, and that symbolic value is usually recorded in his language and art. Consider the statements "solid as a rock," "strong as an ox," "delicate as a rose," and "sly as a fox." Consider paintings of a sunset or sunrise, of a turbulent or calm sea, of a pastoral scene, and what they symbolize. Notice the symbolic difference between catching a trout and catching a marlin, or the difference between killing a lion and killing a jackal. And what values are men operating on when they select such emblems as doves, eagles, and wolverines for their crests? Much can be learned about man's values, both his hierarchy of values and conflicting values, from a study of the natural objects he bestows with symbolic value.

The point of all this is, of course, that the study of values is in a real sense the study of man. He is the only animal capable of thinking beyond his immediate drives and a presented stimulus. He can consciously modify his behavior in preferred ways. He expresses those preferences through his behavior and through his symbols. To know man, to predict how he will behave, or to change his behavior, one must know what he values. That should be the content of a humanities course.

A humanities program should take up where the disciplines leave off. Let the mathematicians teach their symbols and how to use them. Let the chemistry teacher, the biology teacher, the home economics teacher, the shop teacher, the art teacher, and the music teacher do the same. Yes, and even let the English teacher teach the knowledge and skills involved in using language in its communicative and expressive contexts. But once those teachers have done, let the humanities teacher lead the investigation of the values associated with the use of those symbols.

Here are some of the questions that might be studied in a humanities course. Is there a natural order in the world? What is to be gained from assuming either that there is a natural order or that there is not a natural order? When did the idea first gain popularity? What effect has it had on man's development? How do modern scientists view natural order? Where in literature can you find acceptance of the idea of natural order? Where in art? Where would modern architects stand on the issue? What are some of the objects man has used to symbolize natural order? What symbolizes natural order to you? If you accept the idea of natural order, what are the implications for the way you live your life? There are, of course, hundreds of similar questions that could be asked about the same topic, all of which would require that students draw upon their knowledge of the past and present and end up with a clearer view of their own values. Whether they change their values or not, they will at least have to identify and consider them. That, I think, should be the main purpose of a humanities program, a purpose that is very different from most of our existing humanities programs.

As chairman of the NCTE Humanities Conference that was held in Chicago last spring, I had the opportunity to look over about a hundred course descriptions of humanities courses being conducted throughout the country, and I also had the opportunity to listen to the assembled teachers discuss what they considered to be the content of their courses. What I found missing in both the written descriptions and the live discussions was any great concern for teaching values. Most existing humanities courses seem to be conceived of as just more of the same survey courses, variously called American studies, cultural epochs, great ideas, or aesthetics.

In most cases, American studies amounts to little more than a new name for the same old content, American history and American literature. The fusion seems to exert greatest influence on the selection of materials. The history teacher teaches those historically important political documents that have literary value, and the English teacher teaches those works of literature that are relevant to America's political and historical development. These courses are usually organized chronologically, and they emphasize those periods with which the particular teachers involved are most familiar. There are, of course, some good things that could be said about American studies programs, but among them is not the fact that they do much to sensitize students to their own humanity.

The same thing could be said for most courses organized by cultural epochs. Although these courses tend to be much broader in scope than American studies courses, they often amount to little more than the study of the modes of expression popular during a particular period. A more comprehensive view of man, including his art, his literature, his architecture, his dances, and his music, is generally given, but the objective is usually to teach the facts, not to evaluate them. Seldom does the study lead to an investigation of the values characteristic of a period or a man, and even less often to a contrastive study of values then and now.

Humanities courses devoted to a study of great ideas have great potential, but if the published course descriptions and teachers' comments are any indication, their potential is seldom realized. In many schools the great ideas course is little more than a chronological survey of the great thinkers of the past, with the emphasis on learning who they were, what they thought, and what they wrote. In fact, this course sometimes goes by the name "Great Books." Far from a study of the social, political, and religious forces that contributed to the genesis of great ideas, or from a consideration of the value-shifts that usually precede and follow the advent of a new idea, these courses are often little more than memory sources for kids who someday might be contestants on the G. E. College Bowl.

A fourth kind of humanities course now popular is one called aesthetics. The popularity of these courses has grown with the influence of the new critics. The new critics assume that a piece of art achieves structural unity through the interrelationships of the parts to each other and to the whole. In order to fully appreciate a work of art, then, one must be able to identify all the parts, see their relationship to each other and the whole, and account for the unity. Some critics talk about levels of response, with the unconscious, "gut-level" response being the lowest and the conscious, intellectual response the highest. The emphasis in these courses is usually on teaching about works of art—their forms, their media, their techniques—so that students will develop taste or, to use Harry Broudy's term, "enlightened cherishing." The very nature of these courses demands that the attention be focused on the object, which is all right so long as after what is "out there" has been comprehended it is used to reflect on what is "in here."

Perhaps I have exaggerated the case against existing humanities courses, but I do not think so. It seems to me that if humanities courses are to have a legitimate place in the school curriculum, they must go beyond the mere teaching of knowledge and skills. Existing courses already so that. The fact that they cut across subject-matter lines and utilize team teaching is not enough to justify their existence.

In our carefully tracked schools where kids of different abilities and interests never get together, we need a forum where students can come together to examine the values that both unite them and keep them apart. Few of us are fully aware of our values or of how our values affect our behavior. Humanities courses could perform an essential service if they would, indeed, force students to recognize and evaluate their values. The easiest way to uncover values is through a study of the symbols that are incorporated in all areas of human behavior. Such a study, I suggest, might save humanity.

Encounter with the Humanities

R. F. Arragon

My purpose is to examine the claim of the late Ernst Cassirer, German intellectual historian and philosopher, that "art and history are the most powerful instruments of our inquiry into human nature" (*Essay on Man*). A similar perhaps not so extravagant claim is implicit in the classification of the study of these fields of thought and expression as "humanities"–a term originating in the description during the Italian Renaissance of the literature of Greek and especially Latin antiquity as the "more humane letters." Their devotees were the humanists, who directed their scholarship to the revival and popularization of the writings of Cicero, Livy, and Virgil and Plato, Herodotus and the Greek tragedians. In these, they found the expression of humanity (*humanitas*), the quality of civilized man, and therefore the means of cultivating this quality. Such literature, the *bonae litterae* of the gentleman and scholar in the universities of the 16th and 17th centuries, came to be the standard works, known as the "classics" since used in the classes of the schools. Today, they are among the "Great Books." They were not limited to what we call literature as *belles-lettres* (that of beauty)–epic, dramatic and lyric poetry, satire and oratory-but included history and philosophy. Note the definition used on the establishment of a professorship of "Humanities" at Columbia University in 1794, which included "the opinions of the ancient philosophers, the religion, government, law, policy, customs and manners of Greece and Rome: the whole designed to explain and elucidate ancient learning and to facilitate acquisition of liberal knowledge."

The emphasis among the Italian humanists, as in this definition, was more upon the good or moral (i.e., the liberal or liberating effects), the love of virtue, than upon the beautiful or what came to be called since the 18th century the aesthetic, though Renaissance humanists did not neglect the importance of the study of classical languages and writings for encouraging the mastery of the means of thought and expression, chiefly on the model of Latin. Rhetoric was, however, not merely for effect. It shaped the thought–as well as the expression, and so the study of classical literature shaped the mind, opening up problems of politics and other fields for exploration and offering worthy models of thought and action.

The Socratic injunction "Know thyself" challenged Petrarch and other early humanists. To know thyself was not only to take stock of one's own capacities so as to make the most successful use of them for a career. It was also to understand the nature of man and to evaluate those qualities which made him worthwhile to himself and to others. To Petrarch the pursuit of literature was an avenue to virtue, and a younger contemporary, Vergerio, after calling those studies liberal "which are worthy of a free man," described moral philosophy as "in a peculiar sense a liberal art, in that its purpose is to teach men the secret of true freedom." The cultivation of the pagan authors was justified by Leonardo Bruni on the ground that "Morals indeed have been treated by the noblest intellects of Greece and Rome." Neither then or later was there any serious difficulty in reconciling Homer and Plato,

Cicero, and Virgil, Seneca and Plutarch with Christian morality. The moral purpose of teaching and reading literature became a tenet of the humanistic tradition which was never entirely neglected and has been revived by recent champions of the humanities as a remedy for the moral uncertainties in the present world.

The term "Good Literature" is, however, no longer confined to that of the ancients. At first, "modern" works were admitted only grudgingly, except as textbooks on grammar or rhetoric or handbooks in logic and philosophy. Erasmus' *Colloquies*, written, like most of the textbooks of the 16th century, in Latin, was an early exception. The writings of Burton and More and of some English poets were recognized as possible university materials but only in a light course for students not taking a degree. With the rise of scholarly interest in English and other languages in the eighteenth, and particularly in the nineteenth century, these literatures elbowed their way into American college curricula alongside Latin and Greek and by the last quarter of the nineteenth century were gaining the upper hand. They too were becoming "classics" and instruments of the purposes Erasmus had described in the sixteenth century: "Without languages and polite learning all branches of study are numb, speechless, almost blind; states languish, and life loses its value; man is hardly man at all."

Such was the educational ideal of the civilized man—the man of the upper classes of the cities of Renaissance Europe and of the landed aristocracy which frequented the cities. It was the ideal set-up both for the courtier of the Italian princely court and for the English Christian gentleman.

Erasmus' word "polite" suggests something more than the love of virtue and even the effective mastery of speech and writing, though the common present application to social relations is too narrow and artificial for the seriousness of this Dutch humanist's use of the word. Yet "polish" in the Renaissance did belong to social manners and to literary style. "Besides goodness," said Castiglione in *The Courtier,* "the true and principal ornament of the mind in every man are letters." They were the source of delight. Letters were not only "good" (*bonae*) but "beautiful" (*belles*). It was a long way to the modern distinction of art from craft and from practical life as the manifestation of pure form, art for art's sake, the aesthetic as a special category of feeling; but an important step had been taken in the distinction of ornamental beauty from goodness in literature.

This century-long development was encouraged also by the change of status given in the Renaissance to the visual arts. They did not at once become "humanities" but they were elevated from the manual to the liberal arts. The Renaissance painter, sculptor, and architect were no longer servants or salaried employees but artists who were given personal recognition and patronage for their special talent by church and nobility, as they seldom were in the Middle Ages. Their activity was theoretical as well as practical, for the principles of perspective and human proportions had to be explored and the mind stored with images, or ideas, of beauty in which were included the examples made available by the discovery of the antique. The arts became *belli arti,* or fine arts, and for education in them there arose in 16th century Italy academies of art, as the rivals of apprenticeship in the master's workshop or studio. The prestige of the artist and of the fine arts was such that an observer's knowledge of painting and sculpture and even some skill in practice, especially in the art of drawing, was recognized as worthy of free men and particularly of courtiers by Castiglione in the book on *The Courtier* already quoted in regard to literature. Similar developments took place in the recognition, patronage, and education of musicians and in the prestige of music as an avocation for gentlemen and an embellishment of the court of a prince. Connoisseurship in music and in the fine arts as well as in literature became a mark of the civilized elite.

Only after the middle of the 19th century (100 years ago) did the fine arts and music enter university and college curricula in America both in professional schools of music connected with universities and, for nonprofessionals, in the liberal arts as courses in history, criticism, and appreciation. In this respect, the arts developed a scholarship comparable to the humanistic scholarship in literature, alongside of which they have taken their place, in one way or another, in the humanities. Scholarship in the arts (in contrast with technique and creativity, whose status as a humanistic field in a liberal arts program is still uncertain) has a surer place among the humanities than even history and philosophy. The last two have drifted away from their Renaissance positions, history having become (mistakenly, I think, and I am a historian) linked with social science by its political and economic preoccupations to the neglect of its humanistic origins and philosophy having claimed a critical sovereignty over all disciplines when it does not confine itself to a positivistic logic and an almost mathematical method of analysis. Moreover, neither history nor philosophy have the aesthetic emphasis that links the various arts with each other. Yet art, history, and philosophy have some points in common that may justify a loose alliance.

Witness what Plato does in *The Apology* of Socrates. This purports to be history, a reconstruction of the trial of Socrates, or rather of his defence against his accusers and plea to the jury of five hundred ordinary citizens of Athens. The oratorical form that fits this purpose enables Plato to slip easily into drama, for we hear not only the colloquies with Meletus, one of the accusers, but through Socrates' words the shouts of the jurors. We follow the very feelings of the Athenians from the way in which he addresses them. The interaction between the accused, the accusers and the jury suggests a dialogue, Plato's characteristic method of exploring philosophical problems. The *Apology* is indeed not simply a courtroom defence but the exposition and defense of a philosophic method and attitude aimed not at acquittal by the jury but at recognition by a wider audience. The speech is pervaded with irony, little calculated to win the votes of the intolerant majority. Socrates handles the charges of impiety and of corruption of the minds of the young with a dialectic close to sophistry that cleverly and contemptuously reduces their advocacy to absurdity and contradiction. On a higher level, he condemns perhaps too sweepingly the Athenian democracy itself.

He says,

Please do not be offended if I tell you the truth. No man on earth who conscientiously opposes either you or any other organized democracy, and flatly prevents a great many wrongs and illegalities from taking place in the state to which he belongs, can possibly escape with his life. The true champion of justice, if he intends to survive even for a short time, must necessarily confine himself to private life and leave politics alone.

He suggests even that he should be awarded not death or a fine but support for life at the expense of the state. Here the irony is serious enough, a matter of life and death, for his claim for the award is the very independence in the search for and testing of truth that made him the gadfly whose destruction was required for the security of the conventionally-minded, those upset by novel questions and ideas. The *Apology* is philosophy as well as history and art, a demonstration of the danger and the greatness of seeking the truth only and of challenging others in the search.

This dialogue is an allegory in a broad sense of the term, through which the reader is excited, puzzled, and moved, perhaps at times to impatience but in the end to admiration, as he thinks the thoughts and feels the feelings of Socrates and of the jurors. Each of us may make the dialogue imaginatively a part of his own experience, and yet the allegory, being only in the imagination and not experienced as the accusers, accused, and the jury would have experienced it, can be an object of study, an instrument of education. The example suggests the nature of the humanistic object and of the *humanitas* which it offers the members of its audience.

Before exploring further the nature of this *humanitas* and its meaning for us, we can summarize the variety of the humanities. Originating with antique literature and including philosophy and history, they have been expanded to take in not only modern literature but the fine arts and music. At the same time the audience has been expanded even more radically with the rise of democracy and of democratic education. The humanities are no longer simply the polish of an aristocratic elite. They are for all who can read or own a hi-fi or get hold of a print or photographic reproduction. We aim, as did ancient Athens, to give a democratic society the advantages of the education of an elite.

The humanistic object is both less and more than "life." It is not even "a slice of life" such as we individually experience. Inner dialogues or streams of consciousness, whether by Henry James, Thomas Mann or James Joyce, are not that. They could not be. The imitation of life by artist or historian (to say nothing of a philosophical system) is not a copy. It is a re-creation in another medium of a part of life, and therefore necessarily is an interpretation. The raw materials of experience are shaped, given an artistic form, a logic, a meaning that may be present in the actual event or situation (I suppose that we should hope they are) but are there not singled out from the apparent chaos of immediate experience, are not evident or obvious to all of us. Of course anyone of us shapes more or less successfully the immediate experience for ourselves. We cannot take it whole; we try to be selective and to make some sense of it. But the artist, the historian, the philosopher, seeks to give it a stable, enduring form, as you or I might see for our own eyes in a diary. This form objectifies the experience in the act of interpreting it. It frames it, so to speak, as an object which can be contemplated. In doing so, the creator of the object intensifies the experience by selection and concentration. The irrelevant is left out, or should be. For that which is included should be made relevant so that attention is not distracted from whatever unity of action, thought, and feeling the artist, historian or philosopher has sought to give his object by the form to which he has shaped it.

Eugene Delacroix, the French romantic painter, wrote in his diary over a century ago (20, October, 1853): "The type of emotion peculiar to painting is, so to speak, tangible ... you enjoy the actual representation of objects as though you were really seeing them and at the same time you are warmed and carried away by the meaning which these images contain for the mind—(They) are like a solid bridge to support your imagination as it probes the deep, mysterious emotions, of which these forms are, so to speak, the hieroglyph." Delacroix goes on to say that the hieroglyph "becomes in the painter's hands a source of most intense pleasure—that pleasure we gain from seeing beauty, proportion, contrast, harmony of colors in things around us, in everything which our eyes love to contemplate in the outside world, and which is the satisfaction of one of the profoundest needs of our nature." "The power of painting," he says later, is that "if it has to record but a single moment it is capable of concentrating the *effect* of that moment." It should be clear that Delacroix was not advising the exact imitation of nature. This he considered cold. The artist was inventor leaving his imprint upon his work (Sept. 2, 1854). What was sublime was what the painter's imagination gave to the presentation of emotions through the images drawn from nature.

By tangibility Delacroix was referring to the physical actuality and the immediate sensuous impact of the image directly before us in painting and sculpture. His specific purpose was to distinguish the visual arts from poetry and music. In these other arts and especially in literature the image was, he thought, not perceived except in connection with the idea. It was abstract and mental, not physically present as on canvas or in bronze or stone. The emphasis on tangibility has had radical consequences not foreseen by Delacroix. His successors have in the century since he painted and wrote developed the tangibility of painting at the expense of the recognizable images of things in the world about us. These have disappeared for the sake of the sensuous surface of line, color, texture, and volume. Such surface is itself an interpretative imitation of nature, a limited but perhaps a self-sufficient one. Delacroix might well have observed that music and poetry also have their own kind of tangibility, an auditory one, which today has been likewise emphasized as physical sensation abstracted from recognizable themes and emotional content. It is not surprising, however, that the painter gave close attention to the physical means of his own art while confining his comments on the others to the emotional experience.

Yet, as his words and works show, he was not content in painting with tangibility alone. It was for him "full of mystery" and revealed "deep emotions." He did not neglect the idea in the literary and historical subjects of which he made much use or in his criticism of earlier painters. The sensuous experience must not lead us to forget the humanistic importance of meaning and feeling, without which we would not have the *Apology*, to say nothing of dramatic, lyric and narrative literature, vocal and probably most of the rest of music, religious and other representational painting and sculpture and even non-objective art.

But I join Delacroix in his emphasis upon tangibility, not only because I delight in the sensuous surface but because, in a sense broader than his concern for the physical immediacy of the image, tangibility is a prime feature of works of the humanities. Artistic and historical imitations of nature and of man in any art are not copies, but they have the concreteness of nature and of life. They select and organize but they do not reduce experience to scientific or philosophical generalizations. In one way or another the actual is present in the created object. We experience it in its concrete immediacy as an individual poem, picture, drama, history, string quartet, even philosophical treatise—a particular interpretation of man and of the world. It has the richness of actual life, heightened by artistic integration given by its artistic form. We may find in it, it may even have been intended to have, a message, a precept, a lesson handed down from the past. It may serve as an exemplar of a doctrine, a policy or a strategy. Yet its humanity will be lacking if this is all it has. *The Apology* may be a defence of freedom of inquiry, and of speech; but in its dramatic presentation it raises the broader issues of responsibility to a free conscience or to a conventional piety, of the usefulness of verbal dialectic and questioning to challenge one's neighbor's beliefs, and of the conflict of loyalty to oneself (in Socrates' case to his *daimon* or guiding spirit) or to the state. Socrates accepted both with his own distinctions of when and where they applied. In the *Apology,* he said, "Well, supposing that you should offer to acquit me on these terms (that I give up spending my time on this quest and stop philosophizing), I should reply 'Gentlemen, I am your very grateful and devoted servant, but I owe a greater obedience to God than to you; and so long as I draw breath and have my faculties, I shall never stop practising philosophy and exhorting you and elucidating the truth for everyone that I meet.' And so, gentlemen, I would say, 'You can please yourselves whether you listen to Anytus or not, and whether you acquit me or not; you know that I am not going to alter my conduct, not even if I have to die a hundred deaths.' " Compare with these declarations his refusal to escape as defended in another of Plato's dialogues, the *Crito.* There is in the irony, even in these dialogues, an ambiguity, or at least a complexity of values, of emotional and rational responses.

So too in all works of art, history, and philosophy. Thucydides' narrative of the Peloponnesian War between Athens and Sparta became from the experience of its author, as general and political leader, a study of the state as power and of the disastrous effects on politics at home and abroad, indeed the irony of the empire. Cervantes in *Don Quixote* used the parody and chivalric romance as an opportunity to spread before us the panorama of Spanish life in the age of Philip II, especially on the seamier side, as well as to play upon the ambiguity of reality and illusion, of the ideal and the practical. A Beethoven symphony or quartet is less adapted to verbal analysis, but it repays, indeed requires, careful study. Nor is this completed by a merely literal examination of its themes, rhythms, harmonic changes and their place in the structure. Behind the often surprising complexity of the structures lie the sensuous and emotional effects of the tempos, the modulations, the conflicts in the development of the themes, their repetition and variation. These are continuing sources of excitement and delight. Something similar is true of Picasso's use of the mask in both of his paintings of the *Three Musicians* and that of the mirror image in the *Girl of the Mirror*, symbolic images which bring us back to ambiguity and irony. And lest I seem, even with *Don Quixote* on my list, too serious-minded (though *Don Quixote* is one of the most broadly humorous as well as one of the most profound of books), why not add *Alice in Wonderland* and Charlie Chaplin's early films!

Of course, our responses vary in accordance with the experience we bring to the work of art. The result varies from person to person and for the same observer from day to day. We cannot be passive. We participate in the re-creation of the work of art in our eyes and ears, in our feelings and thoughts. As the work of art is an imitative interpretation of life and nature or at least of the artist's emotions before life and nature, so the observer's experience is an imitative interpretation of the work of art, in reference of course consciously or unconsciously to his view of the world about and within him. As Delacroix said (in the passage cited already) of "the impression that the arts produce on sensitive natures," "I firmly believe that we always mingle something of ourselves in the emotions that seem to arise out of objects that impress us. And I think it is probable that these things delight me so much only because they echo feelings that are also my own. If, although so different, they give me the same degree of pleasure, it must be because I recognize in myself the source of the kind of effect they produce."

It is not strange that the spectator sees what he has already the capacity to see. What is true of the life going on about us everyday is true of paintings, symphonies, dramas, and histories. We understand in accordance with our state of mind and emotion and with the resources of experience that we bring to them. The passive receptor receives only on the wave-length he is turned in on, but passivity is not enough. We can try more than one wave-length. The situation or the work of art we are facing is "so different" (as Delacroix says). It offers something new and yet we can approach it only from that which is old. If a painting is a bridge between the artist's and the spectator's minds, the spectator must take an initiative in crossing it. He must engage in exploration to discover a fresh experience for himself in the painting, poem, history or musical composition that the artist, author or composer has shaped from his effort to interpret *his* experience of the world. If there is any paradox in this, it is the paradox of learning. In such discovery lies the excitement of the humanities. It stimulates and extends the imagination.

The other evening I was reading a short story by Thomas Mann. I was at first put off by the artificiality of the style until I recognized that it suited the characters as the glove should fit the hand. My interest rose until it was capped in the climactic scene of the communion of the two romantic figures in love with art rather than each other as the woman exhausts her fading life playing the piano score for *Tristan and Isolde*. My recollection of the art of the Liebestod, vivid from my youth, supported the art of the novelist and gave me the moving images of these pathetic, not quite tragic, persons doomed to frustration. Here was, it may be, a problem, among others, of too precious, too affected a view of the humanities.

Such ventures need not be a solitary enterprise, especially in school. Early imaginative voyages of discovery in the humanities are likely to be uncertain in method and direction. What is often called "private reading," that is, purely personal interpretation, may be narrow and distorted. It will neglect some points and exaggerate others. It profits from being compared with the opinions of others. They may correct obvious misconstructions of the evidence. They will more surely add to the breadth and depth of the "reading" by suggesting different ways of looking at the work of art. These lead to discussion among students and teachers. Ideas are tested and modified. The interpretation becomes richer, perhaps more complex, more subtle. This process is in the very nature of the humanities, as interpretations of human situations. These situations and the interpretations of them are inexhaustible in their possibilities, and their ambiguity and variety are reflected in the efforts of readers and spectators to understand works of arts, of history, and of philosophy.

Teaching, or, as I would rather say, learning and discussion, is not for the dictation of the meaning of a particular painting or of the evaluation of it. Taste is not to be imposed. It can be developed only by the experience of the student. There is no final judgment, no conclusive answer for all men and all times to the questions of meaning and value, no summary for the note-books. This is one cause of the fascination of the humanities. They continue to challenge inquiry. At least the great works do, and this may be the criterion of greatness. There is more to be seen on each viewing or reading or hearing. All possibilities are never quite explored. New ones open up as we and our times grow older.

As I wrote on another occasion, "Such inquiry demands sensitive, imaginative, and thoughtful appraisal of evidence, of logic, of aesthetic effectiveness, of motive and passions, of social goals and individual responsibilities, of moral and metaphysical principles, to name a few of the matters involved in an interpretation of the *Apology*. The outcome is likely to be some disagreement between members of the group and some uncertainty on the part of individuals, but these results contribute more than facile unanimity to the maturing of sympathetic and critical judgment, if there is awareness of the grounds of disagreement and uncertainty, such as the inadequacy of evidence, differences of psychological theory or distinctions in aesthetic and moral values. Similar responsible judgment of men's acts, expressions, and situations is badly needed in the practical affairs of individuals and of society."

The last sentence brings us back to the quotation from Cassirer with which I opened. "Art and history are the most powerful instruments of our inquiry into human nature." Knowledge of human nature, including the desires, ambitions, values, behavior of ourselves as well as of others, helps to determine our goals and to guide our action and to put some reason, some realism perhaps some idealism into them. Such knowledge is of course not gained solely or indeed largely from art and history. It is handed down as tradition from our ancestors to us and to our society and is qualified and added to, if we are sensitive, by our day-to-day experience of what goes on around us.

Tradition is deep-seated and pervasive. It is in our methods of rice culture and our religions, in our tools, including of course languages, and in our ideas, that is, in the technology and in the humanities. Much of tradition is beneath the surface. We are scarcely aware of what our parents, teachers, priests, friends—the generations behind each of us and also our own contemporaries—hand on to us in the way of habits, outlooks, values. We seldom examine them, and yet they have shaped us and given us our identity as persons and as peoples. They are what we sometimes call the dead-hand of the past, but without them we should not, indeed could not, be what we are here today.

Fortunately we are not so closely tied to the past by tradition as the word implies. Traditions are so mixed, in Europe and America as in the Philippines, that they act in contradiction to each other—family habits with technological change, everyday language with that of science, personal and political obligations, and the different cultural strains-that we are forced to recognize the difficulties and to make decisions. A dead-hand of which we are conscious, especially if it tells us different things, is no longer a despotic master. We are given a chance to try to select and to reconcile the best of various worlds.

It is this consciousness that Cassirer calls "knowledge." For the enlightenment of this consciousness, he appeals to art and to history. As the imitators of life they are the interpreters of tradition, its continuators and evaluators. They encourage and help to guide its transformation neither cutting loose from, nor staying behind in, the past. Through them the past is never quite out of date. The artists, the historians, the philosophers, such as Cassirer himself, are continually re-interpreting man and his world for their own generation or perhaps for the generation yet to come. And, while they are doing this, and partly because they are doing it, we spectators are reinterpreting the paintings and sculpture, the music and drama, the poetry and fiction, the histories and philosophies of yesterday and centuries ago and are holding on to what they still have to say to us. Plato created in the *Apology* an image of Socrates that is at once human and ideal, a figure against which to measure and imaginatively to extend our cautious selves.

The humanities are mirrors of discovery, discovery of ourselves and of other men, of our own society (yours or mine) in its complex heritage and of other societies. As we look in the mirror of a work of art or history, we engage our senses and imagination and through these our emotions and ideas. Our responses and our questions reveal our state of mind and feeling, necessarily so, for, as I have indicated already, we understand it in the terms of our fears and hopes, our desires and values. Otherwise we never get beyond the surface, if even that far. Then in turn the process of interpretation, the give-and-take between the painting, the string quartet or the history and ourselves tests and refines, broadens and enriches these fears and hopes, desires and values, and, I hope, the conduct of our affairs that stems from them. We should as a result know more about what we and others are like and what we and they are capable of, for better and for worse.

The Creative Expressions of Man

Prudence Dyer

We shall define the humanities as the creative expressions of man. The study of the humanities, therefore, embodies a consideration of the skills essential to creating the expressions of man as well as those necessary for understanding and interpreting these expressions. Within the humanities we may identify components such as art or literature, each with subdivisions; for example, drawing, painting, and sculpture, or drama, essay, and poetry. Each of the works of art reflects both the creator and the forces at work on the creator. Each is an expression of man—of his joy, his concern, his sorrow, his anger, his search, his exultation. Man has created his art for the purpose of expressing some idea or feeling, and each work of art reflects his values and his ideas. The structure of the humanities encompasses, therefore, the study of the ideas and values held by man, his artistic means of expressing them, as well as his compulsion to express them.[1]

A Model. If this be the structure of the humanities, what might the goals of humanities programs reasonably be?

Charles Keller has suggested that the goals outlined by a Fraser, Michigan, high school staff for its humanities program might serve as a model for other programs:

1. To approach teaching and learning with an experimental attitude and with renewed enthusiasm.
2. To involve the student in learning for the pleasures and satisfactions of learning itself and in dealing with ideas for their own sake.
3. To provide a unifying element which the student may utilize in the integration of separate subjects.
4. To understand, to become familiar with, and to appreciate the great achievements of man.
5. To deal with issues that are important to the student as well as to all men of all time, such as: the search for beauty, truth, values and ideals, man's place in the universe, identity with nature, relationship with society, importance of creativity.
6. To assist the student in gaining a more complete awareness of the world around him.
7. To raise questions rather than to give answers.[2]

Somewhat different are the objectives developed by Henry W. Ray for the sixth-grade classes at the Shelmire Elementary School at Southhampton, Pennsylvania.

1. Help them develop a concept of the meaning of the word *humanities.*
2. Arouse in them new dimensions of interest which would be reflected in their

[1] Further discussion of structuring programs appears in Prudence Dyer, "Structuring and Evaluating Humanities Programs."
[2] Charles Keller, "Humanities and the Social Studies." (Mimeographed, 1966).

choices of reading materials, television programs, and motion pictures.
3. Help them to see themselves as human beings in the world of humans.
4. Deepen their insights in respect to other culture groups—all cultures have their humanities, some quite different from ours.
5. Provide a different orientation in the arts—causing them to see painting, sculpture, architecture, dance, poetry, films, etc. as expressions about and reactions to man himself, his natural and his social environment.[3]

Other programs outline still different objectives. The K-12 program, developed in the James A. Garfield schools in the Institute mentioned earlier and discussed at the second New York City Conference on the Humanities, classifies the objectives in terms of pupil behavior patterns that are outcomes of the humanities programs. These outcomes are grouped according to those behavior patterns the pupil will know and exhibit and through what he can do or be or become.

1. The child should KNOW
   a. certain selections
   b. specific techniques
   c. content appropriate for his age or academic level.
2. The child should DO such things as
   a. discuss how an idea or emotion or theme is expressed in the arts in various media
   b. see, hear, and feel how the spirit of humanity has been expressed in man's arts and institutions.
   c. respond creatively and critically to the works of others
   d. create his own work (art, music, dance, poetry, fiction, drama) developing an idea or a concept.
3. The child should BE
   a. aware of kinds of artistic expressions (classic, contemporary, popular)
   b. sensitive to each individual's expression of his ideas—not only of recognized masters, but also of his own and of his peers
4. The child should BECOME
   a. appreciative of a variety of leisure reading, listening, and other forms of self-expression
   b. committed to patterns of meaningful leisure activities
   c. discriminating in his tastes
   d. conscious of the dignity of man
   e. sensitive to his kinship with all humanity.

Each of these schools, in developing objectives for the programs, expressed similar ideas; each, however, expressed objectives unique to its own situation.

---

[3] Ray in William A. Jenkins, "The Humanities and Humanistic Education in the Elementary Grades," in Albert H. Marckwardt et al., *Literature in Humanities Programs* (NCTE, 1967), p. 38.

Therein lies the strength of these programs—the unique development appropriate for the particular school or district.

Designs for the Humanities. Programs—like pictures—have different compositions, even while working toward similar objectives. Several dominant designs become apparent as one surveys the many programs now in operation. In fact, the design of humanities courses formed the framework for NCTE's National Conference on the Humanities in School Programs in May 1967. The recurring patterns emerged from a survey conducted by NCTE of some seven hundred secondary schools reported to be conducting humanities courses. Only fifty-six per cent of the schools responded, but from these schools NCTE tabulated the following organizational patterns (as reported at that time) for the content of humanities courses:

26% Culture Epoch of Western World
15% Great Ideas,
14% American Studies
13% World Cultures
9% Aesthetic Structure
8% Great Books
4% Great Themes
11% Other

We shall look briefly at some programs illustrating these several approaches.

The Aesthetic Structure has been utilized both in the elementary and secondary programs of humanities. Kent State University School (Ohio) developed its twelfth-grade program in this fashion. Studies in painting, music, writing, or dance furnished the framework for studying *composition. Design* in any period, such as the Classic, might be illustrated in architecture, drama, or sculpture. *Conventions* of ꜱoetry, sonata, spire, and proscenium arch might be illustrative of still another era, ꜳnother emphasis.

Elliott Eisner of Stanford University reported yet another variation on teaching ꜳe aesthetic structure in humanities courses at the 1967 ASCD Conference. He told of his experiences in teaching *form* with the aid of inexpensive cameras and film for each pupil. The children took pictures of basic forms from several angles, in order to experiment with perspective. A circle might be snapped as a row of wheels lined up in a bicycle rack, or a manhole from the angle of a kneeling child. A cylinder might be a silo taken from the ground, the tree, and the barn loft. A rectangle, stacks of lumber from an end view, or bricks, or freight cars at a rail siding. The instructor in the class also used projectors in two's and three's to show his slides taken on the same assignment, with perhaps more sophisticated angles. As the children compared the same "subject" or form taken by themselves, their classmates, and their teacher, they began to develop a sense of form, design, and perspective, both from looking at basic art forms and from producing them.

The Cultural Epochs approach is easy to visualize, and it seems to be a logical method for initial humanities courses, particularly for teams of teachers. As the teams work together through several years, other patterns usually emerge. But this is a beginning. It is easy to visualize how a team of teachers could organize studies around the art, music, literature, architecture, dance, and dress of Renaissance man or the Minoan culture.

A Major Works approach also responds well to a beginning team. An opera, a ballet, a cathedral a fresco, a constitution, or a novel would lend itself to an understanding of that work as a type of expression of man. Methods could emerge for studying other similar works in small groups or independently. Cleveland, Scarsdale, and some Michigan schools are working within this framework.

American Studies, as outlined by Charles Keller at the Seminar at the NCTE Conference in Houston in November 1966 (and a week later at the NCTSS sessions in Cleveland) serves as an illustration of a concentrated study of any region, from Midwest studies to South American studies. He advocated these because we need to know more about the United States than mere political history and the "safe" literature of the anthologies in order to understand the nature—the humanity—of the American man and woman. Keller reported:

In many an American Studies course or program only an English teacher and a history teacher will be able to cooperate, but teachers of other subjects may be involved. Puritans and Puritanism come alive in one American Studies course when they are considered not only historically but also through their literature and through a novel such as Nathaniel Hawthorne's *The Scarlet Letter,* and a play such as Arthur Miller's *The Crucible.* The students go on to consider their own religious beliefs.

Or Thomas Jefferson takes on new dimensions when he is studied not only as a diplomat, secretary of state, and president, but also as architect, writer, and seeker after an American national identity. The Transcendentalists stand with the Jacksonian Democrats in the 1830's. And I know of one American Studies course now in the planning which will follow an eighth grade to the Civil War American history course, and will begin with a reading and discussion of Mark Twain's *Huckleberry Finn.*

The effects of post-Civil War Industrialism can be studied not only politically and economically but also in literature, art and architecture. And music and art can be used effectively to throw much light on the 1920's.

If I were a principal of a high school, I would have an art teacher and a music teacher with no more than three courses each. The rest of the time they would "float"—be available. Under such circumstances a really good American Studies course could be developed. "What is an American?" Crevecoeur asked in his *Letters of an American Farmer* back in 1782. This question should be constantly raised and answers ventured in American Studies courses. In American Studies courses there can be the interplay of the various disciplines which is badly needed in our altogether too segmented curricula.[4]

World Cultures, like American Studies, could be a continuing study in the schools according to Francis Shoemaker, speaking at the 1967 New York City Conference on the Humanities. Dr. Shoemaker contended that there are really only four

[4]Charles Keller, *op. cit.*

cultures: Classic and Judeo-Christian, Islamic, Hindu-Buddhistic, and African. He suggested that the cultures of Europe, North, Central, and South America, Australia, and the Philippines could be studied simultaneously through the use of the Bible, derivative myths, and symbols. For an understanding of Islamic cultures (from Moritania, Africa, through Morocco, the Sudan, Iran, and Indonesia), he suggested a study of the land and water management of these regions as the key to the leadership and imagination of the people, the Koran as the basis of understanding their ethics and law, their architecture as the central expression unifying art and ideals of the people, and their education as the foundation of what Americans think of as Islam today.

For the Hindu-Buddhistic analysis (including Ceylon, India, Cambodia, Thailand, China, Korea, Japan), he suggested a touchstone approach, using Indian materials as a guide to later understanding of Chinese or Japanese studies. He mentioned a focus concentrating on pre- and post-independence attitudes, arts, and ideas as expressed by Indian or part-Indian writers themselves, such as Kamala Markandaya *(Nectar in a Sieve)* or Aubrey Menen *(Dean Man in the Silver Market)*. What are the tension points in the behavior of the characters? Where are the new role models? He further suggested extended consideration of the contemporary simultaneity in the post-modern world as focus for study: 1945 Hiroshima, Communist China of the 1940's, and the 1947 Indian Freedom.

For African studies he suggested analysis of arts and music, as well as a study of Alan Paton's *Cry the Beloved Country* or *Too Late the Phalarope* or Maxwell Anderson's *Lost in the Stars* as a dramatic adaptation of *Cry the Beloved Country*.

Not only the students, but also the teachers would be studying and learning in this approach.

Great Ideas or Values as an approach to the humanities offer structure for study at all levels in the schools, both vertically and horizontally. Great ideas and values burst from the expressions of man, whether sophisticated or naive, whether classic or contemporary, whether old or young. Great ideas may explode from the television screen or the movie projector, from the library shelf or the corner newsstand, from the symphony hall or the cellar coffee shop, from the art gallery or the latest pop recording. We may not "tune in" to these media quite so easily as we do to books and classical recordings, but if we try, our efforts may enable us to communicate with those who feel we are out of touch with reality and therefore, undoubtedly, over thirty.

Great ideas—man's expression of his values—span the ages and assume added dimension in the lives of the students. For example, one high school class of seniors engaged in discussions of Plato's "God and World" from *Timaeus*, "The Creation" of Hesiod from *Theogony*, "Zeus" from *Oedipus Tyrannus* of Sophocles, the story of creation from *Genesis*, "Creation" by Johnson, "On What Base" of Taylor, "The Creation of Adam" by Michaelangelo, Hayden's "Creation," and Milhaud's "La Création du Monde." Other students investigated ideas of creation in the Eastern cultures, while still others examined aspects of Darwin's *Origin of the Species* (and, of course, *Inherit the Wind)*. Then the students moved to a consideration of *creation* itself—creation of poetry or pottery, the art of the masters and of the masses, songs of the so-called classic composers and the spontaneous extemporizations of the jazz man and the guitar strummer. And there were opportunities for individual creative activities in the medium of each student's choice.[5] This portion of the senior program introduced the year for examining Man's Search for Truth, which was designed as the culminating study of man's values, outlined below.

Suggested Concepts and Themes for Humanities Studies
(From a Tentative Working Paper, James A. Garfield Schools
Garrettsville, Ohio, June 20, 1966.)

Kindergarten—Work and Play
  Work, Nature, Personal Habits, Transportation, Safety, A Tiny Introduction to Archaeology, Holidays
Grade One—Love
  Family, Friends, Pets and Toys, Kindness, Helping, Community, Holidays
Grade Two—Friendship
  Loyalty, Bravery, Honesty, Kindness, Justice, Helpfulness, Sharing, Holidays
Grade Three—Ourselves
  Individuality, Integrity, Imagination, Curiosity and the Past, Curiosity and the Future, Brotherhood
Grade Four—Others
  Homes and Folk Art, Kinship, Respect for Others, Service, Enemies, Prejudice, Ignorance, Responsibility
Grade Five—Liberty and Justice
  One Nation Under God, Liberty, Life, Pursuit of Happiness, Justice, Equality
Grade Six—Mystery of Man in His Expanding World
  Restless Spirit, Curiosity, Creativity, Cooperation, Faith, Life
Grade Seven—Sources of Power
  Dedication, Determination, Knowledge of Right, Response to Challenge, Duty, Humor
Grade Eight—Ingredients of Personality
  Resourcefulness, Courage, Justice, Mercy, Tolerance, Responsibility
Grade Nine—Heroic Ideal
  Classic, Chivalric, Romantic, Modern
Grade Ten—The Spirit of American Man
  Frontier, Freedom, Personal Responsibility, Tragedy, Humor, Searching
Grade Eleven—Man's Outward Reach
  Man—Teller of Tales, Man and Woman, Family and Society, Nature, Beyond
Grade Twelve—Man's Search for Truth
  Classic Ideal, Church and State, Humanism, Romanticism, Modern Man, Post-Modern Mind

In our effort to escape the shackles of the anthology, and in our freedom to select complete works in paperback, we sometimes forget the power of a tersely

---

[5] An introduction to the study of Man's Continuing Search for Truth—an outgrowth of an earlier thematic literature approach. Prudence Dyer, "An Expression, a Possession and a Dream," *English Journal*, (September, 1964), 443.

stated idea as content for humanities study—perhaps an idea from a small band of a popular recording, a title of a book, a movie, a poem, a news story from a city or a campus or a country in turmoil. Ideas for humanities courses or approaches are as infinite as the ideas of man's mind.

A Critical Look. With all the variety, we wonder and often ask, how do we evaluate? How do we know the effectiveness of what we are doing?

The initiation of an extensive, unified study of the arts of man requires consideration of certain questions regarding the design of the program and the establishment of criteria for it—whether for grades or not (and that is a local question). Such questions should deal with (1) the school's program, (2) the objectives for that program, (3) the teachers' approaches, and (4) materials and evaluation of the individual student.[6]

Evaluation is one problem. What are the others? Carl Ladensack, summarizing the Humanities Seminar in Houston, called attention to two others:

Some members of the panel expressed concern that humanities courses could easily become too undirected and undisciplined. Certainly the teachers must find ways of engaging the students in meaningful pursuits of what works of art are saying and ways of preventing the courses from becoming erratic, uninformed discussions of the type that the student enjoys without adult supervision.

Perhaps the greatest problem is that of deciding which materials to include and which to exclude. Works used in existing courses range from classics to current popular ones; the emphasis in most courses is on great works of established worth, but many teachers find their best success in starting with contemporary novels, poems, plays, paintings, and music. Critics of humanities courses point to the overly-ambitious programs which sweep blithely over several centuries of work every two weeks. The study group seemed to feel that a few works, studied in greater depth and somehow related to each other, are most valuable to the student. If he can learn that the painter, composer, architect and writer are engaged in kindred activities and that men throughout the ages have been so engaged, he will be better equipped to look at and to listen to new works.

Other problems arise in staffing the programs and providing planning time, particularly for team efforts. The NCTE survey mentioned earlier found that 49 per cent of the courses in the responding schools featured team teaching, 29 per cent had individual teaching for a whole course, and 11 per cent had "turn" teaching, a succession of individual teachers for various units or components.

Still further problems concern the administration of the program by departments. The survey showed that English departments accounted for 49 per cent of the courses in the humanities, a combination of English and other departments accounted for 30 per cent, and 13 per cent arose from social studies, art, or history departments. Only 3 per cent originated in independent humanities departments.

---

[6] A fuller discussion of evaluation of humanities programs and students in such programs appears elsewhere in this volume: "Structuring and Evaluating Humanities Programs," and Sheila Schwartz "If English Is Well Taught, Is There a Need for Humanities Courses in the Secondary School?"

Scheduling, too, presents problems, but certainly the gravest problem with the most far-reaching consequences is the fact that programs are provided for 57 per cent of the "gifted" pupils but only 3 per cent of the so-called slow achievers and only 10 per cent of the "terminal" students. This, I believe, is wrong. It is a trend we must re-examine and reconsider.

Meaning. Meaning in any work of art gives us insight into more than the surface problems, more than the organization, more than the materials, more than the medium. What of man and his humanity? What of the student's understanding of how crucial man and his humanity are to all civilization? Sensitive artists through the ages have cried out against man's inhumanity, but has man always listened? Have we even allowed the children to listen? Let us recall for a moment some of the warnings from the great minds from the ages: we remember bestiality personified in Creon, ruthlessly destroying Antigone; Goneril and Regan ravaging their father and sister; Henry VIII slaughtering Thomas More; Jack and his gang rapaciously destroying Ralph, Benjamin Brittain's weeping over ravages at Hiroshima in his *War Requiem*. None of these works, perhaps, hits with more force than Lasansky's *Nazi Drawings*. In a series of thirty pencil drawings, the artist reviews the horror of the bestiality of the concentration camps, the impotence of the established church, the suffering of the innocents, and finally the butchering self-destruction of the master butcher himself. Many who saw the exhibition agree that it was powerful, moving, frightening and as they discuss it, they become concerned with what they read and see and hear today from Asia to Africa from California to Michigan to Washington. Is man repeating with savage and ravenous appetite what repels him to remember? Is society withdrawing in dismay, feeling impotent to change the jungle's law of survival or the retreat of hundreds of youth into the ghetto of drugged oblivion? Have poets and authors and artists become intoxicated with the ugly and depraved? Or are they trying to arouse the concerned and the bewildered? Lasansky recalls the horror of another era in order that all might remember:

> Dignity is not a symbol bestowed on man, nor does the word itself possess force. Man's dignity is a force and the only *modus vivendi* by which man and history survive. When mid-twentieth century Germany did not let man live and die with this right, man became an animal. No matter how technologically advanced or sophisticated, when a man negates this divine right, he not only becomes self-destructive, but castrates his history and poisons our future. This is what the Nazi Drawings are about.[7]

And that is what humanities programs are about: that all might examine and know that the study of man and his dignity is a force—the force by which all humanity may survive.

---

[7]Mauricio Lasansky, *The Nazi Drawings*. The Mauricio Lasansky Foundation, 1966, p. ii.

Aesthetics and Humanities Education*

Ralph A. Smith

Introduction. As this volume illustrates, humanities programs can be discussed in many ways. This essay presents an approach that underscores three key notions: (a) the idea of an aesthetic form of understanding; (b) the use of aesthetic exemplars as principal objects of study; and (c) a concept of criticism that is relevant to rendering exemplars meaningful.[1] The discussion will be seen to involve the application of aesthetic theory to the task of clarifying problems of humanities education.

An "aesthetic exemplar" is any object perceived as having a high degree of aesthetic value and significance. While clear instances of such objects are the great masterpieces of fine art, an exemplar approach is not necessarily confined to their study. Great works are often large and difficult, and to engage them appropriately requires highly developed powers of discrimination. In the early and middle years of schooling the attainment of a genuinely critical appreciation of fine art is obviously beyond the capabilities of students. Yet just as obviously there are many works which, while not termed "classic" or "great," still deserve attention. The reason for using exemplars as key instruments of instruction turns on their strategic importance in initiating students into the type of learning under consideration.

For purposes of this essay, then, "the humanities" will mean the same as "aesthetic exemplars" in contrast to the subjects of history, philosophy, religion, mathematics, or the physical and social sciences. These subjects do not exemplify the form of understanding that is the major concern of exemplar study.[2] Since,

*I am indebted to the editor for an opportunity to present in revised form ideas contained in various articles. Accordingly, I am grateful for permission to reprint parts of "Patterns of Meaning in Aesthetic Education," *Council for Research in Music Education*, Bulletin No. 5, 1965 (revised 1967); "Aesthetic Education: A Role for the Humanities Program," *The Record*, Vol. 69, No. 4 (January, 1968), 339-54; and "Aesthetic Criticism: The Method of Aesthetic Education," *Studies in Art Education*, Vol. 9, No. 3 (May, 1968), 13-32. I have also included material from Ralph A. Smith, *An Exemplar Approach to Aesthetic Education: A Preliminary Report* (Urbana: Bureau of Educational Research, 1967). This latter study was performed pursuant to a contract with the United States Office of Education, Department of Health, Education, and Welfare, Project Number C-3-6-061279-1609.

[1] The importance of exemplar studies has been persuasively articulated in a number of writings by Harry S. Broudy. See, e.g., Chapter 13 of *Democracy and Excellence in American Secondary Education* (Chicago: Rand McNally & Co., 1964), written with B. Othanel Smith and Joe R. Burnett, and "The Role of the Humanities in the Curriculum," *Journal of Aesthetic Education*, Vol. 1, No. 2 (Autumn, 1966), 17-27. It is best, however, to construe my own efforts as a modified version of exemplar study.

[2] The roughly equivalent expressions "forms of understanding," "ways of knowing," "realms of meaning," or "disciplines of thought and action" have been used by several writers. In preparing this article I have found most helpful Solon Kimball and James E. McClellan, Jr., *Education and the New America* (New York: Random House, 1963); Philip Phenix, *Realms of Meaning* (New York: McGraw-Hill Book Co., 1964); Harry S. Broudy, "The Structure of

however, facts and principles from diverse domains are often needed to understand exemplars, the use of such knowledge is not ruled out. The point to be made clear is that what is being advocated is not the study of a cluster of academic disciplines. Rather, the stress is on initiating a student into the aesthetic form of understanding—a mode of understanding that draws on a number of arts and sciences but which cannot be reduced to any one of them. A form of understanding may also be called a "way of knowing" and for convenience the shorter expression "aesthetic knowing" will be used in this discussion. Accordingly, an aesthetic exemplar approach to education in the humanities essentially involves teaching the way of aesthetic knowing. Since knowing implies a relation between a knower and what is known, exemplars constitute one component of the knowing situation.

It is further helpful to say at the outset that the process of engaging exemplars parallels the procedures of sensitive and cultivated critics. It is not that professional expertise is the goal; it is rather that the procedures of the critic provide illustrations of the kinds of competences that the student in exemplar study is expected to approximate. The actual progress that students make will depend upon variables relative to particular contexts of schooling. If exemplars constitute one component of the knowing situation, the student as aesthetic knower constitutes the other.

While an exemplar interpretation of humanities education rests primarily on a conception of knowledge that postulates different forms of understanding, it is also grounded in a social analysis, in assumptions about the role of art and aesthetic experience in human existence, and in a theory about the ways in which school learnings are used in adult life.

Contemporary dislocations caused by the dissolution of traditional cultural norms are documented in scores of studies and need not be detailed here. It is sufficient to note that the changes accompanying the transition from a traditional rural to a modern mass society have greatly complicated the tasks of achieving social integration and personal identity. Asserting control over the processes of institutional decision-making has also become problematic, including the control of decisions that affect the aesthetic character of the environment. Insofar as manner is increasingly preempting substance in campaigns of dissent and reform, the role of the aesthetic in contemporary life is further evident in the various styles of "youth culture" and "the new politics." Moreover, the handling of censorship questions, expecially issues turning on problems of violence, obscenity, and pornography, entails aesthetic analysis and judgment as much, it seems, as moral appraisal. It is

Knowledge in the Arts," in Ralph A. Smith (ed.), *Aesthetics and Criticism in Art Education* (Chicago: Rand McNally & Co., 1966); Harry S. Broudy, B. Othanel Smith, and Joe R. Burnett, *Democracy and Excellence in American Secondary Education, op. cit.*; Jerome Bruner, *The Process of Education* (Cambridge: Harvard University Press, 1960); Paul H. Hirst, "Liberal Education and the Nature of Knowledge," in Reginald D. Archambault (ed.), *Philosophical Analysis and Education* (New York: The Humanities Press, 1965); Israel Scheffler, *The Conditions of Knowledge* (Scott, Foresman and Co., 1965); and Louis Arnaud Reid, "Knowledge, Morals, and Aesthetic Education," *Journal of Aesthetic Education,* Vol. 2, No. 3 (July, 1968), 41-54.

thus not surprising that educational critics are urging a basic re-evaluation of the kinds of things schools should teach today. This much is certain: at a time when the principle of the sovereignty of personal taste (*de gustibus non est disputandem*) is being generalized to domains formerly governed by publicly accepted criteria, a renewed emphasis on teaching for enlightened judgment is clearly called for.[3]

To restate the general aim of an exemplar approach: exemplar study has as its major goal the development of the disposition for enlightened judgment and evaluation in the aesthetic domain of human experience. Knowing how to deploy a variety of critical techniques is believed relevant to the attainment of this goal. Aesthetic knowing is enlightened whenever judgments and evaluations are supported by reasons which show either that objects have a certain character or that they are worthy or unworthy of acclaim.

Assuming then that exemplar study implies a learner who goes beyond sensuous pleasure to express judgements and give reasons for what he sees, hears, or reads,[4] the next question turns on the distinctive form and content of aesthetic knowing. Or, in slightly different terms, granted that the ideal of enlightened awarenesss involves something like the building of aesthetic "maps" on which learners can plot their experience, in what degree of detail and sophistication should such maps be

[3] The *de gustibus* issue, however, is not lightly dismissed. Aesthetic judgments have an obvious subjective aspect, yet they tend to be couched in strongly assertive language. Kant noticed this peculiarity of aesthetic judgment and tried to explain it. "The judgment of taste," he wrote, "requires the agreement of everyone, and he who describes anything as beautiful claims that everyone *ought* to give his approval to the object in question and also describe it as beautiful. Further, this claim to universal validity so essentially belongs to a judgment by which we describe anything as *beautiful* that, if this were not thought in it, it would never come into our thoughts to use the expression at all. . . ." This is true, Kant observed, despite the fact that beauty needs to be defined as "that which pleases universally *without a concept*," which means that there can be "no objective rule of taste which shall determine by means of concepts what is beautiful." Here, then, is Kant's famous antinomy of taste. As formulated by D. H. Parker, it consists of "Thesis—the judgment of taste is not based on principles, for otherwise we would determine it by proofs; antithesis—the judgment of taste is based on principles, for otherwise, despite our disagreements, we should not be quarreling about it."

Kant, seeking to explain this persistent claim to objectivity in matters of taste, appealed to another feature of aesthetic experience: the fact that aesthetic contemplation is free from outside interests or ulterior motives: ". . .since the person who judges feels himself quite *free* as regards the satisfaction which he attaches to the object, he cannot find the ground of this satisfaction in any private conditions connected with his own subject, and hence it must be grounded in what he can presuppose in every other person. Consequently he must believe that he has reason for attributing a similar satisfaction to everyone. He will therefore speak of the beautiful as if it were a characteristic of the object and the judgment logical. . . ." The Kant citations are from "The Critique of Judgment," anthologized in Karl Aschenbrenner and Arnold Isenberg (eds.), *Aesthetic Theories* (Englewood Cliffs, N.J.: Prentice-Hall, Inc., 1965), pp. 189, 177, 180, 186, 176. The Parker quotation is from *The Principles of Aesthetics,* 2nd ed. (New York: Appleton-Century-Crofts, Inc., 1946), p. 103.

[4] The phrasing is borrowed from Lucian: "A work of art requires an intelligent spectator who must go beyond the pleasure of the eyes to express a judgment and to argue the reasons for what he sees." Quoted by Harold Osborne in *Aesthetics and Criticism* (London: Routledge and Kegan Paul, Ltd., 1955), p. 5.

constructed? Selecting a destination for exemplar studies, or specifying the nature of its distinctive content and enterprise, is a necessary precondition for any intelligent scheme of teaching and learning.[5] But maps or enterprises can vary considerably in detail, size, and serviceability.

For example, compared to the large-scale maps of life that seek to assure continuous growth and development, there are the more limited maps of schooling that guide students over relatively short and well-marked paths. Ideally, of course, school maps should productively feed into life maps, but the point to be emphasized is that irrespective of the way in which the link between school learnings and their use in adult life is conceived, schooling is best evaluated by how well it achieves its more limited objectives.

Consistent with the foregoing, an exemplar approach accepts an interpretation of liberal education that is comprised of general and common studies. "General" implies studies designed for the nonspecialist, whereas "common" means that the subject matter taught does not vary from learner to learner. The problem of individual differences can be handled by varying the level of complexity and difficulty at which content is taught. Why a general and common education? Because it is only through liberal education that a student comes to understand the various ways of knowing evolved by man. Vocational or specialized training at too early an age inevitably stunts the growth of mind. Furthermore, full participation in contemporary culture requires induction into all, and not merely a selection, of the basic modes of knowing.

The Uses of Learning. Regarding the uses of learning, it is possible to distinguish two major perspectives or frames: an Interpretive Perspective and an Applicative Perspective.[6] Interpretation and Application have different ends but each involves the use of four different types of learning: associative, replicative, interpretive, and applicative.*

In the Interpretive Perspective orientation of only a limited degree of detail, complexity, and sophistication is sought. It is the perspective of the nonspecialist who, having interpreted a situation as calling for a particular form of understanding, proceeds to associate, replicate, apply, and further interpret elements in the situation. The nonspecialist does not really "solve" problems; his lack of expertise

---

*There is perhaps redundancy or awkwardness in saying that both Applicative and Interpretive Perspectives for using school learnings involve interpetive and applicative uses of schooling. Some help may be received by using capitalized expressions for the major perspectives (Interpretive Perspective and Applicative Perspective), and lower-case expressions (associative, replicative, interpretive, and applicative) for the uses of learning in general. Nonetheless, it is intelligible to say that an individual responds to a situation by putting an interpretation on it (however instantaneous). That is, he interprets a situation as one calling for a certain form of understanding, the special context of awareness determing how elements should be associated, replicated, applied, and further interpreted.

[5] I touch here on the so-called "behavioral objectives controversy." For further remarks and references see my "Goals, Purposes, and Objectives," *Journal of Aesthetic Education*, Vol. 2, No. 2 (April, 1968), 5-8.

[6] For a detailed discussion of the uses of learning, see Harry S. Broudy *et al.*, *Democracy and Excellence in American Secondary Education, op. cit.*, Chapter 3.

does not permit him to "apply" the necessary repertory of knowledge and skills. In other words, for the nonspecialist orientation occurs up to the point where interpretation shades into application, this latter process being the special talent of the expert. Since the concern here is with general education, we need not discuss the Applicative Perspective. Again, exemplar study aims at teaching how to build aesthetic knowing maps within the framework of an Interpretive Perspective. But this is only a beginning. How, more specifically, are learnings used interpretively?

The first thing to notice is that within the Interpretive Perspective learnings vary markedly in their explicitness, ranging from the apparently unconscious or random (associative), to automatic (replicative), to very deliberate (applicative), uses.

1. We speak of the *associative* uses of learning when anything whatsover comes to mind as the result of cue stimulation. As associative learnings are largely unconscious or random, it is difficult to teach for their explicit use. Still they constitute an important matrix of meanings in exemplar study, being operative when a person responds to the connotations of figurative language in literature, or when he senses the allusions conjured up by visual and auditory forms. Once again, there is probably not much instruction can do about unconscious associations. Conventional, conscious associations, on the other hand, are less troublesome since they can be learned like anything else. Associative learnings have sometimes been called concomitant learnings and appear to figure in what Michael Polanyi calls tacit knowing.[7]

2. The *replicative* use of learning involves repeating operations in much the same manner as they were originally learned. This type of learning is relied upon prominently in exercising the skills of reading, writing, and calculating, skills which typically get overlearned to the point where their instances are more correctly regarded as replication than as application. Another illustration of replication is the parroting of facts and judgments precisely as learned, a type of response often interpreted as not using learning at all, although what is usually intended is that automatic replication of skills and knowledge is not very significant. Yet replication should not be denigrated. The question is not whether to replicate, but rather, how do automatic facilities and the replication of information contribute to the more reflective activity of interpretation?

3. Finally, there is the *interpretive* use of learning, a process related to application but less specific and detailed. In exemplar study, for instance, whenever a student provides a general explication of a work's meaning, the process may be called interpretation. The interpretation may be marginal or incomplete, or it may be irrelevant or inappropriate. But then this is the point of exemplar studies; to render interpretation more complete and cogent by infusing it with the peculiar controls of the aesthetic form of understanding.

[7]For two recent discussions of Polanyi's work that have a bearing on humanities education, see Harry S. Broudy, "Behavioral Objectives and Tacit Knowing," in Ralph A. Smith (ed.) *Aesthetic Concepts and Education* (Urbana: University of Illinois, 1969), and Cyril Burt, "Personal Knowledge, Art, and the Humanities," *Journal of Aesthetic Education,* Vol. 3, No. 2 (April, 1969). A good introduction to the idea of tacit knowing is Polanyi's *The Tacit Dimension* (New York: Doubleday, 1966).

Justifying Exemplar Studies. Reference has been made to enlightened judgment and evaluation as necessary conditions for aesthetic understanding or knowing. It was said that these approximately synonymous notions are central to a conception of liberal education that emphasizes the goal of a critical appreciation of different ways of understanding human experience, and that such critical appreciation is prerequisite not only for the full development of mind but also for full participation in contemporary culture. But are these defensible goals for schooling? Is the attainment of a critical appreciation of aesthetic culture *that* important?

To be defensible, a justification of exemplar studies must supply satisfactory answers to such questions. It should, however, go beyond explaining the function of art in the life of the individual and society and show that schooling is required to realize this function in a large proportion of people.

What do the individual and society stand to gain from exemplar studies? It is at this point that the discipline of aesthetics, at least philosophical aesthetics, becomes relevant to justifying and teaching an exemplar approach, for aesthetics typically inquires into the function of art and related issues.[8]

To ask if art has a *positive* function immediately locates analysis in a problematic area; the question stubbornly defies attempts at mapping and precise description. Few aestheticians are prepared to say that art is trivial, but wherein its importance lies is still a matter of debate.

To begin, it is frequently remarked that it is after all futile to inquire after art's function. Art, it is claimed, has no function; it is prized for its intrinsic value, and beauty is its own excuse for being. But one view holds that intrinsic value cannot belong to an object; rather it is confined to states of mind or human experiences. Works of art are thus valued *ex*trinsically, which means that they are instrumental to a type of experience variously called aesthetic enjoyment, aesthetic pleasure, or aesthetic satisfaction. Therefore, what is really prized is aesthetic *experience*.

Intrinsic value can further be distinguished from inherent value. This is ascribed to an object when an object's potential to lead to aesthetic experience is correlated with its aesthetic value. Inherent value is also different from the incidental side effects of works of art that are not correlated with aesthetic quality.[9]

---

[8]It is useful to distinguish three types of aesthetics: *scientific* or *psychological aesthetics,* which typically inquires into what happens when persons express aesthetic preferences or otherwise respond to aesthetic phenomena under experimentally controlled conditions; *analytical aesthetics,* which typically attempts to bring order and clarity into our thinking about a large number of critical concepts, such as form, style, metaphor, etc.; and *synoptic* or *programmatic aesthetics,* which, being synthetic and comprehensive in character, tends to collect scientific and analytical insights into an interpretation of the role of art and aesthetic experience in the good life. These latter two types are more properly regarded as *philosophical* than as psychological aesthetics. A good specimen of the first type is C. W. Valentine's *The Experimental Psychology of Beauty* (London: Methuen Co., Ltd., 1962); of the second, Monroe C. Beardsley's *Aesthetics: Problems in the Philosophy of Criticism* (New York: Harcourt, Brace, & World, 1958); of the third, John Dewey's *Art as Experience* (New York: Minton, Balch, and Co., 1934). The latter is now available in a Capricorn paperback (1958).

[9]See Beardsley's *Aesthetics: Problems in the Philosophy of Criticism, op. cit.,* pp. 571-76, and "The Aesthetic Problem of Justification," *Journal of Aesthetic Education,* Vol. 1, No. 2 (Autumn, 1966), 29-39.

Granted, however, that exemplar studies lead to intrinsically enjoyable experiences, this does not necessarily provide a justification for including such studies in the schools. Still to be settled is whether aesthetic satisfaction is intrinsically *valuable.* Is aesthetic experience *worth* having? If so, on what grounds? These are thorny questions. Yet a great deal of testimony suggests that aesthetic experience is in fact valuable and worth having. In acknowledging this testimony, however, we should not expect to find that it attributes a single, specific value or function to aesthetic experience.

The Value of Aesthetic Experience. A great deal of life requires subordination to two crushing demands: one is the need to appease the appetites and assure survival; the other requires responsible adherence to moral imperatives. In the aesthetic domain, however, these demands can be dampened. Here man can freely manipulate colors, shapes, sounds, and many other aspects of reality that don't defy him in the way intractable matter does. He is also largely beyond the jurisdiction of moral imperatives, as his judgments tend to be guided by criteria of aesthetic fittingness and not ethical propriety.

Such characteristics are often singled out by advocates of "play" theories of aesthetic experience. As F. E. Sparshott has noted, the leading ideas of play theories underscore the moral freedom of art versus the moral responsibilities of ordinary life, contemplation versus appetite, excess energy versus toil and fatigue, and appearance versus reality.[10] But play theories, while attractive, suffer liabilities: the term "play" has undesirable connotations in a practical context such as schooling and the concept of play does not credit aesthetic experience with sufficient significance.

Play theories might be said to provide only the general ground rules of aesthetic experience. What we further gain from aesthetic experience is a vivid awareness of a thing's richness and particularity. Only when absorbed in the perceptual presence of an object, remarks Iredell Jenkins, are we making "the personal acquaintance of some feature of the environment that before was only an entry on a filing-card." In such moments, "we are brought back to the concrete body of the world, and our experience of particular things becomes rich and intense."[11] Thus art not only gives vent to the free play of man's mind, it also augments his consciousness of the world. Of course, it does not take exemplars to achieve this kind of awareness—anything will do so long as it is aesthetically regarded. Yet it is obviously the case that works of art are especially fine vehicles for exhibiting particularity and may, in addition, perform a still further function: they may provide a special form of knowledge.

The knowledge question in art has been called the radical epistemological question,[12] the only thing that keeps aesthetics alive,[13] and also the one on which

[10] *The Structure of Aesthetics* (Toronto: University of Toronto Press, 1963), p. 207. Also see Sparshott's essay "Play" in R. Smith (ed.), *Aesthetic Concepts and Education, op. cit.*

[11] *Art and the Human Enterprise* (Cambridge, Mass.: Harvard University Press, 1958), p. 233.

[12] Monroe C. Beardsley, "The Humanities and Human Understanding," in T. B. Stroup (ed.), *The Humanities and the Understanding of Reality* (Lexington: University of Kentucky, 1966), p. 11.

[13] Sparshott, *The Structure of Aesthetics, op. cit.,* p. 262.

philosophers of art most sharply divide. Certainly the issue is as old as aesthetic inquiry itself, having concerned Plato in his famous attacks on certain kinds of art. On any model of scientific inquiry, of course, the arts do not qualify as knowledge. Art is not science and aesthetic knowledge is not scientific knowledge. What then is the nature of art as knowledge? First it should be noted that the conception of knowledge accepted in this discussion does not depend on any *particular* theory of the cognitive status of art. It merely posits that it is possible to have rapport with things in different ways and these different ways may be called ways of knowing or forms of understanding. Nonetheless, it is useful to distinguish between discursive (propositional) knowledge and nondiscursive (nonpropositional) knowledge. This distinction is featured in the writings of Susanne Langer whose theory will be sketched here in order to show how one well developed philosophy of art attributes cognitive import to art.

Langer's theory[14] has two parts. She explains what is known through art and also the process which gives rise to an object's cognitive content.

The theory turns on an interpretation of the image-making propensities of the human mind and the vital function of mental images: "...we apprehend everything that comes to us as impact from the world by imposing some image on it that stresses its salient features and shapes it for recognition and memory."[15] Images are important because they help us order the raw sense data received from the external world and they also appear to perform a similar office with regard to all passages of sentience.

Life processes set up tensions and resolutions within the organism, some of which rise to what Langer calls the "psychical phase," i.e., they are felt. They are not felt, however, merely in some dim, vague fashion; rather they are apprehended. To be apprehended feelings must be structured for recognition, and it is the peculiarity of human sensibility to record itself in images and to do so according to certain principles of representation. In other words, just as imagination abstracts the semblances of external objects, so it also imposes form on the felt tensions of life processes.

Imagination presumably operates in all individuals, but it is the artist who can project images of feeling into visible or audible form. Consequently, "the work of art is not a 'copy' of a physical object at all, but the plastic 'realization' (Verkwirklichung) of a mental image. Therefore the laws of imagination, which describe the forming and elaboration of imagery, are reflected in the laws of plastic expression whereby the art symbol takes its perceptible form."[16] The work of art, according to Langer, is an objectification of feeling. She has also referred to it as a symbol, and as such a work of art symbolizes, represents, or "stands for" a particular feeling. As a symbol it shares its logical form with the mental image of feeling. This morphological identity between the feeling and its artistic

[14]Susanne K. Langer, *Mind: An Essay on Human Feeling,* Vol. I (Baltimore: The Johns Hopkins Press, 1967).

[15]*Ibid.,* p. 59.

[16]*Ibid.,* p. 95.

representation is possible because the artist is constrained to follow the laws of representation according to what the primitive, spontaneous mental image had fashioned.

It can thus be said that "the work of art presents a form which is subtly but entirely congruent with forms of mentality and vital experience, which we recognize intuitively as something very much like feeling. . . ."[17]

The intuitive recognition of feeling in a work of art does not mean *having* that feeling. The essence of sadness is apprehended not at times when persons are sad but when they are presented with an artistic image of it. Furthermore, art, while a special kind of symbol, does not have a structure similar to language in which interchangeable atomistic elements are manipulated according to the logical rules of grammar. Each work of art is unique, self-sufficient, untranslatable, and indivisible. Verbal discourse is unsuited to symbolize its vital and emotional content. This is why Langer calls art a nondiscursive form of knowledge.

So far as the cognitive status of art is concerned, then, it can be said that the function of art is to articulate the individual's own life of feeling for him, to make him conscious of its elements and its intricate and subtle fabric.

Summary. The arguments offered in defense of assigning an educationally meaningful function to art may now be summarized under three headings: aesthetic enjoyment, aesthetic particularity, and aesthetic knowledge.

1. *Aesthetic enjoyment.* Works of art (exemplars) function instrumentally toward the provision of experiences which are intrinsically desired; they offer worthwhile, desirable opportunities for being pleasurably engaged.

2. *Aesthetic particularity.* Aesthetic pleasure accrues within a qualitatively distinct type of experience. This aesthetic experience is self-enclosed, disinterested, and unrelated in large to considerations of utility, associated trains of thought, or theoretical speculation. These characteristics of aesthetic experience give rise to two value claims of educational interest: the value of the free exercise of man's mind, and, more important, aesthetic experience as a precondition for perceiving the particularity and richness of objects.

3. *Aesthetic knowledge.* It was then suggested that through the contemplation of the perceptual properties of exemplars, something further may be added to awareness, a kind of nondiscursive knowledge.

But now, how does one appropriately engage an exemplar?

The Form of Aesthetic Knowing. David Hume once wrote that "in many orders of beauty, particularly those of the finer arts, it is requisite to employ much reasoning in order to feel the proper sentiment; and a false relish may frequently be corrected by argument and reflection."[18] These comments set the stage for the following discussion.

Again, knowing is a relation between a knower and the known. Each component of the knowing situation contributes something to the situation: the former a

[17]*Ibid.,* p. 67.

[18]H. D. Aiken (ed.), *Hume's Moral and Political Philosophy* (New York: Hafner Publishing Co., 1948), p. 178.

propensity for knowing and latter certain objective properties that hold out the possibility of knowledge. While the human or attitudinal component of knowing is less tractable to analysis, the object known submits to scrutiny, judgment, and evaluation.

In other words, knowledge plays a role in aesthetic response because it is possible to obtain information about the objects and phenomena in aesthetic experience. Relevant knowledge about the object of aesthetic knowing is important in exemplar studies because such knowledge may be used to (a) justify immediately felt satisfaction since certain features of the exemplar can be identified as the sources of aesthetic enjoyment; (b) intensify original feelings of enjoyment because analysis would reveal the object to possess more aspects than perfunctory acquaintance had disclosed; and (c) engender satisfaction where none was present prior to an appraisal of the object.

On the view, then, that some understanding of the object is possible in aesthetic experience, and that such understanding influences aesthetic judgments, what kinds of knowledge are most likely to make understanding more enlightened, intense, and justified? This consideration shifts the discussion to an account of critical activity, for it is the enlightened critic who typically enables others to have more meaningful aesthetic experiences, who knows works of art in the special way required.

Aesthetic Criticism: The General Method of Humanities Education. The account of critical activity to follow is neither original, exhaustive, nor, I think, controversial. Recent classroom research, however, suggests that the nature of criticism is not sufficiently understood.[19]

Critical activity may be described in terms of overlapping phases which contain statements ranging from the cognitively certain to the cognitively less certain, beginning with description and phasing into analysis, interpretation, and evaluation. The division is open to challenge since the terms are used ambiguously and the boundaries between phases are not always precise.[20]

1. *Description.* By and large description involves naming, identifying, and classifying, a kind of taking stock which inventories cognitively establishable aspects of a work of art, e.g., knowledge concerning the type of object (triptych, symphony, work of prose fiction, etc.), information about the materials and techniques used, and knowledge of the extra-aesthetic function of the work when

---

[19] See B. Othanel Smith and Milton O. Meux, *A Study of the Logic of Teaching* (Urbana: Bureau of Educational Research, n.d.), p. 64.

[20] Especially relevant in understanding the nature of critical activity is Morris Weitz's *Hamlet and the Philosophy of Literary Criticism* (Chicago: University of Chicago Press, 1964). Weitz takes the criticism of Hamlet as a paradigm of what criticism is and isolates the following modes: description, explanation, evaluation, and poetics (aesthetics). For a study that identifies categories of response derived from the posture that the writer takes toward his work, see Alan C. Purves (with Victoria Rippere), *Elements of Writing About a Literary Work: A Study of Response to Literature* (Champaign, Ill.: National Council of Teachers of English, 1968). Purves isolates the elements of response active in engagement-involvement, perception, interpretation, and evaluation. Also see Beardsley's review of this study in the *Journal of Aesthetic Education,* Vol. 3, No. 2 (April, 1969).

this is relevant. This category would further comprise art-historical data, and in the case of representational works, knowledge of mythology, cultural history, or whatever is required to identify the subject matter depicted.

Descriptive knowledge of the foregoing types is often depreciated because so-called art appreciation courses frequently fail to go beyond this level, or at least so it is often said. Assuredly, memorization of dates and names and drills in the identification of period styles and artists fall short of the general goal of humanities education. Yet descriptive information of the right sort is important. Relevant descriptive knowledge interrelates with the other, more properly aesthetic, phases of criticism and thus enriches the total critique. Lastly, it is conceivable that ability to talk with cognitive assurance about the descriptive elements of works of art, even though they are not necessarily the most aesthetically relevant, may give teacher and student greater confidence to venture into more ambiguous and unchartered territories. It is awkward when an instructor doesn't know the difference (say) between the virtues and the vices in a work of religious art.

2. *Analysis.* This involves a close look at the components, elements, or details that make up a work, the larger groups or complexes into which they are composed, and the relationships they sustain. Analysis in art is not a mere enumeration or cataloging of components; it cannot be done in a meaningful way without at the same time describing and often characterizing what is singled out for inspection. The distinction between "description" and "characterization" introduces different ways in which parts, complexes, and regional properties can be talked about.[21] Such considerations further introduce the complex notion of aesthetic qualities, concepts, or predicates—a topic that invites analysis of the terms, particularly adjectives, that figure importantly in critical activity.

a. There is a first group of predicates so matter-of-fact and uncontroversial that it probably is not proper to consider them as aesthetic concepts. A color may have a certain degree of saturation, a musical note a given pitch, a shape a geometric configuration, a word a conventional meaning, and so on. These characteristics, which anyone whose sensory and mental apparatus is not impaired should be able to perceive, are literally in the work. Ascription of such characteristics is normally accompanied with the certitude distinctive of propositions cited in support of fundamental knowledge claims. That an element is crimson, circular, cylindrical, or a high C is not usually subject to further confirmation.

b. The next class of predicates typically finds employment in distinctively aesthetic contexts but may also be used in other situations, e.g., words such as "harmonious," "delicate," "graceful," and many others. Here agreement among critics is still substantial but by no means unanimous. Some persons may detect subtle rhythms where others utterly fail to do so. Similarly a feature appearing "graceful" to one critic may appear "flaccid" to another. Indeed, one cannot always decide whether terms like "delicate," "garish," or "harmonious" are used to

---

[21] The distinction between "description" and "characterization" is for convenience. "Characterization" implies the pointing out of aesthetic qualities, whereas "description" notes the more literal properties of objects.

describe or characterize, whether they are closer to the cognitively certain or to the cognitively uncertain end of the spectrum of critical statements. Once more, it is sometimes impossible to maintain sharp and clear distinctions. Nor is it always necessary to do so.

c. There is another, more properly aesthetic, group of characterizing predicates which cannot be certified through simple inspection. They do however have one thing in common: their normal application lies in a different modality of experience; hence to ascribe them to works of art is to use them metaphorically. Thus critics speak of "strident" colors, "luminous" tones, "lugubrious" movements, "taut" story lines, or "stern" passages, to take only a very few simple examples. While often construed as a source of perplexity, it should not be concluded that talk attributing such aesthetic qualities to works of art is necessarily fuzzy and imprecise. Of matters metaphorical some relatively reasonable things can be said.[22]

(1) In the first place the metaphorical use of terms is predicated upon identifiable features in a work of art; aesthetic judgments containing such terms need not report grossly idiosyncratic impressions. Although it may be thought that "violent" does not properly characterize a certain component or pervasive regional quality, when this term is used people generally understand what is meant. Critics, moreover, can offer good reasons in support of such an aesthetic judgment; i.e., they can generally explain why an object has a certain quality.

(2) Furthermore, divergent judgments are usually not poles apart but seem to lie along a qualitative range. For instance an arrangement of elements may be called "restful" by some and "monotonous" by others, but it is highly unlikely that such elements would be characterized as being "turbulent." and a concept of aesthetic knowing requires only that we can speak intelligently about matters of relevance and appropriateness. Charles Morris once remarked that Stravinsky's *Rites of Spring* may induce different interpretations, but no one suggests that it connotes a quiet brook, lovers in the moonlight, or the self's tranquility.

(3) It is also pointed out that the use of metaphorical language is neither estoteric or unnatural. As Frank Sibly has noted, the shift from literal to metaphorical uses of words is due to "certain abilities and tendencies to link experiences, to regard certain things as similar, and to see, explore, and be interested in these similarities. It is a feature of human intelligence and sensitivity that we do spontaneously do these things and that the tendency can be encouraged and developed. It is no more baffling that we should employ aesthetic terms of this sort than that we should make metaphors at all."[23] Moreover, the propensity for metaphor, or what is sometimes more loosely called colorful language, is doubtless developed at a very early age by emulating the actions of parents and peers, a fact perhaps fraught with unexplored educational consequences.

Some additional remarks about the analytical phase are in order. It should be

---

[22]See Frank Sibley, "Aesthetic Concepts," in R. Smith (ed.), *Aesthetics and Criticism in Art Education, op. cit.,* pp. 332-42.

[23]*Ibid.,* p. 339.

clear that the characterization of elements and relationships in a work of art already shades over into the next, the interpretive, phase. Furthermore, as remarked earlier, descriptive and characterizing terms are, in many cases, normative as well, thus anticipating the evaluative phase. In most contexts words like "harmonious," "unified," and "graceful" tend to have positive connotations, while "shrill," "harsh," "unbalanced," "disjointed," etc., seem to be not only descriptive characterizations but negative judgments as well, though not always. In a great deal of modern art criticism the judgments "harsh" and "shrill" have positive connotations, owing to that peculiar tendency of contemporary sensibility to assert intensity of expression as a norm.

3. *Interpretation.* The proper concern of this phase is to say something about the meaning of a work of art as a whole, as distinct from an interpretation of its parts. Judgments of this sort are sometimes the first ones made, which is to say they are not always preceded by descriptive and formal analysis. But to justify or support interpretations a critic will often resort to description and analysis. Such activity may indeed have the effect of amplifying, modifying, or even radically altering a viewer's, listener's, or reader's own interpretation.

Since interpretation is often taken as the most meaningful and enriching phase of transaction between a percipient and a work of art, just what and what not to expect from it should be indicated. Interpretation, it is suggested, should probably not be attempted where human significance is obviously irrelevant, e.g., in the case of works primarily concerned with pattern and decoration. Further, the impression should be avoided that interpretation is merely a summing up of what is found in analysis. The interpretation of a work of art as "an image of lonely despair" seems to follow logically from the characterization of its components as "somber," "drooping," "mournful," "dark-hued," "slow-paced," etc. But not necessarily.

For instance, normative connotations of interpretive ascriptions may be altered when elements characterized negatively (say) as "unbalanced," "top-heavy," or "murky" are perceived as necessary to a forceful expression of "menace" or "impending disaster." Original characterizations may also take on ironic or distrubing twists when details which one would normally call "gay" and "sprightly" are seen as essential to a "sinister" or "anxiety-ridden" mood. The sixteenth-century work of Hieronymus Bosch come to mind. His "Garden of Delights," e.g., is hardly delightful. Moreover, the modern style of Surrealism in painting, literature, and now film trades on such devices to create queasy and unsettling qualities. The work of the expressionist composer Schonberg is also said to have used nineteenth-century values of unreality and modish display in the service of an ultimate seriousness.[24] All of this is merely to indicate that while the citing of analytical findings in support of interpretations is required by responsible criticism, the manner in which interpretive judgments emerge from analytical ones is sometimes complex and not always productive of general agreement.[25] Perhaps this

[24] George Steiner, *Language and Silence* (New York: Atheneum, 1967), p. 130.

[25] For further discussion of some of the logical problems involved in moving through the phases of criticism, see Brian S. Crittenden, "From Description to Evaluation in Aesthetic Judgment," *Journal of Aesthetic Education,* Vol. 2, No. 4 (October, 1968), 37-58.

is one reason why certain works of art continue to have appeal: their infinitely rich forms continually give rise to new interpretations when seen from a different angle of vision.

If the connection between interpretation and analysis is often ambiguous the relationship between the subject matter of a representational work and its message or content is of course even more so. It is a good rule to say that a critical response is inadequate if it offers as an interpretation a mere recapitulation of subject-matter description. Content, it may be said, is a kind of distillation, abstraction, or compaction of the character or import of whatever is depicted or portrayed. And often it is in the more significant works that striking discrepancies are found between what the work ostensibly represents and what it is interpreted to mean, or what it is said to be a metaphor or image of. A clear-cut case is Masaccio's "The Tribute Money," a mural that is impressive not because it depicts a particular biblical episode (in itself not high in the hierarchy of biblical events). Rather, it is impressive because it shows the dignity and worth of the individual, a meaning supported by the manner in which Masaccio individuated the various figures in the picture and fixed their spatial and psychological relations. An aesthetic interpretation of "The Tribute Money" thus delivers the judgment that the picture's significance resides in its image of human nobility, such image being the essential import of what is depicted, i.e., its content in contrast to its subject matter.

4. *Evaluation.* The term as used here implies an assessment of the merit of the work of art in question. The simplest kind of verdict asserts that the work is good or bad, based upon an examination of its aesthetic qualities, say, its degree of unity, complexity, intensity, or some combination of these qualities.

As for import or significance, the only acceptable aesthetic evaluation is one of sufficiency or deficiency. A work may be judged sufficiently expressive to reward contemplation, or, as in the case of certain elaborate and technically brilliant productions, it may be dismissed as shallow, insignificant, not worth the percipient's time. To praise or condemn on the basis of *what* a work says, however, is to make a moral or cognitive, or extra-aesthetic, and not a distinctively aesthetic evaluation. To condemn or praise a work *because* it depicts (say) moral decadence would be a case in point. An aesthetic evaluation, however, would arise from an assessment of the work's parts, complexes, relations, and regional aspects, the overall interpretation of which might give rise to the kinds of content statements previously referred to. Since, however, moral and cognitive judgments will be made by teachers and learners anyway, and rightfully so, it is no use ruling them out of humanities education. Indeed, it is necessary to know how to handle them in order to understand better what is involved in aesthetic judgments. The only stipulation would seem to be that teachers and learners understand that works of art can be judged from different value perspectives.[26]

---

[26] For a discussion of different types of judgments, see Monroe C. Beardsley, *Aesthetics: Problems in . . .*, *op. cit.*, Chapter 10. Also "The Classification of Critical Reasons," *Journal of Aesthetic Education*, Vol. 2, No. 3 (April, 1968), 55-63.

There are at least two ways in which even a work that rates high in aesthetic value and significance may yet draw a negative critical assessment. One is to find it derivative and unoriginal; there simply are too many things like it around. Secondly, an aesthetically good work may be denounced when it fails to serve whatever extra-aesthetic functions it may have. Paul Rudolf's Art and Architecture Building at Yale may be a case in point; it is purportedly interesting to perception, yet students are said to complain about working in it.

Another pair of evaluative terms are "successful" and "unsuccessful." Now "successful" and "good" are almost equivalent. But to ascribe lack of success to a work appears to mean that certain expectations were not fulfilled. This could refer to the artist's intentions: he did not achieve what he set out to do. Speculations about what the artist had in mind, however, are sometimes difficult, if not impossible, to verify, and for purposes of aesthetic evaluation it would seem that the work itself provides most of the necessary information. If "unsuccessful" indicates that a work is not quite what it might have been, then some description of what would have constituted success should be expected.

Lastly, critics will frequently sum up their reaction, the nature of their experience with the work, with such terms as "interesting," "impressive," "challenging," "stimulating," "dull," "preposterous," etc.[27] In other words, an assessment of the value possibilities of a work may be rounded off by a statement about the nature or intensity of the response, and the latter is not always predictable in light of the former. It is perhaps one mark of the enlightened aesthetic observer that he can recognize a work's value potential, endorse it, and even recommend it wholeheartedly to others, yet say it's not his cup of tea. This is perhaps the highest degree of impartiality one can hope for. But there are still problems.

Even if the foregoing constitutes a reasonable and acceptable description of critical activity, it does not explicitly prescribe content or procedures for doing criticism. Needed is a comprehensive set of concepts and critical techniques as distinct from critical phases.

Very briefly, some content that might be used to help develop critical capacities are the concepts (or topics) of medium, form, content, and style. These are some of the more inclusive notions. Regarding *form,* the principles of harmony, balance, centrality, and development may be mentioned, aspects which can be displayed by the devices of recurrence, similarity, gradation, variation, modulation, symmetry, contrast, opposition, equilibrium, rhythm, measure, dominance, climax, hierarchy, and progression. In addition, somewhere in instruction such topics as symbol, meaning, truth, intention, and metaphor should be dealt with.[28] The generality of

[27]See the distinction between "emotion-arousal" and "recognition of emotional quality" words in R. W. Hepburn, "Emotions and Emotional Qualities: Some Attempts at Analysis," in Harold Osborne (ed.), *Aesthetics in the Modern World* (New York: Weybright and Talley, 1968), pp. 81-93. This volume is a collection of essays from the *British Journal of Aesthetics.*

[28]Any standard anthology of aesthetics will reveal a sense of the topics currently structuring the field; e.g., Monroe C. Beardsley and Herbert J. Schueller (eds.) *Aesthetic Inquiry* (Belmont, Cal.: Dickerson Publishing Co., 1967). This volume is a collection of essays from the American *Journal of Aesthetics and Art Criticism.*

content from one art to another should not, however, be taken for granted lest a spurious unity be imposed on materials. Content as transfigured subject matter, i.e., the subject as presented in the medium of the materials, is an important and accepted idea in the visual arts, but more problematic in music. And it's an open question how to talk about the significance of some examples of nonobjective and abstract painting. Does a Mondrian or a Kandinsky, or a work of "op" art, have either content or subject matter? It depends on how the terms "content" and "subject matter" are used. Further, as noted earlier, content or expressiveness may be marginal or inappropriate in arts relying on abstract patterns, and the question of the medium presents difficulties in poetry. How important, e.g., is the sound of poetry, the timbre of the spoken word? Should even some novels be read aloud? And how after all is the term "form" to be used? Does it simply mean the same as structure or design, i.e., the elements in any kind of relation? Or is it a normative concept implying something achieved and valuable, as it does in several theories? Awareness of some of these important differences among the arts has prompted one philosopher to organize his discussion of the arts such that painting and music are examined together with respect to their descriptive aspects, separately with respect to problems of interpretation, whereas literature is a separate topic altogether (except in dealing with critical evaluation where most judgments, it is claimed, can be supported by making appeal to a fundamental set of canons).[29]

Regarding critical procedures or techniques, again as distinct from critical phases, recent studies of the critic's activities suggest methods and procedures for teaching.[30] These techniques have been described as involving approximately seven moves or tactics.

Very briefly, there is (1) the *pointing out of nonaesthetic features.* Examples would be "Notice these flecks of color. . . ." "Did you see the figure of Icarus in the Breughel?" "Notice how he has made use of the central figure." The idea, of course, in mentioning or pointing out nonaesthetic features is that by indicating one thing the learner is encouraged to see something else, presumably more aesthetically relevant. Then there is (2) the *pointing out of aesthetic features and qualities.* In doing this the critic simply mentions aesthetic qualities. "See how nervous and delicate." "The landscape is barren." "Feel the vitality!" Simply mentioning the quality may do the trick, achieve the perception in the learner. There may also be (3) a *linking of remarks about aesthetic and nonaesthetic aspects.* This, of course, is quite common. "Do you notice how the horizontals give a feeling of tranquility?" "See how the red adds to the intensity of expression." Something has already been said about the metaphorical use of terms in criticism, but the (4) *use of genuine metaphors and similes* may be noted. "The light shimmers, the lines dance, everything is air, lightness, and gaiety." The critic may also (5) *make use of contrasts, comparisons, and reminiscences,* e.g. "It has the quality of a Rembrandt." "In the Botticelli the edges of forms are stressed as lines, whereas in the Rubens there is a tendency toward fusion and interplay." The (6)

[29] Beardsley, *Aesthetics: Problems in. . . , op. cit.*

[30] Sibley, "Aesthetic Concepts," *op. cit.,* pp. 336-39.

use of repetition and reiteration is another tactic, as is (7) *making use of expressive gestures.* This latter is merely to say that nonverbal behavior may help: a sweep of the arm, a dip of the body, a certain facial expression.

It is important to note that there can be no guarantee that such techniques will be successful in bringing others to see, hear, or feel what is to be experienced, for critical skills and procedures cannot be equated with a method which, when followed conscientiously, ensures success, i.e., a perfect judgment or appraisal: there is no such thing in the aesthetic domain. The teaching of categories, concepts, criteria, and procedures, though seeming to be the only way to make sense out of what can be known in a work of art, constitutes merely the *conditions* for aesthetic knowing, not knowing itself.

But, it may be asked, how can it be determined whether a student is developing as an aesthetic knower? It is suggested that initial evidence of growth in this direction is to be found in written and oral responses to works of art. With respect to the problem of authenticity two things may be said. First of all, excessive parroting, or what was earlier called the "replicative" use of learning, can be avoided by selecting works for test responses which are sufficiently different from the ones used in trial demonstration yet similar enough to allow learnings to be used "interpretively." To deal with the discrepancies that are bound to occur in student responses, clues may be sought in the appropriateness of the reasons given in support of various types of judgments and evaluations. A sense of what is reasonable and appropriate, however, can come only with experience; hence critical competence must be fashioned over a relatively long period of time. Actually, what differentiates the very good from the inferior in student responses is not difficult to discern. Once again, one thing to look for is the organization of critical statements, the ways in which descriptive, analytical, interpretive, and evaluative remarks are interrelated. Neither would one want to overlook the peculiar interpretive moves made in critical ventures. The use of apt comparisons or especially fitting figures to portray a work's qualities, or the dramatic development of a critique leading perhaps from an explication of the role of minor details up to the characterization of the import of the whole, are interpretive characteristics which help a teacher to determine whether responses represent low, average, or high degrees of sensitivity. They are what set expert interpretations apart from those of the novice.

Concluding Remarks. The justification for an aesthetic exemplar approach to humanities education rests on two foundations: the first upholds the need to develop a critical appreciation of the aesthetic form of understanding. Otherwise the growth of mind is stunted and full participation in contemporary culture is denied. The second support derives its strength from a commitment to the ideals of freedom and responsibility. Since works of art have the capacity to influence thought and action, humanities education creates the conditions for rational reflection about an important domain of human activity. If it is granted that art can inform as well as distort perception, then it becomes just as important to be free from error and illusion in the aesthetic domain as in any other.

Humanities in the High School:
The Wave of the Present

Charles R. Keller

Last July, in an art class in our Summer Institute in the Humanities at Williams College, two paintings of four men engaged in a card game were shown on the screen. One was an example of nineteenth century realism, an artist's almost photographic representation of the game; the other was by the post-impressionist Cézanne. In the one it was all there for me to see, to memorize, even to copy. In the other was an invitation to search, perhaps to find, certainly to think. One was factual; the other concentrated on the essence of things, not on outward appearance but on the "form beneath."

Immediately I thought of our present, fact-dominated, separate-subject courses as compared with the interdisciplinary humanities courses which are appearing in schools here and there throughout the country. The nineteenth century was an age of facts. In Charles Dickens' *Hard Times,* Mr. Gradgrind called for "Facts." "Facts alone are wanted in life," he said. And facts are what he and his contemporaries got during much of the century—in art, music, literature, and education.

Art has moved from realism through impressionism and post-impressionism—there was the Cézanne—to the modern and the contemporary. Music and literature have done the same. But education is in many ways, I believe, still nineteenth-century. As I looked at and pondered those two paintings, I wondered whether the appearance of humanities courses is—at a much later date than in art, music, and literature—an important step toward an impressionistic and post-impressionistic period in education. Certainly we need such a movement.

At this point a definition is in order. Negatively, the humanities are those areas which are not included in the sciences and the social sciences. But I like to be positive. The humanities then embrace—and I think the word appropriate—literature, languages, history, music, art, and philosophy. Originally the humanities meant only the classics; the list of subjects has been properly lengthened. In broader terms, the humanities acquaint man with the thoughts, creations, and actions of his predecessors through the ages and mankind around him. They tell him about his roots and his origins and his neighbors. They impel him to ask questions and to seek answers to them: Who am I? Where have I come from? What is the meaning of life? What can I do to become and remain an effective, responsible member of society? They have to do with making man more human.

The humanities include creativity in the areas which have been mentioned. Poets, playwrights, artists, architects, musicians, philosophers, most historians—they work in and deal with the humanities. They have something to say, and they say it in various ways. We badly need more such men and women. We also need people who can read, listen to, see, and feel intelligently the things which other people have created and who can then act responsibly—the more so in an era when there is and will be more leisure time than ever before in history.

Importance of Humanistic Approach. I urge the humanistic approach in all teaching, in all learning, and in all living. This approach puts man at the center of things, provides him with needed strength outside himself, and gives him confidence that men make history, that men can "ride things" and not things men. Ralph Waldo Emerson epitomized the essence of the humanities when he wrote, "Every revolution was once a thought in one man's mind, . . . every reform was first a private opinion."

The essence of the humanities came alive for me, too, in a talk given last February by Miss Evelyn Copeland, Curriculum Consultant in English in Fairfield, Connecticut. Miss Copeland began her talk by quoting from Lewis Carroll's *Alice In Wonderland*:

The Caterpillar and Alice looked at each other for some time in silence; at last the Caterpillar took the hookah out of its mouth and addressed her in a languid, sleepy voice.

"Who are you?" said the Caterpillar.

"This was not an encouraging opening for a conversation. Alice replied, rather shyly, "I—I hardly know, sir, just at the present—at least I knew who I was when I got up this morning, but I think I must have changed several times since them."

Then Miss Copeland continued:

In talking with you about the humanities in the schools, I take my text—three texts, in fact—from the fifth chapter of *Alice In Wonderland*:

"[They] looked at each other for some time in silence," for there must be silences; "Who are you?" for any study of the humanities must be a voyage in self-discovery; and "I must have changed several times since then," for something does happen to us when we study the humanities.

Study of the past is very much a part of the present. Knowledge of what men have thought, said, written, created, and done in the past throws considerable light on the present and future. In the humanities is found not escape into the past but strength for the present and the future. A man should identify himself with the past in the way which Emerson highlighted when he wrote:

There is a relation between the hours of our life and the centuries of time. . . . I have no expectation that any man will read history aright who thinks that what was done in a remote age, by men whose names have resounded far, has any deeper sense than what he is doing today.

From a study of the humanities will come: a knowledge of the values which have stood the test of time and which give men convictions and the courage to stand by and for them; a desire to search for truth which is badly needed in the United States where pragmatism is the prevailing philosophy; an awareness of the excitement of life which can lessen the boredom which is too much with us; roots that give stability; and examples of human courage and accomplishments which may prevent disillusionment. Involvement in the humanities—as creator or as creative listener, looker, and reader—will, I contend, enable a person not only to meet the unexpected and the unusual in his life but also to do something even more difficult—to live, day by day, with the expected and the usual.

With the humanities defined—is "defined" really the word—I turn to a consideration of my topic: "Humanities Courses in High Schools: The Wave of the Present." I believe that these interdisciplinary courses represent one of the most important and the most heartening developments in American education. And there are enough of them in existence and on the way that it seems appropriate to call them "the wave of the present."

These courses constitute a needed challenge to the present separate-subject-dominated curriculum. Knowledge is now compartmentalized in the familiar five-classes-a-day, five-days-a-week pattern. Subjects have little relation to one another. Fusion of knowledge, when it does occur, results more from accident than from design. The student's day, week, and year are mad scrambles as he moves from subject to subject, usually learning without being involved, frequently simply overcome by the continuous exposure to unrelated subjects. Compartmentalized education may have fitted a simpler, more unified era when fewer people had much formal education. It must be questioned in a more complex, atomistic, disunified period when so many human beings are restless, mobile, unconcerned about others, and without standards of value. Humanities courses have come at an appropriate time.

Interesting is the fact that these courses have no set pattern of organization or content. In one high school, for instance, a team of six teachers, two of English, two of history, and one each of art and music, has set up and developed a double-credit course. In another high school, a history teacher, an English teacher, and an art teacher work together in a single-credit course; in still another an art teacher and a music teacher cooperate. There are also one-teacher courses, with teachers of other subjects invited in from time to time as lecturers or discussion leaders. And it should be remembered that some schools have set up humanities *programs* of various kinds on Saturdays, on afternoons after school, and during free periods—without any credit.

In some courses different historical periods are considered chronologically. In others man and his relations to basic concepts and institutions are discussed: man and beauty, man and society, man and the state, etc. I know a humanities course that is called "Man and Ideas" and another which is entitled "Exploring the Arts." Students may listen to a lecture on Brahms or discuss Greek tragedy. They may consider in one course nineteenth-century thought and in another Plato and *Lord of the Flies.* This absence of pattern should continue as courses and programs multiply. Essential is the existence of a situation in which students and teachers are concerned with fundamental human values and are asking the basic questions which I mentioned earlier.

Important, too, is the fact that humanities courses are being developed both for able students and for students who will not continue their education beyond high school. Students in college have reported favorably on their high school courses—as an awakening experience and as good preparation for work in college. At the present time most courses are for this kind of student, but people are beginning to see the peculiar value of the adventures in ideas, provided by humanities courses, for students who are not going to college.

Worthy of note, too, is the interest shown by a few people in humanities courses for students before high school. Last year in one school a course flourished in the sixth grade. This year a similar course has appeared in the fourth grade.

There was a time when I spoke out strongly against school courses in the humanities. I had the jaundiced view of a college teacher of history, entrenched in a discipline and impressed by the difficulties which such courses had encountered in colleges. Furthermore, teachers always seemed to crowd too much into these courses, and some of the teachers just were not competent enough. Things have changed, and I have become a champion of good humanities courses when they do not try to cover too much and are taught by capable teachers. Why do I feel as I now do? Let me suggest some answers.

1. Humanities courses deal with important ideas and values rather than just with facts. More easily than in single-subject courses questions can be raised rather than answers given, and education can really be discovery. Integration of subjects and the accent on ideas make education more meaningful—both for able students and, just as importantly, for students who are not going on to college. Students become really *involved* in humanities courses. They develop new interests; they learn not just facts but something about themselves. The raising of the question, "Who am I? " makes a difference. Here is a chance for some of the much-needed self-identification. Learning comes alive when students are involved, when what they are studying has real importance for them as individuals.

2. Because they deal with ideas and values, these courses help to develop both scholastic competence and social conscience. In recent years the emphasis has perhaps been on the former. Here the balance is restored.

3. Art and music present new forms of communication and enable some students to learn and to enjoy learning as never before. It is good for high school students to learn how and why men create. Some will become creative themselves while others will profit from an understanding of the creative processes.

4. In humanities courses there can be such good reading, looking, and listening. Textbook-leaning is not possible, for textbooks do not exist. Writers are read, not books about writers and their writings; works of art are studied, not books about them; music is understood, not just appreciated.

5. In humanities courses is a form of team teaching, less "trumped up" than is sometimes the case in separate subjects.

6. Students enjoy learning as never before when they realize that their history teacher, for instance, is learning perhaps as much as they are when the art teacher, the music teacher, or the English teacher performs. Learning is best when it is a shared activity of this kind.

7. Humanities courses in high schools will have important effects on education in the earlier years of school and in college. There will be less gathering of inert facts and more getting at the essence and the meaning of things.

Humanities courses in high school—in such quantity that they are called "the wave of the present"! They will increase in number. Accordingly, some warnings are in order. Courses should be set up only when teachers are ready to give them. Careful planning and preparation must come first. Teachers must *know* their subjects and related subjects; they must not just *feel* an interest. School boards and committees should give teachers free time while they plan and begin to give these courses. Teachers must avoid trying to *cover* too much. Courses should be post-holed with a few periods and a few ideas studied in depth. Students must have time for discussions and for independent work. The more learning there can be for learning's sake rather than for grades and credits, the better. No overnight miracles will be performed. Failures should be expected.

In planning a course, teachers may borrow ideas from others, but they should never pattern a humanities course on somebody else's course. Such a course must be indigenous in the school where it is set up, adapted to the faculty and the student body.

I have been reading a spate of novels, seeing a spate of plays, in which men and women are trying to find out who they are, endeavoring to become whole people. They keep probing into their pasts—frequently without success. I live in a world in which many of my fellow human beings are simply escaping from reality or vainly seeking self-identification. I keep wondering whether involvement in humanities courses will cause people to raise basic questions at an early age, to live self-consciously, to bring their pasts with them.

A Commission on the Humanities has published its *Report*; a bill recommending the establishment of a National Humanities Foundation has been introduced into Congress. We should cherish this new interest in the humanities and strengthen it through exciting courses in schools. We should do so on a "both-and," not an "either-or," basis with science and mathematics. A knowledge of science enables us to live; a knowledge of the humanities enables us to live well. Then as the Commission's Committee on the Schools indicates, "we may hope for citizens who are educated in the full sense of the word—interested, informed, inquiring, tolerant." And then we may hope that education will take another step out of the nineteenth century.

Real emergence from the nineteenth century will come however, when, as Professor Fred Stocking of Williams College has suggested, "the curricula of American secondary schools will themselves be large, clearly departmentalized Humanities courses."

Nonperformance Music Classes in Secondary Schools

Marguerite V. Hood

Without question, American secondary schools emphasize instrumental and vocal performance in music to a far greater extent than they do the more academic, nonperformance experiences. In spite of this, however, we do have a large and important segment of the music education in our secondary schools devoted to classes which do not have the purpose of learning music for performance, but rather concentrate on the hearing of music and the study of music history, literature, and theory. There is frequently, it is true, some singing and playing of music by the pupils in these academic classes, but such performance is only for the purpose of increasing the understanding of the music being studied or helping the boys and girls to learn how to play and sing together informally.

In the lower grades of the secondary schools, when pupils are twelve to fourteen years of age, most schools in our country have a required music class, often called general music. The activities of such a class include many of the musical experiences I have seen used in schools in England and western Europe: hearing and learning about standard music literature, old and new, by means of phonograph records and books; and studying musical notation and theory, usually in connection with songs being sung or music being played on informal instruments such as classroom percussion instruments and those of the recorder-flute type. There is no one pattern or standard curriculum for such classes, but they do represent a variety of nonperforming music experiences.

Older pupils in some high schools have the opportunity to study music history and literature quite intensively, and also to study music theory and harmony, often with emphasis on creative writing of their own compositions.

All of the classes mentioned have been rather typical nonperformance offerings in American schools for many years. There is, however, a recent development in our schools which is unique. It is a new type of class called *humanities*. In the humanities class, music is only one of several subjects included, although it is usually a very important subject. Because this is a relatively new area in our schools, it is important to discuss it in some detail here.

While humanities classes (or related arts, as they are sometimes called) have been in existence for many years in a few places, they have suddenly increased in popularity and importance within the last ten years. The humanities class is a special kind of school experience which is sometimes taught by one teacher, but more often by a group or team of teachers, each of whom is a specialist in history or philosophy or in one of the areas of creative expression in literature (drama, poetry, novel), music, fine arts (painting, sculpture, architecture, and related arts), or dance.

This type of class is so new in our curriculum that there is no clearly developed, uniform pattern of instruction for it at present. The purpose of such a class, however, is generally agreed upon by the schools. Most of these teachers take as their aim the development of understanding on the part of American youth that there is a close relationship between these areas of cultural expression—the fine arts, music, literature, and dance—and that they cannot be isolated from one another or from the study of history by being put in separate compartments; that a true understanding or appreciation of any of them rests on a knowledge of this interrelationship.

Philosophers and creative artists in all fields have spoken through the years about the importance of recognizing the relationships between cultural areas, but in most of our schools there are still barriers between the various subjects, and most teachers concentrate only on their own narrow specialties while they teach. Except where an individual teacher has the vision which impels him to recognize the importance of areas other than his own, each subject is likely to be totally unrelated to the others in the minds of both teachers and pupils. As a result, our boys and girls often do not develop an understanding of the breadth and depth and richness of human culture.

The subjects included in the humanities classes are those which deal with different facets of *man as a human being,* and with the development of his *ideas* through the successive periods in the history of the world, with the factors which have influenced those ideas and with the cultural creations which have grown out of them. The humanities classes attempt in a variety of ways to make our young people aware of this important interrelationship and to give them an intelligent basis for appreciation and evaluation of all cultural areas.

Sometimes humanities classes are taught with emphasis on the ways creative artists—composers, painters, sculptors, architects, poets, dramatists—use certain aspects of *form*; how they achieve unity, variety, repetition, contrast, and balance in their works. Sometimes the classes study the ways the creative artist uses the materials, ideas, and techniques available to him for emphasizing an idea, telling a story, or expressing an emotion.

Such experiences, where all the arts are studied and compared, enrich the cultural background of the students. In addition, because some of these arts are expressed primarily through things that are seen, others through sounds heard, and still others through communication by means of words, individual differences in learning habits among students may be served. Some boys and girls apparently comprehend new ideas most easily if the first presentation is a visual one. Some others grasp an idea more quickly if it is presented through the ear. And, still others understand ideas presented with words or verbal expressions most easily.

It is possible, for instance, for an intelligent youngster to be unable, at first, to hear and comprehend the way a composer has organized his musical ideas or used his thematic materials. The study of poetry with certain types of word patterns, repetitions, and changes in rhythm and line, may help such a pupil to hear and understand the repetition and contrast in music in forms such as rondo or theme and variations. The use of the ostinato, whether in old music, jazz, or electronic music, becomes a clearly discernible technique for some listeners when a similar use of a repeated background chant using words is heard in drama or poetry.

Just reading the simple, poetic, antiphonal expression found in the Bible in Psalm 136, will sometimes clarify for a bewildered (and therefore probably uninterested) student the way a composer has used themes in some music being heard. For classes which use English poetry, poetic rhyme schemes such as those of Shelley in "The Cloud" or of Robert Frost in "Stopping by Woods On A Snowy Evening" are fascinating and revealing in a study of patterns in artistic creation. Many languages have similar poetic resources. Similarly, understanding the ways a composer achieves balance in using his melodic, rhythmic, and harmonic ideas is sometimes easier for the beginning student if he sees visual examples of the varying techniques used in painting and architecture to achieve balance. Thus, a comparison of the simple, basic ways by which balance was produced in architecture such as a Greek temple, a Florentine Renaissance palace, and an example of Frank Lloyd Wright's cantilever architecture is helpful in such discussions.

In contrast to the above teaching techniques, many humanities classes are organized around a central core of historical study. In such cases, the content of the course is organized chronologically and follows the sequence of historical events, but the art, music, and literature of each period become a part of the historical study, as expressions of the time.

Thus when the history of the period of the middle eighteenth century in Europe is studied, the class also has the opportunity to become acquainted with some of the literature, art, and music of that time. Whether one calls this period late Baroque, early Classical, or Rococo, certainly the music of such composers as Rameau, Haydn, and Mozart can add to our understanding of the people and life of the time. Also, the paintings of Watteau, Fragonard, Boucher, and Gainsborough; and novels like Richardson's *Pamela,* Fielding's *Tom Jones,* and Goldsmith's *The Vicar of Wakefield* can serve in the same way to add richly to our knowledge of that period. And all of these help provide an introduction to the period which follows at the end of the eighteenth century and the beginning of the nineteenth century.

Other periods of history can be enriched in the same way—Renaissance, Baroque, Impressionistic, and Contemporary. Granted that not all products of any period fit neatly into a pattern, there still is, at any time in history, one group of style characteristics which is noticeably dominant. The most expressive artist is the one from whom we can learn the most about how to interpret his period. Why? Because he knew both the creative impulses and the life of his time.

Musicologist Curt Sachs once wrote, "Analysis can show that each generation has shaped its cathedrals, statues, paintings, and symphonies in the image of its will and dream exactly as emotion will shape at once the features, speech and gestures of a man, to indicate one mood, one act."[1]

These are some of the types of experiences which our humanities classes attempt to provide for students. Unfortunately, to date, most of these classes have concentrated principally on Western arts, music, literature, and history. More and more, however, there is a growing recognition of the importance of including the history and cultural creations of all areas of the world in this type of study. The interest and enthusiasm of the growing group of ethnomusicologists has helped improve this situation considerably.

When we consider the administration of a humanities class in a high school, we immediately recognize some special problems. One of the most difficult problems is that of organizing the team of teachers. This group must be able to plan together and work together amicably. The members of the team must not only be specialists, each in his own area, but they must also be interested in the other subjects included in the course and be willing to study in many fields outside of their own, since

---

[1] Curt Sachs, *The Commonwealth of Music* (New York: W. W. Norton Co., 1946).

obviously, a teacher cannot function well on such a cooperative team if he knows only his own subject. They must be willing to cooperate (and sometimes to compromise) in order to make the course a true joint activity. In considering the music part of the course, we must recognize that not all music teachers have the time or the interest to make these adjustments. However, those who teach humanities classes almost always report this to be a wonderful and rewarding experience.

Materials and equipment for teaching are also important. Audiovisual materials are particularly valuable for use in teaching a humanities class. A good library of phonograph records is important. Many fine motion pictures are available and one company, Encyclopaedia Britannica Films, is producing a series of films designed especially for secondary school humanities classes. In addition, slides, filmstrips, and color reproductions of famous works of art are also used in the classrooms.

In such a course as this, three approaches are important in teaching: (a) auditory—tone and rhythm in music and poetry, (b) verbal—word imagery in imaginative literature, and (c) visual—color, line, and texture. However, these are all essential, whether we teach a special class called humanities or just a class limited to some phase of music. And we need, all of us, everywhere, to consider the great importance of making this art of music live in the future lives of the young people we are teaching. Performance of music is important and wonderful; no one doubts this. But performance alone is not enough. Music and the other arts are super-communication channels. They have helped express man's thoughts and feelings and dreams down through the ages. The next generation should learn to understand this communication of the arts as one of the rich and lasting forms of human expression. The late Will Earhart once said: "The failure, so far as there is a failure, in teaching music education, is in teaching that subject in a vacuum, in not connecting and coordinating it with all other areas of human interest and experience."[2].

Cultural Democracy and the Humanities

Ewald B. Nyquist

For the next few minutes I am going to talk about the school's role in the achievement of a cultural democracy, man's highest aspiration. I shall use the terms "humanities" and "performing arts" interchangeably with the understanding that the second is a limited part of the first.

A cultural revolution is well on its way in American society and especially in New York, which already has rich resources and civil leadership aggressively active in bringing the arts within the mainstream of everyday life. The universality of the arts

[2]Clifford V. Buttelman, ed., *Will Earhart, A Steadfast Philosphy* (Washington. D. C.: MENC, 1962).

and the attainment of excellence in a political and economic democracy are not mutually exclusive.

Waning provincialism, provoked by increased affluence, a better educated population, a heightened concern for greater international understanding, and marked mobility, is a root cause of the cultural explosion. It is probable, too, that the new interest in the arts and the humanities is generated by a need to redress the value imbalances characterizing a technological society which is too preoccupied with system and mass production; with means, not ends; and which emphasizes bigness, impersonality, the denigration of the individual, and increased specialization, rather than meaningful human contact.

There have long been scoffers—frequently rooted in the older cultural and aristocratic traditions of Europe—who have challenged the capability of democracy to attain high standards of excellence in the arts. In the past, we must admit, there has been ample reason for such skepticism.

At the same time, there have also been in our midst those of great faith who have believed that democracy—with its ideal of universal education—is not only capable of producing superlative art, but of ultimately producing a far broader audience than any other form of society has ever done.

Next to his own inner resources, both the creative and the performing artist need more than anything else appreciative and comprehending audiences, and such audiences do not spring from nowhere: They must somehow be developed: the mind, the heart, the thirst, and the anticipation.

To develop this hunger for the arts, an individual must have assimilated a certain amount of knowledge and be given the opportunity for direct exposure to the creative arts. The earlier in life that such exposure takes place, the better for developing thinking, analytical people, and enduring and appreciative audiences. One thinks, for instance, of the custom so common in some of the European centers of culture—where parents and grandparents take very young children to the opera or the symphony, and make lifelong devotees of them. There it is a kind of family ritual, inducting them into the audience and the wondrous mysteries of the art. In this country, we too frequently leave the children home with the babysitter when we visit the art museum or go to the theater.

But many of us have come to realize that the ultimate test of democracy lies in the quality of the humanistic and artistic life it engenders—and supports. What we are after, in the last analysis, is a *cultural democracy.*

We hope to prove that the common denominator of democracy is not necessarily a low one. We are seeking to demonstrate that there is no basic incompatibility between democracy and high artistic standards. As I said earlier, the universality in the enjoyment of the arts and excellence in democracy are not mutually exclusive goals—they are one and the same. Now is the time, if ever, to demonstrate this. We have achieved the greatest economic abundance in our history, and its widest distribution. We are at long last engaged in the process of completing the social and political equalization of all segments of our society.

The flowering of a widespread popular desire for the finer things—in short, a true appreciation of the humanities and the performing arts, permeating the total fiber of our civilization—is what will make the long historic struggle and the materialistic progress finally worthwhile, in the larger and nobler sense.

The means of attaining this cultural democracy is fundamentally education, and it is now becoming our self-appointed task.

To quote a sentence from the recent Rockefeller Panel Report on the Arts:

The effective exposure of young people to the arts is as much a civic responsibility as programs in health and welfare.

A recent annual report of the President of the Rockefeller Foundation is relevant here:

...the testimony of almost everyone with firsthand experience in the arts seems to underscore the fact that organization, continuity, and leadership are needed to cultivate the proliferation of creative modes of artistic endeavor, the aggregate of which is what we call culture and whose widest availability makes a cultural democracy.

The State Education Department believes that it can provide organizational leadership in order to promote the objective with which we are concerned during this Convocation. We are engaged in a number of programs and projects which collectively suggest a strong commitment to the development of a Statewide program in the humanities and the performing arts. This morning I should like to tell you of just a few of these.

First, our Curriculum Development Center undertook a writing project two years ago, to strengthen humanistic education in the schools. The first major accomplishment was the preparation of *The Humanities—A Planning Guide for Teachers.* This endeavor was aided by the advice of outstanding humanities leaders around the country.

The initial objective was "to develop a course of study in the humanities for the 12th grade level." The wisdom of broadening the effort was soon seen, however, and the material included was made meaningful for other than just the 12th-graders.

A policy was adopted that gave complete responsibility to the local school to design its own humanities program to suit its unique needs. The material was devised as a planning guide rather than as a prescriptive, narrowly focused, State-sponsored course of study. All secondary schools in the State received copies of the *Guide.* Schools which already had humanities courses are using the *Guide* to expand or enrich their present offerings. Many others are setting up faculty committees to study the *Guide* and plan their humanities programs. The approaches are diverse.

The preferred methods used in humanities classes are:

1. *Conceptual.* General objectives are determined and experiences involving the great masterworks of man are selected. Hopefully, the student arrives at the discovery of a basic concept through his own inductive activities.

2. *Creative.* The mere accumulation of factual data will not necessarily aid the

student in realizing his own potentialities. Through performance (writing, speaking, discussion, painting, or composing), he freely expresses ideas and tests them against teacher, peer, and masterwork.

We know that much of humanities education is strongly dependent upon aesthetic experience. And the vehicles for such experiences are most desirably found in primary sources. In order for the student to approach an art form most beneficially and to derive meaning from it, the ideal situation is one in which he views the actual rendition—the play performed rather than simply read; the ballet witnessed on stage rather than filmed; the painting, sculpture, or architecture itself, instead of a reproduction; and the musical work heard "live" rather than recorded.

Naturally, this method of study does not discount secondary source materials. The electronic communications media we now have—motion pictures, television, recordings—play an influential role, to be sure. But there is a sharp and subtle difference between the electronic performance and the "live" performance. Despite Marshall McLuhan, the medium is not the whole message. A mechanical presentation must, by the very nature of the medium, be distorted. The human voice is different, when heard first-hand, from an electronically reproduced or amplified one. A dancer appearing on a television screen is distinctly different from the very same dancer performing on a full stage, with music in the pit and theater lights creating aural and visual effects of great beauty. A musician facing a real audience and commanding the whole of that audience's attention behaves quite differently from one who is conscious of the eye of the television camera but not of the human response of the listening group.

Our students are inveterate, seasoned mass media viewers of unending performances of varying quality. We are, after all, dealing with students who represent the first generation brought up on television. It is the Now Generation, one used to instant experience, instant fantasy, and instant wisdom. If these students are left to their own untutored tastes, without guidance and inspiration, they are frequently likely to choose the tawdry on television and to settle for jukebox mediocrity in music. We in education should strive to create audiences who seek and respond to live performances of the highest professional quality.

The ideal circumstance, needless to say, is for a child to grow up in a family environment that is cultivated and arts-conscious, so that he is exposed to the arts from his earliest years, just as he is to the spoken language. Unhappily, this is the exception rather than the rule in our culture. And the mechanical media help mightily to bridge the gap, even with their shortcomings.

We must teach our students to have a rich repertoire; which is another way of saying a large cultural appetite and a wide education. To accomplish this requires continued exposure, with appropriate preparation, follow-up, and hopefully a large degree of personal student involvement. Students will be hospitable to what is familiar and comfortable, just as we all are. But we must also give them the opportunity to discuss, to analyze, to see and listen to the strange, the novel, and the new.

By such exposure, accompanied by appropriate instruction in the school program, children become potential future audiences for ballet—and for the other performing arts to which they are now being introduced in the schools: symphony, music, opera, and theater. Some will even be inspired to assume careers in the realm of the arts, for their knowledge of what is possible has been enlarged and the range of their choices has been expanded. And this is what education and freedom are all about. The job of education is to remove ignorance. Freedom is the exercise of enlightened choice, the opportunity for self-control and self-direction.

In education we are always searching for exemplary models with which to augment classroom instruction. What better exemplary models can we possibly find than real, live artists—writers, painters, performing artists. They are dynamic—not static—models. They are a vivid illustration of what learning is and of what teaching is. Not only do their writings, paintings, and performances, when properly presented, fire the imagination of students—children being especially susceptible to ideas, color, movement, and sound—but the pupils absorb something beyond those observable elements. Artists, by their obvious dedication to quality, their continuous practice in search of the perfection of their skill, their sympathy and regard for the efforts of the beginner, their downright unending hard work, their honest self-criticism, exemplify the best principles of the psychology of teaching and learning. We would have to look far to find more dramatic examples of the "exemplary models" we constantly seek.

Whenever possible, it would be a rewarding experience for students to observe an artist-in-residence at work, to talk with him about his art form and his methods of achieving his goals, or to watch a short rehearsal session of dancers. I know of no learning situation that is comparable. And I think we could expect that students, exposed to this kind of dedication to the mastery of skills, would bring back into the classroom a greater understanding of and respect for what the teacher is trying to do and what they, as students, should do to acquire the skills they need.

I could take as a text a paragraph written lately by a prominent New York critic:

If our children are taught to look upon culture as a natural part of their lives, if they grow up exposed to music, theater, and art, they will support it in their maturity. But that will involve an explosion in pedagogical philosophy, from kindergarten through college, that would make the "cultural explosion" appear like a pea-shooter against an atomic warhead.

Let us, indeed, take realistic note of the fact that only some 30 percent of the teachers of literature and arts in the schools of this country have ever *personally* seen live theater. Consider the fact that the actual boxoffice public for the performing arts—that is, for symphony concerts, plays, opera and ballet—is derived from a very narrow segment of our society; mainly the affluent, the better educated, and frequently (for want of a better word) the "social" element. Consider the fact that not more than four percent of the population used the 20 million tickets purchased for such performances in a recent typical season. Consider that, while the paying audience for symphony in the United States has been increasing over the years, it has actually lagged behind the growth in population, proportionately.

In other words, the question has recently been raised: Just how much of an explosion is the cultural explosion? It has been raised, soberly and statistically, by a study commissioned by the Twentieth Century Fund, conducted by two eminent Princeton University economists, Professors William J. Baumol and William G. Bowen. The report was published just last year in book form, entitled *Performing Arts—The Economic Dilemma.* This is a book which cannot be ignored. The professors detect no convincing evidence of a grass-roots upswing in actual public support of the arts in the nation as a whole; and find that what has been happening during the past 15 years is "little more than a continuation of past trends." But, for all their statistical cold water, these gentlemen admit that there exists an "air of excitement and growth" in the performing arts and related areas which augurs well for the future.

The Baumol-Bowen report is, in effect, a sequel to the Rockefeller Panel Report of 1965, which was published under the title of *The Performing Arts: Problems and Prospects.* I heartily commend both of these books to the attention of all the participants of this workshop.

I do not think it amiss, in our expanding program of humanities and performing arts in the schools, to set as one of our goals the creation of future audiences which can help to encourage a more secure footing for the performing arts than they now enjoy. And I am thinking Statewide—not just of Lincoln Center, where the usual wild scramble for tickets puts this workshop in a truly favored position. Along this line, it seems pertinent to quote this passage from the Rockefeller Panel Report:

The creation of a propitious environment for the arts depends primarily upon the education of a people. Any significant increase in demand for the arts will derive only from a citizenry that has come to love them and to depend on them. Furthermore, the pursuit of excellence in the arts, without which their expansion is meaningless, grows only from a general public recognition of what constitutes high quality. Mediocrity is the menace that lies inherent in egalitarianism. The only weapon that can be used to combat it is education; and again, not a mediocre education but one that produces an appreciation of form and a basic concern for the things of the mind and spirit. Obviously this cannot be accomplished quickly. But if it is to be accomplished at all, there are steps to be taken now and in the years immediately ahead. The habit of attendance is based on a strong sense of need—and without a sense of urgent necessity on the part of the people, the performing arts will always remain peripheral, exotic, and without any true significance. Therefore, the habit must be acquired young; it is probably not too soon to begin at six. After all, at that age boys are learning how to play baseball. Music and dancing and playacting come naturally to children at that age. This can easily be translated into the pleasures of seeing and hearing others perform. . . .

The report continues:

The self-contained classroom prevailing in elementary schools for several decades has worked against the development of an effective program of instruction in the arts. We need more and better trained teachers in the arts, particularly at the elementary school level. School administrators need to be made more aware of the place of the arts in a balanced curriculum and the necessity for providing not only adequate time during the school day but also the materials and equipment needed for an arts program. . . . *The American School, in general, should show greater imagination, initiative, and responsibility than it has in bringing art to the school and the child to art.*

I am reminded of this comment on the schools and their previous lack of regard for the arts by what Sam Goldwyn used to say about movie critics: "Don't pay any attention to them. Don't even ignore them."

Finally, I should like to quote from a recent article on art education by Professor Melvin Tumin of Princeton University:

In the present sorry plight of education in general, one can point to the most egregious failure of the current schools—the failure to be concerned with goals of education beyond those of limited cognitive skills. Other goals can be named. They include the acquisition of a satisfying self-image; a capacity to live with differences; a vital interest in participation as citizens; sound emotional development; and a continuing refinement of tastes and sensibilities.

And, he might have added, a capacity for self-criticism.

. . .it may very well prove to be the case that a whole new concept of education, education for creativity, or education for taste and sensibility, or combinations of these and others, in which many disciplines join hands, may be the new and broader vision of things to come and curricula and processes to develop.

But our schools are moving, and moving strongly, in these directions. This is most emphatically true of the schools of New York State. The State Education Department is now deeply involved in developing programs in the humanities, including major programs for bringing the performing arts directly to students—as well as taking students to the performing arts. In this activity, we are working closely with the New York State Council on the Arts, with the Lincoln Center for the Performing Arts, and with the new Saratoga Performing Arts Center.

In the spring of 1965, the Lincoln Center for the Performing Arts and the State Education Department joined forces to provide performances of music, dance, and drama for a present attendance of over one million in junior and senior high schools in all parts of the State. This joint program was designed to be a "curriculum-related activity." This meant that schools could use education funds for this new and important phase of the humanities program. For the first time in the United States, the performing arts were presented in schools in an organized program under the auspices of a State Education Department.

The program of humanities and performing arts, upon which the Department is now so seriously launched, is designed to enrich the curriculum and to be an integral part of the regular educational program. Let me tell you of some things we have in mind:

1. The development of a model humanities program, with the aid of consultants

drawn from educational institutions in the State and the nation, the tryout of this program in pilot schools and the publication of the worthwhile elements of the program for other schools to adopt.

2. An intensive Statewide survey of humanities programs to determine characteristics and practices of schools conducting such programs.

3. A new museum project in which teams composed of teachers, administrators, and museum specialists will hold a series of brainstorming sessions to evolve creative ways in which schools can work with museums. A document presenting these ideas will be produced for the schools of the State.

4. Continuation of our pilot Museum-Lincoln Center Project involving 50 upstate school districts in performing arts and planned museum visits to the Museum of Modern Art, the Metropolitan Museum of Art, the American Museum of Natural History, the Hayden Planetarium, and Lincoln Center. This pilot program will launch its second year in September and will be used to create a Statewide network of such activities.

5. A Statewide program of 10 regional Performing Arts Festivals for students at all levels of the school system—from elementary to adult—now in the planning stage.

6. Institutes and workshops for teachers and administrators, with nationally known performing artists at the Saratoga Performing Arts Center. These were begun last summer and will be continued this summer, in July and August.

7. A project which will bring great film classics to school children throughout the State—still in the planning stage.

8. This Convocation which is being attended by 800 teachers, administrators, performing arts coordinators and school librarians, and which is designed to move us into the next major phase of the program's development—the determination of specific and practical ways of further integrating the humanities and the performing arts into the total curriculum.

Our activities have already generated so much interest and demand for assistance and participation from schools and related cultural agencies that we are now in the process of providing a permanent focus for our cultural concerns by establishing within the Department, at the direction of the Regents, a Division of the Humanities and the Arts. This Division will function in a leadership role by developing our expanding program and supplying the Statewide services required to implement it successfully. The former art and music units of the Department will become bureaus in the new Division.

The functions of the Division, in addition to art and music education, will include:

1. Close liaison with humanities and performing arts groups.

2. Continued planning and cooperation in the development of materials prepared by those groups for use in the schools.

3. Development of a Statewide network of humanities and performing arts programs in elementary, secondary, and adult education programs.

4. Integration of the humanities and performing arts into the related instructional programs developed by the Department.
5. Cooperation with the Department's curriculum unit to insure infusion of the humanities and the performing arts into the curriculum.
6. Cooperation with the State University and other institutions of higher learning in the development of regional performing arts programs and teacher training programs in the humanities and the arts.
7. The conducting of conferences and workshops such as this one for teachers, administrators, and school librarians.
8. Establishment of a humanities and performing arts laboratory in the Department for the use of teachers and school librarians throughout the State.

I truly believe that we stand today on the threshold of an exciting fresh epoch in which the humanities and the arts may recapture some of their ancient importance—some of that quality of celebration through which, in olden times, entire communities expressed their happiness, their faith, their allegiance to the best in themselves and to the universe in which they lived.

Humanities and Verbal Communication

Alan Sapp

This problem of the relationship of the arts and humanities is a fascinating one, indeed. It is my daily experience to have to deal with these questions—to see where they are inter-related and where they are not inter-related. It seems to me important to understand where humanities, in the traditional sense, stop, and where arts begin.

I'd like to give you several basic philosophical tendencies that I have about the relationship of the arts and the humanities.

First of all, I think that they are coexistent, coequivalent, and represent two immensely important but different aspects of mankind's need to receive communications and to express himself in communications. Humanities, for me, mean the great world of letters, the great world of verbal communication, and the great world of man's efforts, in language and in letters, to say what he has to say—to criticize, to ennoble, to give it fortification, to make a record, to make a prophecy. The arts have an equally important communicative side, but it is symbolic. I don't mean to say that words are not occasionally symbolic or that language itself, as gesture, and language as symbol, is not terribly critical. The two obviously intermesh in many ways, but it is the symbolic aspect of communication through the arts that has always fascinated me. It is the balance between communication by words, by letters, in literature, and the communication through art, visual or in music, which is so important to keep related and separate.

Let me give you an anecdote of this year which I think is very relevant to the discussion. The State University at Buffalo, of which I am a part, has been going through a massive, total reorganization, and in such times of reorganization, all the administrators and faculty reexamine their premises and their assumptions. They reexamine the bases from which they speak. The question of whether arts and humanities should be allied, should be kept together administratively, or made distinct, was a very crucial one. The incoming president and many of my colleagues, particularly my colleagues in music, insisted that music should become part of a faculty of art; that it should have an independent identity; that it should function professionally; it should be discrete; it should have its own traditions and its own mores; it should have a faculty different from the faculty of letters and differently recruited, differently rewarded, and with platforms of different types of expressions. I alone resisted this current. Over the course of the years it was really part of my job to define why I thought that the humanities and the arts needed to be together.

I started off, as I said, with the first of these philosophical premises that the arts and humanities are coexistent in any context which one wishes to draw—the academic context, or the much more important context of our daily existence. Yet they both involve values, and they both involve the kinds of values without which civilization, no matter how affluent, will be meaningless. And I was queried, of course, about why the training of a professional musician, of an actor, of a drama critic, of a painter, of a sculptor seemed to be rather significantly different from the training of a poet, of a writer of novels, of an essayist; certainly different from that of the classical scholar; certainly very different from that of the numismatist or the Byzantine expert. Therefore, why?

Well, it seems to me that the arts, operating in a framework merely of replication and recreation, suffer desperately from the critical leavening influence of the creative people and the reflective people. I like to think not of scholars and creative people but of the reflective and active people in letters. I think that it is an impoverished kind of art which does not mirror conflict or the relationships that come up every day with humanists. Humanists are safer, generally speaking, since they have a long history in Academia and a distinguished position in cultural history. Any history of culture deals extensively with humanistic aspects but not so much with the contributions of the arts. Therefore, the humanists need the artists because the artists are the prophets, the critics, the iconoclasts, the "messy" people—the people with the internal heat, with the anger channeled and not dissipated, with worries which are capable of expression, with the sense of new beauties in the old world.

To move to my second basic premise, how are some of the ways we in education can bring into our orbits, our spheres, to make part of our lives and part of the lives of the students around us, some of the rage, some of the excitement? To use that wonderful phrase which kept cropping up in all the recent meetings that I attended, how can we make sure that we are all "turned on," once in a while? "Turning on" implies that for some of the time we're "turned off"; and there is a sense in which the arts, perhaps through the cool rage that I speak of, turn us on. But how can we do this? Well, my second premise is obviously that art has a terribly significant role in the context of general humanistic education, of providing us with the moments when we are "turned on." When we, in a sense, lose ourselves.

I think this phrase "turned on" means many things. It's a colloquialism, and it can have a vulgar meaning—hyper-excitement of the moment which is ephemeral and passive—or it can have a more profound meaning. It can have the meaning basically of forcing us to split, forcing us to reexamine ourselves, and forcing us to burst out of ourselves. We need it perhaps more than the young people in whom the effects of being "turned on" are more obvious.

Art turns us on. Beauty has always turned us on—turned us on to a moment of sudden awe, turned us on in the sense of blinding experience which transforms our lives, turned us on in the sense of an experience which makes us start to question everything we believed in up to that point. Beauty turns us on in the sense that we have suddenly a query where there was no query before, the sense of inquiry about the fundamentals of our artistic convictions, our critical credos; where we, in a sense, come face to face with an order which we have not previously been willing to deal with or which we have dealt with only in terms of hearsay. So, I think that art is necessary to turn us on.

Why have we been turned off? If we can be turned on by art, where have we been turned off? Well, we are narcotized, not by drugs, but by the constant experience, particularly visually, of vulgarity. We are narcotized by a blanket of sound which threatens to atrophy our ears altogether. I don't know which I detest more—the piledriver and all its relatives, which raise the level of noise in decibels to the point at which it affects my nervous system; or the quiet, low music which is meant not to be heard but which is ubiquitous, which we cannot escape anymore. I don't know which is worse. Both serve to narcotize us; both serve to lull or hammer our receptive organs into a kind of passivity. How do we react? We turn ourselves off. How do we react to the incredible visual vulgarity which is so documented everywhere—the vulgarity of signs, the vulgarity of all those creations which are commercially justifiable and esthetically horrendous? Well, we turn ourselves off. We stop looking; we stop seeing. And I submit that when we stop seeing and stop hearing and listening, we become less; we become much less, and we become therefore incapable of transmitting our value systems. So when we're turned on, what is happening is that that decision, that defense which has been necessary to keep us going through life is punctured for a moment.

So, art does turn us on, and it turns us on in a different way from the experiences of literature and the humanities, because the impact again is symbolic. Therefore, I would suggest that art is the kind of communication which is perhaps more direct. I will not say more discreet, or more refined, or more persuasive, or more didactic, or more elegant, but I will say more direct. I think that those students of communication who are concerned with the communicative aspects of the arts have come to at least one acceptable conclusion—that it is a kind of communication which is extremely direct and to which we are really very vulnerable, very open; that our defenses are more easily pierceable, so to speak.

A cool response, a response which is either absent, hostile, or neutral, is immediately perceptible to anyone on stage; whereas, a warm response or a hot response is equally clear and equally important in the quality of the performance. Any good professional can overcome negative input, and a great performer can rise to heights we can hardly describe if the response is hot. What the nature of that response is I do not know, and secretly I hope I never find out. And I hope that nobody ever figures out a way to measure, through some occult laser beam or radar machine, what it means to be here and to register the response collectively of an audience. It is one of the mysteries.

And the word "mystery" brings me to the third of my philosophical premises about art and the relationship of art and the humanities. Art and humanities must coexist. Art has the function of turning us on, of making us see again the wonderful phrase of James Sweeney: "Art washes our eyes." It makes us see again. It cuts away all the defenses we have.

My third point has to do with mystery. In a way, magic is not very fashionable. This is a scientific, rational age—a quantifying age. But at the same time I can't help thinking that the artist in our time is something like a magician. He causes wonderful, mysterious, and miraculous things to happen. One of the prime reasons for bringing into our context the artist is that he is a form, sometimes not so overt, of magician. There are, of course, white magicians and black magicians. There are magicians who cause damage, and there are magicians who are wise and good. If there is magic, there is strong and good magic; there is strong and not so good magic.

One of our problems as we delicately move, like a slow barge up the river, toward the acceptance of the inclusion of the arts in our curriculum, of the presence of artists in our schools, on our campuses, in our regional districts, in our towns, through our activities as members of arts councils; one of the important things is the distinction between the good and the not so good kinds of magicians. But certainly there always ought to be the awareness that an artist is in fact a magician. This is a metaphor, and I don't want to push it too far, but I think it's a very important metaphor because it again tends to differentiate one very important aspect of the arts from important aspects of the humanities. We don't know quite what to do with magic—we're uneasy about it. If we think it exists at all, it exists in fairy books in a distant kind of land. I would only suggest that you explore the notion that there is in fact a magic.

If magic means the capacity to cause change miraculously, then many of the performing and creative artists around us are magicians. I don't want to get into the matter of taste and the kinds of things that are best, but I would make a little plea. When I came in, I walked down the aisle to hear a discussion which sounded to me as if there were problems about some of the new music going on. I would say this: Let us err much more in the direction of sponsoring and accepting the new and the unpredictable, the present, the prophetic, than we err on the side of an overbalance of that which is safe and which has been conserved. It has been my experience, time and time again, that art is created from the problematic, the experiment in magic which might or might not succeed, where the formularies are a little imperfect, and where we don't know quite what's going to happen in the transformation. It might turn out to be a dog, or it might turn out to be a castle. We're not quite sure. It is in such cases that the young are apt to be most perceptive. They have not been told, and I hope they are told less and less, what is good, what is bad. The presence of a group of young performers doing a piece of music which is very new is apt, from an efficiency standpoint, to penetrate, to cause the eye to be washed, because they are seeing something which they are translating immediately into terms which are not verbal.

Young people are not critics yet. They are not interested in being able to talk about a work of art to somebody else and therefore maintain status. They are interested in experiencing it in its own terms. I think one of our biggest jobs is to make sure that whatever we do in our activities, there is a very large measure of the new, the controversial, the problematic, and the questionable. In other words, all those possible reservoirs of the kinds of magic which will turn people on, make them see, make them hear, make them responsive.

Part II
The Humanities and the Contemporary Scene

The previous section attempted to define the humanities. This section demonstrates why there has been a great upsurge of interest in this field. The underlying theme of each of the articles is that students are searching for a way of dealing with unanswerable moral questions that cannot be dealt with through nonconfrontation or through the advances of technology and science.

Prigmore sees the contemporary need for the humanities as a result of our society's emphasis on the purely utilitarian, which produces people "not unlike mechanical robots which perform the same useful duties over and over in a mechanical manner, void of any creativity, perceptivity, or emotional involvement."

Frank, phrasing the question as "Why Moderize the Humanities?," answers that "the humanities and arts are central to the humanization of man." The modernization of the humanities is becoming increasingly necessary because ' we are witnessing the breakdown and disintegration of much of the traditional beliefs and expectations by and for which man has lived for centuries." Frank hopes that the modern humanities idea may give rise to a new Renaissance or a new Enlightenment and "thus carry on the humanistic ideal of man's unending quest for meaning and for fulfillment of his ever-rising aspirations."

Cornog, describing man's estrangement from himself, sees a need to restore man's humanity through the subject matter of the humanities. It is science, he believes that has been contributing to the diminishing of man and that has caused the present state of crisis. "I hold," he writes, "that the way back to true reverence, manhood, and meaning is through the arts, philosophy, religion, and poetry."

Greene sees the coming of the humanities to the foreground as motivated by the contemporary need to redefine the human being in terms of "individuality, not of essences. "This individuality she finds implicit in the humanities because they "image a plural world...[in which]...manifold ways of seeing and knowing and being, exist." It is the humanities that offer a range of choices to the individual and thus enable him "to create what he will be" and to "become an organization of possibilities."

Fox believes that the humanities movement is an answer to the school's failure to teach moral and ethical values. "The schools," he writes, "have avoided a duty that is expressed in the goals of every curriculum, that of serving the needs of society. Such neglect implies an unfounded belief that the students will absorb, by some mysterious osmosis, the standards of decent, responsible behavior." He adds that there is no place but in humanities courses for students to discuss such questions as "Who am I?" and "What am I here for?" "If the Humanists can teach our young people the secrets of such men as Socrates, Jesus Christ, Nathan Hale, and Albert Schweitzer," Fox states, "they may be teaching secrets more valuable than the polio vaccine, the transistor, or rocket fuel."

Shoemaker also sees a need in our society for a pattern of values and for a process that leads not toward things, but toward people. The large sums of money spent on science after the Russians launched Sputnik made us strong, but not safe. The Cold War and the problems related to it "left unsolved most of our social and human problems." The humanities are now needed to give us a sense of direction toward humaneness.

Dearing's article, although concerned with humanities education for college students, is equally applicable to the secondary school. He sees the humanities as the answer to the grave problem of preserving the independent, original, and creative personality in the age of automation. "Recent events," he points out, "have illustrated dramatically and tragically the residual barbarism in our civilization." Humanities education is the means he sees that will help us to produce a society in which we have neither the small dictatorial elite of 1984 nor the misery of the masses of that same book. It is humanities education that can help humanity to find the middle way between these two extremes.

Philosophy and Content in a Comprehensive Humanities Program

George T. Prigmore

Too often the average person is prone to think of aesthetic appreciation as some peculiar pursuit engaged in by people of wealth, leisure and sophistication, who have nothing better to do with their time. Equally often aesthetics are condemned for lack of utility and dismissed with the statement: "What can you *do* with it?" A rare exception is the practitioner of the arts who can sustain his livelihood through the performance of his skill; and generally suspect is the person who expends a large sum of money toward the purchase of a good painting, piece of sculpture or tenth row seat at a symphony concert. The same amount of money spent to purchase a set of golf clubs, a 50-yard line seat at a football game, or a new color television set goes un-noticed and certainly un-condemned.

Obviously the golf clubs can be used, but what use has the sculpture? The seat can be used from which to watch the football game, but how can one *use* a painting? The television set can be watched, until the life of the picture tube is used up, but what use is the concert? The answer to these questions belies a dichotomy in our thinking, an anachronism that must be dispelled. The answer is to be found not in use, but in values. And values provide the balance in our lives with utility. Values make possible good judgment and logically ordered lives. Values provide variety in.life and understanding of what it means to be a human being. The intense concentration on the development of utilitarian skills at the expense of aesthetic experiences produces people who are not unlike mechanical robots which perform the same useful duties over and over in a methodical manner, void of any creativity, perceptivity or emotional involvement. Perhaps this over-emphasis on developing the so-called "useful" is what prompted the great Spanish cellist Pablo Casals, on the eve of his 91st birthday last December 30th, to lament: "We have forgotten too often that we are human beings. . .in these times of tremendous technological advances man appears to have forgotten humanity."

Our schools must share responsibility for this imbalance. Particularly in the past three decades we have become preoccupied with the teaching of mechanical skills in various content areas and we have ignored or slighted their applications to life situations and manifestations. A few illustrations will point up this problem. (1) We want our students to learn to read, but we give them reading practice in literature which we "assume" they can relate to their own lives and experiences. (2) We expect a modicum of the school population to be able to provide twenty-minutes worth of palatable entertainment between the halves of the football games, and seem to ignore instruction in music appreciation for the remainder of the student body. (3) Hopefully, enough students will enroll in arts and crafts classes to make it financially practicable to employ a teacher. Better is it, if that person can also take a few classes in commercial arithmetic to fill out his teaching day. (4) The social studies teacher is pleased if his students have acquired a portfolio of important dates, names and places, and can accurately recite from memory the preamble of the Constitution. (5) Since each student is required to enroll in English each and every year, the minimum expectation is that he learn a certain amount of patience and perseverance.

The anticipation from all this is that the high school graduate will be able to synthesize all of the bits and pieces from various subjects into a logical understanding of human values and their development; thereby becoming able to compete in a society fraught with complexities of cause and effect and personal choice. Perhaps the manifest frustrations of our young—and not so young—result from an over concentration on the utilitarian and insufficient attention to the aesthetic experiences, which are themselves only distillations of man's yearnings to escape the daily utility of living. Ironically, the artistic output of any cultural period cannot escape that utility, but becomes the pure essence of it.

Every culture known to inhabit the world has developed some form of artistic expression. Early man developed stone and bone tools for utility, yet each artifact is characterized by form or ornamentation representative of the maker's search for beauty. The walls of the cave dwellers were decorated with primitive paintings. Later tribes amused themselves around the evening fires with story-telling—an elementary form of literature—and with rudimentary music performed on crude drums and pipes. There is no need for the designs on the clay pottery and a woolen blanket is no warmer because of its intricately-woven and colorful pattern. One of the most universal forms of aesthetic expression is the decoration of the human body: clothing, jewelry, cosmetics and other devices, all with the sole purpose of beautifying the person. Before the advent of recorded word, man began to compose apostrophies to human and natural beauty and these literary expressions took the forms of myths, legends, tales, songs, verses, etc. Ancient cultures were quite simple, however, and it was possible for the "Sabertooth" man to integrate the demand for utility and his longing for beauty into a simultaneous endeavor. Today, our fragmented curriculum poses problems which make this fusion almost impossible.

The problem is not insurmountable, though. One solution may be found in a re-alignment or re-organization of the present curriculum offerings such as is implicit in a Humanities program. This is not offered as a panacea, nor does it guarantee that every graduate of an extensive Humanities program will possess idealistic humanistic values. There is evidence, however, that a good Humanities program offers the student a better chance of developing into a well-balanced individual.

It is not my province here to recommend a specific design for a Humanities program. This will be left for another time. However, we should consider some general aspects. Humanities is an attitude, an attitude which provides for the students a wide range of experiences in an integrated manner, leading the learner in the formation of personal judgments, tastes and values. Essentially, the focus of the

Humanities centers on those six universal issues which have confronted mankind since the dawn of time and which are oblivious to mental capabilities, race, religion, occupation, geography, or any other artificial boundary. Three of those issues have to do with search: the search for Truth, the quest for Beauty, and the yearning for Freedom; the other three issues are concerned with man and his association and identification with Nature, with Society, and with some Supreme Being. The exact organization of these themes into a course of study is flexible to fit the local demands of staff, equipment, materials, objectives, and other considerations.

The attitude of the Humanities offering is one of interrelated fields or inter-dependence between different content fields. There are no other mandatory requirements. I have consulted with many schools regarding the design of Humanities programs and I have yet to find it impossible to set up a program of this nature because of facilities and equipment. Certainly dear to the heart of any fiscal agent is the fact that a Humanities program need not require any large outlay of money. It is not necessary to have collapsable walls between classrooms, large lecture halls, modular scheduling, or locally available museums, concert halls, and ballet troups. It *is* necessary for the various members of the teaching staff to want to work together. A typical Humanities "team" might consist of an English teacher, a social studies teacher, an art teacher and a music teacher. Collectively, the four teachers would decide on the nature of a given unit of instruction, the objectives and attitudes to be expected of the students at the conclusion of the unit, the materials to be employed, etc. Individually, each teacher would be primarily responsible for the content in his respective area. Each would draw parallels between his area and the others. All would *lead*—not dictate—the students in their search for answers.

At present it is not an exaggeration to find the history teacher covering the American Civil War in the spring semester, while the English teacher may have taken up the literature of that period the previous October. Worse is the study of the English Renaissance in the tenth grade and the literature of the same period two years later. In both cases the students are exposed to no art or music from these periods. History is a record of the culture of any country during any time period. The manifest distillation of the culture is to be found in its literature, music and art, architecture, drama and dance. Can we expect our young people to develop thorough understandings of our heritage, when they are exposed to only one-third of it? Can we expect them to develop value systems when we exclude from them two-thirds of the total heritage? The answer is painfully obvious.

We have fragmented the curriculum and kept it narrow and restricted in scope. Particularly does this indictment apply to the secondary schools, grade years when the students need more involvement with what it means to be totally human. Instead of more, they get less. At this time when students should learn to use freedom, there is more regimentation. When learning and experiences should assume unity, we pervade their schooling with greater diversity. They should be developing internal controls, values, judgments and discipline; yet, they are faced with imponderable external forces and dicta. Just when these young people plead to be individuals, we run them through vast computers and test batteries and label the extrusion at the end of the process much as the USDA purple-stamps a beef carcass: Choice, Good, Commercial. Once the label has been determined, the track is established and the resulting herd becomes "my slow group," "the H section," "our red students," "C.P.'s," etc. These are not individuals; there is no personal identity for them. The herd moves from cell to cell at the command of an electronically automated bell, ringing with authority in C-sharp minor. The most perplexing thing about the ubiquitous bell is not its harsh tonal quality, but the realization that it implies—in fact, demands—cessation of learning in one content area and commencing of learning in another. I remember with some dismay overhearing a student of mine remark with relief—upon hearing the bell—"Thank goodness I'm through with English for the rest of the day." We had been discussing Voltaire that week and coming to grips with the problems of Candide in his search for a better life. We understood Pangloss and we added the adjective *panglossian* to ɔur vocabularies. But, when the students left my classroom, Candide and Pangloss stayed behind with the other relics of the English department and that concept—so vitally important in the development of the human race and especially in America—remained unrelated to the real world of mankind. We could have traced the same idea in the art of Gauguin, the photography of Steichen, the Ninth Symphony of Beethoven, the cathedral at Mont St. Michele, the writing of the Declaration of Independence, the invention of the wheel, the applications of electricity, and the practice of medicine. That year we didn't. The following year we offered our first Humanities course: That course was predicated on the assumption that if you place students in the midst of facts, they memorize and hopefully regurgitate accurately on test day; however, if you immerse students in ideas, they learn and learn and keep on learning.

Our youth of today are bright and privileged as never before in our history. But the world facing them is filled with pitfalls and complexities and frustrations which trouble them deeply. They cry out for help and guidance and leadership which will prepare them for living fruitful lives of self-fulfillment and realization of dreams. A person would have to be grossly unperceptive to deny the powerful internal currents surging in our young people. The symptoms range from subtle questions and concealed longings to more blatant restlessness, alienation, drugs, sex, campus rebellion, crime and other expressions of valueless lives. The challenge is laid. It is up to us to accept it by expanding our curricular horizons, unlocking our lockstep of yester-year, altering our attitudes about the learning process in terms of proven results, and forsaking our jealous possessiveness for one content area. There is nothing more difficult to take in hand, more perilous to conduct, or more uncertain in its success than in the introduction of a new order of things. The old order is established and certain: its conduct is mechanical and boring; its result is one of increasing decadence.

What is the challenge? We must "pollute" the air of the English classroom with good music and "desecrate" the walls of the history room with great art. And if we really try, we will no longer be able to walk into a vacant room and be able to announce its subject affiliation. It will have lost the aroma of facts and data and lectures "about" some isolated subject. It will have become an idea center, where students grapple "with" concepts in broad contexts, where the aspects of "problem-solving" are more realistic in terms of the choices facing adolescents, and where the "proper study of mankind is man." Idea immersion develops sensitivity, and heightened sensitivity leads the individual to greater perceptivity, deeper insights and intensified feelings. When we find ourselves in conflict, these heightened sensitivities help us find our way out of the maze. Life is not unlike that mythological Labyrinth built by Daedalus. It was filled with twisting, diverging and criss-crossing paths. The resulting confusion always led to doom at the hands of the Minotaur. It is the dedication of education to provide our people with the skills and thought processes which would allow them to avoid the confusions and dooms of living. This is what the humanities is all about: the human-ness of man, his problems, his ideas, his conflicts, his experiences, and his solutions. These are what we must give our students an opportunity to "soak" in. There are two notions implicit in this word "soak." There is the concept of time. One semester or one year of immersion in a highly concentrated Humanities brine will not produce a well "pickled" human being. He should be aged in the Humanities pickle barrel throughout his schooling. Secondly, small cucumbers make just as good pickles as big ones—although different kinds and through different processes. The small ability student can profit from a Humanities program equitably with the big ability student. The process—that is, instruction materials and techniques—is different and the end result is different. The point here is that a Humanities program should not be reserved for the intellectually elite.

As I began with a consideration of aesthetics versus utilitarianism, I should like to close with a return to a brief reminder of the balance in life offered through experience in the arts of music, literature, painting, sculpture, architecture, dance and drama. It is contained in a statement of Clement Greenberg in an article entitled "The Case for Abstract Art." "I think a poor life is lived by anyone who doesn't regularly take time out to stand and gaze, or sit and listen, or touch, or smell, or brood, without any further end in mind. Simply for the satisfaction gotten from that which is gazed at, listened to, touched, smelled, or brooded upon."

Why Modernize the Humanities?

Lawrence K. Frank

We must find again what it means to discover, to aspire.

Art and literature, theology, and science are the three symbol systems by which man has imaginatively created his many different cultural worlds and, in a few cultures, has continued his search for new meanings, symbols and his enduring goal values. With the invention of new concepts and assumptions about nature and human nature, the development of new insights and sensibilities and the delineation of new areas for commitment and devotion, the prevailing climate of opinion has been altered; man has enlarged his awareness and learned to perceive the world and himself in new ways.

In our western European culture and subcultures, we can trace a succession of these changing climates of opinion, each of which has made an enduring contribution to western ways of living, especially when, as in the Renaissance period, earlier and almost forgotten manuscripts, arts, philosophy and mathematics were rediscovered.

Life Tasks. From his earliest beginnings, man has been confronted with a number of persistent life tasks, problems which can never be finally solved but must be faced anew in each generation as long as he exists as man. Each successive age in our western culture has attempted to reformulate these persistent problems and to offer answers in terms of its contemporary orientation, which a succeeding age has partly, if not wholly, superseded with its own proposals. Thus we have a cumulative record of how western man has viewed the universe and his place therein and has sought a new image of the self for guiding his living, feeling and thinking. These survivals from the past span the whole range of our recorded and recoverable past. They cover a gamut from the earliest and more primitive to the contemporary orientation, but all express man's creative imagination and the operations of his reflective mind focused upon these basic concerns and aspirations.

In the humanities we find what the artists, poets, story tellers, dramatists, historians (continually remaking our past), the scholars and the philosophers have offered on these basic themes, utilizing the concepts and assumptions of their age to provide a world view and a philosophy of living that has been translated into these various artistic media, especially poetry and religious beliefs, and, more recently, into science. As biology and paleontology provide man with his history as a product of organic evolution, so the humanities provide man with his cultural history, showing how he has tried to humanize his mammalian organism and create a symbolic world for human personalities.

When initially produced the arts and humanities were creative challenges and bold improvisations upon the persistent themes of man's basic concerns. They were the fruits of living experience, of imaginative creation and, above all, of passionate convictions, usually expressed esthetically to evoke feelings and to win acceptance in the face of resistant tradition and often rigid institutions. Later generations found in these a version of their own perplexities and aspirations and also a source of renewed courage and dedication to the enduring goal values of western culture which the more sensitive and creative attempted to restate in terms more congenial to, and congruous with, their own age.

Clearly the humanities and arts are central to the humanization of man. Yet how they should function in formal education has become, as this issue of *Educational Leadership* indicates, a focus for critical discussion and often acute controversy. To say that the scholars have almost ruined the humanities for education may seem outrageous and indefensible. However, the scholarly analyses and dissection of the arts and literature of the past and their conversion into formal subject matter have transformed what was a genuine esthetic experience into a body of systematic knowledge, and a series of intellectual tasks of mastering the fruits of scholarly investigations and historical interpretations. While officially students may be encouraged to read and to enjoy poetry, drama, the novels and stories of the past, they are impressed with the primary importance of the cognitive, scholarly approach to what they read and they realize that for academic approval they must be concerned, not so much with the meaning and human significance of what they read, but with memorizing actual words and phrases, dates and other minutiae derived from scholarly investigations. Here we see an expression of the educational conviction that every student is a potential recruit to the discipline or profession of the teacher and therefore must be taught and compelled to learn what the scholar has found to be essential to the practice of his discipline. It is as if no one were permitted to ride in an airplane until he has mastered the theory and practice of aerodynamics, nor encouraged to admire and enjoy plants and animals without having to learn their full evolutionary history.

A New Climate. Modernization of humanities is becoming increasingly necessary as we recognize the contemporary emergence of a new climate of opinion generated by new and radically different concepts and assumptions and altered perceptions of the world and of man, as presented in the arts, literature, science and even in religion. We are witnessing the breakdown and disintegration of much of the traditional beliefs and expectations by and for which man has lived for centuries and the development of new awareness and deeper insights, many of which are now almost overwhelming, but will gradually become a part of our esthetic and intellectual orientation. Thus while we can and must emphasize the continuity with the past we must also recognize the acute breaks with tradition, the actual or apparent discontinuities by which human advance takes place.

Despite the almost overpowering display of confusion and disorder in all our lives which is being portrayed by contemporary poets, dramatists, novelists, painters and sculptors, musicians, dancers, and architects, these creative persons are also carrying on the basic tradition in humanities of seeking new meanings and finding enhanced significance in human living. Where and by whom will our students be introduced to these contemporary productions and learn to recognize that they are carrying on the aspirations of their predecessors while endeavoring to be responsive to the needs and the opportunities of their time as their predecessors served the ages in which they lived?

We should realize that in the future, when historians and scholars look for understanding of what happened in the 20th century, they will seek for light in the arts, poetry, drama and novels of our present today, where the creative imagination of our gifted writers and artists is struggling to resolve their own and the public confusion, seeking new ways of dealing with these disturbing conditions and persistent questions that cannot be resolved by appeal to the past. These future scholars will also carefully examine what was being communicated by radio, TV, phonograph and tape recordings, comics, illustrated magazines, and especially by advertisements, the whole range of so-called mass communications, in and through which we of today are exhibiting both our dismay and our hopeful search for escape from our perplexities. Again we may ask where, when and from whom are students to find some orientation, some ways of understanding and evaluating these contemporary communications to which they are continually exposed?

At the risk of being dismissed with scorn by many educators, we may say that the tasks of education today are not primarily to teach "the best that has been known and thought in the past," but to orient students to the present and especially to the future in which, as adults, they will live and actively participate, assuming the various roles and carrying on a variety of activities that are both relevant and necessary in their lives, as their predecessors have done throughout the centuries. If the humanities are to fulfill their responsibilities in contemporary education they must indeed be modernized so that the scholars' nostalgic love for the past does not deprive students of learning about the present as a product of that past and as the matrix of the future. Years ago, Otto Rank, in his *Modern Education,* remarked: "We cling to the past, not because we are in love with the past but because we are fearful of the present"—and, we may add, terrified by the future, so that it is both comforting and reassuring to focus on what has passed.

The modernization of the humanities, as approached in this context, is not a petulant dismissal of the past or a rejection of history and scholarship; rather it is a plea for recognizing that we may pay our debt to the past only by doing for our day what our predecessors did for their time, thus carrying on their aspirations, but being responsive to our contemporary world and the emerging new climate of opinion, just as the significant contributors to our western culture were responsive to their climate of opinion. Equally important, modernizing the humanities may be interpreted as helping students to experience contemporary literature and the arts and also those of the past as esthetic experiences, not treated as so much subject matter to be memorized for examinations dealing primarily with the cognitive, historical aspects of what they have read and seen. It is hard to avoid the suspicion that the humanities have had a large snob appeal, insofar as it has been a mark of superior social status to recognize literary allusions and to be able to quote the classics, and thereby exhibit one's superiority to the untutored mass.

Man as Observer. But if education is to be genuinely concerned with the human personalities of its students, it should also provide a wide range of nonverbal education so that students will develop the awareness, the sensibilities, and the capacity for enjoying the actual world around them and not be limited to intellectual and symbolic communications alone. We are all exposed to a variety of sensory overloads, especially of symbolic and verbalized messages, and at the same time, we suffer from sensory deprivations, cut off from the many sensory cues for maintaining our dynamic stability and normal functioning as personalities.

With the rise of modern science we are suddenly realizing how frequently the teachers of the humanities have lacked, not only a concern for but even an awareness of the role and functions of science. Usually they have thought of science in terms of "facts" derived from empirical investigations and of rigid laws and far-reaching, but unhuman, generalizations. Apparently such teachers do not realize that contemporary science is considered, by at least the advanced scientists, as essentially a symbol system which, along with mathematics, enables man to communicate with the universe and to relate himself cognitively to events.

Contemporary science has abandoned the 19th century conception of a wholly mechanistic world, with rigid boundaries, operating with unfailing cause and effect and subject to immense forces.

Rather, the intent of science today is to develop a system of postulates and assumptions with which to observe and perceive and to interpret events, recognizing that the scientist-observer is in the picture and that whatever he observes and interprets is patterned by his basic conceptions, his criteria of creditability, and the use of the symbols he employs for communicating with others and for reflective thinking. Indeed, it is not too much to say that we are seeing the emergence of a scientific humanism which is restoring man as the observer and the interpreter of observations, to the center of the universe as it is now scientifically conceived. To perpetuate the split between *Two Cultures*, as described by C. P. Snow, is not only an anachronism but an imposition of wholly misleading viewpoints upon young and trusting students.

For almost two hundred years we have lived upon the fruits of the Great Enlightenment of the 18th century from which we have derived the guiding models for educating our children, organizing and operating our national government, carrying on our economic, financial and commercial activities, and trying to order and manage our social living. These 18th century models were essentially Newtonian and have now become not only obsolete, but frustrating and self defeating. Thus the great task we face is to do for today in terms of contemporary science what was done by Locke, Hume, Adam Smith, Bentham, and the French philosophers, who used Newtonian science to formulate the then new models and theories for the guidance of human living. Moreover, the poets in the 18th and 19th centuries reflected Newtonian science, the conception of natural law, and the belief in the rationality of the human mind. The modernization of the humanities, therefore, may find a highly appropriate and entirely relevant pattern in what was done in the 18th century, but must now be undertaken again in terms of modern science and the problems of the 20th century world.

Another task for a modernized humanities program is to reduce, if not eliminate, the nationalistic, often chauvinistic, emphasis and to orient students to an understanding of the many different cultures around the world, each with its symbol system and language and its often unique design for living. If we are to avoid the imposition of a monolithic world state, we should prepare our students to live in a world community as an "orchestration of cultural diversities," each of which is to be recognized and its integrity respected and maintained as an expression of the creative imagination of the human race. For this, of course, the teaching of foreign languages must be rescued from their customary pedantic presentation and humanized as modes of communication.

Perhaps we can speak of modernizing the humanities as primarily an attempt to shift the emphasis in teaching from factual information to a communication of the meanings and significances of materials being presented and especially to help the student to "live at the height of his times," as Ortega y Gasset has expressed it, capable of participating in this most exciting of all times in which every individual has both the privilege and the opportunity actively to participate.

Likewise, modernizing humanities may be approached through greater recognition of individual cognitive styles or "learning by discovery," that is, encouraging each student to gain understanding by his own idiosyncratic recognition, interpretation and acceptance of the materials being presented, as contrasted with learning a fixed body of facts and demonstrating their mastery on examinations. This in no way denies the importance or excludes the possibility of training future scholars who must learn these facts and historical material and be prepared, so to speak, to "dehumanize" the arts and literature as a biologist must be prepared to dissect the living organisms he studies.

Finally we may say that the humanization of knowledge is essentially a process of communicating analogically the basic concepts and assumptions, the patterns of perception, and of presenting a variety of models for direct experience, as far as possible, whereby a student learns to orient himself and to summate, coordinate, integrate or orchestrate what he is learning. If education is to be more than the training of future scholars and scientists and professional workers, we must thus humanize what we teach so that, as personalities, students will be helped to learn to live in our contemporary world, neither wholly ignorant of the contemporary world nor completely immersed in the past.

The "humanities idea" today may be as fruitful as was the earlier humanist movement that brought into European education the larger concern for human living and achievement in this world and gave rise to the succeeding period of the Renaissance. Or the humanist idea may generate a new Enlightenment and thus carry on the humanistic ideal of man's unending quest for meaning and for fulfillment of his ever-rising aspirations.

Teaching Humanities in the Space Age

William H. Cornog

My theme is simple and direct. It is a prime task of teaching in the H-bomb and space age to aid the restoration of man, the ending of man's estrangement from himself. My argument is that for more than a century by reason of the apotheosis of science and the coronation of progress, man has lost his way and is in flight from his humanity. My thesis is that poetry is more important to our salvation than rocketry, and that the person is more important than the people. I hold that the way back to true reverence, manhood, and meaning is through the arts, philosophy, religion, and poetry, all of which were at one time central to our schools and teaching.

With a prophetic power appropriate to a poet, Emerson wrote a century ago:

> There are two laws discrete,
> Not reconciled,
> Law for man, and law for thing;

The last builds town and fleet,
But it runs wild,
And doth the man unking.

The tragedy of our time is that the law for thing *has* run wild and man *has* been unkinged.

And the dreadful irony is that science, which is a glorious expression of man's human mind, and therefore truly one of the humanities, has put man's continued life on earth in gravest doubt and jeopardy. Science, which has helped man to escape many bondages of body and spirit, bids fair now to inclose him in a final bondage to itself. The law for thing reaches out to encompass the law for man and draws man down into undifferentiated and indifferent nature; and physical-chemical laws are held to determine not only the digestion but the imagination of man.

Contributions to the diminishing of man have been coming in from scientific sources for a long time. Bruno, Copernicus, and Galileo destroyed the classical horological universe, though theology burned one of these to death with temporal fires and threatened the other two with fires eternal. These learned astronomers shrank God's theater for man to a cooling speck of mud orbiting an ancient and very minor star.

But for Renaissance man, and for seventeenth- and eighteenth-century man, this smaller stage sufficed; man was still man and earth was enough. Western culture could still look back to Greece and Rome, Sinai and Bethlehem. We had our roots still; we knew whence we came and still depended for our earthly as well as the soul's salvation upon the saving grace of ancient virtues.

As late as the early nineteenth century, the young romantic poets of England were exalting the spirit of man. Shelley could write that magnificent last stanza to his epic *Prometheus Unbound:*

> To suffer woes which Hope thinks infinite;
> To forgive wrongs darker than death or night;
>   To defy Power, which seems omnipotent;
> To love, and bear; to hope till Hope creates
> From its own wreck the thing it contemplates;
>   Neither to change, nor falter, nor repent;
> This, like thy glory, Titan, is to be
> Good, great and joyous, beautiful and free;
> This is alone Life, Joy, Empire, and Victory.

And Shelley could cry, almost with a shout:

> The world's great age begins anew,
>   The golden years return,
> The earth doth like a snake renew
>   Her winter weeds outworn:
> Heaven smiles, and faiths and empires gleam,
> Like wrecks of a dissolving dream.

And the gentle Keats knew the centrality for man's spirit of the uplifting power of beauty. You know the opening lines of *Endymion:*

> A thing of beauty is a joy for ever:
> Its loveliness increases; it will never
> Pass into nothingness; but still will keep
> A bower quiet for us, and a sleep
> Full of sweet dreams, and health, and quiet breathing.
> Therefore, on every morrow, are we wreathing
> A flowery band to bind us to the earth.
> Spite of despondence, of the inhuman dearth
> Of noble natures, of the gloomy days,
> Of all the unhealthy and o'er-darkened ways
> Made for our searching: yes, in spite of all,
> Some shape of beauty moves away the pall
> From our dark spirits.
>
> For one short hour; no, even as the trees
> That whisper round a temple become soon
> Dear as the temple's self, so does the moon,
> The passion poesy, glories infinite,
> Haunt us till they become a cheering light
> Unto our souls, and bound to us so fast,
> That, whether there be shine, or gloom o'ercast,
> They always must be with us, or we die.

We have died a little: Man has lost some of his humanity since Keats wrote those lines. Thirty years after he wrote them, Karl Marx and Friederich Engels published the *Communist Manifesto.* Eleven years after the manifesto came Darwin's *Origin of the Species.* The dignity of man, and the worth of the person suffered devasting assault. Darwin's theory not only did violence to orthodox religious beliefs about man's special God-given place in the order of nature. Social Darwinism, the application of the jungle law of survival of the fittest to man's economic and political affairs, justified man's exploitation of fellow man both at home and abroad. The law for thing, having claimed man for its creature, seemed all that need be read both to explain and sanction his behavior. Marxism, though it sentimentally presented itself as the means of liberation for enslaved and exploited masses, at root never intended more than a change of masters, from the few to the many, from the ruling class to the ruling mass. The Sunday *New York Times* recently had an interesting account of a recent action of Mr. Khrushchev, dated Moscow, June 29, 1963:

Premier Khrushchev has urged the expulsion from the Communist party of Victor P. Nekrasov, a Soviet writer who has been accused of bourgeois objectivism in reporting on his visit to the United States. On June 21 at a plenary meeting on ideology of the party's central committee, Mr. Khrushchev asserted that Mr. Nekrasov had failed to adhere to the party line. The party should get rid of such people who set their personal delusions above the decision of the party, which represents the entire great army of single-minded people, the Premier said.

Thus under communism the monster dragon-god, the people, engorges itself on persons. Marx, who was no scientist, was never embarrassed by lack of evidence to support his application of the law for thing to the government of states and nations. An insupportable hypothesis, eloquently urged upon men and women who stand in want of both bread and faith in God or man, can seem to have the authority of natural law. It is not surprising that men by the millions have sold their souls for bread, for the solace of a state religion, for the trivial creature comforts provided by the good shepherd, Science. Who else but the state is buying souls today?

When men sell their souls cheap, it is fair to conclude that they do not value them. If they do not value their identity and dignity as persons, they must have been persuaded that men are nearer relatives of the algae than of the angels. The image of man at least partially advanced by Freud has certainly served to make this identification with the lower rather than the higher increasingly plausible. At least the Freudian ethic calls question whether man can make boast of the powers of reason and will, driven as he is still by the strong subconscious animal within.

Man has had cause in the past hundred years to embrace despair, turning in flight from his humanity. The flight begins, so far as one can say any theme in art or literature has a beginning, with the note of doubt and melancholy in the nineteenth century in the mid-Victorian poets and becomes almost a rout in the poetry and art of our time. The despair is at times a posturing despair, as in Swinburne's *Garden of Proserpine:*

> From too much love of living,
>   From hope and fear set free,
> We thank with brief thanksgiving
>   Whatever gods may be
> That no life lives for ever;
> That dead men rise up never;
> That even the weariest river
>   Winds somewhere safe to sea.

Or it can be a ringing affirmation of the sensitive mind in full revolt at the meaninglessness of man's life, as Arnold expressed it in *Dover Beach* (1867), which concludes with that magnificent stanza:

> The Sea of Faith
> Was once, too, at the full, and round earth's shore
> Lay like the folds of a bright girdle furl'd.
> But now I only hear
> Its melancholy, long, withdrawing roar,
> Retreating, to the breath
> Of the night-wind, down the vast edges drear
> And naked shingles of the world.
> Ah, love, let us be true

> To one another! for the world, which seems
> To lie before us like a land of dreams,
> So various, so beautiful, so new,
> Hath really neither joy, nor love, nor light,
> Nor certitude, nor peace, nor help for pain;
> And we are here as on a darkling plain
> Swept with confused alarms of struggle and flight,
> Where ignorant armies clash by night.

By the end of the Victorian era, revolt had hardened to cynicism, such as Thomas Hardy expresses in his poem "Hap," which ends:

> Crass casualty obstructs the sun and rain
> And dicing Time for gladness casts a moan;
> These purblind Doomsters had as readily strown
> Blisses about my pilgrimage as pain.

But at least in the depths of Hardy's pessimism he speaks for man, and revolt and cynicism and despair are human emotions. Man "troubling deaf heaven" with his "bootless cries" is still man.

It is not until our time that man's dehumanization truly begins. The theme is pervasive in art and literature, but again it is a poet, I think, who expresses it best. T. S. Eliot says it in *Ash Wednesday:*

> Because these wings are no longer wings to fly
> But merely vans to beat the air
> The air which is now thoroughly small and dry
> Smaller and dryer than the will;
> Teach us to care and not to care
> Teach us to sit still.

We are the generation, by now the scond generation, of the Hollow Men, for whom Eliot writes the epitaph:

> This is the way the world ends
> This is the way the world ends
> This is the way the world ends
> Not with a bang but a whimper.

What is the quality of hollowness in men? There is no person there. What has happened to the person? He has been superseded. One of the people moved in—a citizen, a worker, a consumer, an economic unit, a political multiplicand, Mr. So and So, little more than a statistic. Why did this happen? Because no one told the fellow in early youth that it was important to be a person, to be himself. No one taught him how to grow to be himself, to be a person. By a perversion of education he was taught to be a co-operator, a committee member, a joiner. He was vocationally trained for any vocation except the only one that matters—the vocation of being a man.

Why was he so taught? Because society, and what passed for educational philosophy therein, thought he ought to be well adjusted and no burden and no nuisance. Because collective man, in civilized society as in tribal society, is distrustful of persons. Because the hollow men became admired and hollowness rewarded, and wholeness became regarded as eccentric, deviate, and suspect.

It is a curious phenomenon of our unquiet time that much of our art eschews the human form or reduces it to abstraction or caricature; our sculpture distorts the human body, making heads small and torsos large, and both occasionally full of holes. Our artists seem at times in full flight from humanity, and our poets and novelists in full flight from the norm of human behavior. Even so conservative a poet as Edna St. Vincent Millay can write, "Euclid alone has looked on beauty bare."

The clockwork cosmos of man's age of faith was early shattered by science. His place in the hierarchy of living things as a favored creation of the Deity has now for some time been in doubt. The possibility of knowing himself, or governing himself when he does, has been called into serious question by at least a quasi-scientific psychology. Uprooted from faith, his free will and proud reason often denied, bemused by gadgets his science has given him for comfort and joy, and terrified by the weapons science has stored for his destruction, Western man has lost himself, his center of meaning. There will be peace in the world, no healing of the division within the family of man, until man himself is whole again.

What shall a man do, what shall he be taught, in order to restore himself, to restore his soul? Can the discoverer of the law for thing, discover or rediscover the law for man? Can the geometer, the measurer of the earth, find his own dimensions? Can the tool-maker and builder build a house for himself not of wood or stone? Can the world's best weapon-maker and destroyer find a reason and a way to live with himself in peace?

The unexamined life, said Socrates, is not worth living. We in our time agree. We would like to examine our lives, to explore the nature of man singly and in society. Since science is the peculiar genius of our age, perhaps science can do the testing and charting for us. Thus we have come to the position of depending upon science not only for a better world of things but for a world of better men. We have developed social sciences, after the model of the physical sciences, and by these we hope to weigh, measure, define, and manage men. We have taken a header into human engineering, probing with depth interviews and searching questionnaires into the behavior of voters and consumers. When we know enough about what makes people tick, we say, we can make cash registers ring and production lines roll. When we know enough about propaganda techniques and mass indoctrination, we, can control whole nations and preserve them in bondage very scientifically.

If this view of man is right, education will become unnecessary. If man is as malleable and manageable as matter is, we can treat him as an accountable reliable political integer; and the science of statistics will tell us a good deal more about man than Chaucer or Shakespeare. If man is merely a macromolecule, we have only to analyze his structure to understand and thus control him. We shall engineer his consent, even to the proposition that he is nothing but a macromolecule.

Happily, the social sciences remain very inexact sciences, and man retains a scope for mystery and discovery and an outside chance to be himself. The computers twinkle and whirr in a closing ring around him. The brave new world of card-sorted identities following controlled behavior patterns may soon take over all of us insolent and intractable variables. But the machines, who serve the law for thing, will not get us if we keep our own circuits open, speaking the language and knowing the law for man.

What is that language, and where is that law? We have only to consult our own intelligence and memory, and the cloud of witnesses to the dignity and the immeasurability of man. And we the teachers bear the heaviest obligation to summon these witnesses who speak the language and describe the law for man, and among these we must call upon those who speak with the greatest authority and grace. We teachers, if we are worthy of our profession, have heard these testimonies and know that it is our joyous task to let them be heard in our schools.

Who has spoken for man? Poets and prophets, artists and philosophers, those who have made music and the songs and the dances, and those who described the nature of man in history and story. Among this distinguished company of exalters of the spirit of man, pure science has a proud place, and mathematics is as eminent as music. A brilliant mathematician friend told me that he once asked his professor of mathematics at a European university why he had chosen to study mathematics. There is only one answer, said his teacher: For the honor of the human mind.

To what labors shall we turn our human minds in school? To the man-centered studies surely, and not to the child-centered, the whim-centered, the play-centered, or even the community-centered. Your community and mine is this earth. Your past and mine goes back to apes and fishes, but also to Aeschylus and Socrates, Michelangelo and Shakespeare, Montaigne, Cervantes, and Bach. Homer and Newton are our countrymen, and to whom do Aristotle and Einstein now belong?

In this diminished world, lesser allegiances than these or preoccupation in our schools with the trivia of daily life, personal or communal, give a mean and narrow compass to man's emotions and thoughts or press him to listless mediocrity from which flat plane his farthest reach is to opiates and palliatives for his tension and boredom. Only the studies which celebrate the humanness of man can truly help any man to find his bearings in the world and identify himself as a man.

Walter Pater concludes his essay on Pico della Mirandola in his book, *The Renaissance*, with this sentence:

For the essence of humanism is that belief which he seems never to have doubted, that nothing which has ever interested living men and women can wholly lose its vitality—no language they have spoken or oracle beside which they have hushed their voices, no dream which has once been entertained by actual human minds, nothing about which they have ever been passionate or expended time and zeal.

If the proper study of mankind is, as Alexander Pope said, man, the practical educator, who usually does not want to lose a minute from the fun of shaping men in his own faceless image, nervously asks, "Can we find a place for the humanities at a time like this?" He has heard the call for more engineers and scientists and he wants to tool up the educational machine to catch up with Russia's rolling production line.

Asking whether the humanities are practical is like asking, "Do I have to be a man?" The answer is, "Not necessarily, but you have some ties with the human race as a kind of hereditary circumstance, and it has been said that it is worth while trying to be one." The second question from the timorous educator or pupil is not stated directly, but if it were it would be, "What's the next best thing?" Well, the next best thing to being a man, my child, my primitive, is to stay what you are, a child or a primitive. Some people remain so all their lives innocently, harmlessly, and effectively. Some, it is true, get as far as adolescence and taper off from then on to senility, whence it is easy retrogression to second childhood. No, no one has to be a man. There are ways of making a living and passing the time on a pretty advanced anthropoid level.

The harried defenders of humanism and apologists for the arts have in present controversies advanced many good reasons for the study of the humanities. The reasons are really quite simple. First, man has never quite been able to escape himself, try as he may by dodging into crowds, immersing himself in mass emotions, performing en masse social and religious rituals, enjoying public entertainments, rushing about, getting and spending. Self-consciousness remains his peculiar heritage, and he is fated to have the capacity to regard himself and to know that he is alone. His loneliness, his selfness, keeps crowding in, and the questions come and keep coming: Who am I? Why am I here? Where did I come from? Where am I going? Only man asks these questions. And each man has to find the answers—some kind of answers, for the questioning is insistent. Unless he finds the answers for himself, he rings hollow not to the world alone but to himself also. He must discover the law for man, or as much of it as will make life reverberate with some few decibels of meaning.

Second, man's hold on freedom, his recently won political and economic freedom, is precarious. He cannot remain free and grow to full manhood, or he will not want to, unless he gains some idea of what it is to be a man. The only way he can do that is to read the record of man, the minutes of the previous meetings, in the poets and artists, the prophets and historians.

Finally, the poets and artists especially have given us the means of drinking the life of man to the lees, and living many more lives than one. The study of the language of man adds to the dimensions of life, to its breadth and depth. This is important, since we cannot do much about its length, although science has offered to do something about it, both ways, with antibiotics in one hand and megaton bombs in the other.

At the end of his book, *The Renaissance,* Pater quotes Victor Hugo saying that we are all condamnés, all under sentence of death with indefinite reprieves. The question is: How shall we spend the interval?

Some [says Pater] spend this interval in listlessness, some in high passions, the wisest at least among the "children of this world" in art and song. For our one chance lies in expanding that interval and getting as many pulsations as possible into the given time. Great passions may give us this quickened sense of life, ecstasy and sorrow of love, the various forms of enthusiastic activity, disinterested or otherwise, which come naturally to many of us. Only be sure it is passion, that it does yield you this fruit of quickened, multiplied consciousness. Of this, wisdom the poetic passion, the desire for beauty, the love of art for art's sake has most. For art comes to you proposing frankly to give nothing but the highest quality to your moments as they pass and simply for those moment's sake.

The plain fact of our nature is that we as men have no choice but the endless search for truth and beauty, the unremitting pursuit of knowledge and wisdom. Again, for me, the poets have spoken this law best, and the language of poetry is the most eloquent manner of speaking the language of man. Let a Stuart poet, Henry Vaughan, speak first, and then two gentlemen of the theater in the reign of her majesty, Queen Elizabeth I. Henry Vaughan's poem is simply entitled "Man."

> Weighing the steadfastness and state
>   Of some mean things which here below reside,
> Where birds like watchful Clocks the noiseless date
>   And Intercourse of times divide,
>   I would (said I) my God would give
> The staidness of these things to man! for these
> To his divine appointments ever cleave,
>   And no new business breaks their peace;
> The birds nor sow, nor reap, yet sup and dine,
>   The flowrs without clothes live,
> Yet Solomon was never drest so fine.
>
>   Man hath still either toyes, or Care,
> He hath no root, nor to one place is ty'd,
> But ever restless and Irregular
>   About this Earth doth run and ride,
> He knows he hath a home, but scarce knows where,
>   He sayes it is so far
> That he hath quite forgot how to go there.
>
>   He knocks at all doors, strays and roams,
> Nay hath not so much wit as some stones have
> Which in the darkest nights point to their homes,
>   By some hid sense their Maker gave;
> Man is the shuttle, to whose winding quest
>   And passage through these looms
> God order'd motion, but ordain'd no rest.

And then you will recognize this speaker as Hotspur, in the first part of *Henry IV:*

> Oh gentlemen! the time of life is short!
> To spend that shortness basely were too long
> If life did ride upon a dial's point
> Still ending at the arrival of an hour!

Finally, Marlowe's mighty line:

> Our souls whose faculties can comprehend
> The wondrous architecture of the world
> And measure every wandering planet's course,
> Still climbing after knowledge infinite
> And ever moving with the restless spheres,
> Will us to wear ourselves and never rest.

This is the language of man, which in its beauty of form as well as thought, describes the nature of man. The law for man, which this and other great poetry expresses, is that he has no choice, he must seek the truth, the truth about both man and thing, or he dies to himself, violating his nature.

It is to the expounding of the law for man in its noblest expression that this noble and sometimes holy profession of teaching must now rededicate itself. The law for thing which built town and fleet, and now builds H-bombs and missiles, has declared man unkinged. Our mission as teachers is the restoration of man.

So much for the argument.

There are two major questions I would ask, to test the propositions I have advanced. The propositions are (1) that only by according full stature and puissance to the humanities in our teaching can we prepare men to know themselves as men and if not as brothers, at least as fellow earthlings on a very mortal coil and (2) that only by such knowledge can the species survive in the one world to which science has delivered it, under the sign and portent of the mushroom cloud.

The first question is: Does the dichotomy described by Emerson as the law for man and the law for thing force the dichotomy described by C. P. Snow as the two cultures? In other words, though there may be two laws discrete, are science and art or science and poetry natural or only accidental, that is, cultural polarities?

The second question is: What is the basis of the assumption that the restoration of man as the central concern of education and the ending of man's estrangement from himself is a necessary, to say nothing of a sufficient, condition of his survival?

The paradox inherent in the first question is that the more of an artist, a creator, a scientist is, the greater the affirmation he gives to Emerson's concept of the transcendental nature of man. Man is never more remote from the undifferentiated reality of things than he is in the moment of discovery or creation of laws for either man or thing.

Bronowski in his remarkable essay on "The Creative Mind" in *Science and Human Values* describes science thus:

> All science is the search for unity in hidden likenesses.

And further,

> The progress of science is the discovery at each step of a new order which gives unity to what had long seemed unlike.

But then he goes on to make this revealing analogy to poetry:

When Coleridge tried to define beauty, he returned always to one deep thought: Beauty, he said, is "unity in variety." Science is nothing else than the search to discover unity in the wild variety of nature—or more exactly in the variety of our experience. Poetry, painting, the arts are the same search, in Coleridge's phrase, for unity in variety. Each in its own way looks for unity in the variety of human experience.

But the worlds of science and the humane studies meet in more than method and intent. They meet in the consanguinity of scientific and literary humanism. Snow thinks that the characteristic bent of scientific though is future-mindeness. Scientists above all, in his view, are oriented to the future; one gathers that he believes they have really pre-empted it. Humanists, on the contrary, are past-oriented, and are sort of backing into the future.

This is not in my opinion a true contrast. The message of the humanities is dominantly hope; humane studies encourage a faith in man's power to reshape, remake his world, himself, his destiny because they reveal both the power and the variety of his creative spirit.

The legend over the portals of Dante's Hell is "Abandon hope, all ye who enter here." The condition of hell is hopelessness, which is to say the loss of will to live, to strive, to "wear ourselves and never rest."

And Goethe's spirit of evil, Mephistopheles, is above all the spirit which denies, the spirit of negation, whose wager with that prototype of the scientific humanist, Faust, is that Faust's restless inquiring spirit can be beguiled by a surfeit of pleasures to say to the passing moment, "Verweile doch, du bist so schön" ("Stay, thou art so fair").

The faith that man not only can but must remake the world is the central faith shared and sustained by both science and the humanities. The possibility of doing it—man's power to do it—has been much enhanced by the insights man has gained not only into nature but into his own nature and into human societies or cultures. Never in his history has man been freer to change the world and never has he had at hand more powerful or dread instruments of change.

The late Clyde Kluckholn of Harvard in his splendid book, *Mirror for Man,* writes:

In the 18th century a Neopolitan philosopher, Vico, uttered a profundity which was new, violent—and unnoticed. This was simply the discovery that "The social world is surely the work of man." Two generations of anthropologists have compelled thinkers to face this fact. Nor are anthropologists willing to allow the Marxists or other cultural determinists to make of culture another absolute as autocratic as the God or Fate portrayed by some philosophies. Anthropological knowledge does not permit so easy an evasion of man's responsibility for his own destiny.

Kluckholn goes on to quote Lawrence Frank:

"Now man is beginning to realize that his culture and social organization are not unchanged cosmic processes but are human creations which may be altered. For those who cherish the democratic faith this discovery means that they can and must undertake a continuing assay of our culture and our society in terms of its consequences for human life and human values."

The quality and kind of what Frank calls "a continuing assay" will depend ultimately upon the validity of the weights or values we use to measure our culture or society against both the reality and the possibility of life for man. History tells us that many times false weights have been cast into the balance and human life has been cheapened, or its worth denied. Cultural relativity, and consequent relativism in defining good and evil, have weakened faith in man's capacity to judge values and have consequently been thought to have weakened morality. On this point Kluckholn again has a perceptive comment:

While breeding a healthy skepticism as to the eternity of any value prized by a particular people, anthropology does not as a matter of theory deny the existence of moral absolutes. Rather, the use of the comparative method provides a scientific means of discovering such absolutes. . . .
Anthropology has given a new perspective to the relativity of the normal that should bring greater tolerance and understanding of socially harmless deviations. But it has by no means destroyed standards or the useful tyranny of the normal.

And later Kluckholn quotes F. S. C. Northrop's generalization, which to me echoes both Plato and Spinoza:

The norms for ethical conduct are to be discovered from the ascertainable knowledge of man's nature, just as the norms for building a bridge are to be derived from physics.

But bridge-building is child's play compared to building an ethic for the family of man. It was Einstein who remarked that the wide gap between what man had learned and could do about the control of nature and what man had learned and could do about the government of himself and society was accountable by the fact that physics was so much simpler and less complex a field of knowledge than politics.
Yet if both poetry and science are the search for unity in variety, and if there is an ethic discoverable by either or both which can unite and justify the family of man, all studies humane and scientific can encompass such discovery, each in the orbit of its relevance to the nature of man.
Bronowski, whose essay, "The Creative Mind," I have already quoted, writes in his second essay, "The Habit of Truth":

A society holds together by the respect which man gives to man; it fails, in fact, it falls apart into groups of fear and power, when its concept of man is false. We find the drive which makes society stable at last in the search for what makes us men.

So, the discovery of the universal ethic is not enough. If it had been, the injunction of the prophet Micah would have been enough: "What doth the Lord require of thee, O man, but to do justly and to love mercy and to walk humbly with thy God?"

What is required is not the moral injunction which purifies the heart, but what Bacon calls "the inquiry of truth, which is the love-making or wooing of it," by which the mind is opened to light and freedom.

I give Bronowski the last word:

Poetry does not move us to be just or unjust in itself. It moves us to thought in whose light justice and injustice are seen in fearful sharpness of outline.

What is true of poetry is true of all creative thought. And what I said then of one value is true of all human values. The values by which we are to survive are not rules for just and unjust conduct, but are those deeper illuminations in whose light justice and injustice, good and evil, means and ends are seen in fearful sharpness of outline.

It is in the seeking of those deeper illuminations of human values and the human spirit that the humanities have special power to inform the mind and refresh the soul of man.

There is no more to be learned about the arts of war. Perfection has been achieved. Indeed with grotesque illogic it can be said that the ultimate has been surpassed; the military establishment has acquired the capacity to overkill. The hardware is ready and the delivery schedules have been plotted on both sides.

So be it. School still keeps. Now about the arts of peace. Hand me that bit of chalk. . . .

The Humanities and the Public School: "You Must Change Your Life"

Maxine Greene

There is a poem by Rainer Maria Rilke called "Archaic Torso of Apollo" which deals with a confrontation between man and a work of art. The response described is strangely like a familiar response to talk of introducing the humanities into the public schools:

> We did not know his legendary head,
> in which the eyeballs ripened. But
> his torso still glows like a candelabrum
> in which his gaze, only turned low,
>
> holds and gleams.

The humanities once suggested something awe-inspiring, élitist, suspect to many educators. The very term conjured up visions of Renaissance Humanism and its classical ideal, its emphasis upon a predominantly "literary" education for what can only have been an aristocratic few. The curricula prefigured by the Commissions meeting in the 1890s were intended for the many, a majority of whom would be "children whose education is not to be pursued beyond the secondary school." What relevance could Prince, Courtier, or even Christian gentleman hold for them?

The humanities were, therefore, diluted and broken down. They entered the curriculum in fragmented form; English, civics, spelling, and the rest were inlaid in random order, like discrete but matching pieces of glass. The terminology changed as the years went on; there were reclassifications, reformulations, occasionally a "design." But the humanities as traditionally known—and the general education associated with them—were given over to the universities. It is only within the last few years that they have been seriously considered as subject matter for public schools. And suddenly, before the schools have quite accommodated themselves, we find ourselves with an Arts and Humanities Act upon the books, with what might be conceived as an effort to legislate into existence a regard for the "humane."

The Act defines categories by establishing two autonomous endowments: one for a Foundation on the Arts; the other for a Foundation on the Humanities. The Humanities, according to the Act, now officially encompass language, literary history, philosophy, archaeology, history, the criticism and theory of the arts, and social sciences "with humanistic content." That this cluster of disciplines holds implications for public schools is made to appear self-evident. The availability of grants, the proposals for Institutes, the proliferation of Seminars and Symposia on the subject make it entirely clear that a "humanistic" revolution is about to be launched, to complement the "scientific" curriculum reform.

But the peculiar history of discourse about the humanities has left a residue of questions and made it difficult for educators to know even now what stance to take. For almost fifty years, the language of "humanism" was appropriated by those disinterested in public schools or hostile to science and secularism—men desiring a return to the old, burnished ideals of "character and intellect," the True, the overarching Good.

There were, in the first place, the literary critics who espoused what they called the "New Humanism" in the years after the First World War: Men like Irving Babbitt, Albert Jay Nock, and T. S. Eliot took eloquent public positions in opposition to egalitarianism, romanticism, naturalism, materialism, to a mass culture embodying "mediocrity." Eliot's great and influential poem, "The Waste Land," presents a modern world grown arid through loss of faith and rejection of the values of the past. It is not accidental that "the Dog" described as "friend to men" should be interpreted as a symbol for science or naturalism, preventing the second blooming of belief:

> "That corpse you planted last year in
>   your garden,
> "Has it begun to sprout? Will it bloom
>   this year?

"Or has the sudden frost disturbed its
    bed?
"Oh keep the Dog far hence, that's friend
    to men,
"Or with his nails he'll dig it up again!
"You! hypocrite lecteur!—mon semblable,
    —mon frère!"

For shelter from that "sudden frost" of sceptical empiricism, Eliot recommended a reaffirmation of tradition. To his reader (his "hypocrite lecteur"), to his fellow poet, he said that a man should write with the "feeling that the whole of literature of Europe from Homer and within it the whole of the literature of his own country has a simultaneous existence and composes a simultaneous order." It was within this order, clearly one created by the humanities, that education was to enable the few to live.

Like Eliot and his "semblables" in spirit were the neo-Thomists, men like Robert Maynard Hutchins and Mortimer Adler, who saw themselves as "rational humanists," hoping to fashion a curriculum in accord with a pre-existent "order in the intellectual realm." Hutchins was writing in the full pride of traditional humanism, for example, when he warned that "the cults of skepticism, presentism, scientism, and anti-intellectualism will lead us to despair. . . ."

These were the men who claimed the humanities as the very substance of their cause. In an essay called "Education and the Humanities" (*Daedalus*, Winter 1959), Douglas Bush summed up two decades of their conversation by suggesting that "one way of approaching the nature and function of the humanities is to indicate the nature of the forces that oppose them and are opposed by them." And what were those forces? The "lower" or the material interests of human beings; the "sophisticated vulgarity" of contemporary mass culture; the domination of science; specialization, mechanization, and a "democratic religion" defined as "the worship of commonness."

In the meantime, the public schools were attempting to meet the unprecedented challenge of mass education, to find a way of equipping diverse persons to cope with the complicated world. There were wide swings back and forth from vocational emphases to experiential, from training for citizenship to education for self-realization. It is somewhat startling to realize that, in 1947, the problem of democratic schooling was still officially described as one that could be solved by putting stress on "active and creative achievements as well as an adjustment to existing conditions." This was the unfortunate "life adjustment" phase, happily short-lived. The ends of popular learning were not yet conceived in terms of cognitive skills or initiation into subject matter fields: The "high premium" was placed on "learning to make wise choices. . . ."

The post-war attack upon the schools was in large measure generated by "life adjustment," an approach both conservatives and progressives (if asked) would be likely to reject. Allied as it was with the long-simmering humanist discontent, the attack polarized the educational domain to such a degree that talk of the "humane," like talk of "intellect," antagonized even those educators whose first commitment had always been to intelligence, to teaching children to think. (There were many, in fact, who had defended the cause of subject matter and "organized" experience along with John Dewey who, writing *Experience and Education* in 1938, had made himself wholly clear. Present experience must "tend both to knowledge of more facts and entertaining of more ideas," he had written. Moreover, experience must be "stretched . . . as it were, backward." And, in language not too remote from the humanist poet's: "It can expand into the future only as it is also enlarged to take in the past.")

The "great debate" petered out in 1957, however, when Sputnik I plunged schoolmen of all persuasions into the effort of curriculum reform. Initiated by members of the learned disciplines who had never before paid heed to public schooling, the movement (ironically enough) achieved many of the ends defined as valuable by those who had spent their lives in public schools. In any event, the polarizing tendencies were halted—or obscured. The day had come for remaking and for redefining terms.

Because of the exigencies of the period, of course, attention was first devoted to subject matters in the natural sciences and mathematics. The humanities, which were in any case more difficult to conceive in terms of "structure," were set aside. After a time, articles began slowly appearing; and discussion hesitantly began. There was talk of the "structure" of literature, of ways and means of teaching the arts to the young. Investigations into "reading" and the state of literacy were undertaken. "Language" became the object of extended inquiries. The vague construct, "social studies," began to give way to "social sciences" as historians and behavioral scientists turned their attention to the concepts structuring their particular fields.

Only in recent months, however, have the humanities (in the "true" sense) come to the foreground. Only now have teachers begun to work cooperatively with scholars and critics, with those committed first and foremost to the integrity of the arts. And this is the reason why the fundamental questions must be framed—the questions having to do with subject matter, meaning, and intent; the questions having to do with the nature of man and the chosen ends of his life.

In what sense is a concept of the humanities linked to a concept of "man"? If the humanities are taken to be "humanistic studies," what precisely does "humanism" mean? Can the humanities be defined most adequately in terms of subject matter, or ought they to be conceived inclusively as "advancing civilization"? Are they to be studied by means of single works or through consideration of what Whitehead called "the curves of history"? Are they to become the occasions for a contemporary quest for meanings, a renewed effort to impose order on the world?

Educators would be committing a kind of "genetic fallacy" if they judged the humanities—or even humanism—in the light of the classic image of man. For the Prince of Humanists, Erasmus, as for other Renaissance scholars, man was defined in terms of his perfection, his fullest realization: He was, in "essence," what he was destined to be. Like their classic forebears, the Humanists conceived man's true end to be the fullest development of his rationality, since it was reason that made him distinctive, reason that placed him high on the ladder of being-reason that brought him near to God. And this was what moved them to combat dogma and obscurantism, to speak of "liberal studies," to strive for the liberation of thought. Only in a state of freedom could the mind of the scholar be released. Only when allowed to speak in many tongues, to read the books of the ages, could the rational man attain his predestined end.

Today, when we consider the human being, we think in terms of individuality, not of essences. We think of open possibility, of realization as a function of culture and social setting, not as a predetermined fulfillment already decided at birth.

The humanities for the existing individual—in many senses free to create what he will be—may then become an organization of possibilities. Not only can he discover a range of potential fulfillments in the literature he reads; he can explore the linguistic behaviors of man, as he learns to put his thoughts in words, and how to make himself clear. He can formulate the kinds of philosophic questions which will permit him to relate himself to what is known—and what is not. Clarifying, criticizing, find his own particular way, he can *create* a perspective instead of *find* one, as the rational humanists used to do. He can fashion his own life order as he seeks out meanings—an order reaching as deeply into the past as T. S. Eliot's, but consciously defined through thoughtful exploration of the history of his kind.

The point is that he must be considered as in some sense unique, in some sense "open," undetermined—free. He must be seen by his teachers to exist in a definable temporal situation, the dimensions of which *he* must learn to relate to through knowing and choosing and concern. The humane studies will become studies *he* may appropriate as he forges authenticity, as he becomes what he may become among his fellows, in a world stretching back in time.

"Humanism," then, when linked to such a notion of man, may become a belief about human life on earth. It may give rise to commitments in the context of that life: commitments to human decency, to happiness, to rebellions on behalf of meaningfulness. It may make possible a commitment to the "visibility" of every man with whom the individual is engaged—not Mankind, not the exemplary Prince, but the single person in his promise and his limitations, the person who can reasonably be granted a measure of justice (as Camus used to say), a measure of freedom, a chance to find a sunny space by the sea.

It would appear to follow from this that the individual must be introduced to the humanities by means of single works, each one offering him a possibility of engagement, an opportunity to inquire, or an occasion for forming his experience and defining what he can be. But there remains as well the matter of perspective, the matter of the organic relation among the subject matters called humane. Alfred North Whitehead may have responded to this more suggestively than most scholars when he said, in *The Aims of Education,* that every child should be permitted to make a few main ideas—"thrown in every combination possible"—his own, that he should be enabled to discover and to understand the past so as to understand "an insistent present," that he should learn how to use what he learns. And then:

The difficulty is just this: the apprehension of general ideas, intellectual habits of mind, and pleasurable interest in mental achievement can be evoked by no form of words, however accurately adjusted. All practical teachers know that education is a patient process of the mastery of details, minute by minute, hour by hour, day by day. There is no royal road to learning through an airy path of brilliant generalizations. There is a proverb about the difficulty of seeing the wood because of the trees. That difficulty is exactly the point which I am enforcing. The problem of education is to make the pupil see the wood by means of the trees.

The wood, the humane order in which educators hope their students will live, must be one young people plant themselves and protect with their own minds and hands. Learning to see through the disciplines and the arts, learning the methodologies of the disciplines and, perhaps, a few aesthetic skills, they may learn to chart their own paths in the quest for meaning. Not every one will chart a straight path nor a scenic one; not every one will learn to appreciate fully nor even learn to see. But, if we keep the thought of possibilities and an open world in mind, those well enough endowed will keep alive the humane studies in their wholeness and integrity; those not so endowed will sometimes have the opportunity to see the wind move in the trees.

Much depends on whether a person exists in the bifurcated universe of ancient times, on whether he persists in envisaging hierarchies in a cosmos predesigned. If he conceives reality to be an analogue of Dante's universe, shaped like a pyramid and culminating in immaterial Form, he cannot but imagine sensuality to be "lower" than rationality; he cannot but place the single and the unitary "higher" than the many and diverse.

If, on the other hand, the individual lives his life in a world of events, if he understands that the orders that exist are the ones human beings have defined, he is able to image a plural world—sensually appealing, theoretically perplexing—where meanings are to be sought. In such a world there can be manifold ways of seeing and knowing, manifold ways of being as well.

The humanities, once integrated in a curriculum for the young, allow for just this manifold. Complementing the sciences, countering aridity, they offer infinite possibilities. The rest is up to the person, acting upon and in the world. Confronting heritage, confronting the humane studies, he can be challenged to become himself more human than before. Rilke's poem, with which we began, renders the effects of such experience when deeply lived; and it may apply to what the humanities, once ushered into public schools, can mean. The poet is talking of engagement, of full exposure to what Apollo (and all he signifies) implies. His last words may be directed to every teacher, every child who can risk a total engagement as he learns: "You must," Rilke says, "change your life."

An Administrator Looks at
the Fine Arts and Humanities

Eugene J. Fox

The American schools have accepted all kinds of responsibilities, the teaching of factual knowledge, the responsibility of providing recreational activities, vocational training, even hot lunches. But our schools have hesitated to accept one responsibility, perhaps the most important of all, the teaching of the differences between such things as right and wrong, morality and immorality, duty and shirking, loyalty and treason, honesty and dishonesty.

For a long time the schools have left the teaching of moral and ethical values to the home and church. But in these times of broken homes and decreasing reliance on the church hundreds of thousands of young people are unable to find satisfactory answers to the questions, "Who am I?" and "What am I here for?" The schools have avoided a duty that is expressed in the goals of every curriculum, that of serving the needs of society. Such neglect implies an unfounded belief that the students will absorb, by some mysterious osmosis, the standards of decent, responsible behavior.

Many of us in teaching and administration have hidden behind the excuse that democratic schools should not teach religion nor the Bible. But, after all, honesty, loyalty, duty, kindness, courtesy, respect, are not religious matters, they are matters of social behavior and, as social institutions the schools must be concerned.

At every level of the educational curriculum, elementary, secondary, and college, we are concerned. Even the conservative Association for Supervision and Curriculum Development showed its awareness of changing needs when its choice for a theme in 1967 was "Humanizing Education—the Person is the Process."[1]

Although most educational administrators are aware of needed changes they are also aware that they are dealing with human beings and are, therefore, cautious about changes.

Teachers on the other hand, feel that their own academic area is the most important and should receive the most support. But a curriculum maker must plan for the greatest benefit of the most students. To arrive at logical judgments he asks himself, and others, many questions. Among these questions he asks. . . :

1. What are the student needs?
2. Are the courses meeting the needs?
3. What changes, if any, should be made?

Since my topic is on the Fine Arts and Humanities, I will direct each of the three questions to those areas and, if possible, I will try to find the answers.

First, however, I would like to clarify what I mean by Humanities. There is a great deal of confusion and misapprehension about the word. Sometimes

[1]Robert R. Leeper, editor, *Humanizing Education; The Person in the Process* (Washington, D.C.: ASCD, 1967).

Humanities is taken as the study of being a humanitarian, sometimes it is taken as a study on the Humane Society. Recently I received a letter from an official in the department of education in a neighboring state stating that, so far as he knew, no school in his state offered a single course in Humanities.

A legal definition of Humanities is given in Public Law 89-209, the National Foundation of the Arts and Humanities Act of 1965, which defines the Humanities as including, but not limited to, "the study of: language, both modern and classic; linguistics; literature; history; jurisprudence; philosophy; archeology; the history, criticism, theory, and practice of the arts; and those aspects of the social sciences which have humanistic content and employ humanistic methods."[2]

The word "humanistic" is more important than the naming of the courses in Humanities. A course may be taught by the "scientific method," as well as by the "humanistic method." The scientific method works with objective materials that are capable of precise measurements, but the humanistic method must work with the human individual and his search for purpose, for beauty, for identity. Science tells us what man can do, but never what he should do.

When I use the word "Humanities" it will include the Fine Arts. Now, let's ask the first question. What are the student needs that the Humanities should serve?

There seem to be five student needs that the Humanities should be serving.

The first one is the need to understand another human being, even an enemy. All of us need to appreciate and tolerate the thinking of another. In a world of exploding population and some 3,000 languages, unless we find the means of understanding and tolerating each other, suspicion and war may destroy us. The other two areas of a liberal education, the Sciences and Social Sciences, do not help us with this need. The sciences are concerned with measurable facts and the social sciences are concerned with social groups: the Humanities, then, must meet the need to appreciate, tolerate and even love one another.

The second need that the Humanities must serve is the need to preserve and hand down the heritage of mankind. Future generations may find even more comfort, pleasure, and knowledge in the works of Shakespeare, Beethoven, and Van Gogh than we have found.

It's not difficult to imagine a young lady of the 21st century, sitting on the moon looking at the earth and saying "Romeo, Romeo! Wherefore art thou, Romeo?"

Our great, great grandchildren may see a painting by Da Vinci or Millet and be stirred to kindness or hope or inspiration.

Music, also, should be preserved so that it may go along with our first colonists on Mars. I must admit, however, that some of our modern music seems hardly worth preserving. And if I should be the one to choose the musical instruments to be preserved for posterity, my grandchildren would never have to hear an amplified guitar. However, the Humanities need to preserve the past, for the humanist must look at the past, in order to see and guide the future.

The third need is the need that our students have to develop an ability to criticize, evaluate, and choose. Each one must evaluate and choose his own friends,

---

[2] The complete text of Public Law 89-209 may be obtained by writing to the Superintendent of Documents, Washington, D. C.

his purposes and his way of life. As I said earlier, we have neglected this need terribly. Osmosis cannot replace a good teacher. And although we strongly believe and defend the rights of man, we must show our children how to choose correct behavior. If society says that stealing is wrong, then we must insist that the young know it is wrong. If our society says that a young man must register for Selective Service, we will allow that young man to study, even criticize the law, if he pleases, but we must teach him that breaking a law is wrong and not a matter of choice. Certainly we do not wish to dictate another person's way of life, but we would be at fault if we did not tell that person which way of life is socially acceptable and which way is not. Some 10,000 young men defied our laws last year and escaped across the border into Canada, in order to dodge the draft.[3] Many of "society's children" are growing up without strong moral beliefs, without the security of a religious faith, and without understanding why they should obey social laws. Juvenile crimes in the United States have increased 62% since 1960.[4] Many young people think of their lives as meaningless existences that may soon be destroyed by a cobalt bomb. After listening to the drop-outs and the potential drop-outs with their feeling that "no one cares,"[5] we can hardly blame them for having rather hopeless, nihilistic attitudes toward the future in a society that has dehumanized them before they finish school.

A fourth need that the humanities should be serving is what John Dewey and others have called the "impulse life."[6] This is the need that the students have to wonder, to imagine, to seek knowledge. Without intellectual curiosity, man becomes no more than a machine in an industrialized society. Even our brightest students are showing a decrease in curiosity. Psychological studies of college students majoring in the sciences and engineering show the majority of them to be conformists, "polite, conscientious, duty-bound, and conventional."[7] Those tested show an avoidance of originality in preference to accepted procedure. Given a problem they work hard at it, but they feel their work is dull and only "assembly lines of science." They are inclined to abandon efforts of "intimate human involvement and, on the other hand, turn their attention to the more approachable and comprehensible world of impersonal things." These are our brightest young minds, and they are content to become more like their machines and less like humans. This impersonal, incurious attitude has spread and it seems to be the fashion to avoid becoming "involved" with other people's problems. The scientifically detached method of observing only real and measurable substances

[3] Bill Davidson, "Hell No, We Won't Go," *The Saturday Evening Post* (January 27, 1968), p. 21.

[4] John Edgar Hoover, *Crime in the United States* (Washington: U. S. Government Printing Office, 1967), p. 2.

[5] Educational Planning Service, *Curriculum and Administrative Study, Roswell Schools* (Greely: Colorado State College, 1967), p. 45.

[6] Christian Bay, "A Social Theory of Intellectual Development," in Nevitt Sanford (ed.), *The American College* (New York: John Wiley and Sons, Inc., 1962), p. 1003.

[7] Carl Bereiter and M. B. Freedman, "Fields of Study and the People in Them," in Nevitt Sanford (ed.), *The American College* (New York: John Wiley and Sons, Inc., 1962), p. 563-580.

have made things that can not be taken out and measured seem to be of little importance. Therefore, justice, honor, and truth appear to be unworthy of serious curiosity.

Even the humanists have been affected. Historians find themselves interested in collecting documents, maps, data, facts, and things that can be measured, if only by the ton. More time has been spent on researching the plots to assassinate Abraham Lincoln than has been spent on the study of his thoughts and writings.

The *Phi Delta Kappan* magazine recently carried an article by Edgar Bruce Wesley entitled, "Let's Abolish History Courses."[8] Mr. Wesley points out flaws in the teaching method of what he calls "facts, facts, facts."

Other humanities reflect the technological influence. Foreign language teachers are using language laboratories, films, and tapes; English and Music teachers are using overhead projectors and record players. The machines are certainly valuable tools for the teacher, and with new programming materials, the machines will become even more valuable. But we must take care that we do not train our students to be only passive spectators of T.V., movies, and life itself. If the medium is the message, and the medium is a machine, then logically, the message cannot be human. The medium may inspire curiousity and imagination in our students—to a point. When that point is reached however, the student needs the message from living, human beings.

The fifth need that the Humanities must serve is a very intangible, but powerful one, the need to create and enjoy beauty. Aesthetics are not as impractical as many pragmatists would have us believe. We see the expression of this need in the color and design of homes, buildings, clothing. Most of us have admired, and even spent money on beautiful things. We enjoy the design of a Ford Thunderbird, the sound of Al Hirt's trumpet, the colors in a Peter Hurd painting, and the human emotions in a Hemingway novel. Even as children most of us felt the need to create our own beauty and we smeared water colors, or wrote poetry, or squeaked away on a violin. As we grow older we still get pleasure out of playing *Chopsticks*, growing roses, and modeling clay figures. The need to create and enjoy beauty does not disappear with age.

It's hardly necessary to ask, are the Humanities courses meeting the student needs? The answer, I'm afraid is, "No." The Humanities are not serving the needs of the students. Only a moment's thought reminds us of the profoundly disturbed generation coming up through our schools. Each day we see the hippies, the flower children, the rebels, and the drop-outs. Educational administrators and counselors, who work with the problem students, are aware of their dissatisfaction and restlessness and their intense need for purpose and identity. No, the Humanities are definitely not serving the needs.

And now the third question, "What changes, if any, should be made?" Obviously, if the Humanities are not meeting the needs, changes should be made. But what are they?

[8] Edgar Bruce Wesley, "Let's Abolish History Courses," *Phi Delta Kappan* (September, 1967), p. 3-8.

Forty percent of all college students in the entire world are in American colleges.[9] These students come from high schools where they have spent, if Dr. Conant's research is correct, from a third to almost one-half their time in subjects claimed by the Humanities.[10]

Should the students be given more time for Humanities in their high school course of study? Perhaps, but perhaps not. Increased time is not nearly as important as changes in content and teaching methods. English and foreign languages taught as simple basic skills in communication are not true Humanities. Neither is political and military history. In fact, the student may be getting no Humanities at all, except in literature and, if he takes the courses, in Music and Art.

Of course teaching methods are changing and have been changing since The Saber-Tooth Curriculum came out and poked fun at those who were teaching a "collection of traditional activities" that were worshipped as education.[11] Some courses however, have been slow to discard some of their useless, traditional activities. These courses should be evaluated as to the needs and whether the needs are met. Vague, general goals should be weighed against the needs and be made more specific. Dreamers have to wake up sometime and I suppose that is why we have administrators, so that they can act as alarm clocks.

Humanists, psychologists, educators, and even politicians are working to develop better programs in the Humanities. This support and interest has been slow in coming.

A few years ago, educators and learned societies became alarmed at the swing toward science and engineering that had been brought on by the National Defense Education Act of 1958. Professors and students, drawn by grants and job opportunities, abandoned other areas to work for urgently needed scientific and technological knowledge. The results have been almost unbelievable. Millions of dollars and millions of brains have advanced the sciences; the electronic industry, the computer industry, all the technological and industrial areas; and we have become, what John Kenneth Galbraith calls "the Industrial State."[12]

In 1964 the Commission of the Humanities, supported by twenty-four learned societies recommended the founding and the funding of a national Humanities Foundation.[13] The Humanities Act of 1965 was passed to provide aid and encouragement for the Humanities and arts. Councils were established, Humanists were put to work, summer institutes were formed—even administrators were invited; and money became available for study and research. Clark Kerr stated that the Humanities, "the ugly duckling or Cinderella of the academic world is ready to

[9]College Entrance Examination Board, *The Challenge of Curricular Change* (New York: College Entrance Examination Board, 1966), p. xii.

[10]James B. Conant, *The Comprehensive High School* (New York: McGraw Hill), p. 23-65.

[11]Harold Benjamin, *The Saber-Tooth Curriculum* (New York: McGraw Hill Book Co., Inc., 1939).

[12]John Kenneth Galbraith, *The New Industrial State* (Boston: Houghton Mifflin Co., 1967).

[13]The American Council of Learned Societies, *Report of the Commission on the Humanities* (New York: The Commission of the Humanities, 1964), p. 1-15, especially p. 9.

bloom."[14] I question his use of "bloom" in use with "duckling" and "Cinderella," but I certainly do not question his meaning.

Now let's examine ten curricular changes that are being made, or soon will be made in the Humanities.

1. Less emphasis on grammar rules in the teaching of English and foreign languages, with more emphasis on oral and written expressions of ideas and feelings.
2. Less emphasis on plots in literary works and more emphasis on the moral and human values.
3. Revision of the teaching of History, with more attention to the humanistic content and less on military and political chronology.
4. Less imitation of European art and music, with more original and independent creativity.[15] Our artists would not need to go to Paris or Milan to study, nor should they feel inferior to the artists of the past or present.
5. Less emphasis on the passive appreciation of music and art, in favor of more individual activity and training in critical ability.
6. New courses in interdisciplinary Humanities. Many high schools are already offering such courses with favorable results.[16]
7. The use of machines, team teaching, and new scheduling techniques to free more teacher time for small discussion groups.
8. More school time for the students to explore, read, talk, exchange ideas, and even, I hope, to day dream.
9. Coordination of course planning by elementary teacher, high school teacher, college teacher, and administrators. The student is a single individual and his education should be a continual and sequential process, not pieces of a jig saw puzzle that he must try to fit together after his graduation.
10. Deliberate and planned teaching of philosophy and ethics. If the purpose of education is to affect the way people actually live, the teaching of ethical values is probably the most important area of teaching. Science has given man the power to destroy himself, a humanities course that does not aim at self control betrays man.

These are the ten changes that administrators will soon be considering when they look at the Fine Arts and Humanities. There are other changes developing, some less involved with courses of study and more concerned with the individual's development. For example, counselors are working with new ideas and techniques developed by the humanistic psychologists.[17] The changes that are in process

[14]Clark Kerr, "The Frantic Race to Remain Contemporary," in Robert Morison (ed.), *The Contemporary University: USA* (Boston: Houghton Mifflin Co., 1966), p. 25.
[15]For more complete discussion on the development of American art, see John A. Kouwenhoven, *The Arts in American Civilization* (New York: W. W. Norton & Co., Inc., 1967).
[16]Charles R. Keller, "Interdisciplinary Humanities Courses," *NEA Journal* (January, 1968), p. 19-20.
[17]For fuller discussion of Psychology working with the Humanities see Frank Severin, *Humanistic Viewpoints in Psychology* (New York: McGraw Hill Book Co., 1965).

promise much. But, from past experiences with new programs, I must point out that anger and disappointment are inevitable. We have come to expect tangible results almost immediately from the sciences. I am far from certain that the Humanities will be able to hand out pat answers to student questions such as, "Who am I?" "What is truth?" "Why am I alive?" But if the Humanities and the Arts can help a student find his "Why," for living, he will be able to endure almost any "How."

And if the Humanists can teach our young people the secrets of such men as Socrates, Jesus Christ, Nathan Hale, and Albert Schweitzer, they may be teaching secrets more valuable than the polio vaccine, the transistor, or rocket fuel. Perhaps the cliche that "the Humanities are necessary, maybe, but not very useful" will be changed to necessary *and* useful.

Seven Aspects of the Humanities Movement

Neille Shoemaker

A very important curricular and sociological fact of recent years is the resurgence of the humanities. The traditional emphasis on the humanities, which was a major theme in the history of American education in the nineteenth and early twentieth centuries, receded after World War I. The shift away from the classics and the movement toward vocationalism and mass education are a major part of the history of education since the 1920's. World War II assisted in disorienting our culture from the classics. The Greco-Judaic culture, which sustained the upper class in America in the eighteenth and nineteenth centuries, was not adequate for mass education. The continuing industrialization of our society, the larger emphasis on the world of business, and the consequent emphasis on vocational education moved us further from the traditional pattern of the humanities. The inadequate support of public education, both at the financial and intellectual levels, likewise caused a decline in the humanities. Increased numbers of students who could not be educated within the traditional curriculum caused a greater emphasis on craft and skills education and further accelerated the drift away from the humanities. The long years of the Cold War have given us a weapons complex and placed survival ahead of living.

A day of decision was reached after Sputnik. We were led to believe that all we needed for survival was a greater emphasis on science. Large sums of money and much educational emphasis were placed on scientific education as a part of national policy. We educated our citizens to live in an age of higher weapons and created a national psychology of the cave. The national policy of underground shelters grew out of the psychology of fear. Science, which had made us strong, had not made us safe. The Cold War and the resultant emphasis upon science as a tool of war left unsolved most of our social and human problems. Fighting communism became more important than ending the blight of the cities.

Within the past three or four years some spectacular changes have occurred in the national attitude toward unsolved problems. We have realized that our national education policies were incorrect. The humanities, the traditional emphasis in our curriculum, are now looked on once again as being essential at all levels, local, state, and national. It has been recognized that the humanities are needed to give us a sense of direction and a pattern of values. A change of immense implication has taken place. Not only has there been a reoccurrence of emphasis on the traditional humanities; there has also been a shift of definition of the humanities, so that now we are speaking of the subject not just in terms of the classroom but in terms of the social scenes of community life, including the inner cities. Humanities is no longer just art and music and literature. It is these and much more. It is religion and philosophy and sociology and anthropology and psychology and even the physical and natural sciences. It is an idea that addresses itself to unsolved problems. It is a philosophic attitude to support the tools of the social scientist. It is a value pattern that emphasizes humaneness. It is a concept that leads toward humanitarianism. It is a return to the Renaissance concept of humanism. It is a process that leads not toward things but toward people.

There are seven major aspects to the current humanities movement.

1. The first fact in the current movement is that it covers all areas of study from graduate school to the kindergarten. The focal point has been at the high school level. Currently, the chief emphasis of the movement is in the grade school and the kindergarten. The movement is making inroads at the undergraduate and graduate level, but because of the traditional departmentalism, the humanities are still tangential to most college curricula. The traditional concept of the humanities—that is, a hodge-podge of art, music, and literature—has a place in the college curriculum. The new humanities, however, have not made any considerable progress at the college level. It is safe to say that when a change occurs in the humanities on the college campus, it will occur not because of faculty and administrative leadership, but because of student pressures. The students desire a new curriculum; the faculties, in the main, would be quite content to proceed in their traditional patterns of tight departmentalism.

On the other hand, the elementary and high schools have been quite willing to experiment and to evolve new forms. The experiments in the humanities at the kindergarten level are very encouraging. If anything has been learned about the humanities through the current emphasis across the country, it is that humanities for high school seniors is no longer adequate. The humanities must be a life-long process; consequently, it is very hopeful that many programs across the country are being initiated at the kindergarten and elementary levels. We have also learned that the humanities for the college-bound only is no longer adequate. The humanities must be for all students, and not just the potential elite. Again, it is encouraging that the current movement is programming for all students and not just for the college-bound.

An underlying philosophy of the change in the humanities is that the entire movement is related to value patterns. The humanities constitute a way of thinking. This is far removed from the traditional data-oriented course. If the humanities are to be meaningful in developing value patterns, obviously students must be related to the program before they are seniors in high school. Most things are learned better if they are learned early. In the language emphasis after Sputnik, it was discovered that French can be learned better at the fourth-grade level than at the tenth- or twelfth-grade level. Likewise, we have discovered during the current humanities movement that many subjects that were thought to be for juniors and seniors only actually are more meaningful if offered to first- and third-graders. A highly successful program offered by the Humanities Institute of Baldwin-Wallace College is anthropology for third-graders. Still more successful is anthropology for first-graders.

It is safe to predict that a major development in American education is the moving of subjects downward in the curriculum. Cultural anthropology, sociology, languages, foreign studies, and other disciplines of the humanities will increasingly be offered at the lower elementary grades, and even at the kindergarten level.

2. A second major fact in the current humanities movement is that it encompasses many academic disciplines. The definition of the humanities has moved much beyond the traditional concept of art, music, and literature. It now includes the social sciences and the physical and natural sciences. It is currently accepted that anything that is humane or that might lead toward increased humaneness rightfully belongs with the humanities. This emphasis of the movement is gaining in momentum. At the present time many high schools have science units built into their humanities programs. A recent conference sponsored by the Humanities Institute of Baldwin-Wallace College on the humanities and the physical sciences proved to be of great importance to the schools. It seems clear that during the years ahead several of the sciences will become a part of the humanities and will be greatly influenced by them. Those sciences that relate to the daily and general welfare of the people may well be labeled the humane sciences. The philosophy of the humanities and the interest they express in the welfare of mankind can be related to the sciences. Both disciplines may be redefined in a new concept of public welfare.

It makes no sense at all to think of the sciences and the humanities as being unrelated and belonging to exclusive academic disciplines. They are, in fact, quite inclusive. Those branches of the sciences that relate to human welfare must become, and in fact are becoming, a part of the humanities. The study of water and air pollution cannot be approached by the sciences alone, because a solution to these problems relates not only to the sciences but to sociology, political science, aesthetics, housing, and the many phases of the public welfare. The sciences relating to agriculture, medicine, birth control, and the military are also related to morality, philosophy, aesthetics, political science, and all phases of the social sciences. The humanities are no longer academic subjects of the ivory tower but have come down into the market place and are a part of the daily lives of people. Sociology is essentially a study of the social fabric of society, but so is a Shakespearian play or a character portrait by Rembrandt. Poetry today is as closely connected with a street of poverty as is a sociological welfare statistic. Communication and languages, part of the humanities, are a part of both the traditional humanities and the traditional social sciences.

Thus, across the nation the departmental boundaries are breaking down in the humanities movement, and many disciplines now are a part of the humanities.

3. A third emphasis in the humanities movement deals with non-school organizations. These include churches, women's clubs, welfare organizations, and inner-city action groups. This is one of the most hopeful signs in the humanities movement at the present time. Traditionally, we have put education in the hands of the schools. Many non-school institutions now are deeply involved in American education, particularly in the humanities. This is especially true in the problems involved in urban affairs. The churches, which historically in America have been largely pulpit-oriented, are now involved in action programs. It is quite clear that government agencies cannot solve all of the problems of the ghetto. It is equally true that city school systems, case workers, and the foundations cannot solve all of the problems. The humanities, being value-oriented, unselfish, and concerned with the individual, are beginning to exert leadership in urban situations. The humanities are more oriented toward problem-solving than they were in the past. The operating philosophy of the humanities has an advantage over that of the case worker. The philosophy speaks to the unmet needs on a long-range basis, as distinguished from the emergency philosophy of relief organizations.

It is most likely that interpersonal guidance and spiritual fulfillment are more important than monthly rent. Several very important programs in the humanities are under way in ghetto conditions. These are not connected with any school and are not offered for credit. This is not the place to spell out the programs in detail, except to state that the humanities can operate outside of the traditional school setting.

4. A major movement in the humanities is that the emphasis is increasingly placed on the individual. Emphasis is placed on involvement, upon fulfillment, upon independent study. There is every indication that the great emphasis on the humanities at the present time will assist in changing the traditional structure of the high school and college curriculum. Less emphasis will be placed on the classroom and more upon out-of-class activities, seminars, independent study, travel, and research.

The humanities are particularly suited to this type of emphasis. In fact, it is the humanities more than any other area of study that are taking the leadership in moving away from the traditional classroom structure. In the lecture method people may be herded into a classroom and fed a body of data. In the humanities this is less necessary and less desirable. The humanities must speak to the individual, and the individual must be permitted and encouraged to proceed in part on his own initiative. The programs being developed over the country in the elementary, secondary, and college levels are moving toward individual performance, and the teachers are becoming counselors, advisors, and resource people rather than dispensers of factual data. An increasing number of programs are taking place outside of the classroom and even away from the school building. Students are going either individually or in small groups to all parts of their communities for the information they need. They are using the business establishments, newspapers, museums, theaters, churches, and slum areas as their operating geography. Travel out of the city, even out of the state and out of the country, is becoming a vital part of humanities programs. Likewise, the computer and resource centers, both at the schools and in other locations, are being used in humanities programs.

The modern student is action oriented. He is less interested in the sit-down type of class; he is less interested in being told what to do; he is less interested in the prescribed curriculum. A project that he himself creates, either individually or in cooperation with a small number of his friends, is of more concern to him than a course that the school system prescribes. This trend is increasing and will become a major fact in curricular procedure in the future.

It should be pointed out that this free-wheeling system of independent study, travel, research, and creative projects is as adaptable to the fifth-grader as to the twelfth-grader. A strong case can be made that a fifth-grader is more capable of proceeding in this type of program than is the twelfth-grader. This is likely due in part to the fact that the fifth-grader has been mistrained for fewer years than has the high school senior. A major development of this trend is the breaking down of class distinctions. In the past, the sophomore was quite distinct from the freshman, and the senior high student was quite distinct from the junior high. These distinctions are increasingly less evident, and the humanities have played a major part in the breakdown of the boundaries.

Psychologically, this phase of the movement has many advantages over the traditional system. Students are permitted to be more creative and to exert more initiative. They are called to an earlier maturing. They respond well to the natural interest in involvement. They are less the victims of bad teaching that abounds in the school systems. They can isolate pockets of interest for maximum development. They are partly engaged in self-teaching, which is the highest form of the teaching art. They can proceed at their own pace.

This phase of the movement is receiving maximum emphasis across the country and well may be the major breakthrough in the humanities. It places the emphasis where it should be, namely, upon the individual and not upon the teacher, the subject, or the school system.

5. Closely allied to the point above is that of creativity. Greater emphasis is being placed upon individual expression in the arts, music, writing, and the like. It is most likely that an important course in the curriculum of the future will be one on private meditation, a type of philosophic retreat. The emphasis on social interaction in areas of civil rights and war protest is finding its counterpart in personal and philosophic interaction. More attention will be placed on the thought of the individual student, and less on the acquiring of data.

Of course, the private meditation will not be the major emphasis in individual creativity. This will find expression in the traditional arts of all types. The main point of emphasis, however, is on creativity in the arts and not the mere historical study of the arts. Traditionally, the humanities have been presented from the historical and factual points of view. This is no longer satisfactory to the students. As was mentioned above, students want action, they want to do something. They are no longer willing to be fed a steady stream of data; they are less willing to share their time with thirty other students in a class; they want to create, perform, experiment, and fail, if need be. They are less interested than formerly in being told about the arts; they are more interested in getting on the stage and acting than in sitting at a desk and reading a book about the theater. They do not wish to study the history of costuming, but instead wish to make costumes for their parts in a play. They are willing to act in a play written by Shaw or O'Neill, but some of them want to go to the next step in creativity and write their own plays. The same is true in the other arts; students want to compose, play music, create the dance, paint and draw. They want to relate the history of these art forms to their own private creations. They are more interested in studying their own writing than that of Hemingway or Faulkner.

As a consequence, a vast movement in the creative aspects of the humanities is under way at all levels from the kindergarten to the undergraduate college. Some of the programs are becoming part of the curriculum, but many elements are still tangential to the main offerings of the school systems. If the students can survive the controlling and limiting effect of the system, they may be able to create a modern renaissance of student art forms. In the programs that have been most successful, the guiding factor is that the students themselves have created their own programs. The teacher takes on a new dimension. The teacher becomes more of a resource person, guidance counselor, and individual tutor. The results of the first few years of this type of humanities program are extremely gratifying.

The key concept here is that the creative aspects of the humanities are a vital part of a humanities program, and are not to be confused with the traditional extracurricular activity—they are a part of the curriculum. Likewise, it must be clear that this is not a program essentially for upperclassmen or for the highly talented. A major fact of the movement is that students at all levels are participating, and that the non-talented and semi-talented are as important in the movement as are the talented. It is highly gratifying that so much outstanding art of all types is coming from the talented students. It is likely, however, that of much more importance is the self-development that is being experienced by masses of the untalented. One group may be creating the arts; the other group is perhaps creating the students.

6. Increasing interest is being placed on intercultural experiences. Non-Western studies are being placed in the curriculum. An art history course, for example, has traditionally dealt with art of the Western world. In the future, such a course will include the Middle East or Far East also. Likewise, the economy, sociology, philosophy, and other disciplines of the non-Western world will be included in humanities programs. The humanities will also be more intercultural within the framework of traditional Western culture. Exposure to other cultural patterns and subcultures is increasingly important in the study of the humanities. A major service of the humanities during the past decade has been to introduce the non-Western world to Western-oriented curricula across the country. Even today many academic programs at the grade, high school, and the college levels are slanted entirely toward Western culture. In most colleges and in elementary and high schools a study of art, literature, music, history, and the like mean a study of those disciplines from the Western point of view. Even a college course labeled "world literature" in most colleges today is a history of Western literature. A study of

urban problems normally means a study of the problems of New York, Chicago, or some other American city. It rarely means a study of urban problems of Cairo or Calcutta.

Fortunately, this concept is changing. Across the country schools at all levels are instituting non-Western studies, either as a separate course or as a unit in some other course. Fortunately also, the emphasis is not entirely at the upper levels. A study of Oriental religions is now very popular at the fifth-grade level. Sociology, anthropology, history, art, philosophy, and religion are becoming popular subjects from the third grade up to the senior year at the undergraduate college level. All of these subjects are a part of the humanities movement. The schools are beginning to discover what the airlines and international communications discovered long ago; the exchange of students between countries is increasing. Student travel likewise is becoming more important as a part of a school program. Materials dealing with the non-Western world are now readily available and are being used across the country. The great movement of non-Western studies, which was largely initiated by the graduate schools after World War II, is now being felt down to the first grade. It seems quite clear that in the future an entirely different type of student will enroll for college work. He will be more knowledgeable of other parts of the world and better informed than his counterpart of the present generation. Again, all levels of students are included in the program. The third-graders are as apt in studying the non-Western world as are the seventh- or the twelfth-graders. As in other parts of the humanities program, some of the emphasis is upon independent study, special projects, travel, and research. The non-West program came late enough to escape many of the harmful effects of the traditional curriculum.

7. The entire emphasis in the current humanities movement is people-centered. More emphasis will be placed on the activities of people within their sociological setting. The humanities may succeed in identifying and solving human problems that the social sciences, using other tools, have not been able to solve. The sociologists or the economists, operating alone in their traditional disciplines, have identified urban problems and have brought data to bear upon the subject, but these disciplines have not solved the problems that the data identified. It will be up to the humanities to solve the human problems growing out of poverty, inadequate training, overpopulation, and inadequate housing. When moral values are added to statistics, the solution of a problem may be more likely. The knowledge of medicine may be listed as science, but the physical and mental ailments of people will not be solved by the scientific knowledge of medicine, but through the humanitarian application of healing and well-being for all people. The concepts that make the best society come from the humanities. These concepts include moral values, aesthetics, humanitarianism, human rights, and similar philosophic ideas. The information and data dealing with many of these concepts come from other disciplines, disciplines that in the past have been entirely removed from the humanities. The major opportunity of the humanities in our time is that they may give the necessary leadership and thought to the fields of technical knowledge, so that human problems may be solved.

It seems most likely that the decade that began in 1965 will be known as the age of the humanities. It is most likely that if this occurs, another Renaissance will be underway. When the humanities received major emphasis from the fifteenth to the seventeenth centuries, a great Renaissance of culture, literature, art, politics, and geographic exploration was created. All the great ages in the past have been times when the humanities received maximum emphasis. A major resurgence of the humanities may indeed create another Renaissance.

Education for Humane Living
in an Age of Automation

G. Bruce Dearing

In many of our increasingly anxious discussions of the role of what we traditionally have called "the humanities" in contemporary higher education, our councils have been beclouded and baffled by confusions in definition. "Humanistic Education" is not limited to the standard courses in classical language, literature, the fine arts, and the subjects normally offered in departments or divisions familiarly classified as Arts or Humanities as distinguished from Sciences and Social Sciences. And I do not wish to subsume all knowledge under the rubric of "Liberal Education" and to argue that it is at least as easy to teach Sanitary Engineering humanely and as an humanistic discipline as it is to teach Middle High German. However, it is possible to draw a distinction between general education and specialized education, between education and training, between the liberal and the vocational, and between the humanistic and the technological or technical. I do not aggrandize the one and disparage the other, for each is inescapably necessary to anyone who seeks to be effectively human and humane in our society. We are dealing here not with polar opposites, but with separable, if not wholly discrete elements of the activities which are going forward in our colleges and universities and inside the heads of those who are listening, reading, observing, and reasoning in whatever context. I shall concern myself with those elements of education which I take to be general, liberal, humanistic, and educative.

If I am asked to outline the proper shape of humanistic education for an age of automation, I would begin by quoting the construction arrived at by the hard-working Curriculum Committee of the School of Arts and Science, University of Delaware, after a full year of deliberation and debate. One reason I like it so much is that it turned out to be the statement which I had written for the undergraduate catalogue two years earlier and which the school committee happened upon after being unable to agree on any alternative formulation. Although it sounds a bit ambitious, it still is an earnest essay in expressing what many of us deeply believe about the mission and purpose of higher education:

Courses and programs are designed to help the student to organize his experience meaningfully and to acquire perceptions, skills, and attitudes which will assist him in achieving a full and satisfying life as a contributing member of society. The school seeks to develop in its students a heightened awareness of all aspects of human environment, intellectual curiosity, respect for fact, perception of the complexity of truth, skill in reasoning, and concern for integrity and logical consistency.

Contributions of the humanities include the development and refinement of systems of value, of aesthetic appreciation, and of a viable world view. The humanities should provide, also, an acquaintance with the heritage of both Western and non-Western cultures, and increased skill in communication, both verbal and non-verbal. Contributions of the social sciences include the acquisition of historical perspective; acquaintance with facts and concepts relating to social organization and patterns of inter-action among individual persons and groups; and the development of an informed concern about practical, moral, and ethical issues in the structure and operation of society. Studies in this area aim toward emancipation from provincialism and naive ethnocentrism; refinement of concepts of causality in the social realm; and the development of understanding in the recognition and resolution of intra-personal, inter-personal, intra-group and inter-group conflicts. Offerings in mathematics and the natural sciences are directed at the development of skill in quantitative thinking; acquaintance with the basic facts and concepts relating to the physical universe; comprehension of, and respect for, the approach to knowledge through experimentation; and direct experience with rigor and precision in perception, description, and manipulation.

In the face of the Twentieth Century explosion of knowledge, only that graduate can be considered educated who has developed the tools, techniques, and attitudes for continuing education. In recognition of this fact, a premium is placed on individual initiative and self direction. The University cannot successfully educate students who merely present themselves passively to be *taught;* it can provide an environment in which a well-motivated student may *learn* up to the full limits of his capacity.

Let me expand upon some of the implications of this statement. One of the things anyone who teaches both college-age students and adults in a continuing education program quickly discovers is that older students have more experience, and they organize it differently. But if an education does not immediately and materially assist in the organization and interpretation of life experience, it seems to me to be of questionable value. Moreover, it is by no means enough to acquire information (which, unfortunately, is too often the primary, or even the only, commodity given much attention in the plan of courses of instruction). We need to sharpen all our perceptions, to see, hear, and even to taste, touch, and smell many material and immaterial environments with greater accuracy, precision, and joy or revulsion than those who are only partially educated and, therefore, only partially alive and incompletely human. We need to acquire learned skills not merely to recommend ourselves for gainful employment as typists, draftsmen, or chemists, but to permit us to communicate effectively, to establish acceptable and satisfying social relationships, and to facilitate our continued growth. And too often we overlook the importance of attitudes, whether recognized and consciously evoked or instilled, or developed and communicated without intention or recognition. Consider, for example, the attitude of fear and distaste toward mathematics which is communicated to so large a majority of our elementary school children by teachers who themselves have a fear and distaste for a body of knowledge and for techniques with which they are uncomfortable and uncertain. Or consider the attitudes toward academic honesty which have scandalized so many secondary schools and colleges in these past years and which are properly so grave a concern of the society at large.

We express our concern for alertness and awareness, which is essential if we are to adapt to change, recognize opportunity, respond relevantly to threats and dangers, and experience anything to the fullest. We must be curious if we hope to continue learning. We should respect fact and love truth, recognizing that any truth worth comprehending, like any woman worth knowing, is infinitely various and inexhaustibly complex. We should have learned how to reason and, if possible, how to think, recognizing that there is an important place for the irrational, the intuitive, and the inexplicable in the most penetrating thought, as Jerome Bruner has pointed out so winsomely in his "Essays for the Left Hand." And however unfashionable the idea may be at present of a faculty concerning itself with the personal values of its students, I ally myself with those who believe that both precepts and examples of integrity, consistency, and magnanimity should be available to, and even urged upon, the college student.

I do not claim all the virtues as the exclusive property of the humanities. Such studies are traditionally concerned with preparing a student, in Matthew Arnold's phrase, to "see life steadily and see it whole," or in Gordon Keith Chalmer's phrase, "Not merely to think, but to think in relevant terms about things that matter." However, concepts of the good are as much a property of history or sociology as of philosophy or literature; beauty belongs as much to mathematics as to art history, and truth both transcends and eludes all our formulations and organizational patterns. We do too little and should do more straightway to introduce significant aspects of non-American and non-Western cultures into our curricula, particularly in the humanities and the social sciences. Also, while agreeing with the critics of higher education that our products exhibit too little skill in communication, such as writing and speaking, I earnestly would urge the importance of non-verbal communication—the visual arts, the performing arts, and the language of gesture and of the eloquently unsaid.

The direction which our society appears to be taking with increased interdependence, increased interaction, and, therefore, increased opportunity for choice, conflict, and decision seems to place a premium upon literacy in the sciences of anthropology, sociology, psychology, economics, and politics. Recent events have illustrated dramatically and tragically the residual barbarism in our civilization as well as its potentialities for dignity, nobility, and the rational approach to complex social problems. A world of automation will be a world of groups in any case, whether or not it is possible to preserve the separate, distinct, and distinctive humanity of the individual.

We recently have discovered, to the dismay of some and the delight of others, that mathematics is as basic to the current understanding and development of economics, music, and sociology as it is for physics or engineering. We have begun to tell one another, and at least in part to believe, that scientific illiteracy in our technological age is as indefensible as religious or literary ignorance and indifference have been in former times. Surely, one who expects to live alertly and in a significantly contributing way in an age of automation needs to know something of the physical universe he inhabits and of the techniques of dealing with unyielding and unforgiving reality with rigor, precision, and a healthy respect. One does not have to be an astronaut to get in trouble with a lawful universe if the calculations are off or the reasoning is imprecise. I have heard an astronaut quoted as reflecting in the midst of the pre-launch tensions that everything below him had been provided by a low bidder. Other moments of truth have been and will be approached in analogous ways by managers, political leaders, administrators, and all others with responsibility for action. They should be able to hope that rough approximations, easy generalizations, inviting self deceptions, the almost fine and the nearly true, have little part in the analyses, constructions, and predictions on which they must stake much that they value. We hope and believe that the necessary rigor and precision can be cultivated by a student's experience in quantitative thinking and experimental procedures.

Finally, we feel that higher education is not coextensive with the undergraduate or graduate years and that passive submission to teaching is a poor way to spend those years. It is alleged that most engineers become obsolete in a cycle of from five to 10 years and either must be re-educated continuously or continually if they are to perform their proper functions. I am prepared to assert that both our general and our specialized education are subject to obsolescence if we have not learned how to continue to learn throughout our lives.

One of our most difficult problems is that of determining whether we really are talking about the education of an elite who shall be governors and directors, or undertaking the education of an eligible majority or the whole society. The curricula we cling to were designed originally for governors and professional men. It may be that such curricula are but ill-adapted to the needs of those who shall be making decisions only for themselves and not for others. It may be also that we do a disservice to a man if we educate him for power and authority and he finds not only that he has no one to command or govern, but that he has not even a role in which he can contribute. What Napoleon could ever be happy either in Corsica or on Elba?

We must recognize in ourselves some extraordinarily incongruous and inconsistent attitudes toward work. Most of us are the inheritors of the 19th-century "gospel of work" and have thought with Carlyle that "work is worship." At the same time that we spend many of our days in quiet desperation, we dream of lotus land, plan feverishly for vacations and retirement which seem but rarely to live up to expectations, and recognize, if we do not identify with, Auden's "unimportant clerk" who writes "I do not like my work" on the pink official form.

It has been widely and shrewdly remarked that in our time a traditional pyramid has been overturned. Where once the mass of people toiled that a few might live in ease and luxury, it now appears to be not only possible but probable that a few among the most gifted and able shall work long hours without stint so that their numberless inferiors can vegetate in indolence and ease. The evidence of this shift is everywhere, and it is unmistakable. In many large organizations it appears that overtime work and harassing pressures are not merely the responsibility, but the privilege and the symbol of status of the major executive. Indeed, in many management and administrative circles it appears that a kind of "cult of overwork" is consciously fostered. We all can think of leaders in government, industry, and education who make it a point to arrive early at the office, work beyond regular hours, and regularly take home a briefcase full of work. In an essay in *Vogue* (October, 1963), David Ogilvy chillingly recounts the devices he has employed to pervert the Protestant Ethic and to insure that his subordinates will feel guilty for every moment they are not actively working at their jobs. The implication is that the men who really count will choose to work all the time and that the no-account majority is, by nature, indolent and will work as little as it can get away with.

One of the most striking effects of automation, and of the advanced technology which has made it possible, is the denial of work to the unskilled or semi-skilled majority and at the same time the piling of excessive loads upon the highly skilled minority. I doubt that we really are prepared yet to face the implications of this new situation.

It seems significant that literary artists, for a surprisingly long time, have foreseen and written prophetically about matters which society only recently has begun to take seriously. In the 1860's, Samuel Butler, in his ingenious fable, "Erewhon," described an utopian society which had recognized and met the problems of technological unemployment by the expedient of destroying all the machines and the scientific advances developed in the 271 years preceding the fateful decision. A similar device is employed in Ayn Rand's more recent "Anthem," where a handicraft economy is reinstituted to occupy the time of the society which otherwise would have lost its purpose and its meaning. In the 1920's, Ryunosuke Akutagawa, in the anti-utopian novel, "Kappa," described the direction he felt the industrialization of Japan was taking: "An average of seven or eight hundred new machines are invented every month, and things are produced on a larger and larger scale with less and less labor. The result is forty or fifty thousand more Kappas thrown out of work every month." The solution arrived at in this romance was that of Jonathan Swift's "Modest Proposal." As the spokesman for the society says, " 'We kill all those workers and eat their flesh. Just look at this newspaper here. This month 64,769 workers have been dismissed, and the price of meat has dropped accordingly.' 'Do they meekly consent to be killed?' I asked. 'It's no use making a fuss,' said Pep, who sat frowning by a wild peach in the pot. 'We've got the "workers butchery law." ' " In the late 1920's, the Russian Eugene Zamiatin, in his satirical anti-utopian novel, "We," described the effects of the mechanization, materialization, and dehumanization of totalitarian Russia. In 1930, Aldous Huxley, in his "Brave New World," developed what is probably the most brilliant and comprehensive analysis of a society in which technology has been carried to its logical conclusion. George Orwell's more recent "1984" owes much to the Russian "We" in its account of a dehumanized totalitarian society.

All of these books are consistent in suggesting that "the most difficult problem that exists today in the civilized world is a problem of the preservation of the independent, original, creative personality," as Gregory Zilboorg said in his 1924 introduction to "We," reiterating in 1959 that "man as an individual, not just as a statistical datum, seems to have lost his value." All postulate the theory that in Zilboorg's words, "most men believe their freedom to be more than a fair exchange for a high level of materialistic happiness. If the present rapid rate of technological development continues, both totalitarian and democratic societies will be involved in this test. As we ourselves pursue even higher goals of materialistic happiness, the complexity of our technological society will increase and exert even more intense pressures for efficiency through the regulation of our lives." The Grand Inquisitor in "The Brothers Karamazov" and the World Controller in "Brave New World" argue persuasively that a regulated, conditioned happiness is the best that can be hoped for by the mass of men in a technological society. The brilliant psychologist, B. F. Skinner, in his novel, "Walden II," seriously proposes the kind of "human engineering" which is anathema to Huxley, Dostoevski, Zamiatin, Akutagawa, Huxley, and Orwell. All reveal a passionate commitment to individual human freedom and express hope that somehow humanistic values can prevail in the face of rampant technology and materialism. Have we any reason to hope that their prophetic fears can be prevented from being fulfilled in all their horror?

The area in which we are weakest and least advanced is that of knowledge of the nature of man, and particularly of man in the aggregate rather than as an individual person. We may be horrified at the progress of the development of techniques for brain-washing and for the manipulation of masses of people by totalitarian powers. However, such techniques are far less efficacious, and far less advanced in theoretical explanation, than we have been led to believe. This seems to be the weakest part of the horror stories presented in the anti-utopian novels, like "Brave New World," "We," and "1984." Perhaps I am merely a naive product of a narrowly and optimistically humanistic education, but I prefer to believe that the human animal is more complex and more resistant to the conditioning than the gloomier of the prophets of enveloping totalitarianism appear to think.

I prefer to believe that it will be possible to develop and to learn new definitions of and attitudes toward work and to substitute the concept of *relevant and humanly significant activity* for the concept of *productive labor* as the primary basis for human dignity and human satisfaction. This may veer perilously close to social philosophies which are not acceptable to a democratic society. However, I cast my lot with those who are seeking a middle way among the extremes of totally engineered and, therefore, no longer fully human happiness in the manner of the "Brave New World" and "Walden II," the totally engineered misery of "1984" and "We," and a chaotic and demoralized society in which only a minority has a basis for the sense of individual worth and significance which alone can make the human condition a bearable estate. I think that education of the kind I have described has a signal contribution to make to the search for this middle way.

Part III
Humanities in the Secondary School

It is in the secondary schools that we have witnessed the major humanities upsurge during the last few years. In New York State alone there are approximately four hundred separate humanities courses, and still the number swells.

The first article, "If English Is Well-Taught, Is There a Need for Humanities Courses in the Secondary School?," was a speech given at a Conference on English Education in 1967. A survey that was part of this speech indicated an overwhelming affirmative to this question on the part of the English teachers who were polled. Dante, studying this same question from the viewpoint of the social studies teacher, concluded that both the humanities and the social studies deserve to be studied but that neither is an adequate substitute for the other.

Glass and Miller, to ascertain the status of humanities courses in the secondary school, distributed two questionnaires. The first was sent to every state department of education in the United States, and the second was sent to each school listed by the state education department as having a good humanities program. Their interesting results indicate that the general area of the humanities remains "an underdeveloped area of the secondary-school instructional program," but may provide the different type of curriculum that will be needed in the schools of the future.

The remainder of the articles in this section explore possible designs for secondary school humanities courses. Shoemaker describes a world-cultures curriculum that "implies the need to find new ways to deal in life-like simultaneity with wide spectrums of materials and values."

Karel suggests the base of fusion of the arts and concentration on development of standards of taste. This design is called the "Allied Arts: An Approach to Aesthetic Education."

Warshaw suggests the Bible as a source book for the humanities from which will grow the student's understanding of allusions in literature, in music, in the fine arts, in media, in entertainment, and in cultured conversation.

Manchel advocates the art film as the basis for a humanities course. It is the best means, he feels, for communicating not only with facts, but with feelings as well. [1]

Diamond describes in detail the instructional resources used to teach the art component of the humanities course at the University of Miami. This article is included because the methods described are completely applicable to the secondary school.

Miller describes several humanities courses in which students seem to have gained a sense of understanding about themselves, the past, and the present world. Stern, also, describes a variety of settings in which students can be led to see the balance in life. In addition to describing successful classroom techniques, she discusses some of the problems inherent in humanities courses. Hipple, examines a variety of organizational patterns and suggests that the best pattern is one in which a set of courses cover various disciplines but are restricted to a few periods of history.

Cauble and Ladensack describe the Scarsdale High School program, Cauble in general terms and Ladensack, more specifically, in relation to one unit based on a Hart Crane poem. Moore describes the Dobbs Ferry humanities program, which is required of all ninth graders and in which each particular era to be studied is arranged into a unit called "creative learning enterprise."

Calisch describes the Elk Grove High School program, which is an outgrowth of a "self-actualization philosophy which supports the freedom to attempt of the school communiy," and Murphy describes a program begun in a Catholic high school.

Bogart, demonstrating the relationship between literature and the humanities ideal, shows a humanistic approach that is concerned with man's central problems as a human being. Izquierdo explains the importance of individual research and small groups in the Auburn High School humanities program.

York bases his humanities course on the applied aesthetics concept of Dudley and Faricy, and Kirk, too, attempts to demonstrate the structural relationships among literature, music, and painting. Stuart and Hunt also describe a humanities program based on the elements approach in which they divide the course into music, visual arts, and literature.

This section closes with an article by Harry Broudy in which he discusses the fact that no two humanities courses agree fully on content, approach, or method of instruction. The principle of selection that he suggests is "enlightened cherishing." This purpose will lead to the selection of materials and methods for programs, and this approach can best be achieved through the identification and teaching of works of unquestioned excellence that help to illuminate the human quest.

---

[1] It is an interesting point in this connection to note that Dr. William Arrowsmith, the major speaker at the fourth NCTE Humanities Conference, which was held in San Francisco in 1969, also suggested the film as the basic instructional aid for teaching the humanities. The film, he pointed out, is truly interdisciplinary and international.

If English Is Well-Taught, Is There a Need for Humanities Courses in the Secondary School?

Sheila Schwartz

The question I have been asked to discuss today is the following: If English Is Well-Taught, is there a need for humanities courses in the secondary school?

This question raises the false premise that the contents of English and humanities classes are interchangeable. But they are not. The question is no more valid than would be the same question with the substitution of the word *art* for *English*.

Despite the fact that there may be some duplication of English materials in humanities courses, the basic goals are different. The basic purpose of the humanities is to acquaint man with the ideas and actions of his predecessors and contemporaries that "have to do with making man more human."[1] To achieve this purpose, literature, language, art, music, or any of the "branches of learning concerned with man"[2] are valid materials for the development of understanding. The traditional content of English courses becomes one tool in humanities courses and is not an end in itself.

This definition suggests that the study of any art form as an expression of the ideas of man is distinctly different from the study of its techniques. Perhaps poetry is a "scientific" study when emphasis is on its techniques, but it may belong to the humanities when the focus is on its use as a vehicle to answer questions about man.[3]

In addition to a difference in goals, there are other reasons why these two areas are not interchangeable. The reasons are concerned with climate, content, the affective side of learning, and the utilization of staff.

The Climate of a Humanities Course. Humanities courses cannot flourish in a traditional mark-centered structure. The pressure of marks and examinations cannot help but inhibit the free association that is essential to creative thinking. If a student is tested on his knowledge of answers, he cannot devote his major concern to developing his *own* questions. He must, instead, concentrate on learning the right answers to the *teacher's* questions. This need to please and appease is antithetical to the humanistic spirit.

If a humanities course is graded, there is little point in giving it. It is no longer a humanities course because the development of ideas cannot be evaluated. No one knows which presentation of an idea will interest a student, or at exactly what moment the epiphany occurs.

[1] Charles R. Keller, "The Wave of the Present," *The English Journal*, March, 1965.
[2] *Ibid.*
[3] *Ends and Issues*, 1965-66, NCTE, p. 24.

The impossibility of humanistic thinking in a pressured mark situation was clearly demonstrated by a 1966 research project designed to find out which literary experiences had helped students to develop self-insight or to answer the basic question "who am I?," which is the core of most humanities courses.

The responses of three hundred English students, in grades seven through twelve, made it absolutely clear that schools not only do not encourage but actually militate against the development of self-knowledge.

I wish that I could include many responses in this paper. However, time will not allow, and so I am including only two samples. The first is that of a twelfth-grade girl. She wrote:

Up until last year, I never entered a classroom expecting to learn about myself. All our education seemed to be interested in was to cram my head full of knowledge and to have me put ahead in as many advanced classes as possible to see how long I could hold out. No one seemed particularly interested in what *I* thought.

But last year, I entered a class which really helped me to understand myself and human nature better. It was my English class. Although my teacher was like any other teacher (which means that I wrote to please him usually, for the grade and not myself), we had fantastic class discussions.

We considered philosophical problems such as "is love stronger than hate" and many others. When topics such as these came up, I was really able to think about such things and by writing papers on them, I was able to collect my thoughts.

We talked about reality and read books which deal with a conformist (*Babbitt*), a seeker of truth (*Huckleberry Finn*), and other fine selections. The teacher seemed genuinely interested in what we thought (a quality which is quite rare from my experience with teachers). Yet, like all classes, it was for a mark. The main thing that matters is what your mark will be—not what you really believe.

The educational system today doesn't give me enough time for myself in the respect of insight.

How can I associate myself with King Charles VIII or $X(2) - AB(3) + Y$? In these classes there is no room and no one really cares what my opinion is. I just have to accept my classes for what they are. Self-insight has nothing to do with it.

Things were the same even in elementary school. What did my first grade teacher care about my developing as a person? She was just interested to see that I could read, to push me on to second grade! Very few attempts have been made evident to me in which the educational system tries to give the student self-insight.

This student believes that all that matters in school is the mark—not what a student really knows or believes. She understands that the necessity for grading is as much a problem for the teacher as for the student.

She has further suggested that for her to undertake humanistic learning she needs a climate in which there is opportunity for good class discussions, a teacher who is genuinely interested in the thinking of the students, and content with which she can "associate" herself.

Another student, echoing the need for a particular kind of climate in which a teacher is able to listen, wrote:

Sometimes in school I find that no one really cares how I do. But it is a glorious feeling when you find out someone really does. One of my teachers and I got to talking one afternoon and I saw that he was really interested in ME.

Not in my compositons, not in my readings, but me! It made me feel that what I do in school is important. I am only an IBM card if that's what people think of me. But this teacher spoke as though he was talking *with* me, not *to* me.

De-emphasis on Literary Works. I have stated that the first essential for humanities courses is a climate that fosters creative thinking and emotional involvement, in essence a climate that is "evocative." A second essential is a de-emphasis on literary works as the major way of understanding the humanities.

Many secondary humanities courses are based on "The Great Books." Some of these books are undoubtedly valuable for humanistic studies, but they can also strangle a course with their institutionalized ideas. Teachers tend to handle them with awe, as if they contained irrefutable answers. In addition, the use of "The Great Books" limits courses to the intellectual elite.

An example of this tendency can be observed in the following description of the St. Louis High School humanities course, a credit course open only to seniors who have an average of *B* or better. In this course:

Themes are taught and take about two weeks each. They are based on the required books. (There are 18 required selections, 12 of which are from the first year of The Great Books Series) .... The class procedure follows a pattern of the student's reading the book, writing an analysis of the content, and ending with a group discussion in a conference-style atmosphere.[4]

It seems evident that the focus of this course is not on the use of literature to illuminate humanistic ideas but, instead, on the literary selection itself.

Another, similar humanities course is based on the question "who am I?" In this course nine periods are studied as an aid in understanding this question. The literary works on which the course is based are the following:

1. The Hebrews (*Bible* selections)
2. The Greeks (Plato's *Republic*)
3. The Medieval Age (Dante's *Inferno*)
4. The Renaissance (*The Prince*)
5. The Baroque (*Paradise Lost*, Books I, II, IX, X)
6. The Enlightenment (*Candide*)
7. The Romantic Age (*Sorrows of Young Werther*)
8. Impressionism (*Lust for Life*)
9. The Modern Age (*The Stranger*)[5]

[4] The New England Association of Teachers of English, "The Humanities," *The English Leaflet,* P. O. Box 256, Wellesley, Massachusetts, Fall, 1964, p. 54.
[5] *Ibid.,* p. 51.

Now, I submit that the twenty-five to thirty "able seniors who are strong in English and reading" who take this course may read every one of the above books and still come out by the same door wherein they went. It may be part of every cultured person's background that he have some familiarity with these books, but because of their lack of affect, I do not believe they help a student to better understand "who he is." And once again, the students who are not "strong in English and reading" are excluded from the course.

It occurs to me that the use of "The Great Books" for humanities courses is the result of a basic confusion in which it is assumed that exposure to literary excellence will lead to humanistic understanding. We know, logically, that this is not true. Members of the Inquisition read the Bible, and many Nazis were well-read.

Two years ago I had the opportunity to discuss literary heroes with Bruno Bettleheim in his Orthogenic School at the University of Chicago. He expressed the opinion that Hamlet, as a hero, has little meaning for today's students. Bettleheim, who had experienced the horrors of Auschwitz, felt that Hamlet was useless. At the end of the play everyone is dead and nothing has been accomplished. I then asked Bettleheim which literary figure he believed to be a representative model for our times, and he told me, Lewis Eliot, the hero of the C. P. Snow books.

I mention this incident here because I had read and rejected the works of C. P. Snow as good examples of the nineteenth-century novel. As an English teacher I could never have thought of substituting even the best of Snow's books, *The Masters*, for *Hamlet.* But to illustrate man in society in our time, Lewis Eliot might indeed be a better figure than a prince who sees ghosts and finds his mother's marriage to his uncle incestuous.

Howard Mumford Jones, in discussing this problem, warns that there is a tendency in using "The Great Books" "to twist the original occasion of a book into a coarse facsimile of our own problems."[6] He points out that the past is not the present and says that contemporary *Angst* (or "identity crisis") is not the same *Angst* suffered by Lucifer or Job.

In a famous Jules Feiffer cartoon, we see a man in dark glasses lying on a couch talking to his analyst. He says:

After all I was raised away from home. How was I to know this guy was my FATHER. I mean, all right, so I KILLED him, but I didn't know he was my father. And then I meet this dame. How could I know who she was? Is it MY fault I like them MATURE? All right . . . so I MARRY her. But did I know she was my MOTHER? It's not like I was sick or something . . . .

As the man feels his way out with aid of his cane, he says:

O.K. I'll come back next week. I'll bring my daughter . . . . You can talk to her. Boy has SHE got problems.[7]

---

[6] Howard Mumford Jones, "Uses of the Past in General Education." paper delivered at the Advanced Administrative Institute, Harvard University, July, 1965.

[7] Jules Feiffer, *Sick, Sick, Sick.* New York: McGraw-Hill, 1958.

I am referring to this cartoon as evidence that certain works of antiquity may not be relevant and may be fit topics for satire in this computer age. I doubt, however, that anything satirical could be made of *The Trojan Women.*

All the above is not intended to imply that no great books can or should be used in humanities courses. But the books should be used *only* as one tool and not as ends in themselves.

Flexibility in Methods and Materials. A third essential for humanities courses is a flexible approach to methods and materials. Unorthodox materials can be employed to understand humanistic questions.

It is not necessary to study complete works in humanities courses. For example, there is a record called *Brecht on Brecht*[8] from which one or more of the short bands can be used. In the band called "Means and Ends," Brecht gently mocks people who lead unexamined lives. He tells of his neighbor who plays music in the morning by which to exercise. Why does he exercise? In order to become strong enough to beat his enemies downtown at work. Why does he do this? In order to eat. Why does he eat? To become strong enough to do his exercises.

"If he exercises to go downtown to beat his enemies in order to eat and get enough strength to do his exercises," Brecht asks, "then why does he eat?"

This brief excerpt need not be substituted for the *Nichomaechean Ethics*, a popular text for humanities courses, but it might have more immediacy for a study of "what is the good life?" than does Aristotle's work.

Another brief fragment from this same record, called "Burning Books," could be used for a study of "what is truth" or of "man and society." Here, Brecht tells of a poet who finds that his books are not on the list of books to be burned by the Nazis. He is furious.

"Burn me," he scolds, "Have I not always reported the truth in my books? And now you treat me like a liar. I order you to burn me."

Experimental use of media can also be incorporated into a humanities course. For example, Tony Schwartz is at present conducting an experiment at the Dalton School with a group of students whom he has trained to use portable tape recorders. One of the first assignments given to the students was to "write" their autobiographies through sound, in essence to find out "who am I?" through sound.

To do this, the students interviewed and taped everyone who had been part of their lives since birth. The difference between doing this and writing a conventional biography was amazing. It was, for example, the difference between saying "he laughed" and hearing a laugh. If you read the words *I was a big baby*, it is quite different from the fond voice of a loving mother saying, "He was such a big baby."

The students were asked if they preferred to write their autobiographies in words or "write" them in sound, and all the students preferred the latter. Some of them said that they were finding out about themselves by listening to what other people said about them and by how they said it. One student added, "Words are a symbol of what is real, but sound is really there."

Cartoons and magazines such as *Mad* can also be incorporated into a humanities

---

[8] Brecht on Brecht. 2 LP's, Columbia Records, No. G21278.

course. This month's *Mad,* for example, has a selection entitled "Stoccly and Tess," which is a sad but hilarious satire on the Negro predicament in our society today.

Jules Feiffer, the cartoonist previously mentioned, has an excellent cartoon to illustrate the question "where am I going?," a typical humanities question. A boy stands, holding a baseball, and thinks:

Eleven years old and I can't play baseball. Where did the time go? What have I done with it? Eleven years old—huh—that's still not very old. It's not like I was THIRTEEN. I STILL can learn. I can PRACTICE! Learn all the ANGLES! Maybe take a few evening courses. Why I've got a whole LIFETIME ahead of me.

Caught up in hope, the boy gaily tosses the ball into the air. It drops; he fails to catch it, and it rolls away. He walks off sadly into the distance, saying:

Eleven years, eleven years . . . shot to hell.[9]

Why do I think this would be good material for a humanities course? Because it has immediacy and affect. It is related to the real concerns of students. For example, this is what an eighth-grader wrote in answer to the research previously referred to:

No one incident has told me that I'm a complete flop. I guess it was as soon as I was exposed to the world that I knew. All through school it was reproved again and again. I guess maybe when I couldn't write good compositions, I realized that I'm not as good and smart as I thought.

Content for humanities courses need not always conform to the highest established artistic standards. A good discussion of values can begin with the ad that asks if it is true "blondes have more fun." Student work also is valuable.

The following poem was written in an eighth-grade class. When I asked if I might copy it, the teacher was surprised. "It's not really a poem, you know," she told me. Maybe it is not a poem, but I would find it more valuable as a starting point for a study of "who am I?" than either *Candide* or *Sorrows of Young Werther,* which were mentioned above as ways of studying this question.

On Being Fourteen

Fourteen is confusion
  eight feet tall

                     too tall.

Just a decision
  after whose making
leads only
        to another
Shoult it be Janet or Phyllis?
  the dance

              or the party?

[9] Jules Feiffer, *op. cit.*

Fourteen is indecision
Like an umpire who hesitates before
                                        a call

Fourteen is like a fire in the room.
It flickers,
                            it strains,
It cannot quite make it
                            and appears to die out

But
    as suddenly as it died out
                flares up again,
To fight the never-ending
                onslaught of
                            the life-sapping rain.

Fourteen is wild parties
                which
are only   really
imitations of parties told by
    a fifteen year man.
Fourteen is a cigarette,
                a flat-chested girlfriend,
an empty wallet
                                        problems
        unsatisfactory answers.
                Fourteen is long hair

                        looking cool
                in front of "the girls"

looking for fights

                                    hoping you don't
                                        find any

Fourteen feels tough
            talks big

                                    looks small

shows off
            to envious twelves and thirteens
        who wonder what *he's* got
    Fourteen is holding tears
            that
once in the safety of one's own bedroom
    can flow their course in steady streams
    on pillows
                            stained from the past

Fourteen is taking your first drink
        cause you want to be
                    "one of the boys"

    holding back the disgusting feeling in
your stomach
                the burning in your throat
    'cause you're fourteen
                        going on twenty-five

Fourteen's wearing your letter
  to show the girl who's wearing your ID
                        you're the fourteen year old
                                        Jim Taylor

Fourteen is wondering
                What am I?
Why am I?   Where am I?
                Why does it happen to me?
                Why can't I be like the rest?
Fourteen is one wish
        "My only wish is that
                                    I wish I were——"
Fourteen is having to be old
    Yet

                        in reality
                            wishing that so much had not
                        been put on your shoulders
and wishing

                                sixteen would
                                        hurry up
or twelve
                                would come back
                                        once again.

Humanistic understanding cannot develop without reference to the real world of the child. The flexibility in the choice of materials and methods that I advocate is one way to bring the school world and the real world together.

Team Teaching Essential. A fourth requirement for humanities courses is the team-teaching approach. Few teachers are familiar with disciplines other than their own. Interdisciplinary knowledge has not been a desired goal for secondary school teachers.

I would like to illustrate the need for a team approach with the Encyclopedia Britannica film *Early Victorian England and Charles Dickens*.[10] In this film, we hear the words of Sarah Gooder, an eight-year-old girl who worked as a coal carrier in the mines. Her pathetic words help to illuminate the Victorian era for us.

Because of our traditional fragmented subject organization, information about child labor would have been studied in a social studies class and not in an English class with the study of Charles Dickens. A teacher treating Dickens might know little about Charles Darwin, George Stephenson, Florence Nightingale, or the Great Exhibition at the Crystal Palace, all of which are part of the Victorian cosmology.

In order to encompass all relevant subject areas, teachers from different disciplines must join in a team-teaching approach. This provides not only the rich background needed for humanities courses, but also a humanizing experience for teachers. Teachers are able to observe their colleagues for the first time. And the

---

[10]Lesson 2 of *The Novel,* four filmed lessons in the Humanities. EBF. (Lesson 1: *The Novel*; Lesson 3: *Great Expectations*; Lesson 4: *Great Expectations*, II).

interaction involved in teaching humanities courses forms a completely new basis for the establishment of professional relationships.

Emotion as a Desired Goal. My last essential for a humanities course is the establishment of emotion or affect as a desirable goal. Our schools bottle up emotion. Crying is weak and laughter is disruptive. Edgar Friedenberg, in describing the fundamental patterns of high schools as ones of "control, distrust, and punishment,"[11] adds that "one thing a high school student learns is that he can expect no provision for his need to give in to his feelings, or to swing out in his own style, or to creep off and pull himself together."[12]

But it is the emotional involvement that finally drives a point home. In New York City, Beckett's *Waiting for Godot* was an intellectual experience for the *avant-garde*. But when it was presented at San Quentin, it was a searing emotional experience for the inmates. They did not have to bandy sophisticated phrases about the meaning of the play. The horrors of marking time and the hopelessness of waiting for death were familiar images to them.

Teachers in general appear to be afraid of emotion. Most of us know how profoundly we were moved by *Death of a Salesman*. Yet I have witnessed many classes in which neither teacher nor students showed any emotional reaction to this. The same teacher may have wept when it was recently reshown on television, but something happens in the classroom. Emotion is completely contained because it is feared.

In a humanities course affective learning must be regarded as equally important as cognitive learning. To obtain this acceptance of emotion, teachers are needed who are sensitive, receptive, and lacking in pedantry or false pretensions. They must be able to laugh but must know when not to laugh.

I recall an adult education class with whom I was working on *Antigone*. One woman took a violent dislike to the heroine.

"That Antigone," she railed. "Just like my daughter-in-law. She doesn't care how she upsets people as long as she gets her way."

This woman was emotionally involved. If I had cut off her emotion and asked her to give me just the facts, the affective side of her learning experience would have been denied. *Antigone* would have become for her merely a typical intellectual exercise.

But using her emotion as a starting point, the class continued on into discussions of freedom, responsibility, civil rights, and the law versus the individual conscience. The question of burning draft cards was also raised. This play was 2500 years old, but it had aroused emotion, and consequently it was not dead.

As a further illustration, I would like to cite my teen-age daughter, whom I recently observed weeping over *David Copperfield*. When I recounted this to a teacher friend a few days later, my daughter was present.

"Oh, I stopped crying after the first day," she said. "After that I had to really start learning the book for a test."

---

[11] Edgar Z. Friedenberg, *Coming of Age in America.* New York: Random House, 1965. p. 36.
[12] *Ibid.,* p. 32.

In Conclusion. In 1967 a questionnaire was sent to five hundred English teachers, distributed throughout the United States, to ascertain their feelings about the new wave of the humanities.

A summation of this survey indicates the following: 78 per cent of the respondents are familiar with humanities courses, although only 34 per cent have had direct participation in them. Eighty-eight per cent indicate a need for such courses, 39 per cent feel that the humanities should be incorporated into English classes, but 52 per cent prefer a separate elective course. Sixty-four per cent believe that all students should be admitted to these courses, but 26 per cent prefer to limit them to the gifted students. Sixty-seven per cent believe that these courses should be taught by teams, but 38 per cent apparently believe that the individual teacher is capable of teaching humanities courses. Seventy-two per cent believe that humanities courses are needed, whether or not English is well-taught.

It is evident that humanities courses are not just a passing fad. It is essential, therefore, if they are to achieve the dynamic and creative change in the secondary schools for which they have the potential, that the ideas related to climate, materials, affect, and utilization of staff, which have been discussed in this article, be incorporated into them in the early stages of planning.

The Humanities, History, and the Goals
of the Social Studies

Harris L. Dante

The boundary lines between the humanities and the social sciences are most debatable in regard to history, which may properly be regarded as both. History is a science in that the historian has a method for gathering data and evaluating his evidence. History is not a science in that it is less precise and definitive in its generalizations and in its ability to predict, although this is a relative matter as far as all of the social sciences are concerned. History does have some particular disadvantages. The historian works with circumstantial evidence. His chief witnesses are out in the graveyard and cannot be summoned back for cross-examination. Important evidence, as well as witnesses, may be missing, and others may attempt to deceive him. However, a knowledge of the past is essential to the social scientist, and history has valuable contributions to make in any attempt to understand the present.

History is also properly one of the humanities because its expression is the view of a particular historian and hence dependent upon his interpretation and philosophy. As Theodor E. Mommsen has noted: "History is neither written or made without love or hate."[1] Moreover, the great history that has stirred men's minds and exerted a lasting influence has also been great literature.

---

[1] Theodor E. Mommsen, quoted by Herbert J. Muller, "The Uses of the Past," in Robert F. Davidson *et al,* editors. *The Humanities in Contemporary Life.* New York: Henry Holt and Company, 1960. p. 593.

This is not to say that history cannot contribute to the social sciences or that historians have not made use of empirical studies, including psychology and psychiatry. History long ago ceased to be merely past politics, and many historians have recognized the close relationship their studies have with both the humanities and the social sciences.

The historian likewise believes that subjecting man to quantitative analysis is far from conclusive, and that all social scientists, while they may not have to comment on the human experiences as the historian does, have to recognize that they themselves are men. There is a place where the social scientist has the objectivity of any scientist in handling his data, and draws conclusions based on the evidence which permit of few exceptions. When the social scientist, however, comments on his data and interprets it he is often confronted with the same value problem as the historian.

History perhaps has a unique role to play. Many historians and professional educators alike have suggested that history could be the coordinating link between the humanities and the social sciences or the all-encompassing subject in a social studies program.

The pedagogical problem presented by history is that its relevance to the student's understanding of contemporary society is seldom understood by students, retention of factual information is often meager, and that in view of the amount of curricular time given to history, diminishing returns set in as students go through a repetitive cycle of regurgitation. The dubious generalizations found in history textbooks and the limited results proportionate to the amount of curriculum time devoted to history are arguments that have been made many times.[2] Moreover, many behavioral scientists have stated that history has relatively little predictive value and are critical of the generalizations of history as applied to contemporary society to the point that they would make an effort to exclude history from the social studies curriculum.

It is true that one cannot go back into the Civil War period with a Gallup-poll type interview, but many understandings related to contemporary society require more than quantitative analysis since they deal with man, his motives, his changeability, and even the part played by historical accident. Moreover, the kind of analysis given above seems to miss the point that there are various levels of generalizations and that while some may be less definitive than others, they can, nevertheless, provide the student with some meaningful insights. Thus, the study of the causes of the American Civil War could develop the view that the American political system works through compromise, that our two major parties are made up of divergent interests, and that when men took a stand on a moral issue in 1860 they split the Union.

On the other hand, many political scientists would say the times in which we live are too critical not to face up to them, and we should reorganize the parties along

---

[2] See the discussion in Maurice P. Hunt and Lawrence E. Metcalf. *Teaching High School Social Studies.* New York: Harper and Brothers, 1955. p. 352-354; Arthur S. Bolster, Jr. "History, Historians, and the Secondary School Curriculum." *Harvard Educational Review* 32:56-59; Winter 1962.

conservative and liberal lines, placing Senator Lausche in the same party with Senator Dirksen and Senator Javits in the same party with Senator Kennedy. In any event the student who studies the Civil War in this manner would gain not only an understanding of the conflict itself but would also gain valuable insights into how our political system has developed and how it works.

It is true that historians would not and should not make predictions. At best the historian would say that once before under a set of similar conditions this is what happened and presumably it could happen again. However, human beings often do not react the same way twice in succession, and it is well-known that they pay little attention to the lessons of history.

The great increase in historical knowledge does create a curriculum problem as more factual information is crowded into textbooks and courses. The World History course was pedagogically unmanageable even before the non-Western world was "discovered." Granting that history teachers cannot keep abreast of the scholarly specialization indicated in the 60-some pamphlets of the American Historical Association Service Center and that it is impossible to duplicate all of the offerings that university professors believe should be included, it is generally agreed that a selection must be made. There are many who say that the way out is to study a problem, an idea, or an issue intensively, but there is less unanimity in regard to just what criteria should be used in the selection of content, or at least it has not been made clear to high school teachers.

To summarize the foregoing discussion, there are three general positions regarding the role of history as related to the humanities and the social sciences. The same views likewise apply to the high school humanities course and its relationship to the social studies program. (1) There are historians who would say that history should not concern itself directly with the problems of the contemporary world, that history more properly belongs with literature, art, and music. (2) There are behavioral scientists who agree with this point of view. They would gladly exclude history from the high school social studies curriculum on the grounds that it has little to offer since it has little predictive value and produces doubtful generalizations in contrast with modern practices of the social sciences. (3) There are others who would hold that there are various levels of generalizations, that the differences between historical generalizations and those of the other social sciences are at best relative, and that valuable insights necessary to an understanding of the present can be contributed by historical generalizations.

Any discussion of these positions and the role of history and the other social sciences in the curriculum rests upon the conceptual framework in which one places learning theory and what one believes to be the purpose of secondary social studies teaching. The primary goal of effective social studies teaching ought to be to involve students in the process of reflective thought on issues facing contemporary society. The disorientation of our society is all about us, and the citizenry, products of our schools, are woefully unprepared to deal with the complexities of a confused and complex world. They not only lack the factual background to understand social problems but too often arrive at illogical conclusions based on mere preferences, prejudices, and ignorance. With the very real possibility that we may all be cremated equally, irrational discussion goes on, if any discussion takes place, in regard to the war in Vietnam. Lake Erie, we are told, is one-third dead, incapable of supporting any form of life. Thus the Great Lakes, one of the North American continent's greatest natural assets, is faced with the same pollution that threatens virtually every water resource in the nation. Pictures of the unrest in our large cities show young white hoodlums professing their religious faith by wearing religious medals around their necks while at the same time spewing obscenities and hatred out of their mouths. Many more such examples come to mind, but these will suffice to dramatize the concerns to which the social studies should address themselves.

We have not been very successful to date. Every study that has ever been made has shown that students enter high school and emerge four years later virtually unscathed in regard to their basic attitudes. Their beliefs remain conditioned by their prejudices and their affiliations. They have not learned to examine their values, nor have they learned to think critically and independently.

If we have failed, it is because we have not really tried. Most social studies teaching has been largely narration, description, and exposition. Teachers have avoided the introduction of value conflicts into the classroom. The school has remained too far removed from life. This is really what John Dewey was all about. Dewey advocated that the schools meet the needs and aims of an urban industrial society. The education he had in mind was wedded to the idea of progress on the assumption that the functional relationship between the school and the problems of society was clear. An understanding of TVA, for example, requires full analysis, and the student in learning the facts of life will recognize that efforts by the federal government on behalf of the Negro probably came more out of manpower studies than out of humanitarian impulses.

It is all right to theorize on how to teach advanced placement students, but society now demands that we educate individuals whom we have traditionally said cannot be educated. To the extent that conservative viewpoints are represented by the classical tradition, they are reflecting a culture that has passed, and we are not arguing here against verbal, conceptual, abstract learning. There have always been teachers in the "good old days" who dealt with ideas rather than memorization of isolated factual material, and likewise no modern teacher would say that the so-called activity or experience program should take the place of reflective thinking. The knowledge which is taught must not be mere information' but must be prudential, actively involving the learner. It could be observed that scholars of all ages have always had meaning for their own times. The emphasis on classical studies had a functional purpose in the sixteenth and seventeenth centuries because Latin was the language of the scholar, the clergy, and the professions. Today, whatever is taught in the social studies classroom must survive the test of current verification. It must have some relevance for the present. This does not mean an abandonment of ancient history, nor does it mean a current events lesson "every Monday." In the well-known words of Whitehead: "The understanding which we want is an understanding of an insistent present. The only use of knowledge of the past is to equip us for the present."[3]

Historians have always recognized that their chief purpose has been to interpret the past to their own generation. This is why each generation writes its own history anew. Thus in the depression years of the thirties we built the Jefferson Memorial and wrote of "Robber Barons" while in the affluent society of more recent years historians have emphasized the accomplishments of businessmen and have rehabilitated Alexander Hamilton. The past must be used to serve the present. The question is, how can a knowledge of the past be used to clarify issues, to encourage the search for truth, to resolve conflict and to advance great ideals for today? To this end the selection of facts should have a high degree of workability with the hope that they will carry forward to other problems.

If the background of information needed to form useful concepts is important for understanding the world in which we live, the methods of inquiry which students are taught may be even more crucial. The year 2000 A.D. which has seemed to belong to the realm of science fiction is in actuality only a short 33 years away. We are in a very real sense preparing students to live in a rapidly changing world, and we ourselves have very little notion of the kind of world it will be. If this is true then it becomes quite clear that the best way we can serve students is to teach them a method of inquiry which will give them some basis for making choices when they are confronted with two or more alternatives. While insisting that content and method cannot be separated, the method of inquiry may in the long run be of greater significance than any given set of facts with which students may be involved at any given moment.

The term "problem" has lost much of its meaning because it has been used in a variety of ways, but we take the position here that all teaching should be reflective involving students in content and in various problematic situations. Teaching then must relate to learning theory with the teacher himself committed to reflective thinking, skilled in its use and insistent on reflection as the test by which any technique is measured. Facts must be learned in a context in the social studies which again relates to purpose. We make an assumption that students have had certain experiences or that they understand the facts with which we wish to deal. In many instances, however, they have been exposed only to ideas related to folklore and they have not learned to assess critically what they read. Far too many students assume that it must be true because it is in print. The specialist, whether he be a college professional historian or a capable scholar-teacher in the high school can see relationships among the social sciences and the relevancy of given content to the present which the high school student may not see. The causes of the Civil War may be a challenging intellectual experience for the specialist, who has studied this issue in depth. Whether or not it is a problem for the high school student will depend upon how he looks at it.

Problematic teaching in this sense then would mean that the facts of history and

<hr>

[3] Alfred North Whitehead. *The Aims of Education.* New York: The New American Library of World Literature, 1949. p. 14-15.

the other social sciences would be brought to bear on issues having contemporary social significance. Using the method of inquiry, which has been described, facts would always be taught in relationship to other meaningful facts which are relevant to the goal to be achieved. Facts would be used in establishing generalizations right now and this is the way the student would learn. They would not be stored away for use at some future date. Utility and relevance to the student would be apparent as the facts learned would hence always be accompanied by understanding and purpose. Retention would be longer. Teachers should introduce value conflicts into the classroom with the student being encouraged to question the basis for his own value system and examine critically competing values. Issues would be studied in as many different frames of reference as possible and decisions made between alternatives on the basis of a study of the facts in the case, the consideration of consequences, and preferential criteria.

High school humanities courses in most instances quite properly emphasize culture and aesthetic goals rather than the purposes which it has been indicated ought to be of primary importance for a social studies program. It is evident enough why some would remove history from the social studies and place it in the humanities. Here, history, allied with literature, can play a dominant role, whereas history as part of a social studies program, focusing on contemporary issues, could pose a pedagogical problem.

A humanities course would naturally not include any of the social sciences, and in many instances other subjects compete for equal time with history and literature. Professional journals abound with articles describing humanities courses built around English and some in which history is excluded.

In a number of instances humanities courses as originally conceived did not include any history taught in a systematic manner, with history and the history teacher added after the course had been taught for one year.

It is quite likely that educational conservatives or even political conservatives might prefer to see history taught as one of the humanities or even to have humanities courses replace the social studies program. This would be on the grounds that the school's chief mission should be to pass on our cultural history and that in any case, the schools have no business engaging in controversy. One result would be that any treatment given to economics, for example, in a history course, taught as one of the humanities, would probably be only incidental.

Thus the history and literature of the Great Depression taught narratively and supplemented with the music and art of the period would probably do little to strengthen the current unreliable precarious understanding of modern economics. There would probably not be suffcent time, even if the teacher were competent, to explore the many economic concepts that are related to the history of these times. Thus, regardless of the extent to which Roosevelt did or did not accept Keynesian economics, it would be important for students to learn how the New Deal experience proved modern economics pragmatically. The lasting results of the New Deal, including the economic stabilizers placed under the economy; the degree to which a changed philosophy regarding the role of government relative to the economy came into being; the understandings and instruments which have been developed to predict and to cope with downswings in the business cycle, would all have a part in correcting the folklore of economic illiteracy and help to develop understanding of the many economic paradoxes that add to the confusion of the laymen. Such are the interrelationships between history and the other social sciences which a culturally oriented course would certainly minimize.

Some high school principals have confused cultural studies and social studies to the point where they actually believe they have strengthened their social studies program by replacing a social studies offering with a humanities course. Moreover, if a humanities course, which is an interdisciplinary team-teaching program, competes as an elective with a social studies course involving one or more of the social studies taught by a single teacher, it is clear which would win out. The humanities course involving several teachers and several disciplines, would be the innovating course. It would attract not only the more talented students, but also the more talented teachers.

Humanities programs can offer students an exciting and rewarding experience. History quite properly should be involved in a humanities course, but it should not be taken from the social studies curriculum. Both the humanities and the social studies deserve to be studied, but neither is an adequate substitute for the other.

Humanities Courses in Secondary Schools

Carolyn A. Glass and Richard I. Miller

Is there an increased interest in teaching a course in the secondary schools that is generally called the humanities? Are more secondary schools incorporating this course into the instructional program? Where? How? What content comprises the course? How do the teachers like the course? How about the students? These questions and others have prompted this study. Very little evidence is available on what has been called "the humanities movement."

One can list many reasons why a secondary-school course on the humanities might be expected to develop. These include: a growing concern about the effects of mechanization and mass society, with accompanying tendencies of alienation both from oneself and from society; a view that man's rich intellectual and cultural heritage is not being explored by young people; the Hegelian-like view that the humanities can help counterbalance the increasing emphasis on vocational education; and the belief that man, the full man, should be the goal of education—the thinking, believing, acting, and feeling man.

Given conditions that are favorable to the development of the humanities, has this development, in fact, taken place? To help constructive thinking about this question, this background paper will take two approaches: the results of two questionnaire surveys are outlined, and some conditions are discussed that favor development of humanities and some obstacles are mentioned. A personal note concludes the paper.

I. Questionnaire Surveys

Two questionnaires were constructed. The first one was sent to every state department of education in the U.S.A. as well as to the equivalents in the territories. A 100 percent response was received on this questionnaire.

Following up information received on the initial questionnaire, another questionnaire was sent directly to each school that was listed by state departments as having good humanities programs. This questionnaire sought information about the nature of the program.

Description, analysis, interpretation, and evaluation of answers to these two questionnaires form the basis of this report.

The three questions in the initial questionnaire were:

1. Has the State Department published materials, articles, etc., relating to this area of interest?
2. Is philosophy or any course (Humanities, Great Books, etc.) taught in any secondary school system in your state?
3. As you see it, do you believe interest in this area has *decreased* or *increased* in the past five years, and how about the future?
   (Increased–I; Decreased–D; About same–S)
   1960-65; interest evident
   1965-70; interest expected

The Role of State Departments in the Humanities Area. The first question was designed to determine whether state departments of education were publishing materials, articles, etc., relating to this area of interest. Of the 54 replies received, five (9.3%) answered "yes," 47 (87%) said "no," and two (3.7%) did not reply. The five that have published articles or teachers' guides on humanities courses for high schools are: Florida, Missouri, Pennsylvania, Puerto Rico, and Virginia.

An analysis of the responses on the first question would lead one to conclude that state departments have not taken an active part—with the exception of Pennsylvania—in establishing humanities programs in their states.

Secondary Schools Offering a Humanities Course. The second question sought to learn (a) whether the state departments of education knew about humanities programs within their states, and (b) what schools they would list as having good humanities courses.

Of the 54 replies received on the question about whether philosophy or any course (Humanities, Great Books, etc.) is taught in schools of their state, 31 (57.4%) answered "yes", 20 (37%) replied "no," and 3 (5.6%) indicated that they had no knowledge of such a course being taught in their state.

The reliability of these replies may be open to question on the basis of discovering two schools offering humanities courses that were in states that answered "no."

The pattern of answers do indicate that the humanities programs are filtered throughout the United States and its territories, with such states indicating humanities programs in their school systems as Alaska, Arizona, California, Hawaii, Kansas, Mississippi, New Hampshire, North Carolina. The greater concentration of courses does seem to fall within the eastern half of the country and specifically the northeastern section. This is evidenced by affirmative replies from such states as: Connecticut, Massachusetts, Michigan, Minnesota, New Hampshire, New Jersey, New York, Ohio, Pennsylvania, Vermont, Wisconsin.

The third question probed into state departments' estimations of the direction in which interest in the humanities is moving. One part of the question asked for an indication of interest evidenced from 1960 to 1965. Of the 54 replies, 37 (68.5%) answered "increased," 13 (24.1%) "about the same," and 4 (7.4%) made no indication.

Another part of the question asked for interest expected from 1965 to 1970. Of the replies, 43 (79.6%) answered that an increase was expected, 5 (9.3%) about the same, and 6 (11.1%) gave no indication.

In listing factors that were instrumental in determining the state departments' estimation of state interest in the humanities program, the results were correlated in two ways. First, the relationship between those states giving a "no" answer in question two and the amount of interest indicated; and second, the comparison between the amount of interest indicated and reasons or factors given for the conclusion.

Of those 20 states replying that no humanities course was being taught in their state, all but three (Canal Zone, New Mexico, Virgin Islands) gave an indication of interest in this area. And the Canal Zone gave as reason for its conclusion that humanities had not been discussed.

Such states as Idaho, Iowa, Maine, Oklahoma and Oregon indicated that interest in this area either was about the same from 1960-65, or they expected it to continue about the same in the future. One factor given in this conclusion was that their curriculum was being revised but in the direction of the vocational areas; while another said that they hoped to move in this direction with the addition of an English consultant to their state department of education.

The greatest number of states replying "no" to question two indicated on question three a present interest in this area or an expected interest. This category includes such states as Arkansas, Colorado, Illinois, West Virginia. An increasing stress on academic excellence and a concern for enrichment programs for the gifted were two reasons listed for the anticipated interest.

Of the 31 states replying "yes"—that a humanities course was being taught within their school systems—all states indicated an increase in interest either at present or in the future. Some factors listed as instrumental in their estimations were: more attention paid to the individual needs of the learner, national publicity and conferences reflecting new interest in this type of program, and a need to bring about a balance in the curriculum. While these reasons were dominant, others were given: Nebraska stated that such materials were being read and discussed in a larger degree in their state as a result of Project English; a new emphasis upon literature and history is evident with a tendency to identify the "educated man" with great books; requests made to the state departments from schools systems for information in this area have increased; and finally, one state department replied that "apparently this is another of those cycles that education and society must go through. Usually takes a decade to get it out of their system."

It would appear, in conclusion, that those states having a humanities program within their school systems are more aware of the scope of such a program and of its value for education. They also seem to be taking part in establishing such programs in many instances, particularly from an indication of requests made to the state departments by the school systems for information about this area.

As one would expect, the large secondary schools dominated the scene—schools between 1700-1800. Schools with an enrollment from 300-600 were generally special or college-preparatory schools.

The larger schools would be the logical ones pioneering this field with greater faculty specialization and more instructional flexibility.

Respondents were asked to check one of the following course titles: Humanities, Philosophy, or Great Books. In some cases other titles were written in, such as: Society and the Arts, American Civilization, Arts and Man, Essential Ideas, and History of Western Thought.

The vast majority of high schools with a humanities course indicated it was entitled "Humanities" in their curriculum. Several schools offered a philosophy course—usually an introductory course or one on ethics. Other schools listed a Great Books course, either in their school curriculum or as independent study.

The humanities offerings appear to be rather evenly distributed throughout the United States. A course dealing with the Great Books appeared most frequently in school systems in such states as Delaware, Minnesota, and Texas. And the philosophy course appeared in a few school systems in states such as: Delaware, New York, and Washington.

Respondents were asked to indicate whether materials presented to the students were in the form of a concepts course (Freedom and Man, God and Man, etc.); Allied Arts (Music, Art, etc.); or Philosophy (original works or textbooks).

The types of materials most frequently listed came under the heading of the Allied Arts or a combination of concepts, allied arts, and philosophy. Those schools which offered a philosophy course included readings of original works and a type of concepts course.

For the majority of secondary schools, the humanities course is defined as a study of the allied arts or a combination of the allied arts, concepts, and philosophy.

A vast majority of the school systems reported that their courses in the general area of the humanities had been initiated since 1960. Some school systems in New York and Washington indicated that humanities programs were started in 1954 and 1955. Large school systems in Minnesota, New Hampshire and New Jersey indicated that humanities courses were initiated in 1957, 1957, and 1955, respectively.

The respondent was asked to indicate whether the students enrolled in humanities courses were: intellectually superior, juniors or seniors, or if the course was open to all students.

In comprehensive high schools, the humanities course is limited to juniors and/or seniors, and in many cases to the superior student. The college preparatory high schools likewise offer the humanities course primarily for juniors and/or seniors with no emphasis placed upon the superior student.

The great books course, both in the comprehensive and college preparatory high schools, is usually open only to juniors and seniors. The philosophy course in these same types of schools, is open to juniors and/or seniors, with emphasis placed upon the superior student.

Respondents were asked to indicate the professional training of teachers for such a course. The following suggested specialties were given: English major or minor, philosophy major or minor, special certificate, or other.

The majority of the teachers employed in teaching the humanities courses were either English majors or minors. Those who taught a philosophy course were either history or philosophy majors or had some graduate or under-graduate training in philosophy. The great books teacher seemed most frequently to have an English major.

The major trend among those schools having a humanities course, and particularly one which used the Allied Arts as source material, was toward team teaching. The average course in the humanities was taught by four teachers, frequently with majors in English, art, music, and history or social studies. Team teaching is also being used in some school systems in New York State which offer a philosophy course. Team teaching seemed most prevalent in school systems in the states of New York, Pennsylvania, and Washington.

On the second questionnaire, the individual schools were asked whether they had "any means of evaluating the relationship between student interest in this course and his further study?"

The majority of school systems reported that they did not have means of evaluating student response at the present time, primarily because their humanities programs were relatively new. The main source of information used by schools indicating some evaluation was interviews with college students returning to visit their high schools. According to these reports, the students believed that further study in the arts and humanities came as the result of interest stimulated by the humanities course in secondary school.

A final question to individual schools asked for an evaluation of the humanities course. Of the 51 individual schools answering this question, a substantial majority took evaluation to mean whether the course was good or bad. With one or two exceptions, these evaluations were glowing. Typical comments include: "very valuable to students," "one of the most exciting courses ever offered," "received with considerable enthusiasm," "fills a great need," and "exceptionally stimulating to the students."

Some responses were analytical rather than evaluative, with such comments as: "broadens horizons in vocational thinking," "great need for a balance in the curriculum," "for about top 15 per cent of student body." "sharpens critical thinking and reading scope," and "biggest problems are qualified teachers and enough time for planning."

In general, the greatest value from the humanities courses in the sampled secondary schools seemed to be in helping to broaden the curriculum and in widening the horizons of college-bound students. Also, several schools indicated that the course helped to develop critical thinking and to broaden the outlook toward the arts.

II. Some Observations and Conclusions

This section is based upon a selective survey of the literature, the two questionnaire surveys, and first-hand visitations of a small number of secondary-school humanities programs. More appropriately, this section should be entitled "Some Informal Observations and Tentative Conclusions." More research and study is needed in order to fortify or modify many points that will be raised subsequently.

Three Themes Supporting Humanities Programs in Secondary Schools. At the start of this paper, several reasons for the current development of humanities programs were listed. This section will be addressed to some additional factors that favor the humanities movement.

1. *Increasing mechanization and complexity in living requires greater intellectual and cultural expansions.*—Stephen Vincent Benét recognized that man might be dominated by his inventions when he wrote of the machine as—

> The great, metallic beast. . .
> The genie we have raised to rule the earth,
> Obsequious to our will
> But servant-master still,
> The tireless serf already half a god. . . .

To counterbalance tendencies toward greater mechanization and complexity, the schools need to offer opportunities that will help youngsters think about aesthetic and cultural experiences— the humaneness of man. As Jacques Maritain has written:

The Humanities are those disciplines which make men more human, or nurture in man his nature as specifically human, because they convey to him the spiritual fruit and achievements of the labor of generations, and deal with things which are worth being known for their own sake, for the sake of truth or the sake of beauty[1]

2. *Awakening sense of values on part of today's youth requires opportunities for intellectual probing.*—The abundant response of American youth to the Peace Corps and other service-type opportunities has deflated some pessimistic views of today's

---

[1] Quoted in: Clifton Fadiman, "The Role of the Humanities in Secondary Schools." An address given in Miami, Florida, November 23, 1962, p. 7.

youth. Harold Taylor has pointed out that the "new generation" is often misunderstood by those of the "older generation, especially among educators, who have not themselves had the experience of direct involvement with the situation of the world. . ."[2]

Where in the secondary school program does youth have an opportunity to examine values? Social studies could provide some opportunities in this area of study although one seldom finds this to be the case.

In an age where science and technology play a vital role, the vast scope and rapid production of knowledge tends to leave little time for discussing philosophical and moral aspects of many critical developments in modern life. Educators are asking the question, "What can the schools do to help the students develop a sense of values without being dogmatic?" The humanities course offers one answer to this question. Clifton Fadiman argues that in terms of equipping students to meet demands of the adult world, this direction is important:

A great work of art, properly taught, performs work on the teenager; and—this is what somehow he must be taught to feel—it performs it more efficiently, more economically and even more lastingly than most of his so-called "practical experience," The Humanities *force* him to grow up. They are not a nosegay to put in his buttonhole as a mark of culture. They are, or should be, as much a part of his life as his relations to his family or the career he will later choose for himself.[3]

3. *Increasing interest in self-realization evident among youth requires opportunities for individual and group introspection.*—In Hamlet one finds these lines:

. . . What a piece of work is a man! how noble in reason! how infinite in faculty!in form and moving how express and admirable! in action how like an angel! in apprehension how like a god!

Literature courses may brush over such well known passages, but how often does the already crowded course outline allow probing analysis of such thoughts? A humanities course allows one to see oneself by viewing others, and by relating oneself to great men and women and to great ideas. A primary role of the Humanities is to entice and stimulate young minds into exploring the human experience through what man has written or done. A great painting, for example, is an eloquent statement speaking across the ages about human feeling and insight. And about the music of Bach and Vivaldi, Secretary-General Hammarskjold once said, "They have a beautiful way of creating order and perspective in one's mind."[4]

Three Obstacles to Expansion of Secondary-School Humanities Programs. This section will touch upon three problems or conditions that will continue to inhibit growth of this area.

[2] Harold Taylor, "American Idealism, 1965," *Saturday Review,* 48:16 (June 26, 1965).

[3] Clifton Fadiman, *op. cit.,* p. 7.

[4] Richard I. Miller, *Dag Hammarskjold and Crisis Diplomacy* (New York: Oceana Publications, Inc., 1961), p. 17.

1. *Inadequate teacher preparation.*—If the humanities program is to enjoy continued growth and interest, some provisions for special teacher preparation will need to be considered. At the present time, someone with a special interest in the area is given the course to teach. Interest is a vital prerequisite, but so is content competency. Even a cursory study of the background of teachers who offer the humanities course and the content of the course will reveal a high correlation—as one would expect. Is there a core of subjects or knowledge that should be included in the humanities, or is any approach as good as any other?

Encyclopedia Britannica Films is in the process of making a series of films on the humanities, and the University of Georgia has developed an interesting and provocative series of films for the general public on the great issues of mankind. Films can be particularly useful in in-service programs that are pointed toward developing competencies for teaching humanities courses in secondary schools. The in-service area offers excellent opportunities for the humanities area.

2. *Curriculum fullness.*—In describing the "creeping curriculum," Ole Sand has said, "Never has so much about so little been taught to so many!" Where does a humanities course belong in the secondary school?

Thus far, the course is predominantly an elective course for bright junior and senior students. If it is good for this group, is it also good for average students? Are we selling short the below-average students by assuming they could not master the content or they would not be interested?

The newness of the humanities course has not allowed time for curriculum specialists to analyze the course with respect to the total school program, and experimental programs in this content area have been very slow in getting under way. The expected future growth of the humanities will need to reckon with curricular fullness, and an intelligent reckoning will require more research and experimentation.

3. *Misconceptions about the humanities.*Too often the secondary school humanities course is a series of loosely related anthologies, with little analysis and with little inductive learning. Reading and knowing Shakespeare is one thing; understanding him is another. With understanding can come increased insight into human motives and behavior, the poetry of language, the power of words, and the historical parade of human events.

One suspects that a great many of the teachers offering humanities courses are doing a good job, but not an outstanding one. A good teacher has half the battle won, but the other half is mastery of content.

Some excellent programs have been developed—programs that have carefully considered what should be included in a humanities course. Three such programs are mentioned:

A report on the work of the Pennsylvania Committee on the Humanities has been published and will not be repeated here.

The Lexington, Massachusetts, high school developed a project called "A Pilot Project in the Study of Mankind." The statement of purpose for the program is as follows:

... the over-all objective was the development of a greater awareness on the part of the student of his relationships to mankind as a whole. A second purpose was to enable the student to become more objective toward himself in the perspective of other people immediately about him. A third was to place the student in a position where he could view the ideas, values, and aspirations of his own culture against a wider circle of different cultures. Still another objective was to help the student seriously consider whether or not there are common concerns shared by men everywhere—concerns which in turn, could provide the foundation for a world community[5]

The evaluation of the results of this project are interesting from the standpoint of a reasoned optimism about the future of such programs:

The project was subjected to various techniques of evaluation which, although imperfect demonstrated to our satisfaction that students of high school age will respond to a searching examination of the great issues of our time, and that their own values will often be broadened to include more regard for their common interest with people everywhere on earth.[6]

A third humanities program, started in 1964, was offered to two classes of sixth-grade students in the Shelmire Elementary School of Southampton, Pennsylvania. It included one semester of a study of man's relationship to nature and the arts. It was considered to be quite effective. The rationale for offering such a course is stated in the following goals:

1. Help develop a concept of the meaning of the word "humanities."
2. Arouse new dimensions of interest, which would be reflected in choice of TV, motion pictures, and reading.
3. See themselves as human beings in a world of humans.
4. Deepen insights in respect to other cultures.
5. Provide a different orientation in the arts—expressions about and reactions to man himself.[7]

These two surveys leave many important questions unanswered. Obviously a great deal more study is needed before sufficient data is available for effective decision-making about curricular aspects of teaching about the humanities in secondary schools.

III. A Personal Note

The school of tomorrow should be as different as tomorrow itself. But for all the brave words about change and innovation, a pitiful harvest remains in prospect

[5] Richard G. Lyons, "Philosophy and Anthropology in the Study of Mankind," *Social Education,* 28:405 (November, 1964).
[6] *Ibid.* p. 406.
[7] Henry W. Ray, "The Humanities in Elementary Education," *Social Education,* 27:459 (December, 1964).

unless we think differently and act differently about what is known of the future. As an example: The so-called Seven Cardinal Principles of Education listed "worthy use of leisure" as a major objective. Developed in the Model T age, the relevance of this objective continues to escape the structural inertia of that social institution known as the public school.

The general area of the humanities remains an underdeveloped area of the secondary-school instructional program. The Bible admonishes us: "Man does not live by bread alone," yet the current concern for vocational and technical education, adrenalized by billions in federal money, will very likely have profound effects upon the public school. Hopefully, the as yet unseen future trends in vocational education will move toward the broad sense of "all education as vocational preparation" as well as the narrow view of job preparation. The cause of democracy will be weakened if the latter pays no more than lip service to the former—and the odds do not look favorable at the moment.

Unless those in professional education can move ahead more imaginatively and courageously, directions for the future will not be theirs to influence significantly. Already unmistakable signs of shifted control are evident. The role of academic scholars in major cirriculum studies has been the vital catalytic factor in success of these efforts, and increasing action of state legislatures in instructional matters speaks both of their impatience with educational conservatism and of sense of frustration over lack of vigorous leadership by educators.

Educators may be standing at some sort of crossroad. American education is the best ever—make no mistake about it. More children are being educated better than ever before. But the question we should be asking is this: "Is it good enough for the future?" A future in which the forces of specialization, complexity, impersonalization, international relations, and knowledge expansion may be expected to continue—indeed accentuate—their divisive and invidious onslaught upon development of the whole man. C. P. Snow's two, indeed two dozen, cultures are everywhere as we continue to be basically unconcerned upon separation of art and intellect or with the early Greek belief in "mens sana in corpore sano"—a sound mind in a sound body.

Is our education good enough for the future we want? President Kennedy caught the essentiality of the relationship when he said: "I do not know whether or not the Battle of Waterloo was won on the playing fields of Eton, but I do believe that the future of our nation will be decided in its classrooms."

New Dimensions for World Cultures

Francis Shoemaker

We are currently engaged in a second revival of the Humanities in American education. Many of us participated in the first one during the fifteen year period before War II, when within the remarkable growth of broadfield Humanities, Social Science and Natural Science course in General Education programs in colleges and universities, the Humanities brought together previously scattered offerings in literature and other arts, and frequently history, philosophy and religion, predominantly of Western Civilization.[1] Today's revival constitutes a comparably dramatic growth in American high schools of courses variously titled Humanities, Culture Area Studies, World Affairs and the like. Central to many is concern for literature and other arts, but almost universally within the total cultural context of other cultures than the so-called Western. Where Western culture is included, a prominent concern is to place it is perspective among other world cultures.

The revivals resemble one another in their search for both breadth and focus in times of cultural crisis. The world-wide Depression and World War II challenged us in then unprecedented measure to testify to the value of the individual in society. We sought the testament in the individually formulated values embodied in the arts of Western Culture. In some colleges—Stephens and Antioch, for example—we used basic aesthetic principles as the focusing factor for the tremendous breadth of material. In other colleges—Columbia and Chicago, to name two—we found focus in selected Great Books as representative of great ideas. By 1940, drawing on the social sciences of history, anthropology, psychology and human ecology—as in Stanford, Colorado State College of Education and Teachers College, Columbia University—we had begun to point up successive culture epochs in Western civilization, each embodying a new and enlarged conception of self in Western man.[2] With each new organizational framework we increased the scope of our material and sharpened the aesthetic focus in philosophy and method.

Today we find many of our definable concepts of self rudely challenged, both abroad in modern pluralistic planetary culture and on home ground in ghetto, campus and complacent suburb. Just as insistently we find ourselves studying to redefine values and redesign course content and patterns of inquiry. Thousands of us are returning from assignment overseas as exchange teachers, Fulbright lecturers and tutors, USIS and USAID technicians and Peace Corps Volunteers. What designs and emphases are we likely to find significant, when everyone in our communities knows that manned satellites sweep over the European peninsula before we can call the names of such epoch embodiers as Sophocles, Dante, Shakespeare, Goethe, Melville, Tolstoy and Steinbeck—and that the United Nations now includes 120 members, half of which are less than twenty years old? Will Eastern Humanities and Western Humanities suffice? Or White-skinned Humanities and Dark-skinned Humanities? Or Greco-Roman-Judeo-Christian Humanities? Or Islamic Humanities? Or Buddhist Humanities? Or African Autochthonous Humanities? Or Humanities based on universal Aesthetic Principles, culturally defined? Or on concepts of imaginitive individuals speaking for or against prevailing and intuited ideas and values of their societies?

[1] Patricia Beesley, *The Revival of the Humanities in American Education.* New York: Columbia University Press, 1940.

[2] Francis Shoemaker, *Aesthetic Experience and the Humanities.* New York: Columbia University Press, 1943. Reprint AMS Press, 1969.

My guess is that many of us lean toward the last of these, but that we also want a serviceable design within which to observe and compare these ideas and values. With this in mind, I would like to explore one such design which, after thirty some years of teaching Humanities in the United States, has begun to take shape through my day-to-day involvement in international education in Latin America, Africa and Asia. The process that Matthew Arnold calls "artistic simplification" leads me to think of the nations of the world as constituting four major world cultures. The nations comprising each world culture share common and differentiated values. They participate in the contemporary world through common and differentiated patterns of symbolization. It is their fundamental values and symbol systems that both provide and denote their integrity. While the nations in each world group share some geographic proximity, it seems important to designate them by terms that suggest their centers of loyalty and devotion rather than their geographic location. In consequence, I find it helpful to think of our own world culture as Classico-Judeo-Christian, and simultaneously of two other world cultures as Islamic, and Hindu-Buddhistic-Taoist, and the fourth as African Autochthonous—to suggest a world culture in the making.

Redefining "Western". In using the geographical term "Western" to designate our world culture, we have for the most part limited ourselves to Europe and the United States; we have ignored the linguistic, political, religious, literary, educational and familial ties of Latin America with Mediterranean and Biblical cultures. And the continent of Australia, with its rich new literature, we have yet to relate to its Anglo-Saxon origins. In the Classico-Judeo-Christian culture design, then, I would suggest that we include Europe, the Americas, Australia and the Philippines. And there can be little doubt that the great books of "Western culture" notwithstanding, the most pervasive formulation of values for this world culture exists in the Bible in its many versions and derivative myths and symbols in art, literature, music and architecture.

It is momentarily staggering to think of adding to an already overambitious content any concern for Incan art or Caribbean music, Mexican painting, recent Latin American novels in English translation, the architectural promise of Brasilia, or Randolph Stow's prize novel of Australian life, *A Haunted Land*,[3] or Leonard Casper's *New Writing from the Philippines*.[4] But I take courage from the publication in April of William H. McNeill's *A World History*[5]—not because it is a tremendous *tour de force*, but because it exemplifies the principle of simultaneity. Application of this principle, plus judicious use of touchstones in selected art mediums will permit us, I believe, to help students intensify the quality of their experience and heighten their feeling for the reality of their study.

Knowing the Middle East. As we move on to consider the second world culture within this planetary design we realize that a number of schools have introduced new courses with titles resembling "The Middle East." If we follow the lead of such

---

[3] See *The Journal of Commonwealth Literature*. No. 1, September 1965.
[4] Leonard Casper. *New Writing from the Philippines; A Critique and Anthology*. Syracuse: Syracuse University Press, 1966.
[5] William H. McNeill. *A World History*. New York: Oxford, 1967.

a geographic designation to its farthest dimensions, we immediately list twenty nations, speaking several major languages, but all sharing in the inspiriting precepts of the *Holy Koran.*

Islamic world culture today stretches over 160 degrees of longitude, from the Islamic Republic of Mauretania on the Atlantic coast of Africa, across Morocco, Algeria and Tunisia, skirting the northern provinces of Mali, Niger and Chad into the whole of the Sudan and then throughout Egypt, Arabia, Jordan, Lebanon, Turkey, Iraq, Iran, Afghanistan, Pakistan and the Republic of Indonesia—with an additional 50,000,000 Muslims in India. The history and geography of this vast area shows pervasive problems of land and water management that are directly related to food supply and national and regional self-sufficiency. The frequency of reference in the *Holy Koran* to "gardens underneath which rivers flow" helps us to read this great book with something of the 7th Century Arab's ear for metaphor and survival.

With no prior study each of us can read the A. J. Arberry[6] translation of the *Holy Koran* or *Aspects of Islamic Civilization* and find himself caught up in the 7th Century return to monotheism, the security of a new legal structure, and a strenghened code of ethics. He can virtually feel himself cleansed of tradition-bound depravity when he reads

There is no fault in those who believe and do deeds of righteousness. . . .God loves the good-doers.

A thoughtful reading of this key literary document of Islam can bring our students to understand, with Bernard Lewis in *The Arabs in History,* that "Islam . . . was not only a system of belief and cult. It was also a system of state, society, law, thought and art—a civilization with religion as its unifying, eventually dominating, factor."[7]

Architecture provides another symbol of culture for Islam. It introduces us to the sequence of the culture epochs of national leadership—Arabian, Egyptian, Persian, Turkish, Moghul, with Egypt bidding again today for primacy. From the Alhambra Palace in Spain to the Taj Mahal in India magnificent structures reveal superb engineering, artistry, and affluence. Palaces and citadels reveal the brilliance of princely society, and congregational mosques and their decorative themes (of course devoid of painting and sculpture) speak of "a religion of triumph in success, of salvation through victory and achievement and power."[8] And today, alongside the ubiquitous Hilton Hotel, each country is making its own adaptation of international architecture.

Islamic Perspectives. The educational system provides a third perspective on the unity of Islam. This will be particularly true for those who can assume the point of view of the Islamic student in his own country, not that of the American scholar gathering data in comparative education. From grade one every child throughout

---

[6] A. J. Arberry (trans.). *The Koran Interpreted.* New York: MacMillan, 1956.

[7] Bernard Lewis. *The Arabs in History.* New York: Harper and Row, 1960.

[8] Wilfred Cantwell Smith. *Islam in Modern History.* New York: New American Library, Mentor MT 537, 1957.

Islamic culture memorizes sections of the *Koran*. He later reads parts of it in his national language; but he also studies Arabic in which to recite the *Koran*; he studies his nation's history and geography in the context of Islamic history; he studies calligraphy as an art form, and other arts and crafts. Knowing the fairly uniform curriculum, we can ask ourselves what Islamic humanities contributes to the young person's development and national pride. What are his feelings of wonder at Islam's replacing the Roman Empire in North Africa and Spain within a hundred years of Mohammed's death in Arabia?—and at the founding of the oldest university in the world in Cairo (enrolment now 50,000) and of other university centers at Aleppo, Baghdad, Teheran and Balkh in Northern Afghanistan while Europe groped through the darkest years of the Dark Ages? What are his feelings when he learns that Greek culture and science reached Europe through Arabic-to-Latin translation?

When he reads George Sarton's *History of Science*, how does he respond to the tribute that ". . .from the point of view of the development of mankind as a whole, the Arabic-Islamic culture was of supreme importance, because it contributed the main link between the Near East and the West, as well as between the Near East and Buddhist Asia"?[9] What kind of perspective does he gain on himself when he compares the descriptions of Arab character by 15th Century historian, Ibn Khaldun, and those of 20th Century social scientists, Edward T. Hall and Daniel Lerner? How does he regard the tragedy of the leveling of the great cities of Afghanistan, Iran, Iraq by Ghengis Khan between 1220 and 1260? And the elimination of 1,000,000 Muslims in Spain at the end of the 16th Century? Does he recall that 900 years elapsed from the sack of Rome to *The Divine Comedy*—and that today his culture may be on the threshold of a new age after only 700 years of recuperation from holocaust in Asia and 350 years in Spain?

This kind of historical perspective is valued in Islamic culture. Islam's greatest modern poet Mohammad Iqbal writes,

> What is history, O stranger to thy-
> self?
> A tale, a story or a fable?
> No! It makes thee conscious of self
> Capable in action and efficient in
> quest!
> Sharpens thee like a dagger on the
> whetstone
> And then strikes thee on the face of
> thy world?[10]

Historical information is readily available to students in the paperback editions of such books as Bernard Lewis's *The Arabs in History* and Wilfred Cantwell Smith's *Islam in Modern History*. Direct approaches to other humanities are available in T.

[9] T. Cuyler Young (Ed.). *Near Eastern Culture and Society*. Princeton: Princeton University Press, 1966.
[10] K. G. Saiyidain. *Iqbal's Educational Philosophy*. Lahore: Muhammad Ashraf, Sixth Edition, 1965.

Cuyler Young's *Near Eastern Culture and Society,* and James Kritzeck's *Anthology of Islamic Literature.* [11]

Again it is instructive to read six more lines of Iqbal to let him reinforce the thought that education may open the key window on Islamic culture.

> What is the school-master?
> An architect of the souls of men!
> How attractively has the phi-
> losopher, Qaani,
> Remarked for his guidance:
> "If you will have your courtyard
> flooded with light,
> Do not interpose a wall in the path
> of the Sun. . . ."[12]

The Hindu-Buddhistic-Taoist. Hindu-Buddhistic-Taoist world culture is the third in this brief exploration. It involves twelve countries: Ceylon, India, Nepal, Tibet, Thailand, Burma, Laos, Cambodia, Vietnam, China, Korea and Japan—in all of which, according to F.S.C. Northrop in his monumental *The Meeting of East and West,* Buddhist culture is a major and persistent component.[13]

Buddha had completed fifty years of teaching a thousand years before Mohammed was born. As happened in the later recording of the teachings of Christ and Mohammed, groups of Buddha's one-time Hindu followers assembled after his death and set down from memory the canon of the *Tripitoka.* This is now the basic document of Hinayana Buddhism in Ceylon, Thailand and Burma; its literary, artistic and philosophic continuity in India is evident in the much repeated *Jataka Tales* of the rebirths of Buddha, the symbolic representations of his life and work in the temples of Sarnath and Sanchi, and the codes of law and humane conduct inscribed on the pillars of Asoka and abbreviated in the *chakra,* or the Great Wheel of the flag of modern India.

At a later date other philosophically-inclined disciples of Buddha set down in the form of discourses with Buddha the *Surangama Sutra.* This is the major document for Mahayana Buddhism in Tibet, China, Korea and Japan. With its sustained discussions of mind and perception we may find that it leads us in the direction of what Northrop calls the undifferentiated aesthetic continuum of Chinese Buddhist and Taoist painting, and the Sumiye and Haiku of Japanese Zen. What new aesthetic will emerge from Chinese Communism we may sense presently.

But the close reading to arrive at these discriminations can be very dull reading for high school students. It seems more important that they take Hindu-Buddhis-

---

[11] James Kritzeck. *Anthology of Islamic Literature from the Rise of Islam to Modern Times.* New York: New American Library, Mentor MT 666, 1964. For further reading: *Islamic Literature,* An Introductory History with Selections by Najib Ullah. New York: Washington Square Press, 1963.

[12] Saiyidain, *op. cit.,* p. 39.

[13] F. S. C. Northrop, *The Meeting of East and West: An Inquiry Concerning World Understanding.* New York: Macmillan, 1960, Chapters X, XI.

tic-Taoist relationships as a given, and then briefly, in impressive visual maps and graphs, grasp the simultaneity of parallel culture epochs in the three major secular components of the Hindu-Buddhistic-Taoist world culture, India, China, Japan, and in turn, their relation to contemporaneous culture epochs in other world cultures. This could bring students quickly to the modern context of three world cultures.

The striking fact about contemporary India, China and Japan, of course, is that they entered the present epoch at almost the same time: Hiroshima (1945) for Japan, Independence (1947) for India, Communist dominance (1949) for China.[14,15] It seems essential that we continue to deal with them simultaneously in their modern phase. Their own interrelations multiply, with India and China disputing territorial boundaries, Japan according to Hajime Nakamura, diligently researching the roots of its own Buddhism in India, and India using Japan as a national model for its developing education and industrialization.[16] As we come to know more about Buddhist humanities and their Indian, Chinese and Japanese components, we may well develop a touchstone approach to the diverse factors in this world culture. Let me sample here one or two aspects of such an approach, using Indian material primarily and touching lightly on possible leads into Chinese and Japanese culture patterns.

Indian Emergence. Pre-Independence Indian education was largely set by an English Government document known as the Macaulay Minute. This called for the education of persons, "Indian in blood and color, but English in taste, in opinion, in morals and in intellect." There was little room in this system for Indian geography and ecology, Indian archaeology and history, Indian mother-tongues, or indigenous art.

But in the twenty years since Independence, India has moved dramatically on all these cultural fronts. As in our efforts to achieve empathic identification with Islamic culture through the eyes of Islam's youth, so may we with Indian culture. To further what India calls "national integration," each of her sixteen states teaches the physical and economic geography of each other state. Each State Education Ministry maintains a science institute, which helps youngsters to observe indigenous flowers, trees and birds rather than memorize the characteristics of English daffodils, oaks, and robins. The Indian Archaeological Survey has become the largest national archeological endeavor in the world—virtually lifting an inspiring national history from the prehistoric sites of Harappa and Mohenjo-daro. from Buddhist stupas in Sarnath and Sanchi and the temple caves of Ellora and Ajanta, from such Muslim tombs as the Taj Mahal, and fortress cities like Fatehpur Sikri, and even from the consciously preserved monuments to British governors and kings. Dance groups—Bharatanayam, Kathakali, Manipuri, Kuchipudi, Odissi—travel among the states, reembodying traditional values in regional classic forms. Comparably in literature, Indian youngsters recite the *Koran,* read and retell the

---

[14]Lin Yutang (Ed.). *The Wisdom of China and India.* New York: Random House, 1942.

[15]Hajime Nakamura. *The Ways of Thinking of Eastern Peoples.* Japanese National Commission for UNESCO, 1960.

[16]Hajime Nakamura. *Japan and Indian Asia, Their Cultural Relations in the Past and Present.* Calcutta: Firma K. L. Mukhapodhyay, 1961.

Jataka Tales of the rebirths of Buddha, the animal stories of the *Panchantantra,* tales from Kalidasa, the epic of the *Ramayana,* and the historico-philosophic drama of the *Mahabharata* with its religious center in the *Bhagavad Gita.* The classic Indian humanities become part of a living present from which India is consciously constituting her modern synthesis.

One of Nehru's great interests was the founding of the Children's Book Trust to develop a children's literature for India. Little has yet come from the Book Trust that provides modern role models for modern children. But last year the Sahitya Akademi published a book, *Contemporary Indian Short Stories,*[17] one from each state, that sets a good example. And since 1964, following the work of Professor Constance McCullough as a member of the Teachers College, Columbia University advisory team, young authors are learning to look at their village communities and to write stories about today for school primers. Also, I venture a guess that increasing American interest in the Indian Tolstoy, Premchand, will lead to the reprinting of many of his short stories and novels, both in English and in Indian languages.

Modern Indian Art Forms. Film, it seems to me, may play a unique role in Indian humanities. In the hands of Satyajit Ray, of course, it provides a realistic mirror for Indian youngers—quite different from the four-hour productions of the Bombay and Madras studios. But those of us who have taught Humanities in its western form look at all Indian film from a special perspective. We know that the high degree of consciousness of self in Classico-Judeo-Christian culture dates from Gutenberg and subsequent preoccupation with the printed word. Millions of Indian people are illiterate in print but fully literate in film. They are coming into their literary heritage through sound-color film. There are implications in this for the development of Indian national personality. It may, indeed, develop along lines of much greater social conscience than characterizes the privatism of our culture. Both G. Morris Carstairs' *The Twice born*[18] and Nirad C. Chaudhuri's *The Continent of Circe*[19] provide us with psychological insights for reading Indian literature.

Humayun Kabir writes in *The Indian Heritage,* "The modern world is instinct with the urge for a new and impatient life. To the old tradition of unity of life has been added the new demand of equality and justice...."[20] There are intimations of this in much of contemporary Indian literature, certainly in the many biographies and writings of Gandhi and Tagore, which seem to be "musts" in any program we develop. But there are also novels such as Khwaja Ahmad Abbas' *Inquilab,*[21] which deals with the freedom movement; Raj Anandi's *Coolie,*[22] which cuts deeply into values of aspiration, injustice and denial; Khushwant Singh's *Train to Pakistan*[23] and *Mano Majra.*[24] which treat the

[17]*Contemporary Indian Short Stories.* New Delhi: Sahitya Akademi.
[18]G. Morris Carstairs. *The Twice Born,* A Study of a Community of High-Caste Hindus. London: Hogarth Press, 1961.
[19]Nirad C. Chaudhuri. *The Continent of Circe,* An Essay on the Peoples of India. London: Chatto and Windus, 1965.
[20]Humayun Kabir. *The Indian Heritage.* Bombay: Asia, 1960.
[21]Khwaja Ahmad Abbas. *Inquilab.* Bombay: Jaico, 1955.
[22]Mulk Raj Anandi. *Coolia.* London: May Fair Books, 1962.

inanities of partition; and Thakazhi Pillai's *Chemmeen*,[25] which examines young love thwarted by custom. And R. K. Narayan's new book, *The Vendor of Sweets*,[26] asks us to look again at the conflict of the generations with an overlay of the conflict of world cultures,[27]

Our responsibility to our students, it seems to me, is to help them with the criterial questions with which they can continue to read the increasing amount of Indian literature available. What, for instance, are the tension points in the behavior of characters? Do they arise because characters are using ancient epic heroes as role models? Or because literary characters may have had no modern role models from which to learn the consequences of varied behavior patterns? And—perhaps most important—what new role models are contemporary Indian literatures of print and film creating for Indian youth?

There is some likelihood that painting will become the major expressive form for Indian youngsters. For the past thirteen years the Shankar on-the-spot painting contests and the Shankar International Children's Art Festival have enlisted hundreds of thousands of perceptive interpretations of environment and human relations. Indian children seem to come closer to self understanding through painting than through literature.

In architecture, India has tried her hand at two all-new state capitol cities, Chandigarh in the Punjab and Bhubaneschwar in Orissa—answering affirmatively Le Corbusier's and Lewis Mumford's insistence that our old cities are not redeemable. With public school providing extensive experiences in virtual space in painting, we may expect a new generation of city planners to come into university programs in engineering and architecture, bringing a new respect for Indian traditions in tropical shelter and their relation to human survival.

Simultaneous with our study of touchstones in Indian culture it should be possible to observe comparable touchstones in Japan and in China. Unless we press ourselves to perfect this kind of method we will continue the vast culture lag that characterizes much of contemporary education.

Japanese Touchstones. Turning to Japan we can, as in India, look at education as a key to national culture. The address of Japan's Education Minister, Abe Yoshishige, to the U.S. Education Mission, March 8, 1946, eight months after Hiroshima, provides a starting point, but one quite unlike the English Macaulay Minute.

After this miserable defeat. . . .Our people have suddenly turned their eyes on education and become keenly aware . . .that the present condition of our country is due to errors and defects in education, and also to [our] low cultural standard . . . as individuals. . . .[28]

[23] Khushwant Singh. *Train to Pakistan.* London: Four Square Books, 1961.

[24] Khushwant Singh. *Mano Majra.* New York: Grove Press, 1956.

[25] Thakazhi S. Pillai. *Chemmeen.* London: Victor Gollancz, 1962.

[26] R. K. Narayan. *The Vendor of Sweets.* New York: Viking, 1967.

[27] Milton Singer, (Ed.). *Traditional India: Structure and Change.* Philadelphia: American Folklore Society, 1959.

[28] Herbert Passin. *Society and Education in Japan.* New York: Teachers College, Columbia University and The East Asian Institute, 1965.

... the characteristics of a tradition that is still alive among the people should be respected. Thus I would like to ask America not to deal with us simply from an American point of view. . . .America as a victorious country, is in a position to do anything it pleases with Japan. I hope I am not making too bold in expressing the wish that America may not avail herself of this position to impose upon us simply what is characteristic of America or of Europe. . .if this is. . .the case. . .I fear that we shall never be able to have a true Japanese education . . . firmly rooted in our soil and which can work on the inmost soul of the . . . people.[29]

Leads for understanding of the "inmost soul" of Japan, pre-war and contemporary, are opened to us in *Approaches to Asian Civilizations.*[30] edited by Theodore de Bary and Ainslee Embree. But we come much closer in Ruth Benedict's war-time analysis of Japanese culture patterns, *The Chrysanthemum and the Sword,*[31] and UNESCO's post-war *Without the Chrysanthemum and the Sword,*[32] a study of personality structures and values of young people. Focus on personality orientation sharpens in L. Takeo Doi's essay, "Amae: A Key Concept for Understanding Japanese Personality Structure."[33] The social science perspectives of these and other studies[34] inform our reading of 17th Century dramas of Chikamatsu and 20th Century novels of Tanizaki. They prepare us for cross-cultural insight into Japanese popular culture as reported by Hidetoshi Kato,[35] and as reflected in the UNESCO anthology of *Modern Japanese Stories,*[36] and Donald Keene's *Modern Japanese Literature.*[37]

Chinese Touchstones. To this simultaneous approach to Indian and Japanese humanities we need to add comparable concern for Chinese humanities, starting with the now available *Red Book* of Mao Tse Tung and moving to the excellent new book of Liu Wu-Chi, *An Introduction to Chinese Literature.*[38] It will be no surprise that Chairman Mao, as early as 1942, was demanding "a unity of politics

[29]*Ibid.*, p. 277.
[30]Theodore de Bary and Ainslee Embree. *Approaches to Asian Civilizations.* New York: Columbia University Press, 1964.
[31]Ruth Benedict. *The Chrysanthemum and The Sword.* New York: Houghton-Mifflin, 1946.
[32]Jean Stoetzel. *Without the Chrysanthemum and the Sword,* A Study of the Attitudes of Youth of Post-War Japan. New York: Columbia University Press, 1955.
[33]L. Takeo Doi. "Amae: A Key Concept for Understanding Japanese Personality Structure," pp. 132-140 in Robert J. Smith and Richard K. Beardsley, *Japanese Culture, Its Development and Characteristics.* Chicago: Aldine, 1962.
[34]John W. Hall and Richard K. Beardsley. *Twelve Doors to Japan.* New York: McGraw-Hill, 1965.
[35]Hidetoshi Kato (Ed.). *Japanese Popular Culture.* Rutland, Vt.: Charles E. Tuttle, 1959.
[36]Ivan Morris, *Modern Japanese Stories, Anthology.* Rutland, Vt.: Charles E. Tuttle, 1961.
[37]Donald Keene (Ed.). *Modern Japanese Literature.* New York: Grove Press, 1960.
[38]Liu Wu-chi. *An Introduction to Chinese Literature.* Bloomington, University of Indiana Press, 1966.

and art, a unity of content and form, and a unity of revolutionary political content and an artistic form of as high a standard as possible."[39]

Matching theory with talent, Lao She provides insight into a new Chinese national personality in the conclusion to *Richshaw Boy* (1938) with this paragraph:

The face-saving, emulative, dreamy, self-seeking, individualistic, robust, and great Hsiang-tzu. No one knew how many funeral processions he had attended for others, nor was it known when and where he would bury himself, this degenerate, selfish, luckless product of the sickly womb of society, the wayworn ghost of individualism.[40]

African Autochthonous Humanities. In sub-Sahara Africa, new nations date their independence within the last ten years; remaining ones expect theirs within the next ten years. Political newness is matched with the newness of visible and transmittable formulations of African values. Vigorous and prolific literature is either newly created by a new generation of writers or newly transcribed directly from the story tellers. In consequence, as W. E. Abraham says in *The Mind of Africa,* "Our interest in our own cultures is not historical and archeological but directed towards the future. . . ."[41]

Dr. Abraham's personal cultural roots are in Ghana, but he speaks for the fifty nations of Africa which are trying to heal what he calls the "multiple wounds" of diverse European exploitations and to find the "Agreement which would draw the skin together and give Africa a continental outlook."[42]

Here again it seems to me that entry into African culture through African education is particularly appropriate. One of the key books studied by Nigerian youth for the Nigerian Secondary School Certification Examination is Chinua Achebe's *Things Fall Apart*.[43] The beginnings of modern African humanities for Africans and for us must include this classic effort of an author to get life into form for his people, who have witnessed personal deteriorations and tribal disintegrations from the incursion of commercial, political and missionary interests. *Things Fall Apart* renders into highly charged form Abraham's factual account in "Paradigm of African Society" of tribal social-religious-aesthetic values.

As in other world cultures, education is being looked to to provide the personality resources to fuse the finer qualities of tradition with the most promising aspects of modernity. At this juncture the center for this synthesis seems to be the concept of *the African personality* ". . . that complex of ideas and attitudes which is both identical and significant in otherwise, different

[39] O. Edmund Clubb. *Twentieth Century China.* New York: Columbia University Press, 1965.
[40] Liu Wu-chi. *op. cit.,* p. 275.
[41] W. E. Abraham. *The Mind of Africa.* Chicago: University of Chicago Press, 1962.
[42] *Ibid.,* p. 115.
[43] Chinua Achebe. *Things Fall Apart.* New York: McDowell, 1959.

African cultures. . . ."[44] Philosophically, "the African personality" seems to share something with our own conception of transactional participation in environment. The African thinks much about the world but not, indeed, as the world inside which he finds himself, but as the world of which he forms a part.[45]

Aesthetics and Culture. Nothing is more central to the realization of the African personality than comprehension by us and our African friends of the culture-based characteristic of any aesthetic. In the well-intentioned vandalism of missionaries, countless thousands of objects of art were destroyed. A little anthropological understanding would have shown that for peoples without writing, normal expression of values is through art—through, as Abraham writes, ". . . the timeless, immemorial, silent, and elemental power so characteristic of African traditional art. Indeed this is the main reason why it is not lifelike in a representational sense. Forms had to be distorted." He continues, "In art there was a moral-philosophical preoccupation which led it to portray a forces of the world, and to portray a force it is essential that it should not be treated like something assimilated, and consequently like something overcome, as the rendering of it in life-like figures would have been."[46]

It is obvious that we have a lot of exciting study ahead of us as we add a wholly new aesthetic to our understanding, or, following Susanne Langer's lead in her latest book, *Mind: An Essay on Human Feeling*,[47] search out the biological bases of art forms in world cultures, including the African Autochthonous.

Scholarly organizations will be increasingly helpful to us. The University of Leeds publishes *The Journal of Commonwealth Literature*.[48] The Association for African Literature, based in Fourah Bay College in Freetown, Sierra Leone, publishes its *Bulletin*[49] replete with perceptive reviews of current literature of all types. The Department of English at the University of Ibadan is behind *New Approaches to African Literature*,[50] a comprehensive bibliography and commentary.

These organizations are essentially extensions of the modern aesthetic of African authors. Onuora Nzekwu's *Wand of Noble Wood*[51] reflects the self-conscious effort to use literature to make Ibo society understandable to

[44]W. E. Abraham, *op. cit.*, p. 39. For further reading: Alex Quaison-Sackey, *Africa Unbound, Reflections of an African Statesman. New York: Praeger, 1963.*

[45]*Ibid.*, p. 46.

[46]*Ibid.*, p. 111. For further reading: Janheinz Jahn. *Mantu, The New African Culture.* New York: Grove Press, 1961.

[47]Susanne Langer. *Mind: An Essay on Human Feeling.* Baltimore: Johns Hopkins Press, 1967.

[48]Arthur Ravenscroft (Ed.). *The Journal of Commonwealth Literature.* Leeds, England: Heinemann Educational Books. (Annual).

[49]*Bulletin of the Association for African literature in English.* Freetown, Sierra Leone: Department of English, Fourah Bay College. (Annual).

[50]J. A. Ramasaran. *New Approaches to African Literature,* A Guide to Negro-African Writing and Related Studies. Ibadan, Nigeria: Ibadan University Press, 1965.

[51]Onuora Nzekwu. *Wand of Noble Wood.* New York: New American Library, Signet D 2262, 1961.

English-speaking audiences. And Chinua Achebe goes the distance in making his art an integral part of African cultural evolution. In an essay entitled "The Novelist as Teacher" he writes:

> Perhaps what I write is applied art as distinct from pure. But who cares? Art is important but so is education of the kind I have in mind. And I don't see that the two need be mutually exclusive.

In a recent anthology a Hausa folktale having recounted the usual fabulous incidents ends with these words:

> They all came and lived happily together. He had several sons and daughters who grew up and helped in raising the standard of education of the country.

As I said elsewhere, if you consider this ending a naive anti-climax then you cannot know very much about Africa.[52]

It is not only the self-conscious author who has access to emerging ideas of social conscience though. In contemporary African literature, read in the spirit of inquiry, we can put down a number of test cores to assay the quality of values being nurtured in the culture. William Conton's *The African* affords one example. After years of provocation by an unreconstructed bigot, the narrator of this story has a perfect opportunity for vengeance. He writes:

> He lay very still as I stood over him, and as the first drums began to send their throbbing message out across the night it was pity I found in my heart for him, not hate. I stooped quickly, lifted him gently, and bore him through the easing rain to the safety of his home.[53]

There can be no summary to this exploration of a potential organizational framework for the study of world cultures. There can only be projection into the methods it implies. It implies the need to deal with parts only in the context of wholes. It implies the need to find new ways to deal in life-like simultaneity with wide spectrums of materials and values. It implies the need for staff and students to work together at their respective levels of inquiry. It constitutes a new opportunity to demonstrate that scholarly method is an integral part of teaching method.

---

[52]John Press (Ed.). *Commonwealth Literature, Unity and Diversity in a Common Culture.* London: Heinemann Educational Books, 1965.

[53]William Conton. *The African.* New York: New American Library, Signet D 1906, 1960.

Allied Arts: An Approach to Aesthetic Education

Leon C. Karel

Historians are always quick to point out that the date assigned for the close of an era is never an exact one. The end of any particular period is usually set at the year in which the earliest signs of the next period can be plainly detected. People living in such times are rarely able to sense these changes. Only much later do they wake up to the fact that things have altered, and many times it is a rude shock that precipitates the awakening. At the risk of being presumptuous, I predict that the 1960's will be the time designated as the close of one era of art education, and the start of another. This is when, it will be said, the earlier concepts of isolated courses in the several arts gave way to a unified arts program at the secondary level. This is when the arts began an upward climb from the entertainment-public-relations-activities-showmanship level to that of an academically respected segment of the curriculum.

Signs of Change. These future chroniclers may well point out portents of change which we should have been able to see but did not. First, there was the heavy reliance on art courses to please the public throughout the 30's, 40's and 50's, as one condition for remaining in the curriculum. Music departments became regular booking agencies ready to provide anything from a soloist to a chorus for any occasion. Civic groups relied more and more on the schools for pageantry and parades. Dramatics hinged almost solely on the "class play" in most schools. The dramatic work presented was invariably a "crowd pleaser," never controversial or obscure. In visual art study there were always posters to make or banquet tables to be decorated. Throughout these decades, serious art education was always second to pleasing others outside the school.

Second, there was the growing separateness of the arts in the school curriculum. Throughout the decades of struggle on the part of drawing, painting, and music to win a place in the program, a third art, English, had become firmly established. But somehow the teachers of literature never recognized their kinship with the other arts. The gap between literature and music, both so intimately involved with aural and temporal factors, was especially noticeable. Third, the arts were not only separated, but were incomplete. Especially conspicuous by their absence were two arts of particular importance to American young people, architecture and cinema. Until the early 60's, generations of high school graduates entered adult life knowing little about either of these arts to which America has so greatly contributed.

Fourth, the school arts became mutually exclusive, competing for the student's time, and effectively preventing him from getting any sort of broad, general aesthetic education. Music very often enlisted the talented youngster as early as the fourth grade and so completely controlled his elective time that he had no opportunity to work in the visual arts or dramatics. Closely allied with the constant pressure on the arts to keep the public happy was the consequent trend toward channeling students into this effort. As instrumental music groups became more and more professional in their playing and pageantry, recruitment for students was pushed into junior high and then grade school. A not infrequent youngster would thus be carefully nursed along for as many as eight years of specialization on a musical instrument, his instructors knowing that he would have no use for his hardwon skill upon graduation. Meanwhile, of course, his education in music as an art suffered.

Fifth, a danger sign curiously ignored during the 60's by educators in the arts was their decreasing hold on the young people in the schools. Enrollment in music, art, and dramatics enterprises failed to keep pace with the rapid rise in school population. Each year a larger percentage of the total pupil enrollment was untouched by art experience of any significant sort. A further omen was the shift of the best students away from the arts and into the "solids." Art educators reacted by blaming everyone from local guidance people to college entrance boards. Few thought to compare the intellectual challenges of the class play or the half-time formation with those offered by the new math or foreign language. Fewer still found means to offer art as an intellectual or aesthetic challenge.

Here then were the signs of an approaching change. This change might have been gradual except for the impetus provided by an academic race with the Russians. From that moment on, the schools were fair game for public criticism, and following criticism came the shock of legislation. It was this which awakened art educators to the realization that perhaps an era had ended. Local school boards legislated some art programs out of existence and sharply cut back many more. Budgets were reduced in many schools, with art funds now going to other subjects. Finally came the major blow for which the nation's art educators should have been prepared. One state legislature enacted laws to prescribe the required courses for the high schools of that state. The arts were left out as a graduation requirement and were given extracurricular status. The consternation which the California legislature's action caused is proof that art and music teachers were not alert to developments in their respective fields.

What was changing was the view that art education should be based solely on production and performance. This notion had been so widely adopted that few art educators could have suggested any other kind of approach. The whole profession had been geared to an acceptance of art learning in which drawing and painting were the chief activities, to dramatics teaching devoted entirely to the staging of plays, and to music education whose sole outlet was in singing and playing. This viewpoint somehow manged to ignore the quite obvious fact that the adult rarely ever acts, paints, or plays an instrument. Instead, he watches movies and television, observes paintings, and listens to music. The skills needed for intelligent viewing and listening were simply not being taught anywhere in the arts curriculum!

A New Approach. One new approach designed to correct the deficiences of arts instruction was started in 1963 with the publication of a curriculum guide by the State Department of Education in Missouri. Entitled *The Allied Arts: A High School Humanities Guide for Missouri,* this book described a course designed to steer aesthetic education in an entirely new direction. It offered the following features:

1. An inclusive course which dealt not only with painting, literature, and music, but sculpture and architecture as well. In addition, areas of city planning and creativity were included.

2. A five-day-a-week, two-semester class which made use of outside readings, assignments, projects, and examinations. Grades would require the same kind of mental effort as in other courses—rather than motor skills, performances in public, or any of the other grading practices of which the arts, rightly or wrongly, had been suspect.

3. A fusion of the arts, not simply separate arts crammed into one course. This was done by concentrating upon the basic similarities among the arts, and upon their unifying principles. The concept of "subject" in the arts, with its interesting variations of realism, distortion, and abstraction, was used to introduce students to the course. Other general topics such as "function" and "medium" followed. The "elements" and "forms" common to the audible and visual arts were taken up as was "style."

4. A concentration on the development of standards of taste. The customary drama, music, and art activities did little or nothing to prepare students to say what was good or bad in the arts. As a result, the younger generation had come to accept the simplest sort of musical and dramatic fare in movies, TV, and the world of popular music. The new course tried to encourage the student to develop standards of his own through showing him what the arts are and letting him make gradually more complex judgments of them.

5. A course designed for all students, not just those with performing or creative talents. As such, the Allied Arts Course was aimed at the future "consumer" of the arts, and it dedicated itself to assisting him to become a more intelligent viewer, listener, and user of the arts. In this way, it could serve the total student population, including the performer and creator.

6. A general education art course, around which the previously separated disciplines could group. Previously, art was the only curricular field in which no general course was offered. There were "general science" and "general history" of course, in each of which all students learned something of the whole field. Even physical education had its general offering, but art began and ended in specialized courses. Furthermore, in those established general courses, students were being taught to think in ways appropriate to the area represented. The "scientific method" was introduced in one case, and the "historical method" in the other. But never was the student taught the "aesthetic method" of approaching the world about him.

Primary Problems. In formulating a new approach there were many problems that had to be faced. One of these appeared at the very outset in choosing among alternative paths to follow. The question concerned the methods of uniting the arts in a single course, the other possibility being that of a historical combination.

Prior to 1963, a scattering of high schools, especially in the East, had experimented with a "humanities" approach to integration. The arts were brought together in historical eras, with the purpose of illuminating man's heritage, his great ideas and achievements, and his constant search for truth, beauty, and meaning in life. A long-standing program of humanities workshops and John Hay fellowships popularized this approach. The Missouri planners, though admiring this kind of course wholeheartedly, decided against it for the following reasons:

First, it was using the arts to teach history and philosophy, and, worthy as this may be, it still does not help the student to think aesthetically, to make aesthetic judgments, or to raise his own standards of taste. Second, it was concentrating its study on the past, when what is so sorely needed in America is an awareness of the present-day world of the arts. A historical approach inevitably must concentrate on great masterworks—painting, cathedrals, symphonies, statues, or plays. Allied Arts can, and does study industrial design, domestic architecture, jazz, movies, television, urbanization, and fashion. These may not rank in aesthetic importance with the Parthenon or *Hamlet*, but they are more meaningful to the student of today. It should also be kept in mind that the Greeks achieved their artistic triumphs by becoming passionately concerned with the aesthetic quality of their own daily lives, not by studying the arts of the Egyptians before them.

Having made their decision, the committee charged with writing the guide could go ahead. It is of interest to note the comparative swiftness with which Missouri's project was brought to completion. One year from the time that the work began the guide was finished. Several factors account for this, among them the fact that Missouri is one of a handful of states with a single Supervisor of Fine Arts Education, rather than separate art, music, and English supervisors. Thus a group could be appointed to work on the problem without having to consult autonomous officials who often have a specialist's view of their own fields and who tend to cooperate somewhat reluctantly. The task of writing the curriculum guide was assigned to two members of the committee, both of whom were teaching such a course at the college level. The rest of the group served as consultants, proofreaders, editors, and so on.

Secondary Problems. With the publication and distribution of the guide, the committee faced a second round of problems. One problem area centered about the need for explaining the new course to administrators, teachers, and the general public. The other problem dealt with the preparation of instructors. Both were attacked simultaneously but will be described separately for the moment.

A curriculum guide is effective only to the extent that teachers are guided by it. With such a new concept being advanced, it was doubly important to reach the teachers with explanations and assistance. Four approaches were used.

1. Through the professional teachers' associations. Missouri's art educators have the customary art, music, and English associations. The first move came from the Missouri music educators, who included an Allied Arts session on their state convention agenda. In the following year, this group invited the presidents of the state art and English groups to speak, possibly the first time the school arts had

officially come together even on this limited scale. Both art and English associations reciprocated with Allied Arts sessions in their meetings. In each meeting of the large State Teachers Association thereafter, an Allied Arts program was planned. In 1965 the people present at this meeting formed the Missouri Teachers of Allied Arts and Humanities Association, which now plans meetings of its own, and is developing projects for promoting instruction in related arts in Missouri. From state association meetings, the Allied Arts idea has spread into regional and national meetings, so that in recent years it has become a familiar topic among art educators.

2. Through publication. The new area was described in articles published in the state education magazines, the professional journals, and even in the metropolitan newspapers. Art editors in both the Kansas City and St. Louis papers were generous with publicity about the venture. Both the State Department and the author's own college sent information on request. The curriculum guide was also sent free to anyone who requested a copy until the flood of requests made this practice too costly. It was then placed in a publisher's hands.[1]

3. Through clinics and conferences. Since 1963 there has been an annual Allied Arts Clinic held for instructors in the new area. Demonstrations, methods, and materials are featured and plans made for future meetings. The State Teachers College held a national Allied Arts Workshop in the summer of 1966 which attacted art educators from states as far apart as New York and California.

4. Through other organizations. With the interest shown in the school curriculum by parents and citizens, the Allied Arts found a fruitful avenue for publicity in civic groups and parent-teacher associations. It was found that parents were often more receptive to the idea of such a course than were the art educators themselves. Speeches before such groups at the local and state level found adults well aware of what they had missed in their own aesthetic education.

As for the preparation of teachers, here was problem which required a much longer time for solution. On the one hand there was the curriculum guide with no teachers trained to implement it. On the other there were the teacher-training institutions with no foreseeable market for any people they might educate in Allied Arts. The solution arrived at was a compromise. For the first few years, the State Department of Education would permit any teacher with an education degree in art, music, or English, and sufficient hours in one of the other two areas for a minor, to try the new course. In the first year, 11 schools made the effort. In 1964, according to the department's tally, 26 schools took up the new program, and in 1965 the report showed 64 schools. A check of these figures indicates that some schools were really teaching something other than a related arts course, but the trend was unmistakable.

Early in 1964, Missouri State Teachers College in Kirksville announced an "Allied Arts Certification Program" designed to prepare instructors in the new

---

[1] Alfred M. Sterling and Leon Karel, *The Allied Arts: A High School Humanities Guide for Missouri* (Marceline, Missouri: Walsworth Pub. Co., 1963).

area. It was open to candidates for the degree of Bachelor of Science in Education, with a major in either art, English, or music. The reasoning behind this requirement was in part practical and in part philosophical. Practically speaking, an "Allied Arts major" was risky because few schools would employ a full-time instructor in this area for many years to come. Therefore, the graduating college senior had better possess a degree fitting him for the more usual sort of public school position. It was also thought that the graduating senior would need a special area of concentration in order to hold his own in a world of specialists. The specialization provided by a major would result in a degree of professional competence denied a "generalist."

The certification courses prescribed by the Teachers College began with a two-quarter general art course something like the one laid out in the curriculum guide, but at a higher level. It then went on to require broad courses in art, music, and theatre appreciation. Following this, basic techniques courses in each area were specified, ranging from drawing and design to music fundamentals, and so on. Capping the whole effort was a senior philosophy seminar in aesthetics.

At the time of this writing, several dozen students in all three areas are "in the pipeline" working their way toward the certification goal. Already their presence has made itself felt in the college, for this is a new kind of student. Never before have art instructors had senior music and English majors in their courses, nor have teachers of music had to face the penetrating questions of majors in other fields. The interchange of ideas has been most fruitful, and it has been discovered that deficiencies in techniques can be more than made up by mental awareness of basic structures and elements. As students cross boundaries, faculty too are being brought together in ways seldom achieved earlier. Regular staff meetings of the art, English, and music instructors involved in the Allied Arts program are now planned. A sort of inter-arts education is being shared by these people, who themselves were trained as specialists.

The preparation of Allied Arts teachers was faced with still another problem. Should the secondary schools be urged to employ team-teaching for this course, or would it be better to assign it to a single instructor. With the publication of the guide, a policy was gradually shaped which led to the decision in favor of the individual teacher. The committee did not categorically disapprove of the team-teaching approach; it did point out its weaknesses.

For one thing, the team is an expensive proposition to urge upon an administration already burdened with budget problems. To function properly, the team must all be present all of the time, so in effect the course will cost three times as much as an ordinary one. Second, a team is still made up of specialists when what is wanted is the veiwpoint of the generalist. Integration of the arts through their common principles is sought, and this can scarcely be done by presenting music first, then poetry, then painting, followed by architecture, and so on. One person is needed who can bring these principles to light and integrate the arts about them. Third, even where a team of teachers does catch the spirit and works into a true general education approach, there is always the possibility of one or more members leaving, whereupon the team has to be carefully rebuilt with new personnel. A final consideration may be the most telling argument of all. In offering the related arts course we are in effect saying that each student should learn about all the arts, yet in offering a team of teachers we admit that we have no instructor who can teach all the arts. Surely under such circumstances the teaching profession can produce adequately trained people.

In this connection, an argument has often been advanced to the effect that teachers in each art have a difficult enough time trying to master their own subjects. How, then, can any one person be expected to master all three, and others in addition? Will not superficial instruction emerge as a result? The answer must be, yes, of course, if the allied arts course is conceived as five specialized art courses rolled into one. But it is not that at all. Precisely the same kind of instructor is needed here as in a general science course. Such a person is not trained as a specialist in physics, chemistry, biology, geology, astronomy, and botany. Instead he is trained in teaching youngsters how to approach phenomena scientifically, how to observe with the scientist's precision and emotional detachment, and how to proceed from observable facts to careful deduction based on those facts. He teaches the principles of scientific thought, not the separate sciences.

By the same token, the Allied Arts instructor teaches young people how to observe and listen aesthetically. He introduces them to line, color, texture, and to pitch, timbre, meter, volume, and rhythm, among other things. He teaches them to think with emotional commitment and to concern themselves with matters of taste, value judgment, and discrimination. He is teaching aesthetic thinking rather than music, sculpture, painting, architecture, drama, and dance. Such teaching, of course, may be superficial. On the other hand, the properly trained instructor can make the Allied Arts a vital experience for students, one concerned with matters vaoided in traditonal offerings.

A Testing Program. A program of such radically different nature must be launched with a great deal of faith that it will succeed. Once under way, however, faith is no longer sufficient for guiding its progress. Some kind of measurement is necessary. Toward the end of the second year of the course in Missouri, an assessment was attempted. A test was administered to nearly 200 high school students enrolled in Allied Arts courses in four Missouri high schools.

The test consisted of five sections, one for each major art area. It was designed to measure the accuracy with which these young people could analyze works of art in each area. Test folders contained five painting reproductions, five pictures of architecture, five of sculpture, a poem, and several paragraphs of prose. In addition, an orchestral composition on tape was played three times. Questions were designed to require direct perception of the works. They were not the kinds of questions which could be answered correctly by one who had read the art and music columns of weekly news magazines. Sample questions will illustrate the approach:

1. In which painting is radial design most prominent?
2. Which building would most likely contain ribbed vaulting?
3. In the poem, what symbols are used for "death"?

4. What happens between (voice numbers) four and five in the music?
5. In which statue is texture part of the expressive quality?

The questions were multiple-choice because of machine scoring requirements, and the total examination time was one hour. The scoring computer was programmed to differentiate between the highest quarter of the group (on total performance) and the lowest quarter. If a question was missed by a majority of low performers and answered correctly by most of the top group, it was assumed that the question had value as a test item.

Results were far better than the four question-writers had expected. Top and middle-group students proved able to grasp the essentials of art elements, structures, and meanings in all five areas. Questions which would have been considered suitable for college majors in art, music, and literature were found to be well within the grasp of these high school students. The pilot test does not, of course, contain sufficient data to warrant any sweeping claims. It does, however, offer tentative evidence that the Allied Arts course is accomplishing what its planners hoped for, an aesthetic understanding of the arts on the part of high school students. At this writing, further interpretation of the test scores is being made, and plans for its extension and improvement are under consideration.

The Growth of a Concept. In the three years since the course made its appearance, the idea of the related arts approach has spread with unexpected rapidity. Visible proof of its growing importance is the establishment of projects similar to Missouri's in several state departments of education. New York has had such a committee at work and has produced a detailed Allied Arts-Humanities-Great Ideas Guide for schools of that state to follow. Pennsylvania's Department of Public Instruction is at work on a curriculum development project in this area, and Florida has held a statewide conference in related arts education. The inauguration of *The Journal of Aesthetic Education* promises to stimulate understanding and analysis of the many problems new programs are generating.

As searching questions are being asked of the arts, a pattern of answers begins to emerge. For one thing, nobody is satisfied with the small proportion of students now reached by our present program—all agree that every student needs aesthetic education. For another, the consensus is that one new course will not solve our problems. It will take a new philosophy of aesthetic education. For a third, the program must begin as the child enters school and continue in one form or another so long as he remains there. Finally, whatever is done must be aimed at providing lifelong value, not a terminal skill for which there is no adult outlet. Without a basis of aesthetic sensitivity offered somewhere in the curriculum, the citizen remains ignorant of the arts about him, and the professional in one of the arts remains a specialist. Neither can do much toward raising the general level of culture. Up to now, the specialist-teacher has gone into the lower schools to teach his special field to students who, in turn, have gone to college to become specialists. Now, however, the cycle has been broken, and it is this small break in the process that must eventually change the course of aesthetic education.

Studying the Bible in Public School

Thayer S. Warshaw

Is it possible in public schools to study the Bible, not as a religious book, nor even as a literary work, but as a source book for the humanities? The over-publicized Johnny may follow the adventures of Ulysses by reading the *Odyssey* in school; he may become acquainted with the noble Brutus by reading *Julius Caesar* in school; but he will not find out about King David or Joseph's coat or Paul of Tarsus by reading the Bible in school, simply because the Bible is rarely studied there. Nor will he learn about David, Joseph, and Paul anywhere else, according to the evidence.

One piece of evidence is contained in answers to an unannounced test given to five classes of college-bound eleventh and twelfth graders in a community generally regarded as above average, culturally. Several pupils thought that Sodom and Gomorrah were lovers; that the four horsemen appeared on the Acropolis; that the Gospels were written by Matthew, Mark, Luther, and John; that Eve was created from an apple; that Jesus was baptized by Moses; that Jezebel was Ahab's donkey; and that the stories by which Jesus taught were called parodies.

The test consisted of 112 rather simple questions selected to discover whether these pupils were familiar with at least the most commonly known Biblical names, stories, and quotations. The results were, to say the least, disappointing. 79% could not supply the last word of the expression "Many are called, but few are *chosen*." 84% could not furnish the last word of the familiar "The truth shall make you *free*." 63% did not know the last word in Isaiah's "They shall beat their swords into *plowshares*." 84% were unable to say that "A soft answer turneth away *wrath*." 88% did not know that "Pride goeth before . . . a *fall*." 74% could not give any reasonable last word for the following statements: "God tested Job by making him ＿＿＿." And a full 93% could not complete the well-known "The love of money is the root of all *evil*."

This evidence is certainly dismaying, but an experienced high school teacher needs no such test. Let the English teacher begin the study of Nobel prize-winner John Steinbeck's *The Pearl* with an examination of the book's second paragraph, which begins, "If this story is a parable, perhaps everyone takes his own meaning from it. . . ." Nine-tenths of the pupils do not know even what a parable is, much less that in one parable a man "sold all that he had" for "one pearl of great price." Perhaps next time the book is Hemingway's Nobel prize-winning *The Old Man and the Sea*, at the end of which the old man staggers up a hill carrying a heavy mast across his shoulders, stumbles several times, and finally collapses on his bed with his arms outstretched and his hands and forehead showing his recent injuries. Not a soul in the class makes an association until the teacher points to it; and even then most of the pupils take their cue from the quicker ones. Or finally, let a class in social studies or in English examine Alan

Paton's great novel of South African apartheid, *Cry, The Beloved Country,* in which the main character, a religious leader, has a son named Absalom who rebels against him and dies by hanging. Again the pupils can make no association. The teacher wonders what his responsibility is—to the child, to the community, to himself, and to the piece of literature.

Should the public schools teach the Bible? In the sectarian clamor over that question, the voice that pleads the case of the humanities cannot be heard. The Bible is indeed a religious book, but it is also a part of our secular cultural heritage. To keep it out of the public schools because it is controversial and because the public cannot trust the good sense of both the teacher and the pupil to treat it as part of the humanities is a simple but questionable judgment. A knowledge of the Bible is essential to the pupil's understanding of allusions in literature, in music, and in the fine arts; in news media, in entertainment, and in cultured conversation. Is he to study mythology and Shakespeare, but not the Bible? Is it important for him to learn what it means when a man is called an Adonis or a Romeo, yet unimportant for him to be able to tell a Jonah from a Judas?

Last year at Newton High School two of my English classes read the Bible. They had read Shakespeare's *Macbeth,* as usual. They had studied Greek and Norse mythology, as usual. What more appropriate—though more unusual—than to go on to the book that pupils would need far more than either Shakespeare or mythology for an understanding and appreciation of their culture? Such a study was indeed unusual; the Bible has not been in the high school curriculum, even for its great literary passages, in Newton, Massachusetts, for many years.

By reading a few short stories, of which the pupils could make no sense because they could not understand the allusions, they had been made aware of the need for a background in the Bible. They again felt the need when they were unable to interpret some political cartoons I showed them from current newspapers. As a clincher, they both demonstrated and observed their own inadequacy to meet that need, in their humorous but pathetic performance on the pretest described above. The evidence was convincing and they wanted to learn.

At the outset, we came to an understanding on two points. First, we would not discuss meaning or interpretation. The pupils were made to realize that such questions as how to reconcile the two versions of the story of creation in Genesis could not be brought up in class; pupils were to take such questions to religious authorities. Secondly, we would use the King James Version (KJV) solely because that was the form in which the pupils would meet Bible quotations in their reading and in everyday life—as a glance at Bartlett's *Familiar Quotations* immediately proved.

Both points were involved when a pupil quoted scholarly authority in questioning the correctness of the KJV at Isaiah 14:12: "How art thou fallen from heaven, O Lucifer." His Bible at home read, "How art thou fallen from heaven, O day star." Wasn't his translation more accurate? Couldn't he memorize the "correct" one instead?

The answer was obvious: we were not interested in that kind of correctness; we were interested in knowing the words that have influenced our literature. It is just because the KJV uses the name Lucifer in that passage and because Luke 10:18 says, "I beheld Satan as lightning fall from heaven," that Lucifer has become another name for the devil in our culture. For every person today who thinks of Lucifer as the Roman god of the morning star there are a hundred who think of Lucifer as the devil. In Milton's *Paradise Lost* Lucifer is one of the fallen angels: "Pandemonium, city and proud seat of Lucifer" (Bk. X, line 424). From Milton, again, "proud as Lucifer" has become part of our stock of familiar expressions. For these reasons the class had to learn the quotation as it appears in the KJV and leave questions of accuracy to theologians.

A similar question arose over whether 1 Corinthians 13:13 was to be memorized as "faith, hope, and charity," as in the KJV, or as "faith, hope, and love," as in later versions. Regardless of the merits of one or the other interpretation, the quotation that the pupils would meet in literature and in conversation would almost invariably be the "faith, hope, and charity" of the KJV. Once again, our interest was in the version that is the source of our familiar quotation; accuracy of translation and appropriateness of meaning were irrelevant.

Class Procedures. Our procedure was simple. Three times a week the pupils had assignments in *The Holy Bible in Brief* (Mentor, 50c), which contains excerpts from the KJV. Because some favorite Bible stories (Cain and Abel, for example) and commonly used expressions ("Am I my brother's keeper?") are omitted, these regular textbook assignments were supplemented by other passages. Pupils had the choice of looking them up in Bartlett, for quotations, plus any Sunday school book, for stories, or else in the complete KJV.

Also three times a week the pupils had a five-minute quiz to test their knowledge of what they had been assigned: quotations to complete, names to identify, and incidents to remember. These quizzes were corrected, graded, returned, and used for brief instruction sessions. In these sessions I linked as many passages as I could with literature, music, and art. As we went along, the pupils heard about Melville's *Moby-Dick,* with its Ishmael, Ahab, and Elijah; Thomas Mann's *Joseph And His Brothers;* Rosini's *Moses in Egypt;* Mussorgsky's *Josua Navina;* Michaelangelo's *Moses;* Milton's *Samson Agonistes;* Saint-Saens' *Samson and Delilah*; Honneger's *Le Roi David;* Faulkner's *Absalom! Absalom!;* Bathsheba in *Hardy's Far From The Madding Crowd;* Gounod's *Queen of Sheba;* Marc Connolly's *Green Pastures;* the popular "Shadrach" and "Jezebel"; Verdi's *Nabucco;* MacLeish's *J. B.;* Massenet's *Herodiadae;* and Da Vinci's *Last Supper.* And they learned the origin of such expressions as the patience of Job, a doubting Thomas, a Nimrod, a Judas, a Jonah, a Lazar, an Ananias, and the Adam's apple.

A lighter touch was provided by good-humored reports of anonymous "boner" answers to the regular quizzes: Israel extended from Dan to *dusk,* the Gibeonites were hewers of wood and drawers of *pictures,* sufficient unto the day was the evil *eye,* man could not serve both God and *Merman,* and the word was made *fresh.*

So much for the pupils' day to day acquaintance with the Bible through regular assignments and quizzes. In a few special class periods they had other experiences, through audio-visual materials. One day we had a concert. First, there was the recorded voice of the city's Supervisor of Music singing "Little David Play on Your Harp," as he enthusiastically cooperated in the project. Next, the pupils were able to recognize the voice of Sammy Davis, Jr. singing " 'Tain't Necessarily So," with its "little David was small, but Oh my!" Then, having heard the Negro spiritual and the song from the folk opera, we listened to Judith Anderson's dramatic reading of the story of David and Goliath. That gave us three different forms of expression based on the same Biblical passage. A fourth medium rocked the room as Harry Belafonte shouted the gospel song "Noah." Next, the pupils sat enraptured as Joan Baez complained her folk song about Moses. A sixth genre using the Bible for text was represented by the opening aria of Handel's *Messiah.* During this oratorio passage, as in the case of the Anderson reading, the pupils followed the words in their books.

Two other periods were devoted to viewing slides, one set based on stories in the Old Testament and one on episodes in the New Testament. Again the emphasis was on variety of forms of expression and excellence of performance, as we covered a span of time from the thirteenth century to last year. There were canvases by Titian, Rubens, Veronese, Tiepolo, Rembrandt, El Greco, Murillo, Brueghel, and Bosch; murals by Michelangelo, Donatello, Verrocchio, and Bernini; reliefs by Brunelleschi and Ghiberti; engravings by Dürer, Doré, and Lucas van Leyden; movie stills of a Hollywood Biblical epic; and a three-in-one package—an Aubrey Beardsley print illustrating Oscar Wilde's *Salome,* a drama that was also the inspiration for Strauss' opera.

These three sessions, showing the Bible in music and the visual arts, constituted most of what was done in class. We devoted no time to interpretation of the text. Instead, we spent the time between the quizzes on the more usual aspects of our course of study: critical reading of poetry (some with Biblical allusion) and the art of effective writing.

Some of the pictures, which the city's Supervisor of Audio-Visual Instruction helped make into slides, and some of the recordings were brought in by pupils. In their enthusiasm they also brought materials from their reading. One student found in his U.S. history textbook an 1884 political cartoon depicting James G. Blaine as Belshazzar at a feast with William Vanderbilt and Jay Gould, complete with the warning handwriting on the wall, but with no word from the author explaining the allusion. Another boy discovered in his U.S. foreign policy textbook a 1932 cartoon opposing cancellation of European war debts, showing a man (Europe) with one pocket bulging with money (for armaments) and one pocket empty and turned out (for war debts). The caption, "Does one pants pocket know what the other is doing?" was an illustration of how a Biblical quotation may come to reverse its meaning. The original, from the sermon on the mount, says, "When thou doest alms, let not they left hand know what they right hand doeth." In context, it urges self-effacing charity. But today, as in the cartoon, the saying usually implies that it is prudent to distract attention from a bad deed by doing something sympathetic at the same time.

Other political cartoons came from today's newspapers and magazines; and we found humorous cartoons and comic strips with Biblical quotations or allusions, as well as news items about "good Samaritans" who picked up hitchhikers and about praise that should be rendered unto Sid Caesar. All these were made into transparencies that were thrown on the screen in the front of the room—sometimes for discussion, sometimes for a quick laugh, but always as a reminder of the many points at which the pupils come into contact with the Bible in daily life.

What were the results? The 41 pupils in my two eleventh grade classes had scored 22% on that initial test of 112 questions. At the halfway point—upon completion of the Old Testament—and again at the end of the nine-week unit, we had full-period review tests. The test on the Old Testament consisted of 267 questions, of which some pupils got only two or three wrong. The average was 86.5%. Eleven weeks later, one class was given the same test again, without warning. The average performance showed only a 16% loss in recall. For the 310 questions on the New Testament, the average performance was 92.3%; two pupils got them all: Cohen and O'Connell.

Much to our satisfaction and surprise, not one complaint from a parent or other member of the public came to the school principal, the department head, or the teacher. It was surprising if only because ours is a large school that draws from widely differing backgrounds. A teacher comes to know his pupils fairly well in the course of a school year. I know that there were in my classes devout Catholics; Reform, Conservative, and Orthodox Jews; Protestants of several denominations; and nonbelievers, from the listless to the atheistic. Those parents and clergymen from whom I did hear, either directly or indirectly, were enthusiastic about their children's new knowledge and ability to use it. A few parents good-naturedly protested that they themselves were being forced to study the Bible more intensely than ever before; they had either to defend themselves against the insufferable superiority of their more knowledgeable offspring or to help their children memorize what were becoming all too familiar quotations. Within the school considerable excitement was stimulated. The librarians reported with satisfaction that paperback excerpted Bibles were going fast and that the reference copies of Bibles, Bartlett's *Quotations,* and Biblical encyclopedias were in unusual and intelligent demand. Administrators and fellow faculty members told of Biblical quotations in student conversations. Other teachers expressed interest in using the same materials with their classes—just as, in my classes, I had used materials created by my colleagues.

The greatest source of satisfaction, of course, was the pupils themselves. Nearly every day some pupil made a discovery that he had to share with the teacher or the class. Movie, book, and song titles were especially popular. One boy even brought in some jokes that couldn't be understood without a knowledge of the Bible. He was proud to add a medium of Biblical allusion that the teacher had overlooked.

Results and Reactions. The pupils were given a chance to express themselves on paper. They wrote, in class, on the general topic "Studying the Bible," though they were not limited to a discussion of our course. Some took a look at the question of religion in the public schools, a subject we had never discussed. "I believe there is a difference between teaching and studying the Bible. To me teaching the Bible means looking at it in a religious sense, while studying the Bible means looking at it as a part of literature. I feel that teaching the Bible should not be done in public schools but studying the Bible should." The terms he uses are significant: he feels that he is learning rather than being taught. Another pupil wrote, "Studying the Bible could be most interesting if there weren't so much talk about reading it in schools today. I'm not saying that it isn't interesting, but I think that it would be more so if there weren't all this controversy over the separation of church and state. But by studying the Bible purely for the historical or literary point of view, we have overcome these reasons for not allowing the reading of the Bible." And a third: "Today especially, when the Bible—and whether or not to read it in schools—is seemingly forever in and out of the courts in our country, how can a person form an intelligent opinion if he doesn't even know what is inside the covers? Since the laws of our land are based in part on those in scripture, doesn't it seem reasonable that it would profit a person to study the book (the Bible) that has had such an effect on our country?"

Some told of their religious attitudes and initial reservations to our course on the Bible. "At the start of the course on the Bible I felt that it was not only purposeless to study it as part of literature, but also somehow morally wrong. . . . I no longer feel this way. . . . I am now immediately aware of Biblical reference in books that I have re-read many times without noticing the references." A representative of a different tradition had similar qualms: "My first thoughts of studying the King James Version put great doubt in my mind as to the place of the Bible in school. I received permission to read the Protestant Bible and really enjoyed my Bible course in school." A member of a third group expressed his introduction to the New Testament thus: "True, in class the principles of 'separation of church and state' and 'keep religion out of the public school' have been strictly adhered to. . . . Yet, in any Biblical study, exposure of the pupil to theological doctrine is in my opinion both inevitable and valuable. . . . Even the most unwilling student, having been thus exposed, would find it extremely difficult not to emerge with some idea of what the word 'Christian' ideologically connotes. I do not condemn this added knowledge; in fact, I greatly value it. I do not consider it necessary to discuss the merits for one living in the midst of a predominantly Christian country to have some understanding of Christianity. . . . Thus this study for me has been two dimensional. It has helped me to feel at home both in and out of the library."

Still others told stories that ranged widely in what they felt they had gained. "My mother is always quoting things she learned from her mother, and I can now answer her with one from the 'other side.' For instance, my sisters were quarreling; and my mother finally got mad when the fight came to blows, and she told the older one to 'turn the other cheek.' Immediately I jumped up and called out, 'An eye for an eye and a tooth for a tooth!' " Said a second "Not only does one seem more intelligent to others when one recognizes a Biblical reference, but it makes one (speaking for myself) feel educated and slightly different from every other junior in high school. It gives me a feeling of superiority and a thrill of pleasure to find that I read and understand more fully." A third tied the subject to a poem she was analyzing: "As Chapman opened the door to Homer for Keats, so the Bible can broaden the meaning of things we read, hear, and see. . . . Not only do I find places where the Bible passages are used, but I have opportunities to use some myself in conversation. In many cases my statements have not been effective, mainly because many people do not recognize the allusions. They are missing all that I used to miss."

Should the public school teach the Bible? A teacher wonders what his responsibility is to the student, to the community, to himself, and to the humanities.

Movies and Man's Humanity

Frank Manchel

It is quite clear that those who teach a humanities course are involved with the formidable task of helping humans to become human. Such competent teachers are rare indeed. Not only do they take their professional obligations seriously, but they also make it a point to be sensitive to the interests, concerns, preoccupations, and activities of the age in which they live. Furthermore, these dedicated individuals search for some understanding of how one becomes and acts human; that is, how to develop not only a person's respect for himself and for other people, but also his sensibilities for animals, institutions, entertainment, tradition, and values. For them it is what an individual feels about the world around him that forms, as Professor Joseph Church has pointed out, "the stuff and substance of his consciousness and keeps him oriented to reality."[1] So I want to begin by stressing the importance in a humanities course of the human concern with communicating not merely with facts, but with feelings.

From this point, we can move rather easily into the area of the arts. Who of us involved in the humanities has not witnessed the value of having students engage in an artistic experience? Which of us would deny that an individual's unique response to a work of art leads him to formulate his attitudes about the pressing issues of equality, justice, truth, morality, and responsibility? It is precisely because the work of art stimulates a student to think critically about his convictions that the humanities are so vital to the well-being of the world's mental health. And it is precisely because motion pictures are one of the most influential arts of our time that they rightly deserve a place in any humanities curriculum.

[1] Joseph Church, *Language and the Discovery of Reality* (New York: Vintage, 1961), p. 210.

Before we go any further together, I want to stress the profound distinction between an audio-visual aid and a commercial feature film. The former is a useful tool for presenting information and for stimulating learning. When intelligently applied to a particular situation, the a-v film is a very effective instrument. The feature film, however, is not an instrument for conveying factual knowledge. It is primarily concerned with entertainment and art. Both film types belong in the school. No one would deny that the EBF series on the humanities is an excellent example of what worthwhile materials can do to provide youngsters with an enriching class. Yet there are still teachers who have not recognized the value in showing movies like *Nothing but a Man, The Pawnbroker,* and *Odd Man Out.* This essay, therefore, is intended to emphasize the importance of having such feature films in the humanities class, not as visual aids but as works of art in their own right.

Another necessary distinction needs to be made between the schools of yesteryear and those of today. In bygone days our educational institutions were heavily print oriented. Books did their job well. But this is not true any longer. Print cannot meet all the demands of a new age. We live in a multi-media world. Within the past hundred years man, through his technological genius, has produced new languages of sight and sound. These revolutionary modes of communication have significantly influenced our human behavior, that is, they have helped shape our attitudes, opinions, and actions. In particular, the motion picture has had a marked effect upon today's young people. For example, Kenneth Clark, Executive Vice-President of the Motion Picture Association of America, issued these statistics in June of 1968:

It is estimated the average young person being graduated from high school today has seen 250 commercial feature films in theaters, and the equivalent of 7,500 two-hour feature films on television, for a total of 7,750 features. The time that the graduate has spent in the classroom in 12 years is by comparison, the equivalent of 5,400 feature films, or 2,350 fewer.[2]

Professor W. R. Robinson puts the case another way:

Anyone doubting the predominance of visual images as a vehicle for storytelling need only consider recent estimates that the typical college Freshman in 1966 had seen five hundred movies, twenty times the number of novels he had read, and had put in fifteen thousand hours watching television, more time than he had spent in school to that point. . . .These figures become yet more impressive when supplemented with those of film attendance, which ran [in 1965] around ten billion in the United States, the Soviet Union, and China alone. . . .The fact that images and movies have many uses besides storytelling simply adds gratuitous evidence in support of the observation that the life of the

[2]Kenneth Clark, "Foreward," *Exploring the Film* by William Kuhns and Robert Stanley (Dayton: Geo. A. Pflaum, 1968).

mind today receives its nourishment primarily from visual rather than verbal sources.[3]

In light of such statistics, in recognition of the need for students to examine their experiences and understand how they are affected by them, and in view of what the humanities program represents, movies have a definite place in the curriculum. If teachers want their students to grow emotionally and intellectually, then suitable motion pictures must be shown and discussed in the schools in order that young people can evaluate their critical faculties and increase their individual imagination.

So much then for the rationale for inclusion of movies in a humanities program. Let me turn now to a popular humanities theme—man's inhumanity to man—and suggest how motion pictures could be used.

Here, too, a word of caution needs to be sounded before we proceed any further. Basic to the problem of educating people to be human is the development of the mind's faculties, those intellectual and imaginative strengths without which no work of excellence can be achieved. Thus, in teaching about movies, the instructor needs to stress the distinction between seeing and perceiving a film. As the late Robert Gessner stated in his invaluable book *The Moving Image*: "Seeing is an optical capacity, while perception is an awareness, involving visual intelligence and visual sensitivity."[4] To put it another way, we study films in the schools to examine our reactions to specific situations and to increase our sensitivity to art, and not to memorize names, dates, and facts.

This is our setting: students who are interested in movies, teachers who encourage free responses to important works of art, and a thematic unit whose major objective is to involve young people in the world's perennial cultural and social issues.

Nothing but a Man is a wonderful movie to use in such a setting because its chief appeal lies in a young black man's frustrating attempts to achieve basic, human dignity in a Southern, white man's world and in the meaningful way adolescents react to his problems.[5] Furthermore, Duff Anderson's story provides a teacher with a unique opportunity to arouse students' sensibilities to the shameful conditions of black people in our society and, more important, to the fundamental problems of maturity and adult responsibility that each of us needs to understand in order that we can become "nothing but a man."

The movie begins by depicting Duff's life as a railroad section hand in a small town not far from Birmingham, Alabama. Although the job provides most of the men with a tolerable freedom and a tentative economic security, Duff wants more for himself than to be an irresponsible outsider in a white culture. Here is a

[3]W. R. Robinson, *Man and the Movies* (Baton Rouge: Louisiana State University, 1967), pp. 3-4.

[4]Robert Gessner, *The Moving Image: A Guide to Cinematic Literacy* (New York: E. P. Dutton & Company, 1968), p. 20.

[5]The film is available from Brandon Films, 200 West 57th Street, New York, 10019, and a study guide has been prepared, including pictures, script excerpts, and suggested bibliography.

notable place to start students developing a perspective about why some black men are cynical and willing to tolerate their substandard existence. A mature adult would understand that there are several layers of reality to the scarred men who move in the shanty world of poverty, pool halls, and prostitutes. The student, young, impressionable, and inexperienced, might not be able to look backward from the present predicament to what made these section hands what they are; for that matter, he might not be able to imagine ahead to his role in helping to remove a moral cancer in our nation. What better place to begin asking significant questions about the profile of black men today,[6] why Duff is different from the disgraceful Negro stereotypes of the past centuries, and how these differences are revealed cinematically.

But it is one thing to want to escape from the shiftless realm of the section gang, and quite another to make a place for yourself in the white man's bigoted community. Duff finds this out when he begins to court a Negro preacher's daughter. Although both Josie and he feel they can build a meaningful life together, Reverend Dawson objects. Their differences are clearly articulated when the two men meet in the Dawson living room. The preacher is worried about how Negroes should speak to white men, about getting better Negro schools, about going slowly in integration, and about maintaining the proper amount of humility in a white, Southern town. Duff, on the other hand, cannot understand why there have to be separate schools for colored children, how a black man can live honestly yet avoid trouble, and why it is so important for black people to go to church for guidance. As he says, "seems to me us colored do a whole lot of church goin'. It's the whites that need it real bad." Consequently, Duff, in order to become a man, has to leave his friends and ask his girl to choose between her family and her lover. This particular episode requires a responsible discussion about Reverend Dawson's position. It is not enough to dismiss him as an "Uncle Tom." And an intelligent teacher will oppose any tendency to reduce the issues to clichés and superficial condemnations.

While Josie is making up her mind, Duff goes to Birmingham to visit his illegitimate son and his own drunken, one-armed father. The environment in which the child is being brought up the emotions between the two grown men, and the ugly conditions under which black people are forced to live in the ghettos of the large city should awaken some strong sense of repulsion in the audience. Heaven help us if they don't.

Seeing the possibilities that are open to him if he remains rootless, Duff decides to marry Josie and try to build a better future for himself. The newlyweds move into a decrepit shack in the restricted Negro area, and Duff gets a job in a sawmill. (Here is an excellent opportunity to contrast the squalor of the Andersons' initial marital life with the intensity of their love; hopefully, students will realize the horror that many decent human beings are subjected to.)

---

[6] James A. Banks, "A Profile of the Black American: Implications for Teaching," *College, Composition and Communication*, XIX : 5 (December, 1968), 288-296.

It is not long before Duff notices the difference between the relative independence of the wanderer's life and the servile role expected of black men in a white-controlled community. When he questions why things have to be that way, one spineless Negro worker turns Duff in to the white foreman for being a union organizer. But the supervisor gives him a chance to stay on the job; "I just want you to tell these boys here you didn't mean what you said 'bout stickin' together 'n all." Duff is too much of a man to sacrifice his honor for a moral eunuch, and so he loses his job.

Now Duff becomes a marked man in the white world, and the only jobs open to a "troublemaker" are bellhop, delivery boy, or cotton picker. Out of his own sense of shame for what he is and what his son-in-law is fighting against, Reverend Dawson gets Duff a job as a grease-monkey in a filling station. Even here, the scum of the streets try to degrade him with racial insults and smutty comments about Josie. After showing remarkable restraint, the black man answers the human trash. The cowards, in turn, threaten the filling station's owner with the loss of his business unless he gets rid of the "white-eyed nigger!" Once more, Duff refuses to compromise with his integrity. Although many of the situations may appear conventional to enlightened individuals in the audience, the naturalistic visual effects of racism do shock the overwhelming majority of unconscious Americans to a vivid awareness of the deplorable situations throughout this country. This particular motion picture serves as an excellent *beginning* for developing student awareness about such matters as Duff's options, a boss' responsibilities to his employees and to his family, and a society that not only allows such conditions to exist, but in too many instances encourages them.

In anger, confusion, and frustration, Duff abandons his home and his pregnant wife. He travels to see his father, but finds the pathetic forty-odd-year-old man fatally ill. Leaving behind him a wasted life, Will Anderson's pitiful span of years and his death suggest to Duff what he has to expect if he does not have the courage to fight for his rights, regardless of the difficulties involved. So he returns to Josie, taking with him this time the young boy whom up to now he has denied. Whether or not Duff succeeds remains an open-ended question. But the fact is that he is now enough of a man to try.

Mainly, *Nothing but a Man* is entertainment at its best. The film-makers *re-create* the sordid relationships that can exist between whites and blacks, parents and children, husbands and wives. The movie *diverts* attention away from ourselves and our personal problems and involves us in the difficulties of other human beings for which we must share a responsibility. And the motion picture *reminds* the audience that all men are entitled to human happiness.

The Pawnbroker also serves as a reminder of our responsibilities and the sordidness of the world in which we live.[7] This time, however, the audience views the effect of man's inhumanity to man from the perspective of one who had happiness, had it torn from him, and has become less than human.

Director Sidney Lumet's movie skillfully illuminates the consequences of

---

[7]The film is available from Audio Film Center, 34 MacQuesten Parkway South, New York 10550.

cruelty and injustice on everyone involved in mankind. But it does not excuse anyone from facing up to life. In fact, Lumet has argued that the film's major theme is "that regardless of how brutal life is, one must go on."[8] Even before the screen credits are given, the contrast between what was and what is becomes clear to the audience. We are shown a country picnic (projected in slow motion to signify the past), specifically to illustrate the blissful existence of Professor Sol Nazerman, his wife, their two young children, and his parents. Suddenly, the shots are frozen. Quickly the speed and scene shift to the present, twenty-five years later. The differences in Sol Nazerman, now a pawnbroker, are startling. Visiting his dead wife's obnoxious and vain relatives in a suburban area, he sits rather than stands, listens rather than talks, dissuades rather than encourages. Not only do we realize that the director's method of flash cutting will serve to contrast the past with the present, but also we are alerted to an unusual man's loneliness.

The story's main action takes place in the present, set in the milieu of Spanish Harlem. Most of the attention is focused on this wretched Jewish pawnbroker who has only physically survived the horrors of a Nazi concentration camp while his loved ones have been brutally exterminated. His spirit, his will to live, seem broken. He apathetically conducts his affairs, insensitive to the world around him. He closets himself in an area that he despises, works for a black racketeer whom he detests, and considers the pathetic people who frequent his shop as scum, creatures that just exist. Gone are his former beliefs in religion, science, politics, and philosophy. Now all that interests him is money. Talking with his apprentice, who looks up to the older man, Sol bitterly explains what life is all about: "Money is everything."

But no man can exist for very long half alive, blotting out his past and his basic human feelings, and Sol Nazerman is constantly reminded of this fact. When he gives a minimal loan to a desperate pregnant girl forced to pawn her worthless engagement ring, he cannot forget how once he witnessed helpless prisoners extend their arms across barbed wire fences while faceless Nazis barbarically pulled the rings from the lifeless fingers.[9] When Sol passes a school yard where a street gang is savagely beating a defenseless boy, he cannot blot out the memory of his best friend helplessly pinned to a barbed wire fence being chewed to death by merciless dogs while Nazerman remained incapable of doing anything about it. When a frightened prostitute attempts to seduce the pawnbroker by baring her breasts, he cannot repress the image of being forced to watch his hopeless wife waiting to be raped by a Nazi officer. A subway ride triggers his mind, and he cannot avoid recalling the boxcar where forlorn prisoners accidently trampled his son to death because he was just too weak to carry the boy any further. Time and time again, both Sol Nazerman and the audience come to sense that a man cannot escape his past, and that as long as he is alive he must learn, whatever the pain, to live with the intolerable.

[8]Sidney Lumet, "Keep Them on the Hook," *Films and Filming,* 11:1 (October 1964), p. 17.
[9]For a valuable examination of the film's technical strengths and weaknesses, read the Spring 1966 issue of *Film Heritage.*

There is a danger not only in a man becoming apathetic, but also in his acting apathetically toward those he meets. "Thus," as Gordon Gow comments, "the woman who would help the pawnbroker is debilitated, and the apprentice who would gain from the pawnbroker's help is thwarted and driven to crime."[10] Students have much to gain from discussing the nature of moral decay and its effect on everyone else.

Adolescents might also benefit by comparing and contrasting the two films. For example, certain characters in both movies try to copy the white man's values: Reverend Dawson seeks middle-class respectability; and the apprentice, Jesus, brute power and material success. It is interesting to look critically at the visually white emphasis in both men's homes, especially as symbolic representations of their lives. It is also useful to compare the manifold expectations of all the young men, particularly those of Duff and Jesus. Each wants to improve his position, forcing a break with friends and traditional patterns. Though the values are different, the consequences are evident. Another similarity is the basic concern that the main characters have for the welfare of others. Both men go through a series of painful experiences before they are able to accept adult responsibility. Duff becomes aware of his maturity only when he recognizes his obligations to his son and to his wife. Sol begins to be reborn as a man only when he recognizes his role in the criminal life of Spanish Harlem and when he feels some emotion for his apprentice. By examining these kinds of contrasts and comparisons, adolescents might cultivate a better understanding of themselves and of a suffering humanity.

Because of Sir Carol Reed's Belfast setting, his audience may find *Odd Man Out* a more difficult film to become involved with.[11] But this sensitively created screen masterpiece about a hunted and fatally shot revolutionary graphically portrays the issues connected with man's inhumanity to man. The cinematic story of a wounded man's fatal flight through the dark streets of a city and how he affects the lives and fortunes of those he meets is a classic examination of society's need to develop charitable feelings. The late and famous film critic James Agee wrote:

This night city is civilization; on that intricate stage a wide variety of people try to help or hinder or capture the fugitive. Many of them are selfless in relation to some idea of passion or conception of their own duty; not one is capable of the selfless charity it would require to deal with this hounded, doomed soul purely for its own sake.[12]

What more useful and valuable example, therefore, can we have in a humanities course than an artistic movie designed to examine the pressing issues of morality, justice, truth, love, and knowledge?

[10] Gordon Gow, "The Pawnbroker," *Films and Filming* 13:3 (December 1966), p. 6.
[11] The film is available from Contemporary Films, 267 West 25th Street, New York, New York 10001.
[12] James Agee, *Agee on Film, Vol. I: Reviews and Comments* (New York: Grosset and Dunlop, 1967), p. 268.

In using Johnny McQueen's tragic steps to expose man's relationships with his fellow man, Reed begins by showing the fatal robbery where the hero accidentally kills a factory employee, is mortally wounded, and then cowardly abandoned by his companions. Up to the unexpected murder, the question of the group's cause and justification for crime is avoided. The issue of right or wrong is purposely ignored. Now, however, Johnny has gone beyond political disagreements, and each person he comes in contact with must decide what to do about him.

First, the members of the organization are faced with the problem of jeopardizing their activities or trying to rescue their leader. The issues of loyalty, honor, friendship, and courage are argued, played off against each other, and finally carried to their various consequences.

Second, the law is faced with the responsibility of bringing a criminal to justice, yet at the same time understanding the hunted man's anguish and his loved ones' futile rescue efforts. As a result, the police are sympathetically depicted. The head constable warns Katherine, Johnny's girl, to stay out of this hopeless situation. "He belongs to the law. That is the truth. Admit it. If you don't, and if you stir a hand to help him get away from us, you'll be in trouble."[13] After the police leave, Grannie also warns the young girl, reinforcing the positive aspects of the law. She explains that this tragedy has happened over and over again. "I have seen the men go out looking like he did, and I have seen the women set off to look for them. But they never found them. . . .What is the sense in runnin' towards trouble when you know you can't mend it?" Nevertheless, Katherine goes. The question is—should she? It is not easily answered. Although the police are eventually proven right, Reed shows their very humane intentions.

Third, everyday people face the moral dilemma of what to do about Johnny's frantic efforts to escape. Two ladies find him in the gutter and then bandage his wounds; a cabdriver unwittingly drives him through the police barricades, and then leaves him to go in search of help; a barge captain agrees to hold his boat until midnight so that Johnny can escape; and a tavern keeper hides the fugitive in order to avoid trouble with either the police or the organization.

But the strangest human lot of all are the three twisted souls who try in the end to use Johnny to further their own interests. An ex-doctor cares for the man's wounds only as an excuse to demonstrate his former skills. A demented artist props the weak fugitive in a studio chair so that he can paint the sufferings of mankind. And a weasel of a man maneuvers Katherine and Father Tom into promising him money in return for information about Johnny's whereabouts.

Each one fails in his own way to provide charity for the sufferings of a fellow human being. Thus, in his desperate attempt to escape, Johnny McQueen comes in contact with the interests, concerns, and preoccupations of those involved in society. In so doing, he shows us something of ourselves, and we are the better for it.

[13] All quotations are based on the printed script in *Three British Screen Plays: Brief Encounter, Odd Man Out, Scott of the Antarctic,* edited by Roger Manvell (London: Methuen & Co., 1950).

Unlike *Nothing but a Man* and *The Pawnbroker,* which emphasize their themes through the actions of a single, main character, *Odd Man Out* underplays the individual problem in order to remind us of mankind itself. But in so doing, Reed also demonstrates how important art is in making a motion picture. Although the other two movies have much to recommend them thematically, *Odd Man Out* is a director's triumph of sight and sound.

This brings me to the final point in this essay: the necessity to understand the relationship between art and entertainment. So far the emphasis has been on plot, theme, characterization, setting, and related literary values. But a motion picture contains much more than these traditional entertainment features. It also involves a skillful blending of visual and audio effects, a sensitive eye for composition and projection, and an awareness of how the actual film experience can be meaningfully created. I have no quarrel with those who wish to begin their humanistic studies by engaging students' free responses to the movie experience. But I refuse to accept the argument that nothing else needs to be done. Quite the contrary is true. Adolescents need to be helped to develop critical standards. Notice, I did not say critical judgments. Students have to learn how to ask significant questions and not how to passively accept authority. This will require their knowing something about film history and technique in order to better appreciate the differences between what is being done and what can be done.

And as far as teachers are concerned, they must realize that every worthwhile educational experience broadens and enriches our lives. They must see that the advantages of using movies in a humanities program are as richly diverse as humanity itself. By approaching their responsibilities honestly, I have every hope that they will offer fresh and expanded evidence of why movies are one of the most marvelous art forms of our age.

The Humanities Course: Instructional Resources

in the Teaching of Art History

Robert M. Diamond

The teaching of art history—painting, sculpture and architecture—is one of the major components of the Humanities course at the University of Miami. For most of the students the course consists of one television lecture, two seminars, and one two-hour writing laboratory each week; enrollment in both the freshman and sophomore years totals about 2,000 at each level. Content includes a broad survey of literature, drama, philosophy, music as well as art history.

From the inception of the program emphasis has been placed on developing an effective and interesting learning sequence. From 1963 to 1966 the Instructional Resources Center of the Office for the Study of Instruction with the Humanities

Department explored the entire range of new teaching tools and techniques. With both resources and a support staff available, the key question became: what was the most effective and efficient manner in which each subject could be introduced to so large a number of students?

The problem was particularly critical in the art history area since a majority of the faculty had their teaching strength in literature and therefore could not be expected to provide maximum instruction in art history without assistance. Furthermore, specialists in the area although present on campus, were not available to devote major portions of their time to the Humanities program.

This article will attempt to describe the various applications of the instructional media within the art sequences of the course. It should be noted that throughout the project a major effort has been made to provide the faculty with both maximum resources and maximum flexibility of choice. Use of the materials within the seminar was always left to the instructor.

A. Overhead Transparencies. The overhead projector has, in recent years, been the most rapidly growing instructional tool in the United States.[1] Teachers find it easy to use, extremely portable and effective. During the three-year period, more than 200 new transparencies were designed for use in the Humanities courses with approximately 40 relating directly to the teaching of art. The majority of these transparencies were designed specifically to promote discussion or help answer questions within the seminar sessions. To cover the 80 or more seminar sections that meet twice weekly in these courses, duplicate copies of transparencies were made and complete sets placed in each of the eight seminar rooms. To further expedite use, overhead and slide projectors were kept permanently in each room.

The art transparencies were of two basic types:

1. *Comparative Sculpture:* Each of the 11 transparencies in this series was developed to illustrate and compare two or more types of sculpture. On the transparency each piece of sculpture was identified by title, approximate date of construction, and the period of art to which it belongs. To assist the teacher, additional information concerning dimensions, art medium and present location of each work along with some detailed analysis for use with discussions was provided in the instructor's resources guide developed for each course.[2]

The particular pieces of statuary included in this series were chosen for two basic reasons: (1) they exemplified many of the general characteristics of the type they represent; and (2) they exhibited subtleties of style which could be analyzed by those instructors wishing to approach the pieces as individual works of art. To highlight similarities and/or differences, the pieces on a single transparency usually represented like characteristics in like situations.

[1] Eleanor P. Godfrey, "Factors Associated with School District Adoption of Five Instructional Techniques," Bureau of Social Science Research (Washington, D. C.) 1966.

[2] A more detailed description of the faculty guide will be found in "Instructional Materials within the Seminar"–Report No. 18, Robert M. Diamond, Office for the Study of Instruction, University of Miami, July 1965.

2. *Architecture and Design:* Transparencies in this series illustrate floor plans, cross sections, illustrations of various types of columns as well as comparative styles of design. Also included is a single transparency with overlays showing the step-by-step historical development of the Greek Theater.

B. Slides. For each course a series of slide kits was also prepared. In the process of developing these kits, an attempt was made to provide the highest quality possible. Rather than photographing reproductions in books, the University was able, for the most part, to secure slides made directly from the original art work. The sources from which these slides were purchased included major museums and galleries in both the United States and Europe. It should be mentioned that there are two problems inherent in purchasing slides directly from foreign sources: (1) several months are usually required for delivery, and (2) orders are sometimes filled inaccurately.

If the cost of purchasing multiple copies of slides directly from the original source proved prohibitive, a single copy was obtained and duplicates made from it. Often, however, top quality slides could be purchased for prices well below the cost of duplication (as low as 17 cents). In several cases, double frame filmstrips were purchased and then cut and mounted as 2 x 2 slides. By this technique, it was possible to obtain excellent slides for less than 15 cents each.

The slides themselves fall into three basic types—entire picture, entire picture with related details, and reconstructed details or diagrams of compositions.

In the instructor's guide, faculty are provided with the name of the artist and the title of all the slides, plus any additional information on the reconstructed details and diagrams of composition that might be helpful. When known, size, medium, and present location of all works of art reproduced in the kits also are included. For much of the project a complete set of slide kits was placed in each seminar room. Later, because of the disappearance of several kits, a check-out system was instituted.

C. Television. Over the course of several years the use of television has seen the greatest amount of change. At the beginning of the project, students viewed two television lectures a week. These were devoted primarily to philosophy, literature and music. In 1965, the number of lectures was reduced to one with emphasis being placed on the four areas which the faculty felt could be most effectively covered by this technique, namely, art history, drama and music.

At first, the entire area of art was relegated to television with the seminars serving solely for follow-up discussions. This approach slowly changed as greater use was made of the art gallery, the overhead transparencies and the slide kits. During the spring semester of 1966, for example, students in the sophomore course viewed outstanding lectures on post-impressionism, engraving and modern painting. In these instances, emphasis was placed either on demonstrating a specific art technique or presenting an outstanding lecturer who otherwise would have been unavailable to the large number of students involved. It is the hope of the department that, in time, all television lectures will be of this high quality.

It should be noted that in the Learning and Instructional Resources Center of the University of Miami, it is possible to use colored slides within a television presentation. However, this use is somewhat limited by the fact that vertical slides cannot be effectively used and that many faculty members prefer not to mix color and black and white. Since six large lecture rooms may be viewing a lecture at the same time, the use of colored slides requires six copies of each slide which presents both scheduling and budgetary problems.

D. Programed Instruction in the Art Gallery. The one approach that has perhaps created more excitement than any other was the recent experiment in which students were programed through a learning sequence in the University's art gallery. Here, students, working independently, were taught fundamental concepts about Renaissance art in an extremely effective and efficient manner. The objectives of the approximately 25-minute branching program were achieved, the students were enthusiastic and an additional resource was used advantageously without increasing the work load of the faculty.[3] As a result of this project, an entirely new approach to teaching certain aspects of art within the Humanities program becomes available.

The Humanities course at the University of Miami, although fairly unique, is not exceptional in its aims or in its content. What is unusual is the concerted effort to utilize a wide variety of instructional tools and techniques in the particular teaching configuration that will be most efficient and most effective for each subject area. Problems still exist but the program has come a long way from the original course which was nothing more than learning sequences built around television. Today an attempt is being made to combine all the available resources—faculty, art gallery, slides, transparencies, television, program instruction, live plays and concerts—with the various teaching configurations—large group presentations, seminar discussions and independent study—into a quality program for a large number of students.

The Quest for Values in a Changing World

Bernard S. Miller

John Patrick's play, *The Teahouse of the August Moon,* deals with the fortunes and misfortunes of two U. S. Army of Occupation officers, Colonel Purdy III and Captain Fisby, as they try to build a school house in Okinawa. Captain Fisby, an associate professor of humanities, has failed miserably in every position he has held while in the military service. When Fisby complains that perhaps he was not cut out to be a solider, Colonel Purdy explodes:

Purdy: Captain—none of us was cut out to be a solider. But we do the job. We adjust. We adapt. We roll with the punch and bring victory home in our teeth. Do you know what I was before the war?
Fisby: (hesitates unhappily)—A football coach?
Purdy: I was the Purdy Paper Box Company of Pottawatomie. What did I

---

[3] A detailed description of this experiment can be found in "Programed Instruction in an Art Gallery"—Report No. 27, Robert M. Diamond, Office for the Study of Instruction, University of Miami, April 1966.

know about foreigners? But my job is to teach these natives the meaning of Democracy if I have to shoot every one of them.

We can be amused and reject this simple-minded, military method of establishing democratic values, but when values are considered in our schools, too often the teaching is based on compulsion rather than commitment. Because we are older, and stronger, and society has decreed that education is compulsory, our students come to school, they listen, they learn, they regurgitate the facts we have made them memorize for our examinations, and they leave.

Far too many of our captive students pass courses and pass through courses without becoming involved in the meaning of the subject. We place so much stress on what students have to learn that they have too little time to discover what they themselves want, believe, and value. George Santayana commented years ago that never before have men known so many facts and been master of so few principles.

The problem is not new. Early in the seventeeth century Comenius protested against the way in which teachers try to impose values by preaching:

Most teachers are at pains to place in the earth plants instead of seeds, and trees instead of shoots, since, instead of starting with the fundamental principles, they place before their pupils a chaos of diverse conclusions. . . . [The schools] have taken no trouble to open the fountain of knowledge that is hidden in the scholars but instead have watered them with water from other sources.

How can we "open the fountain of knowledge" and have students recognize that values which have stood the test of time have meaning for their own generation? Does it make sense to believe that in a rapidly changing world, some values should not be changed? What kinds of learning experience will encourage young people to act as though human beings are closer to the angels than to the animals?

I believe with those who say that values are not taught, they are caught; I subscribe to the proposition that if we wish to develop character in our students, we should have a large supply of it ourselves.

Virtually every school system is prepared to present a list of goals, a statement of beliefs and values, whenever the question is raised. Values we have aplenty. Lists of school goals and values will be found in the teacher and student handbooks and often inside an impressive frame in the main school corridor. What are these values? Generally in first place are the skill values of reading, writing, and arithmetic. Such values as a belief in the United States of America, a faith in democracy, respect for property and human rights, tolerance, good health, and character development are also to be found in most school philosophies.

Our school systems can make a tolerable case for our success in developing skill values, but the headlines in newspapers each day provide painful testimony that both north and south of the Mason-Dixon Line, the commitment to ethical values is, at best, inconsistent.

Both the Declaration of Independence and the Constitution of the United

States stress the sacredness of life and liberty as hallmarks of humanity. One would suppose that after so many years these values would be as much a part of every American as breathing out and breathing in. Laws are a legitimate way to express the moral conscience of a community. But to write our beliefs into laws, or to inscribe them on the facades of public buildings is not enough. I quote from the trial proceedings in Jackson, Mississippi, as jurors were selected to determine whether Byron De La Beckwith, a fervid segregationist, murdered Medgar Evers, Mississippi field secretary for the N.A.A.C.P.

"Do you think," asked the prosecutor, "it is a crime for a white man to kill a nigger in Mississippi?" The prospective juror was silent. "What was his answer?" asked the judge. "Nothing, Judge," said the prosecutor. "He's thinking it over."

Emerson has observed that "a man is what he thinks about all day long." The values we acquire come not from memorization of words or events; they come from living and identifying with people around us. Young people in particular, who seem to be attracted to the latest thing, need models of greatness, models of what man at his best can be. Too many girls consider it a sign of womanhood when they dye their eyelids green, their nails red, and their hair yellow. Too many boys think they are men when they drive too fast, drink too much, and need a shave. We may bemoan such surface values, but for some girls and boys, these are the adult cultural images with which they identify.

Nor will young people pay more than lip service to a value system that permits no questions to be raised, that insists that the only purpose in study is to learn and to obey. The truth may set us free, but what is truth for one generation may be old-fashioned nonsense for another. Values to be viable can not be embalmed and set apart for reverent worship. When a new generation in a changing world is unable to have a choice in determining values, the values lose their vitality. Young people will not readily accept a life of death.

Last year a group of distinguished professors assembled at Boston University for a symposium on values. On and on, and round and round went the talks. Seeking to bring the discussion down to earth, the chairman asked: "Is it possible to say, 'These are the values that we should be reaching for in schools'? And, if so, how do we know we are working on first rather than secondary priority values?" Professor Theodore Brameld, assessing the temper of his colleagues and the times in which we live, replied, "That is an exceedingly embarrassing question, and I suspect that we will do everything we can to avoid answering it."

Finding general agreement on what values to stress and what to subordinate is an endless task. Indeed, some will even object to so-called noncontroversial values like good health. The story is told of a teacher who got downwind in a rural Kentucky schoolhouse, took a short whiff, and promptly sent Farmer Brown's two children home for a bath. Back came the children with a note from their Pa. "I send my kids to school to be taught. Your job is to teach them, not to smell them."

I intend neither to teach nor to smell values with you. Instead, I propose to give examples of classes in which students seem to have gained a sense of understanding about themselves, their past, and their present. In diverse but meaningful ways the important questions posed by Dr. Charles R. Keller, the director of the John Hay Fellows Program, were being asked: "Who am I? What is the meaning of life? Where have I come from? Where am I going? In what do I believe? Why?" Teachers in these classes were more interested in involving than impressing the students, and in the process the students discovered values for themselves.

We go first to a new high school in the San Francisco Bay Area. In this school, teachers and students in English and history have been scheduled back-to-back so that, when appropriate, the English and history teachers can work together for a double period with the same students, or they can divide the class and the lessons into other combinations. The nature of the work determines the organizational pattern from day to day, not the other way around.

On the day of my visit, the two teachers and 30 eager students were having a grand time discussing symbolism in Hawthorne's *The Scarlet Letter.* "Why," asked the English teacher, "did Hawthorne choose the name Pearl for Hester's illegitimate daughter?" Answers ranged from a detailed explanation of how oysters create pearls as a result of an irritation, to the comment that Hawthorne wanted Pearl's children to have a mother-of-pearl.

When the dialogue moved from symbolism to Calvinism, the history teacher related the concept of justice in *The Scarlet Letter* to the stern Puritan ethic of the Massachusetts Bay Colony. Not one student could find any kind words for the strict, predeterministic, Calvinist philosophy. After the members of the class had finished congratulating themselves for living in our more enlightened twentieth century, the students heard the following:

Perhaps you are right when you all insist that the Puritan ethic, with its alternatives of Hell or Heaven, with its demotion of man's will to a subordinate role, with an eternity hanging upon each act, with no possibility of salvation after sin, did present a truly tragic way of life. You say that today we are better adjusted, broad minded, relativistic. But our lives lack the greatness of a tragic dimension. Today an analyst can explain the behavior of Hester, and Dimmesdale, and they can be exonerated from blame for their actions, but somehow the world seems a little stale, flat, and unprofitable, a world in which actions, instead of having eternity hinge upon them, have no consequences.

The silence in the room could be felt as the teacher continued:

If Puritan beliefs make for repressed and frustrated human beings, I invite you to formulate an ethical system which would be an improvement. In an essay you will be writing on this theme, be certain to explain why our modern world, so air-conditioned, neon-lit, and superhygienic, has led to so much frustration, repression, and violence.

Then from the English teacher, "Would you want to spend some time on ways in which to approach a problem in writing an essay of this kind?" Thirty voices chorused "yes," and the class moved enthusiastically into composition work. In this class the teachers were succeeding in opening the eyes and minds of students, not just in loosening their tongues.

We move from the West Coast to an up-state New York high school English class where the students were required to read and report on four novels from the Victorian period. Some students, of course, consider any reading contrary to the child labor laws. One student handed in a report which showed that she had gained more than knowledge. Here, in part, is what she wrote:

These novels have shown different people in different situations. They have explored the cruelty of children, the ignorance of so-called intelligent adults, the love between two young people, the distrust and dislike between brothers and sisters, and the disgust that certain types of people inspire. . . .These novels have been helpful to me; they have shown me how not to raise a child and how to understand and tolerate younger children. Possibly more important, however, is the idea that is produced in these novels; the idea that I may be very much like these adults.

And then the teen-ager made an observation that illustrates how the arts can give us maturity beyond our years. She wrote:

The most important aspect of these novels is self knowledge. In the difficult process of growing up, getting to know oneself is the hardest, most frightening, and saddest experience in life. These novels have helped me to see myself and have shown me some of the possible things I can do with my life.

We shift from high school to elementary school students and to a seven-year-old reading *The Wizard of Oz*. Suddenly the child exclaims, "Golly, I think the Scarecrow does have a brain. He's the one who thinks of all the ideas." The teacher replied that this was an interesting thought and then asked what she thought of the tin woodsman's search for a heart. The child looked for a moment and then, you could see the flash, it was so plain, "I think he already has a heart," she said. "He feels sorry for the animals, and cries." And then the girl went on, exploring the idea further in relation to the Lion, and the whole group combined. "Dorothy's friends," concluded the girl, "are like some of my own friends who are always complaining about not having things that they really have." Observed the teacher: "If a seven-year-old can discover, explore things, and make value judgments in this fashion, how absurd we are as teachers to interpret the reading for them."

In contrast, I recall visiting a first-grade class and listening attentively as the boys and girls had a wonderful time identifying the hours, half-hours, and 15-minute periods on a large cardboard clock. When the students wished to go on to identify individual minutes and seconds, the teacher brought the lesson to a halt. "You learn about minutes and seconds in the second grade," she said.

We are now in Rochester, New York, where students are discussing Sir Francis Bacon's essay on revenge. The teacher quotes Bacon, "Revenge is a kind of wild justice," "Perhaps," suggests the teacher, "justice is a kind of deliberate or rational or conscious revenge. Perhaps justice, or at any rate punishment, cannot be justified at all with complete certainty." The students talked about utilitarian and retributionist theories of punishment, the efficacy of punishment, and when they were mad enough either at the teacher or at one another, they were told to start writing. "When the papers were returned the next day," the teacher has written, "they were not superb, but they did show a genuine effort to think through a knotty, philosophical problem."

In Garfield High School, Seattle, Washington, the concepts of justice, loyalty, and human values are approached by comparative studies of how other civilizations and cultures dealt with these issues. To illustrate that what seems to be justice is not always justice, the students are shown the films, *Les Miserables* and *The Ox-Bow Incident*. Then they read what Plato, John Milton, John Marshall, and Judge Learned Hand had to say about justice. After their smug preconceptions have been thoroughly upset, the students write a paper on their concept of justice.

On March 13, 1964, *Life* magazine ran a feature article entitled "The Rewards Of A Great Teacher." The great teacher cited was Mrs. Henrietta Miller, chairman of the history department in Chicago's Senn High School, and (of course!) a John Hay Fellow. Here are quotations from two of the 150 students she greets each day in her five classes:

I hate this class, I positively hate it; it's too interesting—it makes me work.
She's always asking 'Why?' 'Why?' That makes you do the same thing to your fellow students.

Reports the education editor of *Life;*

Mrs. Miller refuses to go over the factual "story," as she calls it. "Why should I spend my time giving students what they can get in books?" she asks. "I always take the position that we are learning together and I must never slip into the role they expect me to play—the superhuman being who can meet all their questions with the truth." Instead, Mrs. Miller fires back her own questions.

Three teachers in different school systems in the West Cleveland area noticed that high school students in their respective schools were brought together only for athletic events. "Why not for academic events as well?" they asked. And then they acted. Two hundred eleventh-grade students from five high schools—Bay Village, Berea, Fairview, Midpark, and Rocky River—were invited to attend an afternoon and evening series of Humanities Seminars. The first session was on Thomas Jefferson. Prior to the meeting, the students read suggested material by and about Jefferson. At the seminar the students heard a Jeffersonian scholar lecture on Jefferson, and then they divided into groups of ten for dinner and discussion. The second Humanities Seminar was on "Thoreau," the third on "The Role of the American Artist."

So enthusiastic were these juniors about the Humanities Seminars, that this year, as seniors, when they heard that the new Humanities Seminars would be limited to juniors, the students insisted on starting a Humanities Seminar for seniors. When I attended the first Humanities Seminar for seniors in October, I heard a philosopher, Professor Alburey Castell, talk on "The Humanities Give You The Modern World." The students had read C. P. Snow's *Two Cultures,* and the discussion on the conflict between science and humanism, and between man as a maker or a product of destiny, was both spirited and worthwhile.

"Not to know the principles and presuppositions on which we act," said Professor Castell, "is to be naive." I am happy to report that many of the seniors cited examples to show that human beings were not ruled entirely by outside forces and pressures. They were inclined to say about man, not with Pavlov, "How like a dog," but with Hamlet, "How like a God."

You may comment that these examples involved students from relatively secure communities where the desire to learn, to think, to succeed in school by really trying, is self evident. How about students who come to school with no love for learning, who are our "sit-ins" and at an early date become our "drop-outs"?

I take you to such a school and to a classroom filled with so-called slow learners. The teacher was unaware of my pending visit until the principal brought me to her classroom door. I asked if I could observe her class. She was less than overjoyed. "This is a very slow class," she protested. "We are not doing anything you would find of interest." But my foot was in the door and I would not be moved. Reluctantly, she allowed me to enter.

More than 30 students were in the room. And what students! One glance and I knew that here were boys and girls not fated for intellectual greatness. What were they doing? Reading *Huckleberry Finn.* The teacher asked why Huck's father smashed the furniture in the room and tore to shreds the clean clothing given to him by the kindly judge. Several hands went up. One burly youngster indicated that the old man was drunk and didn't know what he was doing. "Why would Mark Twain put such an episode in the story?" asked the teacher. Again hands went up. "He just wanted to show that getting nice stuff ain't enough. You have to learn to appreciate good things or you'll go right back to being a bum." The boy who gave that answer will not go to college—he may not even graduate from high school—but I like to believe that reading and discussing *Huckleberry Finn* in this class has helped him understand himself and, his own world a little better; he has become a better human being.

In a letter we later received from this teacher she told more about her program:

We use no grammar text, realizing that the teaching of formal grammar to slow students is frustrating to both them and the teacher. Their retention is limited and their grasp of the material practically nil. Instead we give them many short writing assignments and concentrate on correct spelling, complete sentences, and interesting presentation. Both good and poor papers are duplicated for class discussion, and the emphasis is put on finding something to praise. Some reading is done in class. As you know, if the teacher can be excited by a book, she can pass this excitement along to the pupil and make him eager to read ahead.

Here is a teacher who exposes a student's intelligence rather than his ignorance. She knows with E. E. Cummings that one times one is still one and she makes certain her students will come in contact with ideas and values that will help them grow.

We are now in an overcrowded classroom on Long Island. Most of the boys are majors in auto mechanics, the girls in office practice and beauty culture. They are reading an abridged version of John Steinbeck's *The Pearl.* In answer to the teacher's question, "What does *The Pearl* mean to you?" one student replies: "All of us wish for a pearl. But I think he's trying to show that you don't get all you want even if you have a pearl." And from another student this summary: "Some things are more important than making money."

In an industrial community in central Ohio, a history teacher helped eighth-grade students as they read haltingly, almost painfully, from Plato's *The Apology.* The way some of the words were pronounced would make Socrates wish to die again. "Was Socrates a nut to prefer death to freedom?" the teacher asked. One student observed that Socrates would rather die than switch. Most of the answers indicated that the students understood why, at times, a human being may set greater value on law than on life.

In the Fall 1964 issue of *The English Leaflet* is an article by two teachers describing their humanities program for non-college-bound sophomores. Here is not the usual watered-down curriculum; instead, we find the emphasis is on challenging intellectual assignments, on substance rather than survey, as the means of affecting the students' self-image. The teachers have written:

How do we know what the students learn from the course? Term tests and final exams ... tell us whether the pupil has anything to say, whether his imagination and intellect have in any way been aroused. . . .Most important are the questions a student begins to ask us. . . . If he sees that the ideas we discuss are interesting enough, relevant to him, thought provoking, and worth asking questions about, we think he is moving toward our goal. For his questions show when his attitude toward school, education, and himself are changing. We hope the course opens new possibilities for the pupil as an individual, that it begins to affect his aspirations, taste, attitude, and self-awareness so that eventually he may acquire satisfaction in his work and in his leisure. We are hoping for much but we have no right to strive for less if we really believe what we teach: that for better or worse, man is a creature with potential.

Certainly the humanities—history, literature, music, art, philosophy—can expose students to the whole spectrum of values and help them see for themselves the relationships between past, present, and future. Edmund Burke believed that "the individual is bound to his past and committed to the future by ties which though light as air, are as strong as links of iron." And it is to the humanities we must turn to understand why Walter Lippmann has written that "young men die in battle for their country's sake and . . .old men plant trees they will never sit under."

Humanities courses are important, but like a civilization, a school is more than a sum of its courses. It is an atmosphere, a mode of conduct, a spirit that can add powerful elements to the values derived from an education. A school system needs teachers and administrators who will provide the mood for learning as well as the tools for learning.

Harold Howe, writing on the topic "Schools and Character Development," has observed that "the school's contribution to character growth is determined first by who teaches, secondly by how he teaches, and only thirdly by what is taught." Humanities courses in and of themselves offer no panacea for strengthening ethical values in a society. I emphasize this point because too often in our country we are offered a simple solution for all our ills—pass a law or add a course.

Nor can we rely entirely on divine faith to preserve and enhance values. You know the story of the parishioner who came running to his religious leader in a state of great excitement. "Something most unusual has just happened!" he exclaimed. "A man on crutches walked into the Temple, went to the altar, said a prayer, and then threw one of his crutches away. He said a second prayer, and he threw his other crutch away." "A miracle right in our Temple!" rejoiced the religious leader. "Where is this person? I want to meet him." Replied the parishioner, "He's still there in front of the altar—flat on his face."

In the final analysis then, the quest for values begins and ends with the teacher. Not too many miles from here a teacher was asked to appear before the Board of Education and justify why she assigned and discussed in class Harper Lee's *To Kill A Mockingbird*. The teacher gave the following reply to the question, "Why do you choose to teach *To Kill A Mockingbird?*"

When I teach this book, I look at my students and hope that they and I will learn to be like Atticus Finch, to meet ignorance, hatred, prejudice, not with more ignorance, hatred, prejudice, but with understanding, goodness, love. . . .

Students respect Atticus because he is an adult who practices what he preaches. More than ever today young people are questioning us as adults when our lives do not measure up to our words. . . .

I have spent over half my life working with young people in school and in church and working with language, the miracle that makes us human. It is through language that we think, communicate, express our ideas, and transmit them down the years. Why study literature? Because it is one of the humanities—one of the ways by which man expresses his beliefs, his hopes, his understandings. The study of literature helps us to develop an understanding of ourselves and others without having to experience directly every aspect of life. . . .It helps us to develop values, ideals, a sense of purpose, an understanding of what life is all about. I consider this book a superior resource for such development because the basic idea of the book is that prejudice poisons the mind, and that the only cure is understanding. . . .

The school board voted unanimously to continue using the book. No students had to be shot to understand why some values that have stood the test of time made sense for their present and their future.

Humanities: From Aeschylus to Antonioni

Adele Stern

The wonder is that we speak of humanities at all. The greater wonder is that we speak of humanities *programs*, as if what we have been teaching all along is not about humans, as if someone suddenly discovered that music and painting and sculpture and literature have something to do with each other, as if we are only now learning that the bright-eyed, restless natives in mustache and mini-skirt may have human qualities: the curiosity of Oedipus, the values of John Proctor, the loyalty of Antigone, the passion of Othello, the drives of Macbeth.

Curiously, one hears the word *humanities,* receives invitations to humanities conferences, reads of the proliferation of humanities programs—curiously, because this is happening at the same time that the federal Congress cuts the appropriation to the National Foundation on the Arts and Humanities by $700,000 from last year's budget, 10.5 million dollars less than was requested for 1969. A paradox indeed when one reads the figures in money allotted to the National Science Foundation and the expenditures for the military action in Vietnam.

"I hear that you have a good humanities program at your school," the weekly letter remarks to me, "May I have a copy of your curriculum?"

Indeed, humanities is taught in our school. In almost every English classroom, I know. And in the music class, the art class, the history class, the French class, I hope. And in the classes of all these disciplines that meet together in some sort of pattern, somewhat different each year. The question that gives me pause is the one about curriculum. Shall I send the summary of what was read in the American studies classes in 1966, or shall I send the list of projects completed by individual students in world ideas in 1967? Are these our curricula? This *is* what has been written down after the fact, after the students and teachers in their curiosity have decided what to study and what to talk about, what to read, what to investigate. Do these lists show what the students have learned, what has touched their hearts and minds piercingly, if briefly, to emerge sometime in the future as strength and value? Hardly. A humanities course should involve students' whole personalities, and this is the part that is not written down anywhere.

Fashion is spinach, and *one man's meat is another man's poison.* And so it goes with humanities programs

One school gathers up four teachers: English, history, art and music, gives them a mutual planning period, a budget for paperbacks or perhaps one of those new, brightly illustrated humanities anthologies, a back-to-back schedule, and the kids are fed the history of the world from Ulysses to the Yippees in ten easy months. Lecture, lecture, lecture, while the kids do math homework in the last rows of the auditorium; a few humanities films (preinterpreted and predigested by a national expert), a field trip or two, tests and papers, even some small group discussion. A humanities program.

Another school takes its brightest lights, college prep all the way, and announces that senior English for these select will now be called humanities. The music teacher and the art teacher will lecture to the classes once a month to show, for example, the relationships between Renaissance music and art and Renaissance literature. The reading list is as long as the sandwich menu in Oscar Davidson's restaurant in Copenhagen. Dante's *Inferno* (the Ciardi translation) is covered in five class periods. A sprint from Plato to Pinter. Humanities program.

The latest fashion in humanities programs is to start "where it is" and to "tell it like it is." The year begins with a field trip to *Hair*, or *Your Own Thing*, and students read and analyze *The Invisible Man* and *Manchild in the Promised Land* (if they are not banned by community disapproval). The art studied is a repetition of Campbell soup cans and the digestive system of a 1929 Ford. The film is a screening of *The Graduate*, and the teacher, barely past the thirty-mark, feels self-consciously a swinger. Some time during the year *Moby Dick* gets squeezed in, and maybe *The Scarlet Letter* and *Huckleberry Finn*. And the students speak, are spoken to, and write. They may even sculpt and paint and sing ballads accompanied by their guitars. A humanities program.

There are infinite patterns and philosophies of what humanities programs are or should be. Are the examples I have given valid programs? Surely, and surely not. They could be the most deeply felt, vigorously broadening experiences for student and teacher alike. Or they could be cardboard lessons, revealing little, touching few.

The magic key is the teacher and the lock he unlocks through his choices and his questions.

I know of a program that involved ten students and a teacher doing things together after school and on Saturday afternoons—visiting museums, listening to concerts, attending a play, reading anything and everything that came to their attention, and talking—lots of talking, teacher and students together, listening to each other, kids saying what they really are thinking and feeling, not what they think the teacher wants them to say, not playing the mind-reading game for the answers on the weekly quiz. Students remembering the exquisite moments of insight, the brilliance of beauty recognized and transforming, the heat of exposure of thoughts at the same time personal and timeless. This is a humanities program.

I have been part of a club, after school on odd Thursdays, when students who had read the books they did not have time for in class, books by Kazantzakis, D. H. Lawrence, Hermann Hesse, Alan Ginsburg, Catullus, C. S. Lewis, Boccaccio, discussed them and reveled in the discussion. Books that might not have been *allowed* in class, books that opened minds to the glory of man as well as to his misery, to the humor of human life counterpointed with its sadness. Poetry read aloud by students who loved the poems, emotions revealed for the first time by students who rarely spoke in the box we know as the classroom.

I know of a humanities program, not so named, that took place in a tenth-grade English class when the virtue of having diagrammed ten sentences faithfully according to curriculum instructions was rewarded by a teacher—vital, glorious, dynamic, beautiful (at least to her students)—with the reading of her own poetry, the playing of her own compositions on the left-over piano, the small seminars in which the boys and girls discussed and discussed, argued and clarified, shrieked with laughter and groaned with dismay. It was a noisy classroom, and the door was firmly closed against the hall lest other students learn what a good time was being had by all. Here, the boys and girls were experiencing the *shock of recognition*—that learning need not be arduous, that learning had something to do with people.

This is what humanities is all about. People. Given a class of kids—all kinds, shapes, forms, colors, ages—given a place to meet—the lawn, the auditorium, a carpeted study, any place wherein to create a humanities studio—access to hundreds of books, records, tapes, paper and pen, paint and clay, a piano and film—given freedom to travel on buses and trains, to visit museums, factories, gardens, the theater—given all this and a teacher (even one slightly over thirty) who is alive, compassionate, honest, awake, unthreatened, loving, educated, sensitive, caring, a real human being who thinks of each kid in her class as another human being—given the freedom to GO, and you have the beginnings of a humanities program.

Then come the choices. What to teach? Does it really matter what the content of a course in humanities is if the result is to create a voracious hunger for literature and theater and music in the student?

Why *Medea* over *Oedipus*? Why *Lear* over *Hamlet*? Why analyze the score of *Boris Godunov* and Mussorgsky's use of the whole-tone scale if students are not going to go to opera ever in their lives? Might it not be better to have them humming the tunes from *Carmen* and dying to see the pageantry of the performance? Curriculum choices are frequently handed down from bureaus in central offices somewhere in the state. In humanities programs this must not be the case. The choices must be those of the teachers involved and of the students involved with the teachers. And the choices must be ones that lead to *mind expansion*. What is read, and seen and heard in the Humanities program must be understood to be only the visible part of the iceberg. The aims of every Humanities course must be to arouse voracious appetites for more of the same, dissatisfaction with what one knows, curiosity about what one does not know, concern about what is and what might be.

Which brings me to *questions*. If the teacher is to continue with the "who did what to whom and where?" question, forget it. If the question probes "why?," "how?," that is more like it. The most challenging aspect of teaching, I suppose, is the content of the questions a teacher asks. Never is this more important than in the humanities course, which is, after all, a course about the revelations of human life in all times and all places, and the motives for human behavior, complicated as they are, require penetrating, challenging questions. A teacher is as good as his questions.

So, we have it: a teacher, some choices, and some questions.

Then, what is the problem?

The problem is that we have hang-ups! Take the attendance. Check to see if books are covered. Be sure to choose books that will not offend anybody. Give the kids grades. Everybody must be in the right place at the right time. The classroom must be quiet. A teacher must stand in front of the room. The halls must be unpeopled. Forty-five minutes is the right amount of time for all lessons. Twenty-five makes a perfect class size.

Oh, yes. Lots of hang-ups (with apologies to the Commission on English and the authors of the new criticism): teach language, literature, and composition. How does a poem mean? Not, what does a poem mean? The medium is the message. Never discuss anything controversial. *Cover* the material. Cover, cover, cover. Don't get too involved with your students. A composition a week.

Oh, yes, we have hang-ups. A school is not a democratic institution. Teachers are dispensers of information. Movies and television belong in the local theater and living room and do not teach the kids anything.

That last one is the biggest hang-up of all. While we are talking about humanities, we had better do some talking about film, in the local theater and in the living room and in the classroom. We had better recognize just how much the kids are learning from this plastic medium, and just how much of it they absorb and believe and act upon. And we had better believe it. We might recognize that a good film can be a humanities program in itself, with the merging of human disciplines as never before in any art—dance, literature, music, philosophy, painting, drama, sculpture. And that one can learn the skills of criticism as well from discussing a television program—and I don't mean a documentary or ETV—as one can from discussing *Pride and Prejudice*.

Our hang-ups reveal our gaps, generation gaps to be sure, communication gaps, political gaps, space gaps, technological gaps. The widest gap of all, the one that should be most meaningful to those of us who want to teach humanities, is the gap between what is school and what is life. Our students have been so trained that if anything meaningful is taught in school or discussed in class, they feel immoral, incurably wicked. What do they think about after they leave our control? Drugs, sex, religion, commitment, student dissent, black power, hair, Aristotle Onassis, Julian Bond, *I Spy, The Invaders, Mission Impossible, Peyton Place*—hardly subjects for the classrooms, we are still told, but subjects that involve our students totally except for the few hours we pull the reins on their brains.

There are other gaps in the school, too: gaps between the white students and the black, between the smarties and dummies (whatever euphimism we use to describe the lowest classes in our track system), between the vocal and the quiet, the athletes and the egg-heads, the math department and the English department, the sciences and the social studies. Gaps galore.

I say that a humanities program is the place where all the gaps can be closed.

It should be so constituted that the teacher and the students learn together, that all kinds of *kids* have the opportunity to participate–the college prep and the life prep, the language oriented and the manually oriented. It should be the place where the student who has done beautiful term papers but has never held a paint brush can feel the joy of color on canvas, the squish of soft clay through his fingers; where the would-be mechanic and the future senator discuss *prejudice* and *power* and the SDS; where the auditorium becomes a little theater for the revealing of ideas and emotion and cooperation. It should be the place where students gather to talk *to each other* about each other, about books, of course, but about films and television programs, and about issues, about life. Life that is, more often than not, humdrum, but that has, during its course, moments of ecstacy, feelings of joy, experiences of excitement and wonder. Life that is–as has often been said, but not recently–after all, worth the struggle.

I look at the newspaper and read of one big, bloody battle after another; I listen to the radio and hear one biting roar after another; I watch television and view one violent act after another. I am middle-aged. I know that battles have always been fought, that people have always been cruel to people, that misery has stalked the world from the beginning of counted time. But I have also listened to Steinbeck and Dylan Thomas. I have read Melville and Kafka and Yeats. I have seen the islands of Greece and the mountains of Spain. I believe what I have read and seen and felt; the gorgeousness of the earth, the perfectibility of man, the wonder and miracle of growing life. And it is my duty, in the humanities class, to lead my students to know the balances of life, for if I do not do this, where will they learn that man is great and good and proud and wise? That when Antonioni is saying man is lonely, he is also saying, let us love. That Euripides is questioning man's gods and marveling at man's strength. That Faulkner is begging us to look around and recognize the strengths in nature that will prevail. Where will they learn that everything a human being does–his song, his marble, his words–reveal what he is, and that this revelation has been repeated and repeated from the beginning to the now? Where will he learn all this if not in the humanities class?

The Humanities in the Secondary Schools

Walter J. Hipple, Jr.

What is a humanities course and what ought it to comprise? The broadest and simplest answer to this question is that a humanities course embraces several of the disciplines traditionally called humanistic: history, the various forms of imaginative literature, the visual arts, philosophy, and music. The essential thing is not simply that these things be studied, but that they should be studied *together*; it is the combination of these disciplines into one plan of study which makes the course interdisciplinary. But why, it may be objected, should a course be interdisciplinary? Why should not each subject be taught with stress upon the integrity of its materials, the uniqueness of its methodology? The principles of construction of a novel are quite different from those of a sonata; the beauty of a painting is radically different from that of an aria; a philosophical dialogue has precious little in common with a dramatic dialogue. Each of the nine Muses has her own province and attributes, and we can serve the Muses best by helping students to see each in her distinctness.

Yet there is something to be said on the other side. The compartmentalization of knowledge in modern education is more often lamented than remedied. Even in high schools, where radical specialization is not possible, the several departments of knowledge may remain wholly separate. They may never fuse into that coherent matrix of principles and information, tastes and attitudes, which constitutes intellectual culture. Interdisciplinary courses, provided they are rigorous and not vague, broad but not vacuous, are an evident remedy for the disintegration of knowledge. And this is a powerful argument for offering courses which, like humanities, bring the separate parts of knowledge together. Such a generalization is in itself vacuous, however, unless it can be more precisely specified.

Matthew Arnold once remarked that "The civilised world is to be regarded as now being, for intellectual and spiritual purposes, one great confederation . . . whose members have for their proper outfit a knowledge of Greek, Roman, and Eastern antiquity, and of one another," and he declared that the nation which best equipped its people with that outfit would make the most intellectual and spiritual progress. He was sharply taken up by the scientist-philosopher Thomas Henry Huxley, who supposed, though wrongly, that Arnold intended this statement as a blow at the pretensions of science—that by knowing Greek and Roman antiquity, for instance, Arnold meant simply knowing Sophocles and Virgil; that by the modern nations knowing one another Arnold meant simply that Englishmen should know Racine and Goethe. Arnold was therefore obliged to explain himself more fully. "When I speak of knowing Greek and Roman antiquity as a help to knowing ourselves and the world," he wrote, "I mean more than a knowledge of so many portions of authors in the Greek and Latin languages. I mean knowing the Greeks and Romans, and their life and genius, and what they were and did in the world; what we get from them, and what is its value. . . .I understand knowing [Greece] as the giver of Greek art, and guide to a free and right use of reason and to scientific method. . . .I understand knowing [Greece] as all this, and not merely knowing certain Greek poems. . . ."

Arnold was right. The object of studying ancient literature is not merely to have the experience of reading a play by Sophocles or an epic of Homer. These experiences are good in themselves; but they should also lead to something further. They ought to form part of our integrated conception of a way of life—a way of life which included the Parthenon and the "Discobolus" as well as Sophocles and Homer, which included philosophers like Plato and mathematicians like Euclid, a way of life that embraced all sides of human nature. To know the Greeks, or any other epoch, in this way is to acquire more than a literary polish; it is to gain insight into a view of the world and man, a view that is fruitful in interpreting and enriching our own lives.

This is part of our object in the humanities: to know the Greeks, or the men of the thirteenth century, or of the eighteenth, in such a way that this knowledge becomes part of our own intellectual character and has an influence upon our lives. To know any epoch in this fruitful way requires that we know their philosophy and their sculpture, their drama and their music, their history and their poetry, and their science—and to know all these things as aspects of one civilization.

The matrix of time and space, of history and geography, which the average student possesses is grossly inadequate to organize and clarify his other knowledges. Many students may think that the *Divine Comedy* is a work of the Renaissance, or that Wordsworth was writing in 1700, that Mozart lived in the nineteenth century, or Michelangelo in the Middle Ages. Such errors are more than isolated cases of mistaken fact. They betray radical misunderstanding of the whole course of development of the human spirit. The man who errs thus does not truly know his place in world culture, nor can he easily be emancipated from the provincialism of his time and place. To be sure, many of our students will be saved from these errors by the happy circumstance of not knowing what the *Divine Comedy* is and never having heard of Mozart. But this is not the salvation we require. Our aim is not to be free of knowledge but to be free *through* knowledge. To be free from the shackles of our time and place in the world is to understand where we are, why we are here, what we have gained and lost in getting here, and whither we might go now. To understand this means to know the history and geography of our civilization; and this is one of the values of a general course in the humanities.

One also currently hears much about the necessity of redressing the balance between the sciences and the humanities. One cannot sympathize with declamations on this subject which are simply reactionary and seem to regret that men know more science than they used to. Knowledge is in itself always good, both because it gratifies the fundamental spiritual appetite of curiosity, and because it serves to organize the other facets of our lives and to bring them into harmony with reality. Students ought to study science, even more than now falls to their lot. But such improvement in scientific training need not be made at the expense of the humanities. The past decade has seen significant improvements in the way the sciences are taught, whereas matching advances have not been made in the teaching of the humanities. A new mathematics begins to permeate our school systems, a mathematics which puts first principles first and which makes much of the logic of mathematical reasoning, thereby making problem-solving more rational and efficient by grounding it in a more fundamental understanding. A new physical science begins to integrate physics and chemistry by stressing the methodology of science and expounding the principles fundamental to the various physical sciences. A new biology is making its appearance. These advances in curriculum forward the cause of science not by absorbing the student's time to the exclusion of other subjects, but simply by teaching science better. The way for humanists to redress the balance is by teaching their subjects in new and better ways. An interdisciplinary program in the humanities could compensate for any overemphasis upon science, or upon vocational preparation, not by doing away with other subjects, but by itself exerting a more powerful influence upon students.

Humanities courses thus help to remedy the fragmentation of knowledge and to promote intellectual culture; by placing us in the history and geography of civilization, they free us in some measure from the bondage of local and temporary viewpoints, free us for intelligent self-development and action; and they restore the balance of our educational system by counteracting the ever-greater impact of the sciences and the pressures of vocationalism. There is yet a fourth advantage: integrated courses in the humanities afford a convenient avenue for introducing into the secondary curriculum subjects now almost entirely neglected.

Although hundreds of high schools in the United States currently teach philosophy, this number should be increased. Two kinds of philosophical study seem appropriate at the high-school level. One is the study of logic, the other the reading of some of the less intricate works in the substantive branches of philosophy—in ethics, for instance, or metaphysics. The study of logic is most effective when affiliated with the study of mathematics or language. But the second kind of philosophical study can best be introduced in a humanities curriculum. Clearly, any study of the Greeks that does not include Plato or Aristotle must be incomplete. All men, Coleridge declared, are born either Platonists or Aristotelians. Even a high school student might realize the truth of Coleridge's dictum if he actually reads and discusses a dialogue of Plato or part of a treatise by Aristotle. High school students can be shown that these ancient writers are discussing problems which agitate students in the twentieth century: the grounds for believing or disbelieving in immortality, what makes an act right or wrong, how one can know a fact and be sure that he knows it, or how the claims of individuality and of social responsibility can be harmonized. A statue by Praxiteles, a dialogue of Plato, and a play by Euripides represent the same civilization; all have something to say to our intellect, taste, and feeling; and we have not thoroughly studied the Greeks if we leave out the philosopher. Nor have we understood the Middle Ages if we have never read a page by a medieval theologian, nor the eighteenth century if we have never read Hume or Rousseau, nor the twentieth if we have not scanned Bertrand Russell or Jean Paul Sartre.

Much can be said in favor of teaching an actual philosophy course in the senior year of high school, a course devoted for an entire semester to reading a number of philosophical works adapted to the intellectual level of high school seniors. Let us have such courses. But let us also introduce philosophy into integrated courses in the humanities so that it can be seen as one aspect of civilization, affiliated with other aspects.

Another subject largely ignored in the secondary schools is art history. The visual arts are very often the most obvious point from which to grasp the character of an epoch. They are certainly the easiest and most obvious way to study the development and evolution of civilization. In the time required to study closely a single play by Shakespeare, one can canvass the whole sweep of Renaissance and Baroque painting. In the time required to analyze a single symphony by Beethoven, one can scan two centuries of architecture. And the study of art history is essential for developing the taste of students. One learns to see the beauties of architecture, to distinguish good from bad design in the buildings that daily envelop us, by studying the manifold styles of building from ancient times to the present. Nor will an understanding of architecture ever come from practical exercises in the art studio; the principles of the art are found in buildings—in the Pantheon, the Cathedral of Chartres, Rockefeller Center. And one simultaneously learns more than architecture in such study: one learns the variety of human culture that can give rise to such diverse expressions.

In painting, sculpture, and the beauties of nature too, the same principles of form and line and color, the same expressions of character and feeling are to be found. Practical work in the art studio, to which art education is now largely confined, does little to awaken the student's sensibility to the manifold styles in which beauty may be found. Indeed, the instructors of such exercises, since they themselves are often practitioners in a particular style and may be insensitive to and intolerant of other styles, often restrict rather than enlarge the student's visual sensitivity. If the instructors are enthusiastically contemptuous of art works that have subject matter, as is frequently the case, the result may be to restrict the student's moral sensitivity as well, by teaching him to be systematically blind to the insights into human character and feeling, and into the expressions of external nature, which painting and sculpture afford. One of the great organs of human education, education both of the moral and the aesthetic sense, is largely lost to us because our educational system does not employ the vast resources bequeathed to us by the ages of art.

Music history also suffers in the usual high-school curriculum. In any humanities course, music ought to be correlated as far as possible with the other materials of the course. If the course is chronologically organized, time can be set aside during the study of the classical and medieval worlds to treat the grammar of music and to train students in the reading of simplified scores, a skill which greatly facilitates this study of music. "The grammar of music" implies not only an understanding of what a theme is, what different meters are, and the like, but also architectonic principles—the nature of a fugue, of theme-and-variations, of a sonata-allegro movement, and so forth. Then, beginning with a brief presentation of medieval music, this aspect of culture can be brought into relation with the others. The difficulty remains, to be sure, that music of the eighteenth and nineteenth centuries bulks larger in the repertory than the visual arts of those centuries. But if the material in the grammatical phase of the musical instruction is aptly chosen, the student will already have learned some works of Bach and Mozart, Beethoven and Chopin, works which he can fit into the cultural continuum he will study later as examples of Baroque, Classic and Romantic styles.

The final justification for the introduction of humanities courses into the secondary schools is, then, that such courses create an opening through which a number of subjects valuable for intellectual, moral, and aesthetic development can be introduced into the curriculum.

Some passages in the discussion thus far have presupposed a course that is chronologically arranged, a course in cultural history. This is not, of course, the only mode of organization for such a course. No subject is taught in a greater variety of fashions than integrated courses in the humanities. In general, however, four modes of organization prevail: by arts and genres, by aesthetic aspects or categories, by topics, and by chronology and culture. The first of these modes, organization by arts and genres, tends to separate the materials—literature, art, and music being taught in distinct blocs and often by different personnel. Such a program has its values; but they are for the most part the values of a course in art appreciation, plus a course in music appreciation, plus a course in the appreciation of literature. Much is to be learned by combining a group of dramas of contrasting kinds, for instance, and treating them together to elicit both the characteristics of drama generally and the distinctive traits of these particular kinds; or by simultaneously studying the problems of Grecian and Gothic architecture, Baroque and contemporary architecture, stressing both the persistent problems of architectural design and the variety of possible solutions to these problems. Added to these separate values, if such a course is well taught, will be a sense of the analogies between the arts—the insight, for example, that the plot of a novel functions somewhat like the sonata form in a symphonic movement or like the pyramidal composition of a painting of Virgin and Child. Similarities in style can also be studied: the student can perceive that the "Laocoön" is akin to Berlioz and the "Discobolus" akin to Beethoven, both in the way the formal components are handled and in the kind of expression exhibited.

But analogies among the arts can be better handled in a course organized by categories or by chronology. The term "categories" means such aspects of works as subject, style, function, and structure. In some categories, discussion might naturally dwell at especial length on particular arts: the problem of *subject,* for instance, would be prominent in treating non-objective painting or program music, that of *function* in architecture. Other categories would be of great importance in all genres: the *structure* of a *pietà* of a sonata-allegro movement, of a philosophical dialogue, of a tragedy. So too with *style.* But discussion of style (like discussion of ideology) leads very naturally to chronology, to the correlation of styles, or of ideological content, with the broad movements of cultural and intellectual history. It is not enough to see that rhythm as a structural element enters in some sense into both painting and music; we make fruitful use of such an analogy only when we observe that the rhythms and symmetries of a Mozart symphony have much in common with those of a painting by David, and that the rhythms and symmetries or asymmetries of a symphony by Berlioz are like those of a painting by Delacroix. This last insight, however, suggests the importance of distinguishing a Classic from a Romantic style, and if one pursues this thought, he is immediately in an historical framework.

The third kind of organization, by topic, is perhaps the most common of all, but its disadvantages are serious. This plan consists of imposing a dialectical schematism upon the various materials of the course; polarities such as "The Individual and Society," "God and Man," "Freedom and Authority," "Man and Nature," and the like are employed as the fundamental rubrics. Handled with subtlety and flexibility, such polarities can often afford insights into individual works and synthesize diverse materials. But dialectical schematisms tempt one to simplify and distort the particular works in order to make them fit the categories, or even to employ the categories as a device for promoting some favorite taste or point of view. And in any event, this approach diverts attention both from the formal characteristics of the works studied and from the historical context in which the works subsist.

For situations where only one humanities course can be offered, the historical organization insures that the materials of a given culture will be studied together. One might learn more about the drama or the symphony by studying these in isolation, but he would learn less about civilization. The student needs to see the stream of civilization as a whole and to grasp his place in that stream. Teachers can more easily cross-index a historical course by topic or genre than elicit the character of an epoch in civilization from materials scattered through a course that is organized non-historically. Meaningful comparisons between a Greek play, a Shakesperian tragedy, and a drama by Ibsen are possible even if the three works are separated by several months in presentation; but grasping the coherency of Greek or Renaissance or Victorian culture would be difficult if some aspects of those cultures are omitted wholly and others are treated only in alien contexts. Historical organization integrates the materials of the course and reinforces that matrix of time, space, and development within which any cultural fact, including our own existence, ought to be seen.

The Teaching of Integrated Courses. The chief temptation to abandon the historical organization results from team teaching. When a team of specialists teaches a humanities course, they can more easily budget their time and coordinate their efforts when each handles his specialty in a block and from his own viewpoint. But team teaching is not always the best way to treat a humanities course. It has its advantages, to be sure, and it is often the only feasible method. A given faculty may include members who are qualified in their separate disciplines but none of whom considers himself to be adequate in the other disciplines of an integrated course. And more positively, the team affords a greater variety of personality and approach; the student's interest may be better maintained, and he may gain more insights if one instructor lectures and another conducts discussions, if one instructor is devoted to formal analysis and another to explication of a work as an expression of a culture or as a treatment of a human problem, and so forth.

But team teaching does not guarantee that the diverse subjects of the humanities program will be adequately related, even when the various members of the team attend each other's class sessions. The facets of the course have not entered into one consciousness to be seen and felt as parts of one civilization, of one way of living, of one way of seeing the world and man. The instructor himself should certainly accomplish what is expected of his students! If they are expected to comprehend the Greek way, or the spirit of the Renaissance, or of the modern world, so should he! One may argue that the members of the instructional team *will* understand these matters, but that understanding and teaching are not the same, and the shoemaker should stick to his last. This objection takes too pedantic a view of teaching! The teacher who is exploring an area outside his own specialty has a sense of adventure and enthusiasm which may be infectious. True, he may err; but his freshness may compensate for his naiveté. Students will be working alongside a more developed mind that is undergoing the same experience they encounter—entering fresh territories and assimilating them to the kingdoms already conquered.

The objection that an instructor may know a subject yet not be prepared to teach it, rests on a false premise: that one can possess knowledge in the abstract and yet be unable to apply it. One would be absurd to argue that he understood the law of cosines but could not solve the problems in trigonometry that involve that law. It is equally absurd to argue that a humanities instructor may understand Greek art without being able to teach it. What one understands clearly, one can teach. Either, then, the members of an instructional team do not understand the various materials of the course, in which case the student is asked to accomplish what his professors have not managed; or the instructors do know those materials, in which case they can and should teach them, and in so doing share the intellectual experiences of their students.

The minimum requirement for a team of instructors is that each instructor teach part of the materials that fall in the province of every other. The English teacher ought to try his hand at analyzing the "Last Supper"; the musician should debate the issues of a Platonic dialogue; and so on. This does not imply that an instructor wholly unversed in literature attempt to teach Sophocles, or that one who has had no training in art try his hand at Michelangelo. But any mature and interested person can sufficiently train himself to play his part in a cooperative teaching effort—that is, to participate in the work outside his own specialty. A team should not be merely an aggregate of individuals, each performing separately, but a group working together, reinforcing and learning from one another.

Still, it is no doubt best that people giving instruction in the humanities actually have had some formal instruction themselves, and this article will outline what such instruction might comprise. Anyone preparing to teach a humanities course ought to have had a course of the kind he will be teaching. This implies at least one full-year humanities course. Usually such courses are pitched at the sophomore level in college; their staffs often have superior qualifications and certainly have broad interests; and the students who voluntarily enroll in such courses are generally above average. If the course is historically arranged, so much the better—especially if the student studies world history previously or concurrently.

But what should follow this broad introduction to the humanities? It will *not* do for the student to follow up his survey with a random selection of courses in literature, art, music, and philosophy. To be truly useful, such courses should fit together into a pattern, the part of which support each other. But no one can hope to cover uniformly the history of Western culture—its *belles lettres,* its philosophy, its architecture and painting and music. The ideal must give way to the possible. The best compromise is to elect a set of courses that canvass the different disciplines but are restricted to a few periods of history. One can acquire a fair understanding of eighteenth-century culture, for instance, from a cluster of three courses. A course in *belles lettres* need not be a survey; indeed, a course concentrated upon the eighteenth-century novel or eighteenth-century poetry would be at least as valuable. Then a course in the art of the eighteen century—perhaps in Rococo and Neo-Classicism in France. Or a course in the classical period of music would fit in well. And any thorough study of the age would be incomplete without some knowledge of philosophy, without having read some works of Voltaire, Rousseau, and Hume.

Two periods of cultural history studied in this way, especially two strikingly contrasted periods, will equip the student with the breadth that he needs to work in an integrated program. But perhaps the integration itself is still missing. A cluster of courses in the eighteenth century, for instance, ought to be crowned with a seminar that is itself an integrated course. Such a seminar might be devoted to the later eighteenth century in Britain. It could canvass Hume, Gibbon, and Burke (the greatest of British writers of philosophy, history, and political rhetoric); the novel and didactic and lyric poetry; architecture from the Palladians to Robert Adam and Chambers and Nash; painting from the time of Kneller through Hogarth to Reynolds and Wilson and Gainsborough; landscape art from William Kent to the picturesque school at the close of the century. Such a course naturally presupposes that the students have previously acquired knowledge of some aspects of the period; it attempts to present a comprehensive picture of an entire cultural complex. Music has been omitted, to be sure, because there is no British music of distinction in the eighteenth century. The lack could be supplied in another seminar: the international Romantic movement, for example, would comprise Berlioz and Schumann alongside Delacroix and Turner, Wordsworth and Hugo.

The exact course prescription for a student taking an interdisciplinary minor in humanities and majoring in one of the humanistic disciplines might be as follows: (a) A broad humanities survey, two semesters in length: six hours; and (b) Two periods of concentration, each comprising a course in the history of the period, one in the art or music of the period, one in the literature, plus an integrated seminar embracing all aspects of the epoch: twenty-four hours—but only eighteen chargeable to the minor, since at least six hours will fall within the major preparation. A third item could be added to the preparation as an elective: a course in aesthetic theory that would both provide models of philosophical analysis and enhance critical sensitivity to the visual, musical, and literary arts. "Aesthetic theory" implies theory as developed systematically by philosophical writers. Santayana's *Sense of Beauty* would serve as an instance—but, of course, more than one of the many alternative systems ought to be examined. Systems of criticism in the various arts may also be canvassed in an aesthetics course, but ventures into criticism should stay closely tied to general and systematic principles. Wölfflin's *Principles of Art History* is an example. Courses in "appreciation" and applied criticism are not aesthetic theory.

It may be objected that although the foregoing prescription proposes preparation in only two disparate periods of cultural history, the candidate thus prepared will teach other periods as well. But to study two periods with sufficient thoroughness to get a sense both of the analogies and the diversities of the different aspects of a given culture enables the student to examine other periods by himself and in the same fashion. After all, education is not only the imparting of knowledges; it is the inculcation of skills, and above all, the skill of extending one's own education. Provide the student with models of analysis and synthesis, and if he has the intellectual initiative without which he can neither be educated himself nor educate others, he can carry on.

We should attempt to do no more, in principle, even with the student who is majoring in interdisciplinary studies. One cannot cram into a four-year program all that a student would need to know to be conversant with all sides of Western culture in all epochs since the Greeks. The humanities major would survey three periods instead of two; but he, too, would be presented only with incomplete models of the structure he must complete for himself in a lifetime of study and experience. If one postulates an area major of fifty-two hours in the humanities, it might comprise the following: (a) A broad humanities survey: six hours. (b) A sequence of history courses canvassing Western civilization from the ancient world to the present: twelve hours. (c) Literature courses—not broad surveys, but detailed studies in particular periods, so selected that one falls in each of three periods of concentration: nine hours. (d) Art history and music history, selected as with the literary studies: nine hours. (Music history becomes pertinent for a secondary-school teacher only with the Baroque. Art history could be recommended for Classical, Medieval, and Renaissance periods, but either art or music for more recent periods.) (e) Three integrated seminars in the periods chosen for concentration: nine hours. (f) Aesthetic theory: three hours. (g) Other philosophy courses, selected to reinforce one or more of the periods of concentration: four hours.

Such a major concentration in humanities for secondary-school teachers is at present hypothetical, although in a few years humanities courses and programs may become so numerous and extensive that appointments can be made specifically to teach them. The immediate need, however, is certification of minor programs adapted to teachers whose primary appointment is in one of the humanistic disciplines and which will better equip such teachers to contribute to humanities programs. It is also true, however, that a considerable number of teachers already established in their profession have come to be engaged in humanities courses, often as members of a "team." What can such persons do to strengthen and broaden their own training? If such a teacher still has his master's program ahead of him, the answer is easy. The rules for certificates requiring the master's degree vary from subject to subject and from state to state. But consider the case of a teacher with a B.A. (or B.S.) in English in the State of Indiana. His master's program requires eight hours in English and suggests (but does not require) four hours of professional courses. Eighteen hours would be available for establishing what one might call a "graduate minor" in humanities, time enough to fit in two clusters of courses concentrated in two periods of cultural history. One can assume that a graduate English student can prepare himself in the *belles lettres* of other traditions; the problem is to provide the training in the ancillary disciplines. Such a student might choose a concentration in the ancient world: ancient art, Greek philosophy, and an integrated seminar in the Hellenistic period. Or he might concentrate on the nineteenth century: nineteenth-century painting, work on some group of nineteenth-century philosophers (perhaps the British Utilitarians), and an integrated seminar in Romanticism. Such a battery of six courses would be a very good outfit for a humanities teacher, and most graduate departments will readily give permission to students zealous enough to be thus preparing themselves for interdisciplinary work. Certain kinds of music courses may presuppose too much "theory" for the outsider; but a distinguishing feature of the humanities in general is that there really are few prerequisites. Any intellectually mature person can work competently in a graduate course in Shakespeare, Aristotle, or the Italian Baroque.

A teacher who has received his master's degree and desires only to strengthen or broaden his competences by further university study could in the progress of a few summers outfit himself in just this same way. The two axioms that dictate the design of a program under whatever conditions and stipulations are *breadth* and *integration.* A derivative theorem is that preparation should ordinarily consist of clusters of courses which are unified by cultural epoch and which include integrating seminars.

Breadth and integration are, indeed, both the method and the end of these interdisciplinary studies in the humanities. To respond to and be knowledgeable about painting and architecture, music and poetry, fiction and philosophy, the course of history and the beauty of nature—and to form from all these responses and knowledges a system and a pattern that is one aspect of a coherent personality—this is the goal.

Humanities: Why and How

Courtenay V. Cauble

In an address on the humanities which he recently gave in Cleveland, Carl Ladensack, who is a member of Scarsdale High School's English Department and who has been in on our humanities program since its inception three years ago, alluded to the controversy over whether specialized or general education is more desirable. He went on to say that by its very nature high-school education is general and will continue to be so for a long time to come. He compared the high school's curriculum to a smorgasbord, the student being the diner who samples many dishes without taking a great deal of any one and who follows a recommended procedure, taking light appetizers first, meatier dishes next, and finishing with further helpings of whatever pleased him most. Mr. Ladensack's analogy is an apt one and, I think an encouraging one at a time when specializing seems essential to success from a material point of view. Someone has said that we are in danger of producing a generation of trained workers, admirably prepared to fill a cubbyhole, but sorely unprepared to fill the role of heirs to Western culture. I believe that is what a friend of mine meant the other day when she referred to an acquaintance as "a completely uneducated Ph.D." I do not believe she was conscious of being a snob; she simply thinks of an educated man as much more than just a brilliantly trained engineer.

We must be practical, however. The age we live in encourages specialization just as the Renaissance encouraged its men to learn as much as possible about as many things as possible. It is a good thing in such an age, then, that the high school is a smorgasbord, both because it provides the student, who must ultimately specialize, with a variety of dishes to taste, from which he may choose, and because we know that there is more to being educated than just being well prepared to do one's job. We know that many of our students are like the boy who dropped by my office the other day to tell me he is grateful for the humanities program, that he plans to specialize in mathematics in college and knows that he will have a very limited amount of time to devote to other interests. He was obviously sincere in his belief that the course awakened him to new pleasures and meaning in life. It is our awareness of the possibility of this sort of awakening which makes us feel that it is our responsibility to offer students this course. A great deal has been said about educating "the whole child," so much in fact that many of us have come to cringe whenever we hear that particular bit of jargon. But I think there is something to be said about awakening the whole experience of the child so that he will be able to profit from the legacy of the past and the gift of the present which are his if we can help him to develop a sensitivity to them.

It has always seemed unfortunate to me that studies are often divided into two groups, the "practical" or "useful" arts and the "humanities," as if there were something either impractical or useless about the humanities. Civilized man has never chosen to live without art, music, literature, and drama, and this seems to me to indicate that they are indispensable, and therefore eminently practical. They have little to do with the survival of the body, but they have a great deal to do with the survival of the spirit, and few of us would deny that having one without the other would be a hollow achievement. The arts are important and relevant to the individual. Although he can survive without them, he cannot do so in good health.

The phrase "important and relevant to the individual" brings me specifically to our humanities course at Scarsdale, why we have it and what we try to do in it. We believe we have always had very fine courses in literature, music, and art, and our decision three years ago to have a humanities course was certainly not a response to an inadequacy in our teaching of any of the separate disciplines. We felt that by bringing them together under one tent and approaching them in a particular way we could accomplish something that could not be accomplished in any individual course in music or art or literature. The importance and relevance of the arts to the individual come from the fact that all of them are ways man has found to express and communicate to others something in his deepest nature which needs to be expressed and can enrich others through its communication. Perhaps this is the most important way in which the arts are related: they are all vehicles of communication of one kind or another. Our humanities course is, in a sense, a course in communications. It is this emphasis, in part, which justifies our crossing of departmental lines.

As English teachers, we all know that the most basic thing we do in teaching literature is to try to get the student to relate to his own experience whatever it is he is reading. If he is unable to do this, chances are his reading will be meaningless to him. But if we can get him to see that literature has some practical value for him, we can be fairly sure that he will go out of our classes encouraged to continue reading, that literature will be one of those objects Walt Whitman talks about which the child will look at with wonder or love or dread and which will become a part of him. He will have come to appreciate literature because he has seen that it has some practical significance for him. I recently heard an English teacher say that he has come to believe the time has passed when we can expect to be successful teaching literature, especially poetry, to high-school students on an appreciation level. Although there are a few students who have a sensitive enough ear to be able to revel in the beauties of language and rhythm and thought, most young people today, my friend continued, remain coldly untouched by anything for which they can find no practical value. I was shocked at first, but later it occurred to me that to appreciate means in one sense to understand, and that to understand any art a person must know why it is made, how it is made, and what it means. To appreciate, in any other sense, is either gushy sentimentalism or merely lip service. What I mean is that appreciation comes after understanding, that understanding is a by-product of learning, and that learning has to be motivated. What my friend was getting at, then, is that, whether we like it or not, most young people today have to be motivated by an appeal to their intelligence, to their sense of the practical, rather than to their romantic sensibilities; they must be able to see some practical significance in a learning object, some relevance to them. It is along such practical lines that we have fashioned our humanities course.

Because we are still experimenting, we limit our enrollment to 30 students selected from all of the members of our senior class who express an interest in being part of the program. We may soon open the course to juniors, and we are offering a summer humanities institute this year as an experiment with children from the ninth and tenth grades.

Our guidance counselors and faculty play an important part in the selection of our students. Information about the course is made available to members of the junior class, and those students who are interested discuss the program with their counselors. In some instances the counselors will approach students who have shown a particular interest either in English or in one of the arts. From a final list, which has included the names of as many as 90 candidates, the coordinator of the humanities program, with the advice of the counselors and each student's teachers, selects 30 juniors to make up the next year's class. We feel that the first criterion for participation must be student interest. No effort is made to limit the enrollment to students who are superior academically. As a matter of fact, we like to have as nearly representative a group as possible. Because of the nature of our experiment, the other major criteria for student selection are good character and sincerity. I would say that most of our present humanities students are only average academically, but they are an outstanding group of honest, sincere young people.

The students who are chosen are given no assigned study halls. We provide them with a place to study, if they wish to do so, and with a specially equipped humanities listening and reading room where they may listen to recordings from our humanities collection or read assigned or suggested material or just something they are interested in from our growing collection of books dealing with philosophy and the arts. They are scheduled for a 45-minute humanities session five times a week, although there are weeks when we choose to hold only four or even three sessions. By the end of the second month of school, each student has selected an independent project on which he will work for the remainder of the year. He knows that he, with the guidance of the faculty member or other person who has agreed to serve as his advisor, must produce a thorough piece of research work demonstrating a real understanding of some artist or composer or writer or style by a given date towards the end of the year. He is often encouraged in his work, but never pushed. We have had very few violations of our honor system, very few disappointments, and many gratifying and exciting experiences with our students and their work. One of our important objectives is the encouragement of responsibility and independent research and study. There are some risks involved in giving high-school students so much freedom, but we feel that no gain can be made without risk. The rewards are often great. Last year, for example, a boy who was only a mediocre student in all his other subjects became so involved in the work of Jackson Pollock that he read every book and article he could find on the artist, corresponded with Pollock's widow, visited numerous museums and galleries, read extensively in the writings of Sigmund Freud, engaged an art authority to tutor him, produced a report on the development and meaning of Pollock's style which was worthy of publication, and decided to make art criticism his life's work.

Our approach stems directly from a desire to make the humanities course a practical one with an emphasis on the arts as means of communication. The course is taught by a team of three teachers, one each for literature, music, and art. To enrich our presentations, we bring in guest speakers from time to time from our own faculty, from Scarsdale, and from the New York metropolitan community, and make as thorough a use as possible of the museums, galleries, theatres and concert halls in the New York area, arranging field trips whenever they are of help to us.

Because we are anxious to show how the arts are expressions of basic, never-changing feelings, drives, and needs, we ask the students to do a bit of precourse reading during the summer. At present we are using these works: Sigmund Freud's *Civilization and Its Discontents,* Carl Jung's *Modern Man in Search of Soul,* Soren Kierkegaard's *Fear and Trembling,* and parts of Sir James Frazer's *The Golden Bough.* We begin the year's discussions with consideration of this summer reading with an especially close look at Freud's and Jung's evaluations of the relationship of art to the human mind, both conscious and unconscious, their commentaries on the needs and basic problems of man in modern society, and Jung's interesting if controversial ideas regarding the "collective unconscious" as the source of mythology and spontaneous symbology in the arts. *The Golden Bough,* of course, is itself a convincing documentation of recurring primal symbolism. This sounds formidable, but it all falls into place when we are able to return time after time to the summer reading for clarification of meaning in many of the literary and artistic works which we discuss during the course. The discussions of the relationship between the innermost mind of man and his artistic productivity make the students cognizant of a profound underlying meaning which many critics feel is a valid part of much art. We do not belabor the point, but we feel that we would be doing our students a disservice in a course designed to awaken them to significance in the arts if we left this important area unexplored.

We proceed from the discussion of the summer reading to a consideration of classical mythology, because it provides a rich fabric of meaningful narrative in itself, because it has been drawn upon so consistently by artists and writers, and because it gives us an opportunity to explore artistic manifestations of some of the archetypal symbols which Jung believes spring from the collective unconscious mind of the human race.

After this introduction, we begin the formal presentation with a consideration of the elements and organization of each of the arts in the belief that it is as unreasonable to ask a person to try to understand and appreciate a painting, a literary work, or a piece of music without the proper vocabulary and comprehension of form in each medium as it is to ask him to grasp the meaning of a sentence without the requisite vocabulary and understanding of grammar. Next, we deal with subject, with what a work can be *about* in each of the media. This is an excellent opportunity to illustrate the ways in which the arts are *not* alike and especially to dispel the notion that a painting, piece of music, or other art work which does not represent what we might call a literary subject is meaningless. From subject we go to function, with special reference to changing function in art due to such influences as photography, television, the concert hall, and the museum. Our next unit, style, deals with the ways individual stylistic traits can shape works of art and with the ways the tastes of an age can influence the arts. We deal mainly with the Neoclassical and Romantic periods and with some of the stylistic trends of our own century. The purpose is not to show a development or to cover the arts historically, but to demonstrate how different personalities and different attitudes towards life and towards the arts affect individual works, making them in some ways alike and yet unique. We end our formal presentation with an attempt to arrive at a few meaningful criteria for judgment. Guest speakers at this point very nicely demonstrate to the class that judgment is to a degree a matter of personal taste. But there are certain criteria, such as sincerity, honesty, appropriateness to the medium, genuine feeling as opposed to sentimentalism, which can be demonstrated. Each of the formal units of the course offers the instructors opportunities to present selected works for intensive reading, listening, viewing, study and discussion. We deal not only with recognized masterpieces, but freely with examples of excesses in all the arts in an effort to develop in our students the ability to discriminate between what is genuine and what is not. Although we do not deal with the humanities primarily by periods, we are anxious to show that there is much to be admired from every age, and that fault in the arts comes not from any particular trend that tastes take, but from the excesses into which any trend may lead. We especially stress the importance of both an emotional and an intellectual response to art, the importance of understanding that there can be no art without feeling and no art without form.

The teaching team retires for the final two months or so of the course to give the students an opportunity to present whatever they have been able to learn in their independent study and research. We all feel—students and teachers alike—that some of the most valuable insights and some of the best teaching come from this part of the program. Although it would be dishonest of me to suggest that there are no poor presentations, I can honestly say that many of them are exciting, even inspiring. Most of our students accept the challenge of the responsibility we expect them to take upon themselves and respond in terms of a mature effort. They emerge from the program, we feel, having learned much about the arts, about research techniques, about organizing and handling their time, about their fellow men, and about themselves. We like to think of our course not as a dessert, but as a nourishing main dish on the smorgasbord.

Brooklyn Bridge: A Good Jumping-Off Place

Carl Ladensack

Recently a vistor came to Scarsdale to inquire about current developments in our English program, and as part of her visit she attended a humanities class. She was a mature woman with many years of teaching experience as well as a desire to remain informed about new ideas and practices. While discussing the humanities curriculum before class began, I described the course as an attempt to relate the various arts (painting, sculpture, music, drama, and literature) to one another and to develop understanding and appreciation of man's artistic endeavors. The woman exclaimed gleefully, "We used to have that. We called it auditorium." And I was sent back thirty years in memory to my own class called auditorium in elementary school, and I remembered the prints we saw, the plays we produced, and the music we heard. A great truth arose out of the vistor's exclamation the current trend toward humanities classes resembles the programs that used to be such a vital part of American elementary education, programs that often engaged a variety of teachers in a common effort and aroused the enthusiasm of children and adults alike. These qualities, the cooperation and pleasure, are among the vital contributions of the humanities awakening.

Today I am going to try to illustrate some of the ways in which the Scarsdale humanities program is organized and operated to generate that curiosity and enthusiasm. Our course is structured around a series of topics we adopted from a humanities text that we no longer use. Basically, we try to lead the student to discover a relationship among the arts in their subjects, elements, organization, style, and function. To accomplish this goal, we study works in each of the disciplines and help the student to see that though the medium may be different, the basic purposes and ideas are similar. Hart Crane's "To Brooklyn Bridge" will serve as a good example of our method and objective. Earlier this year, while teaching "To Brooklyn Bridge," I mentioned to the class that I had been invited to give this talk today and that I planned to use the poem as a basis. After class one of the boys stopped and said, "Hey, Mr. Ladensack, you know, for your talk you've got a good jumping-off place." Although I prefer not to pursue all of the implications of the boy's comment, I did find a title and an approach to the topic there.

To Brooklyn Bridge

How many dawns, chill from his rippling rest
The seagull's wings shall dip and pivot him,
Shedding white rings of tumult, building high
Over the chained bay waters Liberty—

Then, with inviolate curve, forsake our eyes
As apparitional as sails that cross
Some page of figures to be filed away;
—Til elevators drop us from our day. . .

I think of cinemas, panoramic sleights
With multitudes bent toward some flashing scene
Never disclosed, but hastened to again,
Foretold to other eyes on the same screen;

And Thee, across the harbor, silver-paced
As though the sun took step of thee, yet left
Some motion ever unspent in thy stride,—
Implicitly thy freedom staying thee!

Out of some subway scuttle, cell or loft
A bedlamite speeds to thy parapets,

Tilting there momently, shrill shirt ballooning,
A jest falls from the speechless caravan.

Down Wall, from girder into street noon leaks,
A rip-tooth of the sky's acetylene;
All afternoon the cloud-flown derricks turn. . .
Thy cables breathe the North Atlantic still.

And obscure as that heaven of the Jews,
Thy guerdon. . .Accolade thou dost bestow
Of anonymity time cannot raise:
Vibrant reprieve and pardon thou dost show.

O harp and altar, of the fury fused,
(How could mere toil align thy choiring strings!)
Terrific threshold of the prophet's pledge,
Prayer of pariah, and the lover's cry,—

Again the traffic lights that skim thy swift
Unfractioned idiom, immaculate sigh of stars,
Beading thy path—condense eternity:
And we have seen night lifted in thine arms.

Under thy shadow by the piers I waited;
Only in darkness is thy shadow clear.
The City's fiery parcels all undone,
Already snow submerges an iron year. . .

O Sleepless as the river under thee,
Vaulting the sea, the prairies' dreaming sod,
Unto us lowliest sometime sweep, descend
And of the curveship lend a myth to God.

—Hart Crane

Basic to my feeling is the idea that any one or all of the major topics of our humanities course can be illustrated in almost any genuine work of art if one has a complete understanding of his goals. Hence, I feel that I can use "To Brooklyn Bridge" to illustrate what a poet writes about, what materials he uses in his writing, how he organizes those materials, what the product does for him and for the reader, and how that work relates to other art forms. Although I want my students to feel that they are making great discoveries—and frequently they do—I realize that most works we will study in a humanities course have been examined and re-examined by experts. How then can a teacher make the student feel that he is engaged in a dynamic pursuit of new ideas? I believe that it can be accomplished in part by giving the student a few facts and then asking him questions about the application of that knowledge to a new subject. I especially like to follow this method in reading a poem without giving the author's name. Short stories, novels, and plays almost always carry with them prejudices deriving from the author's reputation that get in the way of a fresh reading. Hence today we will talk about a poem that can be easily duplicated and studied without having to fear that the student will be parroting what he has found in Monarch notes. The poem could be approached in many ways, but because I want to relate it to other art forms, I would begin with a simple series of questions about the poem. What does it seem to be about? The title indicates that the poem is concerned with Brooklyn Bridge; however, we see instead gulls, water, the Statue of Liberty, ships, pages of figures, file cabinets, elevators, and cinema screens before we turn to the bridge. And then we do not find an actual description of the bridge; instead, we are given effects that the bridge conveys, uses to which it is put, and metaphoric descriptions. We see a man about to commit suicide from it; we note its proximity to Wall Street; we view the city from its shadow. Thus the student is led to conclude that these fragments have some meaning beyond a mere representation of the bridge through the medium of language.

Most students are willing to begin their study of art with an acceptance of the premise that the artist is serious in his intention to convey some meaning. The poem offers an excellent means of analyzing images as objectifications of abstractions. We have a series of seemingly scattered images surrounding a central image of a bridge. What does it all mean?

Because I am theoretically using the work as part of an American studies program, I might at this point digress for a while to elicit from the class a few generalizations about American character, values, attitudes, etc.: America is a land of freedom, freedom that takes multiple forms; America was founded in part on a desire for religious freedom; a concomitant of our love of freedom is the extension of a sense of dignity and worth to people of all social levels, with special emphasis on the importance of the laborer; in pursuit of the American Dream, America has reached great heights in industrial development. These ideas lead us back to the poem to see if they are a part of Crane's thought. The general discussion of America's love of freedom may enable the class to suggest that Crane is contrasting true and false freedom in his opening stanza, in which he presents images of gulls dipping, pivoting, "shedding white rings of tumult, building high/Over the chained bay waters Liberty—." Eventually someone will suggest that for Crane the bridge is a symbol of freedom, because the bridge is a study in motion and stillness. The idea is easily confirmed with the line

Implicitly thy freedom staying thee!

Our problem then becomes one of reconciling the rest of the imagery with this idea. For example, how does a suicide relate?

Here a discussion of the particular medium in which the artist is working is valuable. The student should be led to greater sensitivity to language by this experience. Why has the poet chosen the particular works that he has used? How does the sound of the poem convey his meaning? Does the punctuation or capitalization of the poem serve any special purpose? The suicide is called a *bedlamite.* No great imagination is necessary for a student to offer an explanation of the etymology of the word, and in his explanation he may use the word *asylum.* Here is another path to follow. Can the bridge be offering asylum or escape to someone deeply troubled by the pressures of modern life in his "subway scuttle, cell or loft?" Is there any other fragment in the poem to indicate that Crane believes man seeks escape from his daily routine? Inevitably, someone will offer stanza three as an example: the movies, "panoramic sleights," invite the "multitudes" who are "bent toward some flashing scene" after elevators have dropped them from their day spent over pages of figures in offices. The word *bent* reveals the intensity of their desires, which are not satisfied by the cinematic escape. Only the bridge seems to be a satisfying experience, so satisfying that Crane deifies it in his very first reference to it. Why then does he not continue to capitalize *thee* in the rest of stanza four? In response to this question I have had students offer the idea that it is Crane's way of bringing God down to earth and transforming spirit into flesh. It is an idea I hesitate to reject and one we shall have to reconcile with the concluding stanza.

Having established symbolic meaning to the bridge, we can begin to expand its meanings beyond that first, relatively assigned interpretation. What else can a bridge mean? Stanza eight offers a clue that we have a celebration of American industry and its mastery of materials. Perhaps at this point a report on research into the history of the bridge is appropriate. Washington Roebling's struggles to convince backers, the spectacular deaths of workers hit by lashing cables, Roebling's loss of health, his wife's aid in continuing the work while he was paralyzed, his son's assumption of supervisory duties after Roebling's death, all work to impress the student with the fantastic accomplishment of building the bridge. But most impressive to them is the fact that it was the first great suspension bridge and that a suspension bridge at that time was "an act of faith." Then I tell them about the ironic circumstances of Crane's living in the very room at 110 Columbia Heights from which Roebling had supervised construction of the bridge. The student must not, however, be allowed to settle for the easy idea that Crane is merely celebrating America's industrial accomplishments, for that explanation leaves too much of the poem unread. Hence we must look further for more meanings. This search for additional meanings also helps in establishing that the metaphor that develops into a symbol is vast in its power of suggestion, and that multiple meanings may coexist in a figure.

One additional interpretation rises immediately in response to the question of what relationship the bridge has to the workers who built it. For those workers it is a monument:

> . . . Accolade thou dost bestow
> Of anonymity time cannot raise:
> Vibrant reprieve and pardon thou dost show.

This section often stimulates a discussion of man's desire for immortality and the various forms of expression that the desire takes. Depending upon the backgrounds of the students at the time, we may develop some fairly sophisticated statements about the creative urge, the perishability of man, and the persistance of art. Thus the student is learning about the function of art.

Perhaps the question that leads to the fullest understanding of the symbolism of the bridge concerns the author's attitude toward it. When I ask the students to give me words and phrases that show how Crane feels about the bridge, I am given, "O harp and altar," "how could mere toil align thy choiring strings," "condense enternity," "lend a myth to God." The reverential attitude is evident. We discover that the bridge has a transcendent symbolism, that it represents everything that joins, that it carries a faith in something absolute. The poem no longer is simply American; rather it is universal in its implications of the value of collective human effort and the relationship of the individual, his achievement with other men, and God. A valuable discussion might arise out of the request, "lend a myth to God." What are myths, and what part do they play in our lives?

So far the poem has been useful as a means of approaching almost all of the major topics that I indicated form the rationale of our course: subject, elements, medium, organization, and function. Perhaps organization has been somewhat slighted, but in class I would probably spend some time on the logical transitions, the cinematic technique of cutting, blending, panning, etc. An understanding of the organization might also arise in trying to establish the style of the poem, its mode of expression. Perhaps the style becomes clearer by introducing another medium. Joseph Stella's *Brooklyn Bridge* is the perfect companion work, for it seems to me to be a translation of the words into line and color. If I flash a slide onto a screen or show a print of the painting and ask the students in what ways the painting relates to the poem, the response is quick and lively. The reverential attitude is the first point brought out. The bridge is painted as if it were a cathedral window. Even the shape of the supports resembles the arch of a Gothic structure. Other parallels to the poem leap out: the "choiring strings" formed by the cables, which are painted in harp-like beauty; the stylized stars "beading thy path"; the city viewed under the bridge. But the additional quality that allows the student to see more in the poem is the upward thrust of the lines of the bridge, which express an aspiring emotion. We see that what has been a very practical construction—a bridge linking busy parts of a city—now takes on a mystical significance as Stella gives us his large, dramatic, personal interpretation "of the beauty of technology." He is not presenting the bridge exactly as it exists, but rather as he sees it or interprets it.

We also see that the abstract style of the picture is similar to the style of the poem. The poem is a series of fragments that are carefully fitted together into a cohesive pattern. Images in the poem are suggested not by careful, full development, but by significant parts that carry in themselves clues to the whole. They are like the cubes, triangles, and other shapes that fit together into the jig-saw of the picture. The two disciplines reinforce each other and show that art movements in different media may be analogous.

This discussion of style may lead to more generalized studies of what creates a style and the relationship of style to the period in which it exists. The class would easily identify the poem and the painting as moderately modern. If it is useful, I might give them the name *futurist* to identify the characteristics of Stella's work, but I would want the label to serve only as a quick means of identifying the characteristics that make it futuristic. To gain better understanding of style, I would eventually contrast the poem and the painting with other poems and paintings, preferably on the same or a similar subject. By examining the way in which several artists view a common subject, the student learns to look carefully at the parts that compose a work. Hence he is better prepared to look at other works and is building a foundation for real judgment rather than a superficial statement such as "I like it" or "I hate it."

Ultimately, the student may even offer the idea that the poem itself or the picture is a figurative bridge. For the artist his work is an attempt to transcend his environment and its limitations. Whether he is trying to reach God by it or merely trying to convey to other men something of his vision, the art is his means of bridging the gap. The gaps may be in time, space, or understanding, but the work of art is useful in uniting all. The works of the past serve in the present to inform us of the people of the past. Works of other places tell us of the people who dwell there. We see at the basis of art throughout the ages common elements of man's search for meanings in his life. We find that he has always used art as a means of trying to convey what cannot be expressed in scientific language—the mystery of life. I would hope that they would discover, as Joseph Conrad wrote in his preface to *Nigger of the Narcissus,* that

the artist appeals to that part of our being which is not dependent on wisdom: to that in us which is a gift and not an acquisition—and, therefore, more permanently enduring. He speaks to our capacity for delight and wonder, to the sense of mystery surrounding our lives; to our sense of pity, and beauty, and pain; to the latent feeling of fellowship with all creation—and to the subtle but invincible conviction of solidarity that knits together the loneliness of innumerable hearts, to the solidarity in dreams, in joy, in sorrow, in aspirations, in illusions, in hope, in fear which binds men to each other, which binds together all humanity—the dead to the living and the living to the unborn.

Where do we go from this topic? Perhaps these works may be the beginning of a larger study of American achievement as a topic for art. Perhaps they could stimulate a study of the importance of the city in human affairs. What part has the American city played in shaping the American consciousness? Perhaps the study could be a springboard into the past and the influences that created the American character. Any one of these topics could be used for either a group or an individual project. Humanities courses inevitably suggest more questions rather than give tidy answers. Therefore, each subject studied becomes a jumping-off place for the next one, and hopefully the student's mind will never come to a final stopping-off place.

Humanities 9

Elmer Moore

Foreword. This original article was written in 1965 preparatory to the establishment of a ninth-grade humanities program. Although it is now 1969, the validity and the logic of the article have changed little. I have taken the liberty of adding a few footnotes and a brief evaluation after four years of observing the program in action.

Rationale. That one learns by doing, and that learning is an active process, are hardly questionable. It is equally valid to assert that a large part of the activity in a pupil-teacher situation should be on the part of the pupil, if he is to be the learner; if both pupil and teacher are to learn there must be proportionate activity on the part of each. It is this thinking that determines the method of this humanities program.

The overlapping of subject matter presented in separate disciplines and the segmentation of historical and philosophical movements into isolated subject areas have long troubled many educators. It is too much to expect that a student will relate the "Battle Hymn of the Republic" and "Dixie" sung in an eighth-grade music class with the literature of Crane, Timrod, and Whitman studied in an Eleventh-grade literature class with the history of the Civil Was covered in a twelfth-grade American history course. Little provision is made for learning the real motives for the Civil War. Graphic arts representations of this period are seldom presented, and rarely within the context of a unified study. The cultural situation of the Southern way of life, states' rights issues, economic overtones, and ethnic complexities (the full impact of which is hardly realized one hundred years later)[1] are seldom combined into a depth study of the Civil War. The same is true with nearly every significant era of man's development.

Recently there have been many hopeful moves toward the unification of subject areas. This humanities program seeks to correlate the art, music, literature, and history of particular ages into a single unified study.

The dilemma of the survey versus the depth study must also be faced. A thorough study of the history of America 1900-1930 would take an entire school year; literature of this period warrants the same study. Specialization in one era in one subject discipline will hardly result in the broad background needed by high school students. Likewise, time limitations prevent the survey course from providing the necessary depth in any one particular age. Neither approach provides for the crossing of subject-matter lines necessary for an over-all understanding of any particular period.

Educators realize that not all students possess the same interests. Not all are

---

[1] By 1969 the impact referred to is much more recognizable in the numerous ethnic complexities that have blossomed into very ugly flowers.

interested in the same subject, the same area, or the same depth. But each student needs an over-all background or survey of a particular area of study and should have ample opportunity and encouragement to specialize in as much depth as desirable in an area of his choosing.

Another problem in education has been the slow, unwilling, or disinterested student, usually relegated to some form of "dumping ground," such as the so-called business, agricultural, vocational, opportunity, or local program. Each of these programs has academic merit, and to shunt the apathetic student into any one of these areas helps neither the course nor the student. The separation of the less academically inclined students into a special or different program often results in a stigma that exists throughout high school. Once in such a program, a student is rarely inspired to excel. It would seem, therefore, that all students should be afforded an opportunity to discover the same basic material on various levels of difficulty or intensity.

Considering these factors—the need for a learning situation involving an active learning process, an interdisciplinary study of related subject areas, a necessity for both depth and survey study, and a desire to consider student ability, interests, and needs—teachers and administrators at Dobbs Ferry High School conceived the present Humanities 9 program.

During planning, careful consideration was given to the question of what a ninth-grade student should know. It was felt that all the factual learning in English, history, math, or science would be superficial unless the student had some real reasons for pursuing such facts. This does not imply that facts are unimportant, but the association of many facts as well as the knowledge of how and when to apply them is as important as knowing the facts themselves. Therefore, it was felt that a student should first understand the culture or society in which he must apply his learnings. This orientation was termed self-group awareness, and the development of self-group awareness was set down as one of the basic objectives of this program.

Activities are planned to encourage students to consider such questions as "Who am I? Why am I here? What is my purpose? How will I fulfill my purpose? Where am I now with reference to my goals? In what direction shall I proceed?" A consideration of what man is, and how he became as he is, provides a larger frame of reference for questions of this type.

Exercise in communications skills, an awareness of the chronology of man's development, and the realization that particular problems persist throughout many specific stages of man's development comprise the remainder of the over-all objective for the ninth-grade program.

An introductory unit raised the question "what are the humanities?" and dealt briefly with a look at comtemporary man. This led to the question of how man evolved as he did. A chronological study is "post-holed" at the primitive, Greek, medieval, Renaissance, and modern periods, culminating with another look, this time in more detail, at contemporary man.

Organization of Units. Each particular era to be studied is arranged into a unit, better termed a "creative learning enterprise".[2] Units consist of an introduction, a pre-test, an over-all objective, contributory objectives, activities and materials, sharing activities, evaluation (a post-test), and follow up activities. These units are sequential and cumulative.

An introduction to a unit provides an overview of the era to be studied. This should provide motivation and direction. A pre-test is employed to determine what a student already knows about a particular culture prior to a study of it. The over-all objective should state in inclusive yet specific terms the over-all purpose of a particular unit, for example, "An understanding of the survival of primitive man," or "An appreciation of the humanistic importance of the Greek culture."

Both over-all objectives and contributory objectives are stated in terms of understanding, appreciation, or awareness (really behavioral changes) attainable in degrees. Perplexing for the statistician is the fact that these degrees of attainment are not always measurable. Still, they are observable.

Units are planned to last from four to six weeks each; most of this time is spent in carrying out the activities leading to the attainment of each specific contributory objective. The attainment of the contributory objectives leads to the fulfillment of the over-all objective. (See diagram on page 241.)

Provision is made for each student, working with a group of from three to five fellow students, to pursue any specific area of a unit in as much depth as he can master. Each group is also responsible for sharing its learning with all other groups. Effectively carried out, this process affords each student an opportunity to study an area of particular interest, represented by a particular contributory objective, in as much depth as he chooses; in addition, it provides each student with a survey or overview of all the other areas of the study (the rest of the contributory objectives). Sharing activities (wherein students share the knowledge they have attained in specific areas) can be reinforced and substantiated by the teaching team, whose task during sharing activities is to help correlate and facilitate assimilation of the abundance of material presented. These culminating activities should be particularly rich and varied, because it is here that students gain an understanding of areas of study other than the ones they pursue in depth. This broad understanding is necessary for satisfactory attainment of the over-all objective.

Method. Humanities 9 is planned as a series of creative learning enterprises or units, therefore, as in any good program, careful advance planning is essential. An over-all goal or objective must be clearly stated and understood by both teachers and students. Contributory or shorter range objectives likewise must be clearly stated and understood. The activities or means of attaining these objectives should also be clear, specific, and flexible. However, aside from a clearly stated and

------

[2] "Creative learning enterprise" is a term propagated by Dr. Robert Bream, Education Department, Lehigh University. Units are creative in that they provide for means and methods as unique and different as the teachers and students can create. The reason for the association is learning. The activity in which people combine their efforts for the mutual advancement or betterment of all is called an enterprise.

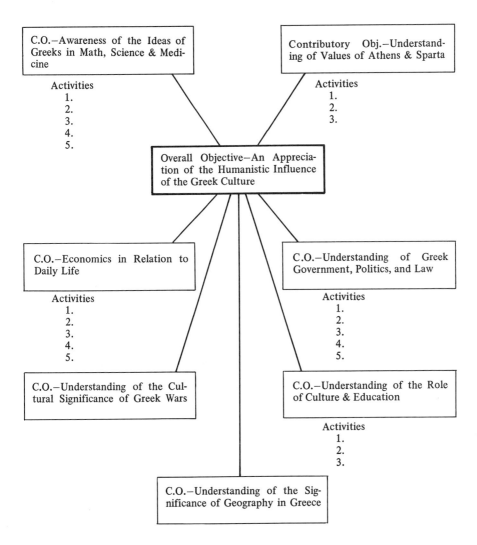

understood goal and a clearly prescribed direction for attaining it, method is primarily up to the teacher.

Considering the abundance of material available on educational method, it is probably trite to emphasize student involvement. But this is one of the essential ideas of the program. The story of the professor who dreamed he was giving one of his lectures and woke up to find that he was illustrates this point. Although the so-called lecture method has merit, it should be used sparingly.

However, so long as a teacher has the objectives of the program clearly in mind, understands thoroughly the direction he must follow to reach these goals, and recognizes the necessity for a great deal of active student involvement, he may choose any method that will effectively meet these criteria. Group lectures, individual instruction, independent study, various team presentations, small group discussions, and small group lectures are all among the possible methods utilizable in such a program.

Scheduling. The scheduling of this program is at once simple and complex. To set aside a time block of three consecutive periods, assign four teachers and 120 ninth-grade students to them, and introduce an interdisciplinary course may seem easy. But here the simplicity ends.[3]

Groups of class size (twenty-five to thirty students) are assigned to each teacher for homeroom purposes (attendance, morning announcements). Then those students who are carrying out activities in groups must meet with their respective groups, and those who are assigned to developmental writing (within the context of the unit) must meet with the writing teacher. Lecture groups must meet with lecture teams. Some students work on art projects in the art room, some do research in the library, and some meet with special teachers. (A library large enough to accommodate a major portion of the student body is a boon to programs like this.) It is no wonder that some students become confused and roam. The teaching team members must coordinate group work, individual instruction, lectures, films, and library periods on their schedules.

Teacher schedules should be prepared first and revised each week as the program advances. A teacher's weekly schedule may look like this:

Teacher A (English)

◄───		HOMEROOM DUTIES		───►
Preliminary Discussion Gps. A-E	Planning Gps. A-E	Gp. A	Dev. Writing 20 Students	↑ Open ↓
Film— All Students Auditorium ↓	Dev. Writing 15 Students ↓	Gp. B	Gp. E	Dev. Writing 20 Students
		Dev. Writing 25 Students	↑ Open ↓	
	Dev. Writing 20 Students ↓	Gp. C		↑ Open ↓
Follow-up Discussion Gps. E-J		Gp. D	Dev. Writing 20 Students	Weekly Evaluation Gps. A-E
◄───		Team Planning		───►

[3] Scheduling was our biggest problem when the program was put into action. We learned to permit our academic objectives, rather than administrative expediency, to determine our schedule (within reasonable limits) and still reschedule each student many times throughout the year. The topic of really flexible scheduling would require several books.

A student assigned to teacher A's homeroom group may be scheduled as follows:

Pupil 1 - Group B

Homeroom - Announcements				
Pre. Disc. Teacher A	Planning Teacher A	Meet with Teacher D	Meet with Teacher B	Discussion with Tchr. B
Film Auditorium	Research in Library	Meet with Teacher A	Group Work	Dev. Writing Teacher A
		Group Planning		Meet with Teacher C
		Group Work		
Follow-up Teacher C				Weekly Evaluation Teacher A

Larger group presentations and lectures should be scheduled first, on both the teachers' and students' schedules. Time spent in planning with the students should result in a clearer understanding of goals and objectives by both pupil and teacher. Plans should include the purpose of a study, the nature of the activities involved in such a study, materials needed, plans for evaluation, as well as the amount and sequence of time devoted to the study,

This is undoubtedly the most difficult part of the program. Teachers who have planned their own lessons, centered around themselves as propagators of learning, are most reluctant to include the student in their plans. It is disappointing to see teachers who, uneasy with pupil-centered activities, dissolve groups into teacher-centered classes without really being aware of what they do.

The Role of the Teacher. Teachers are responsible for providing an overview of each unit, establishing direction for objectives and activities, and getting students started on their specific activities. The teacher should move from the leadership role into that of advisor and resource person as soon as possible. Each teacher on the team also serves as a specialist in his particular field, so that groups or students with particular needs in art, music, social studies, or writing will have help readily available.

As though this weren't enough, teachers are responsible for guiding students to plan carefully their presentations or sharing activities. They must constantly meet with groups that are inclined to "get off the track," establish and maintain direction in independent study, and regulate pressure on students, as well as determine the structure of various areas studied.

Teachers also plan team presentations, combining their ability in various fields into a unified demonstration or lecture-discussion. Planning and coordinating such a program as this requires at least half of each team member's school day, and provision to make all members of the team available for this planning time is essential to the success of the program. Locating and obtaining materials is also a great time-consuming activity, and teachers must be provided with such time.

Because of the nature of such a program, only those teachers of superior ability, exceptionally wide background, almost unlimited flexibility, and tremendous dedication should be considered for team membership [4]

The Role of the Student. Students in Humanities 9 play the same roles as students in any other program. They are essentially learners; they take notes, answer questions, memorize material, and take tests. In addition to learning facts, however, they seek concepts, associations, and relationships among the various problems of man. A student may be a group leader, responsible to the group and his advisor and charged with getting the members of his group to carry out their activities and attain their objective. He may be a process observer, responsible for helping the group chairman stay "on the track," or a recorder who chronicles the group's progress. A student with an unusual background in a particular field may become a resource person and share his talents with other groups or the entire class.

One of the unique elements of this program is that it involves all ninth-grade students. But this precludes neither homogeneous nor heterogeneous grouping. Homeroom groups are arranged alphabetically, work group arrangements are based on interest, discussion groups are arranged according to group topics, and writing groups are organized by ability. Groups change often. A conscious effort is made to vary the composition or groups as frequently as desirable, and all groups change with each new unit.

Considering the many possible roles created by this program, no student ever need repeat the same role in the same group.

Emphasis is on activity, and the student who cannot adjust to the class, work group, discussion group, or grade group has the opportunity to elect independent study. Here he pursues a specific area of study determined by himself and his advisors. The guidance department stands by to hold group counseling or individual counseling sessions with the pupils who do not seem comfortable in any of the aforementioned patterns.

Afterword. The 1968-69 version of Humanities 9 is little different from the 1965 program. Structure and organization have remained essential elements of the program. A cinema series and a humanities newspaper *Man Alive* have been added. A-V materials and advices are widely used and have embellished the program greatly.

Humanities 9 is not a panacea. It has meant much hard work and far more preparation than any other program known to me or to any of our team members. Most of our students enjoy humanities and indicate that they learn more and better than in any pervious program. But a few of the disinterested and apathetic remain disinterested and apathetic. A summary of our evaluations of the program indicates,

---

[4] I suspect that the greatest single problem in any program is personnel. Classicists, traditionalists, and progressives have been among the successful teachers in this program. The success or failure of any classroom learning situation is determined by the personality of the teacher in the room.

among other things, that students read more material from a wider field than previously; that they write more and improve their skills in written and oral expression through the utilization of the skills in real situations; that they are delighted with the study of philosophy and anthropology, as well as with newspapers and films that are an essential part of the program; that skills in learning fact as well as the basic communications arts are developed and enhanced; and that students do become concerned and involved in the basic problems of values and obligations that have perennially beset all man's civilizations.

Humanities at Elk Grove

Richard Calisch

From the moment it opened in September 1966, Elk Grove High School was intent upon assaulting the shibboleths. An exciting climate of freedom to attempt pervaded the school. Encouragment of self-actualization on the part of faculty members led to interesting innovations in school procedures and class room styles. Among the ideas to spring from the faculty was the desire to concentrate at least a segment of the curriculum upon the nebulous "discipline" known as the humanities. Realization of this suggestion was made not only possible but natural by the fact that the school had abandoned the traditional departmental lines of organization and was operating under a divisional T/O in which departments were combined into larger administrative units called division. In one case, Art, English, and Music comprised the English-Fine Arts Division. At the outset, then, the term humanities was defined, temporarily at least, by pragmatic consideration. If Elk Grove were to concentrate on the humanities, it would commence within the "humanities" division.

Very quickly faculty interested zeroed in on three aspects of a humanities thrust: a humanities course, a humanities resource center, and a series of co-curricular activities to be sponsored by the division. As is always the case in matters involving public education, a series of meetings was held. Attendance at these meetings, however, was entirely voluntary: only the interested showed up. Because of this, action started swiftly. Social science teachers were brought into the discussions as understanding of what was to be accomplished developed, and out of these expanded meetings in December, 1966, came the Elk Grove Two Year Humanities Plan—a big name for a logical development.

The Plan. The plan involved three phases: planning, which was to be completed by September, 1967; operation, which will continue through the 1967-68 school year; and evaluation and refinement, which will be completed prior to September, 1968. At that time it is hoped that the results of the plan will become permanent additions to the Elk Grove *modus operandi.* The plan had and has as its aim the institution at Elk Grove High School of a course in the humanities, a humanities resource center, and a series of co-curricular activities related to the humanities.

The Course. The first step in the program to plan and institute the humanities course was to initiate correspondence with schools having quality humanities programs. From twenty-five institutions came brochures, pamphlets, course outlines, and other information, each piece of which was studied carefully by those faculty members who were working on the humanities program. Needless to say, much of the information was to prove invaluable as the Elk Grove plan matured.

Step two involved a "dry run" of the humanities course approach (involving ideas gleaned in part from the information received from the twenty-five cooperating schools) in the existing fine arts appreciation course. This course, taught by an art teacher, and a music teacher, was informally modified for the spring semester in two ways. An English teacher was asked to give six lectures on literary works and the format was changed from chronological art-music history to a thematic approach involving three historical periods. The theme chosen was "The Hero in Art, Music, and Literature"; the periods chosen were Greek, Renaissance, and Modern. As a result of this one semester trial, several decisions were reached: the theme chosen was judged to be too restrictive to sustain over a whole year; a social science teacher was needed to supply the social and historical background to the arts; the course was felt to require more than one hour a day; and a full scale planning session was deemed necessary to pre-plan the course so that the four teachers would be aware of each other's materials, methods, and interests.

Consequently a four week summer workshop was convened during June and July of 1967 to plan the humanities course for the following year.

The four teachers who had expressed interest in teaching the course, one of whom had attended the NCTE Humanities Institute in New York in May, met daily for four weeks. At the end of that time they had devised the outline of what they thought would be an exciting course. Primary to it were to be three questions which were selected to serve as the basis for instruction. They were:

1. What has man over the ages thought and felt about himself?
2. How has he expressed these thoughts and feelings?
3. How do these thoughts and feelings affect the man of today?

Four cultural periods were selected: Greek, Renaissance, 19th Century Romantic, and Modern (post World Was II). Each of these periods was to be examined in the light of the three questions. Included in the first quarter, for example, would be study of the Greek City-State, religion, the philosophies of Plato and Aristotle and the history of the "Golden Age". Along with this the students would read Aeschylus's *Agamemnon*, Sophocle's *Oedipus Rex,* Homer's *Illiad,* selected myths, a dialogue of Plato, and a selection from Aristotle. In addition they would see slides of works by Greek sculptors and architects and hear and discuss music based on mythological themes. Always these works would be discussed in terms of three key questions.

The course would meet two hours a day and would be limited to forty seniors of average level or above. The literature and history teachers would trade off the first hour, the art and music teachers the second. A tentative, flexible day-by-day course outline was devised by each teacher and correlated with those of the other three. In addition, over 100 books were examined in order to determine which works of literature could be most advantageously used. Films were previewed and music selected. By the end of the workshop the humanities course, called HUMEX (*ex*perimental *hum*anities) was ready to begin operation. After a year the course will be evaluated, revised, and refined if it is to become a permanent part of the curriculum at Elk Grove High School.

The Resource Center. A simultaneous step in the Elk Grove humanities involved the establishment of a humanities resource center, a combination library, A-V room, and lounge where the students could gather to study, read, listen, or view surrounded by a wealth of books, magazines, slides, records, and art reproductions. A project listing the resources was written and submitted under the terms of Title III of the National Defense Education Act; it was subsequently accepted and the materials were purchased and placed in a class room which had been set aside. A committee of ten students was selected by the student body to act as administrators of the room; its first activity was to give a dance at which enough money was raised to purchase comfortable chairs and a few magazine tables for the center. The committee also helped during the summer to catalogue all the resources. The room opened in September, 1967, and is now available all day to all students and faculty. It currently contains about 800 books, 200 records, a large collection of art reproductions and slides, three phonographs with earphones, a slide viewer, and pegboard wall space for exhibits of student art work. The room also serves as a pleasant place for small groups to meet, for poetry readings, and sing-alongs.

The Activities. The third stage of the Elk Grove plan involved establishment of a popular series of activities related to literature and the arts which would supplement the school programs. This phase of the program was put into action during the school year 1966-67. Expansion of the high school field trip program to include evening and Saturday trips and a weekend excursion was the first step. Trips were taken to theatrical and motion picture productions playing in the Chicago area: *Fiddler on the Roof, The Glass Menagerie, Spoon River Anthology, The Taming of the Shrew,* and *Othello.* In addition, a group of forty-four students and two teachers and their wives visited Springfield, Illinois, to see the Lincoln shrines, Vachel Lindsay's home, and the Edgar Lee Masters country near Petersburg. Other groups took Saturday trips to the University of Chicago to participate in the humanities seminar series.

Trips, however, were not the only form of co-curricular activities sponsored by the English and Fine Arts Division.

A series of eleven afternoon and evening presentations was initiated in February, 1967. These included feature films based on great dramas—*Desire Under the Elms, Cyrano de Bergerac, Kiss Me Kate;* a group of short films of an experimental nature; a choral concert by the high school singing groups; a group of readings and monologues by the forensics league; and lectures by teachers and local guests on such subjects as *The History of Chicago Architecture* (with slides), *Spiritual Aspects of Shakespeare, A Short History of the Movies,* and *The Life and Works of*

Leonardo da Vinci (with slides). These sessions were generally well attended and are being continued during the 1967-68 school year.

This three part program has been the result of the efforts of many people: teachers, students, administrators, and members of the community. It has cost money; both district and government funds have been made available to the project. Many people have put time and cooperation and effort into it, but the program has, at least at this point, been successful primarily because it originates with the people who were to be involved and only those people became involved who were interested. The Humanities program at Elk Grove High School is just one result of a self-actualization philosophy which supports the freedom to attempt of the school community.

A High School Humanities Program

Owen J. Murphy, Jr.

A unique program begun at St. Bernard's Central Catholic High School during 1965-66 has convinced many people in the Fitchburg, Massachusetts area that "top scholars can be graduated from high school."

The words are those of the Rev. Martin P. Donahue, headmaster of St. Bernard's and the driving force behind the school's new humanities program. But the idea was echoed by teachers, pupils, and parents as the first year of the program was discussed and evaluated during the summer months.

Briefly, the humanities program at St. Bernard's presents to selected students the entire background of their 20-century culture in an integrated four-year course of studies. The core subject is world history, broken down into four chronological parts. It incorporates as part of the basic study of history, studies in art, architecture and literature, art appreciation and music appreciation, religion and philosophy, politics, and geography. Class lectures in the program utilize visual aids, movies, and slides to a great extent. There are frequent invitations to visiting lecturers and field trips to nearby museums.

Success in the program, Father Donahue explains, "depends on the student's ability to read. The students now taking part in it have been invited to do so. Their ability to read—and comprehend—was the deciding factor in selecting each student."

Parents Can Participate. "In planning the overall humanities program, we did not intend to inaugurate something only for the "elite" student, although the basic program is directed toward the student of superior reading ability. As we anticipated, we have already found that everyone in the school—faculty as well as students, and even the community at large, particularly parents of students in the program—can benefit from it. For that reason," he continued, "we have already begun studying ways in which variations of the basic program could be offered students with a lesser proficiency in reading and ways in which more adults could benefit more directly."

Parent participation in the program last year was mostly indirect, he explained. This year we plan to have a lecture one night each week, specially for parents of students in the humanities program, in which the materials covered by the students in class during that week will be explained to the parents. This will be in addition to the public lecture program given last year for faculty members, other students in the school, and parents of all students in the school, by guest lecturers in the humanities program.

Last year 40 of the 279 members of the class of 1969 were selected to take part in the humanities program. These same 40 will continue the course as sophomores this year; in addition, 79 of the incoming class of 260, will begin their humanities studies. Each freshman and sophomore in the program will take all other required courses with their classmates. However, freshmen will follow the humanities program in place of the world history course, while sophomores will take it in place of an elective subject.

Until last year, all students at St. Bernard's the largest high school in the diocese of Worcester, studied world history as a required subject in the freshman year. "Then we received permission from the Massachusetts Department of Education to substitute the first part of the humanities program for the world history course," Father Donahue said.

"We do anticipate some scheduling problems as the program continues," he explained. "The problem will not be in finding time for the courses in the schedule, since the humanities students will take these courses in place of other electives. Rather the major problem we foresee now is what to offer these students, for example, as an English course in their junior year in place of the "tired" course in literature we have been offering all students in previous years. Certainly, these students will not be content with an uninspiring course."

Presentation of the humanities program is chronological. Freshmen study the history of man from prehistoric times through the fall of the Roman Empire; sophomores study the period from the Middle Ages through the Renaissance period; juniors continue from the Renaissance to the early part of the 19th century; and seniors cover the period from the early 1800's to the present.

"This chronology is logical." Father Donahue explained, "because what we are trying to do is 'integrate the cultural advance of mankind' including the whole 'historical complex'—that is, how people lived and what they thought and how they expressed their mode of living through the fine arts. We hope that the student will acquire for himself a point of view sufficiently broad in outline to discern those factors responsible for his place in Western culture."

The course presentation is broad and diverse utilizing class lectures, outside reading and term papers, field trips to museums, studies of films, slides and recordings as well as lectures by "visiting" members of the faculty and guest lecturers on specific subjects. "We felt such an approach would provide opportunities for the students' development without overemphasizing any one area of study."

"What we are trying to do," Father Donahue emphasized, "is to teach the students to think with a sense of history. This interrelationship of period history, literature and the fine arts lays such a foundation."

Although the emphasis in the program is on Western culture, the course does not give a "vacuumed approach" to the subject. It integrates ideas from all cultures showing the student that man of any period owes his mode of living to a continuum of life's facets.

Father Donahue decided to incorporate such a course into St. Bernard's curriculum soon after he was transferred there from a smaller diocesan high school. He had worked with such a program on the college level at St. Michaels's College in Vermont, where he was graduated and had taught modern languages for seven years before beginning his studies for the priesthood. While some American high schools, public and private, offer "enrichment programs" which study different aspects of the humanities concept, "to our knowledge this is the first total program on the high school level," he stated.

The inauguration of the humanities program does not mean that some "peripheral courses" taught at St. Bernard's in the past, such as art or music appreciation or other history courses, will be dropped. They may even be expanded for the benefit of students who are not enrolled in the humanities program. The humanities students will study these subjects as part of their total program. Only two of St. Bernard's 31-member faculty actively teach the program: Charles McManus, who teaches history and English, is coordinator, while Sister M. Virginia, P.B.V.M., teaches the classics. However, all the other teachers, nine laymen and laywomen and 20 Sisters, have felt its effects in their own classes. Therefore, the school plans to expand its in-service training program on the humanities material for all faculty members, because each teacher is exposed to students in the program in other classes—and exposed to his questioning. In addition to taking part in the in-service programs and attending lectures by visiting authorities, every member of the faculty is expected to have read every one of the books assigned to students in the humanities program.

Extensive Reading Program. Last year alone, when only one class was taking the course, the outside reading list included ten titles: the Bible; the Oedipus Plays of Sophocles; the Great Dialogues of Plato; *Antigone* by Jean Anouilh; Homer's *Iliad; The Confessions of St. Augustine;* Thucydides' *Peloponnesian Wars,* and Bulfinch's *Mythology.* The text book for the course for each of the four years is the *Record of Mankind* by Roehm, Buske, Webster and Wesley.[1] Also each student owns a supplementary text, the *Intellectual and Cultural History of the Western World* in five volumes.

"Could freshmen in high school devour all of that, in addition to the demands of their other courses?" Father Donahue was asked.

"They had no trouble at all," he answered quickly. Then he proceeded to read some critiques of the course given by the students themselves at the end of the school year last June. The only major (and almost universal) criticism was that there was "too much note-taking during class hours." Father Donahue believes the criticism was justified from high school freshmen who are not used to note-taking.

[1] Published by D. C. Heath & Co., Boston.

As a result, the teachers are planning to mimeograph most of the notes this year, giving them more time to go into explanations in the classroom.

The films used with the course have been prepared by the Harvard and Yale faculties in conjunction with Encyclopaedia Brittanica. St. Bernard's obtained them from the Massachusetts Council on Humanities. The slides, mostly of great treasures and remains of ancient cities, have been "acquired from wherever we could get them," he said.

Brings Culture to Community. The young priest noted that the "side effects" of the program on school life "have been amazing." Other students' interest in art has been profoundly affected by visiting lecturers such as Rabbi Harold Roth of Fitchburg, and by several others who have addressed faculty members, other students and parents in addition to the humanities students. The field trips to such places as the Worcester Art Museum and the Boston Museum of Fine Arts, in which only humanities students participated, have also had a profound effect. "The humanities students started giving art classes in the cafeteria after they made the trips," Father Donahue smiled.

More cooperative efforts with other schools in the area have been another effect of the new program. Other educators in the area have been invited to present programs and to give their advice and reactions to the course also, and all teachers in the Fitchburg-Leominster area have been invited to the monthly public lectures given by experts who had already addressed the humanities students in their classroom. Thus far, all the schools in the region, public and private, have been represented.

Such meetings are important not only as an educational tool, but because they have helped dispel the idea that Catholic schools are not interested in what other schools are doing. "We are vitally interested," he stated.

Another by-product of the course was the inauguration last year of "St. Bernard's High School civic and cultural series," which projected the school boldly into the civic life of the community. Last year the program included the presentation of Handel's *Messiah* by the Worcester Orchestra and Chorus, and the Lenten presentation of Bach's *St. Matthew's Passion,* by them and the Worcester Oratorio Society. A pops concert was held in the spring at the school's football stadium. Although students in the humanities program had no direct role in the presentations, all attended. Father Donahue believes that as the program continues through the high school years "these students will plan a vital role in encouraging their follow students to become more ambitious in all extracurricular activities."

Although the syllabus for the program will not be complete until it has been in operation at least four years, "we are most encouraged by the first year—and especially by the students' and Parents' reactions to it," Father summarized. "Some students—and some parents, too—had difficulty in adjusting to the program at first, but the students' critiques at the end of the your showed that they knew what it was all about."

One said: "It is a different and interesting approach to history." Another wrote: "It showed me how to understand what I read and how to allocate my time."

"This is what it's all about," Father Donahue stated. "We become too narrow by giving a course in history without incorporating into it all the other things that made that history. These students are seeing history, not as something alien, or as a series of hard-to-memorize dates, but as a documentation of life."

Literature and the Humanities Ideal

Max Bogart

Literature, instead of being an accessory, is the fundamental *sine qua non* of complete living. *Arnold Bennett*

In recent statements certain educators have urged the schools to return to an emphasis on form and technical analysis in the teaching of literature. Essentially their thesis is that English teachers have been obsessed with the emphasis on ideas, and, in their zeal, they have overemphasized content and neglected the study of form to the detriment of the student. At times the attack is so vehement that one would think that the humanistic tradition is the path to illiteracy and corruption.

Were it possible to separate substance and form, it is at best a wavy line of division, and where and how is it to be drawn? The return-to-technical-analysis proponents claim to have discovered a national trend in their direction; however, in examining the polls for evidence of this momentous movement no significant data were found.

Nevertheless, it is asserted that the trend is with us, but is it not difficult, if possible, to "return" to an approach which, unfortunately, many teachers did not leave? Many classes today are cluttered with definitions of quantitative meters, heroic couplet and similar earthshaking, cogitative matters, but too often the content of the story, essay, poem or play, is absent. In the teaching of literature it is not, according to Coleridge, the acquisition of "lifeless technical rules—but living and life-producing ideas . . ." that is important.

In today's world rather than to "return" to where we now stand, we are in need of a resurgence of the humane values in the teaching of literature, an approach which we have neglected or subordinated to drudgery, mechanical and, in general, threadbare and meaningless trivia. The requisite is not for greater emphasis on technical analysis but to transcend the mechanical elements toward a deeper concern with the responses to the human condition its thought patterns, value conflicts and social predicaments. And we desperately need the classroom setting in which the student will be encouraged to read and to react to these stimuli for ". . . the subject area in the curriculum which deals most obviously with the inner life of man since it is a direct reflection of that life, is literature. . . ."[1] "What is needed

---

[1] Board of Education of the City of New York. "Balance in the Curriculum: The Role of the Humanities in the High School Literature Program." *Curriculum and Materials,* Vol. XV, No. 3 (Spring 1961), p. 9.

for every student is a program which quickens the senses, turns sight into insight, and above all, gives him a sense of worth as a human being."[2]

This is not to deny the value of literature as an aesthetic experience; it does mean that *the* essential function of literature, in the words of Samuel Johnson, is to teach the art of living. A modern literature program, based on this principle, will serve as an extension of the student's experiences and as an instrument of articulation for his values, attitudes and emotions. How are these to be dealt with where technical analysis is the center of attention?

If the humanities ideal is to be emphasized, the literature program's materials and goals will require a reappraisal. Certain schools presently include a humanistic approach; others claim such programs with lofty aims described in courses of study, but, unhappily, these are not transmitted to the classroom. The humanities approach is not presented as a panacea, as the solution, to the multiproblems of teaching English. (Need we be reminded that current practices have not produced the desired results?)

A Vital Link. The teaching of literature is a vital link in preserving and communicating the humanistic tradition in our technological society. It serves both civilizing and utilitarian functions. Cognizant that specifics in aim, method and content will vary, to achieve the humanistic ends a literature program will provide students on all grade levels, elementary and secondary, with materials that:

Stimulate their growth, self-development, and understanding of others through literary experiences that sensitize them to the extent and variety of human affairs because a primary task of literature is "to lay bare the foundations of human emotion";[3]

Focus on materials that connect with the lives of young people, books that reveal, clarify and illuminate reality, that reach different readers in different places, giving them a "lens on life" from many angles of vision;

Broaden their aesthetic perception, sensibility and understanding of the miracle and beauty of the creative process;

Raise their levels of aspiration through contact with literature that involves readers in the moral life, thus combating moral illiteracy by exposure to what is noble, compassionate and faith-provoking;

Explore not only the contributions of their own culture but the ideas and values from varied cultures by studying foreign works in translation, thereby discovering the sense of human connection;

Expose them to literature that will cultivate the lifetime reading (and thinking) habit, for such an approach will "probe our prejudices and presuppositions, challenge our premises, and test the basic assumptions of our business, moral and political codes";[4] and

Serve as a counter-movement to the mechanistic approach to literature by teaching for meaning, and, not to be minimized, for enjoyment and delight.

Suggested Principles. Without presuming to prescribe an entire curriculum, the

---

[2]*Ibid.,* p. 10.
[3]Max Lerner. *Ideas Are Weapons.* New York: The Viking Press, 1939. p. 409.
[4]William O. Douglas. *An Almanac of Liberty.* New York: Dolphin Books, 1954. p. 41.

following principles, which James A. Michener advocated, are worthy of consideration.[5] (The readings are suggested only; where they are inappropriate to a particular program, the teacher will know many meritorious books that treat the central idea.)

1. "People are the aim and end of life. Teach the supremacy of people over machines, political systems, economic systems, or any other systems. People are the focus of our interest, our only hope." (This may be illustrated by teaching Tolstoi's *Anna Karenina* or *War and Peace,* Camus' *The Plague,* Dickens' *Great Expectations* or the stories of Jesse Stuart.)
2. "People are endlessly complex, endlessly superb." (Balzac's Père *Goriot,* Dostoevski's *The Brothers Karamazov* or Faulkner's *Intruder in the Dust.*)
3. "But people are sometimes endlessly confused and evil." (The short stories of Poe, Shakespeare's *Macbeth* or Koestler's *Darkness at Noon.*),
4. "Optimism has not yet been discredited. Students need contact with sensible optimism; desperately they need it." (Paton's *Cry, the Beloved Country,* Hemingway's *For Whom the Bell Tolls,* Saint-Exupéry's *Wind, Sand and Stars* or White's *Charlotte's Web.*) The simple themes in these books "acquire a majestic dignity. It is this dignity we must show our students lest they fall into the sinful indignity of thinking their world to be a gruesome and lost place."
5. "Society is worth studying. Students should be encouraged to read the great fictional studies of our national life." (Wolfe's *You Can't Go Home Again,* Lewis' *Main Street* or Steinbeck's *The Grapes of Wrath.*)

How will these principles be accomplished? The school program must offer a reading program with a wide variety of choice, subjects which have meaning to the young reader, careful teacher guidance and encouragement of pupil initiative.[6] This kind of program will provide units on the individual, intergroup relations, the American heritage, the great traditions of western civilization, and similar subjects. Such units are now taught in many schools.

In addition, provision must be made for the study of world literature, not only to introduce young people to the important writers of the non-English speaking world, but as a cultural vehicle for gaining insights into and understanding of the peoples of the world, the art-for-art's sake school to the contrary. Why world literature as one aspect of the humanities ideal? An exclusive diet of British and American literature, regardless of its excellence, is ill-balanced and it may cause literary and cultural anemia. There is no isolated literature and the curriculum has an obligation to make the student cognizant not only of his national heritage but also of the republic of letters, which is international.

The Best Plot. The humanistic approach concerns itself with man's central problems as a human being; often we learn more about human beings and "the depths within" from the creation of the great literary artists than from the "professional" writers on the subject. "A human being," John Galsworthy once

[5] James A. Michener. "Idealism Today."*Books in Their Courses,* Vol. 10, No. 2 (April 1949). p. 3.

[6] Lou LaBrant. *We Teach English.* New York: Harcourt, Brace and World, 1951. p. 263.

said, "is the best plot there is." Although literature presents masses, many writers' main concern has been the individual, and in their tales what counts is the insight into the human heart. Perhaps this is best represented in the simple words of Joseph Conrad, writing about Lord Jim: "Because of his feelings, he mattered."

In the present period of history, filled with illnesses of the spirit, chaos and violence, we must cling to this ideal—the sense of the worth, uniqueness, dignity and importance of the individual, despite the current malaise of confusion, cynicism and conformity which has created erosive patches of anti-humanism. The business of the writer, Anton Chekhov wrote in a letter, is to stand up for man. This is evident in the many literary works that attack ignorant dogmatism, blind prejudice, barbarism in all forms, and prove over and over again that man is not an absurdity.

The daily newspapers are filled with headlines on South Africa. But what journalist has presented a document comparable to Alan Paton's *Cry, the Beloved Country?* We read about the tragic struggle of the Jew in Europe, but where do we find in the social science tomes the variety and depth of experiences comparable to those narrated by I. J. Singer, Isaak Babel and John Hersey in *The Wall?*

The fate of the "little man," living on the edge of survival—where is this theme better portrayed than in the writings of Giovanni Verga, John Steinbeck, Honoré de Balzac or Giuseppe Berto in *The Works of God?* What psychologist has analyzed the problems of growing up in greater detail than Sigrid Undset in *Kristin Lavransdatter* and Roger Martin du Gard in *The World of the Thibaults?* The plight of the Negro in our society is diligently described in the books of Richard Wright, Ralph Ellison and William Faulkner. Which professional philosophers and historians have explained our immediate era as meaningfully as Albert Camus, Thomas Mann, Jules Romains and Franz Kafka? And so it goes. These are but a few of the elements covered in a humanistic approach to literature—one means of interpreting and illuminating human behavior.

A Balance. Further, a basic requirement of this program is the balance of books of the past and contemporary works. Without disparaging the older "classics" the age of a literary work is not the sole or primary means of determining its suitability for use in a particular school or for a particular student. "A work of art no matter how old and classic is actually, not just potentially, a work of art only when it lives in some individual experience."[7] By assigning materials that interest and stimulate our students we will provide them with live education. Ultimately what matters, when young people read a book, is its power, how and why they respond to the experiences, and the lasting effect of the work.

If it is true that the depth of feeling and cerebral awareness the reader experiences determines a book's value, then we must include works that challenge and even provoke us! This means the reading of so-called controversial materials for the kinds of learning that bridge the school with the outside world. A major fault of our schools is that "they try to teach only that which is not controversial. When anything passes the point of being controversial, it no longer matters, except as

[7] John Dewey. *Art as Experience.* New York: Minton, Balch and Company, 1934. p. 108.

history. This keeps both teachers and learners pawing over material that has lost its significance."[8] On occasion the literature teacher must, for the very survival of the curriculum, turn to books that do not fall into the categories of safe, wholesome or noncontroversial. The fact is that many students now read "controversial" books and periodicals outside of school—why not discuss such materials openly and objectively in the classroom? Failure to recognize and to act on what we know about our students' reading habits and social behavior will perpetuate an unreal and sterile curriculum.

Literature must keep alive the sparks of idealism, human decency, hope, belief in a better world, and dedication to the goodness of mankind. . . .Let our students be trained in commas, and mathematical formulas, and chemical analyses, and historical understandings. But above that vocational training, let them be shown that sensible idealism is more needed today than ever. Let them meet in their teachers people who are not afraid to affirm the great humanist values, for I believe that it is upon those values that we will build a strong society.[9]

The Auburn High School Humanities Program

Sandra Izquierdo

In the summer of 1967 I wrote a proposal for a pilot humanities program with the assistance of Auburn University's Educational Media Center staff; it was funded by the federal government under a Title III mini-grant. The program was incorporated into the curriculum of Auburn High School, and fifty-six tenth--through-twelfth graders with basic, average, and above-average abilities enrolled in the course in September of 1968. I direct and coordinate the program with the help of a co-teacher, Mrs. Rose M. Moore, and a secretarial assistant.

Approach: As this is a pilot program, the teaching methods have constantly been varied in accordance with evaluations by teaching consultants, the humanities staff, and the students themselves. Basically, however, a chronological approach has been used to examine the growth of Western man, beginning with the medieval period. The dominant aspects of each period have been selected for special study to illustrate the "mood" of that period. Ultimately, the students have been able to use this background to relate the humanities to themselves as individuals and to their twentieth-century society. An emphasis has been placed on the student as a "learner" being more important than the teacher as a "teacher." The students are encouraged to voice their feelings concerning subject material, consultants, methods of teaching to which they respond best, and so on.

Materials, Equipment, and Facilities: The humanities program has its own small library of books (the students also have access to the school library and the Auburn University library), records, art prints, slides, and recording tapes. As the mini-grant

[8] Earl C. Kelley. *In Defense of Youth.* Englewood Cliffs, N.J.: Spectrum Books, 1962. p. 124.
[9] James A. Michener, *op. cit.,* p. 5.

did not provide funds for the purchase of equipment, the Educational Media Center has loaned the class a film projector, tape recorder, slide projector, and portable stereophonic system. The class has the use of a regular classroom and a small auditorium.

Class Schedule: Flexibility is much in evidence in this new program, and there is no rigid class schedule. The basic structure is as follows:

Monday and Tuesday: Large group lectures by Mrs. Izquierdo or a class consultant
Wednesday and Thursday: Small group sessions
Friday: Independent study

Consultants and Field Trips: Consultants are chosen for their knowledge of a particular subject and for their ability to relate well to the students. Usually, when a single consultant is invited to lecture to the class, he does so on a "lecture day"; however, at various times during the year, a whole week has been set aside for several consultants to come at once and be "in residence." Occasionally, night sessions with consultants have been scheduled for the purpose of informal question-and-answer seminars. Field trips are taken by the class when it is necessary or deemed important to see the consultants in their own element.

Independent Study: In a class of so many students where such a great deal of material is to be covered, it was felt that there would be too little opportunity to give the students any more than a general orientation to the humanities. An answer to this problem is the independent study program. Here each student may make an in-depth study of any particular phase of the humanities or any specific period in history in which he is interested. Each semester a paper is presented on the topics of research, and an oral report is given to the rest of the class. This part of the program has been most rewarding in that it has given an opportunity for each student to become an "expert" on a particular subject. Often a student is called upon by other students in group discussions to serve as a "consultant." The slow learners in the class, many of whom have never been "good" at anything in their school careers, have gained a great deal of confidence from this phase of the program.

Small Groups: One of the most interesting aspects of this program has been the use of the small group situation. For the purpose of discussion the students have been divided into six groups of approximately ten students. With the help of a group specialist from Auburn University every effort has been made to insure that the members of each group are compatible and cooperative. Group leaders were selected and instructed on how best to lead their groups. There is a minimum of supervision when the groups are in session. The discussions are oriented primarily to the topics of recent lectures, but the students are allowed to let the subject of discussion go where it will. It is of great importance for the students to learn to think and express themselves freely; they are encouraged to use a logical approach rather than an emotional one.

Related Activities: A state-wide humanities workshop that I coordinated with the cooperation of the Alabama State Department of Education was held at Auburn

High School in April of 1968. Teachers interested in beginning new humanities programs attended. The primary purpose was to promote this interest, to give the teachers an opportunity to hear about humanities programs in other states, to give them practical information about setting up new programs, and to analyze various approaches to teaching the humanities.

As a result of a visit I made to Connecticut high school humanities programs, plans were made for an exchange visit of eight Auburn High School humanities students and seven students from high schools in Connecticut.

This day book was written to keep a record of the development of the program. Its sole purpose is to inform teachers interested in humanities courses of the changes in student attitudes, teaching methods, and a few of the successes and failures that occurred throughout our year of experimental teaching.

Small Group Discussion. Many educators think of the small group in terms of size alone (from ten to fifteen students). Our concern with the small group, however, is not primarily with group size; rather, we are concerned with the behavior of the group members and with the role of the student as well as the role of the teacher. In the small group, communication must be free and open; anxiety must be minimized. Intrinsic rewards are of the utmost importance to the students. The students must feel free to discuss what is meaningful and real to them and the context of their lives. There should never be overt teacher direction or interference. The small group should always be considered a student endeavor and, therefore, student-controlled.

Objectives: The objectives of the small group are (1) to give the students an opportunity to inquire, reflect, create, and modify, (2) to make learning active instead of passive, (3) to encourage active leadership and participation by all members of the group, (4) to clarify points presented in lectures, (5) to encourage individual questioning, (6) to strengthen basic skills in self-expression, and (7) to have the student become more independent of the teacher.

Procedure: There is no set pattern for a small group discussion. Many approaches have been made this year in order to find the best solution for meeting the needs of the students at Auburn High School. Because these students did not have an opportunity to express themselves in their previous traditional classroom setting, we have had a difficult time in persuading them to talk openly. Almost all of our students had *never* been in a small group discussion. They did not know what to say or how to react.

Our procedure has evolved from the technique of allowing students to submit questions of importance, through having teachers offer suggested topics, to starting with a ten-minute lecture by a teacher on current controversial articles from newspapers, magazines, or other media to stimulate some reaction. These are only a few of the methods we have tried. We have had to experiment all year long, both to encourage the students in regard to self-expression and to find the best stimuli for discussion. Because we feel that it is important for men to communicate effectively if they are to resolve their differences and live in harmony, we have worked especially hard on this part of our program. It is the phase of our program that has given us the most trouble this year. It has been a slow, tedious, and sometimes frustrating procedure, but our students are now able to express their views intelligently and often participate spontaneously in impromptu small group discussions.

Evaluation: There has been no attempt on our part to make an empirical evaluation. We have allowed the students to evaluate themselves. We have followed all of their suggestions and recommendations for group improvement. We have allowed them to run the whole show. We have never made a change that they did not suggest. Without their help and cooperation this phase of our program would have been a failure. Whatever we as teachers have gained from this experience we owe to our humanities students; it is they who have taught us!

Independent Study Program: The class period on Friday of each week is designed as independent study day. Students attend just as they would for regular class. After roll check they are given unstructured time to work as they choose.

Independent study is an activity motivated largely by the student's own aim to learn. Students engage in activities independent of other students and in large part independent of teacher direction and supervision. Activities include reading, writing, listening to records and tapes, viewing slides and films. They are expected to investigate, examine, question, and discover. Because independent study emphasizes the individual's role in learning and personal responsibility to it, it implies that all students possess potentialities for initiative, self-discipline, productivity, and self-evaluation.

Objectives: Some of the objectives of the independent study program are (1) to develop the independent, self-directed learner, (2) to provide an opportunity for self-expression and independent research, and (3) to enable the student to investigate full and undisturbed any area of interest the humanities may stimulate.

Participation: All students enrolled in humanities participate in the independent study program. They write a paper each semester based on their research. The paper is presented orally at the end of the semester to the entire class, using visual aids. This replaces a final exam.

Areas of Study: Independent study may be done in any area discussed during regular humanities classes, for example, music, art, history, or literature. The program affords the opportunity for students to explore in depth any area pertaining to the humanities that is of special interest to them.

Teacher's Role: The teacher's goal is to become increasingly dispensible as students develop more responsibility. We expect our students to grow in self-analysis, self-correction, and self-direction. Individual conferences are set up with students to determine the extent of their progress and to discuss their problems. If the student needs help of any kind on his project, he may request additional conferences with the teacher or with consultants.

Evaluation: The independent reports are read by us. They are evaluated according to the degree to which they have been researched comprehensively. Then oral reports are given at the end of each semester. If students are to be successful in the independent study program, they must possess the ability to accept individual responsibility. They must also have the potential for intellectual curiosity. Each student is evaluated on attitude and performance according to his ability.

Notes on Starting a Humanities Course

Roy York, Jr.

The ways of teaching a humanities course are practically limitless, but to date one of the best organizational possibilities is found in *The Humanities: Applied Aesthetics,* by Louise Dudley and Austin Faricy.[1]

Areas of inquiry in this interrelated arts course, which may be presented as units, are arranged cumulatively in an order of increasing complexity: subject, function, medium, organization, style, and judgment. If the maximum degree of integration is desired, it is likely that only one instructor will teach the course. If the ultimate in skillful specialization is wanted, other teachers may participate. For example, three regular instructors, one each in music, literature, and the visual arts may be joined by as many guest specialists as desired. All regular staff members, however, should be present at every class meeting.

The first meeting, it is suggested, should provide an introduction to at least two related masterpieces or historic exemplars of art—e.g., Stravinsky's *Le Sacre du Printemps* and Picasso's *Les Demoiselles d'Avignon.* Before the class is ready to hear *Le Sacre,* some special preparation is helpful. Photographs of Stravinsky and Picasso and relevant information pertaining to their work; prints of paintings by Picasso, and perhaps Sargent, Gauguin, and Henri Rousseau; reproductions of sculpture by primitive peoples and by Modigliani and Epstein; and a copy of Zola's *La Terre* might be displayed. This exhibit should remain on view throughout the duration of the unit. After brief preliminary references to the display, the class might hear Thomas Sherman's recorded musical program notes for *Le Sacre.*[2]

Using the titles of the various episodes as guideposts, the class could then be presented with an abridged, seven-minute version of O'Connell's notes from his *Victor Book of the Symphony.*[3] O'Connell devotes considerable attention to the dancing as a clue to the significance of the music. He begins in this engaging manner:

First Tableau
Adoration of the Earth

A desolate valley lies shadowed between barren hills that crouch above it like great brooding beasts. In the foreground is a mound of earth, and partly surrounding it a semicircle of great stones, and poles surmounted by the heads of wild animals. On one side is a group of young girls and on the other young men; all are quiet in thought. . . . A bearded Sage, bowed under the burden of years, comes forward and approaches the dancers. The girls circle around him as he leads them toward the mound of earth, which he ascends with dignity. . .here the men arouse

---

[1] Third ed. (New York: McGraw-Hill, 1960).

[2] *The Rite of Spring–Stravinsky,* Musical Program Notes, Music Appreciation Record MAR H3014 (New York: Book of the Month Club, Inc.).

[3] Charles O'Connell, *The Victor Book of the Symphony* (New York: Simon and Schuster, 1941).

themselves...and the adolescents begin their primitive dance.... There is constantly increasing excitement both in the music and among the dancers. . . .

Now the stage is set for a performance of *Le Sacre.* I prefer the verve of Ormandy's interpretation.

At this point in the orientation unit, a synoptic survey of the entire course is provided. This abbreviated tour is designed to assist the students in long-term planning as well as to promote a feeling of interested or, as I have found in most classes, eager anticipation. The slightly abridged Dudley and Faricy chart provides in a glance a precise view of the five major arts to be studied together with six basic areas in which each art is related to the others in the order in which the units will be presented.

	Music	Literature	Painting	Sculpture	Architecture
Subject					
Function					
Medium					
Organization					
Style					
Judgment					

Brief references to the units are coordinated with appropriate emphases on some of the basic principles that underlie and are common to all of the arts.

Subject (What is it about?):
a broad word for whatever is represented in a work of art
Function (What is it for?):
a definite, practical, and usually utilitarian purpose or usefulness
Medium (What is it made of?):
the material used
Organization (How is it put together?):
Skeletal structure:
the overall arrangement of the materials
Organic structure:
the interrelationships of the elements in a work of art
Style (What is its temper? Its mood? Its personality?):
the distinctive manifestation in art of a coherent spiritual outlook (Greene)
the distinctive or characteristic manner of presentation, construction, or execution in any art (Machlis)
the totality of devices and procedures that determine the artistic language (Machlis)
Judgment (How good is it?):
analysis, using subject, function, medium, organization, style, and questions dealing with judgment alone:
Honesty (Is the work sincere?):
Scope (How much has the artist attempted?):
not the same as size or length

Level of meaning (Is the work superficial or deep?):
  one or more than one level of meaning
Truth (Has the artist shown the essential truth of the subject?):
  the essential nature of the thing
  rightness (Is it *right*?)
Magnitude (How great is it?):
  shallow or deep
  important or unimportant
  great or trivial

These principles are applied in brief outline to *Le Sacre* and to *Les Demoiselles* by means of a few concentrated statements. To assist in these applications I have drawn chiefly upon the scholarship of Machlis, Murphy, Sherman, Canaday, and Fleming.[4]

Le Sacre du Printemps
The Rite of Spring

Subject:

  the religious rites of prehistoric man in propitiation of spring, culminating in a human sacrifice (O'Connell notes)

Function:

  a ballet originally, thus functional
  concert version—a nonfunctional piece derived from a functional one

Medium:

  3 flutes, 1 or 2 piccolos, 1 alto flute, 4 oboes, 1 or 2 English horns, 1 or 2 clarinets in D and E flat, 3 clarinets in B flat and A, 1 or 2 bass clarinets, 4 bassons, 1 or 2 contrabassoons, 8 French horns (2 interchangeable with 2 Wagner or Bayreuth tubas), 1 trumpet in D, 4 trumpets in C, 1 bass trumpet in E flat, 3 trombones, 2 tubas, 4 tympani, bass drum, tambourine, cymbal, tam tam or gong, antique cymbals in A flat and B flat, triangle, guiro, strings

Organization:

  Skeletal:

    concert version probably should not be called a symphonic poem, as it more nearly approximates a miscellaneous suite, that is, a suite in 13 episodes, which, separated from their scenic titles, are so many symphonic pieces in rondo or song form, unified by a common stylistic method

  Organic:

    rhythm by numerical progression, polyrhythm, multirhythm, polytonality mixed in the tonal structure, musical nationalism, percussive use of dissonance, extraordinary orchestral imagination

---

[4] Joseph Machlis, *Introduction to Contemporary Music* (New York: Norton, 1961); Howard A. Murphy, *Form in Music for the Listener*, 2nd ed. (Camden, N.J.: Radio Corporation of America, 1948); Thomas Sherman, *op. cit.*; John Canaday, *Metropolitan Seminars in Art*, Series One and Two (New York: Metropolitan Museum of Art, 1961); William Fleming, *Arts and Ideas*, rev. ed. (New York: Holt, Rinehart and Winston, 1963).

Style:
> *Stravinsky's personality:*
>> the type of orchestra he used and especially the imaginative and original effects he obtained
>>
>> the seemingly inexhaustible rhythmic invention
>>
>> in short, the transfer of the dynamic and elemental force of primitive music into sophisticated musical form—neo-primitivism

Judgment:
> *Honesty:*
>> an authentic expression of Stravinsky's musical imagination:
>>> no sentimentality
>>>
>>> Stravinsky's efforts are directed toward achieving an unmistakable "rightness" in the music in expressing genuine musical ideas

> *Scope:*
>> Stravinsky succeeded brilliantly in giving us a composition of major proportions and achieved the difficult task of providing various views of prehistoric primitive man participating in a fundamentally vital religious rite—the propitiation of spring—culminating in a human sacrifice

Level of meaning:
> we can merely wonder what lies beneath this surface of striking originality not only in program but also in one compositional stratagem after another

> *Truth:*
>> Stravinsky rises to great heights in capturing the essential truth, the essential nature—in a word, the *rightness* of this music for the purpose of mirroring his program, e.g.:
>>> the sharply angular melodies
>>>
>>> the complex polyrhythmic textures
>>>
>>> the brutal accentuations
>>>
>>> the geometrical movements of the dancers
>>>
>>> a masterly realization of the spirit of savagery

> *Magnitude:*
>> the beginning of modern music as we know it
>>
>> introduced or developed compositional techniques that have become the standard methods of the greater part of contemporary music—especially contributions to rhythm and to use of the orchestra

Les Demoiselles d'Avignon
Young Ladies of Avignon

Subject:
> the title does not refer to the town, but to Avignon Street in a notorious section of Barcelona
>
> a composition of five nudes and a still life, with drapery in the background
>
> the title seems to have been suggested by a friend as a joke

Function:
> an intellectual exercise in abstraction
>
> a prodigious effort to discover new means of expression, not for the sake of their newness, but to increase the scope and intensity of the art of painting for Picasso,

a self-imposed labor of creative analysis—was not exhibited until thirty years after it was completed

Medium:

oil on canvas—96 3/8" by 92½"

Organization:

Skeletal:

formal arrangement of the figures suggests the angular rhythms of a primitive dance

Organic:

a discordant picture, not only in the violent way in which it ruptures,fractures, and dislocates form but in the disharmony of its own parts. On the left, the standing figure is posed in a standard attitude of Egyptian and archaic Greek sculpture. But by the time the right side of the picture is reached, this formality has given way to a jagged, swinging, crashing line, and the African mask makes its impact with full force in the grotesque faces.

not only the proportions, but the organic integrity and continuity of the human body are denied here

resembles a field of broken glass

pronounced contrasts of color and texture

Style:

these nudes possess a savage aggressiveness:

the three on the left are angular distortions of classical figures

the two on the right, with their violently dislocated features and bodies, have many barbaric qualities of primitive art

Picasso used primitive art as a battering ram against the classical conception of beauty

this painting, although technically ambiguous, is decisively the beginning the cubism

the was in Picasso's art between:

classical and primitive

abstract and figurative

ideal beauty and the grotesque—oppositions which he has often exploited creatively and which he has the power to weld into a convincing totality in the single canvas

Judgment:

not an unqualified success in every way, but undeniably a landmark

a painting which, as much as any single work, redirected the course of twentieth-century art

chief fault—the young experimenter (age twenty-six) was not able to solve the conflict between reality and abstraction. Here abstraction has merely deformed the figures, and the deformations are not of a kind to clarify or intensify our reaction, as in the case of expressionism.

When it seems helpful to do so, reference can be made to these principles and their applications in analyzing and judging any work of art.

Fleming, in his *Arts and Ideas,* (see footnote 4) invites our attention to the remarkable resemblance of a mask from Itumba in the old French Congo to the head of the figure in the upper right of Picasso's painting. The jolting contrast between the violence of the Picasso (1907) and the serenity of Sargent's exquisite painting the *Windham Sisters* (1900) is pointed out by Canaday (see footnote 4). And in Sherman's recorded musical program notes, one experiences a similar outrageous shock when an excerpt from *The Rite's* "Glorification of the Chosen One" is juxtaposed with a contemporary passage from *An Elegy* by Saint-Saëns.

Attention is then directed to Henri Rousseau's *Charmeuse de Serpents* (*Snake Charmer*). This painting, with its exotic jungle background, appears as a cover for the Monteux recording of *Le Sacre* and can be misleading for students in a high school humanities class. We know that this Rousseau is one of the best known of the French untaught painters, a so-called primitive painter. On the other hand, we know that in *Le Sacre* Stravinsky is a sophisticated neo-primitivist—a highly trained composer writing in a style best labeled as neo-primitivism. The subject matter in both the Rousseau and the Stravinsky is of a primitive nature; but this aspect is the only safe one to consider in comparing Rousseau's painting with Stravinsky's composition. Apropos of *Le Sacre*,[5] the recorded commentary by Stravinsky concerning the history of this musical landmark provides approximately sixteen minutes of highly recommended listening.

Appropriate cognizance is also taken of the fact that Jacob Epstein's massive primordial statue *Adam* and Zola's strong, naturalistic novel *La Terre* may, together with *Les Demoiselles*, be thought of as counterparts of *Le Sacre*. Tischler feels that the

... statue symbolizes fertility in the sense of the Old Testament. Compression of form, reduction of the presentation to essentials, omission of all ornamentation, short motifs and utmost tension, and the power and primitive quality that results—all closely parallel the technics employed in musical expressionism and neo-primitivism.[6]

One commentator tells us that

If there could be a counterpart to *The Rite of Spring* in literature, it would be Zola's *La Terre,* the novel that horrified France a generation before. Zola's theme and Stravinsky's are basically the same: The human animal and his dependence upon the soil; the more primitive the man, the more fierce becomes his struggle to live, to reproduce, to scratch and tear the means of living from a fecund but unheeding earth. Frankness was essential to such a theme, and both artists met it manfully; but in so doing, each shocked a generation which still clung to the sentimental illusions of romance.

I have found that the use of such dramatic material as *Le Sacre, Les Demoiselles, Adam,* and *La Terre* readily captures the interest of senior high school students. The evident flavor of importance and, except for the Zola novel, of immediacy, has much appeal.

[5] Columbia Masterworks, DL 5505.
[6] Hans Tischler, *The Perceptive Music Listener* (Englewood Cliffs: N.J.: Prentice-Hall, Inc., 1955).

As an alternative to *Le Sacre* and the counterparts in painting, sculpture, and literature, many might prefer a different presentation. Thus the first movement of Schubert's *Unfinished Symphony* might be used at the initial meeting of the class while the students follow a skeleton score. Attention might be directed to Sigmund Spaeth's[7] appropriate parallels of the sonata-allegro form with literature: the exposition is similar to the stage custom of introducing the leading characters (melodies), masculine and feminine. The first theme is comparable to the hero, and the second theme to the heroine. The development parallels the plot in a play or novel, and the recapitulation, the reminder of all this material that has been heard, is like the happy or logical ending.

A display of paintings by Giorgione could reveal the great similarity between the characteristics of Giorgione, and this Giorgione of music, Schubert. In their *Music in History* McKinney and Anderson maintain that

> Looking at such pictures as Giorgione's *The Tempest* or *The Pastoral Symphony* gives us the same sort of experience that we get in listening to the *Unfinished Symphony:* both artists are lyricists, the one painting his lyrics, the other drawing them from the depths of some instrument; both held the gift of easy persuasion as a flower holds its perfume and with the same lack of concern as to impulse; both showed the most exquisite feeling in their expression, but neither had any need for story or program for his works; both knew instinctively how to organize materials without making us conscious of the process. Rossetti has described Giorgione's Venetian pastoral as "life touching lips with immortality"; and no better phrase could be coined for describing the essential nature of Schubert's music.[8]

Excellent recorded musical program notes written by Howard Shanet and narrated and conducted by Thomas Sherman enhance this presentation.[9]

When using either the Stravinsky-Picasso or the Schubert-Giorgione material Clifton Fadiman's filmed lesson *The Humanities: What They Are and What They Do*[10] should find a prominent place in the unit. In a pleasant manner, Fadiman introduces the students to the meaning and and significance of the humanities. He says that the humanities are man's *ideas* and *feelings* about life and about himself, recorded in certain definite ways. Music, literature, painting, sculpture, architecture, drama, and the dance are some of the ways in which Western man has recorded his hopes and fears, his joys and sorrows, and his guesses about his place in life. The humanities ask and try to answer certain basic questions. They challenge us to think about our own answers and reveal to us certain underlying patterns beneath life's apparent confusion. When time permits, John Canaday should also address the class in his film *Art: What Is It? Why Is It?*[11]

---

[7] *Symphony No. 8 in B Minor "Unfinished,"* with comments spoken by Dr. Sigmund Spaeth. *Music Plus!* Vol. 1, No. 12, MP-100-12A (RE-33-726). Remington Records, New York.

[8] New York: American Book Co., 1949.

[9] *Analysis: Symphony No. 8 in B Minor, "The Unfinished"–Schubert*, Music Appreciation Record MAR 913A (New York: Book of the Month Club, Inc.).

[10] Series No. 1 (Wilmette: Encyclopaedia Britannica Films).

[11] Wilmette: Encyclopaedia Britannica Films.

These orientation procedures are no longer theory. I have used these and other successfully, but to date the Stravinsky-Picasso-Fadiman approach serves my purposes better than any other.

English and the Arts

Robert Kirk

Ten years ago relating the arts in an English class might have been considered a very unnecessary frill in many high schools, but the climate has changed markedly since then. Humanities courses have popped up in schools all over the nation, and probably most teachers realize the values that can be achieved by bringing the arts into English classes: it would seem unnecessary to defend the practice. Yet perhaps some of the projects that I shall discuss may be novel ones. I think all of them can be adapted to any grade or intellectual level. Some of the projects are major units and some are only incidental, but all of them have been tested for at least three or four years.

After the first few weeks of the school year spent on various organizational procedures and study of certain basic techniques, I open my first short unit on the arts, on a demonstration of the structural relationships among literature, music, and painting. If I have the time, the unit extends over three days; it is not only an exercise in finding relationships, it is also an exercise in logical thinking and in the techniques of conversation.

Prior to the first day's round table discussion, the students are asked to develop a list of ideas on how they would judge a work of art—painting, musical composition, or literary work. When they arrive for that discussion, they find that they are surrounded by paintings and sculpture, paintings on easels, in the chalktrays, and hanging from the walls. Some of them are realistic and some non-objective; presumably some of them are good and some bad.

The discussion involves making a list of ways by which one can analyze a work of art. The emphasis during the first part of the period is placed on the factors of organization in painting: focal point, balance, line, color, mood, originality, period of history in which it was created, texture, the media, and others. The paintings in the room are used as examples. An abstraction is found to have no "picture" but to have a strong focal point, and everything in the painting conspires to point it out; if one blots out a shape in one corner of the painting, the entire organization is thrown off; every item in the work is essential. A bowl of fruit painted in oils has interesting colors and exact balance, but it lacks originality; it looks like any of a hundred other bowls of fruit.

Toward the end of the period, a literary work which the class has recently studied is analyzed using the same list. Hemingway's "Old Man at the Bridge," a story about an old, confused man displaced during the Spanish Civil War, has a strong focal point: the confusion of the man and the meaninglessness of the war to him is conveyed by repetition; every action and statement in the little sketch centers on this point. A definite organization can be found, an introduction, a rising action, crisis, falling action, and denouement, all carefully arranged. There is a mood to the story; the colors are drab grays.

On the second day, the emphasis is placed on music and on one method in which some works of literature and art may be related to it. This time the structure of a movement from a sonata is used as the basis for comparison. As a short movement from a Mozart sonata is played on the phonograph, the teacher diagrams the various themes, their repetition, and variations. The movement has basically an AABBABBAA arrangement or something close to this; that is, the introduction of the first theme and its repetition, then a new theme, a return to the first, variations of the second theme, and a final return to the first. The basic ABA arrangement can also be easily demonstrated with a Beatles recording. And, of course, the arrangement can be applied to a short story, an exposition, or a poem, any example which has an introduction and a conclusion, a theme or key sentence or phrase which is repeated at strategic points throughout the work.

Later in the period, or on a third day if interest and discussion hold up, a third type of relationship can be demonstrated, that of the collage, a composition in which pieces of newspaper, cloth, pressed flowers, wood, or the like are placed on a canvas for their symbolic or organizational effect; there is no picture in the usual sense, only a group of symbols which the viewer puts together in his mind to form an impression. In music one can find parallel compositions in such works as Gershwin's *An American in Paris,* in which approximations of various street sounds are fitted together to give an impression of the tourists' view of the city, or in certain works of Charles Ives, in which parades through a Connecticut village's streets include the shouts of little boys, tiny fragments of New England hymn tunes and folk songs, and snatches of sound from two bands marching against each other—a cacaphony of sound symbolizing American small-town life.

Many works of literature can be compared to the collage. I usually start with Karl Shapiro's short poem, "Auto Wreck," in which many of the sounds and sights that occur when an automobile is wrecked at night on the highway are thrown into a lump to demonstrate the confusion of the scene. The wreck itself is not mentioned; the sound of a siren, a broken telephone pole, an ambulance, a blanket on the ground all convey the picture vividly. While the youngsters list all of the symbols of a wreck that they find in the poem, either one of the more artistic students or I draw the symbols on the blackboard. When the symbols are placed helter-skelter into one square, a collage—a sense of the confusion—emerges; the instance of the poem has been transferred from one medium to another.

There are many assignments, themes, or projects that may develop from this unit. Undoubtedly any teacher can think of examples. However, it needs to be stressed that if the teacher is seriously interested himself in relating the arts, he needs to reinforce the introduction directly throughout the year with other units and incidentally, through the atmosphere in his room and in his vocabulary, to promote an awareness among his youngsters. If art and serious music are new and strange to a student, occasional units involving them will be helpful in reducing the strangeness; but one really must live with something strange before it becomes normal, before it becomes comfortable.

Bulletin boards are one obvious place for incidental teaching. Displays may be reproductions of professional art or originals from the school art department, and they can very easily be related to the literature units in an English class, e.g., charcoal sketches by Kathe Kollwitz of displaced old people in the Germany of the 1930's bear a striking resemblance in style, mood, and theme to the Hemingway story of the Spanish Civil War's displaced people. Professional reproductions, or student drawings of set designs may accompany a unit on drama; a discussion of impressionistic poetry, by impressionist paintings.

Music can also be used incidentally. Each week I bring a different collection of records to school and display them in the chalktrays. During the five-minute break between classes I put a record on the phonograph assigned to my room, place the jacket in a position so it will be noticed, and play it softly without any particular comment. The records may be borrowed by students who simply sign them out and keep them as long as they want. The procedure takes no moments from class time. With some students it may make a marked impression; with the many students who only barely notice the music, the procedure at least has the effect that after a few months the music does not seem odd to them; they accept. When a class accepts art as a part of their curriculum, then a teacher can go on to other projects.

Again, without any direct teaching, these displays of music or art can relate to the literature: I spend a few days of my poetry unit using the poems and autobiography of the contemporary Soviet poet Yevtushenko, whose attitudes and interests are similar to the attitudes and interests of American young people. The recordings played between periods during that week had been sent by a high school-age student from Leningrad with whom I correspond: Russian folk, pop, and serious music played by Soviet musicians. The bulletin board displays include typical Soviet art sent by the same student. The teacher may use this directly in his teaching or simply let it contribute to the atmosphere. If one is teaching *Faust* or *Dr. Faustus,* certainly art and, especially, music displays can contribute. The possibilities for parallel studies are innumerable: Byron's *Don Juan* and Mozart's *Don Giovanni;* a Medieval miracle play, *Noye's Fludde,* with the twentieth-century musical version by Benjamin Britten; *Oedipus Rex* with Stravinsky's choral composition.

The teacher can relate the arts to literature casually through his choice of vocabulary: *focal point, balance, color, texture,* all art terms primarily, can apply to both music and literature. *Fugal structure, crescendo, scherzo* are all terms from music that can be applied to literature also.

Television can be a most helpful aid. In the English department at Lexington High School, a list of 20 or more recommended television programs in the humanities is distributed each week. In some classes every student receives a copy, and the teacher may discuss particular programs for five or ten minutes or simply hand the lists out without comment. It is particularly important that the average and lower-ability students get the list each week; they are the ones most likely to regard *The Beverly Hillbillies* as the highest form of art.

About the middle of the year I usually introduce another short unit that emphasizes both music and literature; one appropriate time is after the classes have completed a drama unit.

If the course of study stipulates that youngsters gain an understanding of the different types of literature, then one way to emphasize similarities and differences among the types is to demonstrate what happens when a literary work is transferred from one medium to another: Goethe's poem, "The Elf King," to Schubert's song version; the Sholem Aleichem short stories to any of the various dramatized versions and finally to *Fiddler on the Roof,* the musical comedy; Shirley Jackson's famed short story, "The Lottery," to the play version or to the ballet based on it.

On the first day of the unit, the class meets in a round table discussion to analyze what happens when a story or novel is turned into a play. A list is made of the characteristics peculiar to each medium and the changes in emphasis that need to be made in the conversion: drama is visual, for example. Dialogue becomes more important than in the original source. The original story must be revisualized as scenes. The class discusses stories that might be candidates for the new form. Then the discussion turns to a consideration of the aspects of opera which might cause further changes in the original form: the problem of condensation, rephrasing of lines to make them suitable for music, a searching for sections of the story that would be possibilities for arias or ensemble singing.

On this first day also, I usually illustrate conversion techniques with a story with which most of the youngsters are familiar. One is Stephen Vincent Benét's "The Devil and Daniel Webster" which was adapted into a play by Benét himself and into a folkish opera by the author and Douglas Moore. It is a good example to use, because it has obvious possibilities as drama. Even in the original story, it is conceived in scenes; it has characters who could be effective on the stage whether they are speaking or singing; there are possibilities for set speeches which would reveal character and make excellent arias. Since the setting is rural New Hampshire, the composer can insert barn dances; the folklore flavor of the story is easy to capture in music.

But the important thing for the non-musical oriented class is to hear examples rather than simply discuss possibilities for relationships. I think it is important that the example be short, partly because of the suspicion of opera many pupils may have and partly because opera is a visual art.

On this first day I like to select one short example from "The Devil." As the youngsters search for the lines that give a clue to the character of Daniel Webster and that might be used to build a character-revealing aria, I point out lines that Moore selected for just such an aria. Then as the pupils follow the libretto on the overhead projector, they listen to Webster's aria from a recording of the opera. They will find that statements made about the lawyer in the original story have been pulled from various sections and placed together in one song, that certain things are repeated for emphasis and to allow for refrains in the aria, that lines are arranged to build to a musical climax, that the style of the music is a bit corn-fed but that, since the original story is also corn-fed, the style fits.

Usually I spend an entire class on one work so that the conversion process can be seen in some depth. Almost invariably I select Benjamin Britten's opera version of Henry James' *The Turn of the Screw.* The plot is Gothic and, at least to me, fascinating because of the horror it engenders; it has been done successfully as a play and a movie under the title of *The Innocents;* it captures very well the slow-moving style of James with its scenes that almost but not quite build up to climaxes but grow to a horrifying crescendo at the end.

Again I use an overhead projector to show the youngsters the long paragraphs in the original novel, the long descriptions that slowly build characterizations. Yet the problem of the composer is to show a characterization almost immediately, perhaps in one brief song. Britten does this beautifully as the little boy sings a six-line song that demonstrates both his innocence and his evil and his own perplexity at the dichotomy within himself. The last scene of the novel is the same as that of the play and opera. The librettist has selected key lines from the James version; and as the class listens to the climax of the opera and follows the libretto, they also see on the overhead projector the chapter from the novel with key passages underlined. The art of condensation is illustrated as is that of recurring themes, common to both literature and music: as the little boy dies in the arms of his governess, a victim of the evil which has tantalized him, the six-line song is sung by the governess herself and the combination of innocence and evil is reemphasized.

Recordings of operas made from novels, stories, or plays abound. Among those listed as available in the *Schwann Catalog,* which lists almost all commercially available records, are the following: Arthur Miller's *The Crucible* in an operatic version by Robert Ward, Lillian Hellman's *The Little Foxes* transposed into *Regina,* Saroyan's *Hello, Out there,* Mark Twain's *The Jumping Frog of Calaveras County,* and Alan Paton's *Cry, the Beloved Country.* Shakespeare is well represented with operatic versions of *Julius Caesar, Othello, Macbeth, The Merry Wives of Windsor,* and two different versions of *The Taming of the Shrew.* Leonard Bernstein has written a fine musical-comedy from Voltaire's *Candide.* The story of *The Odyssey* has emerged into *The Golden Apple,* which sets the story in the period of the Spanish-American War and manages to satirize amusingly both Homer and the music of the gay nineties. And an entire year could be spent on the musical and literary versions of *Faust.*

Poetry is an undefinable type of literature. It is basically musical, because of its emphasis on sounds of word combinations and, often, because of its rhythm. Dame Edith Sitwell, among other poets, has composed in her *Facade* poetry to be half-spoken, half-sung to music devised by Sir William Walton. Dame Edith insists that the poems are almost abstractions, that their main point is to relate rhythms in poetry to music. They are often very funny; they almost invariably set a class to tapping its toes when a recording of the work is played; and they certainly emphasize the musical aspects of poetry.

Poetry is found in prose also: metaphors, similes, personification, alliteration—all the devices may appear. When I teach poetry as a type, I like to emphasize that poetry, unlike the novel or short story, is not a rigidly isolated type but rather a series of characteristics that may pop up in music and prose. There are many examples one can select. At the end of the unit I like to arrange a one-day round table discussion designed partly to confuse the pupils and partly to make them start looking for relationships. As an example, I select prose description that James Agee originally published in the *Atlantic Monthly* under the title, "Knoxville, Summer of 1912," later adapted for the first chapter of *A Death in the Family*.

I open the class by asking the pupils if they would like to read a poem, and then I give them a mimeographed sheet with Agee's work written in paragraph form. The students' reaction, of course, is that this is prose; but when we start finding all of the examples of poetry characteristics in the work, they soon agree that almost every characteristic on our list is illustrated in the essay. After I suggest that we next listen to an actor read the poem, the youngsters hear as they follow the lines on their copies of the work a recording of Eleanor Steber singing Samuel Barber's musical arrangement for soprano and symphony orchestra. He has changed almost no words; yet the essay works perfectly into a musical adaption.

Recordings of poems set to music are, of course, in great supply; and the teacher can suit his selections to the nature of his class. I especially like to stress the prose-poetry-music relationship, however. I do find it important, incidentally, to make sure that youngsters have a text to follow when they listen to recordings. I think television-reared pupils, and teachers too, often need something to look at as an aid to concentration.

All of the projects and units described in this essay have been useful to a large or small degree to me in my teaching. I alter them, add to them, or drop them from year to year, of course, depending on the needs of my individual classes; but in one form or another most of them have sparked some of the youngsters. At the very least, they present the pupils with a fresh way of looking at old subject matter.

The Good, the True, the Beautiful: Experiencing—and Using—the Humanities in General Education

Bessie Stuart and Muriel Hunt

For the past eight years all students at Edsel Ford High School in Dearborn, Michigan, have participated in the civilizing influences of a three-year integrated humanities course.[1] In this course, art, music and literature are treated as man's means of communicating what he has found to be good and true and beautiful. Because this course was carefully planned to meet the needs of the individual as well as those of his society and was introduced as part of the curriculum in a new school, no student as yet has manifested any negative reaction toward this exposure to culture. On the contrary, most students, as they approach graduation, express gratitude for the enriching experiences they have been offered.

[1] The one exception is an ungraded, special education class for retarded students.

Factors which tend to unify the three areas of study for the students are implicit in the arts themselves and in our manner of teaching these arts. Each area is concerned with increasing the range of human experience to which the individual can respond. Each area is concerned with helping the individual to gain access to the experiences of people of other times and of other cultures. Each area is concerned with increasing the sensitivity of the individual to the meaning of his own feelings and to making him aware of the feelings of others. Each area consists of certain elements which the artist must select, arrange and organize in order to achieve both unity through repetition and interest through variety and contrast in his finished product. We study this product and through discussion try to achieve some understanding of its structure and purpose. We teach and learn by probing for answers to leading questions, usually asked by the teacher but sometimes by the students themselves.

This method of teaching, in which the teacher assumes the role of gadfly of the intellect, forces the students to learn what they can from any selection by drawing upon their own resources and sharing their reactions with their fellows. At no point are they told they must like or "appreciate" a painting, a musical composition, or a piece of literature because it is a masterpiece. In short, they are not expected to like or enjoy anything. If they do so, that is an extra dividend. All they are required to do is to understand and to express their understanding in speech or in writing.

From Simple to Complex. Two of our general objectives remain constant throughout the three years. These are communicating effectively and enlarging and enriching the understanding through the arts. The objective which is specific to the tenth grade is understanding the human qualities of the individual. The eleventh grade is directed toward an understanding of cause and effect relationships in human behavior and an understanding of the values of the democratic way of life. The special objective of the twelfth grade is the development of an understanding of the various relationships of man and his world.

Experts who have evaluated our program tend to attribute much of our success in the humanities to the organizing threads which unify the three-year study and give the students a cumulative experience. These threads move from the self to the universal, from the simple to the complex, from the immediate to the more remote, from the concrete to the abstract. Even in a brief summary of the course these threads are readily apparent.

We begin with a quotation from Herman L. Meyers, a mathematician at the University of Chicago: "Communication is by someone to someone for some purpose; it involves a certain medium it is about something, and it has a certain form."

Preliminary discussion is centered on the prepositions *by* and *to* because these denote the directions implicit in any communication—the outward, or expressive, and the inward, or impressive. Since the free flow of ideas depends on keeping the outward and the inward channels clear, responsibility for any interchange is placed directly and equally on both the receiver and the sender. Therefore our students who will be reading literature, listening to music, and viewing works of art, must accept the charge of keeping themselves actively receptive. They must also make themselves meticulously expressive because they will talk and write about what they read, hear and see; they will compose simple melodies; and they will do some creative work in the art laboratory each semester.

If they are to fill satisfactorily the dual role of receiver and sender, they must also understand the significance of the next two prepositions, *for* and *about*. Whereas the second denotes the subject selected by the artist, the first denotes his treatment of that subject. We believe that nothing in the world or outside it is beyond the reach of man's mind and imagination. Our discussion of choice of subjects, therefore, tends to break down any preconceived bias the students may have formed and to broaden their perspective. They discover that subject is secondary to what the artist has attempted to say about it, to his purpose in presenting it.

Areas of Study. Although at this point we have not yet covered *medium* and *form,* we are ready to separate our study into the three areas: music, visual arts, and literature.

Music: In music, taught one 60-minute hour per week, we begin with the medium of sound and the four elements of musical sound—melody, rhythm, tone color, and harmony. Starting with the simple and familiar at the tenth grade level, we listen to short, uncomplicated tunes, such as folk melodies, in which these four elements can readily be heard and easily recognized. During the next two years, longer and more complex music is studied. This includes arrangements of folk music, suites, vocal forms, polyphonic forms, as well as the composite forms such as oratorio, opera, sonata, concerto, and symphony. The last semester covers the chronological development of music from the Gregorian Chant through the Renaissance, Baroque, Classical, and Romantic periods to music of the present day. This historical review serves as a summary and gives the students a sense of the continuity of musical expression.

Visual Arts: In the visual arts, also allotted one hour per week, the medium may be paint, clay, wood, pen and ink, stone, or whatever other material the artist chooses to use. Some of the elements with which he must work are line, shape, texture, and color. Because an important goal is to enlarge the range of art to which the students can respond, care is taken to select examples from a wide range of cultures, styles, and ages as well as media. Again the students begin their study by considering simple, familiar forms. They look at a number of objects such as a brick, an arrow, a salt shaker, a bathroom scale—and try to discover the underlying principles which guide the product designer.

From these small articles they move on to forms which are more complex and more subtle. Architecture, painting, graphics, and sculpture are studied. In most of the sequence, art works are not discussed in chronological order. Instead, a variety of work is studied so that the students may gain insight as to the force of the elements of art and their organization within that work. During part of the third year they trace the development of the French school of painters from the realistic pre-Degas group through Degas, Monet, Renoir, Seurat, Gauguin, Van Gogh, Cézanne, and Picasso, so that they may be aware that both continuity and change are involved in the evolution of art styles. This is followed by a culminating experience in which students bring to an analysis of a print assigned to them their accumulated knowledge of art.

Literature: The remaining three 60-minute periods are devoted to English, with emphasis upon oral and written analyses of the selections studied. The impact of this integration of the arts we believe to be real, as the standardized test results have shown our students to be well above the national expectancy level. In this area of communication, of course, we are working with the medium of words as spoken or written symbols, with the arrangement of words into sentences and paragraph units, and the various forms into which these units can be organized.

In literature also we begin with simple forms—the short story, informal essay, one-act play, and lyric verse. These forms are introduced one per unit in the first four of the twelve units for the beginning year and each is studied in greater depth as the students proceed. During the two following years, the novel, the three-act play, the formal essay, and dramatic and narrative poetry are added.

In addition to this development from simple to more complex literary forms, there is a development of concepts. These begin in the tenth grade with the individual as he is found in contemporary writings and include experiences he shares with all men, the changes brought about in him by his reactions to his experiences, the qualities of character he may develop, and the bases for strengths and weaknesses in his character. The eleventh grade moves into the larger unit of American literature—our moral commitments, our conception of the good life, our deepest loyalties, our standards of excellence, and our abstract goals. The twelfth grade, drawing from world literature, returns to the individual and considers his relationships to nature, to man, and to society.

Writing also is a cumulative experience. Students in the tenth grade begin with sentences and expository paragraphs, advance to longer, more complex themes, and finish in their senior year with research papers and critical analyses. From the beginning, emphasis is placed on clarity of thought, accuracy of statement, and precision of vocabulary. To ensure mechanical skill, all errors must be corrected and rules which have been broken must be quoted before credit is given on any paper.

The Creative Teacher. Although such a carefully structured program might seem too restrictive for a creative teacher, we have not found it so. Each lesson must still be tailored by the teacher to fit his class and his own personality. On the other hand, there is great comfort to be secured in knowing generally what learning experiences the students have had and what objectives they must achieve.

On the other hand, there are serious problems. These are not unusual problems in education since they are chiefly concerned with teacher time and school finances. However, because of the peculiar demands of our curriculum, these are somewhat exaggerated.

Beginning teachers cannot be expected to teach all three areas of the humanities. Rather, they observe as specialists teach their art and music classes. Then, after one or two semesters of observation, they begin to assume responsibility for all three areas—fortified by a weekly conference with the chairman of each of the other two departments. These conferences and extra preparations are a drain on their time and energy. Also, because of the teacher-time involved in this in-service training and team teaching, the program is a little more expensive than a straight English course. However, we believe that the results in human values are of great worth.

When students compose both the words and the music of their school song; when a student watches the raindrops form fascinating patterns on the surface of a newly formed puddle in the court; when students travel 60 miles to an exhibit; when our graduates at the universities extol the merits of the humanities in retrospect; when a student has his composition premiered by the city's symphony orchestra; when students, turned away from a Van Gogh exhibit in Detroit after hours of waiting, return to face more lines in order to have a first-hand experience with great work; when senior folk singers perform "Nancy Hanks," a poem studied in the tenth grade, with a melody and accompaniment of their own creation, we believe we have proof that the program has made its contribution to a little clearer understanding, and perhaps even appreciation, of the good, the true, and the beautiful.

The Role of the Humanities in the Curriculum

Harry S. Broudy

I do not know how many junior and senior high schools now have or are planning to have a humanities program or course. Doubtless, somebody can cite a figure, but if it were ever accurate, it was so only for a moment, because program development in American public schools is a luxuriant rather than a systematic growth. Programs are born, publicized, adopted, and fade away, but nobody, taking the country as a whole, really knows why, when, and where. Nevertheless, the impression is strong, and there is some evidence to support it, that there is much activity in the humanities field, and there is little doubt that the recent establishment of a National Foundation for the Arts and Humanities will stimulate it even more.

Curriculum change in our public schools is not only indefinite in quantity but bewilderingly varied as to form. This is almost inevitable because the common method for developing a program is to have it done by a large representative committee. This body tries to find out what others everywhere are doing, pools all plausible suggestions, and finally makes some kind of selection from them.

As might be expected, no two humanities programs agree fully on content, approach, or method of instruction. Some include all the fine arts, some insist on history, some on philosophy, and some on religion. Some propose to organize the material by periods, some by styles, some by themes. Some intend to utilize teaching teams; some propose to teach all the arts together; some combine all approaches, methods, and contents.

Problem of Selection. There is nothing intrinsically wrong with this lush variety, but often it threatens to choke the program to death. To be sure, the suffocation would be from a surfeit of goodies that the committee insists on stuffing into the program, but suffocation is just as fatal as when caused by any other means. And what little life remains in the patient after the committee is through stuffing it may be snuffed out altogether by an attempt to crowd a half dozen different approaches and methods of instruction into it.

In ancient days the humanities referred to the literature of Greece and Rome,[1] and in the schools only a small selection of classic works were studied. Moreover, a fairly standard way of teaching them was developed as early as 166 B.C. that was used for a long time thereafter.[2]

Today, when we make up a program of the humanities, there are 20 centuries of western civilization alone to be surveyed for possible classics, not only in literature, but in every art. In addition, there is all of contemporary production to consider, so that the danger of suffocation is very genuine indeed.

In these circumstances the principles of selection are everything. Such principles depend, in turn, on the purposes the humanities course is to serve, a point on which there may be divergent views. The situation is further complicated by the fact that even though a school may not list a course called the humanities, it may offer instruction that is supposed to achieve the purposes attributed to the humanities, for example, courses in literature, art, history of ideas, etc. If this is the case—and usually it is—then the claim to curricular time and staff for an additional course becomes debatable; whether or not it is defensible will depend on the distinctiveness of the outcome claimed for the new course, and whether or not this unique outcome is worth pursuing. One significant alternative is to reorganize the existing offerings in literature, arts, history, etc., into a humanities course; another is to replace existing courses with a new one.

I do not know which proposal—adding a new course or reorganizing a number of existing ones—gives the administrator more sleepless nights, but this consideration, cogent as it may be, is less important than the possibility that after all the agonizing reappraisals and reshufflings, after all the abrasive anxieties that such reorganiza-

[1] "Humanities" as meaning arts and letters was used by Cicero and other admirers of Greek culture to refer to the total educational process or the formation of man according to a conscious ideal. (cf. Werner Jaeger, *The Greeks and the Education of Man* (Annandale-on-Hudson, New York: Bard College, 1953), pp. 4-5.

[2] By Dionysius of Thrace who divided the teaching of a work of literature into steps. For a brief description see H. S. Broudy and John Palmer, *Exemplars of Teaching Method* (Chicago: Rand McNally & Co., 1965), p. 23.

As to the extent of the classical studies in literature, the curriculum of the *Gymnasium* of Johann Sturm in Strasbourg in 1565 listed the following works:

Sixth class (11-12 years)—Cicero's longer letters, some of Terence, selections from Aesop, Bishop Ambrose, Martial, and Horace.

Fifth class (12-13 years)—Cicero's *Cato* and *Laelis, Eclogues* of Vergil, and Pauline Epistles in Greek.

Fourth class (13-14 years)—More of Cicero's letters, part of *Adelphi* of Terence, and epistles and satires of Horace.

Third class (14-15 years)—More of Cicero's letters, *Menippus* of Lucian, sixth book of Vergil's *Aeneid*, first book of *Iliad* or *Odyssey* in Greek as well as some of Demosthenes' speeches, odes of Pindar and Horace; some comedies of Terence and Plautus acted out.

Second class (15-16 years)—Interpretation of Greek poets and orators; acted out some of the comedies and tragedies of Aristophanes, Euripides or Sophocles, more Cicero, Demosthenes, and *Iliad*.

First class (16-17 years)—Vergil, Homer, Thucydides, Sallust, and Epistles of St. Paul.

tions or innovations inevitably occasion, things may in a year or two settle back into the very moulds from which they emerged.

We need, therefore, principles of selection of materials and approach that will not jeopardize the humanities program by intolerable and unmanageable plenitude and a concept of the distinctive contribution of the program which will justify either a new course or the reorganization of existing courses.

Revival of the Humanities. The humanities taken in their broadest and most generous intent include works of art, literature, music, sculpture, architecture, history, and philosophy which depict the *human* ideal. This ideal is no more nor less than a conviction that man can transform his animal instincts into something worthy of being called "human," a transformation achieved by intelligence and imagination. By intelligence he can reflect on his experience and by imagination he can expand it, even to the point of changing its quality. Who but man, for example, could transmute feeding into dining and lust into romance? From this cultivation of intelligence and imagination emerges a value system in which some experience is judged to be better or higher than another, an understanding of why this is so, and an obligation to achieve the better and the higher at considerable, perhaps at all, costs.

One great ideal of humanity was worked out vividly and clearly in the Greek poetry, drama, sculpture, architecture, and philosophy. The Romans were enchanted by it and perpetuated it. Since then in various renaissances, the ideal has been revived.[3]

Perhaps the renewed interest of schools in the humanities is a symptom for the need of another revival of this idea and ideal of *humanitas*. In our own time, as in the barbaric ages that prevailed in some parts of the world after the fall of Rome, the human style has become ragged and human self-confidence flags. There is a despair about transforming the crudity of raw animal impulse; there is an even greater despair about undoing the perversions of human nature by the misuse of intelligence and imagination.

We need not recount the already familiar bill of complaints. We are unable to distinguish riches from affluence, to find freedom in our efficiency, to find satisfaction in an age designed to maximize comfort and pleasure. The blessings of large-scale industry turn out to be breeders of great fears of great wars. In sum, we are unhappy not because we lack the ingredients for happiness, but because the ingredients don't add up to it.

Above all, middle-aged parents and policemen are baffled and frightened by their inability to reach the young. They talk of honesty, hard work, chastity, kindness, fair play as if the young must mean by these words what they themselves mean. The polite patience with which such talk is so often received dismays us even more than blatant and unkempt defiance. To the middle-aged generation it looks as if the world belongs to teen-agers bent on wrecking it and themselves.

What does it look like to the young? Who knows? Middle-agers cannot make it out from what teen-agers say, but like the animals who are reputed to be able to

[3] Jaeger, *op. cit.*, pp. 16-17.

communicate with each other in mysterious ways, the young seem to communicate with each other so as not to let the "enemy" know what is really going on. We can only conjecture that to the young it looks as if the world belongs to the stupid, timid, and hypocritical middle-agers who talk about virtue because their glands are tired; who talk peace but wage war; who preach freedom and practice oppression.

In the search for the causes of our troubles some critics have blamed the dominance of science and technology in our culture. This dominance, they argue, has given us great power to achieve ends but not the wisdom to choose ends. The humanities, purporting to deal with values, that is, with the assessment of ends, are suggested as a counter measure to the emphasis on science in both school and society. Hence the revival of the ancient feud between science and the humanities, a feud so well publicized in the recent remarks of C. P. Snow about the two cultures.

Scientists understandably do not like to be regarded as inhuman or their sciences as nonhuman. Knowledge is the human achievement par excellence, and science is our most reliable and useful kind of knowledge. Nor are scientists as men inhuman; they lead lives no worse than others and are as responsive to their fellows as the next man. Accordingly, some educators see no reason for excluding the sciences from the humanities. However admirable such hospitability may be, there is some justification for distinguishing humanistic from scientific studies.

Science *as* science is about a domain of objects, and the goal of science is to discover the laws that explain the behavior of these objects. The import of these objects for the human ideal is precisely what is *not* the concern of science as a science or the scientist as a scientist. Thus the truth about the laws of nuclear fission does not depend on the brotherhood of man or a belief in it. However, insofar as the former is important for the latter, nuclear physics becomes a humanistic concern. So the humanistic study of a science is possible, but such a study is no longer science; and the scientific study of humanity is possible, but it is then no longer humanistic.

Enlightened Cherishing. Now the activities of man that deliberately transmute knowledge, feeling, and imagination into actual or possible value commitments are the fine arts, history in its literary dimensions, and moral philosophy. Religion should be included except when it takes the human quest beyond the human boundaries, but insofar as religion is a human activity and deals with the human theme it belongs in the humanities. It is natural, therefore, to turn to the "value" studies or the humanities as a remedy for the troubles of our times. However, humanistic studies are and have always been in the curriculum, so why is a "new" course suggested? The reasons usually given are that some of these studies, e.g., the fine arts, are not given sufficient attention, or that some, e.g., literature, are not taught for the right outcomes, e.g., aesthetic or moral, or that certain items regarded as classics are not taught at all. It is to meet these deficiencies—real or alleged—that the humanities course is proposed as a remedy.

The humanities course, it is suggested, would deliberately devote itself to the human quest for the right answers to the questions about the good, the true, and the beautiful—about the life that is genuinely human. However, even the standard courses in literature and history claim they do this, so the humanities course must promise something more or different. I would suggest that the outcome we really expect from the humanities course be called enlightened cherishing. These two words encompass both the commitment of the individual to certain values and the standards by which he justifies the commitment. The humanities course will not give ready-made "right" answers to value questions, but properly taught and learned it could enlighten our cherishing by offering to the student exemplars of the human ideal for study and possible emulation. This, I take it, is what we mean by value *education* as opposed to value *training,* on the one hand, and to knowledge about values, on the other. The former produces cherishings that are not enlightened; the latter may not result in cherishing at all.

I believe that many of the courses now available in the high school curriculum are humanistic only in the sense that they give the student knowledge about cherishing. Many appreciation courses, survey courses in the history of civilization, most history courses, and not a few of the courses in literature have been accused of this fault. If this charge is well founded, then something other than this mode of instruction is justified either by new courses or reorganization of old ones that stress the shaping of taste.

However, the cherishing phase of schooling can be unenlightened. Teachers may be inculcating and rewarding preferences without being able to give reasons for them. F. F. Skinner, I am sure, could teach his pigeons to cherish Bach and Mozart in this way. Some, adopting the doctrine that there is no way of disputing rationally about tastes, preclude even the possibility of enlightened cherishing. Some reinforce certain preferences because they are approved by the dominant group in the society. Some are hypocrites professing to love what the critics say is good, but secretly preferring what the popular media extol. Others in the schools, fearful lest the emotional experience be marred by turning the intellect upon it, shy away from all talk of standards, of judgment, of connoisseurship. Still other devotees of the arts brand all efforts to teach art or music or sculpture for appreciation as misguided. There is only one way to teach art they say, and this is to try to make a painter or musician out of the pupil. If the learner is successful he becomes a performer, an artist; if not, he can use what little he has learned to appreciate the performance of others. Those with talent perform and appreciate, those without just appreciate.[4]

If enlightened cherishing is the distinctive contribution of the humanities course to the outcomes of schooling, it should guide the choice of materials and approach so as not to lose this distinctiveness. Two strategic factors in the choice are (1) the fact that habits of enlightened cherishing take time to establish and (2) the

---

[4] All of these variants can be found in any one of a clutch of symposia on the teaching of the arts. Typical is *A Seminar in Art Education for Research and Curriculum Development* which came out of Pennsylvania State University in 1966. The contributions cover everything from highly involved theory about what an artist does to such "helpful" suggestions as bringing in people who as artists will act as Pied Pipers and charm pupils into the "basic mystery of art" and let what may happen in the classroom.

presupposition that there are standards of cherishing which the school is willing to accept and use.

The time factor makes it imperative to keep the number of books, pictures, sculptures, buildings, dramas to be studied small. To avoid the danger of suffocation it would be well to concentrate for longer periods of time on fewer items of study. This means selecting items that pack the greatest potentialities for capturing the interest of the student and for displaying to the student the meaning of the human quest for humanity. Precisely because other courses in the curriculum provide for getting knowledge and for achieving certain skills, the humanities course need not worry lest some "items" be left out. One must reiterate this, because school people are obsessed by the fear of leaving something out that anyone on the committee thinks is important. A committee designing a humanities course would be well advised to have its members vie with each other to omit items rather than to include them.

It is desirable but not imperative for the humanities course not to duplicate too many items already being studied in established courses. For enlightened cherishing, works that are not in every anthology may be just as useful as some of the old standbys, but insofar as the humanities course is unique in spirit, duplication is not a serious problem.

The principle of parsimony should also be applied to the choice of an approach. Courses are now organized on the basis of recurrent themes such as freedom, creativity, search for God, etc.; on styles of art and literature, e.g., classic, baroque, modern; on historical periods, e.g., ancient, medieval, renaissance, etc.[5] In an eagerness to exploit the virtues of all the approaches, various combinations are tried. The objection to these is practical: The greater the number of approaches the more complex the teaching becomes, and the greater the staff resistance. It is just about impossible to combine styles, themes, periods, and the various arts in any one course without driving the already apprehensive teacher to despair. It is better to pick one approach as dominant and allow the others to be woven in as opportunity permits, but not to worry overmuch if opportunity does not permit.

Aesthetic Exemplars. One way of simplifying the approach is to select works that clothe the great themes or ideas of the human quest in artistic form. Not all works of art display or celebrate ideas, but some works of great artistic merit do. The Greek tragedies and those of Shakespeare are familiar examples. They not only tell us about the human quest but seduce us into cherishing it. But some paintings, sculpture, and, to a lesser extent, music exert an analogous power over our cherishings even though they do not deal explicitly with ideas. In other words, the humanities course could limit itself to works of indisputable artistic excellence that display, illustrate, and celebrate the human quest. This would leave out most historical works and works of formal philosophy, but the ideas they express might

[5]For samples of approaches, see the project materials now being developed by the New York State Department of Education and the Educational Research Council of Greater Cleveland.

still be among those celebrated by the works of art that have been selected for study.[6]

One advantage of such an approach is that it enables us to adopt a distinctive style of teaching the course, viz., that of aesthetic analysis.

Poems, novels, epics, myths, paintings, buildings, capture our attention and invite our participation by their formal structure, on the one hand, and by stimulating our imagination, on the other. To become enlightened in our cherishing is to learn to respond knowingly to these selected works of the imagination designed for the imagination: to look, listen, and think as the poet, the dramatist, the moral genius, the painter, and the architect looks, listens, and thinks.

These works of art, that form so large a part of the humanities, can be studied with respect to their sensuous properties, their techniques, their formal design, and their expressiveness. Each of the first three types of characteristics can be discerned, pointed to, and discussed. Given enough time to do these three things with a work of art, there is a fair chance that the fourth quality—expressiveness or meaning—may come through.

Aesthetic analysis is formulable into a teaching method and can be applied to any art form; it is adaptable to various levels of learning readiness, and the results can, I believe, be evaluated with a fair amount of confidence. If well done and for a sufficient time, it should produce enlightened cherishing and a commitment to its importance.[7] This style of instruction can be combined with any of the packagings mentioned earlier, but it promises the most solid results if the number of items studied is kept small and their quality high.

Authority. Sooner or later, if the selection of content is to be justified, the selectors will have to appeal to authority.

Now all authority rests upon the willingness to believe that some propositions are true and some things are good because somebody's word can be taken for it. We trust that word because we believe that the utterer is in the position to know the truth of the matter. One can qualify for such a position in various ways: by being a recipient of a divine revelation, or by having special clairvoyant powers, or by having protected one's judgments from error by systematic study and wide experience. In religion the first type of authority ranks at the top, and for some people the second type seems highly trustworthy, but for most of us most of the time the third justification is the one in which we put our faith when our own knowledge is inadequate.

It is a curious fact that in matters of deepest concern to the human quest there is no agreement as to which of these authorities are valid or that any of them are. This skepticism is based on the wide diversity of values held by people

---

[6]For further discussion of exemplars, see H. S. Broudy, *Building a Philosophy of Education* (Englewood Cliffs, New Jersey: Prentice-Hall, 1961), Chap. 13, and Broudy, B. Othanel Smith, and Joe R. Burnett, *Democracy and Excellence in American Secondary Education* (Chicago: Rand McNally & Co., 1964), Chap. 13.

[7]An interesting summary of psychological studies on some of these aspects of art education is given by Dale Harris in "Aesthetic Awareness: A Psychologist's View," *Art Education,* XIX (1966), 17-23.

at different times and places and by the authorities themselves. What are the consequences of this situation for the study of the humanities?

If there is no basis for any authority, then how are the studies to be chosen? The simplest answer is "At random" or "It doesn't make any difference." And the same answer would have to be made to the question as to who shall make the selection, for the pupil is as much an authority or nonauthority as his teacher. Indeed, if we are really to avoid authority there can be no selection at all, for nothing deserves to be included or omitted insofar as there is no standard for judging what "deserves" is to mean. In other words, any meaningful work in the humanities entails the acceptance of some kind of authority as to what is *good* literature, *good* painting, etc.

About the only kind of authority that can be defended with any hope of acceptance is that of the expert, that is, the person who by systematic study and wide experience has developed a system of ideas by which he can give reasons for his imputations of artistic or moral merit and of human import. But what about the notorious lack of agreement even among the experts in these matters?

1. It must first be said that the disagreement is neither so violent nor so pervasive as is sometimes alleged. Actually the human quest is described with monotonous uniformity by experts to be the life of virtue, of reason, of love, of courage, of self-cultivation, of self-determination, of self-realization. Even the current dramatic "rebellions" against these verities is not a rejection of them but a protest against a culture that makes achievement of them difficult and perhaps impossible.

2. There is a large area of agreement in aesthetic matters so far as technical merit and the formal properties of a work are concerned.

3. Agreement is not a necessary condition for the possibility of expert authority. The greater the agreement, the greater confidence we can place on any expert, and this simplifies matters to be sure. However, the important difference is not between one expert and another, but rather between the expert and the nonexpert, or between enlightened cherishing and arbitrary cherishing.

4. Finally, not all authority is imposed and external; authority can be escaped by catching on to the rules by which the authorities make their judgment and by practicing the rules himself; or even by altering the rules for himself. If anything can put the individual on the road to becoming an incipient authority, it should be the humanities course.

Because there is disagreement among the experts, the schools in their selections of items to be studied are more or less constrained to pick items on which there is a good deal of expert agreement. Yet it would not be inconsistent with this principle to select deliberately items on which experts disagree, because educationally the inquiry into why the disagreement exists could be very rewarding indeed.

As to educators who inveigh against intellectualizing the arts, against indoctrinating children with standards that somebody does not hold, and who in this area, as in no other, insist on the freedom of the pupil to choose his own objects and standards, I would be more impressed by these arguments if they were more sincere or less naive. As a participant in a number of conferences and committees dealing with these matters, I am convinced that the passion for pupil freedom is usually a symptom of insecurity about one's own preferences, and betrays a profound forgetfulness of the extent to which one's own preferences are based on expert authority. Even the passion for pupil freedom is more often than not learned from authoritative figures. One is hard put to know what to think about people who at one and the same committee meeting deny all objectivity to value judgment and in the next breath condemn television and the movies and popular music as inferior to what they happen to regard as "fresh, creative, and exciting."

A school system might therefore take considerable time to ask the proponents of a humanities course or a course in the combined arts to clarify the notion of authority for themselves and to each other. If the consensus is that about taste there is no disputing, it might be well to give up the course altogether, for there are many other resources in the community for forming just any old taste. If the cherishing is not to be enlightened, there is little point in devoting instructional time and resources to value education.

In value education it is probably true that, as C. S. Lewis pointed out, one must stand inside the Way or outside of it, and for those who stand outside of it the course in the humanities is bound to be misguided and even meaningless. What is the Way?

It is the reality beyond all predicates, the abyss that was before the Creator Himself. It is Nature, it is the Way, the Road. It is the Way in which the universe goes on, the Way in which things everlastingly emerge, stilly and tranquilly, into space and time. It is also the Way which every man should tread in imitation of that cosmic and supercosmic progression, conforming all activities to that great exemplar . . . . This conception in all its forms, Platonic, Aristotelian, Stoic, Christian, and Oriental alike . . . is the doctrine of objective value, the belief that certain attitudes are really true, and others really false, to the kind of thing the universe is and the kind of things we are.[8]

It is only when educators believe that the rational powers of man enable him to understand the essence of man and that his will can shape his life accordingly that they can meaningfully search for that essence in what we call the humanities. We can continue the search even if we are not successful, but we cannot in simple honesty go on with it, if we do not believe that the search is itself meaningful.

[8] *The Abolition of Man* (New York: Collier Books, 1962), pp. 28-29.

Part IV
Humanities in the Elementary School

At the present time, few humanities programs for the elementary school exist. This is reflected in the fact that there are so few articles in this area. However, many of the people who have become involved in the humanities believe that the elementary school is where the program should begin. They believe that the self-contained classroom, in which the same teacher is already responsible for the teaching of the different disciplines, is a natural setting for the humanities.

Jenkins finds a basic paradox in the fact that we attempt to educate the whole child in the elementary school through a fragmented curriculum. He suggests that "the humanities might well be the point of focus for bringing together" the whole child. For this program, Jenkins suggests the study of people "in Africa, in India, in Japan, and. . .China," the teaching of philosophy and history on the elementary level, emphasis on "literature as artistic creation rather than on the commonly used approach of finding literal meaning," and development of "imaginative insight." He also states that writing "can become more humanistic by relating it to literature."

Jenkins describes the basic objectives of a humanities program for two sixth-grade classes in Pennsylvania. A more detailed picture of this sixth-grade program in the Shelmire Elementary School at Southampton Pennsylvania can be found in the article by Ray. Some of the questions discussed by these sixth-graders include: "What is human? How is man different from other animals? How does man communicate his thoughts and feelings to others?"

Aspects of this program that were unusual for the elementary school were the sessions devoted to sculpture and architecture.

Two other unusual topics were "nature" and "the dance." In relation to the dance one of the goals was to help the students perceive dance as a means of expressing an idea as well as a form of entertainment. Student reactions to this program and the kinds of ideas inherent in it should provide a strong inducement to other elementary teachers who are interested in this new area.

The third article, by Beckett, describes a Children's Humanities (CHum) program for all students in the first six grades of the James A. Garfield School District. In this program "unneeded rote learning ... (was) replaced with generalizations and concepts presented by means of a humanities approach to the typically fragmented fine arts, language arts and social studies at the elementary school level." A detailed curriculum has been mimeographed and can be obtained from the author of this article.

The Humanities and Humanistic Education in the Elementary Grades

William A. Jenkins

Introduction. Children, like adults, need an understanding of the nature of the reality of the world in which we live. Some scholars say we live in a scientific world. This statement is almost irrefutable. Others say we live in a humanistic world and insist that man's chief problems are humanistic. Such things as getting along with other people, governments getting along with other governments, and so forth, basically are humanistic problems, they say. Perhaps they are right. However, I cannot accept the position which says we live in two distinct worlds, that of science and that of humanities, for I find myself on the side of the angels who insist that things reduced to their utmost essence are humanistic. This is probably true for me since my background has been in the world of letters, and in the world in which one works with other human beings to develop their understanding, their truths, and their knowledge—education. Perhaps it would suffice at this point to say that in my professional endeavors I have sought to understand who I am, where I am, and how I got where I am. I have also endeavored to help others understand who they are, where they are, and how they got there.

Some Definitions. Perhaps at this point I should retrace one or two of my steps and offer not just one definition but several definitions of the humanities, all the while focusing on the work of the elementary school. At their simplest the humanities represent a study of man as a human being. They are the organized study of the history of the human spirit. The humanities are universal, for they present mankind as one. They reflect the dreams of a people, or of all people, which dreams are most clearly mirrored in the arts. Moreover, they provide a hope for the future, which children, like adults, should have, and a picture of the good life, a prime objective of all education. The humanities present the story of man's search for meaning, value, and order. They might even be said to record his search for immortality. Without question they reflect his quest for Beauty, Truth, Freedom, and his relationships with other men. They provide him with the basis for judging the world around him, even when that world is seen through ten-year-old eyes.

A Look at Elementary Education. Over the years the elementary school program has readily been described as schizophrenic, dichotomous, fragmentalized, if not disoriented and misdirected. While placing emphasis on the whole child as an acceptable and noteworthy objective, educators have used as a means for obtaining this being something less than reputable—a compartmentalized, fragmentary approach to knowledge. We have forgotten that ends and means are related; in effect we have tried to get a silk purse out of styrofoam. I should like to suggest that the humanities might well be the point of focus for bringing together much of what we have been seeking, the whole child. A few years ago I would have said that this focal point should be the language arts. I am not yet ready to relinquish that position. If we can develop children who are flexible, fluent, and facile in the use of their native tongue when met in fine literature, or when heard or used in informal conversations, then in my estimation perhaps two thirds of the job of educating them has been accomplished. I still believe, for example, that disadvantaged children can be "advantaged" primarily through literature-language-linguistic endeavors. I am not ready to abandon this position either. May I, then, hedge a bit and simply say that I am willing to have the humanities umbrella raised over the blanket which heretofore embraced the ideal curriculum.

More than a century ago John Stuart Mill said this: "Men lose their high aspirations as they lose their intellectual tastes, because they have no time or opportunity for indulging them; and they addict themselves to inferior pleasures, not because they deliberately prefer them, but because they are either the only ones to which they have access, or the only ones which they are any longer capable of enjoying." Mill's dictum is very relevant here. If the pupils in our classes are addicted only to the Beatles, the Animals, and the Rolling Stones, it might well be that we have given them nothing better. They have filled the vacuum which exists. And if they read only comics or trashy magazines, they are behaving very naturally in filling a void. My position would have to be that we must offer them a wider range of "voidfillers."

The Humanities in the Schools. It is very obvious to anyone who has looked at the humanities in recent years that much more is being done with them in the high school. Perhaps this is natural, but I must insist that it is not right. If elementary school pupils have minimum linguistic ability—if they are able to read with any power and critical ability, if they are able to discriminate in their listening, and if they are reasonably facile in expressing themselves in writing— then I would insist that the humanities approach to knowledge be included in their curriculum.

I am not a student of early childhood education, so I merely have the feeling that this can be done even in the lower grades. With today's emphasis on oral language, much from the humanities may be given to very young children. But I say with great certainty that the humanities belong in the middle grades and up. They belong there not just for the most able students either. The benefits to be realized from such study will be implicit in the balance of my remarks.

The Humanities in Elementary Schools. How may we approach the teaching of the humanities in the elementary school? Perhaps one answer may be found in thoughts expressed by James A. Michener in 1949. At that time Michener said: "(1) People are the aim and end of life. Teach the supremacy of people over machines, political systems, economic systems, or any other system. People are the focus of our interest, our only hope. (2) People are endlessly complex, endlessly superb. (3) But people are sometimes endlessly confused and evil. (4) Optimism has not yet been discredited. Students need contact with sensible optimism; desperately they need it. (5) Society is worth studying. Students should be encouraged to read great fictional studies of our national life."[1]

The disturbing point in this statement is the emphasis which Michener places on *national* life. In too many ways in schools today we overemphasize the western world. My approach to the humanities in the elementary school would include study of people in Africa, in India, in Japan, and yes, even in China today. From this study I would attempt to give my pupils a sense of both the past and the future. It may be heresy to say that one should teach the elementary school child philosophy and history. I don't say it, but this is what I would be doing.

It has been said so often that knowledge is exploding, the statement has lost its meaning. But Jerome Bruner points out that a by-product of the knowledge explosion is our discovery that knowledge is even more interconnected than we had heretofore believed. The approach suggested here would have us capitalize on the interconnections presented by the humanities.

Is there an explosion in the arts? I really don't know. But if there is one, I suspect that it is of very small magnitude. Undoubtedly we are placing more emphasis on the arts in everyday living and in school pursuits. We have learned—or at least many more of us have learned than knew in the time of the Greeks—that we learn humanity by studying humanity. We are aware and sometimes ashamed that in the not too distant past we have studied human fact when we should have been studying human spirit.

The Humanities and Literature. John Galsworthy once said, "A human being is the best plot there is." In teaching literature I have experienced this sensation, as have most of us. I remember attempting with a freshman composition class a few years ago to talk about the emerging peoples of Africa as background for an expository assignment. I failed miserably, and then I suggested that as many of my students as possible read Allen Paton's *Cry, the Beloved Country* and *Too Late the Phalarope.* The results were astounding, and while I was able to improve in miniscule fashion my students' writing ability, I did much to clear the horizon and give them a view of Africa as a country made up of people who had emotions, who experienced events, and who underwent emotional traumas. Our largest success, then, as it must be in an elementary school classroom now, was achieving some understanding about the human condition, "man's lot."

As a medium, literature has the ability to give man a supernature. But it also gives to him who reads the literature a supernature—of understanding, of feeling, of appreciating, of empathizing. With very young children the approach must be different. It is not humanistic to help them enjoy the sounds that they hear, the rhythms which are worked by the words, and the images which they can see with their inner eyes? But let us underscore the thought that emphasis must be on literature as artistic creation rather than on the commonly used approach of finding literal meaning. Yes, I am saying that in the elementary school it is most

---

[1] James A. Michener, "Idealism Today," *Books in Their Courses*, 10 (April 1949), 3.

important that we teach children to read literature, rather than just reading. Santayana said, "Utmost truths are more easily and more adequately conveyed by poetry than by analysis." In my scheme of things, therefore, children should study the most important ideas about human beings in a humanistic context rather than, say, in the social studies, no matter how one approaches them. If the conveyance of ideas is dramatic, the impressions can only be lasting.

Planning Humanistic Study. Where should our humanistic efforts begin? Perhaps with earnest attention to the balance which we give to matters of letters and language in the elementary school. Specifically, with our major language forces directed at reading competence we have slighted the indispensable and distinguishing trait of literature, the imaginative insight which it offers. All other outcomes of literature are dependent upon this. Self-understanding, understanding of others, vicarious experience, and perceptions of morality, to cite four outcomes, depend on imagination. Imagination is critical because it takes one outside of himself, above or below the surface of life, and beyond the routines of daily living. Because this is so, the humanities, and specifically, literature, deserve a central position in the elementary school curriculum. The aesthetic beauty and the interpretation of human experience represent treasures which should not be denied elementary pupils. Without dwelling on the technical aspects which are to be included, and the problem of avoiding using the technical terms with children, the literary experience for children can be a full one only if they encounter the several genre and the use of such techniques and devices as indirection, metaphor, symbolism, and irony. Good teachers have long pointed to the irony in *Mike Mulligan and His Steam Shovel*; the symbolism in *Charlotte's Web;* the indirection in *The Wind in the Willows* and *The Hundred Dresses.* There is a surprisingly large number of such excellent pieces of literature.

The "color me brown"—or yellow, or red, or black—books which have appeared in great profusion in recent years as our national conscience has become aroused to the problems of various minority groups, frequently smack of didacticism. But judiciously chosen and artfully read and discussed, they lead to great insights into man and his problems.

If you have read "Joaby" by Lorrie McLaughlin, a seemingly innocuous tale of a summer friendship between two boys—one white and one black—then you can realize the power of literature for touching the insides of the young. Perhaps it even gnaws there. The whole gamut of racial strife and tensions, of mores and taboos, of symbols of the "ins" and the "outs" are suggested. Read Taro Yashima's *Crow Boy* to a group of third or fourth graders. Or Emily Neville's *Berries Goodman;* or Molly Cone's *A Promise Is a Promise;* or Lois Santalo's *The Wind Dies at Sunrise;* or Barbara Smucker's *Wigwam in the City.* and I have been arbitrary in my choice of problem theme and examples. I merely suggest what might be done with contemporary books, on a contemporary theme, with contemporary children who have great need for developing the greatest possible humaneness and humanity. On the surface my ambitions would appear contradictory, for I am advocating in children's study of literature abolition of the genteel evasion, the gentleman's agreement about subjects that are touchy if not taboo. Need I remind you that when Gulliver first traveled, his journeys were timely? And *Great Expectations,* too, once had a social impact. The artistry in these creations remains today.

Writing, Language, and the Humanities. Writing (perhaps *composing* is a better term) by elementary school children can become more humanistic by relating it to literature. Admittedly much of the pedestrian will remain. There will still have to be vacuous paragraphs about vacations and puerile sentences about pets. But if we are to realize our language objective of going beyond minimum skills to aesthetic understanding and use, this natural connection must be made. Language study in the elementary grades has deteriorated, in my opinion, and the promise of linguistics for improving it has been empty. To cite just one lamentable occurrence, under the aegis of linguistics, some language programs for children now seemingly attempt to teach them all that we ever knew about grammar. There is more formal grammar, not less, in language texts and workbooks today; and the approach is less functional than ever. The decline continues of writing which is creative; poetry remains in disuse. Only occasionally are there reports of a language program which we can applaud. Such objectives as developing children's sensitivity to language, or the knowledge of the social relationships of language, or the pursuit of language as a study of people in action are all too rare. Even recognition by the school of the fact that each of us, even a child, has and uses a second language in his daily and perhaps private endeavors is often ignored by those who set standards for language study.

In 1934 John Dewey wrote: "As long as art is the beauty parlor of civilization, neither art nor civilization is secure."[2] He defined art simply as "intensification of the ordinary." The suggestions just given for changes in language study and writing exercises are neither radical nor revolutionary. Nor do they imply an abandonment of the goal of excellence. A different type of excellence is called for. The rigor of study in the grades will be no whit lessened. Artistic approaches to the study of language, composing, and literature are not luxuries. They are sound pedagogy. The earlier assertions that art is the vehicle for the imagination and that children's imagination must be nurtured should be repeated here. These approaches are sound psychologically and socially.

A study of art in its broadest sense is essential to balanced study of any cultural development. We have all studied literature at two levels: as a creative entity and as history of the artist and his age. My suggestion, then, is that language and composing be approached similarly.

Teacher Education and the Humanities. Let me at this point make a comment or two about teacher education. Professor Harry Broudy says that "humanistic study to make good its claim. . . needs both humanistic content and humanistic teaching."[3] Without a doubt the elementary teacher has to synthesize knowledge, and of all teachers he has the greatest opportunity to do so. But though he is

[2] John Dewey, *Art as Experience* (New York: G. P. Putnam's Sons, 1959), p. 344.
[3] Harry Broudy, "Symposium: Science 'Versus' Humanities in the School Curriculum: A Philosophical Analysis of the Present Crisis,"*Journal of Philosophy,* (November 6, 1958), 987-1008.

criticized in some quarters for not doing it, I think he must not imitate in his teaching what his collegiate colleague does in his class. Liberal collegiate education has not turned out significant numbers of humanists; is not humanistic in approach or content; is not, in a word, justified in casting stones. The elementary teacher, therefore, should devise his own approaches.

Recently I read of a program in the humanities developed for two sixth grade classes at the Shelmire Elementary School at Southhampton, Pennsylvania. The program had these pupil objectives:

1. help them develop a concept of the meaning of the word *humanities*
2. arouse in them new dimensions of interest which would be reflected in their choices of reading materials, television programs, and motion pictures
3. help them to see themselves as human beings in a world of humans
4. deepen their insights in respect to other culture groups—all cultures have their humanities, some quite different from ours
5. provide a different orientation in the arts—causing them to see painting, sculpture, architecture, dance, poetry, films, etc. as expressions about and reactions to man himself, his natural and his social environment.[4]

The program apparently was successful in developing new insights for the children. Perhaps you will be interested in this comment on their experience with the dance:

The dance was the most difficult of the expressive forms to introduce. Almost without exception the concept of dance held by these children was a form of entertainment. Dance as a means of expressing an idea was almost impossible for them to comprehend. Our introduction of this new concept was a simple one. We asked the children to close their eyes and imagine that the sky had descended to a point barely above their scalps. We then asked them to touch the sky gently with their hands and try to lift the sky a little. We told them that if any stars fell from the sky they were to catch them with one hand and press them back into place inside the sky. Gradually, we raised the sky into its proper place. Sixty-five children, rising from their seats in unison, lifting the sky into place, created as beautiful a dance movement as the writer has ever witnessed. . . .

A few years ago when I was working with a group of fifteen teachers-to-be in an integrated program in elementary education, in one sense I was a miserable failure. As instructor, I was required to supervise their student teaching and then in a daily two-hour seminar teach them educational psychology, social studies methods, tests and measurements, and so forth. The subjects were to be related to their student teaching. A number of the required subjects are anathema to me. My students, therefore, learned psychology by seeing the motion picture and reading the children's book, *And Now, Miguel,* by Joseph Krumgold. Some of

[4] Henry W. Ray, "Humanities in Elementary Education," *Social Education,* 28 (December 1964), 459-60.

our social foundations came from Jesse Stuart's *The Thread That Runs So True.*
Our reading and discussion included Doris Gates' *Blue Willow,* Eleanor Estes' *The Hundred Dresses,* and Paul Gallico's *The Snow Goose,* all fine children's stories.

I guess if I were given this teaching assignment today, I would fail once again, for I would do much the same thing. Perhaps I would change only by adding one of the children's biographies of Helen Keller. Great insight about learning problems could be gained here. Perhaps I should do a bit more with anthropological approaches. *Warrior Scarlet* might be an addition. And since my students would do some of their intern teaching with the disadvantaged, we would probably read such books as *Durango Street* and *Queenie Peavy* (I should probably still have to go to a college text on arithmetic methods. I haven't yet found a good story to help me with this subject.)

Some Problems with Teaching the Humanities. The humanities and humanistic teaching in the elementary school pose problems. Let me list just ten of these problems: 1) The humanities are still a part of the leisure tradition in our country. I think we can expect various admirals and classicists to be critical of our efforts. 2) We will have to team teach the subject. Few elementary teachers could handle it alone. Unfortunately, team teaching has not yet been reduced to workable basic principles. 3) Materials for study will have to be locally produced or searched for. Few if any are readily available, even from the newly formed "learning systems" manufacturers. 4) Language arts would have to have a quality rather than a quantity emphasis, and stress would have to be placed on interpretive and analytical approaches rather than on narrative, descriptive, or minimum essential skills. 5) History, or at least historical orientation, would have to find its way back into the social studies. 6) And art and music would have to be taught for understanding rather than for performance or appreciation. 7) I realize that our culture, which places a premium on specialization, will create pressure on the teaching of humanities to become a specialized teaching area. This should not happen. If it should, it inevitably will lead to the teaching of the humanities by these specialists to children as if the children were future scholars. It has happened in other areas, as the scholars value and promote scholarship. Their consideration of the problems of education may very well be only accidental and incidental. 8) Teaching the humanities to slow learners, very young children, or those whose linguistic development has been slow may be problematical. Special considerations are in order here. 9) There may also be a tendency, at least in the literature aspect of the humanities, to restrict study to the classics. I think I have shown earlier that there is available today magnificent new literature for children. Deadwood of other periods, whether in literature, art, music, or sculpture, should be weeded out. 10) Finally, our schools generally operate today on a democratic-egalitarian philosophy. We are here supporting the humanistic outlook which is largely aristocratic in background. I think we should expect conflicts.

I have given but a brief survey of the problems attendant to humanistic teaching and study of the humanities in the elementary school. It was not at all my intention to suggest that the task *not* be assumed. I have merely attempted to think aloud with you to arrive at a gross estimate of the magnitude of the task.

Conclusion. Let me conclude at this point. What are we here advocating? Perhaps Carl Sandburg has said it for us. He wrote:

> There is only one man in the world and
> his name is ALL MEN
> There is only one woman in the world
> and her name is ALL WOMEN
> There is only one child in the world and
> the child's name is ALL CHILDREN

We want to give children this concept, this insight, this knowledge.

Leland Jacobs, one of our foremost scholars of literature for children has also described what we are about. I would like to quote him at length.[5]

1. The arts and humanities explore and illuminate that which is human and humane. . . .

   The arts and humanities explore not only the mind and spirit of the individual but also the bonds, the strains, the communication and communion between man and man.

   The arts and humanities illuminate the human success, the human dilemma, the decisions, the joys, the sorrows, the impulses of man making his living, of men involved in the human endeavor, in the enterprise, of being human.

   In the arts and humanities, man is not a *thing*.

   Man is a drama.

2. The content of the arts and humanities finds its bearings in the explication of the human *spirit* rather than the human *fact*. . . .

   The content of the arts and humanities permits the beholder to "try on" segments of life without taking the direct consequences.

   The content of the arts and humanities gives the receiver a taste of being, for a moment, *universal man.*

3. The ways of knowing in the arts and humanities are distinctly their own.

   One can know logically, linearly, analytically. This is the way of *discourse.*

   One can know feeling fully, aesthetically.

[5] Leland Jacobs, "What Can the Arts and Humanities Contribute to the Liberal Education of All Children and Youth?" NEA *Addresses and Proceedings,* 103 (1965), 47-49.

Both are necessary. One contributes to rational man; the other to aesthetic, feeling man.

4. The language of the arts and humanities differs from the language of the sciences, mathematics, and the social sciences.

In intent, the latter aims at objective discourse, the former, subjective discourse.

In form, the latter depends on sign and signal, the former on sign and symbol.

In effect, the latter leads to logical conclusion, the former to imaginative conclusions.

Both, however, in their own terms, to be effective, must be precise and discriminative.

5. The teaching of the arts and humanities calls for practices that square with the intent and nature of the content—

By stimulation of activity of thought,

By building upon divergence in thinking,

By developing critics and creators rather than regurgitators and imitators.

Perhaps *serendipity* will come from study of the humanities in the elementary school. I should be surprised if it did not. Perhaps like the three Princes of Serendip in the old Persian tale who always found something unexpected when they traveled, elementary educators, too, will be in for a surprise. Perhaps, they, too, will find valuable things not sought for or expected in their journey.

The Humanities in Elementary Education

Henry W. Ray

A program in the humanities was offered for one semester to two classes of sixth-grade students of average ability in the Shelmire Elementary School at Southampton, Pennsylvania.[1] The purpose of the program was to offer the students experiences in the humanities which would (1) help them develop a concept of the meaning of the word "humanities"; (2) arouse in them new dimensions of interest which would be reflected in their choices of reading materials, television programs, and motion pictures; (3) help them to see themselves as human beings in a world of humans; (4) deepen their insights in

[1] Florence Kunkle and Paul Sensenig were the classroom teachers involved, and Charles Walker, Principal of Shelmire School, was a key figure in the inauguration and development of this experimental program.

respect to other culture groups—all cultures have their "humanities," some quite different from ours; and (5) provide a different orientation in the arts—causing them to see painting, sculpture, architecture, dance, poetry, films, etc. as expressions about and reactions to man himself, his natural and his social environment.

Our first session was devoted to helping the children develop a concept of the meaning of the word, humanities. This required a full class period in which such questions were raised as: What is human? How is man different from other animals? How does man communicate his thoughts and feelings to others? Student comments relating to the meaning of humanities filled a long section of the blackboard.

Realizing that almost every child in the class spent a great deal of time watching television, we chose television programs for the topic of our second session. The students were asked to write responses to four questions:

1. What are some of the TV programs you like best? Why do you like them?
2. What are some TV programs you do not like? Why?
3. If you had the money and the power to put on a television program, what would the subject be?
4. How did television come into being?

The children's answers to these questions were most revealing and opened many avenues of discussion. One frequently mentioned reason for liking a program was because it was humorous. We discussed humor and the fine line that might separate humor and tragedy. The students were asked to look for examples of humor in poetry, stories, cartoons, etc., and to try to determine the element which made the item humorous. We viewed an early Chaplin film and talked about the situations which evoked laughter. Slides of selected paintings and sculpture were projected for study. The children's first reaction to the works of certain contemporary artists was laughter. As we explored the paintings, however, their feelings changed. The paintings were found not only to be lacking in humor, but to require a special kind of knowledge for appreciation and understanding.

In each class session we emphasized that literature, poetry, painting, sculpture, architecture, and other fine arts vary because as changes occur in industry and scientific knowledge, the ideas of men also change. It was pointed out that men can express their reactions in methods peculiar to the individual—that all cultures, from the most primitive to the most technically oriented, express themselves according to the use to which individuals put the materials and tools with which they work, and that in each case the quality of the expression can be at a very high level. These reactions vary in aural-visual aspects because men exist in widely differing geographic and social environments, and have different types of tools and different kinds of materials with which to work.

Two sessions were particularly rewarding in the development of the concepts referred to above. The session on sculpture was built around slides of classic European sculpture—figures of the Asian countries, primitive sculpture of Africa, and contemporary sculpture of the Western World. We discussed the "why" of sculpturing as an art form, the uses of sculpture, and the uniqueness of some contemporary abstract sculpture in contrast to sculpture that was realistic in form.

The other topic that seemed to be a highlight of the program was architecture. We looked at a projected slide of a contemporary nomadic tribe living in Afghanistan with nothing but crude tents for shelter. We immediately contrasted this scene with a slide of the Taj Mahal, only a thousand miles away. We discussed man's reasons for building beyond only what was essential to provide shelter. Slides illustrating other forms of Asian architecture were shown, and the artistry and craftsmanship of the temples in Thailand and Japan were noted. Always we returned to the questions: Why are the structures different? What purposes do they serve? Could such building have happened in *our* environment? Our discussion ended with a look at contemporary architecture in America—the skyscraper and the geodesic dome. The relation of science and mathematics to the development of the American contemporary architectural design was introduced.

Two other topics deserve special mention: *nature* and *the dance.* Man and his relation to nature—his being a part of nature, his need to respect nature—these and other concepts were discussed in a class period which featured slides of nature: the phenomenon of light filtering through trees, the architectural quality of developing plants, mushrooms, spider webs, etc. Through the use of slides the children learned to appreciate the beauty of nature as it is available to us today and how easily it can be permanently destroyed. We viewed paintings that had been inspired by nature. Given more time, we would have delved into nature as an inspiration for poetry, literature, and music. But even our brief experience helped some children to look upon nature with a degree of responsible concern.

The dance was the most difficult of the expressive forms to introduce. Almost without exception the concept of dance held by these children was a form of entertainment. Dance as a means of expressing an idea was almost impossible for them to comprehend. Our introduction of this new concept was a simple one. We asked the children to close their eyes and imagine that the sky had descended to a point barely above their scalps. We then asked them to touch the sky a little. We told them that if any stars fell from the sky they were to catch them with one hand and press them back into place inside the sky. Gradually, we raised the sky into its proper place. Sixty-five children, rising from their seats in unison, lifting the sky into place, created as beautiful a dance movement as the writer has ever witnessed. After performing another similar simple activity, we watched a short movie on the art of Marcel Marceau. As a finale, we projected a slide of a painting on the auditorium-gymnasium wall and asked various students to assume the positions and poses of the characters in the painting. They were instructed to imagine themselves to be these people, keeping in mind the mood and tempo of the music which was being played in the background. The activity, performed by children with no background in dance and its forms and meanings, came off beautifully.

One of the final sessions took the form of an evaluation panel discussion. It was hoped that in such a discussion the students would reveal some of their true feelings about the humanities, the effect of the experiences upon their free-reading and entertainment, and, hopefully, some of the intellectual growth that had been stimulated. So many children wanted to discuss their reactions that it was impossible to hear them all within the allotted time, so we asked for written evaluations. The following are examples of the papers submitted.

In the past sessions I have become very interested in the many different fields presented us in the world of humanities. To take the field of architecture, even though my father is an architect, I was not aware of the many, many, various types of architecture that could be presented. The meaning of different types of design and why they mean what they do can be explored to depths I'd never dreamed they could.

The field of art has always meant a lot to me. I've always liked to draw, but I never really have taken the time to "go into the picture" and "explore" it. This has opened a whole new world to me.

The field of nature I have saved till last because it is my favorite subject. The way you are able to find things in cut lumber, bare roots, and close-up photography, all these things are interesting to find in trees, leaves and roots, even weeds.

I have learned to know more about people and nature. It is a lot of fun to find meanings and pictures in different objects. As in art, you can see many things and feel them too, that others may not.

My mind grew bigger and it was a lot of fun learning about the humanities. It is hard to explain how you feel and what you feel when you see a picture, a building, nature, a piece of ice, and almost anything. It is like a story when you can see faces in ice. To me humanities is a new and exciting world that I had never before realized ever existed.

Bringing the study of the humanities into the elementary school curriculum offers hope of accomplishing some things not provided for in many contemporary education programs. For example:

1. It provides an opportunity for the child to see and feel some relationships in the human experience which are important in developing meaningful understandings of all cultures, including his own,
2. It provides the foundation and the beginnings of a system of values essential to good citizenship and personal happiness.
3. It provides an opportunity to develop a sense of tolerance in human relationships and the varying expressions of human beings.
4. It provides a realistic, meaningful vehicle for developing an appreciation of all the arts.
5. It brings together in various ways learnings that have become separated and compartmentalized. The relationships of science and mathematics to developments in architecture are an example.

Provision for the inclusion of the humanities in the elementary school program places a new burden in the laps of school administrators, supervisors, and curriculum directors. It is especially difficult because it does not involve the substitution of one program for another as was the case with "new" math and science. It is a quite different aspect of mental development that is being suggested, and there are no sets of textbooks that can be adopted to do the job. This fact alone will cause many to shun the humanities as a responsibility of the elementary school. Yet the value of and the need for education in the humanities are as obvious as any in the history of education.

The CHum Program for the Elementary School

G. E. Beckett

Every school child today almost literally has the world at his fingertips. By the turn of the century, we are told, air travel will have progressed to the point that it will be possible to reach any place on the globe in not more than two hours. The world of the twenty-first century will indeed be smaller.

For the purposes of education, should we not consider the corollary of this phenomenon? The world of today's students will be much larger. Their personal world will be the earth itself, with a little of outer space thrown in for good measure. There will be few, if any, remote areas on earth. The life space of future citizens will be in the community of continents. Their neighborhood will extend from coast to coast and border to border.

And what of their fellow man in this larger world of everyday living? Again the prognostication has overtones for education. We are told that the world population by the year 2000 will probably be six to seven billion, about double what it is now; the majority will be non-white, non-Christian Asians, and there is no foreseeable change in this ratio.

All of these factors give impetus for meeting the obvious need of the citizens of the future to develop a more comprehensive world view. Communication between cultures will be imperative with the increased interdependence of all men. This will require understanding between all human beings regardless of how different they may think, look, or act. In the words of Jacques Barzun:

The consciousness not alone of the historian but also of the newspaper reader is filled with the presence of dozens of new peoples, new states and *new pasts* which we struggle to understand and assimilate. Africa, the Far East, the South Seas are mingling with out lives. Persons of every color and creed and tradition are on the move, and their ideas also.[1]

The sciences, per se, offer little help in this area because their charge is

[1] Jacques Barzun, *What Man Has Built* (New York: Time-Life Books, 1965), p. 2.

measurable facts and what man can do, not what he should do. The social sciences, in interpreting past and present man in social groups, are naturally concerned with world cooperation and understanding. But it is the humanities that contribute most to appreciation and tolerance of people, so vital in preventing man's self-destruction.

These are some of the aspects that form a general rationale for any humanities program. Let us focus now on a particular school district.

The James A. Garfield school system in Portage County, Ohio, is composed of three small communities in the northeastern sector of the state. It is in a semi-rural area within thirty-five miles of three large cities. However, fewer than 1 per cent of the elementary pupils have ever been taken by their parents to any of the cultural activities offered in Cleveland, Akron, or Youngstown. Fewer than 10 per cent have ever visited any museum in any community with their parents.

Although there are a large state university and a leading private liberal arts college within twenty miles, less than 1 per cent of the pupils have ever borrowed a book or used the facilities of the Hiram College Library or the Kent State University Library. Only about 9 per cent of the pupils have ever attended a play, a concert, an art show, or a lecture with their parents at either of these educational institutions.

In considering the students in the James A. Garfield School District, let us examine the implications of a humanities program for their needs. This community of children resembles all others in their seeking for a personal identity. They need to know who they are, where they have been, and where they are going. They need to know their place in the general scheme of life.

> At times I wonder
> As the world rushes past—
> Is there a place for me?[2]

The teachers, realizing that such things can not be left to chance, seek more effective ways of translating school learning into world living. They know that each student must be equipped for living in the twenty-first century with the anticipated general decrease in working time and the increase in leisure time. A specific prediction is that by the year 2000 the factory labor force will have decreased to a point similar to the shrinking farm labor force of today. As Martin states in "Beyond Technology":

The quest for a more human society has not been alien to our tradition, but it is possible now in a measure not heretofore possible. Nuclear energy and electric power permit men to turn their energies to a thousand broadening and enriching activities that were only luxuries before. Computers, automation, and cybernation free man to be man. Guaranteed subsistence in an electronic age, man can give substance to his life.[3]

[2]Written by a student in the "Living Arts Program" of the Dayton Public Schools, Dayton, Ohio.
[3]Warren Bryan Martin, "Beyond Technology," reprinted from *Motive* in *School Research Information Service,* Phi Kelta Kappa, Inc., Vol. 1, No. 4, Fall 1968, p. 23.

Implicit in all school programs is the hope that these needs will be met. Realizing that these accomplishments do not always occur spontaneously nor to the degree required by our modern society, the Garfield teachers have sought ways of including these broad precepts in their approach to everyday classroom work.

For instance, let us look at the matter of leisure time. The adult models for students spend a major portion of their leisure time in recreation, socializing in bars or indiscriminate and endless television watching. Not that these activities are bad in themselves; it is the exclusion of other worthwhile activities that is undesirable.

The teachers seek to improve this situation by broadening the interests of their students, using the means of exposure to recognized masters and their creative works in fine arts and literature, thereby making possible the appreciation and enjoyment of many cultural activities.

Let us review the rationale for the Children's Humanities or CHum program for all students in the first six grades of the James A. Garfield School District. The knowledge explosion and the need to develop basic skills are recognized. At the same time, unneeded rote learning should be replaced with generalizations and concepts presented by means of a humanities approach to the typically fragmented fine arts, language arts, and social studies at the elementary school level. "The conventional division of the curriculum into subjects is as outdated as the medieval trivium in the Renaissance."[4]

Students need guidance in developing their own value systems. To do this, they need to develop the ability to exercise critical judgment concerning their own thoughts, actions, and work in addition to those of others. They need to have benchmarks for the evaluation of that which has been accomplished by man through the ages, and especially for what they undertake or contemplate doing themselves. The students should learn how to choose their friends and those individuals they will seek to emulate; their courses of action, both personal and those serving their fellow man. They must be able to analyze the possible consequences of their activities and their responsibility for the results—in other words, their choice of a way of life.

This involves making students aware of the attributes contributing to acceptable social behavior in our culture—duty, loyalty, honesty, kindness, courtesy, respect, to name a few. Montaigne put it in these words:

> ... a scholar should be taught to know ... what it is to know, and what to be ignorant; what ought to be the end and design of study; what valour, temperance, and justice are; the difference betwixt ambition and avarice, servitude and subjection, licence and liberty; by what token a man may know true and solid contentment; ...[5]

An important basis for these personal choices is knowledge of the cultural

---

[4]Marshall McLuhan, *Understanding Media: The Extensions of Man* (New York: McGraw-Hill Book Co., 1965), p. 347.

[5]Michel Montaigne, *The Essays,* Great Books of the Western World, Vol. 25 (Chicago: Encyclopaedia Britannica, Inc., 1952), p. 69.

heritage of our society and other world societies. Along with this is the importance of preserving this heritage for the benefit of generations to come.

Another requirement of our students is the development of intellectual curiosity, imagination, and a sense of wonder. In order to meet the challenges that will face them, students must desire to know, be able to find what they must know, and be able to look at things, situations, and events in an unstereotyped way. In other words, the technological influences that will surround and stifle the individual must be overcome.

Along these same lines is the need to encourage and promote creativity as well as the enjoyment of beauty. Before a child can participate in creativity or appreciate the creativity of others, he must first be able to see with a discerning eye and experience the taste or the sight or the sound or the feel of the examples of creativity that are man-made or found in nature. A child will yearn for a story to be read to him only after he has experienced the excitement of hearing a good story or poem well read. He will long to feel a smooth statue or appreciate its form and line only after he has seen it. He will respond to the warmth and compassion of an artist only after he has seen an appealing work of art. He will react to the rhythm of good music or poetry only after his ears become attuned to it. He will lose himself in creative expression of any kind only after he is free to do so. He may recognize beauty only after he has been made aware of what constitutes beauty.

If he has experiences with meaningful art in reproduction or original, if he learns to love some special work or some special idea expressed in several media, then these copies of literature, of art, of music will become a part of his life. Then he will be able to develop appreciations and build a set of values that will be a guide for his achievements.

He will recognize man's need to express his emotions, to solve his problems, to communicate with others through the arts; the inference from the arts, and from history, of the characteristics of the men and cultures that produced these; the examination of how several creative artists in several cultures, and throughout several ages, have expressed the fundamental ideas of man in his search for truth, the quest for beauty, the yearning for freedom—man in his association and identification with nature, society, and a supreme being.

Growing out of this rationale, the objectives of the Garfield CHum program are to guide the students in the development of the ability to:

—recognize and identify representative selections from the fine arts
—pick out the characteristics of the selections they admire
—discuss how an idea or emotion or theme is treated in various media
—see, hear, and feel how the spirit of humanity has been expressed in the arts
—create their own work (art, music, dance, literature, drama) by developing a theme, idea, or concept
—value creative expression, not only of recognized masters, but also of their own and of their peers

—accept the need to develop humanistic attitudes and behavior in everyday relationships
—grasp the significance of knowing people or other races and cultures as a means of developing world understanding
—grow in a sense of kinship with all humanity
—be tolerant and flexible, both mentally and emotionally, in order to meet the challenge of change.

The meeting of these objectives has been greatly assisted by financial aid from the federal government under Titles II and III of the Elementary and Secondary Education Act of 1965. This has made possible the tripling of the number of field trips by students to historical, science, and art museums as well as cultural events in the area. It has helped in the expansion of a book library into a resource center with many forms of educational material and equipment. Teacher training and the production of suitable teaching units would have been much more difficult without this assistance.

An unusual but tangible feature of the program is the CHum Kit, a loosely used term to cover the items of artistic value (art prints, artifacts, small sculpture, etc.) purchased for each student to be studied and then taken home as the beginning of, or as additions to, their own private collections.

Although it is a little early to say the program is an unqualified success, we do know it is a step in the right direction. Students are enthusiastic, parents approve whole heartedly, and teachers are finding that it affects their classroom techniques. One of them remarked, "I am continually amazed at the number of times humanities ideas come to mind in my lesson preparations, even in the areas of math and science."

Part V
Teacher Education and the Humanities

Articles in previous sections have touched on the question of teacher preparation for the humanities. Jenkins, in "The Humanities and Humanistic Education in the Elementary Grades" discussed the problems of establishing workable basic principles for team teaching and stated that few elementary teachers could teach the humanities alone. Hipple, in his article "Humanities in the Secondary Schools," suggested a curriculum for future humanities teachers.

The present section attempts to deal with this subject in greater depth. The initial article, by Schwartz, asks "Who Should Teach the Humanities?" and then hypothesizes five basic personality characteristics for humanities teachers. Screening procedures based on personality as well as intellect are also suggested.

Reinforcing these ideas is the description by Eldridge Cleaver of the saintly teacher Chris Lovdjieff, who was able to reach even hardened criminals in San Quentin prison. The great value of this article is that the curriculum being taught is clearly interdisciplinary and that the personality of the teacher is so similar to the one described by Schwartz.

In Lovdjieff's curriculum it is impossible to put content into discrete compartments. For example, Thomas Merton writes about Harlem, and Cleaver relates his writings to the teachings of the Black Muslims. "What did he teach?" asks Cleaver. He answers, "Everything. It is easier just to say he taught Lovdjieff and let it go at that."

Karel, in "Teacher Education in the Related Arts," writes that the new field of the humanities requires teachers with a "good grasp of the arts in general and of the common three, literature-music-painting, in particular." He adds that this teacher "must possess the depth of a specialist in one field, that is, he must major in either music, art, or literature."

Kuh, writing specifically about the preparation of art teachers, advocates methods that are completely applicable to the preparation of humanities teachers. *"The fine arts,"* she points out, *"cannot properly be separated from the other arts. Painting, poetry, music, the dance, all stem from common roots."* She suggests the elimination of all orthodox art education and the substitution of practical *"workshops in looking for all teachers."* She further suggests that *"the teacher of art be trained as an artist rather than as a semi-therapeutic dabbler."*

Ladensack's article is a report on a humanities study group for teachers and supervisors who were already working in the field or who planned to introduce humanities courses into their school systems. Among the questions that were discussed were the following: how are humanities courses different from English courses?; what are the patterns of humanities courses?; how are humanities courses graded?; how is a good working team selected?; is there any necessary combination of disciplines?; what is the role of the administrator in relation to humanities teams?; how can student success or failure in humanities courses be predicted?; what is the best enrollment size?; how can these courses be prevented from becoming too undirected and undisciplined?; how does the teacher decide which materials to include and which to exclude?; what are the works used in existing courses?; what is the content structure of existing courses?; what are the main objectives of humanities courses?; what kinds of projects should the students develop?; how does student awareness of himself and other men develop?; how are humanities courses organized that are not part of the school curriculum?

Perhaps the most valuable aspect of this workshop was the building by the participants of two units that could be used in humanities courses. Ladensack's detailed explanation of this will be a valuable blueprint for in-service work. He found an interesting phenomenon. As the participants developed their units, the atmosphere became similar to that of a good humanities class. *"The participants stimulated each other in an exchange of attitudes, ideas, and material"* and were able to take these approaches back with them to their own schools.

Block and Lieberman also describe an in-service humanities institute to develop arts core curricula for the elementary school. *"As a necessary prerequisite to the development of new curricula, the institute hoped to change the participants as human beings."* In this, its accomplishments were similar to that of the Ladensack study group.

Houghton, focusing on the teacher from another viewpoint, describes what the teacher must be. The teacher, he says, *"poses the cultural model."* It is this model of human authenticity that allows the student to become more intensively himself. And this is surely the end goal of the humanities.

Teacher Training for the Humanities

Sheila Schwartz

Who Should Teach the Humanities? Let us hypothesize an institution that sets up a humanities major for secondary school teachers at the graduate level. Screening for this program should require the following characteristics as prerequisites for entering the program.

1. The first characteristic is a *tolerance* for *ambiguity*. The humanities teacher cannot function with an emotional need for closure, for neat packages, for the completion of subjects or ideas, or for dependence on examinations. Two anecdotes will illustrate my point. One concerns a student in the Associate in Arts program, the B.A. at night for older students. During preceding classes we had discussed Greek tragedy, and we were at that point immersed in *Crime and Punishment.*

One of my students, a young man of about thirty, suddenly burst out in a querulous voice and asked, "What good is this course if you just raise questions and don't give us any answers?"

When I asked him to illustrate specifically, he referred to a question I had raised about whether or not suffering ennobles. When I explained that I was primarily concerned with Dostoyevsky's view, he insisted on knowing my own. Intrigued as well as astonished, I asked him if he thought that I should impose my philosophy about the human condition on other adults.

His answer, short and unambivalent, was "Yes."

"You're our teacher," he said, "and you're supposed to have the answers."

Accustomed to traditional education, this student was unable to accept ambiguity and was consequently unable to accept the teacher in the role of guide rather than as authority figure. This student would not make a good humanities teacher.

Another of my students was working with a high school class on *Julius Caesar.*

"Was Brutus an honorable man?" she asked.

A student raised his hand and said, "Well—according to his point of view. . . ."

My student teacher interrupted sharply.

"I'm not interested in his point of view," she said. "Simply answer 'yes' or no.'"

This student too would not be comfortable teaching the humanities. Even momentary ambiguity made her nervous.

2. A second essential characteristic is an *understanding of the importance of dialogue or student talk.* I am constantly appalled at the medieval attitude toward oral expression that permeates both elementary and secondary levels. When students do talk, it is not because the teacher sees a value in it but as some kind of passing nod to a dimly misunderstood progressivism. Talk is viewed as a reward that teachers let students "do" when they have been quiet for a sufficiently long time.

307

In a literature project with which I worked last summer at the University of Hawaii's Curriculum Center, a large variety of teaching methods were employed. Nevertheless, at the end of the project, the students uniformly selected conversation and discussion as the method from which they had learned the most.

A teacher who does not see oral language as the vital core of the humanities would not be comfortable in this subject area. A humanities teacher should be uncomfortable with sterile silence rather than with a lively flow of living language.

3. A third essential characteristic is the *ability to see the student as more important* than the transmission of the cultural heritage. The humanities teacher must be aware that many things are happening to a student simultaneously, and quite often the least important of these occurrences has to do with the content under discussion.

Ravi Shankar, the sitar player, in a recent speech described a guru who had taught him a great deal about his difficult instrument. This guru, as is apparently traditional in India, regularly beat his students for lack of skill or for failure to practice. Shankar said proudly that he had never been beaten but the guru was most severe toward his own son. Finally, in anger at his son's failure to practice, he tied him to a tree for seven days, only permitting the boy's mother to visit him with his meals.

After recounting this story dispassionately, Shankar added, "Outside of his work, he was really a very kind man."

This approach may produce players of the sitar, but a person so fanatically involved in his art would not be a good guide for the humanities. To the extent that external conformity of behavior or any one item of content is viewed as of greater importance than the student, to that extent the humanities are not being taught.

4. A fourth characteristic necessary for the humanities teacher is the *ability to adapt to a variety of physical arrangements* in the classroom.

A person who can tolerate only fixed rows of seats cannot teach the humanities. It is evident that one cannot have a conversation with the back of another person. But I go into classroom after classroom in which seats are in neat rows and teachers complain that they can't elicit conversation. When I ask why they don't rearrange the desks, they say that they don't feel comfortable when the desks are not in neat rows. The absurdity of this was fully illustrated to me last week when I visited a school in which a new wing had just been carpeted and soundproofed and yet the seats were arranged in the same precise rows as before.

A humorous example of this fixed-seat pattern can be seen in the last scene of the film *The President's Analyst*. Here, a row of dummy junior executives, plugged into one central intelligence, sit in perfect rows, looking straight ahead, nodding, smiling, and receiving. When unplugged, these well-dressed dummies collapse. Like our dummy students fastened to fixed seats and desks and plugged in to the teacher's desires, those in the film are expected to repeat but not to think.

Humanities teachers must be comfortable with large groups, with a number of small groups working simultaneously, with individuals working alone, and with the expansion of the classroom to the world outside the school.

5. A fifth necessary characteristic of the teacher is the *absence of ressentiment.* This word, defined at its simplest as "free-floating ill temper," was first introduced by Nietzsche in *The Genealogy of Morals* and is the subject of a recent book entitled *Society's Children: A Study of Ressentiment in the Secondary School.*[1]

Ressentiment has been further defined as "a lasting mental attitude, caused by systematic repression of certain emotions and affects which leads to the constant tendency to indulge in certain kinds of value delusions and corresponding value judgments. . . . The emotions and affects primarily concerned are revenge, hatred, malice, envy, and the impulse to detract and spite."[2] A figure in literature who incorporates these qualities is Dostoyevsky's Underground Man.

Ressentiment is of particular danger to the humanities because the kind of student against whom it is usually directed is the creative student whose thought is divergent from the teacher's. And it is precisely this kind of creative thinking which is needed by the humanities. This type of student does not arrive at right answers by "deducing them from established premises, but by an intuitive understanding of how the problem he is dealing with really works, of what actually goes into it. . . . Facts are not simply right answers, but tools and components for building original solutions."[3]

When this intelligent, aware, creative student encounters a secure high school teacher who is both intelligent and happy in his work, the best kind of teaching and learning follows. But to the degree that the teacher is ressentient, "his reaction will be permeated with defensive hostility,"[4] and he will attempt to stop the student from contributing through ridicule or bullying. This is a particular problem for the humanities because

In the humanities and in the social studies, the creative student is both more threatening and more vulnerable. He is more vulnerable because there aren't any right answers to support him. He is more threatening because these subjects, if truthfully handled, are in themselves threatening to the ressentient. It is the job of the humanities and social sciences to get to the root of human experience, which at best means hewing austere beauty out of some very ugly blocks in such a way that their real character is revealed. This is just what ressentiment cannot tolerate. And this is what makes both the humanities and social studies so dangerous in the classroom, for to teach them well is to inquire directly into the essence of human experience.[5]

6. The sixth and last characteristic which I shall deal with here is the *ability to understand the symbiosis between teacher and students.*

[1] Carl Nordstrom, Edgar Z. Friedenberg, and Hilary A. Gold. (New York: Random House, inc., 1967).
[2] Max Scheler, *Ressentiment* (Glencoe, Ill.: The Free Press, 1961), pp. 45-46.
[3] *Society's Children,* p. 9.
[4] *Ibid.*
[5] *Ibid.,* p. 10.

Dorothy Collings, Education Director of UNESCO, made this point in a recent speech. She said that the sickest people she had ever known were those who were one step above the Negro in the South and were directly responsible for keeping Negroes down. "After all," she pointed out, "there are only two ways to keep a man in a ditch. One is to keep your foot in his face. The other is to get down in that ditch yourself and hold him. In either case, where does that put you?"

The humanities teacher must understand that his students can converse only if he enjoys conversation, can be creative only if he is creative, and can continue to grow only if he continues to grow. The classroom climate must be seen as affecting teacher and students equally.

Screening for Admission. I have attempted to describe above six vital characteristics needed by teachers of the humanities. The question may arise here about how we would screen people for characteristics like these which are not really measurable. I would like to suggest that people who are not in accord philosophically will screen themselves out if they understand what is involved in teaching the humanities. This requires careful guidance. One of the reasons that we have so many people in fields that are wrong for them is that they do not gain a correct understanding of the nature of their chosen field until it is too late to change. We must depend on the graduate students who have completed student teaching and may, in addition, have done some regular teaching to make rational decisions about whether to enter the humanities field once they are apprised of all the facts.

For purposes of illustration I would like to suggest a few screening questions that the applicant must ask himself and also discuss with those involved in guidance for this area.

1. Does he feel that there is a certain cultural heritage that every student must have? Will a student be deprived of a proper education without this heritage?
2. Does he reject the idea of working with a team because he likes to do things his own way in the classroom?
3. Does he feel uncomfortable with the seminar approach?
4. Does he feel that the humanities makes no provision for the teaching of skills such as grammar and spelling?
5. Do noise, student laughter, or student sexuality make him uncomfortable?
6. Does he pursue the humanities on his own time through visits to museums and to the performing arts?
7. Can he hold up his end of the conversation in open, honest debate with his students in which student respect and forebearance are not based on his role as teacher?

Of course, the above questions are only tentative and were formulated for purposes of illustration. If a student gets past this initial screening, he must then have much opportunity to see the humanities in action in the secondary school. Then, if after this additional exposure he finds that this is not the field for him, he should have the opportunity to transfer back to his major field without loss of credits. This, of course, would involve total university cooperation, which implies that university colleagues must have the same respect for colleagues in different disciplines as high school teachers must have for interdiciplinary teaching.

The Content of the Humanities. The first part of this paper has discussed the kind of person who should and can teach the humanities. This second part will deal with what should be taught and therefore with the content that the humanities teacher should experience before beginning to teach the humanities.

At the present time there appear to be no two humanities courses that are exactly the same. However, the most prevalent patterns can be identified:

1. *The Elements Approach.* In this approach, literature, art, and music are examined for the factors that make them great.
2. *The Chronological Approach.* This approach typically includes periods such as "The Age of Greece," "The Renaissance," and "The Romantic Era."
3. *The Great Works Approach.* In this approach, literature and art are used to supplement "The Great Books."
4. *The Functions Approach* (also called *The Thematic Approach*). In this approach, the works of man are examined for their statements about the universal aspects of the human condition. Clifton Fadiman, describing this in the EBF film *The Humanities*, says, "The Humanities deal with questions that never go out of style."

My recommendation for the preparation of humanities teachers combines all of the above approaches. To me, the most important aspect of the content is its ability to illuminate the human condition in a way that would be relevant to the high school student.

This is what I mean by a combination of all approaches: Let us assume that we are studying "Satire" through *Gulliver's Travels,* the art of Hogarth and Grosz, the cartoons of Jules Feiffer and Al Capp, the film *Doctor Strangelove,* and the novel *Catch-22.*

My initial selection of the theme (the functions approach) would have been based on the recurrence of this way of perceiving the universe in many different times and places.

I would have selected the above works because I regard them as the best artistic manifestations of this theme (the great works approach).

During my exposure to this unit I would find that my understanding and enjoyment were enhanced through learning something about the world situation that was being satirized (the chronological approach) and something about why these works have value for the study (the elements approach).

This combination is valid for the study of all humanities themes that are selected because they place man in the center. Meaning and relevance come first in this study. For example, if I see a film such as *Cool Hand Luke,* I am at first intrigued by the story and its meaning. Once this major involvement has been established, I will have the impetus to see it again for further study of its elements.

Particularly important for humanities teachers, in addition to study of the four approaches and to the writing of curriculum based on these approaches, is exposure to and some participation in the performing arts. The ASCD recently took a vital step forward in the area of exposing teachers to the performing arts. At their annual conference in Atlantic City, live performances were given for the teachers attending. These included

1. Shakespeare in Opera and Song (The Metropolitan Opera Studio)
2. In White America (The Repertory Theatre of Lincoln Center)
3. Communicating through Creative Dancing (Mrs. Nancy Schuman, North Plainfield High School, Plainfield, N.H., and her troop of student dancers in a creative interpretation)

Future humanities teachers should have a great deal of exposure of this kind. Even if it means travel of some distance, this aspect of their training should be written into the college curriculum.

Summary. I have attempted above to describe the kind of person who should teach the humanities and the type of content to which he should be exposed. Screening plus exposure will, it is hoped, result in teachers who have in common a certain stance. Some of the aspects of this stance are the following. The teacher should be seen as

1. a searcher for truth rather than a transmitter of dogma
2. a guide who will expose students to a variety of alternative and conflicting ideas
3. a person who is receptive to growth and change
4. a creative person who respects the creative process and knows how to foster a classroom climate which will encourage creativeness
5. a reflective person who is capable of playing with ideas
6. a person who respects ideas and people
7. a lover of the arts
8. a person committed to the value of induction
9. a person who would rather uncover ideas than cover facts
10. an optimistic person who looks forward to a teaching career which will be free from boredom because each year's experience will be related, different, and yet cumulative
11. a person who possesses a vast wealth of interdisciplinary knowledge.

The Guru of San Quentin:
"The Christ" and His Teachings

Eldridge Cleaver

My first awareness of Thomas Merton came in San Quentin, back in (I believe) 1959-60. During that time, a saint walked the earth in the person of one Chris Lovdjieff. He was a teacher at San Quentin and guru to all who came to him. What did he teach? Everything. It is easier just to say he taught Lovdjieff and let it go at that. He himself claimed to be sort of a disciple of Alan W. Watts, whom he used to bring over to Q to lecture us now and then on Hinduism, Zen Buddhism, and on the ways the peoples of Asia view the universe. I never understood how "The Christ" (as I used to call Lovdjieff, to his great sorrow and pain) could sit at Watts' feet, because he always seemed to me more warm, more human, and possessed of greater wisdom than Watts displayed either in his lectures or in his books. It may be that I received this impression from having been exposed more to Lovdjieff than to Watts. Yet there was something about Watts that reminded me of a slick advertisement for a labor-saving device, aimed at the American housewife, out of the center page of *Life* magazine; while Lovdjieff's central quality seemed to be pain, suffering, and a peculiar strength based on his understanding of his own helplessness, weakness, and need. Under Lovdjieff I studied world history, Oriental philosophy, Occidental philosophy, comparative religion, and economics. I could not tell one class from the other—neither could the other students and neither, I believe, could Lovdjieff. It was all Lovdjieff.

The walls of his classrooms were covered with cardboard placards which bore quotations from the world's great thinkers. There were quotes from Japanese, Eskimos, Africans, Hopi Indians, Peruvians, Voltaire, Confucius, Laotse, Jesus Christ, Moses, Mohammed, Buddha, Rabbi Hillel, Plato, Aristotle, Marx, Lenin, Mao Tse-tung, Zoroaster-and Thomas Merton, among others. Once Lovdjieff gave a lecture on Merton, reading from his works and trying to put the man's life and work in context. He seemed desperately to want us to respect Merton's vocation and choice of the contemplative life. It was an uphill battle because a prison is in many ways like a monastery. The convicts in Lovdjieff's class hated prison. We were appalled that a free man would voluntarily enter prison—or a monastery. Let me say it right out: we thought the same thing about Lovdjieff. My secret disgust was that in many ways I was nothing but a monk, and how I loathed that view of myself!

I was mystified by Merton and I could not believe in his passionate defense of monkhood. I distrusted Lovdjieff on the subject of Thomas Merton. My mind heard a special pleading in his voice. In his ardent defense of Merton, Lovdjieff seemed to be defending himself, even trying to convince himself. One day Lovdjieff confided to us that he had tried to be a monk but couldn't make it. He made it, all right, without even realizing it. San Quentin was his monastery. He busied himself about the prison as though he had a special calling to minister to the prisoners. He was there day and night and on Saturdays, without fail. The officials would sometimes have to send a guard to his class to make him stop teaching, so the inmates could be locked up for the night. He was horror-stricken that they could make such a demand of him. Reluctantly, he'd sit down heavily in his seat, burdened by defeat, and tell us to go to our cells. Part of the power we gave him was that we would never leave his class unless he himself dismissed us. If a guard came and told us to leave, he got only cold stares; we would not move until Lovdjieff gave the word. He got a secret kick out of this little victory over his tormentors. If, as happened once, he was unable to make it to the prison because his car had a blowout, he'd be full of apologies and pain next day.

Lovdjieff had extracted from me my word that I would some day read Merton for myself-he did not insist upon any particular time, just "some day." Easy enough. I gave my promise. In 1963, when I was transferred from San Quentin to Folsom for being an agitator, they put me in solitary confinement. The officials did not deem it wise, at that time, to allow me to circulate among the general inmate population. I had evolved a crash program which I would immediately activate whenever I was placed in solitary: stock up on books and read, read, read; do calisthenics and forget about the rest of the world. I had learned the waste and furtility of worry. (Years ago, I had stopped being one of those convicts who take a little calendar and mark off each day.) When I asked for books to read in this particular hole, a trustee brought me a list from which to make selections. On the list I was delighted to see Merton's *The Seven Storey Mountain,* his autobiography. I thought of Lovdjieff. Here was a chance to fulfill my promise.

I was tortured by that book because Merton's suffering, in his quest for God, seemed all in vain to me. At the time, I was a Black Muslim chained in the bottom of a pit by the Devil. Did I expect Allah to tear down the walls and set me free? To me, the language and symbols of religion were nothing but weapons of war. I had no other purpose for them. All the gods are dead except the god of war. I wished that Merton had stated in secular terms the reasons he withdrew from the political, economic, military, and social system into which he was born, seeking refuge in a monastery.

Despite my rejection of Merton's theistic world view, I could not keep him out of the room. He shouldered his way through the door. Welcome, Brother Merton. I give him a bear hug. Most impressive of all to me was Merton's description of New York's black ghetto—Harlem. I liked it so much I copied out the heart of it in longhand. Later, after getting out of solitary, I used to keep this passage in mind when delivering Black Muslim lectures to other prisoners. Here is an excerpt:

Here in this huge, dark, steaming slum, hundreds of thousands of Negroes are herded together like cattle, most of them with nothing to eat and nothing to do. All the senses and imagination and sensibilities and emotions and sorrows and desires and hopes and ideas of a race with vivid feelings and deep emotional reactions are forced in upon themselves, bound inward by an iron ring of frustration: the prejudice that hems them in with its four insurmountable walls. In this huge cauldron, inestimable natural gifts, wisdom, love, music, science, poetry are stamped down and left to boil with the dregs of an elementally corrupted nature, and thousands upon thousands of souls are destroyed by vice and misery and degradation, obliterated, wiped out, washed from the register of the living, dehumanized.

What has not been devoured, in your dark furnace, Harlem, by marijuana, by gin, by insanity, hysteria, syphilis?

For a while, whenever I felt myself softening, relaxing, I had only to read that passage to become once more a rigid flame of indignation. It had precisely the same effect on me that Elijah Muhammad's writings used to have, or the words of Malcolm X, or the words of any spokesman of the oppressed in any land. I vibrate sympathetically to any protest against tyranny.

But I want to tell more about Lovdjieff—The Christ.

Chris Lovdjieff had a profound mind and an ecumenical education. I got the impression that the carnage of World War II, particularly the scientific, systematic approach to genocide of the Nazi regime, had been a traumatic experience from which it was impossible for him to recover. It was as if he had seen or experienced something which had changed him forever, sickened his soul, overwhelmed him with sympathy and love for all mankind. He hated all restraints upon the human mind, the human spirit, all blind believing, all dogmatic assertion. He questioned everything.

I was never sure of just what was driving him. That he was driven there could be no doubt. There was a sense of unreality about him. It seemed that he moved about in a mist. The atmosphere he created was like the mystic spell of Khalil Gibran's poetry. He seemed always to be listening to distant music, or silent voices, or to be talking in a whisper to himself. He loved silence and said that it should only be broken for important communications, and he would expel students from his classes for distracting the others by chatting idly in the back rows. In his classes he was a dictator. He enforced certain rules which brooked no deviation—no smoking in his classroom at any time, before class, during class, at recess, or even when school was out; no talking in Lovdjieff's class unless it was pertinent to the subject at hand; no eating or chewing gum in his classroom; no profanity. Simple rules, perhaps, but in San Quentin they were visionary, adventurous, audacious. The Christ enforced them strictly. The other teachers and the guards wondered how he got away with it. We students wondered why we enthusiastically submitted to it. The Christ would look surprised, as if he did not understand, if you asked him about it. If one of the other teachers forgot and came into Lovdjieff's classroom smoking, he was sent hopping. The same went for prison guards. I can still see the shocked expression of a substitute teacher who, coming into Lovdjieff's room during recess smoking a pipe, was told: "Leave this room!"

When you came to Lovdjieff's classes, you came to learn. If you betrayed other motives, "Get out of here this minute!"—without malice but without equivocation. He was a magnet, an institution. He worked indefatigably. His day started when the school bell rang at 8 A.M. Often he would forego lunch to interview a few students and help them along with their schoolwork or personal problems. He never ceased complaining because the officials refused to allow him to eat lunch in the mess hall with the prisoners. Had they given him a cell he would have taken it. After lunch, he'd teach until 3 P.M. When night school convened at 6 P.M., The Christ would be there, beaming, radiating, and he'd teach passionately until 10 P.M. Then, reluctantly, he'd go home to suffer in exile until school opened next day. On Saturdays he'd be there bright and early to teach—Lovdjieff. He would have come on Sundays too, only the officials put their foot down and refused to hear of it. The Christ settled for a Sunday evening radio program of two hours which he taped for broadcast to the prisoners.

His classes were works of art. He made ancient history contemporary by evoking the total environment—intellectual, social, political, economic—of an era. He breathed life into the shattered ruins of the past. Students sat entranced while The Christ performed, his silver-rimmed glasses reflecting the light in eye-twinkling flashes.

He dressed like a college boy, betraying a penchant for simple sweaters and plain slacks of no particular distinction. He burned incense in his classroom when he lectured on religion, to evoke a certain mood. He was drawn to those students who seemed most impossible to teach—old men who had been illiterate all their lives and set in their ways. Lovdjieff didn't believe that anyone or anything in the universe was "set in its ways." Those students who were intelligent and quickest to learn he seemed reluctant to bother with, almost as if to say, pointing at the illiterates and speaking to the bright ones: "Go away. Leave me. You don't need me. These others do."

Jesus wept. Lovdjieff would weep over a tragic event that had taken place ten thousand years ago in some forgotten byway in the Fertile Crescent. Once he was lecturing on the ancient Hebrews. He was angry with them for choosing to settle along the trade routes between Egypt and Mesopotamia. He showed how, over the centuries, time and time again, these people had been invaded, slaughtered, driven out, captured, but always to return.

"What is it that keeps pulling them back to this spot!" he exclaimed. He lost his breath. His face crumbled, and he broke down and wept. "Why do they insist on living in the middle of that—that [for once, I thought meanly, The Christ couldn't find a word] that—that—Freeway! They have to sit down in the center of the Freeway! That's all it is—look!" He pointed out the trade routes on the map behind his desk, then he sat down and cried uncontrollably for several minutes.

Another time, he brought tape-recorded selections from Thomas Wolfe's *Look Homeward Angel.* The Christ wept all through the tape.

The Christ could weep over a line of poetry, over a single image in a poem, over the beauty of a poem's music, over the fact that man can talk, read, write, walk, reproduce, die, eat, eliminate—over the fact that a chicken can lay an egg.

Once he lectured us all week on Love. He quoted what poets had said of Love, what novelists had said of Love, what playwrights had said of Love. He played tapes of Ashley Montague on Love. Over the weekend, each student was to write an essay on his own conception of Love, mindful to have been influenced by what he had been listening to all week long. In my essay I explained that I did not love white people. I quoted Malcolm X:

How can I love the man who raped my mother, killed my father, enslaved my ancestors, dropped atomic bombs on Japan, killed off the Indians and keeps me cooped up in the slums? I'd rather be tied up in a sack and tossed into the Harlem River first.

Lovdjieff refused to grade my paper. He returned it to me. I protested that he was being narrow-minded and dogmatic in not understanding why I did not love white people simply because he himself was white. He told me to talk with him after class.

"How can you do this to me?" he asked.

"I've only written the way I feel," I said.

Instead of answering, he cried.

"Jesus wept," I told him and walked out.

Two days later, he returned my essay—ungraded. There were instead spots on it which I realized to be his tears.

Although Lovdjieff's popularity among the prisoners continued to soar and the waiting lists for his classes grew longer and longer, prison authorities banned his radio program. Then they stopped him from coming in on Saturdays. Then they stopped him from teaching night school. Then they took away his pass and barred him from San Quentin.

I must say that this man has not been adequately described. Certain things I hold back on purpose, others I don't know how to say. Until I began writing this, I did not know that I had a vivid memory of him. But now I can close my eyes and relive many scenes in which he goes into his act.

Teacher Education in the Related Arts

Leon C. Karel

Educators are now witnessing the growth of another new field, one in which music is playing a leading part. This field has been given various names ranging from "allied arts" to "humanities." Essentially it has to do with the concept that all of the arts should be combined and taught as a single course. The spread of such courses in the nation's secondary schools has been accelerating rapidly. In Missouri, for example, the directory published by the Department of Education in 1963 listed 16 teachers in 15 schools teaching related arts courses. In 1964 that number rose to 32 teachers in 28 schools. By 1965, the figures showed 80 teachers in 59 schools. Why is this growth taking place? Obviously students, teachers, and administrators find the course valuable, but on the negative side this means that the present courses in the arts have been found in some way lacking. In briefly examining the present school arts program, one will quickly discover that there are five grave defects.

First, the arts are divided and compartmentalized to the point where they have become almost total strangers to one another. Music and literature, for instance, are very closely related, both being based on sound and time-span. Both use meter, rhythm, tone, tempo, timbre, and other comparable features, yet teachers in each field ignore the other completely. No attempt is made to compare these two arts or to apply lessons learned in one area to the other. In fact, one is led to believe that music and literature teachers do not realize that they are teaching sister arts.

Second, the arts have been guilty of teaching only those students who want to play, sing, act, or paint. For the nonperformers, there is no arts instruction in most schools. This is like saying that nobody may study history but those who have a special aptitude for it. This concentration on performance results in large numbers of students graduating with no art education at all.

Third, by seeking to justify themselves as entertainment features of the curriculum, the arts have allowed themselves to be governed by "what the people want." This is an excellent policy to follow if success in entertaining is the goal. However, no other curricular area has relinquished control of its subject matter and classroom procedures to the public in this way. When the likes and dislikes of the man on the street are catered to, quality goes out the window.

Fourth, the arts have exploited the students, sometimes quote shamelessly. Music has been especially guilty of this. Talented youngsters in the fifth and sixth grades have been urged to study certain instruments for five or six years, knowing full well that they would have no use whatsoever for their hard-won ability after graduation. Thus, the student is serving the musical organization when *it* should serve *him*. Generally, once the student gets into the music program he will largely be excluded from ever learning about dramatics or painting. The student becomes a six-year specialist, and no other discipline in the school curriculum would think of doing this. What would be thought of a science department that insisted on six years of chemistry for the pre-college student? Even the college science faculty would frown on this sort of specialization, yet music departments in colleges apparently approve of their incoming majors having the same type of educational pattern in the music field.

Finally, the music program has not challenged the best in our young people. In a time when science, mathematics, foreign languages, and social studies are coming up with rigorous new approaches, music is still dependent upon a pattern set many decades ago. The college-bound youngster cannot fail to see the qualitative difference between a challenging course in the new math, for instance, and the relatively easy demands of chorus or marching band. Many music directors complain that they can no longer hold their best students. When such youngsters desert music for tougher areas, this danger sign means that school music offerings need to be overhauled.

These, then, have been some of the reasons for students and teachers turning to the new area of related arts. In it they see a wider field for exploration with all of the inter-relationships which make this sort of study so challenging and exciting. They see a course which sets its own standards, has assignments, outside reading, projects, examinations, and incidentally offers a chance of receiving a failing grade. Administrators have said that the habit of giving only high grades for music activities is not good educational practice, and the consequences may be reaped now. And finally the students see a course which does not interrupt serious study in order to prepare for public entertainment, a course open to *all* students, not just a few. They see a new kind of goal before them, one which has shockingly been omitted from virtually all of our art courses in the schools.

This goal is the building of standards of taste, the perfecting of value judgment techniques, and the practice of an "aesthetic mode of thinking." It is precisely here that the new course supplies what has been lacking in the music programs. Up to now, a music student could study for six or seven years and graduate totally unable to tell good music from bad. All the valiant efforts of the music educator have done nothing to raise taste standards in our young people. They are blamed for liking rock-and-roll, but when have they been taught how to understand serious music? The study of such factors as musical form, music literature, and theory is, naturally, a long and difficult process—and the teachers are always too busy getting ready for next week's concert, parade, or football show. But the new course stays on the job and teaches something the student needs and wants to know, namely how to approach serious music, modern art, architectural structures, the cinema, the dance, and so on. These are adult concerns and today's young people are growing up fast.

Up to now, one of the most amazing features in this rapid growth is that it has been virtually spontaneous. Almost all of the teachers have been self-trained, adding the needed competencies to their own major fields, and struggling mightily to stay one jump ahead of their eager students. They must feel much like the music education pioneers of a half-century ago, working hard because they believed in the value of what they were doing, learning as they developed their unique programs.

No movement, no matter how inspired, can continue to grow without formal guidelines, however. Missouri's growth was given firm direction by the state department's supervisor of fine arts education, Alfred Bleckschmidt. It was he who formed a committee to write the *Allied Arts Curriculum Guide* which has had so wide a distribution. Similar efforts have been made in New York under Gordon Van Hooft, in Florida with Richard Warren, and Pennsylvania where Gene Wenner is directing the work. These states are producing guides for their own schools. Ultimately, however, the big burden of sustaining and shaping the movement rests on the colleges who train the teachers. Their programs will be all important in the years to come. What direction should such training take: What problems do these new programs face?

First of all, the new field calls for a teacher with a good grasp of the arts in general and of the common three, literature-music-painting, in particular. This teacher must possess the depth of a specialist in one field, that is, he must major in either music, art, or literature. The reasons here are twofold—he will probably be hired to teach related arts and music, literature, or painting along with high musical potential, he should be guided to the nearest private source of instruction. In answer to the anticipated cries of "What will we do for music at our Christmas Program, or between halves of the ball games?" it can only be pointed out that these are essentially demands for entertainment on the part of the public, and the true business of the schools is certainly not in *that* direction.

The college, then, must walk a thin line between the preparation of the music major to fill the traditional job as it now exists in the schools, and the preparation of a music teacher who is broadly educated in the arts and sees the problem of school music in a new light. The secondary schools are certainly not going to give up their customary musical organizations immediately, nor should they. Perhaps there will always be a legitimate place in the schools for performance groups, but the present aspect of public entertainment must and will be reduced sharply, if not abandoned altogether. The new style music major will be given the customary work in theory, literature, applied music, and education, but he will see this specialized work against a mind-broadening background of basic studies in drawing-painting, in theater, in art history, literary criticism, and aesthetics. His experiences with the other arts will make him a far different music educator, and even if he were never to teach a related arts course, his music teaching forever would be different. Once a teacher sees beyond the narrow specialty of his own field, he can never again adopt the provincial attitude so many music teachers now have. That this kind of training is badly needed in music education can scarcely be disputed. A composite educational record of most music teachers would read something like this: Age 8, takes piano lessons from local teacher. Age 12, begins study of band instrument, drops piano lessons. Age 13, becomes a member of junior high band. Age 15, joins high school band, wins numerous medals for performance in contests, attends summer music camps, graduates three years later. Age 18, enters college as music major, joins band, endures theory and history classes, writes one or two halting compositions and a couple of term papers. Gives senior recital on instrument, graduates, takes job as band director. This same kind of record would be equally valid for the vocal student, or the string player. If further graduate study were undertaken, the sequence would continue in an ever-narrowing pattern, finally producing a highly-trained specialist in some area of music. Such a person would know almost nothing about architectural styles, poetry analysis, the elements of painting and sculpture, the evolution of city planning, the philosophy of aesthetics, the techniques of movie making, or trends in the dance. What is worse, he would see no reason for pursuing such knowledge. He has his music degrees, he is set for life, why be bothered by the rest of the art field?

Perhaps most people would have remained in this state of highly educated ignorance had it not been for a small satellite put into orbit by the Russians. Whatever else one may hold against them, the Russians were directly responsible for making a lot of Americans think about what their schools were doing, a critical scrutiny that is still going on. In recent months it has been the arts that are under fire. People in music education could decide not to change, and such a decision can be made also by the art and English teachers of the nation. But if educators continue to go their separate ways, the decision will be made for us, as it has been already in several states and in many schools. The pressure to upgrade the quality of school arts education is strong. Listen to what the powerful American Association of School Administrators has to say:

We believe in a well-balanced school curriculum in which music, drama, painting, poetry, sculpture, architecture, and the like are included side by side with other important subjects such as mathematics, history, and science. It is important that pupils, as a part of general education, learn to appreciate, to understand, to create, and to criticise with discrimination those products of the mind, the voice, the hand, and the body which give dignity to the person and exalt the spirit of man.[1]

There are many who feel that the first step in revising our arts curriculum must be a general education course for all students which brings the arts together in a meaningful way. This will inevitably lead to a more closely organized administrative and philosophical setup within the arts area at the high school level, with the end result that the teachers of the arts will find themselves drawn together in common interests and goals. The arts, in such a situation, will become stronger within the curriculum and, as the AASA says, will be "included side by side with other important subjects. . . ." When that time comes, the colleges must be ready for the new era with graduates trained to assume the leadership of the arts programs, trained to see broadly what our young people need, and trained to think beyond their narrow special fields. American education has always been able to meet the demands placed upon it by changing times. This new challenge will be met and successfully.

The Art Education Myth

Katharine Kuh

The education of art teachers in American universities is, as a rule, unwieldy, unrealistic, and stultifying. From undergraduate ranks come young hopefuls armed with a smattering of art techniques plus an overdose of bland educational theory and methodology. No sooner out of college than they gravitate to elementary schools, which are generally the chief source of jobs for neophyte teachers. Graduate art education students, on the other hand, strive with almost incestuous enthusiasm to perpetuate their recently acquired knowledge in institutions of higher learning, often in teachers' colleges, where salaries and working hours are more salubrious but where new ideas are rare commodities.

Thus, the younger the child, the less experienced his art teacher. The age levels and blighted neighborhoods that most need creative guidance are apt to inherit precisely the reverse. Add to this the absurd forty minutes of so-called art per week that are allotted the average pupil in many underprivileged public schools and one doubts whether the game is worth the name. Crayons, paint, or clay are produced and attacked so briefly that most of the time is spent getting ready and cleaning up. Only a genius could reach the children in more than routine measure under such circumstances. Too often, bewildered young art teachers or harassed older ones

[1] This document is reprinted in the *Music Educators Journal,* Vol. 52 (November- December, 1965), pp. 37-39.

preside over classes that become virtual cathartic interludes in a dizzy schedule where any hint of experimentation is lost in a welter of discipline. That such instructors might connect the process of making art with the process of looking at it is asking too much. And too much, also, to expect these teachers to relate art to the child's daily surroundings or, for that matter, to have any idea themselves of what place art should occupy in present-day life. Somehow we proceed on the basis that art is good for people, that it is ennobling, uplifting. But I personally suspect that a Chinese boy in a Bowery school was right when he told me that he wanted to study art in order to find out about himself and about the world he lived in.

Moreover, the art education departments that indoctrinate about-to-be teachers have had relatively little contact with nitty-gritty slum schools where many of their students will eventually work. Though art equipment is often good in teacher-training classrooms and studios, it is the curriculum that becomes the *bête noir*. Based on the false assumption that methods are more important than involvement, teacher education too often tells *how* rather than *why*. It presupposes "right ways" and "wrong ways"; it encourages qualitative judgments from young acolytes who have neither the knowledge nor accomplishments to make such judgments.

Not infrequently, three separate art departments compete with one another in the same university, thus splintering a field of study where close interrelationships are basic. Why should the history of art, the making of art, and the training of art teachers be fragmented into autonomous hierarchies? Why, indeed, shouldn't the teacher of art be trained as an artist rather than as a semi-therapeutic dabbler? After all, any teacher worth his salt will invent his own methodology depending on his skills, experience, intelligence, and dedication. The expense of duplicate studios for divided art departments is minor, though wasteful, but major are faculty rivalries. Professors actually begin to stake out certain areas as their own special domains. Petty politics proliferate as art becomes a battleground. Funds, space, prestige, equipment are all excuses for intramural squabbles. And even more serious are the blackouts that often stifle communication between student artists, art history students, design and teacher trainees.

Until recently, I was a consultant to a large Midwestern university where my job was to acquire original works of art, not for a specific museum but for such public areas on the campus as libraries, theaters, meeting halls, dormitories, and classroom lobbies. Our hope was to humanize the environment while introducing the students to art on an intimate level. The collection, which now comprises a sizable group of first-rate drawings, sculpture, tapestries, original prints, and photographs, is both ill-cared for and inadequately used. Some of the finest pieces have been sitting in storage for over two years. A curiously competitive art department, instead of welcoming the original works as valuable study material, actually set up petty road blocks. Far from cooperating with the acquisition program, it discouraged the activity. To my chagrin, I discovered after five years with the university that most of the graduate art students did not even know the whereabouts of numerous important works. For me, it was like dropping pebbles into a bottomless pit.

Distinguished painters- and sculptors-in-residence complained of similar alienation. Students rarely met them. Their names were proudly listed in a promotional folder, but their ideas remained top secret.

It is depressing to look back on the many time-consuming and relatively costly round-tables, panel discussions, seminars, and similar powwows recently devoted to art education in America, only to realize how limpingly change comes to obdurate bureaucracies. If we remember nothing else from the Bauhaus, we should at least accept the fact that all learning operations related to creative processes are indivisible. Making art, looking at it, teaching it, investigating its labyrinthian past are varied facets of one integrated experience. For that matter, the fine arts cannot properly be separated from the other arts. Painting, poetry, music, the dance, all stem from common roots.

Today, the young art teacher-to-be learns a bit about the techniques of painting, drawing, ceramics, prints, collage, sculpture, weaving, and whatever else seems obligatory. There are also timid stints with art history, methods of teaching (ad nauseum), and art appreciation. The latter, by the way, should be promptly scuttled. Children don't "appreciate" art; hopefully they are involved with and in it. And, to be sure, no smorgasbord of techniques ever compensates for in-depth experience. Every child does not need exposure to multiple materials and methods. Far better that he come in direct contact with one enthused artist who follows no rules but his own. At least then the youngster will acquire some understanding of that excitation we call "the creative process."

Recently, I visited a junior high school where the hesitant young art teacher asked the class to make an abstract design out of primary colors. There didn't seem much rhyme or reason for the assignment, but the children dutifully complied. One boy traced the outline of his hand, then added a sixth finger and painted each finger in a primary color; the result was handsome, but the teacher was dismayed because for her the design was not abstract. Had she, however, been a practicing artist herself, she could not have helped but applaud, nor would she have arbitrarily suggested an abstract design. For though abstractions are very much "in" today, they become empty exercises without some organic *raison d'être.*

What can a child be taught about art? He can be freed to enjoy making it. He can be freed to enjoy seeing it. In art there are no final answers; there are only questions that lead to new ways of understanding. For this reason, when I was teaching summer school a number of years ago at the University of Wisconsin, I stipulated that my course appear in the catalogue as a "Workshop in Looking," realizing that the majority of my students would be teachers and would need just such refreshment. But, characteristically, the University powers-that-be willed otherwise. The class was listed as a more acceptable "Survey of Modern Art," though modern art was not its theme.

And while we are on the subject of specific university art classes, it seems inconceivable that such institutions are still dealing with marks and semester hours. How can we grade a young painter's work? Judging from history, often the man most denigrated in his youth becomes the outstanding artist of his period. And the number of hours spent in the studio are also no gauge of ability. Cézanne took months to paint a canvas; Van Gogh took minutes. Both, nonetheless, passed most of their waking hours grappling with the problem.

Of course, the knotty question is whether one can be taught to teach art. Surely the greatest teachers in this field have always forged their own methods from their own convictions, and these methods, doubtless, had nothing to do with prescribed ones. Techniques, it is true, can be learned, but, where art is concerned, it is never techniques that make a teacher. Indeed, they often act as blinders.

I recall a young woman who said she was attending a workshop I was leading in order to learn how to evaluate art qualitatively. This would, I explained, necessitate years of study, travel, and comparative looking. In one short course all we could hope to do was show her how *not* to evaluate, how to withhold judgment. Before any evaluations can take place, one must learn to see, to *see* in terms of immediate surroundings. After discovering a wayward shadow on the wall, a dirty sidewalk, a broken pine cone, a puddle of water, a bird, and after accepting these visual experiences both in and out of context, then perhaps the time has come to face the *Mona Lisa,* to approach this overfamiliar masterpiece with the same sense of discovery. Nor are the woods and sea more absorbing than a ride in the subway, a look through a window, a walk on a crowded street. Here, then, is the crux of the matter. Before any understanding of art can exist, both teacher and student must learn to use their eyes, to look, to take nothing for granted visually.

All we can hope to do, I suppose, is play it by eye. A middle-class suburban school may need different stimuli than a slum one because of local variations, but teachers and children in both can be equally blind. They hear the same dreary art jargon, the same meaningless moral adjectives about nature and beauty. They rarely look; they are inured to listening and being told. In an active New York grade school, the the art instructor was demonstrating how to make artificial flowers. The boys, not unexpectedly, were drooping with boredom. Interchange of ideas was strictly *verboten.* Inane soft music acted as a further narcotic. Conversely, a splendid art teacher in the Bowery, who helped the children relate images of trees to their own nervous systems, was in danger of being dropped because she was unable to pass all the proper methodology tests.

One can be taught mathematics; one cannot be taught to see, but one can be encouraged to look. Seeing comes later. It takes ingenuity, compassion, wonder, and self-confidence to open the eyes of a child. It takes more perseverance to open the eyes of an adult, for here so much first must be unlearned. What it does not take, however, is a plethora of words. Seeing in depth is a composite operation that results from all manner of visual comparisons and from nonverbal as well as verbal communications. To draw an acorn after feeling it, and then again after looking at it, is to know an acorn in double dimensions. To observe a familiar tree from a distance, to approach it slowly so that the tree gives way to branches, leaves, and finally to a bit of bark—this is one way of seeing a tree, a way which may appear oversimple but in fact is not. Like the cubist who represents all aspects of an object, so a photographer might capture the wholeness of a tree through its arbitrarily superimposed parts. It wouldn't be the familiar tree we first saw, or would it?

Why not, then, do away with orthodox art education and substitute in its place practical Workshops in Looking for all teachers? Of paramount importance is the inclusion on a part-time basis of creative artists in our public school systems. The present method of full-time art teaching drains even the most gifted enthusiast. Arriving early each morning and rushing from one forty-minute session to another, the instructor rapidly becomes a robot. And as for those forty or fifty minutes a week—it might be better to write them off in the debit column. "Reading, writing and 'rithmetic" could benefit from a tie-in with the real visual world. After this world is explored, the transition to art is painless, since the two are inseparable.

Early this month the federal penitentiary at Leavenworth, Kansas, presented its Seventh Annual Inmate Art Show. Some 1,600 paintings were on view. If the forty-four works reproduced in the catalogue were typical, then one cannot but wonder what makes these men tick. There were stiff ballet dancers, banal still-lifes, copies of everything from maudlin religious scenes to Toulouse-Lautrec posters; there were slick landscapes and a curious pervading aura of fake buoyancy, but not one iota of personal expression was evident. We would scarcely expect passionate autobiographical outpourings, yet the prisoners might have been encouraged to *see* their own world, painful as it is, and deal with it, at least on some level that betrayed human involvement. For isn't that what art is all about, about what we know, not about what we are supposed to know?

Report on the Humanities Study Group

Carl Ladensack

During the three days of study sessions prior to the 1966 NCTE convention in Houston, Texas, Study Group 1A met and engaged in a variety of activities planned to introduce humanities programs to teachers and supervisors who were unfamiliar with them and to stimulate teachers and supervisors of courses that already existed.

Semi-formal presentations and discussions revealed that the only definite pattern found in humanities courses is that they are interdisciplinary, relating combinations of disciplines that include art, drama, social studies, and science; that the courses are most often taught by a team of teachers or occasionally, by one instructor with aid from visitors; that the courses create an atmosphere that differs from the standard classroom. The courses are generally aimed at upper grades and at the top academic group. The majority of humanities courses offer a chronological study of man's artistic endeavors by using a "post-holing" technique in key periods of accomplishment; others are arranged thematically; still others utilize no organizational framework except the instructor's own enthusiasm for individual works. A characteristic common to all is that very enthusiasm that is, in part, responsible for the atmosphere distinctive to humanities courses.

The humanities classroom differs from the traditional English classroom in its freedom and dynamic quality. Both students and teachers feel freer to experiment, to engage in activities that are not standard practice, and to raise questions that do not have simple answers. The student is an active participant in all of the work. In general, there is more of an exchange of ideas rather than mere lecture and note-taking. Routine is not common; everything from seating arrangements to materials studied partakes of the dynamic quality that the students sense and enjoy. Teachers who have the same students in English classes and humanities classes report a decided change in a student's attitude from one class to the other. The humanities course is conducive to open-mindedness, frankness, eagerness, and accelerated learning.

Although many of the techniques used in humanities classes are applicable to English courses, tradition somehow prevents them from being entirely successful. Tradition determines subject matter taught, attitudes toward the subject, and goals in the course. Teachers and students find themselves unable to escape from the syllabus. The most successful humanities courses thus far are offered in addition to English courses. Therefore, writing drill, grammar, rhetoric, and stress on correctness in communication skills need not be ignored in favor of the pleasures of analysis of some great work. Obviously, the English classroom should enjoy this pleasurable activity also. The humanities classroom, however, is not hospitable to drill work.

During all of our sessions, questions were invited from the participants. Many of the group were curious about grading systems. Mr. McBride, a panel member to whom the question was first directed, responded that evaluating the students' work did present problems because traditional activities and standards are not the norm. He explained, however, that in his course students keep journals and engage in occasional writing projects that allow him a means of judging growth. He continued by explaining that much of the student's progress is evident in what he says and does in class. The rest of the panel at various times expressed similar opinions. Much of the grading in humanities courses is more subjective and intuitive than the grading in courses for which testing methods are well established. Each teacher works out his own system, but no great problem seems to result.

Selecting a good working team is one of the major problems. Discussion revealed that the best method is to allow a working team to develop naturally out of the abilities, interests, and personalities of the available staff. Because no particular combination of disciplines is necessary, the compatible group can come from any area of the staff. Assignment to a team by an administrator interested in establishing a program is frequently unsuccessful. However, administrators can do a great deal to aid teachers interested in planning courses by allowing them free time and making materials available. In some schools the administrators themselves are members of teams, teaching subjects in which they have special competence.

A problem that arises from the difficulty of setting definite grading standards is that of selecting students and disposing of those who are not benefiting from the work. There is no known method of predicting student success in humanities courses, yet most classes are limited in enrollment. Deans and teachers must rely on intuition in accepting applicants. Unlikely candidates frequently flourish, whereas good bets may flounder.

Some members of the panel expressed concern that humanities courses could easily become too undirected and undisciplined. Certainly teachers must prevent the courses from becoming erratic, uninformed discussions.

Perhaps the greatest problem is that of deciding which materials to include and which to exclude. Works used in existing courses range from classics to current popular ones. The emphasis in most courses is on great works of established worth, but many teachers find their best success in starting with contemporary novels, poems, plays, paintings, and music. Critics of humanities courses point to the overambitious programs that sweep blithely through several centuries of work every two weeks. The study group seemed to feel that a few works, studied in greater depth and somehow related to each other, are most valuable to the student. If he can learn that the painter, composer, architect, and writer are engaged in kindred activities and that men throughout the ages have been so engaged, he will be better equipped to look at and listen to new works. Ultimately, training the student to look and listen more perceptively seems to be the main objective of humanities courses.

Two of the main benefits of humanities courses are releasing student creativity and relating disciplines that have too long been compartmentalized. The first benefit is obvious in the products of the courses: poems, stories, plays, movies, paintings, notebooks, and records that students have produced because they felt inclined or inspired to produce. Instead of the usual required themes or reports, students develop projects that interest them. The second benefit is that the student begins to see relationships. History gains meaning as he finds that painting styles and subjects reflect social, economic, and political developments; English literature gains meaning as the student hears romantic music that expresses emotional attitudes kindred to those of Keats, Shelley, or Blake; analyzing the artistry of a poem is simplified as the student discovers principles of organization in music and art that parallel those of poetry. And along with all these benefits, the student is gaining greater awareness of himself and other men.

In addition to humanities courses that are part of the school curriculum, there are programs that are extra-curricular. Some of these programs are club activities; others are part of an assembly program. Many utilize members of the community, such as parents, museum personnel, or anyone else who is competent and willing to share his special knowledge. Even the courses that are offered for credit as part of the school curriculum often use community resources. Many of the classes are scheduled late in the day so that the class can take trips to museums, attend lectures, or work beyond the dismissal bell when interest indicates that continuing the activity is desirable.

The above discussions were merely preliminaries to the real heart of our workshop: sessions devoted to building two units that could be used in a humanities course. Because the participants had available to them samples of courses built around chronological and thematic principles, we suggested topics that were somewhat different. We began as a large group with the topic *woman;* later we split into smaller groups with the topic *the hero.* We began the building of a unit on woman by projecting onto a screen a picture of Gaston Lachaise's "Standing

Woman," a statue in the garden of the Museum of Modern Art. Gradually, the group began to analyze what the artist was saying in this statue. We looked at her and enumerated many qualities before proceeding to slides of works by other artists: Renoir, Picasso, Chagall, Albright, Arcimbaldi. We began to see comparable and contrasting attitudes; the paintings suggested poems and stories in which woman was a central concern. As we talked about the works, we noted a need for knowledge of technique and a desire to know something about the period in which the work was produced. After the slides we turned to a group of poems about women; the poets represented included e. e. cummings, William Butler Yeats, and William Shakespeare. The group discussed the poems as poetry, but frequently a poem recalled an image from a slide that we had seen or some other work that was described. As will happen in any good humanities class, we had some fairly exciting disagreements of interpretation. Finally, we talked of novels and music that would be suitable for the unit.

Halfway through our discussions of the topic *woman,* we digressed for a while on the objectives in our study. We noted that before beginning we had not specified a single objective, but that we were now in fact accomplishing several. We were learning about attitudes toward an exciting and important phenomenon in the world. We were looking, listening, and speaking intelligently and critically. We were developing criteria for judging and interpreting works of art. We were relating one world to another.

In our smaller groups we developed materials appropriate to a study of the hero. An interesting similarity of thought was evident in the reports from both groups. Among the subtopics suggested were definitions of the hero, changes in heroic qualities through the ages, the origins of heroes, the function of the hero in society, the psychological implications for heroes. Both groups were greatly concerned with the hero in contemporary life and suggested appropriate works in which we can trace this continuing figure, such as *Profiles in Courage* and various representations of John Kennedy, who was acknowledged to be the twentieth-century American hero. A good deal of dicussion also centered on the heroic stature of Huck Finn, and Walter Mitty was suggested as a possible starting point for demonstrating the universal desire for heroic qualities and the principles of identification with heroes. One member of the study group demonstrated the possibility of a continuing study of heroes originating with fairy tales in early grades, continuing through myths and epics in the upper grades, and concluding with mature analysis of heroic figures in drama and novels. We suggested such alternate approaches as comparing classic heroes with contemporary heroes or anti-heroes and tracing a single hero such as Prometheus in his multiple appearances in myth, drama, poetry, sculpture, and painting. These groups engaged in truly dynamic exchanges of ideas as one work suggested another, and in an hour and a half we listed enough material to engage a class in concentrated study for more than a year.

One of the concerns of the group was the fact that modern media, such as films, should play in a humanities course. We viewed and discussed uses of Encyclopaedia Brittanica films on *Huckleberry Finn.* We agreed that they were valuable as a starting place for study of the novel, but that there was danger in the possibility that some teachers might use them as *the* study of the novel. Later, Mr. Vedro, a representative of EBF and a member of our group, made available to us a Dutch film distributed by EBF called *Glass*. As a work of art the film makes an exquisite, wordless statement about the artist. It contrasts glassblowers lovingly making bottles with machines that mass-produce them. The musical accompaniment adds to the contrast of the human and the machine. The "plot" alerts the viewer ironically to the dignity of labor, the value of the artist, the dangers of automation, the values of automation, and much more. After the film the group discussed works that the film suggested, such as Galsworthy's "Quality," Huxley's *Brave New World* and Leger's mechanical-looking figures. We noted that, by itself, the film would act as a good stimulus for student writing.

The greatest value in our study group sessions was that they were in themselves a humanities class. The participants stimulated each other in an exchange of attitudes, ideas, and material that will doubtless have effects in the schools represented. The variety of activities, the frequent change of pace, the following of spontaneous interests, the utilization of talents present in the group, and the general enjoyment of study are typical of the humanities classes across the country.

An NDEA Humanities Institute: Developing Arts Core Curricula in the Elementary School

Elaine C. Block and Janet Lieberman

During the summer of 1967, the New York College of Music, in conjunction with Hunter College and the Whitney Museum of Art, sponsored a Humanities Institute to develop arts core curricula for the elementary school. As a necessary prerequisite to the development of new curricula, the institute hoped to change the participants as human beings—their outlook and feelings about art, their understandings of the urban child and his relationships to art. The program of the institute was designed to guide the participants, and in turn their pupils, to develop keener appreciation of sensory stimuli within their environment. They would become more aware of the excitement of the arts and discover within themselves understandings and feelings in relation to the objects and ideas of their world.

The essential humanistic element the arts core curricula would introduce is the uniqueness with which each person views the world and responds to it. To develop humanistically, one must learn to view the environment clearly and to respond freely and honestly to it. One must not only accept but honor the varying ways in which people perceive and express their reactions to their environment.

In most elementary schools, the arts are relegated to a position of little prominence; the creative experience is subordinate. The faculty of the institute felt that greater emphasis on the arts would lead to more stimulating, enlightening, and humanistic experiences for children. New avenues of learning would be opened; new realms of experience would be explored.

Population of the Institute. The faculty of the institute selected thirty teachers and supervisors from six elementary and junior high schools of New York City to participate in the arts core project. The teachers represented varied grade levels and specialities. One group of teachers taught first grade but most taught grades four to eight. There were several mathematics teachers, social studies teachers, music and art teachers, and those who taught common branches. These varied backgrounds were needed so that people within the group could be resources to indicate how their special areas could contribute to arts core curricula. The faculty also hoped to include a supervisor from each school to insure continued administrative support for the new curricula during the school year. Two supervisors joined the group.

Limiting the number of participating schools served two purposes. First, it insured that each school would have a nuclear group of teachers to serve as resources for innovating arts core curricula in their schools. Second, evaluation and systematic follow-up of the participants during the school year was made feasible.

Curriculum of the Institute. The curriculum of the institute followed two phases. During the first three weeks, the group was involved in direct aesthetic experiences. Participants were to develop skills in music, dramatics, art, and photography and to develop greater confidence and sensitivity in these areas. During the last three weeks, students searched for applications of these experiences to their classrooms. As a culminating project, each participant developed an arts core unit to teach his class during the coming school year.

The initiating experience for the students involved the creation of an environment. Greeted with a supply of beaver board, ramps, wooden planks, rope, wire, lights and tape recordings, the participants arranged these materials to suit themselves. As they worked, they interacted to make decisions. They looked, touched, and discovered the qualities and potentialities of the varied materials at hand. They also discovered that arrangement and juxtaposition as well as texture, light, sound, and form had an emotional impact. The experience was perhaps a strange beginning, but it served to free the students from the traditional curriculum content as well as to focus on the arts.

Each student was required to bring a camera with him. Photography was emphasized as an art that plays a large role in the life of the child. Skill in looking at and responding to photographs should open new vistas for the child and place him in a better position both to enjoy and to manipulate his environment. The participants were taught how to take and how to evaluate the quality of their photographs. At the same time they developed materials to be used later in their classrooms. They also realized how cameras can be used to stimulate learning and to make the child more conscious of his environment.

The first photography assignment was to develop a photographic essay on a theme such as "color in New York," "New York is a multiethnic community," "texture," "signs," "food," "feeling tired." One student photographed a sequence using an apple—on a table, under a chair, in a pile of leaves, cut in half, and in water. The sequence could be used in a number of ways, each resulting in a different story pattern. As students experimented with ways to use their slides, they discovered that placing two slides together in the viewer could have additional impact—such as a slide of a small apple seeming to rest within the apple that had been cut in half.

A follow up assignment was to add an additional art form to the slide presentation—music or literature. Slides could develop imagery for the music or the music could add emotional impact to the slides. One participant coordinated haiku poems with slides of an elderly Japanese barber. Some slides were deliberately projected out of focus to increase the impact of the mood.

Another aspect of the aesthetic phase of the institute was a series of sessions on creative dramatics. These workshops emphasized role playing and dramatization. Art and music were integrated with these experiences to heighten the participants' sense of the individual in relation to his environment.

One group of experiences focused on music and movement. A highlight in this series revolved about LeRoy Anderson's "Syncopated Clock." Students learned how to listen and to respond kinesthetically to this music. Rhythm and meter were expressed both in body movement and in drawing. Students then visited the Dorothy Maynor School of the Arts in Harlem to see children responding to the same music in basically the same ways. One student made a photographic essay to accompany the clock theme. Her photographs included clocks at Grand Central Station, clocks on sale in a store window, close ups of the hands of a clock, and signs of time such as "24-hour service," and "repaired while you wait." As the theme of the music changed, she showed slides of a child caught in action on a skate board. With the return to the original theme, she again focused on faces of clocks. The result was a group of materials with myriad possibilities for teaching about music and concepts of time.

Students also attended biweekly lectures at the Whitney Museum. The illustrated talks, "Art in the Twentieth Century," focused on the gap between art history and art criticism. Students became familiar with the exhibit and also learned how to make museum trips meaningful to children.

Additional experiences during the first three weeks also broke through the four walls of the classroom. Students and faculty saw Pinter's *Homecoming,* the film *Blow-Up,* a jazz concert at the Museum of Modern Art and "living theatre" at a Greenwich Village cafe. Discussion on art forms and their impact on society and on the emotional impact of aesthetic experiences followed these trips.

The manner of teaching as well as the content of the institute was a new experience for the group. The faculty worked as a team planning each week and then each day to develop a coordinated program. Several instructors were present at each session, presenting materials from various disciplines, and often presenting various points of view. Sessions were informal and active. The one nun in the class changed to a modern habit because her veil tore too often during class activities.

Assignments for the students avoided standard texts. Students read essays by artists on their philosophy of art. They also read books by Bruno Bettleheim, Malcolm X, and Marshall McLuhan. Assignments also included viewing art exhibits and attending concerts.

The above activities summarized only part of Phase I. It obviously was a crowded three weeks. Participants enjoyed the experiences immensely. They designed, danced, drew, photographed, reacted to paintings, and improvised dramatic situations. Many of the students seemed to have changed basic ideas and behavior patterns. They became more aware of things around them, of each other, and of themselves. They had caught the excitement of the creative experience.

Although not all students felt a change, the faculty felt that the first phase of the institute had been highly successful. The problem now remained of applying these ideas and attitudes to developing the new curricula. Several sessions were devoted to principles of curriculum construction. It was impossible to find model units on the arts to present to the class. Even if adequate ones had been available, it was not our intention to copy or adapt. We hoped students would be free from the bounds of traditional content and form.

The group discussed various principles by which their units might be organized—chronology, theme, culture case study, style, genre and aesthetic elements. Chronology, theme and culture case study which are frequently used to develop social studies units, can easily be applied to the arts. A chronological focus could lead to a history of films or photography or history of the South through its music. Themes such as peace, love, or revolution could be viewed through the arts. The culture of the North West Indians or the African nations could also be studied through their artistic expressions.

The latter three organizing principles—style, genre and aesthetic element—are more commonly used at the college level. With a study of style, children could study symbolism or humor in the arts. Instead of studying a form such as the novel, a unit on the fairy tale, myth or folk tale would be feasible. Color, as a basic element of art, is also a possible unit theme.

During the last weeks of the institute students divided their time between laboratory sessions designed to fit individual needs and individual consultations with the faculty. In laboratory sessions they developed the specific skills in music, drama, art or photography that they felt they would need to teach the unit. In individual conferences they were helped to clarify the goals of their units and to locate appropriate materials. During the final week of the institute both faculty and students evaluated the completed units.

Student Projects: The Arts Core Curriculum. The arts core units were designed for use with classes in inner city schools to which our students had already been assigned. The arts were to be integrated, but not in a forced manner, with other curriculum areas. The sequence of experiences planned for the children was to be logical, cumulative, and to make use of innovative procedures. Several outstanding units were produced.

"You and the Rest of Them" was planned for a second grade class. As her rationale for the unit, the student wrote: ". . . It is important for all persons to understand that they are different from each other, that everyone has needs and desires, that the law exists not so much to stop them from doing what they want as it does to prevent them from being hurt by other people. . . . Especially for this Harlem child, I would want him to appreciate his individual worth."

The unit began by noting the gross and subtle differences in common objects—pencils, bottles, cans, flowers, and animals. Although a cursory glance might indicate that two pencils or bottles might be identical, a slight nick or a rubbed eraser easily marks one from the other. Two jonquils or goldfish have even greater distinguishing features. Poems such as "Feet" and "Hands" by Dorothy Aldis, "Tall People, Short People" by Lois Lenski, and "Teachers" by Eleanor Farjeon reinforced the idea that people are different in many ways. Dramatizations showed how hands can be used in different ways—to string beads, braid hair, play the piano and to write letters, and how feet change as they wiggle toes in cold water, run down hill or slide on ice. Photography was introduced as children took pictures of hands, feet, smiles and glances during the dramatizations. The pictures could then be studied leisurely, compared, and serve as stimuli for creative writing.

Another major idea in this unit was that things may appear to be alike on the outside but may be quite different underneath. Identical containers with different content introduced this idea to the children. Stories such as the *Five Chinese Brothers* and *New Boy in School* further illustrated this concept. Children were also to move to the music of the "Syncopated Clock" to see how differently each responded to the same rhythm and the same beat. Differences also emerged as children photographed the same object yet each chose a different vantage point and different lighting. Drawings on the same theme also emphasized individuality of reaction.

The concluding section of the unit discussed how groups of people benefit from individual differences of each member and what limits on behavior must be imposed for the well being of the group. Sociodramas, discussions of Superman and Batman television programs and the formulation of classroom rules were some of the correlative activities.

Another unit, "Man, the Worker," was directed to an older group of pupils. It emphasized the different types of work needed in rural and urban societies, as well as a comparison of workers of the past, present and future. A Kwakiutal Indian poem illustrated the workers in primitive societies:

> When I am a man, then I shall be a
>   hunter
> When I am a man, then I shall be a
>   harpooner
> When I am a man, then I shall be a
>   canoe builder
> When I am a man, then I shall be a
>   carpenter
> When I am a man, then I shall be an
>   artisan
> Oh father! ya ha ha.

Children were to rewrite the poem in modern context. Other materials planned for this unit included:

Poems:

Carl Sandburg—excerpts from *"The People, Yes."* Untermeyer, "Caliban in the Coal Mines." MacColl, *British Industrial Ballads.*

Records:

"The Death of John Henry." "Sixteen Tons" and "Pay Me My Money Down" by the Weavers.

Photographs:

Steichen's *The Family of Man*

Paintings:

of works by Millet, Van Gogh, Chardin, Degas, Daumier, Bayeux Tapestry and stained glass windows of Chartres Cathedral.

A unit of the Western Frontier focused on legends and songs of the frontier. Songs included: "Chisholm Trail," "Little Joe," "The Wrangler," "The Dying Cowboy," "The Bent Country Bachelor," "In the Pines" and "Sweet Betsy from Pike." Literature included diaries of pioneers, articles from local newspapers as well as such well known books as Laura Ingalls Wilder's *These Happy Golden Years* and Bess Streeter Aldrich, *A Lantern in Her Hand.*

Other units on particular cultures—the Japanese, the Incas and others—used the arts to develop the power of communication. A mathematics unit focused on forms in the environment. Photographic essays were developed to show form in automobiles, furniture, machines, and toys.

Evaluation of the Institute. The six week humanities institute undertook a tremendous task. The goals were to develop arts core curricula and to innovate curriculum patterns using the arts. In order to accomplish these tasks, we had to teach the arts to our students and also teach them how to construct curricula. More basically we had to teach the students to look at themselves and their environment. Most of the students had to look at teaching in a different light.

Such grandiose goals cannot be attained within a six week period. However, students showed growth and desirable change. All were challenged. As the students became more responsive to the arts, they were more willing to try new approaches to teaching. They gained skill in using a variety of techniques with camera, pencil, brush, notes, voice, and body. They also produced materials to use in their classrooms. Their reactions show the impact of the institute.

I think I see what you are trying to do without the traditional push technique. . . . Through stimulation, discussions, experiences, etc., you wish us to look at the world that we live in closer than we used to. It's not easy to fight conditioning and brain washing in order to look at new things to open our cabinet minds.

I am starting to see new vistas in education, the dynamic use of our environment in teaching.

—Going, seeing, learning, moving, feeling, doing, and participating are such learning experiences and yet the odds are that in most classes today, the teacher will be standing up in front of the class teaching.

—This (the camera) is certainly a new way of seeing what was there all the time.

—My reaction to pop art is starting to change. I now evaluate instead of discarding.

The Institute is over
    And many things have we now learned to do—
Move with Music, swing or
Photograph young children or a King.
    'Tis true the play's the thing
To catch the interest on the wind.
We learn to sway and dip and rock
A-A-B-A-A the "Syncopated Clock."
The staff was kind and the elements
So mixed herein that the participants
might stand up and say to the Federal
    Government
"This was an Institute."

Postscript: Invitation from a Student. It was the week before Christmas and the assembly hall had a scattering of boys in white shirts and many adults at their sides. The room was old and square with two small windows and peeling brown-yellow paint. One too-grown-up to be a boy was sitting behind a projector with a mass of slides on the table before him. The gloom-dark room became darker and a teacher sat down at the old upright piano. He played loud and fast and you had to move your feet and hands to the beat. "Peace on Earth Good Will toward Men," the silhouette repeated. A stained glass window hid the wall. The slide shifted to forms of light and color. A youngster in a slouched hat clutched a microphone and sang of his world—one that did not involve others. The slides changed to jagged forms and textures. A blind man entered and begged for alms. The background of an elephant's eye engulfed him.

And the opera continued. Loneliness in the world of people. And the boys read, and they sang, and *they understood.*

The Focus of Humanism and the Teacher

Raymond W. Houghton

Mankind is human, already. In that sense, the millenium is at hand since ... (Robert Ardrey or Mr. and Mrs. L. S. B. Leekey will give us a date any book now).

And, oh, are we human! For we do what humans do, and our human adventures are recorded daily by our gay chroniclers Huntley and Brinkley who, McLuhan-like, bring the collective and instantaneous record into the centers provided by our electric age living rooms.

You got it baby, Mega-murder makes the scene. Doubles and triples is out. What's news is that? Nothing under seven makes the regional wire. And no singles for local coverage even. With rape, maybe.

Wars we got. Little wars at home and in the office. Medium sized wars around and about. Large wars and Mendel Rivers. Whose planes were those, baby? All them people dead, and they ain't even mad at us! They's all so shell-shocked maybe we can blame Haile Selassie.

Halt, who goes there? Friend or foe?

It's only us chickens.

Whammo! Gotcha that time.

I'll fix you up–cheu, cheu, you're all better. Get up or we can't play no more. Wake up! Wake up! I didn't mean to hit you so hard, wake up! Don't you want to play no more?

Read the books. Forget McLuhan! Typography ain't dead altogether. In Cold Blood *describes our very humanness. Read it and come to my masquerade ball. You come as Martin Luther King and I'll be* The Boston Strangler. *See my sailor suit?*

And love is human. Harold Pinter has written of love in *The Homecoming*. A play of love, a reviewer said. The philosopher's wife at once mistress and prostitute and procuress and, "Don't be a stranger."

The Association is careless with terms. *Humanism and human* and humanizing and humanness are not the same. What do you want to talk about? The Association is sentimental. It comes together to talk of goody-goody. Every year we talk of goody-goody and feel good together at Miami Beach and Chicago and Las Vegas and San Francisco and next year East Lynne. We're a road show company of good feeling. For Maslow's psychology is our psychology. We are the cult of peak experiences. "I like ASCDers. They're good people." Our sociology is Paul Goodman's. Why should all kids be middle class? Yeah! Yeah!

The lower class has good values, too. I'll meet you after the discussion group at The Baker for dinner.

Our philosopher is Pierre Tielhard de Chardin, for our view of the world is optimistic. Each day, in some way, we grow better and better.

Our theology is the cult of Democracy and our *modus operandi* is WASP secularism. We are not cynical. We are not angry. We are in a stage of nondirective indifference.

Epoch of Atomism. Humanism has a real meaning to the philosopher. It would seem to refer to those periods in history wherein man has intended to rely on his own resources in his seeking after truth. It has particular reference to that post-medieval era in which, feebly at first, cautiously in retrospect, brazenly in fact, certain charismatics ventured to probe beyond revelation while remaining in basic concert with God and sought truth through their own awareness. Western man flexed against the bonds of Latin to more vigorously reuse the classic repetoire of data. Hebrew and Greek began to re-reveal ideas and direction. Gutenberg's movable type, a technology already over five hundred years old, allowed dissemination through the emerging use of the vernacular. Aristotelian modes of thought were adapted to the seeking after secular truths. The Platonic mode acquired an impetus and the western world bloomed with fresh hope.

Through Erasmus, to Copernicus, to Descartes, and Newton, man came to the belief that he could perhaps, by himself, know all. For it was the simple things that he was learning. The earth was round, and the sun did not rise and set, and mouse dung might not be the best cure for warts, and properly placed prisms let the stars look big and germs look big, and scientific method replaced exorcism, and experimental technique replaced the beatific vision, and empirical data replaced the Catechism, and science became the new god. The western world was hard aground on an epoch of atomism.

Scientism, technology and the tether of sight-oriented literacy replaced the tyranny of revelation as the source of all truth.

In all of its sterile objectivity, the scientific age failed in secular emergence, for a new god replaced an old god and sustained man's distance for humanness.

That is what McLuhan has so beautifully and unemotionally, yet rather fatalistically described in *Understanding Media.* It is the literary focus which makes us "civilized." The opportunity to focus on the sight medium removed us from the tribal stage of total involvement, of reliance on a multi-sensory openness, and brought about rather a highly individual single focus concentration on the very "hot" medium of the printed page, of datum, datum everywhere and not a drop to drink, for most.

The influence of "humanism" in the post medieval period allowed the development of a scientific technological data source for the age of science to be disseminated via the printed page, thus providing the intellectual impetus for the industrial age, which developed as a sub-stage, paralleling the atomistic. Specific application of intellectually derived "truth" allowed more pragmatic minds to corrupt science to technology. Again, with reference to McLuhan, the media of one age merely allow the description of a preceding age. The late seventeenth century and early eighteenth century rustlings of the industrial age merely reflect the pragmatic exploration of an earlier intellectual culture. The increase in "pure" atomistic scientific inquiry through the eighteenth and early nineteenth century paves the way for the full-blown industrial revolution in Europe and in America.

There are obviously parallel factors involved. Max Weber describes a crucial one in his essay, *The Protestant Ethic and the Spirit of Capitalism.* It is to be remembered that Weber ascribes applied Calvinism as providing the rationale for the growth of capitalism. Calvinism supported a belief that heaven and hell were, for each individual, predetermined. Everything was decided, and yet, no one really knew his fate for sure. God probably saw to it that the chosen ones would succeed in the mortal world and hence, the moneyed and achieving individuals were destined for the heavenly reward. But, in that one could never be sure, it was safer to "live the good life," work hard, stay clean, "shape up" and just hope for the best. This belief provided the ideal milieu for the growth of industrial capitalism, for the mill owner was God's child. The workers had less chance, but if they kept their mouths shut and did what they were told they just might sneak into heaven. And the poor were obviously not going to make it at all in this world or the next.

My personal experience as a Republican candidate for Congress in the last election has convinced me that the social Darwinism, popularized in Europe and America by Herbert Spencer and others, which dominated sociological thinking for more than fifty years is still faithfully accepted by the contemporary American upper class. Generations of Americans were conditioned to accept the substance of this belief by learned professors at such noble institutions as Brown and Yale. There is little wonder that the vision of a Great Society strikes with such trauma.

Again, Max Weber in his writings on classical bureaucracy, describes social change as the result of charisma and democratization of ideas. He analyzes and describes the inevitability of the growth of bureaucracy in an industrialized society and the stultifying effects of high degrees of specialization and impersonalness on individuals.

Atomistic Conditioning. If Weber provides the sociological description of the age, the late Professor Raymond H. Wheeler, the first American gestaltist, provides a description of the psychology. Wheeler, much maligned by his fellow psychologists, nevertheless outlined cyclical epochs of alternating atomistic and holistic character. It was obvious to him that the legacy of the scientific-industrial age could be but a closed, confined, restrained dependence on a blind alley, logical positivism, wherein learning was conceived of as atomistic conditioning.

Aldous Huxley described this world, anticipated its frightening outcomes, and lived to write of it again in *Brave New World Revisited.*

Sinclair Lewis naturalistically described it. T. S. Eliot poetically diagnosed it. Innumerable artists and musical composers reflected this world in their wordless creations.

Karl Marx felt it and proceeded to an evolutionary rationale which, when democratized by Engels and Lenin, resulted in a different and more overriding impersonal bureaucracy which, if carried out, would extinguish any surviving individualism.

B. F. Skinner, with his philosophic behaviorism, accepted the inevitability of the atomistic epoch and speculated on how, by joining the system, it might be possible to get it to work to provide his Utopia. *Walden Two,* a fictionalized vision of such a world, results in what Joseph Wood Krutch describes as "a travesty on the good life."

There have been systems and systems, each having charismatic impetus, followed by the inevitable bureaucratization, as ideas, often dynamic and even sensitive, are democratized into inflexible laws to be expanded and enforced.

And throughout it all there has been the protest—the bohemian, the expatriate, the anarchist, the beatnik, the hipster—the whole San Francisco hippie scene with its alternative respondents, its variety of social activists and those feeling pain but withdrawn to despair.

There is the British dissolution, marked by the genius of the Beatles who somehow sense the time, and relate in a kaleidoscopic synthesis of sound and word affirmed by youth, and others. Their *Strawberry Fields, Forever* is real. It is possible to admire their relevance and despise their solution. It is possible to despise everything about the bureaucratic N.B.C. capitalized show of the Monkees. Unlike the Beatles, who had arisen from the depths of Liverpool with an idea which, coincidentally, sold, the Monkees were manufactured by N.B.C. out of money, to look like and taste like the high priced spread.

The Struggle to Be Humane. It is to be sensed that the Beatles have come to despair, which is, paradoxically, good. For their despair is existential like

Kierkegaard, and less like Sartre, like Martin Buber and Blondel and even Niebuhr. For to despair is to have beginning. It is the vital part of the struggle to be humane.

The relevance of all this to the teacher is to be pondered. What teacher? I say. For there are teachers and teachers. In Plato's *Dialogues* the question is asked, what is teacher? The answer comes back indirectly that teacher is one with a knowledge of virtue, and isn't that a kick in the teeth, for who is so vain as to lay such a claim? But such an individual needs no declaimer. He doesn't tell. He is told by the asking. Like Plato, he manifests his knowing in humility and what a need there is for such teachers! In the specifications for each new school should be a flag pole, a teachers' lounge, a separate girls' gym and at least one teacher who is a real human being.

The whole world is crying out for models of how to live. As Arthur Vidich will point out in his new volume, *The Third American Revolution,* a whole generation has grown up without a clean-cut life style model. There is no relevant American image. For many of the old myths "is 'daid'" or without real meaning. And the television ad imagery, featuring the psychic life style of Darien copywriters, doesn't ring true (neither true blue nor true green, with menthol)—and there are those who are not in the Pepsi generation, nor who wish to join the Metrecal for lunch bunch, looking tall and spare and starved to death—a non-crew aboard a toy yawl moving across a sea as flat as the women aboard. Vidich suggests the life style model of the international jet set as perhaps coming closest, or, horror of horrors, the old college professor serving as model with each suburban community living in a student union with chamber music and sociological lectures in the Unitarian church basement. Second generation Americans and first generation college graduates, living in an affluent society must seek a new American Dream, hopefully not Norman Mailer's. They have had little success.

Lack of a relevant cultural image spawns peculiar phenomena. Vidich cites the so-called cat culture, in which Negro urban youth invent a style—a style resplendent with narcotics and violence and indulgence. He reminds of the grotesqueness of image imitation, contrived in artificial desperation.

The young and the old need lessons in how to live. It is at this point that McLuhan is vulnerable to the epithet of fatalist. For while, in an evolutionary sense, the medium is the message, one needs to be reminded of the humanistic idea of man as possessing the potential to select and create a destiny for himself, or his world, for his media extensions are, by McLuhan's admission—nay insistence, appendages, like fingers or ears which can make man more than man.

Teachers must have used derived data to develop virtue, must have themselves moved beyond "subject matter" as ends and have come to, and continuously and continually come to, new syntheses. The teacher must be in equilibrium in terms of his own understanding. He must be in control of his own computer system so that at any moment he can push his totalizer button and be in awareness with his own reality. Teachers must themselves be living and hence, relevant. They must lose the vision of knowing all and become relevant in terms of the dynamics of existence. They need not know much. They, indeed, cannot know much. A limited vision of God might be the image of omniscience in a Being capable of comprehending infinity and, at once, part of it. Man's place in an infinity of knowing is the sustaining of a dynamic relevance in a suspension of knowledge and ignorance, maintaining equilibrium through a process of growth and, hopefully, limited decay.

Teachers must be more than imperfect computers. If teachers are lifeless as computers, they are truly dead like computers. Although it is not to be imagined that computers need stay dead they will extend as culture determines. As of now it suffices that they be so. If we determine otherwise, it will be otherwise. As we live, our extensions may live. If teachers are simply imperfect data sources, they are less than computers, for, in computers, data stored are data stored. It is to be doubted that IBM builds a psychic life into its computers. While the computer perhaps, like man, stores data never used, recall remains imminent. It is the recall mechanism in men and machines that is the crucial factor. Computers do not of themselves bury data. Recall is atomistically precise and articulate. There is no preconscious. There is no slurring or fusion of response. The computer is clean cut. It does not hiccup data into awareness accidentally. If, as principal, I wished to hire a data source, I would call IBM and never the local teacher agency.

If teachers are afraid of computers, and they are, it is because they feel themselves to be no more than computers, not as much as computers, because, as media of the electric age, as extensions of man, they, as we, are culture products of the atomistic epoch. They handle data of the atomistic epoch infinitely better than those they extend.

But let us remind ourselves of one crushing truth. The screaming cry of the approaching 21st century is that education is that which transpires after the last fitful burp of the computer. It is here that the pitiful need for the humane teacher becomes apparent. For the teacher, to be teacher, must move beyond the definition of data source, and stand ready with a vision of virtue. As Professor Pritzkau has pointed out, to make a better teacher, we must first make better humans. By better it may be interpreted that what he means is more human, with a hopeful inclination toward humane, but at least more sensitively human, with all of the connotations therein implied. A sensitive recognition of what it means to be human might be more precise.

McLuhan wisely pointed out that, if one wishes to know what the world is like at any instant in time, one must turn to the artist who senses and describes but hardly can communicate for all to know, for he sensibly refuses to try. Each artist is himself charismatic. He would not have it otherwise, for he realizes, without McLuhan to tell him, that his medium is his message. It is there for those who would suspend their delimited receptors to hear and (not or) see and feel and touch and taste and, through intuitive synthesis, comprehend. The democratization of his message is left to the corrupting influences of critics and professors of education to mash and slice up and atomize into the hot medium of the newspaper column or the convention speech. The artist is cool. You gotta write your own ticket, man.

You can't put it in lists or write formulas with it or program it for the machine. You gotta make that old intuitive leap, baby, cuz Bruner's Bible tells us so.

This writer likes and respects the Beatles because they, as artists, have their antennae up. But he doesn't worship them, for they have no adequate solutions. They just tells it like it is. But McCartney and Lennon are only twenty-five. Maybe they'll come up with something yet. As of the moment they discern and describe, but continue to use their data simply to respond, rather than in a G. H. Mead sense, choose alternatives toward the establishment of their collective minds.

To Be Sensitively Alive. The essence of humanness is to be sensitively alive, to be headed into the wind and in dynamic equilibrium. Professor Maslow really has the story here. Our late friend, Professor Donald Snygg and Arthur Combs have described it, as have others in and out of the Association. But the key is in the words "sensitively alive," for the world is tough, and it isn't just in the saying of it. The "how" beyond, is impossible to describe, but a boat with stalled power in a rough sea might just as well forget it. A sense of humor helps in the sense of George Meredith, in his introduction to *The Egoist.* Aldous Huxley's *Island* provides some clues with his mynah birds conditioned to call out, "Attend, attend!" and his description of the joy of sensitive dying. His characters are all L.S.D. nuts, however.

So the teacher must be, first of all, sensitively alive. Then after the lunch money is collected, and the shades are adjusted, and the floor is swept and the teaching machines have beeped out and the computer has burped its last, education is ready to begin.

This becomes the moment of awful truth, for this is when the teacher stands naked with his knowledge of virtue, and the chips are down. For the cool truth it might be suggested that Philo Pritzkau offers a means and a way. He described it in his volume, *The Dynamics of Curriculum Improvement,* in his discussion of total values admission. A total values admission classroom is one in which all values are admitted for consideration and analysis. The teacher and learner involve themselves in the dynamics of the collective existence. Ideas and values are analyzed and examined. Alternatives are considered and the teacher and students are confronted with their mutual ignorance and genius.

All students deserve this involvement. Everyone is an intellectual when provided with the opportunity for involvement. McLuhan points out that, in the electric age, the emergent cool age, individuals demand involvement. It is the position of Pritzkau and others previously mentioned, and of the speaker, that it has always been thus. As students find the teacher relevant and the school relevant, they will fight to become involved. It is to be suggested that children drop out of school not because they wish to avoid involvement, but because they seek it and the schools deny it to them. There is scarce need to resurrect the phony, grotesque world behind the doors of too many schools. Grotesque, in the Vidich sense that the image of the school is a distorted representation of a world that doesn't exist, a world too often the reflection of a gobbled, mythological never-never land where we wish things were like we really wouldn't want them to be. A land not unlike Mark Twain's heaven, where everyone says he wishes he could go, but where he wouldn't be found dead.

Schools should be places where the perspective of the student is respected, if not accepted. Otherwise he won't come physically, if he can help it, nor mentally coerced.

Join our make-believe world, kid! Distort and corrupt yourself and leave your authenticity at the door and join us in our illusions, or you can't play the game.

The Cultural Model. And then the teacher must have always represented something authentic himself. He must ask the questions and betray himself willingly, and grow. He must, as Pritzkau says, be the first learner. The magnificent joy of teaching is that the teacher should always be the first and foremost learner. As teacher and children become learners together, they attain a higher level of existence almost too exquisite to savor.

The teacher poses the cultural model. It is not a model of himself, but rather the model of human authenticity that allows the student to become more intensively himself—to find his own existence, his own meaning, his own configuration of the universe. It is not sufficient to have the student become like anything, including the teacher.

Borrowing the terminology of Erving Goffman, the teacher is making a "presentation of self," that is alive and sensitive and analytical and authentic.

Teachers should be living, breathing, sinning, sainted, hating, loving human beings.

To be human is to be human.

A warning: There are those who will despise you for it. Some children will despise you as they come painfully to confront themselves. Some teachers will despise you for it in their very humanness. Many administrators will despise you for it, for such schools are difficult to housekeep. Many parents will despise you for it because their children will come to question. Many taxpayers will despise you for it for it will produce changes. The government will despise you for it because it will create enemies of bureaucracy. But you'll come to like yourself better because you won't have to keep looking up the rules of the game.

The "Sirs" of Anthony Newley's *Roar of the Greasepaint* will go out of their minds.

Nelson Algren edited an interesting book called *Nelson Algren's Own Book of Lonesome Monsters.* In the introduction he says:

> In order to make man free we must first understand what man is. And at St. Pa-De Vence, a schoolmaster who once replaced a code of blind obedience, for seven year old pupils, by one appealing to their friendship, received two direct results. The children's painting and writing became as original and lively as possible and the villagers stoned his windows.[1]

Children must be invited to join us in our humanness. It is difficult to share fully the optimism of Bruno Bettelheim. Humanness involves the full spectrum of man's potential. It is to be hoped that the teacher might accept this and

---

[1] Nelson Algren, *Nelson Algren's Own Book of Lonesome Monsters.* New York, Random House, 1962. © 1962 by Nelson Algren.

patiently seek to evoke the live creativeness and joy in children while recognizing the possibilities of hostility, rage, fear and destructiveness.

Algren points out that ". . . whenever you shut a human being out of the world he will, for better or for worse, build one of his own."

Too many have been forced to.

Might it be possible that if we can learn to love Albert DeSalvo we will have no more problems with children?

Bibliography

Nelson Algren. *Nelson Algren's Own Book of Lonesome Monsters.* New York: Random House, 1962.

Truman Capote. *In Cold Blood.* New York: Random House, 1966.

Gerald Frank. *The Boston Strangler.* New York: New American Library, Inc., 1967.

Erving Goffman. *Presentation of Self in Everyday Life,* New York: Doubleday & Company, Inc., 1959.

Aldous Huxley. *Brave New World Revisited.* New York: Harper & Row, Publishers, Inc., 1958.

Aldous Huxley. *Island,* New York: Harper & Row, Publishers, Inc., 1962.

Marshall McLuhan. *Understanding Media.* New American Library, Inc., 1964.

George Meredith. *The Egoist.* New York: Charles Scribner's Sons, 1916.

Harold Pinter. *The Homecoming.* New York: Grove Press, Inc., 1967.

Philo Pritzkau. *The Dynamics of Curriculum Improvement.* Englewood Cliffs, N. J.: Prentice-Hall, Inc., 1959.

B. F. Skinner. *Walden Two.* New York: The Macmillan Company, 1962.

Max Weber. *The Protestant Ethic and the Spirit of Capitalism.* New York: Charles Scribner's Sons, 1958.

Recordings

The Beatles. *Strawberry Fields Forever.* George Martin, Capitol Records. MacLean Music, Inc., 1967.

Anthony Newley. *The Roar of the Greasepaint; The Smell of the Crowd.* New York: RCA Victor.

Part VI
Humanities and the Disadvantaged

This section details the values of humanities education for the disadvantaged and reasons for the failure to offer this area of education to those students who have the greatest need of it. Howard, in his provocative article written in 1966, states that "too little of the education of the disadvantaged has either the content or the spirt of the humanities." Pointing out that the disadvantaged are those who are limited and "the humanities are concerned with liberating man—this void is hard to understand." He makes the important point that even more than content, the humanities suggest to teachers the kinds of attitudes that can best reach disadvantaged students. "De-emphasizing content, they seek not good listeners or good memorizers, but real experimenters, not the empty 'why' but the internalized insight that often comes from manipulation of objects."

Smiley also draws attention to the lack of humanities courses for the disadvantaged. Like Howard, she emphasizes the value of such courses, which "may be of special value in compensating for impoverished environments in home and neighborhood." An additional reason for using such courses with the disadvantaged is "based on emerging evidence of the existence of different learning strengths in different ethnic and social class groups." The humanities may also have particular appeal for students whose life-styles are described as "expressive" rather than as "instrumental." The humanities further serve as a mediator by means of which the alienated may become part of a dominant culture.

Schwartz, accepting the idea that such courses must become part of the curriculum for the disadvantaged, offers five essentials for the success of a humanities program for the disadvantaged.

Murphy and Gross, asking, "Can the Arts 'Turn on' Poor Kids to Learning?," state that the arts "constitute a potent—and strangely neglected—key for unlocking the hearts and minds of deprived youngsters."

Culligan writes about the "cultural illiterates" who are obliged to sample their cultural heritage "through a compulsory exploratory program of music, art, and assorted hobby crafts." He describes a number of ways in which America's secondary schools are incorporating humanities courses into their curricula in order to place non-college-bound students into "a greater and more creative civilization."

Goldstein and Martin present a report on a humanities program for terminal students. In their program they did not aim to have their pupils develop their potential only so that they might impose middle-class aspirations upon them. Instead, they viewed humanistic education "as essential to these pupils' greatest needs; self-awareness and social identity." It is the hope of the authors that this course opens up new possibilities for the pupil as individual.

Teach Them the Arts of Freedom

Lawrence C. Howard

Too little of the education of the disadvantaged has either the content or the spirit of the humanities. Since the disadvantaged are those who are limited, and the humanities are concerned with liberating man—this void is hard to understand. Part of the problem may be that "disadvantage" has been viewed too narrowly as a deficiency of the child, and education not enough as the enlargement of freedom. This brief review of its nature, history, and current focus suggests the humanities should have a central role in the education of the disadvantaged. And since the humanities are the arts of freedom, such a shift may well permit the disadvantaged to help in the re-education of America.

Much is now being written about the concept of "disadvantage" to describe problems confronting the child, or rather certain children. Yeshiva University in New York has a center, using semi-automatic data processing techniques, called IRCD (Information Retrieval Center on the Disadvantaged). The center's director, Professor Edmund W. Gordon, wrote in a recent *IRCD Bulletin* about "disadvantage" when approached as the child's problem.

"Disadvantage," he indicated, is rooted in the condition of poverty and discrimination in which the child grows up. He is in an American subculture, that of poverty or low status, which has inadequately prepared him to function in the middle-class world of employment and suburban living or, in our frame of reference, for functioning effectively in the educational system. Youngsters are "disadvantaged" in the sense that the preparation they receive is inadequate for successful competition in the larger society.

This kind of "child disadvantage" has been described in great detail by Bloom, Davis, and Hess in their new volume, *Compensatory Education for the Culturally Deprived.* They trace what it means to have poverty and discrimination nagging at you; what a limited diet, inadequate clothing, and shelter can mean in terms of a poor start in life; how these can affect the child during the prenatal period. They note the deficits of early childhood in this setting in inadequate perceptual and linguistic stimulation and in a poverty of experience. When such children reach the first grade, school for them is an unfamiliar and frustrating experience. There is inadequate counseling and an absence of appropriate models. They fall behind in grade, especially in reading skills. By adolescence they are the dropouts; they display a decline in IQ rating over time. The education experience simply does not take, and ahead are social problems. This picture of the disadvantaged child has prompted the conclusion that he needs compensatory education, started early and continued relentlessly, and more enlightened programs to focus upon cognitive development, that is, helping him learn how to learn.

The child is said to have a cumulative deficit that he must overcome: he's non-verbal, has a limited attention span, poor time perspective, limited response to all stimuli; he is the product of a broken home, reared under a matriarchy, is inadequately guided by adults; few things belong to him, he's under-motivated, and has a negative self-image. This is the conception of the disadvantaged child.

There is a divergent view. It states that disadvantage is a societal problem, a critical flaw in democratic America. The existence of poverty, rather than a problem of the poor, is seen as a weakness in our economic system—much the same as depressions used to be viewed. Persisting discrimination, especially against the Negro, reveals America's underdeveloped morality. Gunnar Myrdal has called this the American dilemma: mouthing words of high ideals and Christian percepts, but acting in relentless patterns of prejudice toward Negroes. "Disadvantage" then becomes the problem of the "advantaged." It reflects the middle-class preoccupation with the material, and insensitivity to the human, the strong taking advantage of the weak, the power structure corrupted by its own power. Archibald MacLeish, commenting about disadvantaged America more recently, said, "There is vulgarity everywhere. There are pockets of ignorance and hatred—not only in the Deep South. Our relations with each other lack richness and tenderness." The very existence of ostracized subcultures reinforces this view, points up our historic insensitivity to certain groups—not just the Negro and the poor—the Indian, Mexican, and Filipino as well.

Those who stress disadvantaged America reject the economic deprivation thesis. While they agree limited income is important, they tend to emphasize the powerlessness of the poor, how they are socially invisible in the eyes of those more affluent. Compared with himself, the Negro economically is better off today than he was ten years ago. Yet Thomas Pettigrew has shown that disadvantage has grown steadily more acute. Relative, not absolute, poverty and isolation are the rub. Similar in relative positions are the continuing conditions of the disadvantaged when compared to the ever-increasing promises of amelioration: antipoverty programs, civil rights reforms, urban renewal projects. Only by comparisons can one know his own inferior position.

With so little known about the poor and even less about their intellectual development, the cumulative deficit thesis is also questioned. The void is exposed by terms like "cultural deprivation" and descriptions of disadvantage couched in absent middle-class values. Ralph Ellison has also denied the relevance of the Americanization of immigrants of Jewish experience with discrimination as models for understanding the "disadvantaged." In a debate with Irving Howe, he remarked, "Things don't look like that from the black skin looking out."

To be disadvantaged, concludes this view, is to feel the pain of being labeled disadvantaged. It is defenselessness against compensatory programs hastily assembled by those whose true objective is to preserve white neighborhood schools. It is being ministered *at* by social workers who stigmatize "the clients" and, in fact, increase dependency. When ignoring the moral failures in our history, we demand that the disadvantaged overcome their background by rejecting home and family, the disadvantaged protest, "I cannot so easily put aside my identity."

Discrimination is common ground to both views of "disadvantage." Those who emphasize America's flaw point less to overt bars and more to subtle acts that come from "doing things as usual." The words "de facto segregation" have grown up to describe societal discrimination in housing, jobs, and schools. While not supported by laws, their effect is equally deadly. In this connection the compensatory approach in schools can provide no real solution. Schools remain white-controlled and segregation continues to expand. It thus comes as no surprise that civil rights demonstrations are active where compensatory programs are in greatest prominence. The drive for integration is not a drive to enter white schools, but one to broaden the cultural base of all schools for educational objectives. It is also to make them truly public. Quality education, if our goal is a free society, is not achievable for anyone—Negro or white—without the integration of our schools.

When some are barred and others intolerant, mankind as a whole is the loser. It is this understanding that should turn our attention to the humanities rather than to the more prevalent psychological emphasis which seeks to get the child "undeprived" before he gets any "learning." The humanities embrace all learning and skills which accelerate man in his becoming what he can be. It is because the humanities are fundamentally concerned with the human condition and its betterment that they have such high relevance both to a group stigmatized as "culturally deprived" and to a society with pervasive patterns of inhumane behavior.

The humanities, in a sense, have always been concerned with man's disadvantages. Originally they included the *trivium* on words (grammar, logic, and rhetoric), and the *quadrivium* of things (geometry, arithmetic, astronomy, and music). The content has changed since classical times, with secularism, science, and the study of society—but all along a basic unity remains: concern with what men can do, and knowledge to reach those goals. It is understandable that the disadvantaged themselves dwell too much on limitations to be overcome, on the legal-social barriers, and too little on the fruits that will accrue to all when man's wholeness is achieved. It is harder to account for the American Council of Learned Societies' failure to mention the "disadvantaged" in the *Report of the Commission on the Humanities* (1964).

The quest to free man, the historical concern of the humanities, is no less the focus today. The forms this takes, according to Richard P. McKeeon, are those of increasing man's discovery power, refining his ability to use the past, and bringing men to act when knowledge and power are at hand. Thus, in a sense, the concern with the humanities today remains as with the Greeks: the proper human uses of relevant words and things.

The first item, as in Shaw's *Pygmalion,* is better use of words. The art of utterance, the ability to communicate thought with power and fluency, is one of the fundamental needs of the disadvantaged. Behind the words must be experience, the basis of communication. Appreciation of structure and design, comprehensiveness of view, of insight, and of system, come hard without experience. Nor can one be assured these several arts will develop simply by exposure blessed by middle class or social power. It is being read to as a preschooler, having books in the house, the trip to the museum, that are required. Cultural enrichment is that which prompts the child to expand his view of reality; it promotes his spirit of wonder. Thomas Merton writes inside a monastery, Schweitzer in a jungle. It is not things or places so much as systematic discouragement that dries up one's experience.

Words grounded in experience illuminate values. And here, too, is relevance, for the disadvantaged are often told to change their values or else to go and get some. The humanities' approach would require that these demands, these moral judgments, rest in understanding. The first step is to weigh the various perspectives on reality including those of the poor and ostracized. No war on poverty, mindful of the humanities, would have delayed so long before including the poor. Judgments of others, in short, should follow, not precede, inquiry. The task of the humanities, and, one would think, of all good education, is to strive to understand what understanding is. Socrates, for one, believed that knowledge of the good would leave man pursuing nothing else.

Values formulated in words and expressed in action are not enough. There must be style, if one would remain true to the humanities. The esthetic dimension is communication so efficient and action so purposeful that elegance is radiated. The discordances have been removed. Is not the unlovely way the disadvantaged are seen much of the problem? To be known as disadvantaged blocks out much of anything else. The label "problem" increases social separation and may itself justify the mistreatment the disadvantaged receive.

This cursory look at the humanities prompts one to ask what has greater relevance for the education of the disadvantaged. How has it happened that schools of education and social work, rather than those of the liberal arts, have dominated this field?

Even for those still emphasizing the child's needs, there is a large place for the humanities in our schools. It is to literature that teachers should turn to overcome the poverty of experience. Are not Grimm, Carroll, Graham, Aesop the basic readers, and the lifeless *Dick and Jane* at best for suggested-reading lists? Would not the deportment task of teachers diminish if students had ample opportunities for acting out? Drama, a transliterated Greek word, means a thing done. To live up to this meaning is more than talking literary forms or discussing characters. The fine and performing arts are personalized expressions of conflicts, aspirations, and fears. The tense of drama is current—the present working itself towards destiny. *Hamlet* is a poet's construct; his reality is in the reader's mind. It is we who are Hamlet. "More than any other art," wrote Arthur Miller, "theater calls for relevance. The play must convince that this is the way it is now in human intercourse." Drama is a tool for understanding. It permits telling others who the actors are, as well as letting actors know a world beyond themselves. Much great drama, too, is familial. For those who see family relationships as crucial there is limitless material in *Antigone, Agamemnon,* and virtually all of O'Neill.

Much that is familiar can also be found in poetry, because it is concentrated expression of the human mind in rhythmical language. This should be particularly appropriate for the disadvantaged whose attention spans are said to be short, for those for whom nothing but the existential is of interest. There is even more when poetry is set to music, especially in folk songs, spirtuals, the blues, and now the songs of the Civil Rights movement—for they rise out of the disadvantaged themselves.

But more than content, the humanities suggest to teachers attitudes necessary for teaching disadvantaged students. At heart this is belief that freedom is man's proper condition. Carl Rogers's *On Becoming a Person* and Philip Morrison's *Experimenters in the Classroom* draw heavily on this spirit by presenting teaching as the art of liberating the student. De-emphasizing content, they seek not good listeners or good memorizers, but real experimenters, not the empty "why?" but the internalized insight that often comes from manipulation of objects. They see the formulation of questions by students as more important than teacher-supplied answers. Both have high tolerance for the novel. They urge teachers to enter the students' world of feeling and meaning. To see things as the student does requires withholding judgment—the teacher must cultivate openness in himself to see reality in a new way. The attitude of the teacher then becomes one of warmth, interest, respect, and expectation, because the teacher now is learning with the student. The belief that the disadvantaged child has something of value to offer is precisely that attitude of which he is most deprived!

The teacher who would liberate must see student potential at least in equal measure to statistics suggestive of his limitations. Greater use of the humanities would help produce this balance. It would shift the focus—a little—from the failings of the child versus the middle class to the America that could be. In that new emphasis the teacher would see that the disadvantaged have much to teach America, especially about the nature of freedom. It is true that those who have not had freedom are most preoccupied with it. In America the Negro has been concerned with little else. Those with negative thoughts about the disadvantaged should read Frederick Douglas, Henry McNeal Turner, or W. E. B. DuBois; see Martin Duberman's *In White America;* or sing aloud "We Shall Overcome!" The idea that the disadvantaged bring what America long has needed is not new. Alexis deTocqueville in 1831 visited our prisons and wrote the first reasoned account of democratic government in America. In *De la Democratie en Amerique* he pointed out America's problem as being born free and therefore perhaps not knowing the real value of freedom.

To continue to deprecate the disadvantaged child, his home and culture is to prevent the disadvantaged from giving to America what America most needs. The price of this imposed separation, this social ostracism, even—or especially—when accompanied by impersonal compensatory educational and welfare programs, can only bring the social breakdown that Baldwin predicted and Los Angeles now presents in sample form. The approach of the humanities could perhaps turn us away from discordances of guilt and hatred, and toward the harmony of an integrated society.

To be in the learning enterprise with the disadvantaged is in our time an exciting opportunity. The enlargement of freedom is what education is about.

So, educators, drink deep from the humanities, the arts of all—even of disadvantaged—mankind.

Humanities and the Disadvantaged

Marjorie B. Smiley

A growing interest in humanities programs for secondary school students and widespread concern with programs for disadvantaged children of all ages are two of the notable developments in education in the nineteen sixties. But these developments are not usually discussed together, and in a strict sense the humanities are not to be found in programs for educationally disadvantaged students, despite a number of efforts to "enrich" their school work by trips to theatres and museums, and more recently, by offering them out-of-school experiences in music, theatre, graphic arts, and film-making. Is it reasonable to propose that the humanities be included in educational programs for the disadvantaged?

At present it appears that there is little place for the disadvantaged in humanities courses. A recent questionnaire survey of such offerings in secondary schools throughout the country report these courses usually limited to senior high school grades and to above average and academically superior students.[1] Cumulative academic failure causes a majority of poor children to drop out of school before they reach senior high school; of those who remain, many suffer from deficits in reading which bar them from courses typically organized around "Great Books" or equally difficult readings in contemporary literature, the social sciences, and philosophy. Some advocates of humanities programs argue that they should be open to all students, and that upper elementary grade students might also profit from them. Since humanities programs tend to center on themes of universal human interest, and to the extent that they incorporate music and the graphic arts to extend the meanings of the printed word, it is suggested they may have particular appeal to non-academic-minded students.[2] Humanities programs in some schools are open to average students, but the literature to date does not report Humanities courses for students who are educationally retarded. This is hardly surprising, since a survey of special programs in English for the disadvantaged found few such programs which made a point of teaching literature.[3]

Are humanities programs, then, too difficult, or for other reasons inappropriate

[1] Carolyn A. Glass and Richard J. Miller, "Humanities Courses in Secondary Schools," *Educational Theory,* (July 1967).

[2] William R. Clauss, "The Humanities, Not a Course, but a Way of Life," *Clearing House,* (May 1967).

[3] National Council of Teachers of English, *Language Programs for the Disadvantaged,* (The Council, 1965).

in the education of disadvantaged students? Although difficulty, at least in humanities programs centered on the reading of Great Books, is a real obstacle, prevailing notions about and attitudes toward underprivileged and educationally retarded students are probably more important deterrents.

Conant's perception of underprivileged youths as an unemployed and illiterate reservoir of "social dynamite"—confirmed by statistics of disproportionately high unemployment and delinquency rates and below grade reading scores—was a major influence in the legislation for and actual development of poverty programs in education. Preparation for employment and education for basic literacy were given priority in most of the special programs for the disadvantaged; they still constitute their dominant emphases. Within this context literature and the arts find a place only as they are "practical" or, tangentially "recreational." The mastery of reading skills becomes a prerequisite for responsive and creative experiences in the arts.

But the "disadvantage" of poor children generally and of poor children in minority groups especially is more than unemployment and its physical consequences. It is, as well, the disadvantage of spending the first years of childhood in environments which lack the wealth and variety of objects, activities, and types of verbal intereaction which help to develop "readiness" for learning in schools designed for more advantaged children. It is the compounded disadvantage of schooling in schools, themselves less well equipped and staffed than middle class schools, in a system which categorizes and focuses on learning deficits rather than on potential strengths. It is, finally, the overwhelming disadvantage of rejection and consequent alienation by which one loses his very humanity, his self. It is these disadvantages of environmental deprivation, and of cultural alienation which must underlie the humanities in educational programs for poor and educationally retarded students.

Cognitive Development. One of the most significant recent developments in the conceptualization of intelligence has been the shift from earlier views of intelligence as a relatively stable entity, within the dimensions of heredity and developmental norms, to a view in which intelligence is a much more potentially labile product of the individual's interaction with his environment. In this formulation the child's environment, *and the quality of his interaction with it,* have enormous consequences for his cognitive development. Recognition of the importance of these early experiences underlies the educational efforts of Martin Deutsch to provide a "therapeutic" learning environment for children of pre-school age. In Deutsch's experimental classrooms children encounter a wide range of visual and aural stimuli and are motivated to respond actively and verbally to them. Through ordering, comparing, and grouping the objects in this "enriched" world, and through verbalizing his perceptions, the child from a deprived environment is aided in moving from the initial concrete stages of learning towards the representational or iconic stage in which he is able, in Bruner's terms, to deal with larger areas of his environment in relational and analytical constructs.

Perhaps these experiences seem at first glance to have little relevance to a discussion of humanities programs. In fact, it is just such intellectual operations which are essential to teaching and learning in the humanities. For if there is anything upon which spokesmen for such programs are agreed, it is that students must perceive, react to, relate, and generalize their insights about the music, art, and literature presented to them. In these respects, the teaching and learning processes and the choice of interdisciplinary content in Deutsch's prototype head start classes have basic elements in common with humanities programs at more advanced levels. So conceived, the humanities can and should be a part of the curriculum for *all* children from their earliest schooling; for disadvantaged children such a curriculum may be of special value in compensating for impoverished learning environments in home and neighborhood.

An additional reason for thinking that the humanities may be of particular importance in advancing the cognitive development of underprivileged children is based on emerging evidence of the existence of different learning strengths in different ethnic and social class groups. Children from deprived environments who are low achievers in school and in school-related tests may show marked inventiveness and creativity in such non-academic tasks as story telling and responses to Rorschach cards.[4] On the basis of their study of disadvantaged high and low school achievers, these authors suggest that "the schools may be overlooking a possible strength in divergent thinking which even the low achievers possess while over-emphasizing convergent tasks with the right answer."[5] The humanities, because of the possibilities they afford for spontaneous emotional reactions, and the opportunities they present for original, non-stero-typed perceptions, seem uniquely suited to promote intellectual growth in the disadvantaged. Interdisciplinary approaches, variety of art forms, and multiplicity of styles and modes in the humanities inhibit the search for "right" answers, and invite divergent ones.

Furthermore, because the humanities approach and illuminate intellectual content through the arts, they can have special appeal for students whose life-styles and attitudes are described as "expressive." Because, as some observers believe, deprivation and discrimination block the development of confidence in the individual's ability to control his own destiny, Negro life styles tend to be "expressive" rather than "instrumental."

A curriculum rich in the arts and in creative activities should be particularly effective in schools attended by deprived children of Negro and other minority groups. This orientation is often negatively regarded in our society, where aggressive and manipulative behaviors are admired, especially with respect to males. It is not necessary to debate the merits of these contending values, but to agree that we might be well advised to capitalize on whatever characteristics of

---

[4]Helen H. Davidson and Judith W. Greenberg, *"School Achievers from a Deprived Background,"* Associated Education Services Corporation Project No. 2805, The City College of New York under a grant from the U. S. Office of Education, (May 1967).

[5]*Ibid.* p. 136.

low achieving students we are able to identify. Stodolsky and Lesser make a strong case for equalizing educational opportunity by differentiating educational experiences in terms of the different learning strengths of children from different backgrounds.[6]

Cultural Alienation. Another crucial justification for including humanities programs in the curricula of disadvantaged youth follows from definitions of disadvantage in terms of cultural alienation, a condition at least equally characteristic of youth from affluent families. An additional complexity is that many, perhaps still the majority, of economically deprived youth are desperately eager to acquire the goods and skills to enter into the world of the dominant, middle-class society. However, an increasing number of the disadvantaged seem to be turning against these values; these are the culturally alienated, those who seek not only their own power, but their own heritage, a change of culture. What is the role of the humanities in the education of the culturally alienated?

It is easy to turn to the humanities as a mediator by means of which the alienated may become part of a dominant culture. Literature and the arts embody the values of a culture, and they do so powerfully because they carry metaphors which represent a way of life. The patience of Job, the tower of Babel, the Oedipus complex, Faustian man, the Noble Savage, the contending forces of nature and the city, these metaphoric commonplaces of Western culture illustrate and determine our ways of interpreting experience. They constitute a kind of *lingua franca* among those who have passed through a common educational program. Teachers of the disadvantaged frequently complain that their students have no understanding of these and like metaphors. "They don't even know what the American eagle stands for," these teachers lament. The absence of common symbols constitutes a barrier to communication in the classroom, but what is more significant, as cultural historians warn, it signals rifts in a common culture. As Archibald MacLeish puts it, "A world ends when its metaphor has died."

Certainly disadvantaged students—in common with others—should have continuing opportunities, beginning in the elementary grades, for learning, through the humanities, key ideas of our culture. But it would be naive to expect that disadvantaged students or any others alienated from today's world will come to terms with it through exposure to symbols which no longer seem to them truly representative of the world they live in. Underprivileged students will learn the meaning of the American eagle not by being told about it, or by learning its history, or by drawing it, but when a sense of freedom becomes a viable part of their own lives. For young people generally, many of the ideas, and hence the symbols characteristic of the art and literature traditionally included in humanities courses seem irrelevant to their concerns. If the humanities are to speak to the alienated, we must be sure that iconoclastic, revolutionary, even demolitional elements, to use the evocative tags employed by Goldberg, are a

---

[6] Susan S. Stodolsky and Gerald Lesser, "Learning Programs in the Disadvantaged," *Harvard Educational Review,* (Fall 1967).

part of the program.[7] The literary metaphors of *Nausea, Waiting for Godot, and The Invisible Man,* must find a place in humanities programs if they are to speak to today's youth. Unfortunately, even academically successful high school and college students may find it difficult, because of the limits of their life experience, to grasp the serious existentialist literature which carries these metaphors, these new visions of the human condition. To what extent are these works accessible to the alienated who are also educationally retarded, who read reluctantly and poorly, and who, in addition, have learned to distrust the whole world of the school?

Perhaps a true story about a "disadvantaged" youth in a summer Upward Bound program will suggest one answer to this dilemma. The student of the story, a sixteen-year-old Negro youth, had participated in the picture taking activities of a camera workshop in this program, although he had not contributed to discussions in the group sessions conducted by the photographer-teacher. One day he brought the photographer a picture he had taken and developed himself. It was a shot, taken from above, of a grilled manhole cover and crumpled newspapers, some charred by fire, caught between the manhole bars. The boy held out his picture and waited, silently, for a reaction from the photographer.

"Well," said the photographer, pleased that the boy was interested enough to take the initiative in presenting the picture, "it's an interesting design you've got there—the straight lines of manhole cover and the crumpled shapes of the paper—"

"Man," the boy said, "don't you see? Black and White in jail together."

This story demonstrates the vivid and potent imaginative gift frequently observed by teachers who have established situations in which disadvantaged and educationally retarded students can work creatively outside traditional classroom or subject boundaries. The story also suggests that the exploration of graphic images may serve as a powerful introduction to the humanities in programs designed for the disadvantaged. As with literature, of course, it is likely that such students will respond most quickly and deeply to those visual images which represent the world they inhabit, the sensations impinging on their lives. The images of isolation, of violence, of anonymity, and of deterioration in the works of artists like Munch, Leonard Baskin, Henry Moore, Magritte, and Picasso are likely to have more impact on these students, as on today's youth generally, than those of Renaissance painters or classical sculptors. For the same reasons that modern artists turned to the arts of non-literate cultures, modern students may find that masks and totems speak to them. The Benin bronzes as well as, and probably prior to the Parthenon, should be a part of humanities programs for the disadvantaged.

As disadvantaged and academically unsuccessful students are moved by strong

[7]Maxwell H. Goldberg, "The Humanities and the Alienated Adolescent," *School and Society,* (April 15, 1967).

contemporary visual metaphors so are they responsive to the literature of the theatre. Free theatre groups bringing not only *Purlie Victorious* and *In White America,* but also *Waiting for Godot* into Southern rural communities where ill-schooled Negros gathered to see their first plays, report that these relatively sophisticated plays were enthusiastically and apparently perceptively received. Theatre, contemporary ballads, and films are a gateway to the study of literature particularly accessible even to students who are slow and reluctant readers. Those who would bring the humanities to the disadvantaged must be bold enough to begin with and probably to emphasize the modern and the folk, the primitive and the popular. Certainly the uniquely contemporary arts of film and television must be treated as integral rather than as supplementary to such programs.

Finally. Humanities programs for the disadvantaged must capitalize on the kind of creative capacities exemplified by the youth who saw in crumpled newspapers in a manhole cover the common imprisonment of black man and white man. Through photography, film-making, through music, theatre, and dance improvisations and performances, through *making* as well as viewing art even those students who have been shamed by failures in school to believe they have nothing worth saying can have their say. In such activities, if teachers can learn forebearance for students' hesitancy, lack of discipline, and hostility, the disadvantaged can begin to reap the benefits of the humanities as a way of ordering and illuminating experience.

Let the main ideas which are introduced into a child's education be few and important, Whitehead proposed, and let them be thrown into every combination possible. The child should make them his own, and should understand their application here and now in the actual circumstances of his life. From the very beginning of his education, the child should experience discovery. The discovery which he has to make is that general ideas give an understanding of that stream of events which pours through his life, which is his life.[8]

The special value of humanities programs for the disadvantaged, then, lies in their potential contributions to the cognitive development and acculturation of children whose academic achievement is restricted by environmental deprivation and whose development as individuals valuing themselves and their culture is impaired by prejudice, poverty, and consequent powerlessness. Humanities programs for these children should:

1. begin in the elementary grades
2. start with and emphasize graphic arts, music, and theatre if literature in print presents reading difficulties
3. draw substantially on contemporary arts and literature which express the dilemmas and visions of our time
4. capitalize on students' responsiveness to mass media, especially cinema and TV

[8] Alfred North Whitehead, *The Aims of Education* (Mentor, 1952), p. 14.

5. include the literature and art of non-Western cultures
6. rely primarily on thematic rather than formal or historical organization of content
7. involve students actively, creatively in film making and photography, in painting, sculpturing, dancing, singing, acting, and writing
8. emphasize learning by discovery rather than through exposition

There is an incident in Philip Roth's *Goodbye, Columbus* in which a young Negro boy ventures timidly but determinedly into the imposing halls of the New York Public Library at Forty-second street. "Please," he asked, "where is the heart section?" And the perceptive hero of the novel, working at the library, divined his wish and brought him to the section where the illustrated art books were shelved. Day after day, the boy came back to pour over the pictures, especially over the South Sea paintings of Gauguin, where, he noted, there were beautiful people, "like me." In the humanities freshly conceived, disadvantaged students can find their "heart section."

Humanities for All Students

Sheila Schwartz

In 1964, the national need for secondary school humanities courses was given official recognition in the *Report of the Commission on the Humanities*. The opening statement of this *Report* said the following:

The humanities are the study of that which is most human. Throughout man's conscious past they have played an essential role in forming, preserving, and transforming the social, moral, and aesthetic values of every man in every age. One cannot speak of history or culture apart from the humanities. They not only record our lives; our lives are the very substance they are made of. Their subject is every man. We propose, therefore, a program for all our people, a program to meet a need no less serious than that for national defense. We speak, in truth, for what is being defended—our beliefs, our ideals, our highest achievements.[1]

In the above statement, and throughout, the *Report* emphasizes the need of all men for the humanities, and yet, four years later, this is still the *rara avis* of the secondary curriculum. Many schools still have not acknowledged this new area, others have only fragmented courses that are suspended in limbo, and still others regard the humanities as a reward to be offered to only a handful of outstanding students.

The group of students that is in greatest need of the humanities is not getting them. I refer to the disadvantaged, that is, the group of students that has little or

[1]Report of the Commission on the Humanities. *The American Council of Learned Societies, 345 East 46 Street, New York, 10017, pp. 4-5.*

no chance of exposure to the values of the humanities in their past, present, or future lives outside school. Ironically, the humanities is also in great need of these students if this area is to be the source of change and relevance in the curriculum and not merely a reordering of the liberal arts.

There are many reasons why humanities courses have not been offered to these students, but the major one is the fact that a traditional view of curriculum has been applied to this new area. Subject matter has been reorganized and expanded for humanities courses, but subject matter is still viewed primarily as a body of knowledge to be given to students by teachers.

This traditional view of curriculum can be noted easily in descriptions of current courses. In the NCTE's 1968 list of *Annotated Humanities Programs* almost every page describes the students for whom the courses are intended as "above average," "gifted," and as possessing the "highest reading scores." There are no courses specifically for the disadvantaged and *only five* that may possibly bear some relevance. The first, from a high school:

Two-year humanities program organized for general students (juniors and seniors); *some have ability but appear to be lazy, others have minimal ability* [underlining, mine]. Theme in junior section—"The Dignity of Man"; in senior section—"Who Am I?" Objective: translate and interrelate the world of reality and the world of imagination within the following areas—music, language, literature, history, philosophy, art, drama, science, physical education. Relationship between form and function developed. Hope is that each student will shape constructive personal philosophy embracing courage, pride, and purpose toward self and fellow man; that he will recognize and accept values of others in conflict with own. Extensive use of A-V materials.[2]

The irony of this description is evident: "some have ability but appear to be lazy, others have minimal ability. Theme in junior section—The Dignity of Man." What does it mean to "have ability but appear to be lazy"? What does it mean to have "minimal ability" and in what? For a humanities course, one might ask if this means minimal ability to be a human being.

In order to answer these questions it is necessary to ask what exactly is the purpose of humanistic education. Harry S. Broudy, leading theoretician for the humanities, defines the goals in terms of the perfection of certain capacities through learning. These capacities are the following:

(1) that selfhood, or distinctly human existence, has ontological status and metaphysical primacy, (2) that human selves have some degree of autonomy in thought and action and are not merely the reflexive responses to external pressures, and (3) that all human beings have capacities for intellectual, moral, and aesthetic experience that will not be fully developed without education.[3]

[2] Richard R. Adler and Arthur Applebee, compilers, *Annotated Humanities Programs,* NCTE, 1968.
[3] Harry S. Broudy, "Science 'Versus' Humanities in the School Curriculum: A Philosophical Analysis of the Present Crisis," *The Journal of Philosophy,* Vol. LV, No. 23, November 6, 1958, p. 996.

If we agree with Broudy that these capacities are inseparable from existence itself, then for educators to deny to any students a program of self-cultivation that will "preserve the identity and dignity of the individual"[4] on the basis of some unrelated measure of "ability," frustrates the basic purpose of the humanities. For, Broudy continues, human excellence is always constant in form, it is particular only in content.

> The excellent Hottentot and the excellent New Yorker have the same form in that they both represent a development of their human capacities. They are, therefore, recognizable as brothers under the skin, but neither can be mistaken for the other.[5]

The difference between the Hottentot and the New Yorker "lies in the *content* of the cultural materials used in developing the capacities."[6] But they are both human beings and therefore both possess the capacity for humanities education— as does the disadvantaged student.

A second humanities course description follows:

> Latin Heritage course directed to underachievers and inner-city students. Offered primarily for 10th-grade students, open to all students; year's course; during the 1968-69, expanded to 2 years. Team teaching, block scheduling. Curriculum: Greek and Latin contribution to the modern world, famous men of Antiquity, daily life of ancient world, contribution to English language, mythology. A-V material stressed. Taught by Latin teachers and supervised by Foreign Language Department.[7]

Again, to return to my original point, this is viewing the humanities in a traditional way rather than in a way that is appropriate to humanities education. The above course description makes no mention of its goals or of the values on which it is based. It seems doubtful that it is based on any *student* values. The daily life of the ancient world is exceptionally remote even for the most highly motivated students, and it has almost no relevance to contemporary inner-city life. It is evident, in both of the above descriptions, that in these humanities courses the student has a better chance to learn facts about other men than to develop the capacities for intellectual, moral, and aesthetic experience that Broudy attributes to all men.

What then should happen in a humanities course for the disadvantaged? The first essential is a particular *point of view*. The best humanities course for the disadvantaged that I have encountered took place at the Winston-Salem Advancement School.[8] They describe their approach as follows:

[4]*Ibid.*
[5]*Ibid.*
[6]*Ibid.*
[7]Annotated Humanities Programs.
[8]*This school is now located in Philadelphia.*

Providing students with vital, dramatic experiences relevant to their own lives—as a film about prejudice, the story of a man about to die, a painting that expresses a religious reverence toward nature, or a symphony more moving because it was written by a great composer going deaf, as these and many other things are relevant to all our lives—providing students with their experiences through the arts, then provoking and guiding discussion. . . . The method is inductive, or Socratic, proceeding from an immediate experience which the class has in common—a painting, film, symphony—to generalizations they can make about that experience. . . .[9]

The second essential is a *better setting* than is now found in most ghetto schools. The sterile, ugly, comfortless rooms that now exist are antithetical to the very spirit of the humanities. And humanists realize this. A good example of this can be seen in the newest Police Athletic League center in Brooklyn. It is located in a slum, Bedford-Stuyvesant, but once inside one finds pleasant meeting rooms with wall-to-wall carpeting, good lighting, soft, comfortable arm chairs and sofas, and ash trays. The humane director of the Brooklyn PAL, told me: "We all know that color and comfort affect our moods and yet we persist in ignoring the importance of setting for these youngsters. This is the only chance most of these kids ever have to sit in a comfortable room and read or talk." These reputedly destructive ghetto youngsters take exceptionally good care of this beautiful building that they feel belongs to them.

I cannot prove that creative thinking necessarily flourishes in an atmosphere of comfort and freedom, but I would think it far easier to elicit the open conversation that is at the heart of every humanities program in a setting that tells the students that we care about them.

The third essential for a humanities course for the disadvantaged is that it *originate in the real needs* of these students and not in the imaginations of curriculum planners. The course would begin with free and casual conversation in an evocative environment. Psychoanalysts know that they must elicit talk if they are to reach their patients. And the humanities teacher must be as skilled at eliciting and encouraging honest talk as the psychoanalyst. Teachers must have an unfaltering belief that there is value in student talk—perhaps *the* basic value of a humanities course.

Oscar Lewis, the anthropologist, used the talk he recorded as the basis for his fine books on the Mexican and Puerto Rican poor. In *The Children of Sanchez,* he describes his procedure:

In obtaining the detailed and intimate data of these life stories, I used no secret techniques, no truth drugs, no psychoanalytic couch. The most effective tools of the anthropologists are sympathy and compassion for the people he studies. What began as a professional interest in their lives turned into warm and lasting friendships. I became deeply involved in their problems and often felt as though I had two families to look after, the Sanchez family and my own. . . .

[9]From "The Communication Course" of the school.

The Sanchez family learned to trust and confide in me . . . . I did not follow the common anthropological practice of paying them as informants. . .and I was struck by the absence of monetary motivation in their relationship with me. Basically, it was their sense of friendship that led them to tell me their life stories. The reader should not underestimate their courage in bringing forth as they did the many painful memories and experiences of their lives . . . . They have often told me that if their stories would help human beings anywhere, they would feel a sense of accomplishment . . . . [10]

If disadvantaged students are freed to communicate, what would their real concerns be? Claude Brown in *Manchild in the Promised Land* says:

I heard myself saying, "I guess we ain't nothin' or nobody, huh, Dad?" He went on talking like he didn't even hear me, and I wasn't listening to what he was saying either.[11]

And again, I quote Claude Brown in reference to loneliness:

There was no place for me. I felt lonelier in Harlem than I'd felt when I first went to Wiltwyck. I couldn't go back to Wiltwyck—I had been trying to get away from there for years to get back to this. Now it seemed as though "this" wasn't there any more. It really was confusing for a while.[12]

Or we can listen to the words of Piri Thomas in the Puerto Rican equivalent of Manchild, *Down These Mean Streets:*

Man! How many times have I stood on the rooftop of
my broken-down building at night and watched the
bulb-lit world below.
Like somehow it's different at night, this my Harlem.
There ain't no bright sunlight to reveal the stark
naked truth of garbage-lepered streets.
Gone is the drabness and hurt, covered by a friendly
night.

It makes clean the dirty-faced kids . . . .

YEE-AH! I feel like part of the shadows that make
company for me in this warm *amigo* darkness.
I am "My Majesty Piri Thomas," with a high on
anything and like a stoned king, I gotta survey my
kingdom.
I'm a skinny, dark-faced, curly-haired, intense
Porty-Ree-can—
Unsatisfied, hoping, and always reaching.

[10] Oscar Lewis, *The Children of Sanchez.* New York: Vintage Books, 1961, pp. xx-xxi.
[11] Claude Brown, *Manchild in the Promised Land* New York: The Macmillan Company, 1965, p. 95.
[12] *Ibid.*, p. 103.

I got a feeling of aloneness and a bitterness that's
growing and growing
Day by day into some kind of hate without *un nombre.*
Yet when I look down at the streets below, I can't help
thinking
It's like a great big dirty Christmas tree with lights
but no presents.
And man, my head starts growing bigger than my body
as it gets crammed full of hate.
And I begin to listen to the sounds inside me.
Get angry, get hating angry, and you won't be scared.
What have you got now? Nothing.
. . . Unless you cop for yourself.[13]

It is evident that the gap between the kinds of concerns expressed by the young writers above and the content of most humanities courses, is very wide.

The fourth essential is that *the teacher help the student to transcend his own needs and to join the mainstream of humanity.* The student must start with his own concerns but the course is inadequate if it stops there. It must do more than to provide an arena for self-expression. This is where it begins but not where it should end. Talk is useless unless it moves the students to new levels of self-understanding, empathy for others, and orientation to the world.

At San Quentin prison, a remarkable teacher named Cris Lovdjieff taught the kind of humanities program for the disadvantaged that I advocate. He was unaffected, honest, intelligent, and unafraid of his own emotions. He was the kind of teacher essential for the eliciting of basic concerns. His students called him "The Christ." One of them wrote:

The christ performed, in his silver-rimmed glasses reflecting the light in eye-twinkling flashes. He dressed like a college boy, betraying a penchant for simple sweaters and plain slacks of no particular distinction. He burned incense in his classroom when he lectured on religion, to evoke a certain mood. He was drawn to those students who seemed most impossible to teach—old men who had been illiterate all their lives and set in their ways. Lovdjieff didn't believe that anyone or anything in the Universe was "set in its ways."[14]

Lovdjieff's humanistic goal was to move his disadvantaged students beyond their own problems to an understanding of all people. This is how he taught "Love."

Once he lectured us all week on Love. He quoted what poets had said of Love, what novelists had said of Love, what playwrights had said of Love—he played tapes of Ashley Montagu on Love, tapes of Dr. Green on Love. Over the weekend, each student was to write an essay on his own conception of Love, mindful to have been influenced by what he had been listening to all week long.

[13]Piri Thomas, *Down These Mean Streets,* New York: A Signet Book, 1967, Prologue.
[14]Eldridge Cleaver, "The Guru of San Quentin," *Esquire,* April, 1967.

In the essay that I turned in, I explained that I did not love white people. I quoted Malcolm X:

"How can I love the man who raped my mother, killed my father, enslaved my ancestors, dropped atomic bombs on Japan, killed off the Indians, and keeps me cooped up in the slums? I'd rather be tied up in a sack and tossed into the Harlem River first!"

Lovdjieff refused to grade my paper. He returned it to me. I protested that he was being narrowminded and dogmatic in not understanding why I did not love white people, simply because he himself was white. He told me to talk with him after classes.

"How can you do this to me?" he asked.

"I've only written the way I feel," I said. Instead of answering, he cried.

"Jesus wept," I told him, and walked out.

This teacher's response, weeping, was certainly unorthodox, but his disadvantaged students understood that he wept for *them*. His popularity finally reached such a peak that prison authorities dismissed him from his teaching post. But he had achieved something with at least one student, the one who wrote this article. The student wrote:

After he had gone, and it dawned on us that he would never come back, memory of him seemed like the flame of a lamp flickering in the wind. Would it live? It is only now, years later, that I know such memories never die.

Lovdjieff had aimed for the highest kind of humanistic expression and education. Giving himself freely, he had taken his disadvantaged men (and who could be more disadvantaged than the victims of our penal system) and urged them to transcend hate, transcend the moment, transcend themselves to find peace and unity with all men. The prisoners did not always understand or agree with him. When he told them about Thomas Merton, they thought that anyone who would voluntarily seek imprisonment was "a nut." But the knowledge that Merton believed it possible to grow as a human being despite imprisonment, gave added possibility to the prisoners own potential for choice and growth in prison.

For those of us who wish to look, society provides constant examples that the kind of humanities program for the disadvantaged I advocate, can work. Claude Brown, Eldridge Cleaver, Piri Thomas, and Malcolm X are but a few of the disadvantaged who were able to develop their capacities for intellectual, moral, and aesthetic experience when they encountered *relevant* education. Humanities courses, starting where the student is, providing an environment in which he can talk and listen, and then supplying the connections between his problems and those of other men, is one means of providing this relevant education.

In 1966, Lawrence C. Howard, advocating this kind of education wrote:

Too little of the education of the disadvantaged has either the content or the spirit of the humanities. Since the disadvantaged are those who are limited, and the humanities are concerned with liberating man—this void is hard to understand. Part of the problem may be that "disadvantaged" has been viewed too narrowly as a deficiency of the child, and education not enough as the enlargement of freedom...the humanities should have a central role in the education of the disadvantaged. And since the humanities are the arts of freedom, such a shift may well permit the disadvantaged to help in the re-education of America.[15]

Nothing has changed since that article was published. The need is more urgent than ever, but still, the disadvantaged wait. The ideas that I have suggested are indeed simple: a humanities course that begins with relevance, placed in a better physical setting than is now found in most ghetto schools, and designed to link the needs of the students with the mainstream of humanity.

Those of us who believe "that all human beings have capacities for intellectual, moral, and aesthetic experience that will not be fully developed without education"[16] have a responsibility to extend humanities education to all our students. Here and now is our opportunity to "base our educational policy on the most generous and promising assumptions about human nature, rather than the most niggardly and pessimistic."[17]

Can the Arts "Turn On" Poor Kids to Learning?

Judith Murphy and Ronald Gross

Barbara Dean was, in her own words, "generally falling apart" when she joined the Job Corps at seventeen. She'd been making her perilous way alone in the adult world since she was twelve years old, had had only seven years of schooling, and seemed headed for disaster.

As is true at most Job Corps centers, new arrivals like Barbara are expected to devote a certain amount of their time to the creative arts, offered in an easygoing, inviting way. Soon Barbara displayed an unusual ability to express her ideas and feelings both in words and paint. The experience proved an eye-opener for her. "It's given me encouragement instead of more kicks in the teeth. People all of a sudden are different. I am finally somebody". From these initial—and, for her, unprecedented—achievements, Barbara went on to win a scholarship to a California high school. She plans to study sociology in college.

An extraordinary story of success? Of course. Many poor kids aren't turned on at all by the arts: the armor of deprivation is thick, and there's no magic arrow that will pierce it. But Barbara's story is by no means unique. There's remarkable recent evidence, from the Job Corps and elsewhere, that the arts constitute a potent—and strangely neglected—key for unlocking the hearts and minds of deprived youngsters. Pioneering educators, artists, and others around the country

[15] Lawrence C. Howard, "Teach Them the Arts of Freedom," *Saturday Review*, June 18, 1966, pp. 66-79.

[16] Harry S. Broudy, *op. cit.*

[17] William H. Boyer and Paul Walsh, "Are Children Born Unequal?" *Saturday Review*, October 19, 1968, p. 63.

have used this key to interest and motivate such children despite their psychological and academic hang-ups. Appealing directly to their creative impulses can apparently bring children out to a point where they are ready to benefit from instruction in the three R's and the standard academic subjects.

The evidence comes from diverse and scattered projects: until very recently this approach has had virtually no national coordination or support.

*In Los Angeles, the Watts Towers Art Center has for over five years been running free classes for the young people of the community. They come to paint, carve, build, and act.

*On a dingy street in the same sprawling ghetto, every week for more than a year, a dozen or so teenagers and adults have been meeting with novelist Budd Shulberg in a writing workshop. School dropouts and barely educated adults turn out work of sometimes astonishing quality. One man whose job is sweeping out a local bar has had a piece published in West, the Sunday magazine of the *Los Angeles Times*; another has had a television play produced on a national network; and a 55-year old woman, who never got through the eighth grade, has nearly completed a novel based on her childhood in the South—a novel whose drive and emotive power astonish her tutor and deeply move her classmates.

*In Harlem, world-famous soprano Dorothy Maynor, retired from the concert stage, now gives full time to the music school she organized in her husband's parish. Hundreds of improverished children come after school and on weekends to sing, dance, and learn to play instruments.

*In Santa Fe, N.M., a special boarding school supported by the U.S. Government enrolls every year several hundred young people from the nation's "forgotten" minority, the American Indian. They usually arrive silent, repressed, uneasy, and—by accepted academic measures—retarded. Immersed in a curriculum rich in art work of all kinds and keyed but not limited to their Indian heritage, students blossom into individuals, develop self-esteem and pride, and gradually transfer their new-found confidence to mastering the routines of arithmetic and English and the other standard school subjects.

*In Delano, Calif., the striking grape-pickers have formed a travelling theatre. Performing on the tailgate of a ton-and-a-half truck, going out where the field workers are with the message of "Huelga" (the strike), El Teatro Campesiono uses strikers as actors. Improvising their parts as scabs, contractors, growers, and strikers, the performers are helping an impoverished and exploited community to understand and define itself.

*On Manhattan's Lower East Side, the Arts-for-Living Program at the Henry Street Settlement embraces a music school, a playhouse for drama and dance, and a pottery and art school—all designed to reach young people not yet motivated toward the arts nor toward any kind of disciplined study. Experienced artists team up with trained social workers to help children find new ways to express themselves, gain self-confidence, and taste the joys of creation and working together. Theatre and music are the outstanding art forms here. "Pet's House Productions" have gained the favorable notice of the nation's leading drama critics, and—more important—have given the performing youngsters their first experience in fulfilling a recognized and rewarding social role.

Art in Instructional Programs. "The work of these innovators and others have shown that the arts can help educators reach and teach the deprived child," says Kathryn Bloom, director of the Arts and Humanities Program in the U.S. Office of Education. "As a lubricant in the learning process, the arts can motivate and stimulate, reinforce a child's sense of his own worth, and ultimately bring many poverty-damaged children back into the mainstream of education. I'm convinced this may be one of the most important keys in the history of education for unlocking the doors which shut the disadvantaged child out of our educational system."

If Miss Bloom is right, one trouble is that the key is rusty from disuse, and those who would use it effectively need the finesse of an educational Willy Sutton. In most "compensatory education" programs around the country the arts—if represented at all—are provided on a hit-and-run, "cultural enrichment" basis: a concert one week, a museum visit the next. Since the arts rate low in academic status, educators generally don't ever consider using painting, music, and theatre as classroom devices in *instructional* programs, for the poor or anyone. Moreover, the Office of Economic Opportunity—Sargent Shriver's beleaguered H.Q. for the war on poverty—provides virtually no support for the arts in its community-action programs, preferring vocationally-oriented training courses. Private foundations and state arts councils haven't been much interested either. In the few cases where substantial money is available—as under Title I of the Elementary and Secondary Education Act—very few programs have been initiated involving the arts as teaching and learning tools.

One baleful result is that little or nothing is known about precisely how and why the arts can be so potent with the poor. "The teacher who wants to use the arts in this way has virtually no literature to turn to," says Ronald Silverman, professor of art education at California State College at Los Angeles, who is trying to remedy this gap under an Office of Education grant.

Yet the pragmatic evidence piles up, and successful pioneering projects strongly proclaim that there's educational gold in these hills. A closer look at one notable project suggests why.

Ted Katz and Communication. Ted Katz is a young teacher who developed an extraordinary Communication Course at the North Carolina Advancement School in Winston-Salem. (New arrivals often take him for a fellow student and ask the way to Mr. Katz's class.) The school was established at the initiative of Governor Terry Sanford, in 1964, to meet the problem of educational underachievement in the state. Since then a statewide sample of eighth-grade boys of evident ability but poor academic performance has been brought to the institution for three-month stints designed to revitalize their powers of learning. Grants from the state, the Carnegie Corporation, and the U.S. Office of Education have supported the project under the auspices of the Learning Institute of North Carolina.

In a school brimming with talent and imagination, Ted Katz's Communication Course has achieved nationwide renown. Its objective is to "bring life into the classroom" through the arts. The course uses both the popular and the fine arts, including short stories, poetry, films, music, photography, dance, and painting, to excite students about problems relevant to their own lives. Films like "On the Waterfront," paintings by Andrew Wyeth, stories by Hemingway—to name a few examples—thrust into the classroom the most intimate and potent ideas and feelings, in ways which encourage rather than inhibit student response.

From the first day the boys are immersed in art—pictures on the walls, music in the air—a gentle but persistent bombardment of the senses. As a youngster shows signs of interest ("Who is that guy who cut off his ear?"), the teacher responds briefly and to the point.

The method throughout is inductive, proceeding always from an experience which the class has just shared. Discussion is the primary agent of learning. For example, ten brief musical selections are presented, and the boys are invited to imagine the kind of girl each selection brings to mind. Or dance is sneaked in as a form of athletics: how do dancers achieve those jumps and turns so effortlessly?

In writing, the students' papers are accepted at first without criticism: sheer output is the chief goal, in order to permit maximum freedom of expression and imagination. Once the teacher can evoke this, he puts more and more stress on perceptiveness and originality. Only much later does he insist on technical competence.

Thirty-four teachers in public schools scattered across North Carolina are already using the Communication Course through materials prepared by the school. The response is enthusiastic. "I'll never teach any other way again," said one teacher.

Having demonstrated the approach at the Advancement School, Ted Katz recently moved into the mainstream of American education by joining the Philadelphia school system, where he will assist an imaginative new superintendent in setting up a similar program on a three-year experimental basis.

Alarms and Obstacles. Despite the arresting evidence of projects like Katz's, the notion of using the arts to help the poor faces formidable obstacles in American schools. The general neglect of education through art—despite its eloquent proponents from Plato to Herbert Read and John Dewey—has already been noted. The divergent temperaments of artists and educators make for further difficulties. Painters, musicians, sculptors, dancers, actors, and writers—presumably those who are most "hip" to the potency of the arts—are fiercely individualistic and often suspicious of "square" bureaucrats and teachers who they feel dilute or pervert the arts. Conversely, teachers and educational administrators view with alarm the prospect of putting children for whom they are responsible in the hands of "odd" characters who most likely have no demonstrated capacity for dealing with youngsters successfully, and who for sure are not "certified."

It seems clear that the full utilization of the arts by inner city schools would require the re-training of teachers, the waiving of certain certification restrictions to permit use of practicing artists in the program (called for by Commissioner of Education Harold Howe in a recent speech), and the provision of facilities suitable to such work.

But even when these problems have been solved, there's the question of the attitude of poor children to the arts and artists. Here expert opinion is conflicting. Harold Cohen, who has had notable success using the arts with "unreachable" delinquents at the National Training School for Boys, a Washington D.C. reformatory, warns that to these kids "artist" means "queer," and art means either something worth lots of money which is hung in a museum or in a rich guy's house, or what you find in "art magazines" and "art movies."

On the other hand, Melvin Roman, a psychologist and painter working in the South Bronx, out of the Albert Einstein College of Medicine, argues that "the artist-teacher, because of his magical and myth-making qualities, as well as his craft discipline and dedication, is almost inevitably a charismatic figure to adolescents."

Still another difficulty—but this one has its positive aspects—is that the uses of the arts are so diverse. Unlike one of the conventional academic subjects, or a purely vocational course, experience in the arts can have a wide variety of by-products beyond its intrinsic value, ranging from greater self-confidence to more refined taste, from new sensory awareness to an appreciation of the need for self-discipline and hard work, from perceptual skills to motivation for social action. But this diversity can produce arts programs whose purposes are vaguely defined and whose results are hard to measure. It's hard to state, let alone prove, the case for putting money behind the idea of using the arts as basic strategies to promote learning.

And even a clear definition of objectives is apt to be denounced as "cultural imperialism"—the imposition of middle-class cultural and artistic values on the poor. "In my experience with the 'disadvantaged,'" says Francis Ianni, formerly in charge of research at the U.S. Office of Education, "I've seen very few programs in the arts which don't attempt to take the best of what 'we' have to offer in order to help 'them' fit better into our world." (See "Cultivating the Arts of Poverty," *Saturday Review,* June 17, 1967.)

Towards Massive Support. Basic to many of these problems is "green power"—the money to support imaginative, wise, and enterprising applications of the arts to this major national problem. Fortunately, the sources of money seem increasingly—if tardily—receptive to such proposals. The Arts and Humanities Program in the Bureau of Research, Office of Education, held a developmental conference last November which brought together many of the leaders in the field, and later appointed Junius Eddy to the new post of director of programs for the deprived. The intention was to start the word around that federal agencies like the Office itself, and the Arts and Humanities Endowments, were looking for good projects to support. Eddy, who for years worked with the poor in the theatre program at Cleveland's inter-racial Karamu House, feels strongly that now the arts have to be moved from the neighborhood settlement houses and other places, right into the center of the school program for the deprived.

The view is gaining some powerful support. Congressman William Moorhead, a powerful voice for government support of the arts and humanities, said recently that in this area "the schools require more than just the example of a few islands of excellence if they are to achieve the needed progress. They require the massive support which can come only through the interest of national agencies with the resources to work in all the areas of the country, and at all levels of elementary and secondary education." Meanwhile, the private foundations are awakening to the opportunities in this field. For example, the Carnegie Corporation, which helped to support Ted Katz's Communication Course, is now helping New York's Whitney Museum and the Smithsonian in Washington to set up extension operations in the ghettoes.

There are, then, grounds for hoping that an implausible but engaging notion—that the arts can be used to help poor children in significant ways—will be given a fair trial. We may even discover thereby something important about the proper role of the arts in the education of *all* children. It would not be the first time—witness the work of Pestalozzi, of Montessori, of many of the early progressive educators—that new ideas tried out on deprived children demonstrated their worth for all. For poor kids are not that different from everybody else, and what turns them on may very well do the same for all kinds of children. The particular values embodied in the good arts classroom—individual expression and pace, non-competitiveness, learning by discovery—may be a fruitful model for all successful education.

High School and the Cultural Illiterate

Glendy Culligan

Are Plato and Picasso off Limits? Tom Jones, 16-year-old son of a skilled auto worker in Royal Oak, Mich., made a big decision as he entered the 10th grade at Dondero High this fall. Last Spring, Tom's counselor at Clara Barton Junior High told him that with his IQ he ought to think seriously about going to college. For a while, Tom did think about it, but the idea just didn't turn him on. Tom, who can do anything with his hands, knows he can step right into an apprenticeship at one of the big Detroit plants the day after graduation. After three years he can earn $10,000 a year as a tool and die maker and eventually he should be able to equal or top his father's present salary of $16,000. Like his dad, he can buy a split level in a good subdivision, a car, a TV, maybe even a hi-fi and enough books to fill the built-in bookcase in his den. His next-door neighbor, a college graduate, isn't doing any better. Why get all psyched up about a piece of paper that says B.A., if it doesn't pay off?

Tom's counselor has that piece of paper and he earns less than Tom's dad. The counselor couldn't convince the boy. Now he wonders whether Tom will be earning more and enjoying it less as he advances through the contractual certainties of a 20th century industrial career. Will Tom feel "that the universe is a machine and he a small cog in it," Clifton Fadiman's recent description of the plight of 20th century man overwhelmed by technology? Is he "growing up absurd" as another, more iconoclastic critic of education (Paul Goodman) phrased the plight of youth in a depersonalized society? Or, hopefully, is Tom learning something of value, something that will sustain his spirit after the chalk dust of his school has been supplanted by the metal dust of his factory?

In Tom's case, there is hope that 12 years in one of his area's best school systems will leave a residue of interests and ideas. At Barton, Tom was obliged to sample his cultural heritage through a compulsory exploratory program of music, art, and assorted hobby crafts. At Dondero, he intends to make art appreciation one of his electives.

Meanwhile and most important, this fall Tom will share an excellent new literature text with his college-bound classmates, for unlike many school districts, Royal Oak has no elaborate track system and excludes only those with severe remedial reading problems from its regular English course. The new text, just adopted by Royal Oak and a number of other school systems across the country, will present him with a broad cross section of the best in English and American literature, both traditional and modern, and will show him how to take a story or poem apart as he would an engine, in order to learn what makes it (and others like it) work. Unlike his brother Bob, who took English when the stress was on "life adjustment," Tom will study literature for its own sake instead of for what it might teach him about personal relationships. Chances are, when he really understands what makes a poem by Robert Frost or a story by Stephen Crane "tick," he may want to read more.

Although Tom Jones, is a hypothetical boy, he is by no means unique. In Royal Oak, he is one of 48 percent of that city's high school graduates who will leave school permanently after 12th grade. In the Nation as a whole, he is one of a similar percentage: in 1965, 1,442,000 persons enrolled in some institution of higher learning, slightly more than half of the previous year's 2,642,000 high school graduates. If Tom's group is fortified by the large number who dropped out of school even earlier, he becomes part of that current two-thirds of the Nation's youth not destined to attend college.

His counselor knows that Tom, who is brighter than many but not all of his peers, deserves a good general education despite his present anti-intellectualism. Who knows, after all, what he'll decide to do later? Didn't a boy who summered near them in Michigan grow up to win the Nobel Prize for literature though he never went past high school? (Hemingway, 1954) And in 1949 didn't the same prize go to a southern country boy who never even got a high school diploma? (Faulkner, 1949)

Naturally, his counselor sees the case for Tom's point of view, but some educators see Tom in a larger perspective. Speaking as president of the Carnegie Foundation five years ago, John W. Gardner, now director of the Urban Coalition, described the necessity of "toning up a whole society." In a book written to counter some charges against democracy in the wake of Russia's space triumphs, Mr. Gardner, while affirming that we can "be equal and excellent too," listed some necessary conditions for survival.

"We cannot have islands of excellence in a sea of slovenly indifference to standards," he wrote. "In an era when the masses of people were mute and powerless it may have been possible for a tiny minority to maintain high standards regardless of their surroundings. But today...as consumers, as voters, as the source of Public Opinion [the masses] heavily influence levels of taste and performance...."

As evidence of this influence, the American public in 1965 consumed just under $2 billion in books, $637 million in radio and TV programs, $630 million in records, and $1 billion in motion pictures. Since more than two-thirds of the present adult population did not go to college, secondary schools have obviously played a major role in conditioning the choices so powerfully expressed at cash register and boxoffice, expecially in those areas where taste is formed, the areas we loosely associate as the fine arts and the humanities.

Fortunately, the high school that Tom attends, along with many of the Nation's 30,900 secondary schools from coast to coast, have responded to Mr. Gardner's plea for "greatly enlarged ways of thinking" about education, especially in the humanities, although it is impossible to blanket all of the country's 24,446 operating school districts with a single chorus of praise.

If Tom lived in McMinnville, Oreg., for example, he might participate in a unique "music laboratory" where he would be encouraged to compose orchestral music even though he had no idea of making music his career. He would have a chance to conduct his compositions, not as a step toward becoming another Toscanini, but simply as a means of increasing his understanding of the music he will some day hear at symphony concerts. If he lived in Evanston, Ill., he would be able to join one of 47 music-making groups, ranging from string trio to brass ensemble, as a means toward the same end.

If Tom had lived in New York between 1959 and June 1966, he might have enrolled in an intensive "Higher Horizons" program designed not only to improve his language skill through a double English session, but also to sharpen his senses by visits to art galleries, plays, operas, museums, and selected films. This program, initially lauded for its benefits to the "culturally deprived," was later attacked for being watered-down.

If Tom lived in Arlington, Va., he could elect an Art-Music-English seminar in the 12th grade which would count as his required English course but, through team teaching, would show him the relationships between the arts and how, together, they reflect the history of mankind. He would not have to be in a college preparatory track for this, but, to enroll, would need a C-average or better in English.

If he attended one of four Cleveland-area pilot schools this fall, Tom would have no option on a thorough exposure to the humanities. There, an experimental curriculum revision devised by the Educational Research Council of Greater Cleveland requires every student, regardless of his plans after graduation, to take a list of "basics" which includes English, humanities, art, and music, as well as the physical and social sciences and math. This pioneer project reflects the Council's view that "everyone, whether he goes to college or not, should be educated broadly." The program will be applied citywide if its trial run is a success.

These are a few of the ways that America's secondary schools are conspiring to put Tom Jones in what Mr. Gardner called "a greater and more creative civilization." In so doing, they have even had the backing of the Council for Basic Education, which as far back as 1960 stated that "music, art, and literature . . . are not frills" when they provide "appreciation by the majority rather than performance by a few."

At the Council's annual meeting in October 1966, a panel of well-known critics (Paul Hume, Emily Genauer, and Donald Barr) confirmed this view in a discussion of "What Should Be Taught in Art, Music, and Literature." Council board member and panel moderator Clifton Fadiman called these topics "the young student's initiation to the best his species has accomplished." The panel agreed with the Council and each other when they criticized marching bands, sloppy self-expression by student artists, cultural snobbery, and "liberal artsmanship" that rely on teaching big names without regard for quality, and above all "the mish-mash that we call an English course."

In its emphasis on educating future audiences rather than performers, the Council, which has sometimes been at odds with the mainstream of educational thought, now floats at its center.

"Educators are increasingly aware that in the secondary schools, the proportion of outstanding creative talent is necessarily small," says Kathryn Bloom, former director of the arts and humanities program in the Office of Education's Bureau of Research. The Bureau provides seed money for many experiments in creative teaching. "At the same time," points out Miss Bloom, "every child has a right to become acquainted with his cultural heritage. Therefore, emphasis should not be on developing performers, but on educating tomorrow's adults to appreciate the performance of others."

Courses designed to accomplish this goal are already part of the curriculum in some top-grade comprehensive high schools, such as the art and music appreciation courses available to students at San Francisco's Lincoln High School. Others, like Springfield, Vermont's pilot program in "the humanities for noncollege-bound 12th graders" or pilot courses in general music being tested in Cleveland, Ohio, Greenwich, Conn., and Iowa City, Iowa, represent bold and imaginative responses to the challenge of the Elementary and Secondary Education Act. Still others, like the new English course at Royal Oak, are the product of enterprise by textbook manufacturers.

If Tom Jones lived in these school jurisdictions, he would be eligible to take any of the courses just described even though he is a "terminal" student, for today's schools "never put a lid on learning" but instead try to present "a level of culture suited to the ability of the individual" regardless of his present or future vocational aims. Ironically, however, Tom's father's relatively high income and middle-class background would disqualify Tom from some of the most interesting and intensive cultural experiences offered by the schools today. These, like Duluth's projected TV course in humanities, Detroit's after-school "Cultural Enrichment" plan for 66,360 pupils, and New York's huge "Higher Horizons," represent crash efforts to overcome the cultural handicaps which are a by-product of poverty.

In the normal secondary school population, elective art and music programs reach a relatively small number of pupils. Perhaps 15 percent take music, 5 percent, art, in the estimate of Harold Arberg, music education specialist at the Office of Education. OE-financed experiments, such as Ohio State's project "for improvement of teaching art appreciation in the secondary schools," hope to raise that percentage in art. Other educators rest their hopes on "the rash of humanities programs" springing up around the Nation.

Those in Arlington and Springfield described earlier are examples. Three teachers usually pool their skills to present units on Greek, Roman, Medieval, Renaissance, 17th, 18th, 19th, and 20th century forms of artistic expression. One obstacle to their further spread is a national shortage of trained music teachers, according to Dr. Arberg. To get around this, the State of Missouri, after approving such a course for statewide use, sent us a special training program for teachers at Kirksville State College under Leon Karel.

In contrast to the meager consumption of art, music, and humanities courses, English language arts courses have an impact on every secondary school student. Fortunately, according to Sue Brett, the OE's research specialist in English, most educators now concur that every student should have a chance to learn his language's literature, in the amount and depth that he can absorb. No longer is the general English course primarily oriented toward college preparation.

As a result, Tom Jones in Royal Oak, and thousands like him in comprehensive high schools elsewhere, have the same literary exposure as their college-bound friends. If Tom went to a vocational or trade school, however, his opportunity might be more limited. George Sanders, program specialist for OE's Division of Vocational and Technical Education, explains:

"It's hard to sell those enriched courses to kids who know they will have to go out to work at 16 or 18. They're hungry and they're impatient. Their first desire is to learn the basic skills for survival."

Schools face the tough problem of interpreting to such students the need for less immediately useful knowledge. No matter how sensible the theory of higher cultural horizons, it's hard to practice on a limited school budget under pressure from well-meaning but short-sighted students and parents. Where teachers and administrators have local options, as most do, they understandably try to give students what seems needed most: saleable skills.

Another block to the development of high-quality English or humanities courses is the shortage of good texts. Slowness of preparation, high cost of replacement, legislative resistance, all contribute to a chronic cultural lag in this important area. Tom Jones is lucky to get a good new text this year, one which treats literature as a subject of intrinsic interest. Many tattered texts still in use reflect what Arno Jewett of the Office of Education and noted author and editor in the field of education once called the "prophylatic world" of life-adjustment theorists, who subverted literature to the uses of sociology. In that pantheon, Clarence Day ruled the literary roost; he rather than Samuel Butler or Turgenev was considered the authority on life with father. Similarly, books considered too rich or fat for easy digestion were presented as abridged nubs, disregarding both ethical and esthetic considerations, even by those editors who criticize the Russians for rewriting history!

By contrast, Tom's 10th grade reader enlisted poet-critic Mark Van Doren as advisor and reflects his standards. Without recourse to thematic lures like "Family Life" or "Sports and Teams," it is frankly organized to reveal the ingredients that go into a good poem, essay, short story, play and novel. Within the short story section, tales by acknowledged masters like Chekhov, de Maupassant and Katherine Mansfield are arranged to illustrate such technical aspects of the story as conflict, theme, character, point of view, and total effect. Similar texts use equally authentic materials to, in the words of one textbook house, "enable the student to see how a literary work operates."

Although Tom's text was designed for the average student, according to its publisher, it has not been so treated in all school districts that have adopted it. Detroit, for example, bought it for honors classes only; Glen Ellyn, Ill., for some honors and some regular classes.

These divergent purchasing policies reflect a deeper difference in educational philosophy. If, as Dr. Brett believes, educators agree that every student should study at his highest level, apparently they are not yet sure just how high those ceilings are, in terms of specific content. To be excellent, yes; but how excellent seems to be the question. Comparison of curriculum plans from many cities and States collected by OE's Educational Materials Center reveals that Pittsburghers last year were getting Plato and Camus.

The Pittsburgh program was admittedly an experimental one, but it has the widest possible implications. Under an OE grant, the English Curriculum Study Center at Carnegie Tech, one of 15 financed by the Bureau of Research, compiled and tested a stimulating three-year literature-study plan for "able college-bound students."

Retaining a thematic structure rather than one based on literary genres, the plan goes far beyond the usual thematic curriculum in scope and quality. Tenth graders examining "Universal Concerns of Man" rather than provincial concerns of teenagers were introduced to a dazzling sample of world literature, grouped around such topics as "Social Concerns" (Dickens, Turgenev, Ibsen); "Reality and Illusion" (Pirandello, Lagerlof); and "Human Weakness" (Balzac, Pushkin, and Tolstoy).

Although this curriculum was designed for students capable of handling abstractions, such materials clearly have relevance for less competent students who know the causes of social reforms first-hand. Important to the success of such a course, naturally is the manner of presentation. Class discussion, while pointing up literary style, also encourages honest discussion of real ethical problems.

"How does war shatter trust in the authority of elders," was a topic with current pertinence suggested by *All Quiet on the Western Front.* "What problems might an idealist face today?" was asked in connection with *Cyrano de Bergerac.* What would happen to our society if certain of Christ's teachings were carried out more fully in contemporary society was a point raised by the parables.

This last question, recently voiced by one of the Beatles, caused an epidemic of record-burning. It serves as a reminder of the philosophical gap between generations which has impeded education for centuries and still makes communication difficult in the classroom. Teachers whose minds have been stunted by the conventions of another era cannot hope to reach the tough-minded youth of our own "age of anxiety" unless they are willing to cast some obsolete philosophical freight overboard.

Despite that difficulty, prospects for wider application of the Pittsburgh program look good. Erwin R. Steinberg, reporting incomplete results of a follow-up experiment using these materials with an average group of students, says: "We have enough evidence to suggest that, with some modifications, such materials need not be confined to the upper fifth." Already a text based on these materials has been commissioned, possibly for use in 1968.

Taken together, these innovations in the arts and the humanities promise a widening horizon for all the Tom, Dick, and Harry Joneses who will never get to college. By such means, America's schools can bridge the "seas of slovenly indifference" which Mr. Gardner deplored to connect the "islands of excellence," linking them into the broad highway of ideas on which civilization travels.

Humanistic Education for the General Student: A Progress Report

Miriam B. Goldstein and Edward C. Martin

Lest "armed with the full paraphernalia of our technical civilization, they are more innocent of the resources of the human spirit than a stone age savage, surrounded by spiritual forces strong enough to hold his impulses in check or to direct their course into socially approved channels of war or song."

Margaret Mead

"The chief concern of the educator today is to prepare thinkers. His objective is to quicken in all learners the sense of relationships, of present to past and present to future, of individual to group and of individual to the race, which are involved in belonging to humanity." *Kimmis Hendrick* paraphrasing *Frederick Mayer*

Here is the threat and the challenge which lies behind our thinking as we have planned this program. It developed, as such programs usually do, out of a specific need in the school.

In September, 1962, we were asked by the administration of Newton High School to share a class of general students coming into their sophomore year. What had once been a rigorous course in English and history for the commercial student had gradually been watered down to accommodate a new type of terminal pupil who went through school. But there wasn't much left of school, aside from the discipline, grades, and routine, to go through him. Our housemaster suggested that coordinating the two subjects and teaching them in the same room in sequential periods might help us evolve a more realistic and meaningful program for today's terminal pupil. The English department suggested incorporating new studies in language; the history department, the meaning of critical experiences in the human record. But fundamentally they left the matter to us. We did our best in the 1962-63 school year to think, talk, plan, and teach such a course as part of our regular work load. Somehow we, the youngsters, and the course made it to June. By then, we knew several things. This was the most enjoyable lower track class either of us had ever taught. The youngsters had gained something more than they had from our traditional offering, but much of the material we had prepared had to be thrown out or revised. We needed to know more about the type of student in these classes, and both of us needed time to work on the problem of giving the school day positive meaning for the reluctant unacademic learner.

We were given three weeks in the summer of 1963 to do some of the job. In the school year 1963-64 we again shared one sophomore class and Mr. Martin shared a second class with another English teacher. The administration had given us a reduced work load and their hearty endorsement to continue the program through the senior year. The second time round we felt we knew more about the students we were dealing with and had a course of study which made some sense to us and to our students. We have too long neglected these pupils' needs and offer our work in progress as a first tentative step.

The Students*

There is considerable variety and individuality among the youngsters. They are almost exclusively from the lowest socio-economic group in the community. By and large, their failure in school work is due to low motivation and aspiration, specific disabilities in reading and writing, and emotional difficulties. Some are relatively bright. They make up the majority of serious discipline problems and a high proportion of psychological disturbance unrelated to discipline.

Originally their track was a business major offered to girls like Jane, who knew what they wanted in life: essentially a good secretarial job and early marriage. The boys, if there were any in the class, wanted to go into business or accounting. Such pupils wanted high school to train them for work. They came with a record of achievement and motivation to justify their desires. The other

*The complete report includes significant sketches of eleven of the students in the course.

type of pupil, whose pre-high school years showed failure through lack of ability or effort, left school and found a job or went into the service. As a high school diploma has become a prerequisite for all employment and a college degree a prerequisite for most business careers, we find both the unrealistic business major and the reluctant learner in the same track. The common denominator is their frustration and alienation.

And what after high school, the end of their formal "education?" When the girls graduate they will probably seek early marriage, holding in the meantime jobs as car hops, waitresses, super market checkout girls, beauticians, and secretaries. The boys will enlist in the armed services or get jobs as unskilled factory hands, construction workers, super market stock boys, and gas station attendants. Inevitably they face a shorter work week than ever before. Furthermore, as automation displaces unskilled labor, this type of individual is affected first. He leaves school with little education or training and is the first to become unemployable, the last to use his resources during his enforced leisure.

But the picture is not totally discouraging. These boys and girls have emotional and intellectual potential. The job of education is to help the individual see his potential, respect it, and develop it. We have no illusions about the awesomeness of this task and about the socio-economic and psychological forces which mould the self-image, but here is the threat and the challenge. We do not propose to help these pupils develop their potential so that we may then impose middle-class aspirations upon them. In this course we have seen their potential—for good and for bad—as exciting and varied as that of the college bound student, although it may differ in intensity and depth. This pupil can be intellectually creative and imaginative. He can use his mind in a careful and thoughtful way. He can be held to certain academic standards. But he needs psychological help, pride in real achievement, and intellectual content. We regard a humanistic education as essential to these pupils' greatest needs: self-awareness and social identity.

Course of Study

The student's first problem is to orient himself to a new combined history-English program. We begin immediately with two short stories that obliquely distinguish man from other animals. In reading and discussing these stories, the pupil sees history as the study of man's becoming within a society and English as the study of man's becoming through his most characteristic activity, language. In history then, the pupil will be using his native language, English, to think, read, talk, and write of man's experiences. Which have been the most significant in the development of history? How has the individual participated in these experiences? And why have they been significant? In English he will be thinking, reading, talking, and writing not only about man's general experiences throughout history but particularly about man's experiences in language. What is the nature of language? How may he best use it to record his experiences? How may he best share the experiences of others in literature?

Unit I—Man as a Creature with Potential (Time: six to seven weeks).[1] *General Objectives:* In the first unit we explore the idea of man as a creature with potential and the implications of this idea. In contrast with other animals who always *are,* man can *become* something other than what he is. This he accomplishes by the use of his hand and his brain. There is constant interaction between man's potential and his environment. Man's attempt to deal with his environment (i.e., to observe, to explain, to use, and control) resulted in his invention of tools, language, and myth. We "know" what man was like by applying inductive and deductive reasoning to whatever evidence is available. Modern myth and modern science are further evidence of the interaction between man's potential and his environment. This unit establishes the tone and direction of the year's work. We want to get the student thinking about what it means to be human.

Explication: Part 1: The pupil reads stories like "The Far-Sighted Cat," "Lassie Come Home," and "The Peacelike Mongoose," which enable him to differentiate between animal and human behavior. Such stories inevitably deal with sentiment and sentimentality. He compares the text and the TV film of Lassie to see how the TV version has changed sentiment to sentimentality; he examines human interest stories in the daily newspaper. The pupil's awareness of the difference will broaden and deepen throughout his high school years. In Helen Keller's "Three Days to See" he again evaluates the appeal to sentiment. But he also sees the classic example in our time of a human being who would not live on the animal level to which she seemed doomed—who "became"—and became a part of history. Her three days give the student a panorama of man's record of achievement which we call history and alert him to the price and privilege of what we call being human.

Part 2: Films like *The Hunters* and *Nanook of the North* show man coping with his environment through his use of tools. With each invention (tool, language, myth) the student hypothesizes and creates anew. He figures out how primitive man made the tool by making one himself. Using only the natural resources in the vicinity of the school, boys make (and occasionally invent or discover) weapons and agricultural tools; girls, domestic implements and clothing. Having himself faced the challenge to his own resourcefulness, he sees how man devised tools to meet the physical necessities of his environment. In filmstrips the pupil sees the tools man developed as he moved from food-gatherer to food-producer; the relationship between the environment and the invention of each tool becomes clear. The pupil, in order to discover this relationship for himself, concentrates on a clear, inductive description of the tool, on a hypothesis as to what enabled man to make it, and on the significance of the tool to man's future development. These activities, in turn, force the pupil to validate his hypotheses on the bases of evidence.

[1] The class meets for 50-minute periods, four for English and four for history per week. Parts of each unit vary from eight to twelve periods.

For example, one of the readings deals with an archeologist's discovery in a collapsed cave of the remains of a stone age community. One of the victims of the landslide is noteworthy in that he has buck teeth and is missing an arm. The archeologist states that the man probably had his arm mutilated in a fight with a bear, and some stone-age doctor had to amputate the arm. The archeologist concludes that when the man could not hunt, he used his teeth and his one good arm to make tools.

The pupils take the same evidence that the archeologist has found, but they suggest other possible hypotheses. For example, one pupil asked, "Couldn't the landslide have caused the amputation?" But immediately another pupil asked, "Then why wasn't the other arm found?" Another wanted to know, "Then why did the archeologist call it an amputation? It must have been an old wound!" Another pupil hypothesized that the arm had been severed not by a stone age doctor but by a stone age warrior. Similarly they make counter-hypotheses as to whether this man was a tool maker and in particular whether he had to use his teeth to hold his working implements.

Part 3: But the student does not isolate man. Again the contrast between man and beast is heightened when the pupil looks at man as a maker of tools of expression, of those tools necessary for communal life and for transmission of a tradition: language, art, writing. He begins to hypothesize, as he had with earlier tools, about how man made language. As he manipulates the tool in history class, he begins to examine language in his English class to see for himself that it is an oral, conventional system of symbols. Here he leaves behind the concrete (the visible hand with its thumb, the tangible tool) and begins to cope with the abstract (the mental capacity for encoding and decoding and the utterance which can never truly be recalled for examination). The difference between words and things is inescapable when he tries to invent a simple language or modify one. In a film like *The Alphabet Conspiracy* he sees how varied communication has been and still is, what language fundamentally is, and how it differs from animal communication. He also sees how spoken and written languages have different resources and therefore require different abilities as he makes sounds, draws pictures, writes letters of the alphabet, spells words, and composes sentences. From here on, his knowledge of the system called English must deepen rather than become more arbitrary and distant. If this pupil can deal with ideas, he can deal with ideas about language.

In history class meanwhile he applies his knowledge of language to Egyptian writing in its various stages. He recognizes the relation between word and ideogram in *Mother* (*in Hieroglyphicks*) and composes simple rebuses. He soon finds that representation becomes a problem when his ideas grow complex. As he devises his own picture writing for some of the following sentences, he sees the power of the ideogram and of the abstract, arbitrary, conventional symbol. He sees the connection between the *visual* symbol and the *phonetic* symbol.

> The bird is in the tree.
> I think I see a bird.
> The bird is pretty.

> I think I see a pretty bird in the tree.
> I saw the bird.
> The bird saw me.
> I think the bird saw me, etc.

If there is sufficient interest (if other languages are heard in the home, or if there is curiosity about languages of people in the headlines [Russians, Vietnamese, etc.]) we look at their writing systems briefly.

To begin a study of the Egyptian view of the world the pupil learns to read the language of cartography by examining maps of the ancient Near East and drawing one of the Nile River valley. Although his first attempts are primitive, they lay the foundation for continuous and more sophisticated work with maps.

Part 4: The pupil is involved not only with his own hypotheses and creations but also with those of historic man. He reads myths of various cultures which try to account for man's invention of language, for the creation of the universe (Hebrew, Sumerian, Egyptian) and his survival of the flood (Hebrew, Sumerian). As he reads these records of man's efforts to understand the world around him, he sees how geography shapes myth, particularly how the Nile affected Egypt's cosmogeny. He also sees the relationship between myth and religion: how man develops religious beliefs as he tries to order the world about him. Egyptian myth and art reveal the crucial role of religion in Egyptian life. Now he reads myths of many lands, writes his own, footnoting his hypothesis with a scientific explanation (for example, why the leaves turn red or how he caught cold over the weekend). He writes his first special report of the year on a myth of his choice. He retells it in his own words, lists the hypotheses made by the myth-maker, tries to explain and evaluate each.

Part 5: For the rest of the unit, the teacher chooses his area of special emphasis. He may, for example, consider modern myth, modern science, or problems man confronts in today's environment. Two very readable stories for reexamining all that we have said about man as a creature with potential are Steinbeck's *The Pearl* and O'Flaherty's "Two Lovely Beasts."

Unit II—The Individual in Society (Time: six weeks). *General Objectives:* Having explored the notion of man as a becoming creature, in unit two we see man in the context of society. The emphasis shifts from man the maker of tools, language, and myth in a physical setting to the individual confronting his social environment. We deal with individuals in selected societies in the ancient world: with those men and women who were recognized in their times and are still remembered in ours for their deeds, famous and infamous. We explore the various influences of the group upon the choices and possibilities open to a man in that society. What were the controls, the freedoms, the responsibilities, the directions various ancient societies gave their members? We see societies producing the rebel as well as the conformist. We consider what it meant to achieve manhood and heroism in these societies and what it means in today's world. Here the student confronts ideas which hopefully can make him reflect deeply on the individual human condition.

Explication: Part 1: The student reads a simplified translation of the *Iliad*. This version remains faithful to the original yet isolates only the main incidents of the story: the quarrel between Achilles and Agamemnon, Agamemnon's dream, Patroclus's fight with Hector, the duel between Achilles and Hector, and so forth. The illustrations in this edition give the pupil a foretaste of what he will see in the museum, especially among the Greek vase paintings.

The *Iliad* is still not easy for these students. A particular stumbling block is names of people and gods, all of whom need to be recognizable for their essential attributes. These pupils balk at jawbreakers like *Clytemnestra* or *Agamemnon* only until they see that spelling and pronouncing these names involve less trial and error than our everyday words like *sometimes* or *misled*. The pupil also needs help with close reading. Reading aloud in class by both teacher and those students who are willing is another way to bring text and pupil together.

This is the time when we establish the Thorndike-Barnhart Dictionary as the basic language text for these pupils. The pronunciation key, etymologies, definitions, synonymies, parts of speech, illustrations, citations, and type satisfy this pupil's needs—and seem to be a revelation to him. We have said that our primary aim in the sophomore year is to affect the youngster's self-image so that he will want to get help where he needs it most: in the reading which almost invariably is his first taste of school failure. Remedial reading, like other therapy, succeeds when the pupil cooperates. We do not impose another dose of remedial reading, but dictionary work does much for the pupil who needs help with phonics and word study as he learns to *use* a dictionary intelligently. We keep a complete set in the classroom and find ourselves using it almost daily in the course of our work—especially in this unit. Whereas Unit One stressed close observation and critical thinking as key activities in this course, Unit Two stresses the importance of word study and close reading—at least for the next three years.

At the outset the student is told mythical stories of how the war came about: the golden apple of Discord, the judgment of Paris, and the abduction of Helen. Here he is asked not only to recall the myths he has studied in the previous unit, but also to discover whether in these myths there is any historical basis. By comparing maps of Homer's world and the world as it was and by discussing the intertribal warfare of archaic Greece, the student forms some historical hypotheses about the causes of the war. Moving into the story itself, the student confronts the individual in early Greek society: the war heroes Achilles and Hector striving for physical and military excellence and their attendant material and intrinsic rewards—two very different men reacting to and reflecting the society and time in which they live. The student begins by writing simple descriptions based upon careful observation of these men. Then he compares and contrasts them in paragraphs and in class discussions. He studies their actions and motives, debates who was the greater hero, and considers whether such men exist in the contemporary world.

Among Homer's men mingle the gods—human except for their physical excellence and immortality. The comparison between Greek myth and Egyptian myth enables the student to see the different position individuals held in these societies. It also clarifies the Homeric and Egyptian concepts of life and death and man's position in the universe. In sum, the student should begin to understand Homer's world. He should also get a fairly sophisticated picture of Homer's heroes and their position in their society—how they worked within its bounds to achieve greatness and suffer defeat. He can then compare this world with ours, in order to think about our standards of achievement and excellence.

Part 2: After this careful look at Homer's heroes and ourselves, the student reads a description of the Lycurgan system. Here is a society geared to producing an Achilles or a Hector, but with some very important differences. The pupil continues to compare and contrast the relationship between society and the individual in Sparta, Homeric Greece, and our world. Herodotus's account of Leonidas and the three hundred at Thermopylae provides the specific example of the individual who fulfills the Spartan ideal. Questions and discussions of the *Iliad* and the *History* lead to the more challenging question of whether Leonidas was an individual or even a hero, in view of the society from which he came.

Part 3: In class the student sees slides of fifth century Athenian art and reads Pericles's Funeral Oration. As he did with Egyptian art, the student simply describes the details of what he sees. Then he is asked to hypothesize about what kind of society would have produced this art. Once some general notions have been worked out, we read together carefully the Funeral Oration, thus making the notions more explicit. Here is society with ideals more complex than those of the Homeric or the Spartan world. Film strips on Athenian life help the pupil understand the differences. Socrates, a rebel who grew out of Athenian society, serves as the specific example. The student reads a simple one-page biography designed to sharpen his notetaking. He starts to build words from common Greek roots in the selection. With the help of detailed worksheets, he reads I. A. Richards' basic English translation of the *Apology* and sections of the *Crito*. The student must read carefully, concentrating on the action of the trial, conviction and execution. Finally, the student is asked whether Socrates was a product of his society, whether his trial and conviction seem justified, whether Socrates was a hero, and in what sense, compared to the other heroes studied.

As a review of the first two units we visit the Museum of Fine Arts. The sections of particular concern are Egyptian and Greek statuary, Egyptian funerary objects illustrating daily life, and Greek vase paintings depicting the Trojan War and various other myths. We tour in small groups in order to encourage the pupil to linger, observe, and question.

Part 4: The teacher has the choice in this part of taking up any number of subjects related to the general objectives of the unit. For example, a modern eulogy, recalling the epitaph of the Spartan three-hundred and Pericles's Funeral Oration, could bring the students to consider what our society calls manly or heroic. Or sections from *Child of Our Time* could show the student the kind of heroism which emerges from a concentration camp. Anouilh's *Antigone* or personalities in the daily headlines could be used for similar discussion.

Unit III—Man as Part of a Social Group (Time: six weeks). *General Objectives:* In this unit on social status in feudal Europe we look at the individual within a social group. The knight and his lady are our most vivid representatives. The feudal peasant and the monk contrast with the courtly tradition. We see the strong pull of paganism and Christianity in feudal society as well as the system of wordly obligations which was fundamental to the chivalric ideal. Nor do we ignore the difference between the chivalric code and its actual practice. As we look at feudal man, we note not only his function in his own time and class but also the transmission of his ideals to our own society and their inevitable changes. What do *lady* and *gentleman* signify to society? What should they signify to humanity? As part of this consideration we study etiquette in language: what we mean by correct and incorrect, good and bad, and varieties and levels of usage. Throughout this unit we hope the student sees more clearly the realities of social status and appreciates more deeply the dignity of the individual in any social group.

Explication: Part 1: After the contemporary or classical hero of Unit Two, we meet a heroine, Eliza Doolittle. In this remarkable guttersnipe's story lie all of the questions implicit in this unit. Why does she want to be a lady—only to discover she's been a lady all along? And why does her loving pater lament being catapulted into middle-class respectability? Where did we get this concern with the lady and the gentleman? And what do we mean by these terms today?

Eliza's cockney may seem formidable on the printed page, but the dramatic reading, and if possible, a performance of *My Fair Lady*, helps the pupil understand society's concern with outward status symbols: speech, manners, dress, grooming, occupation. As the students see Eliza's struggle and evolving self-awareness, their own clichés and prejudices about social position give way to the facts of language change and variety (social, regional, and temporal) inherent in the play. They test their generalizations against the varieties of usage in their own environment.

Part 2: A film like *The Medieval Manor* or *The Medieval World* takes the pupil back to feudal Europe. In stories like "Gawain and the Green Knight," in a few sonnets of Petrarch, in a prayer to the Virgin, in the wording of the accolade, in Chaucer's motley pilgrims, the pupil begins to understand the medieval mind and temperament: the clash between the chivalric code and its practice; the political, religious, and social role of the upper class within the general milieu. In the Knight he sees the glorification of Lord, sword, and lady.

Slides of the unicorn tapestries, of parts of a bestiary and of a book of hours bring the Middle Ages to life. Vuegraph transparencies with overlays enable the pupil to understand much of Chaucer in the original Middle English. He sees the text, he hears the spoken word, he looks at the picture to check his linguistic hunches. By examining the language in a brief passage, like the introduction to the young Squire, the pupil notes how English has changed in sound, inflection, word order, and vocabulary. The pupils enjoy this. The language is different enough from their own to give them a sense of translation, of dealing with a foreign tongue. Yet it is similar enough to their English to enable them to make intelligent guesses and to laugh off perfectly reasonable analogies that just don't fit, like the gallant Squire's "floyting al the day."

Part 3: The function, ideals, and influence of peasant Bodo and his wife

Ermentrude contrast with those of the Knight and his lady. On a large map the pupil chooses the best locations for the parts of the manor of Bodo's lord: the monastery, the steward's home, the church, the artisans' shops, the huts of the serfs and peasants. Here the pupil realizes the agricultural foundations of feudalism and the function of the peasant in this economic order. Bodo's daily existence becomes the subject of conjecture. How are his prayers and charms related to the pagan and the Christian world of which he is a part? Is Bodo a gentleman? Is Ermentrude a lady? Here the problems of definition confront the pupil irrevocably. Definition of mere objects and tools in unit one proved demanding; definition of abstractions like *lady* and *gentleman* require even more careful explication if our debate is to move in any direction.

Part 4: The ideal of the holy man and the corruption of that ideal emerge as we read the Benedictine Rules, as we meet Chaucer's Nun and Pardoner, as we read "The Pardoner's Tale." Recordings of liturgical music and slides of monasteries reveal the powerful force of Christianity.

Throughout the unit the pupil's imagination is challenged—first in a negative way when he scoffs at the impossibilities in the Gawain story—only to be confronted with some of the marvels of modern surgery. Yesterday's magic becomes today's science but neither could have come to pass without imagination. The pupil applies his imagination to a very simple exemplum, "The Pardoner's Tale," when he is asked to figure out another reasonable conclusion to this story, and to write this alternative story. Here the problems of inevitability and respect for the imagination rather than fancy show the pupil the place of real and unreal, the relationship between story and myth, exemplum and fable.

Part 5: We look at rules of modern etiquette (including school rules) and discuss their antecedents in the medieval tradition. We also consider how modern society has changed the ideals. The teacher can do any number of things to bring the unit into contemporary focus. The quickest would be to read a story like "Sixteen" and let the pupils decide whether the narrator is a lady and the boy a gentleman. Another way might be to observe the breakdown of the feudal system in the Guinevere story (in the musical *Camelot* if possible) or to consider the attempts to retain the chivalric ideal in "A Rose for Emily" or in *The Glass Menagerie.* The anti-gentleman could be studied in films like *School for Scoundrels* or *Lavender Hill Mob.* Throughout the unit we see the relationship between language and character, whether of the group or the individual.

Unit IV—The Individual in the Renaissance World (Time: eight weeks). *General Objectives:* The fourth unit shifts from the previous concern with social status, lady and gentleman, to the seemingly unbounded humanistic individual of the Renaissance. In studying a few Renaissance men in art, religion, politics, science, and literature, we consider the breakdown of the old order and the coming of the new Europe. The variety of these men's experiences suggests the fulfillment of the creature with potential. Not only does he have the potential; he is now aware of it. His society condones and glorifies the individual free from the restraints of the medieval world. But on closer study we see that many of the elements of the old persist. Despite his new-found freedom, the Renaissance man is involved in the potentials and restraints of the new science and technology, the nation-state, the city, and the Reformation. The modern attitude presents modern problems. This unit should pull many of the ideas of the first three units together, putting them into a new context, and preparing for an understanding of the complexities of our own world and times. Hopefully, the student's insight into the individual's position in a complex society is deepened.

Explication: Part 1: After a chapter from Mill's *The Middle Ages* and a film on the Crusades, the student constructs a hypothetical plan of a late medieval city. He compares this plan with the one he drew for the manor in unit three and discusses what changes have taken place: first simple physical changes, then the more complex economic ones. After reading selections from *Don Quixote,* he considers whether this knight errant is a hero, why Don Quixote fails as a medieval knight, and why he is an absurd Renaissance figure. These discussions lead the pupil to see there is more than a physical change to the Renaissance; it is also a complex change in attitude.

Slides and filmstrips juxtapose medieval and Renaissance art. The pupils note the characteristics of each age and discuss the new elements of Renaissance art: perspective, color, detailed background, concern with the body. Then a slide-tape takes them on a tour of Florence, where they can now isolate the medieval and Renaissance elements in a modern city. The consideration of art enables the student to observe concretely the shift in attitude from the Middle Ages to the Renaissance. An E.B.F. film on the Renaissance reviews the change in music and the visual arts. While watching the film the student again has to observe detail—this time especially of music—in order to discuss the differences. Observation is only the first step; the pupil considers how and why these changes came about. And he sees how much of Chaucer; Petrarch, Dante, and Giotto are part medieval, part Renaissance. "The artists are the antennae of the race!"

Part 2: Beginning with the artists Leonardo and Cellini, we study a series of Renaissance men. We read short biographies, see their art work, and consider what makes each a Renaissance man. On his own, the pupil writes a report on a Renaissance artist of his own choice, using as a model for analysis the class's report on Leonardo. He moves from the painter or sculptor to a variety of men: Castiglione, della Casa, Aretino, Shakespeare, the Duke of Urbino, each time reading a short biography and, when possible, some of the individual's actual work. Always he considers the nature of biography and these men's part in what we call the Renaissance world. We look for the most readable translations from foreign languages. We do not use simplified or modernized adaptations of English works.

Parts 3, 4, and 5 in English are devoted to the study of Shakespeare's *Romeo and Juliet* as a Renaissance play taking place in an Italian Renaissance city. The transition may be made through myth, medieval story, or Renaissance city. Much of the play is acted out before the pupils and Shakespeare's English is contrasted with Chaucer's and our own. If possible, we see *West Side Story.* But no matter what the approach, we inevitably face the problems of whether the characters in the play—the Prince, the friar, the parents, the lovers—fulfill their Renaissance roles. We also consider the inevitability of the end, which leads us to problems of motive and structure in the play.

Part 3: In history the student studies the discovery of the world. He understands from Columbus's journal and from medieval and Renaissance maps how the physical view of the world has changed and brought contact with unfamiliar cultures. He sees in Leonardo's notebooks the beginnings of the new science and mechanics. In Galileo's astronomy he sees how the new view of the universe conflicts with the views supported by the church.

Part 4: In history the student moves to a consideration of the conflict within the church, which brought about the Reformation. Luther's protest is another illustration of the Renaissance mind and spirit. Again, lest we establish misleading dichotomies, we take the pupils back to the now familiar square in Florence, where Savonarola's earlier questioning and protest anticipate the Renaissance attitude.

Part 5: In history the student reads short paragraphs from Machiavelli's *The Prince*. From the readings he gets ideas for drawing political cartoons that the class can see on the screen. He discusses the politics of power and the rising nation-state in the Renaissance picture. He considers Shakespeare's prince in *Romeo and Juliet* to see whether he is Machiavellian. If he is, how should he treat the strife-torn Verona? In the end, who should "be pardon'd, who punished?"

Part 6: History and English classes both direct themselves to making a Renaissance daily paper. The local news is the news of each day's happenings in Romeo and Juliet's Verona.

The international news deals with events of the Reformation or the discovery of the New World. Other items are an editorial, a political cartoon based on Machiavelli, a "What's New in Art" column or "New Inventions of the Day," a Dear Abbey column based on the advice of Castiglione or della Casa and so forth. The possibilities for the paper are unlimited: society page, rotogravure, advertisements, sports, and obituary column enlist any and all interests and abilities. The students work in groups or individually, research, create, and pull together all that they have studied about the Renaissance world and its attitude.

Unit V—Man in a Scientific and Technological World (Time: six to eight weeks). *General Objectives:* Unit five emphasizes one of the chief accomplishments and chief problems of man in the modern world: science and technology. The humanistic worldly individual of the Renaissance discovers the powers and possibilities of the natural world and methods of dealing with it, only to discover also that the more he invents and discovers, the more he depends on these inventions and discoveries. The craftsman of the Renaissance finds he is losing his position of responsibility and power to the greater power of technology. Moreover, industrialism and the new commercial order bring the city into being. In this modern city the new technology provides comfort, but it also creates a community with chronic problems. As men view these events, some glorify, others protest what is happening. They are confronted with how to use what has been created for man's benefit rather than his harm. We hope the students will get an awareness of the complexity of the problem and see their potential for personally coping with it.

Explication: Part 1: As transition from the previous unit, the student reads two or three biographical selections, including Cellini's description of his Jupiter; also the short stories "Quality" and "The Coppersmith." At first the pupils resent the Renaissance craftsman's praise of his own creation, but with further discussion they discover the difference between conceit and legitimate pride in craftsmanship. In each of the stories the student meets a craftsman who no longer fits into his society because the new science and technology have taken over or eliminated his work. Reading, writing, and discussion are supplemented by careful examination of hand-crafted and machine-made articles. Pupils also bring examples of their own handiwork.

Part 2: In history the student reads several short descriptions of inventions since the fifteenth century. He considers how these inventions affect man's life. He also recalls Leonardo and Galileo, Renaissance forerunners of modern science and technology. In science fiction and the pupil's invention of some futuristic machine, he considers what are the limits of our use of machines. The most able pupils write short science fiction pieces. As the sharp distinctions between story and myth were observed in unit one, so are they here noted for fiction and science fiction. It is the essential differences that are noted and insisted upon in the pupil's creation.

In English we examine our language scientifically, i.e., we set aside all notions of social usage and concern ourselves with the structure of the sentence, the unit of thought. Grammar does not improve usage, a function of socio-economic background. We try to develop in the student a respect for his current usage and a desire to enlarge and vary his usage, to work toward adult sentences. In unit three the pupil got some understanding of the facts of usage: of the difference between good and bad and correct and incorrect English. Change in his writing and speech habits can come only through imitation, practice, and repetition of standard speech patterns. The pupil is held to a reasonable standard throughout the school day.

But in stressing the development of curiosity and thought in these pupils, we have been experimenting with more than conventions in language; we have been trying to find out how much the pupil can master of the nature of language itself, part of a humanistic education. Having learned something of hypothesizing in mythmaking, of inductive and deductive reasoning in unit one, we now apply scientific method to the study of the English sentence. This work in grammar comes frequently and in small doses throughout the rest of the year. The pupil applies his intuitive knowledge of sentence composing to discover for himself and verbalize some of the underlying rules of the system. Starting with the simple sentence, we work out rules for the simplest of transformations. These pupils find great satisfaction in hypothesizing a rule and seeing if it works in sentences the class writes based on the rule. When it works, we feel fortified; when it doesn't work, we try to discover our error. More often, we realize that we are not in error but that we are confronting the richness and complexity of English and the tentativeness and partiality of scientific theory. The important thing is not that the pupil gets all the facts of language (Who has them, anyway?) but that his questions are sound and purposeful. *Why* and *what would happen if* are the key questions in this unit on science and technology. If there are any practical applications of such knowledge, if the pupils begin to write more mature and correct sentences, so much the better. But we do not confuse using language with knowing it: science has shown us the difference between the two.

Part 3: Here the students study the origin of a modern city as one of the outcomes of the new science and technology and of their effect upon the economy. The growth of London from the sixteenth through the eighteenth century is the example. They read descriptions of this city in poetry and prose, examine maps, see slides of Hogarth, together with examples of the reaction in Watteau. As the students observe details, they formulate generalizations about the nature of the city and relate to other communities they have studied: tribe, polis, manor. How has technology affected the city and the city dweller?

Part 4: Man is now a member of an industrial urban society. What does he think of it? The pupil reads examples of the praise and protest, from Owen's Utopian schemes to Zola's naturalistic exposé, from Whitman's salute to the muse "installed amid the kitchenware," to Marx and Engels's scheme. The pupils have to take a stand in all this praise and protest. Who makes the most sense? Finally they read "Fawn with a Bit of Green" to see one modern reaction to our industrial urban society.

Part 5: The contemporary section deals with the city of Newton. Students take a trip to a local factory, where they can see both handcrafted and mass-produced stages of the final product. They study the industrial development of one section of the city, and few even get the reaction of the involved and uninvolved citizens to this development.

Unit VI (Time: four to six weeks). Unit six culminates the year's work. The teacher is free to develop those concepts or skills that seem to require more time than the first five units permitted or to explore in depth the work that the pupils found most stimulating. At this time of year the teacher's and class's specific interests and enthusiasms are the strongest antidote to spring fever with its attendant straining at the tether and work stoppage. The best way seems to be fairly rapid reading of several full-length books. Pupils enjoy the contrast to the rather heavy dosage of short readings they have had thus far; they are now in a stronger position to read a book. The important thing is to tie together the concepts of the previous units through these final readings. *Animal Farm* provides a good way of looking at the Marxist reaction to industrial capitalism and at man's attempt to achieve the utopian ideal. *The Human Comedy* presents few reading difficulties; yet it takes the class back to Homer's Helen and Ulysses, to Ithaca; into the midsts of the family's problems of survial and endurance in an urban, war-torn world. *The Little World of Don Camillo* enables us to laugh and to look seriously at man in society, at authority and the individual in today's world. The teacher has any number of options in this unit. We know that these three books work with these classes. We should like to hear of other titles that might work well.

Tentative Conclusions

We are expanding this program cautiously beyond the sophomore year. Other teachers are now participating in the designing and teaching of the junior and senior courses. Our general plan is to teach the combined program to one class the first year, to two classes including another pair of teachers the next year, and eventually to offer the program to all pupils in the non-academic course. Consequently, we do not envisage the full operation of this program until 1968.

We have called this a humanistic curriculum because we do not believe a single humanities course or program can do all we have set out to do. It can only begin. Next year we hope to enlist the talents of mathematics, science, physical education, art, and music teachers whose course offerings will enrich our current program for these students. We look forward to the time when the whole school day will add up to something significant to these pupils. Nor are we ignoring their need for some vocational training. The new high school plant should be in operation when we are ready to reexamine our total academic offerings, to scrap those that have not worked, and to enable the pupils to take advantage of some of the work-training programs the community should offer for some part of the school day.

We regard substance as the fundamental means of affecting these pupils' self-image, and we know that the relationship between teacher and pupil is crucial because of the demands of the content. A very pressing need we have felt in the past two years is for a more encompassing program, one that reaches these pupils and their home environments. Communication between home and school is essential for these pupils. Yet theirs are the parents hardest to reach. The present work load of our guidance counselors does not permit the extra time and help these pupils need. This is why we feel a social worker with a rich background in dealing with adolescent problems is a key person. We hope to enlist the services of a social worker this year and to get more attention for these pupils from the guidance department. We also need better communication between counselor, social worker, administrator, and teacher.

At times during the year we have had individual students with such serious emotional problems that they cannot carry on in a classroom situation. For the class's sake, as well as theirs, we would like such a pupil to be removed from the class and to be tutored during these varied periods of stress. The tutor has to be an experienced, understanding teacher who can use our materials. When the student is ready to return, he will be ready to fit more easily into the course and the class.

A special counselor assigned to these pupils would also serve the pressing need of establishing and using valid aptitude, achievement, and psychological tests. Most of the ones we now use are culture-bound; they cannot help discriminating socially against these pupils. Such tests usually relegate these pupils to epithets like: has a short attention span; likes routine; has little creativity, self-direction, or leadership; learns by drill; has limited vocabulary; is baffled by association and generalization; lacks reading ability and curiosity about language; is not interested in the *why;* dislikes abstractions and fine distinctions; fails to distinguish between fact and opinion; cannot be very self-critical or tolerate ideas different from his own; enjoys group activity only when his role is clearly defined; "may do acceptable written work if instruction has been thorough and he has seen numerous examples; does not see deeper significance of a story." (Adapted from W. Myres' "Identifying Students of Superior and Low Ability" in the October, 1960, *English Journal.*) Such judgments tell us what we have done to and for these pupils; but they do not begin to tell us what might and must be done if we are to educate them as human beings.

We have therefore avoided references to statistics as to I.Q. and achievement found in most pupils' folders. These figures only confirm what we already know about the culturally deprived in our society. Until we have more reliable guides as to the potential of this pupil, we assume that excellence—in course content, teaching, and guidance—can do no child any harm. But we must agree on what we call *excellence.* In this paper we have tried to define excellence in our two disciplines. Guidance is not our province. But we can only suggest some of the basic needs lest we aggravate these pupils' deprivation and helplessly see school and society involved in the most costly repair.

Actually, our course grew out of abandoning all preconceived notions about these pupils and asking ourselves what we would ask for any student, realizing that the answers we got had to be relative.

1. Can he be objective?
   Can he develop taste in art and literature?
   Can he be a detached spectator, reader and listener?
   How far can his critical thinking skills go?
   How complicated an idea can he cope with?
   Can he transfer an idea to new areas of study?
2. Can he achieve intellectual autonomy as a result of this transfer?
3. Can he move from a concern with himself to a concern with others?
   Can he move from a concern with the immediate to a concern with the timeless?
   Can he see when he is moving from private to universal concerns?
   Does he value this kind of experience?
4. Can he develop introspection and perspective?
   Can his imagination be aroused?
   Can he transmute as well as transmit our culture?
5. What are the optimum time sequences for his work?
6. What uses of nonverbal material are most conducive to transmission of ideas?
   What technical aspects (maps, charts, slides, films, statistics) are useful?
7. How can his reading and listening skills be sharpened?
   Can he and should he study grammar?

What goals of expression, written and oral, seem reasonable?
8. What extra classroom experiences are most conducive to a transmission of ideas?
9. What are the emotional and other psychological characteristics of these pupils?

Our tentative answers are reflected in this program. The course starts with content, with a concern for the disciplines of history and English. It assumes that these disciplines studied together offer the general student more than the traditional separation in a high school curriculum. In such a combined course based on only the best literature, art and music, the student confronts similar ideas from different angles and, we hope, as a result is better able to understand and study the ideas in depth. He can better grasp their essential relevance to human experience. The student can also acquire reading, writing, thinking, and speaking skills in a more consistent and concentrated manner and be held to a single standard of recognizable excellence. Although the course takes the student in the same direction in both English and history, the essential uniqueness and variety of the disciplines is preserved. The course makes strenuous demands on the student; but if he accepts them, he sees the satisfaction that it brings.

The demands on the teacher are no less strenuous. Emotionally, these pupils drain him. Academically, they offer few returns. His only satisfaction is exploring ideas and feelings that deeply concern and affect both pupil and teacher as human beings.

How do we know what the student learns from the course? Term tests and final exams are not grim, but they are rigorous. They tell us whether the pupil has anything to say, whether his vocabulary is adequate for the saying, whether his imagination and intellect have in any way been aroused. Our best proof, however, is from experiences in class. Most important are the questions the student begins to ask us. We always have our questions ready, but often the pupil's correct answers matters less than his thoughtful question. Their frequency and nature tell us whether he is realizing the aims of the course. If he sees that the ideas we discuss are interesting enough, relevant to him, thought-provoking, and worth asking questions about, we think he is moving toward our goal. No matter how illiterate he may seem, these questions offer the only promise that he will do more, that he has some incentive. For his questions show when his attitude toward school, education, and himself are changing. Other than hard, serious work, we expect no radical improvement in the sophomore year, only the beginning of the change. We hope the course opens up new possibilities for the pupil as an individual; that it begins to affect his aspirations, taste, attitude, and self-awareness so that eventually he may acquire satisfaction in his work and in his leisure. We are hoping for much but we have no right to strive for less if we really believe what we teach: that, for better or worse, man is a creature with potential.

Appendixes

Appendix A: Statement and Recommendation

American Council of Learned Societies

"The Commission on the Humanities recommends the establishment by the President and the Congress of the United States of a National Humanities Foundation. . . ."

I

The humanities are the study of that which is most human. Throughout man's conscious past they have played an essential role in forming, preserving, and transforming the social, moral, and aesthetic values of every man in every age. One cannot speak of history or culture apart from the humanities. They not only record our lives; our lives are the very substance they are made of. Their subject is every man. We propose, therefore, a program for all our people, a program to meet a need no less serious than that for national defense. We speak, in truth, for what is being defended—our beliefs, our ideals, our highest achievements.

The humanities may be regarded as a body of knowledge and insight, as modes of expression, as a program for education, as an underlying attitude toward life. The body of knowledge is usually taken to include the study of history, literature, the arts, religion, and philosophy. The fine and the performing arts are modes of expressing thoughts and feelings visually, verbally, and aurally. The method of education is one based on the liberal tradition we inherit from classical antiquity. The attitude toward life centers on concern for the human individual: for his emotional development for his moral, religious, and aesthetic ideas, and for his goals—including in particular his growth as a rational being and a responsible member of his community.

This Commission conceives of the humanities, not merely as academic disciplines confined to schools and colleges, but as functioning components of society which affect the lives and well-being of all the population. It regards the arts, both visual and performing, as part of the humanities and indeed essential to their existence. The arts differ in important ways from the conventional academic disciplines, but the Commission is confident that in any practical matter affecting the two these differences will readily be recognized and appropriate means devised for supporting each. The Commission further considers that science, as a technique and expression of intellect, is in fact closely affiliated with the humanities. Whatever scientists may learn concerning the physical world is or should be of profound interest to the humanist, just as the findings of behavioral scientists—whether they issue in social theories and inspire social action or merely make humans understandable—fall within the humanist's purview. The natural sciences, the social sciences, and the humanities are of their nature allies.

The Commission warmly supports the statement relating science to other intellectual activity in the report of the President's Advisory Committee of November 15, 1960 (page 3):

> ... While this report centers on the needs of science, we repudiate emphatically any notion that science research and scientific education are the only kinds of learning that matter to America. The responsibility of this Committee is limited to scientific matters, but obviously a high civilization must not limit its efforts to science alone. Even in the interests of science itself it is essential to give full value and support to the other great branches of man's artistic, literary, and scholarly activity. The advancement of science must not be accomplished by the impoverishment of anything else, and the life of the mind in our society has needs which are not limited by the particular concerns which belong to this Committee and this report.

Science is far more than a tool for adding to our security and comfort. It embraces in its broadest sense all efforts to achieve valid and coherent views of reality; as such, it extends the boundaries of experience and adds new dimensions to human character. If the interdependence of science and the humanities were more generally understood, men would be more likely to become masters of their technology and not its unthinking servants.

Even the most gifted individual, whether poet or physicist, will not realize his full potential or make his fullest contribution to his times unless his imagination has been kindled by the aspirations and accomplishments of those who have gone before him. Humanist scholars have therefore a special responsibility in that the past is their natural domain. They have the privilege and obligation of interpreting the past to each new generation of men who "necessarily must live in one small corner for one little stretch of time." They preserve and judge the fruits of humanity's previous attempts to depict, to rationalize, and to transcend the world it inhabits. The arts and letters, and the study of them, are therefore where we look most directly for enrichment of the individual's experience and his capacity for responding to it. Through the humanities we may seek intellectual humility, sensitivity to beauty, and emotional discipline. By them we may come to know the excitement of ideas, the power of imagination, and the unsuspected energies of the creative spirit.

Over the centuries the humanities have sustained mankind at the deepest level of being. They prospered in Greece and Rome, in the Middle Ages, in the Renaissance, and in the Enlightenment. Architecture, sculpture, poetry, and music flourished, and with the growth of colleges and universities the liberal arts took shape as a body of cumulative knowledge and wisdom. In the formative years of our own country it was a group of statesmen steeped in the humanities who fused their own experience with that of the past to create the enduring Constitution of the Republic.

During our early history we were largely occupied in mastering the physical environment. No sooner was this mastery within sight than advancing technology opened up a new range of possibilities, putting a new claim on energies which might otherwise have gone into humane and artistic endeavors. The result has often been that our social, moral, and aesthetic development lagged behind our material advance. Yet we have every reason to be proud of our artists and scholars, and new techniques have frequently served to make their work more widely available; but this is not enough. Now more than ever, with the rapid growth of knowledge and its transformation of society's material base, the humanities must command men of talent, intellect, and spirit.

The state of the humanities today creates a crisis for national leadership. While it offers cultural opportunities of the greatest value to the United States and to mankind, it holds at the same time a danger that wavering purpose and lack of well-conceived effort may leave us second-best in a world correspondingly impoverished by our incomplete success. The challenge is no less critical and direct than the one we have already met with our strong advocacy of healthy and generously supported science. It must be met in turn with equal vision and resolve.

II. America's Need of the Humanities

Many of the problems which confront the people of the United States necessarily involve the humanities. They are of nationwide scope and interest. Each is of concern to every citizen, and the way in which each is solved will be of consequence to him. Among them are the following:

1. All men require that a vision be held before them, an ideal toward which they may strive. Americans need such a vision today as never before in their history. It is both the dignity and the duty of humanists to offer their fellow-countrymen whatever understanding can be attained by fallible humanity of such enduring values as justice, freedom, virtue, beauty, and truth. Only thus do we join ourselves to the heritage of our nation and our human kind.

2. Democracy demands wisdom of the average man. Without the exercise of wisdom free institutions and personal liberty are inevitably imperilled. To know the best that has been thought and said in former times can make us wiser than we otherwise might be, and in this respect the humanities are not merely our, but the world's best hope.

3. The United States is not a nation of materialists, but many men believe it to be. They find it hard to fathom the motives of a country which will spend billions on its outward defense and at the same time do little to maintain the creative and imaginative abilities of its own people. The arts have an unparalleled capability for crossing the national barriers imposed by language and contrasting customs. The recently increased American encouragement of the performing arts is to be welcomed, and will be welcomed everywhere as a sign that Americans accept their cultural responsibilities, especially if it serves to prompt a corresponding increase in support for the visual and the liberal arts. It is by way of the humanities that we best come to understand cultures other than our own, and they best to understand ours.

4. World leadership of the kind which has come upon the United States cannot rest solely upon superior force, vast wealth, or preponderant technology.

Only the elevation of its goals and the excellence of its conduct entitle one nation to ask others to follow its lead. These are things of the spirit. If we appear to discourage creativity, to demean the fanciful and the beautiful, to have no concern for man's ultimate destiny—if, in short, we ignore the humanities—then both our goals and our efforts to attain them will be measured with suspicion.

5. A novel and serious challenge to Americans is posed by the remarkable increase in their leisure time. The forty-hour week and the likelihood of a shorter one, the greater life-expectancy and the earlier ages of retirement, have combined to make the blessing of leisure a source of personal and community concern. "What shall I do with my spare time" all-too-quickly becomes the question "Who am I? What shall I make of my life?" When men and women find nothing within themselves but emptiness they turn to trivial and narcotic amusements, and the society of which they are a part becomes socially delinquent and potentially unstable. The humanities are the immemorial answer to man's questioning and to his need for self-expression; they are uniquely equipped to fill the "abyss of leisure."

III. Problems of Academic Humanists

The American practitioners of the humanities—the professionals, so to speak—are now prevented in certain specific ways from realizing their full capacities and from attracting enough first-rate individuals into their ranks.

There is genuine doubt today whether the universities and colleges can insure that the purposes for which they were established and sometimes endowed will be fulfilled. The laudable practice of the federal government of making large sums of money available for scientific research has brought great benefits, but it has also brought about an imbalance within academic institutions by the very fact of abundance in one field of study and dearth in another. Much of the federal money for science requires a proportionate commitment of general university funds to sustain the higher level of activity in the scientific departments. Students, moreover, are no different from other people in that they can quickly observe where money is being made available and draw the logical conclusion as to which activities their society considers important. The nation's need for balanced education demands that this imbalance be remedied.

In public and private schools important steps have been taken to improve teaching methods in the sciences, in mathematics, and in languages. Similar steps have not been taken in the humane studies, so that a student may often enter a college or university without adequate training in the humanities or, for that matter, a rudimentary acquaintance with them. Sound education requires that the schools open equally inviting doors into all fields of instruction, so that students may discover where their undeveloped talents lie. Today, moreover, young humanists need to be scientifically literate just as young scientists need to be aware of the world outside their specialty. Only a fully educated people will be capable of sound judgment in government, in business, or in their daily lives.

IV. The Humanities and the National Interest

These are our arguments for greater support and stronger development of the humanities. Societies traditionally support those things which their people regard as useful, and governments support those things which are thought to be in the national interest. The question arises: Is it then in the interest of the United States and of its federal government to give greater support to the humanities?

During our national life the activities of society as a whole and of government in particular have been greatly extended. Health was once considered a private problem; it is now a national one. The newer forms of transportation are heavily subsidized and, to some extent, controlled by the federal government. In World War II the federal government undertook an active role in technology and since then, as we have seen, it has greatly extended its activities in the fields of science. Education was once entirely the concern of private foundations or local government, but it has long since ceased to be so.

Traditionally our government has entered areas where there were overt difficulties or where an opportunity had opened for exceptional achievement. The humanities fit both categories, for the potential achievements are enormous while the troubles stemming from inadequate support are comparably great. The problems are of nationwide scope and interest. Upon the humanities depend the national ethic and morality, the national aesthetic and beauty or the lack of it, the national use of our environment and our material accomplishments—each of these areas directly affects each of us as individuals. On our knowledge of men, their past and their present, depends our ability to make judgments—not least those involving our control of nature, of ourselves, and of our destiny. Is it not in the national interest that these judgments be strong and good?

The stakes are so high and the issues of such magnitude that the humanities must have substantial help both from the federal government and from other sources. It is for these reasons that the Commission recommends the establishment of a National Humanities Foundation to parallel the National Science Foundation, which is so successfully carrying out the public responsibilities entrusted to it.

V. The Humanities and the Federal Government

It is an axiom of our intellectual life that scholarship and art are free and must remain free. Like science, they must judge their ends and means according to their own criteria. It is encouraging to note that the federal government in its massive program of subsidy for the sciences and technology has not imposed control and, indeed, has not even shown an inclination to control the thoughts and activities of scientists.

Yet there are special problems with studies involving value judgment. These are at once the aspect of our culture most in need of help and yet most dangerous to entrust to any single authority, whether of church or party or state. A government which gives no support at all to humane values is careless of its own destiny, but that government which gives too much support—and seeks to acquire influence—may be more dangerous still.

We must unquestionably increase the prestige of the humanities and the flow of funds to them. At the same time, however grave the need, we must safeguard the independence, the originality, and the freedom of expression of all who are concerned with liberal learning.

It is the conviction of this Commission that the independence of the proposed Foundation's board will be the best safeguard against interference. If the director and members of the board are men of acknowledged competence and courage, as are the director and members of the National Science Board, there should be no problem of improper control. Moreover, we feel that the Foundation, like the Smithsonian Institution, should not operate exclusively on government appropriations, but should accept grants from the widest range of sources—foundations, corporations, individuals. Plurality of support will generally strengthen the freedom and variety of scholarship in a democratic society.

In addition, we would insist upon the importance of support for the humanities from sources, both public and private, other than this foundation. The day must never come when scholars and artists can look only to the federal government for the help they need; still less should they depend on a single agency. The notion of any one "chosen instrument" of government in this area must be abhorrent to anyone who cherishes the humanities and realizes that if they are not free they perish.

VI. Recommendation of the Commission on the Humanities

The Commission on the Humanities recommends the establishment by the President and the Congress of the United States of a NATIONAL HUMANITIES FOUNDATION to be composed of a *Board,* a *Director,* and a *Staff.* The suggested responsibilities and duties of this Foundation are described in detail below.

VII. The Nature of the Proposed Foundation

1. The Purpose of the Foundation. The National Humanities Foundation should have for its purpose to develop and promote a broadly conceived policy of support for the humanities and the arts. Under the provisions of a National Humanities Foundation Act, the Board should be empowered to determine and carry out its program with an appropriation made by the Congress of the United States. In determining and administering its policy, the Foundation should confine itself to activities exclusively in the fields of the humanities and arts. The Board should have the authority to experiment with ways in which the Foundation's general purposes can best be carried out, but under no conditions whatsoever should it attempt to direct or control the scholarship, teaching, or artistic endeavor which it supports.

The provisions for a National Humanities Foundation which follow are intended suggestively rather than exclusively.

2. The Scope of the Foundation. The Foundation's definition of the humanities and the arts should be broad and inclusive in character. The humanities are generally agreed to include the study of languages, literature, history, and philosophy; the history, criticism, and theory of art and music; and the history and comparison of religion and law. The Commission would also place the creative and performing arts within the scope of the Foundation. As we have said, these are the very substance of the humanities and embrace a major part of the imaginative and creative activities of mankind. (If the present proposal to establish a National Arts Foundation should become law, the Commission hopes that this foundation would be combined with the National Humanities Foundation, or, at least, that the activities of the two would be co-ordinated.) Likewise, those aspects of the social sciences that have humanistic content and employ humanistic methods should come within the purview of the Foundation. It is assumed that the National Science Foundation will continue to be concerned with social science where its principles and approaches resemble those of the natural and applied sciences.

3. Functions of the Foundation. A. It should be a major responsibility of the Foundation to ensure that suitable means are provided for educating and developing scholars, artists, and teachers at every stage of their growth. They must be able to continue their education, to carry on their creative work and their performances, to conduct research, and to improve their teaching. As a corollary, means of publishing or otherwise disseminating the results of their endeavors, both within the academic community and to the public at large, must be available. Grants to properly qualified and endorsed individuals are a fruitful and efficient way to accomplish these ends.

B. The Foundation should, in like fashion, assist organizations concerned with encouraging and developing scholars, artists, and teachers. A great teacher may be important to the humanities apart from his distinction as a scholar or the renown of the institution he serves. The program should therefore be broad enough to include the many schools and colleges in which such teachers may be found.

C. The Foundation should take steps to initiate and promote programs for the improvement of teaching in the humanities and the arts.

D. The Foundation should help construct and equip the buildings of all kinds so badly needed by artistic, cultural, and educational institutions.

4. Means. *A. Support of Individuals:* In the schools, there is a great need to make the humanities relevant to the lives and interests of the students. To accomplish this, students must encounter in their elementary and secondary school classrooms teachers who can awaken young minds to the richness of humane studies. Such teachers are all too rare. A program to support humanistic studies by actual or potential teachers thus offers a promising line of attack on current deficiencies in the schools. The following kinds of support are required:

1. Grants to acquaint teachers in training or already at work with good teaching practices, by offering them the opportunity to observe or join in successful programs and to pursue their own advanced study or creative work.
2. Fellowships for graduate study and for attendance at summer institutes.
3. Support to individuals for experiments and demonstration projects in the schools.
4. Travel grants to give carefully-selected teachers a chance for direct contact with the language, art forms, or other aspects of their subject matter.
5. Fellowships for school administrators to increase their appreciation of the values and responsibilities inherent in humanities teaching.

The Foundation may wish to act directly through individual grants to applicants screened by its own committees, or indirectly through organizations devoted to these same ends in whose selection processes the Foundation has confidence.

In the colleges and universities there is a great need for graduate scholarships and fellowships for the preliminary training of scholars, teachers, and artists at all stages; likewise, for post-doctoral fellowships in the humanities. The selection of individuals to receive these fellowships should be based upon the judgment of committees or juries composed of scholars, writers, and artists whose work has achieved distinction, with the majority of the members still productive.

B. Support of Groups and Organizations: In addition to the authority to provide scholarships and fellowships for individuals, the Foundation should be empowered to make grants to and conclude contracts with any corporate or private body involved in the humanities or the arts for the promoting of research, teaching, performance, and publication. Some examples are:

1. Summer or full academic-year institutes for the training of elementary and secondary school teachers. Such programs should be directed primarily toward improving the participants' knowledge of their subjects, but in addition they should be concerned with developing techniques to bring the humanities and the arts to children of all levels of ability or cultural background.
2. The Foundation should support improved teaching at all levels of education. It should encourage experiments in presentation and organization, including interdisciplinary studies where many fruitful advances may be made. This support should extend to the development of new curricular materials.
3. Facilities.
   a. Buildings. Many cultural and educational organizations in this country stand in great need of new and expanded libraries and space for instruction, research, creation, performance, and exhibition. The Foundation should be empowered to support the planning and construction of such buildings.
   b. Libraries. Good libraries are needed at all levels in all subjects for teaching

and research. Scholars in nearly all humanistic fields deal almost entirely with information preserved and organized in book form, and they therefore need large and complex libraries. Improved methods of instruction are making the library more and more important to the schools as well as the colleges and universities. The habit of using libraries begins in the school, but most school libraries are pitifully inadequate. They must be developed and extended and must be designed to lead students into the local public libraries. Since most public libraries already are incapable of supporting the demands upon them, they too must be more generously supported, not only in the interests of the schools, but in the interests of the general public. Libraries are a source not only of learning but also of pleasure.

Fortunately the recent extension of the Library Services Act can be expected to stimulate the improvement of public library services throughout the country. In this legislation the Congress recognized the need for federal aid on a substantial scale for public libraries in urban as well as rural communities. Each state, in order to derive the maximum benefit from this wise legislation, should establish a comprehensive public library system.

The Library of Congress is the cornerstone of the country's system of libraries and should therefore be strengthened, but this by itself is not enough; all major research libraries should be recognized as integral parts of this system. Each disseminates information on its holdings, each lends and films copies for the benefit of scholars throughout the United States, and each should seek to avoid needless duplication of the others. Under-nourishment tends to force each library to throw all of its inadequate resources into a losing battle to meet the most urgent demands of its own institution. If libraries were adequately supported, however, further achievements in co-operation and even more effective services could confidently be anticipated. Strength and health will enable American research libraries to work together as they must, if scholarship is to prosper nationally and if the record of civilization is to be preserved for coming generations, not only as a memory of the past but as a base for creative thought in the future.

We emphasize that not only should the Foundation be able to assist research libraries but also it should contribute to the development of public and school libraries, which are of equal importance in the cultural life of our people.

    c. Facilities of Exchange and Publication. The Foundation should be authorized to make grants and contracts for the exchange of scholarly and artistic personnel and information both internally within the United States and with other countries. Conferences and publications should be eligible for support, though it is understood that the Foundation should concentrate its subsidies for publication in university presses or in experimental and scholarly works which under present circumstances cannot be financed.

5. Organization of the Foundation. *A. The Board:* The Board of the National

Humanities Foundation should consist of twenty-four members who would be chosen for a term of six years each by the President of the United States, with the advice and consent of the Senate. These persons should be selected for their general cultivation and competence in the humanities as such, in the arts, in education, or in the direction of libraries and organizations concerned with the arts, and they should represent a wide spectrum of American life. Appropriate organizations should be requested to nominate candidates. The terms of the first twenty-four selected should be staggered to permit replacement of one-third of the members every two years.

B. The Director: The Director of the Foundation, who would be a member of the Board *ex officio,* should be appointed by the President of the United States with the advice and consent of the Senate. The Board should make recommendations to the President, and the President ought not to act until the Board has had an opportunity to do so. Because of the Director's vital role in the conduct of the Foundation, the members of the Commission on the Humanities place the greatest stress upon the need to select for the office of Director a man of the highest distinction in the Foundation's areas of concern. He should serve for a term of six years, unless the President should wish to replace him.

C. Commissions, Committees, and Divisions: The Director, with the approval of the Board, should appoint a staff, and the Board should organize the Foundation into divisions appropriate to its work. At the discretion of the Board, each division might well have an advisory committee composed of eminent persons in the field involved. In addition, there should be regional and national committees charged with judging applications for grants. When necessary, the Board might appoint special commissions to make recommendations upon matters of policy.

6. General Authority of the Foundation. The Foundation should be empowered to administer funds through governmental appropriations, through the transfer from other departments of government of funds whose use falls within the scope of the Foundation, and through gifts from private foundations, corporations, and individuals. Such funds should be used by the Foundation in such ways as it sees fit, within the terms of the appropriation, gift, or grant, and under the general provisions establishing the Foundation. It should also be able to contract with profit-making organizations or non-profit-making organizations and to publish or support publication.

Appendix B: The National Endowment for the Humanities and the Classroom

Barnaby C. Keeney

When the President and the Congress charged the National Endowment for the Humanities with the task of developing a broad national policy of support for the humanities, just as they charged the Endowment for the Arts with a similar task for the arts, they did so not to please us, but because they believed that the pursuit of these activities and their consequent use was in the national interest, partly as a means of enriching human life, but also to provide, particularly in the case of the humanities, the knowledge and the judgment on which sound decisions may be made. Before I confine myself to the work of the Humanities Endowment, I should point out that the work of the Arts Endowment is of equal, and perhaps even greater, importance to teachers of English and literature, for one of its principal tasks is to foster the creation and dissemination of the best literature of our day. Perhaps, however, much of what it does will affect your successors, rather than you, but some of its present and proposed programs for poetry and drama in the schools are of great interest to you.

To accomplish its mission, the Humanities Endowment seeks to help humanists to provide knowledge and understanding of what is past and what is abstract, aesthetic, or not material, so that thinking men may realize their full potential through achieving greater perspective and be inspired to a vision of achievement, have the material with which to develop their wisdom, and the time in which to do it, and ultimately to master themselves and their environment, including that part of the environment that we have made ourselves through our technology. These things, taken together, are the ingredients of the nation's spirit, its ethics, and its morality. They are the basis of the judgments of value involved in all important decisions, whether they be public or private. They are bound together by the relevance of man's knowledge and thoughts to his actions.

More specifically, the Endowment seeks to carry out its mission through three channels: first, by providing individuals with opportunities for their own development; second, by supporting the creation and the dissemination of knowledge; and third, by attempting to improve education both in and out of organized educational institutions, or, in other words, in or out of school.

In doing so, we work closely with the Arts Endowment and with the Office of Education. Our task is large and inspiring. The boundaries imposed upon us by fiscal exigency are small and exacting. I, myself, am glad that our budget for this year is very limited, for lack of means forces us to make decisions with great care and to select very carefully from the many proposals that we receive from outside, and the many ideas that are generated from within. I shall not, however, remain happy with this exigency for long, and I hope you will not either, for the teachers of English are a large minority group, larger, perhaps, than mine—New England Yankees—and the country is particularly attentive to the cries of minorities in these days.

Let me speak very briefly of some of our specific programs, or, rather, of our broad categories of programs, and then of some of the specific ones that will affect teachers of English.

The first program, that for the development of individuals, is essentially a fellowship program, through which we seek to provide scholars with the opportunity and the time in which to carry on their researches and to develop their thoughts. It is aimed primarily at university teachers and college teachers, and for two of the three programs a doctorate or the equivalent is almost a prerequisite. High school teachers are not excluded, if they have the doctorate, or if they have unusual qualifications, but we do not expect that we will have much impact on the schools through this program. This is not because we are unconcerned with the professional development of teachers in the primary and secondary schools, but, rather, because we feel that this work belongs properly to the Office of Education. Possibly in the future we shall develop more meaningful programs of fellowships and other opportunities for teachers in the schools, but probably not for some time, and more likely they will be served by other agencies.

The second program is aimed at the development of knowledge, to which the work of the Fellows in the first program will of course contribute. This program is aimed primarily at the professional scholar rather than at the professional teacher. But the assumption is made that the scholar is also a teacher. Again, teachers in the schools are quite eligible, but it is doubtful that many will apply for research grants in the sort of research that we subsidize, but rather will apply for research grants from the Office of Education. Nevertheless, since one of the main objectives of this program is to reduce the time gap between the discovery of knowledge and its application, it will doubtless have a bearing upon the schools through the improvement of teaching materials, including textbooks. A specific example of use to you and to teachers whether they be school or college teachers in this program is the grant to the Modern Language Association's Center for the publication of definitive editions of great American authors. These we hope will quickly find their way into inexpensive form, at least those volumes that are suitable for instructional purposes in colleges and schools, and with the very rapid development of better curricula in literature in the schools, will doubtless be useful in an important way. Possibly *Silas Marner* may yield to a novel such as *Huckleberry Finn,* an event which I and the other founder will happily celebrate. I had to read *Silas Marner* only once. My son dropped out at a different age and he had to read it twice. And it took him two years to recover.

Other programs and books that will be of interest to the schools will emerge from this division, particularly in the field of American history, or, better put, the history of the Americas.

The third program is to encourage the development of the teaching of the humanities in schools, colleges, and universities, and among the public at large, in order that we may bring into all our present activities and thought the wisdom that may be gained from a contemplation of the past. This is probably the most important of the objectives of the Endowment, since it brings the humanities to bear on important questions of public and private life, but it is also the most difficult to accomplish. We hope to help inspiring teachers in schools and colleges to excite the initial interest of citizens in the whole subject of man and his activities and their best expression. We hope to help inspire teachers who are not inspired.

I had thought initially, before I really went into the question, that we should devote a major effort to the development of curricula and materials for use in the elementary and secondary schools, but when I learned of how much has been done toward this end by the Office of Education and other public and private agencies, I concluded that we would be wise to cooperate with them, and especially to seek to encourage the use of what has already been accomplished, and to improve its dissemination. We feel, for example, that many excellent curricular proposals and developments are in local or otherwise limited use, and we feel particularly that the admirable summer institutes, and even the academic year programs, however great may be their effect upon the participants, do not have as considerable a continuing effect as they should, simply because they are a brief and transient experience. We seek particularly to encourage continuing relationships between universities and schools within a convenient geographic area in developing and using the best that can be done in humane teaching and in the improvement of not a few, but all, of the present and future teachers of the humanities in particular regions.

We are trying to find a way into vocational education at the secondary level, or close to the secondary level, because we feel that vocational education will be better if the students are helped to think by the humanities, as well as to know how to do their vocations well. We do not know this way, and we would like help.

We hope to find a way in which the humanities can be made more meaningful to students who are culturally deprived, whether they are in ordinary schools or in the many special programs that are now being developed. My preliminary guess, however, is that art will initially be more meaningful to them than literature.

These are some examples of what we may be able to do to help you in your professional lives. We hope, further, to help you by improving the level of the environment from which your students come and to which they return. Television, movies, and radio, for example, are a very important part of the environment of all of your students and of some of you. It is natural that those who operate these media provide what is wanted at the moment. Enormous sums of money have been spent and more will be spent to improve educational television, as well as instructional television. We feel that this medium is an excellent one through which to present the substance of the humanities and the arts, and with the little money we have, we shall try to prepare material to help humanists tell their story better on television. We are empowered by the Congress to work on talking books for groups handicapped by other disabilities than blindness. One of the most handicapped groups in our society are the commuters who spend from 30 to 60 minutes a day in automobiles listening to the radio or to their car pool. Already three quarters of a million cars will be provided with radios equipped to receive cartridges of recordings which contain selections of the driver's choice. Next year these will be optional on all cars. I have looked at the catalogue of these cartridges. The change in the fare will not be conspicuous. We hope that we can find a way to influence the programing of those so that good music, good literature, good thinking, will become available to the commuter while he commutes.

I hope that our program to improve museums will be of more than peripheral interest to teachers of English, for through good museums the environment in which authors wrote and characters lived, or pretended to live, may become far clearer to the student. None of your students have lived in a rural, unmechanized society. Few ever will. How are they to understand how people lived before 1900, without such museums as at Mystic and Cooperstown, for example? It is our intention to provide opportunities to the staffs of museums to develop themselves professionally. It is also our intention to set up pilot programs through which museums and school systems will be brought together more closely than they sometimes are now.

These are small steps toward our great goal, and all of them are, in their beginnings at least, difficult and complicated. Obviously, the most difficult task of the Endowment is to increase the interest in and the use of the humanities by the citizens and governors of our country, and to improve their access to them. Teachers of the humanities must often be concerned with the past, for their work is by its nature retrospective, but they must also illuminate the present, and in presenting the fundamental knowledge and thinking that makes the humanities, they may serve as guides to the future. As the President put it, the need is not only to enrich scholarship, but to enrich life for all men. If this were the only value of the humanities, it would be sufficient argument for the program. There is, nevertheless, a practical task to be accomplished, namely, for scholars to make available knowledge of the past so that others may learn from historical judgments and from literature that which can greatly assist people in making present and future decisions of value in public and private life.

The secondary need, which must preoccupy teachers, is to assist people while they are young to begin to find worthwhile uses for the ever-increasing leisure they will have as they age. Both objectives depend upon self-knowledge, which is traditionally the ultimate contribution of the humanities to man's life. In seeking to carry out all these purposes, we urgently need your help.

Appendix C: An NCTE/ERIC Report on Humanities Instruction in Secondary Schools

Robert V. Denby

As careers have become more specialized and, usually, more technologically oriented, secondary school courses have responded in kind; and this response appears reasonable and appropriate in the light of our belief that, in order to serve us best, the education we receive must be relevant to the lives we shall lead. However, the more specialized our knowledge, the more concentrated our efforts, and the more circumscribed our personal orbits, the less capable we become of understanding the relatedness and interdependence of the multitudinous specialties, and, consequently, the less able we become of directing our own destinies rationally.

Many proponents of humane studies maintain that an individual may acquire a better understanding of his humanity, as a counter-balance to his own speciality, in a *humanities* course which emphasizes wholes, relationships, and unities. Too, such a course might be expected to counter-balance the growing emphasis upon technology and to place it in perspective with other accomplishments of mankind in society, the arts, philosophy, and religion.

The growing appeal of this proposal seems to be indicated in reports of the establishment of individual humanities courses, the adoption of the "humanities approach" to instruction in former "one-discipline" courses, and the development of curriculums and instructional materials for use in humanities programs. A number of these reports have been processed by the Educational Resources Information Center (ERIC),[1] and it is our purpose in this review to bring a selection of these to the attention of secondary English teachers, supervisors, and administrators who may already have adopted a humanities course or program, or who may anticipate doing so.

Before turning to these documents, this word about abbreviations within the bibliographic citations: MF stands for *microfiche* (a 4" x 6" microfilm card containing up to sixty reproduced pages), which sells for 25¢/fiche; HC stands for hard copy (a photographically-reproduced paper booklet 70 per cent the size of the original), which sells for 5¢/page. These are the two kinds of facsimiles available from EDRS, ERIC's document reproduction service.[2]

* * * * *

Rationales for the inclusion of humanities courses in the school curriculum were considered during a December 1965 conference sponsored by the Association for Supervision and Curriculum Development of the National

---

[1] As of November 15, 1968.

[2] Documents may be ordered by ED number only from EDRS, National Cash Register Company, 4936 Fairmont Avenue, Bethesda, Maryland 20014.

Education Association. The major addresses delivered then were later published as *The Humanities and the Curriculum:*

Berman, Louise M., ed. *The Humanities and the Curriculum.* Washington, D. C.: Association for Supervision and Curriculum Development, National Education Association, 1967. Available from ASCD, NEA, 1201 Sixteenth Street, N. W., Washington, D. C. 20036: $2.00 each, 10 per cent discount on 2-9 copies, 20 per cent discount on 10 or more. Also available from NCTE: Stock No. 36614–$2.00. (Document not available from EDRS.)

Descriptors: *Curriculum, *English Instruction, *Humanities, Audiovisual Aids, English Curriculum, Ethical Values, Fine Arts, Language, Languages, Literature, Philosophy, Science, Social Studies, Vocational Education.

The place of the fine arts, language, literature, foreign languages, and philosphy within the humanities and the relationship of social studies, sciences and vocational education to the humanities is considered. One address, "The Potential of the Humanities and the Challenge to the Schools," and two chapters by the editor, "The Humanities–The Present Scene and the Potential" and "Toward a Sharper Focus on the Humanities," present broad analyses of the humanities. The use of audiovisual aids in teaching the humanities is also discussed. Sources of additional information regarding current developments within the humanities are suggested, and a bibliography of recent articles is appended.

Authors of conference addresses are Edward D. Allen, Paul E. Blackwood, Marguerite V. Hood, Leland B. Jacobs, Earl S. Johnson, James A. Jordan, Jr., Gerald B. Leighbody, Philip Lewis, John U. Michaelis, and James R. Squire. (RD)[3]

Professor Harry S. Broudy (University of Illinois) prominent author and student of the history and philosophy of education, turned his attention to the same subject during another conference:

ED 019 275
Broudy, Harry S. "The Role of the Humanities in the Curriculum." An address delivered at a Conference for School Administrators conducted by the New York State Department of Education, July 1966. Published in *Journal of Aesthetic Education,* 1 (Autumn 1966) 17-27. EDRS PRICE: MF-$0.25 HC-$0.70 12pp.

Descriptors: *Course Content, *Course Objectives, *Humanities, *Humanities Instruction, Art, Classical Literature, Cultural Background, History, Literature, Philosophy, Values.

[3]Capital letters enclosed in parentheses at the conclusion of ERIC abstracts are the initials of the abstractor.

At a time when humanities courses are undergoing reevaluation and development, they must not be suffocated by incorporating into them too many literary works and too many approaches. Selection of works is of paramount importance, and perhaps the best principle upon which to base selection is one which encourages "enlightened cherishing"—the commitment of the individual to certain values and to the standards by which he justifies his commitments. The humanities course can offer to the student, for study and possible emulation, the best exemplars of the human ideal. In choosing materials and an approach, schools must keep in mind that habits of enlightened cherishing take time to establish, and that it is more effective to concentrate on a few works which have the greatest potential for interesting the student and demonstrating the meaning of the human quest for humanity. By concentrating on those works with great artistic merit, the approach used in teaching can be that of aesthetic analysis, which teaches students to read knowingly and intelligently and to respond rationally and imaginatively. (DL)

Dr. Broudy's concern for the nature, quality, and number of books selected for use in humanities courses was shared by Richard Kuhns, writing in a *Journal of Aesthetic Education* article:

ED 019 274
   Kuhns, Richard, " 'Humanities' as a Subject," *Journal of Aesthetic Education,* 1 (Autumn 1966) 7-16. EDRS PRICE: MF-$0.25 HC-$0.65 11pp.

Descriptors: *Humanities, *Humanities Instruction, Art, Classical Literature, Cultural Background, History, Literature, Philosophy.

Since most of the school curriculum is devoted to specialized disciplines, humanities courses provide the opportunity for creating in students an awareness of the unity which exists among philosophy, history, and the arts. Intensive study and class discussion of individual works become impossible, however, when too many books are crowded into a humanities course. As a consequence, the works remain remote artifacts to be "appreciated," but bear no relevance to the lives of students who prefer current literature and other media. Humanities courses can best be devoted to examining the philosophical and literary issues of a limited number of works, for it is in these areas that the works of the past are relevant to today's students. The intensive study of structure and style can be left to specialized departmental courses. Through the active engagement of the student in studying, discussing, and arguing the philosophical and literary issues, the works of the past can become accessible to him and a part of the shaping forces of his life, rather than dead monuments to be honored but never touched. (DL)

During the 1966 Humanities Conference of the National Council of Teachers of English, consideration was given to instructional methods as well as to the rationale, focus, and content of these courses:

Marckwardt, Albert H., ed. *Literature in Humanities Programs.* Champaign, Ill.: National Council of Teachers of English, 1967 (paperbound). Available from NCTE: Stock No. 37105–$1.50. (Document not available from EDRS.)

Descriptors: *Elementary Grades, *English Instruction, *Humanities Instruction, *Secondary Grades, Classics, Composition (Literary), Cultural Awareness, Fine Arts, History, Integrated Curriculum, Intellectual Development, Language, Literature, Program Improvement.

The 1966 National Council of Teachers of English Humanities Conference considered the place of the humanities in elementary and secondary education and the possible focus, content, and methods for presenting humanities programs. In this collection of papers given at the conference, leaders in various disciplines suggest the scope and magnitude of humane studies by exploring: (1) the problems and possibilities of literature, composition, and language in humanities programs, (2) the difficulties of teaching the classics in translation, (3) the work of the National Endowment for the Humanities and its effect upon the classroom, and (4) the need for a special kind of humanistic education in the elementary grades. Other papers present observations and recommendations to clarify the roles of the elementary, junior high, and senior high schools in creating significant humanities programs. The final paper examines the implications of a humanities conference and the importance of understanding human experience in today's world. (JB)

Two surveys have been conducted in recent years by the National Council of Teachers of English to determine the nature and extent of humanities programs established in the United States. Taken together—and both appeared under the same title, *Annotated Humanities Programs*—the reports of these surveys provide an index to the growth of such programs and to the popularity of various approaches and emphases in them:

ED 015 210
Corbin, Jonathan, comp. *Annotated Humanities Programs.* Champaign, Ill.: National Council of Teachers of English, 1967. EDRS PRICE: MF-$0.25 HC-$1.65 33pp.

Descriptors: *Course Descriptions, *English Instruction, *Humanities Instruction, *Secondary Grades, Ancient History, Cultural Education, Fine Arts, Literature, Humanities, Instructional Materials, Philosophy.

One hundred thirty-five United States secondary schools offering humanities programs are listed alphabetically by state. Annotations present descriptions of the approaches to study in the humanities courses (e.g., American Studies, World Culture, Great Ideas). Many also indicate (1) grade levels, (2) school departments administering the program, (3) methods of teaching—by one teacher, by teams, or by a series of teachers from various departments, (4) quality of students participating, (5) amount of credit given, (6) type of course—elective or required, part of sequence or single course of study, and (7) materials and texts used. (JB)

ED 020 453
Adler, Richard R., and Arthur Applebee. *Annotated Humanities Programs.* Champaign, Ill.: National Council of Teachers of English, 1968 (mimeographed). EDRS PRICE: MF-$0.25 HC-$3.35 65pp.

Descriptors: *Course Descriptions, *Cultural Education, *English Instruction, *Humanities Instruction, *Secondary Grades, Ancient History, Curriculum Development, Curriculum Planning, Fine Arts, History, Humanities, Instructional Materials, Literature, Philosophy, Program Administration, Student Characteristics, Teaching Methods.

The humanities programs offered in 1968 by 227 United States secondary schools are listed alphabetically by state, including almost one hundred new programs not annotated in the 1967 listing (see ED 015 210). Each annotation presents a brief description of the approach to study used in the particular humanities course (e.g., American Studies, Culture Epoch of the Western World, Great Ideas, music and art). Many also supply information concerning (1) grade levels, (2) the department administering the program, (3) methods of teaching— individual teacher, team, or a series of teachers from various departments, (4) quality of students participating, (5) credit given, (6) type of course—elective or required, part of a sequence or a single course of study, and (7) texts, materials, and specific activities—field trips, addresses by visiting lecturers, concert and drama attendance. (LH)

Miller and Thomson's survey of humanities courses in Florida reveals some of the difficulties many schools have encountered, at least initially, in instituting the new programs, and reflects some common misgivings of teachers and administrators regarding teachers' preparation as humanities instructors:

ED 016 659
Miller, Robert D., and Allan Thompson. *An Analysis of High School Humanities Courses in Florida.* Report No. BR-6-8361. Tallahasee: Florida State University, 1967. EDRS PRICE: MF-$0.50 HC-$5.45 107pp.

Descriptors: *Course Evaluation, *High Schools, *Humanities Instruction, Course Content, Course Organization, Educational Facilities, Educational Innovation, Inservice Teacher Education, Preservice Education, Teacher Attitudes, Teacher Certification, Teaching Methods.

Information supplied by principals and teachers in response to questionnaires provided study data to assess the 1966–67 status of Florida high school humanities programs. Of 344 schools, 136 offered humanities and humanities-type courses, seven had previously offered them, and four planned such courses. Development of them represented efforts by individual schools to meet local problems and student needs. Of seventy-eight courses, twenty-nine were taught by one instructor, twenty by teacher teams, and twenty-nine by one instructor occasionally assisted by subject specialists. One-third of the courses were structured historically, six thematically, and over half used a combination of structures. Although necessary audiovisual equipment was ordinarily available, large lecture rooms often were not; supplies were usually inadequate; sufficient teacher planning and preparation time was not provided; and class trips were usually impossible. All humanities teachers held teaching certificates and two-thirds had taught for six or more years; however, many teachers felt at least partly unprepared to teach humanities courses, and seventy-one principals believed that too few humanities teachers were available and advocated more inservice training for them. (A copy of the questionnaire utilized in this study and a summary report are appended.) (RD)

In Pennsylvania pilot studies in ten schools tested a proposed curriculum guide for humanities programs during the 1965-66 academic year. The resulting report included reactions of students, also:

ED 016 666

Pennsylvania Bureau of Curriculum Planning. *Universal Issues of Human Life, A Pennsylvania Humanities Report.* Harrisburg: The Bureau, 1968. EDRS PRICE: MF-$.25 HC-$1.20 22pp.

Descriptors: *Curriculum Evaluation, *Humanities, *Humanities Instruction, Course Content, Course Organization, Curriculum Guides, English Instruction, Experimental Curriculum, Grading, Lecture, Pilot Projects, Secondary Education, Student Attitudes, Teacher Background, Teaching Methods, Team Teaching.

Classroom sessions were observed; and school principals, humanities teachers, and small groups of participating students were interviewed. It was found that the humanities course was required in two of the schools and offered as an elective in the remaining eight, that it was taken most often by seniors in a college-preparation program, that courses lasted two semesters, and that classes met two, three, or five times a week. Teachers generally had English or social studies backgrounds, and most had attended a workshop in the teaching of the humanities. All but one of the programs offered some type of team teaching approach. Grades were most often based upon research papers and oral presentations. Students generally rated the humanities course as among the best of the courses they had taken, though they wanted fewer teacher lectures and more guest lectures, student participation, and field trips. (Included in this report are case studies of eight of the ten schools which participated in the humanities pilot study.) (DL)

ERIC has processed reports from three special projects designed to facilitate the introduction of various humanities materials and methods into the secondary school curriculum: CUE (Curriculum Understanding Enrichment) of the New York State Education Department; the River Dell Center for the Promotion of the Humanities of Oradell, New Jersey; and EPOCH (Educational Programming of Cultural Heritage) of the Berkeley (California) Unified School District. Several reports of interest from each are abstracted below:

CUE

ED 010 373

Allen, James E., Jr., *et al.* The CUE Report. Report No. BR-5-0228-A. Albany: New York State Education Department, 1966. EDRS PRICE: MF-$1.00 HC-$1.80 234pp.

Descriptors: *Cultural Enrichment, *Curriculum Enrichment, *Enrichment Programs, *Humanities Instruction, *Information Dissemination, Audiovisual Aids, Case Studies (Education), Cultural Awareness, English, Grade 9, Home Economics Education, Industrial Arts, Instructional Materials, Mass Media, Resource Materials, Sciences, Social Studies, Student Experience, Teaching Guides.

The experiment of CUE (Cultural Understanding Enrichment) was designed to bring the benefits of the arts and humanities to students to enable them to form tastes, judgment abilities, values, and behavioral goals. Specific instructional areas covered were English, social studies, sciences, industrial arts, and home economics. The elements of the CUE system were: (1) curriculum-related resource collections of newer media, (2) guides for media use, and (3) suggested student experiences with the arts and humanities. All CUE system elements were developed and experimentally tested in pilot projects without the necessity for major curriculum change, additional school personnel, or large expenditures of time, energy, and money. CUE remains a program which any school may use (1) as a basis for its cultural program and (2) as a meaningful and profitable way of using instructional media and equipment in the achievement of arts and humanities education. (An appendix was included in the report which described the case studies made in various ninth grade classrooms where CUE materials were used. Another appendix, containing samples of CUE materials, is a separate report, ED 010 374.) (JH)

ED 010 374

New York State Education Department. *The CUE Report, Appendix B.* Report No. BR-5-0228-B. Albany: The Department, 1966. EDRS PRICE: MF-$0.50 HC-$4.75 93pp.

Descriptors: *Cultural Enrichment, *Enrichment Programs, *Evaluation Methods, *Instructional Materials, *Questionnaires, Curriculum Enrichment, Humanities Instruction, Opinions.

This appendix to *The CUE Report,* ED 010 373, contains test forms for student and teacher evaluation of CUE, sample segments of various materials prepared for CUE, and newsletters and news articles which describe CUE projects. CUE (Cultural Understanding Enrichment) was an experimental program designed to enrich the arts and humanities offerings of public schools through innovative uses of instructional media and equipment. (JH)

ED 012 199

Brown, Robert M., *et al. CUE, English Humanities Media Guide.* Albany: New York State Education Department, 1965. EDRS PRICE: MF-$1.00 HC-$2.35 220pp.

Descriptors: *English, *Films, *Humanities, *Instructional Materials, *Video Tape Recordings, Cultural Activities, Curriculum Enrichment, Curriculum Guides, Enrichment Programs, Grade 9, Instruction, Secondary Education, Teaching Guides, Television.

This document, one of a series of media guides, divides the English humanities into eleven different topics covering areas of communication, vocabulary, and world culture. Within each topic is a series of suggested film and television subjects; and a discussion of each includes a synopsis, statement of purpose, suggested preparation of the class, things pupils should look and listen for, and suggestions for follow-up and related activities. A list of producers and addresses is included. (JM)

River Dell Center for the Promotion of the Humanities

ED 014 007

River Dell Regional Schools, *River Dell Center for the Promotion of the Humanities. Oradell, New Jersey.* Oradell, N. J. River Dell Regional Schools, 1966.EDRS PRICE: MF-$0.25 HC-$0.50 8pp.

Descriptors: *Course Descriptions, *High School Curriculum, *Humanities, *Program Development, *Supplementary Educational Centers, Information Dissemination, Inservice Education.

A program being developed for the promotion of the humanities is described. The program grew out of the need to gather and disseminate information about the great ideas of man—the philosophy, religion, art, architecture, and music of peoples in Europe, Asia, Africa, and the Americas. The program will be implemented in four stages: (1) creation of an interdisciplinary course for high school seniors, (2) introduction of a humanities approach to teaching all high school grades in the English, history, language, music, and art departments, (3) development of inservice courses, and (4) information dissemination of the program to serve as a model and guide. Included in the report are descriptions of (1) program development, (2) goals, (3) planning and implementation, (4) materials and equipment, (5) student grouping and levels of instruction, (6) large group instruction, and (7) a tentative outline of course content. (RS)

ED 014 008

River Dell Regional Schools. *River Dell Center for the Promotion of the Humanities. Progress Report on Printed Information, Conferences and Visitations to November 30, 1966.* (Title Supplied) Oradell, N.J.: River Dell Regional Schools, 1966. EDRS PRICE: MF-$0.25 HC-$2.20 42pp.

Descriptors: *Humanities, *Information Dissemination, *Inservice Programs, *Newsletters, *Supplementary Educational Centers, Course Descriptions, Program Development, Program Evaluation.

This report cites the progress and accomplishments of the River Dell Center. Information is presented regarding (1) printed releases, (2) contacts made, (3) inservice courses offered, (4) dissemination of course information, (5) visitations, and (6) inprogress activities. Two regional school newsletters, letters to the New Jersey Department of Education and Bergen County superintendents, and program announcements to country school teachers are included. (RS)

EPOCH

ED 016 741

Monfort, Jay B., *et al. EPOCH-ESEA Project for Educational Programming of Cultural Heritage. Planning Period Report.* Berkeley, Cal.: Berkeley Unified School District, 1967. EDRS PRICE: MF-$0.50 HC-$3.65 71pp.

Descriptors: *Educational Innovation, *Humanities Instruction, *Instructional Technology, *Program Planning, *Resource Centers, Curriculum Development, Educational Objectives, Educational Researchers, Federal Programs, Information Retrieval, Interdisciplinary Approach, Personnel, Program Evaluation, Resource Materials, Summer Workshops.

This report describes the planning stage of a program to enlarge humanities instruction through the use of innovative teaching methods, extensive multimedia resources, and advanced educational technology. A description of the planning grant activities constitutes a major section of the report. Included among these activities are the selection of staff, definition of objectives and educational needs, involvement of subject specialists and curriculum advisers, experimental installation of a demonstration chamber, program development, evaluation planning, dissemination of relevant information, and a summer workshop. It is felt that these activities were generally successful. Procedures outlines for the 1967-68 pilot period involve the development of replicable installations of the demonstration chamber, development of model programs, presentation to students, and evaluation and planning for operation in 1968-69. Press clippings, a planning period calendar, guidelines for the researching, synthesizing of subject areas, EPOCH Data Card information, and other relevant materials are appended. (LB)

ED 016 747

Monfort, Jay, *et al. EPOCH, Educational Programming of Cultural Heritage– ESEA Title III Submission of PACE for Continuation Grant.* Berkely, Cal.: Berkeley Unified School District, 1967. EDRS PRICE: MF-$0.50 HC-$3.00 58pp.

Descriptors: *Educational Innovation, *Federal Programs, *Humanities Instruction, *Instructional Technology, *Program Planning, *Resource Centers, Consultants, Curriculum Development, Educational Needs, Educational Objectives, Educational Researchers, Information Retrieval, Interdisciplinary Approach, Personnel, Program Evaluation, Program Proposals, Resource Materials.

Described in this report is a project which offers interdisciplinary humanities instruction through extensive multimedia resources, innovative teaching methods, and advanced educational technology. The project, still in the planning stage, will ultimately be housed in a scientifically designed resource center where educational exhibits, informational retrieval systems, and special teaching devices will facilitate learning, teaching, and teacher training. In one section of the report such major project activities as the research program, curriculum study, acquisition of resource materials, and search for space and design development are discussed; and in an additional section the pilot program which will emerge from some of these planning activities is described. Also presented are tentative diagrams of the resource center and certain teaching devices. (LB)

ED 016 742

Berkeley (California) Unified School District. *EPOCH, Educational Programming of Cultural Heritage–ESEA Title I Submission to PACE for Continuation Grant. Addendum to Grant Continuation Application, May 1967.* Berkeley: The District, 1967. EDRS PRICE: MF-$0.25 HC-$1.05 19pp.

Descriptors: *Educational Objectives, *Humanities Instruction, *Instructional Technology, *Program Planning, *Resource Centers, Educational Innovation, Educational Needs, Information Retrieval, Interdisciplinary Approach, Pilot Projects, Program Evaluation, Program Proposals.

This addendum to a report on the development of a program to teach and interrelate arts and humanities instruction through the use of extensive resources, innovative teaching methods, and advanced educational technology outlines the activities and goals of the already accomplished planning stage of the program and of the pilot (1967-68) and operational (1968-69) stages. The description of the procedures for evaluating the pilot activities notes the anticipated outcomes, evaluation personnel, and measurement instruments to be used. Projected expenditures as of May 1967 are estimated at $48,610. (LB)

Another humanities project reported is one by the Louisville (Kentucky) Board of Education which emphasized increased dramatics experience for students:

ED 012 831

Neill, Robert, *et al. Student Dramatic Enrichment Program, Evaluation Report.* (Title Supplied) Louisville, Ky.: Louisville Board of Education, 1966. EDRS PRICE: MF-$0.25 HC-$2.25 43pp.

Descriptors: *Cultural Awareness, *Dramatics, *Enrichment Programs, *Humanities Instruction, *Instructional Trips, Cultural Enrichment, High School Students.

The program was organized to integrate dramatic arts experiences with the regular curriculums as a means of heightening the cultural awareness of students and of making them more perceptive and critical viewers. This report, prepared by an evaluation committee, describes (1) the program goals and concepts, administrative problems, and difficulties with ticket distribution that prevented adequate preplanning and class preparation by teachers, (2) the values and defects of study guides that were prepared, (3) the methods used to compare the results achieved by the six student groups that represented different economic backgrounds and levels of participation in the drama program, and (4) an evaluation of the accomplishments for improvements that could make future programs more efficiently conducted and provide greater opportunities for student learning. The committee concluded that (1) there was a lack of general agreement among administrators, teachers, and actors about the philosophy behind the venture, (2) although the program was of value, it was of varying worth to various teachers and their students, and (3) evidence gathered supports the belief that the program generated aesthetic and intellectual enthusiasm in some areas where it had not previously existed. (AL)

Curriculum experimentation by the Twin City Institute for Talented Youth included the introduction of four courses for the academically gifted students in St. Paul, Minnesota, one of which was of the humanities type:

ED 018 413

Twin City Institute for Talented Youth. *Gleanings from a Summer Institute.* St. Paul, Minn.: The Institute, 1967. EDRS PRICE: MF-$0.25 HC-$1.85 35pp.

Descriptors: *English Instruction, *High School Curriculum, *Literature, *Talented Students, *Teaching Methods, College High School Cooperation,

Composition (Literary), Gifted, Humanities, Literary Analysis, Rhetoric, Speaking, Summer Programs, Team Teaching, Twentieth Century Literature, Writing.

In this report to the English Teaching profession, the Twin City Institute Staff describes its curriculum experimentation with academically talented high school students during the summer of 1967. The following courses are briefly discussed in their reports: (1) Composition and Rhetoric, in which theory and practice were balanced and exposition and persuasion were stressed; (2) Humanities, which was organized around two themes—"Man the Hero" and "Man and the Gods;" (3) Literature and Man's Search for Community, in which motifs of alienation, despair, and the search for a place in society were explored in classical and contemporary literature; and (4) Literature of Protest, in which the nature of protest—what prompts and expresses it—was examined in plays, essays, novels, and poems. Each report included an overview, a statement of goals and purposes, lists of materials and equipment used, a presentation and analysis of the structure of the course, dominant teaching techniques used, suggested teacher-preparation requirements, a statement of the implications of each course for regular school programs, and bibliographies of films and of textual and background materials for both teachers and students. (JB)

The next report pertains to an enlarged humanities course for the gifted; it was designed for seventh-grade students in a junior high setting, and was taught during a daily two-period time block:

ED 010 943

Knight, Bonnie M. "Humanities in a Junior High School," *Foreign Language Newsletter* (March 1966). EDRS PRICE: MF-$0.25 HC-$0.40 6pp.

Descriptors: *Gifted, *Greek Civilization, *Humanities Instruction, *Junior High Schools, *Latin, Cultural Awareness, Curriculum Enrichment, English, Hebrew, Instructional Materials, Literature.

A humanities course has been developed for academically able seventh grade students in Branciforte Junior High School in Santa Cruz, California. Students learn English, literature, and Latin, and investigate topics in archeology, cultural anthropology, linguistics, psychology, philosophy, Greek literature and culture, Hebrew literature and culture, and fine arts. They read extensively, write prose and poetry, and edit and produce classical dramas. Unifying themes for the course are The Heroes and Heroines of Literature and the Ethical Concepts of Different Cultures. The resources of the community, the school library, and other courses in the school curriculum are used in developing class projects. After completing the program, students will have investigated elements of three cultures basic to their own—Greek, Latin, and Hebrew—and will have had many significant experiences in languages and classical literature. (AM)